Complicity and the Law of State Responsibility

This systematic analysis of State complicity in international law focuses on the rules of State responsibility. Combining a theoretical perspective on complicity based on the concept of the international rule of law with a thorough analysis of international practice, Helmut Philipp Aust establishes what forms of support for wrongful conduct entail responsibility of complicit States and sheds light on the consequences of complicity in terms of reparation and implementation. Furthermore, he highlights how international law provides for varying degrees of responsibility in cases of complicity, depending on whether peremptory norms have been violated or special subject areas such as the law of collective security are involved. The book shows that the concept of State complicity is firmly grounded in international law, and that the international rule of law may serve as a conceptual paradigm for today's international legal order.

DR HELMUT PHILIPP AUST is a Senior Research Fellow at the Humboldt-University, Berlin. His key research interests lie in the fields of international responsibility, UN law, human rights law and the interaction between international and domestic law.

CAMBRIDGE STUDIES IN INTERNATIONAL AND COMPARATIVE LAW

Established in 1946, this series produces high quality scholarship in the fields of public and private international law and comparative law. Although these are distinct legal sub-disciplines, developments since 1946 confirm their interrelation.

Comparative law is increasingly used as a tool in the making of law at national, regional and international levels. Private international law is now often affected by international conventions, and the issues faced by classical conflicts rules are frequently dealt with by substantive harmonisation of law under international auspices. Mixed international arbitrations, especially those involving state economic activity, raise mixed questions of public and private international law, while in many fields (such as the protection of human rights and democratic standards, investment guarantees and international criminal law) international and national systems interact. National constitutional arrangements relating to 'foreign affairs', and to the implementation of international norms, are a focus of attention.

The Board welcomes works of a theoretical or interdisciplinary character, and those focusing on the new approaches to international or comparative law or conflicts of law. Studies of particular institutions or problems are equally welcome, as are translations of the best work published in other languages.

General Editors   James Crawford SC FBA *Whewell Professor of International Law, Faculty of Law, University of Cambridge*
John S. Bell FBA *Professor of Law, Faculty of Law, University of Cambridge*

A list of books in the series can be found at the end of this volume.

Complicity and the Law of State Responsibility

Helmut Philipp Aust

CAMBRIDGE UNIVERSITY PRESS
Cambridge, New York, Melbourne, Madrid, Cape Town,
Singapore, São Paulo, Delhi, Mexico City

Cambridge University Press
The Edinburgh Building, Cambridge CB2 8RU, UK

Published in the United States of America by Cambridge University Press, New York

www.cambridge.org
Information on this title: www.cambridge.org/9781107010727

© Helmut Philipp Aust 2011

This publication is in copyright. Subject to statutory exception
and to the provisions of relevant collective licensing agreements,
no reproduction of any part may take place without the written
permission of Cambridge University Press.

First published 2011
Reprinted 2012

A catalogue record for this publication is available from the British Library

Library of Congress Cataloguing in Publication Data
Aust, Helmut Philipp, 1980–
   Complicity and the law of state responsibility / Helmut Philipp Aust.
    p. cm. – (Cambridge studies in international and comparative law ; 81)
   Includes bibliographical references and index.
   ISBN 978-1-107-01072-7 (hardback)
   1. Government liability (International law)   2. United Nations. International
Law Commission. Articles on state responsibility.   3. International criminal
law.   I. Title.
   KZ4080.A93 2011
   342.08′8–dc23   2011020307

ISBN 978-1-107-01072-7 Hardback

Cambridge University Press has no responsibility for the persistence or
accuracy of URLs for external or third-party internet websites referred to in
this publication, and does not guarantee that any content on such websites is,
or will remain, accurate or appropriate. Information regarding prices, travel
timetables, and other factual information given in this work is correct at
the time of first printing but Cambridge University Press does not guarantee
the accuracy of such information thereafter.

Contents

Foreword	page ix
Preface	xi
Table of cases	xiii
List of abbreviations	xxiii

1 Introduction   1
  1 The growing role of complicity in international law   1
  2 The approach of this book   4
  3 Clarifications   9

2 Complicity between bilateralism and community interest   11
  1 Complicity and the traditional bilateralism of international law   12
    1.1 Traditional bilateralism   13
    1.2 Third States and the law of neutrality   15
  2 Complicity and the move beyond bilateralism   23
    2.1 Collective security   26
    2.2 Public interest norms   35
  3 Conclusion   47

3 Complicity and the international rule of law   50
  1 The international rule of law   53
    1.1 Preliminary issues   53
    1.2 Individualism or *dédoublement fonctionnel*?   59
    1.3 The material completeness of the international legal order   62
    1.4 The 'climatic' function of the rule of law   65

2	The principle of abuse of rights	69
	2.1 General meaning of the concept	70
	2.2 Abuse of rights as a general principle of international law	71
	2.3 Abuse of rights and the international rule of law	77
	2.4 Arbitrariness, the rule of law and the ICJ	81
3	Abuse of rights and complicity	81
	3.1 State responsibility and the rule of law	83
	3.2 Complicity and the international rule of law	89
4	Conclusion	95

4 Complicity in customary international law   97

1	The evolution of the Article on complicity in the ILC	100
2	Preliminary remarks on customary international law	103
3	International practice on complicity	107
	3.1 Assistance in the unlawful use of force	108
	3.2 The 2003 Iraq war	115
	3.3 Rendition and detention	120
	3.4 Provision of shelter and safe haven	128
	3.5 Military support and violations of international law	129
	3.6 Foreign aid and violations of international law	145
	3.7 Economic cooperation	147
	3.8 Cooperation as consolidation of unlawful events	152
	3.9 UN resolutions and non-assistance	158
	3.10 UN Security Council practice: exonerating practice	162
	3.11 Extradition	164
	3.12 Legal assistance and cooperation	165
	3.13 Other cases: unspecified support	168
4	Governmental statements	169
	4.1 Objection	170
	4.2 Constructive criticism	172
	4.3 Support	173
5	Evaluation	174
	5.1 Standards for establishing customary international law	174
	5.2 Representativeness of the practice	177
	5.3 Consistency and compliance	179
	5.4 Opinio juris	181
	5.5 Remaining uncertainties	186
6	Conclusion	191

5	**The concept of complicity in Article 16 ASR**	**192**
1	Significant, yet incidental?: the scope of 'aid or assistance'	195
	1.1 The discussion in the ILC	195
	1.2 Interpretation of the provision	197
2	The subjective element	230
	2.1 Preliminary remarks	231
	2.2 The discussion in the ILC	232
	2.3 Interpretation of the provision	235
	2.4 Conclusion	249
3	Complicity and the pacta tertiis rule: Article 16(b) ASR	249
	3.1 Complicity and the pacta tertiis rule	250
	3.2 Difficult cases	255
	3.3 Concluding observations on Article 16(b) ASR	265
4	Conclusion	266
6	**The consequences of complicity**	**269**
1	The content and implementation of responsibility for complicity	269
	1.1 Content of responsibility for complicity	271
	1.2 Reparation	274
	1.3 Implementation of responsibility	286
	1.4 Policy considerations for a prospective regime	295
2	Complicit States before international courts and tribunals	296
	2.1 The indispensable third party	297
	2.2 The case law of the ICJ	298
	2.3 Complicity and the indispensable third party	305
	2.4 Essential parties before other courts and tribunals	311
7	**Complicity and aggravated responsibility**	**319**
1	Introductory remarks	319
2	The community interest in the law of State responsibility	320
3	Complicity and serious breaches of peremptory norms	325
	3.1 Non-recognition and non-assistance	326
	3.2 The concept of complicity in Articles 16 and 41(2) ASR	338
	3.3 Further distinctions	345

4	Complicity and obligations of cooperation	352
	4.1 The obligation of cooperation in the ASR	352
	4.2 The *Genocide Convention* case	358
	4.3 Interim conclusions	364
5	Complicity and countermeasures in the collective interest	365
	5.1 Countermeasures in the collective interest	367
	5.2 Complicity and countermeasures in the collective interest	371
6	Conclusion	373

8 A network of rules on complicity — 376

1	Shortcomings of the general and secondary rules on complicity	377
	1.1 Inherent normative weaknesses	377
	1.2 Structural obstacles to holding complicit states responsible	378
2	Special rules and alternative mechanisms	379
	2.1 The use of force and collective security	380
	2.2 International humanitarian law	385
	2.3 Human rights law	390
3	Conclusion	415

General conclusions — 419

1	Summary of the main findings	419
2	Complicity and the international rule of law	423

Bibliography	429
Index	475

Foreword

Until rather recently, 'complicity' was a marginal concept and a neglected issue in international law. The long gestation of Article 16 of the International Law Commission's Articles on State Responsibility of 2001 did not attract much attention. According to this provision, 'A State which aids or assists another State in the commission of an internationally wrongful act by the latter, is internationally responsible.' However, after the terrorist attacks on 11 September 2001 and in connection with the invasion of Iraq in 2003, certain cooperative behaviour by States raised the general awareness of the possible responsibility of States for providing 'aid and assistance'. This awareness, in turn, shed more light on other areas in which States cooperated in a way which raised questions about their implication in the internationally wrongful acts of other States. Today, barely ten years later, the possible responsibility for complicity is one of the most important and difficult issues which arise in the daily work of government legal departments.

This state of affairs alone would justify the timely publication of a monograph which carefully researches and analyses the relevant issues and practice. But the present book is much more than a solid synthesis of practice and the interpretation of an increasingly relevant rule of international law. Helmut Aust also situates this rule within the larger context of international law. He shows that the general prohibition of aid and assistance, as it is laid down in Article 16, is merely one element within a web of more specific primary rules. He also argues persuasively that this prohibition is an expression of a more general legal principle which would guide the interpretation of Article 16. Finally, he demonstrates that the position which international law adopts with respect to 'aid and assistance' is a highly significant symptom of its own state of development, perhaps as important as the concept of peremptory norms.

Helmut Aust's perceptiveness for relevant practice, his mature sense of place and direction, and his talented erudition have contributed to making this book a felicitous example for the mutual enrichment of practice and theory. This is true both for what the book describes – the development of a norm from certain instances of practice which were successfully postulated by academic lawyers to be of more general significance – as well as for what the author does – developing prudent suggestions of how to interpret and conceive a rule within its wider political, historical and systematic context. The book shows that careful empirical analysis and historically informed systematic thinking with respect to a crucial rule of international law, if well done, are not only compatible with each other but ultimately interdependent. Their combination is necessary for the proper identification and development of international law. This book is a most valuable contribution to this end.

Georg Nolte
Humboldt University Berlin
15 November 2010

Preface

This book is a revised and updated version of the doctoral dissertation which I defended at the Faculty of Law of the Humboldt University Berlin in December 2009. As this is a book about complicity, it is only fair to gratefully acknowledge the 'aid and assistance' that I received from a number of people. It should very well be understood that this 'complicity' does not entail any responsibility for errors and misconceptions which can only be attributed to the author.

First of all, I would like to thank my academic teacher, Professor Georg Nolte. He supervised my work as a doctoral candidate. My way of thinking about international law has been deeply influenced by him. I am especially grateful for the academic guidance with which he has accompanied my work so far, as well as for his personal cordiality and warmth. He also initially directed my attention to the topic of this book.

I would also like to thank Professor Christian Tomuschat for being the second examiner of my thesis. I am very grateful to Professor James Crawford for his hospitality at the Lauterpacht Centre for International Law in Cambridge, for an important conversation about complicity in the work of the ILC as well as for the inclusion of this book in the Cambridge Studies in International and Comparative Law series.

Alejandro Rodiles was often the first person with whom I discussed ideas for this book. Our conversations about international law and other issues had a profound influence on this book. Dr Thomas Kleinlein and Dr Mindia Vashakmadze read the entire draft manuscript which benefited greatly from their constructive comments and criticism.

I received valuable feedback on and suggestions for my work from a great number of people, including Gebhard Bücheler, Dr Thomas Burri, Professor Michael Byers, Dr Alejandro Carballo, Christian Djeffal,

Professor Bardo Fassbender, Dr John Morss, Jörn Müller, Nina Naske, Judge Andreas Paulus, Judge Bruno Simma, Paulus Suh, Carla Thies, Mehmet Toral and Dr Annemarieke Vermeer-Künzli. I would also like to thank the participants in the Munich–Oxford seminar in international law of April 2007, the AjV workshop in Munich in October 2007, Andreas Paulus' colloquy at Frauenchiemsee in August 2008 as well as the Visiting Fellows Roundtable in Cambridge in October 2008 where I had the chance to present parts of this work and received important feedback. Finally, two anonymous reviewers at Cambridge University Press provided helpful suggestions and constructive criticism. Nienke van Schaverbeke at Cambridge University Press was a great help in turning the manuscript into this book as well as a pleasure to work with.

This book was written at three splendid institutions. Most parts originated at the Institute for International Law, University of Munich. I would like to thank all members and staff of the Institute for being such a warm and generous community, in particular Christine Schuhbeck-Schmidt. I would also like to express my gratitude to the librarians at the Peace Palace Library in The Hague where I had the privilege to work for two periods of three weeks each. The Lauterpacht Centre for International Law at the University of Cambridge proved to be every bit the inspiring place for an intense period of research and writing I expected it to be. My stays in Cambridge and The Hague were supported by scholarships from the German Academic Exchange Service (DAAD). The doctoral dissertation underlying this book received the Thesis Prize of the *Absolventen und Freunde der Juristischen Fakultät der Humboldt-Universität zu Berlin – Bibliotheksgesellschaft e.V.*

Finally, I would like to thank my family: my parents supported me generously throughout my studies for which I cannot thank them enough. My brother Martin has been an important influence for me as well as a good friend in all times. My wife Johanna is a constant source of love and inspiration. Without her, I would not know what would become of me.

Table of cases

Permanent Court of International Justice

Article 3, paragraph 2 of the Treaty of Lausanne (Frontier between Turkey and Iraq), Advisory Opinion of 21 November 1925, PCIJ Series B, No. 12   238
Factory at Chorzów Case, Jurisdiction, Poland v. Germany, Judgment of 26 July 1927, Series A, No. 9   84, 286
Factory at Chorzów Case, Merits, Germany v. Polish Republic, Judgment of 13 September 1928, Series A, No. 17   277-9
Free Zones of Upper Savoy and the District of Gex, France v. Switzerland, Judgment of 7 June 1932, Series A/B, No. 46   74
German Interests in Polish Upper Silesia, Merits, Germany v. Poland, Judgment of 25 May 1926, Series A, No. 7   74
Lotus Case, France v. Turkey, Judgment of 7 September 1927, Series A, No. 10   6, 51, 60, 92, 247
Phosphates in Morocco, Italy v. France, Preliminary Objections, Judgment of 14 June 1938, Series A/B, No. 74   15
Status of Eastern Carelia, Advisory Opinion of 23 July 1923, Series B, No. 5   309

International Court of Justice

Accordance with International Law of the Unilateral Declaration of Independence in Respect of Kosovo, Advisory Opinion of 22 July 2010, not yet reported, available at www.icj-cij.org/docket/files/141/15987.pdf (last visited 1 November 2010)   6, 68, 273
Application of the Convention of 1902 Governing the Guardianship of Infants, Netherlands v. Sweden, Judgment of 28 November 1958, ICJ Rep. 1958, 55   37

Application of the Convention of the Prevention and Punishment of the Crime of Genocide, Preliminary Objections, Bosnia and Herzegovina v. Yugoslavia (Serbia and Montenegro), Judgment of 11 July 1996, ICJ Rep. 1996, 595   361

Application of the Convention of the Prevention and Punishment of the Crime of Genocide, Provisional Measures, Bosnia and Herzegovina v. Yugoslavia (Serbia and Montenegro), Order of 13 September 1993, ICJ Rep. 1993, 325   347

Application of the Convention on the Prevention and Punishment of the Crime of Genocide, Bosnia and Herzegovina v. Serbia and Montenegro, Merits, Judgment of 26 February 2007, not yet reported, available at www.icj-cij.org/docket/files/91/13685.pdf (last visited 1 November 2010)   3, 9, 93, 99, 226, 236, 239, 342, 354, 358–9, 362–3, 374, 379, 391, 396, 401, 426

Armed Activities on the Territory of the Congo, Democratic Republic of Congo v. Uganda, Judgment of 19 December 2005, ICJ Rep. 2005, 168   264, 378, 385

Armed Activities on the Territory of the Congo (New Application: 2002), Democratic Republic of Congo v. Rwanda, Judgment of 3 February 2006, ICJ Rep. 2006, 5   44, 348, 350

Arrest Warrant of 11 April 2000, Democratic Republic of Congo v. Belgium, Judgment of 14 February 2002, ICJ Rep. 2002, 3   106

Asylum Case, Colombia v. Peru, Judgment of 20 November 1950, ICJ Rep. 1950, 266   81

Barcelona Traction, Light and Power Company Ltd, New Application: 1962, Belgium v. Spain, Judgment of 5 February 1970, ICJ Rep. 1970, 4   35, 41, 84, 321

Conditions of Admission of a State to Membership of the United Nations (Article 4 of the Charter), Advisory Opinion of 28 May 1948, ICJ Rep. 1948, 57   71

Certain Phosphate Lands in Nauru, Nauru v. Australia, Preliminary Objections, Judgment of 26 June 1992, ICJ Rep. 1992, 240   287, 291, 293, 297, 300–1, 307, 311

Continental Shelf, Libyan Arab Jamahiriya v. Malta, Judgment of 21 March 1984, ICJ Rep. 1984, 3   297, 300, 306,

Corfu Channel Case, United Kingdom of Great Britain and Northern Ireland v. Albania, Judgment of 9 April 1949, ICJ Rep. 1949, 4   71, 73, 93–4, 227, 244–5, 281, 285, 290, 295, 346, 378

East Timor, Portugal v. Australia, Judgment of 30 June 1995, ICJ Rep. 1995, 90   8, 303–4, 306–9, 311

Elettronica Sicula SpA (ELSI), United States of America v. Italy, Judgment of 20 July 1989, ICJ Rep. 1989, 15   81, 417

Fisheries Case, United Kingdom v. Norway, Judgment of 18 December 1951, ICJ Rep. 1951, 116   67, 74, 175

Gabcikovo-Nagymaros Case, Hungary v. Slovakia, Judgment of 25 September 1997, ICJ Rep. 1997, 7   74, 279, 287, 366

International Status of South West Africa, Advisory Opinion of 11 July 1950, ICJ Rep. 1950, 128   257

Jurisdictional Immunities of the State, Germany v. Italy, Order of 6 July 2010, not yet reported, available at www.icj-cij.org/docket/files/143/15127.pdf (last visited 1 November 2010)   352

Land, Island and Maritime Frontier Dispute, El Salvador v. Honduras, Judgment of 13 September 1990, ICJ Rep. 1990, 92   297, 300

Legal Consequences for States of the Continued Presence of South Africa in Namibia (South West Africa) notwithstanding Security Council Resolution 276 (1970), Advisory Opinion of 21 June 1971, ICJ Rep. 1971, 16   160, 309, 329, 331, 333, 408

Legal Consequences of the Construction of a Wall in the Occupied Palestinian Territory, Advisory Opinion of 9 July 2004, ICJ Rep. 2004, 136   42, 44, 279, 309, 343–4, 387, 406

Legality of the Threat or Use of Nuclear Weapons, Advisory Opinion of 8 July 1996, ICJ Rep. 1996, 226   28, 67, 309

Military and Paramilitary Activities In and Against Nicaragua, Jurisdiction and Admissibility, Nicaragua v. United States of America, Judgment of 26 November 1984, ICJ Rep. 1984, 392   99, 297, 300, 306

Military and Paramilitary Activities In and Against Nicaragua, Merits, Nicaragua v. United States of America, Judgment of 27 June 1986, ICJ Rep. 1986, 14   84, 106, 221, 244, 263, 387, 388

Monetary Gold Removed from Rome in 1943, Preliminary Question, Italy v. France, United Kingdom of Great Britain and Northern Ireland and United States of America, Judgment of 15 June 1954, ICJ Rep. 1954, 19   8, 245, 298, 300, 378

North Sea Continental Shelf Cases, Federal Republic of Germany v. Netherlands, Federal Republic of Germany v. Denmark, Judgment of 20 February 1969, ICJ Rep. 1969, 3   103, 174–6, 179, 187, 263, 417

Oil Platforms, Islamic Republic of Iran v. United States of America, Judgment of 6 December 2003, ICJ Rep. 2003, 161   275, 290–1, 295

Reservations to the Convention on the Prevention and Punishment of the Crime of Genocide, Advisory Opinion of 28 May 1951, ICJ Rep. 1951, 15   390–1

Treatment in Hungary of Aircraft and Crew of United States of America, United States of America v. Hungarian People's Republic, Order of 12 July 1954, ICJ Rep. 1954, 99   168
Treatment in Hungary of Aircraft and Crew of United States of America, United States of America v. Union of Soviet Socialist Republics, Order of 12 July 1954, ICJ Rep. 1954, 103   168
United States Diplomatic and Consular Staff in Tehran, United States of America v. Iran, Judgment of 24 May 1980, ICJ Rep. 1980, 3   93, 221, 227–8
Western Sahara, Advisory Opinion of 16 October 1975, ICJ Rep. 1975, 12   309

Arbitral awards

Air Service Agreement of 27 March 1946 Between the United States of America and France, Arbitral Award of 9 December 1978, RIAA XVIII, 417   287
Alabama Arbitration, between the United States of America and the United Kingdom under the 1871 Treaty of Washington, reprinted in John Bassett Moore (ed.), *History and Digest of the International Arbitrations to Which the United States Has Been a Party* (Washington DC, 1898), Vol. I, 653   93
Dispute Concerning Filleting within the Gulf of St Lawrence ('La Bretagne') (Canada v. France), Arbitral Award of 17 July 1986 (De Visscher, Chairman, Pharand and Quéneudec, Members), ILR 82, 590   74
Eurotunnel Arbitration, The Channel Tunnel Group Ltd and France-Manche SA v. Secretary of State for Transport of the Government of the United Kingdom and Le Ministre de l'Equipment, des Transports, de l'Aménagement du Territoire, du Tourisme et de la Mer du Gouvernement de la République Française, Partial Award of 30 January 2007, ILR 132, 1   291
Gold Looted by Germany from Rome in 1943, Arbitral Advice of 20 February 1953, ILR 20, 441   299
Island of Palmas Case, Netherlands v. United States of America, Arbitral Award of Max Huber, April 1928, RIAA II, 829   94, 187, 381
Naulilaa Incident Arbitration, Portugal v. Germany, Arbitral Award of 31 July 1928, RIAA II, 1011   288, 366

Phoenix Action Ltd v. Czech Republic, ICSID Case No. ARB/06/5, Award of 15 April 2009, available at www.icsid.worldbank.org (last visited 1 November 2010)   74
Rainbow Warrior (New Zealand v. France), Arbitral Award of 30 April 1990, ILR 82, 499   286

ICTY and ICTR

Prosecutor v. Akayesu, ICTR-96-4T, Judgment of 2 September 1998   226
Prosecutor v. Blaskic, IT-95-14-T, Judgment of 3 March 2000   213
Prosecutor v. Blaskic, IT-95-14-A, Judgment of 29 July 2004   214
Prosecutor v. Furundžija, IT-95-17/1, Decision of the Appeals Chamber of 21 July 2000, ILR 121, 213   213, 346, 398
Prosecutor v. Tadic, IT-94-1-A, Judgment of 15 July 1999   93, 214

European Court/Commission of Human Rights

Agim Behrami and Bekir Behrami v. France and Ruzhdi Saramati v. France, Germany and Norway, Application Nos. 71412/01 and 78166/01, Grand Chamber, Decision on Admissibility of 2 May 2007, ILR 133, 1   223–4, 411
Al-Adsani v. United Kingdom, Application No. 35763/97, Grand Chamber, Judgment of 21 November 2001, ECHR 2001-XI, 79   38, 248, 398
Al-Saadoon and Mufdhi v. United Kingdom, Decision on Admissibility of 30 June 2009, Application No. 61498/08, not yet reported   412
Al-Saadoon and Mufdhi v. United Kingdom, Merits and Just Satisfaction, Judgment of 2 March 2010, Application No. 61498/08, not yet reported   314, 400
Assanidze v. Georgia, Grand Chamber, Judgment of 8 April 2004, ECHR 2004-II, 221   412
Bankovic v. Belgium and others, Grand Chamber, Decision of 12 December 2001, ECHR 2001-XII, 334   409
Chahal v. United Kingdom, Judgment of 15 November 1996, ECHR 1996-V, 1831   400
Cyprus v. Turkey, Grand Chamber, Judgment of 10 May 2001, ECHR 2001-IV, 1   406

Drozd and Janousek v. France and Spain, Judgment of 26 June 1992, Series A, No. 240   240, 407
Golder Case, Judgment of 21 February 1975, Series A, No. 18   58
Ilascu v. Moldova and Russia, Application No. 48787/99, Judgment of the Grand Chamber of 8 July 2004, ECHR 2004-VII, 179   284, 314, 406, 410–11
Issa v. Turkey, Application No. 31812/96, Judgment of 16 November 2004, not reported   412
Loizidou v. Turkey, Preliminary Objections, Judgment of 23 March 1995, Series A, No. 310   407
Loizidou v. Turkey, Merits, Judgment of 18 December 1996, ECHR 1996-VI, 2216   408
Mamatkulov and Askarov v. Turkey, Grand Chamber, Judgment of 4 February 2005, ECHR 2005-II, 293   314, 401
Medvedyev v. France, Judgment of the Grand Chamber of 29 March 2010, Application No. 3394/03, not yet reported   314
Rasheed Haje Tugar v. Italy, Application No. 22869/93, Decision on Admissibility of 18 October 1995, unpublished   130
Ribitsch v. Austria, Judgment of 4 December 1995, Series A, No. 336   218
Saadi v. Italy, Grand Chamber, Judgment of 28 February 2008, Application No. 37201/06, not yet reported   394, 400, 403
Saddam Hussein v. Albania, Bulgaria, Croatia, Czech Republic, Denmark, Estonia, Hungary, Iceland, Ireland, Italy, Latvia, Lithuania, the Netherlands, Poland, Portugal, Romania, Slovakia, Slovenia, Turkey, Ukraine and the United Kingdom, Application No. 23276/04, Decision of Admissibility of 14 March 2006, unpublished   207, 314, 413
Soering Case, Decision of 26 January 1989, Series A, No. 161   224, 314, 395–6, 398
Stocké v. Federal Republic of Germany, Opinion of the Commission as expressed in the Commission's Report of 12 October 1989, Series A, No. 199   407
Tomasi v. France, Judgment of 27 August 1992, Series A, No. 241-A   218

Inter-American Court of Human Rights

Miguel Castro Prison (Peru), Merits, Reparations and Costs, I-ACHR, Series C, No. 160, Judgment of 25 November 2006   325

Myrna Mack Chang v. Guatemala, Merits, Reparations and Costs,
　　I-ACHR, Series C, No. 101, Judgment of 25 November 2003　　324
Velásquez Rodríguez v. Honduras, Judgment of 29 July 1988, Series C,
　　No. 4　　246

GATT/WTO

Mexico – Tax Measures on Soft Drinks and Other Beverages, WT/
　　DS308/AB/R (6 March 2006)　　152
Turkey – Restrictions on Imports of Textile and Clothing Products,
　　WT/DS34/R (31 May 1999)　　152, 313
United States – Import Prohibition of Certain Shrimp and Shrimp
　　Products (Complaint by the United States), Decision of 12 October
　　1998, WT/DS58/AB/4　　71, 75

UN Committee Against Torture

Individual Complaint of Mr Ahmed Hussein Mustafa Kamil Agiza,
　　Decision of 24 May 2005, UN Doc. CAT/C/34/D/233/2003　　316, 401

Domestic courts

Canada

Supreme Court

Canada (Justice) v. Khadr, Judgment of 23 May 2008, 2008 SCC
　　28　　125–6, 167, 248, 317, 414
Karlheinz Schreiber v. Minister of Justice, Decision of 11 December
　　2008, leave to appeal denied, Docket No. 32754　　168
R v. Hape, Judgment of 7 June 2007, [2007] 2 SCR 292, 2007 SCC
　　26　　166–7, 317, 414
Suresh v. Canada (Minister of Citizenship and Immigration), Canada,
　　Judgment of 11 January 2002, ILR 124, 343　　398–9

Federal Court of Appeal

Amnesty International Canada and British Columbia Civil Liberties
　　Association v. Chief of the Defence Staff for the Canadian Forces,
　　Minister of National Defence and the Attorney-General of Canada,
　　Federal Court of Appeal, 2008 FCA 401, Judgment of 17 December
　　2008　　127

Germany

Federal Constitutional Court (Bundesverfassungsgericht)

BVerfGE 75, 1   154, 278
BVerfGE 109, 13 = ILDC 10 (DE 2003)   165, 317
BVerfGE 112, 1 (an English translation is available at www.bverfg.de/en/decisions/rs20041026_2bvr095500en.html, last visited 1 November 2010)   154–5, 344

Federal Administrative Court (Bundesverwaltungsgericht)

BVerwG, 2 WD 12.04, Judgment of 21 June 2005 = ILDC 483 (DE 2005)   118–19, 198, 317, 382

Greece

Multi-Member Court of Levadia, Case No. 137/1997, Judgment of 30 October 1997, reprinted in *Revue Hellénique de Droit International* 50 (1997), p. 595   37, 155–6

Ireland

Edward Horgan v. An Taoiseach and others, Application for Declaratory Relief, High Court (2003 No. 3739P) [2003] 2 IR 468; [2003] IEHC 64; ILDC 486 (IE 2003)   116, 192

Italy

Federal Republic of Germany v. Giovanni Mantelli, Court of Cassation, Order No. 14201 = ILDC 1037 (IT 2008)   156, 352
Ferrini v. Federal Republic of Germany, Court of Cassation (Cass. Sez. Un. 5044/04) = ILDC 19 (IT 2004)   36, 38, 156, 329, 344, 352

New Zealand

Attorney-General v. Ahmed Zaoui, Supreme Court, Judgment of 21 June 2005, SC CIV 19/2004, [2005] NZSC 38   398

Switzerland

Federal Court of Justice, 1B_87/2007, reprinted in *Europäische Grundrechte-Zeitschrift* 34 (2007), p. 571   164, 317
Federal Court of Justice, Mikhail Khodorkovski v. Ministère public de la Conféderation, 1A.29/2007/col., Decision of 13 August 2007, unpublished, available at http://jumpcgi.bger.ch/cgi-bin/JumpCGI?id=13.08.2007_1A.29/2007   166

Federal Court of Justice, P1201/81/fs, Judgment of 15 July 1982, reprinted in *Europäische Grundrechte-Zeitschrift* 10 (1983), pp. 435 *et seq.*   164

United Kingdom

A (FC) and others (FC) v. Secretary of State for the Home Department and others, House of Lords [2005] UKHL 71 = ILDC 363 (UK 2005)   156, 329, 344

R (on the Application of Binyan Mohammed) v. Secretary of State for Foreign and Commonwealth Affairs, High Court of Justice, Judgment of 21 August 2008 [2008] EWHC 2048 (Admin)   157, 317, 404

United States

Anglo-Chinese Shipping Company Ltd v. United States, Court of Claims, Decision of 11 January 1955, ILR 22, 982   291

Abbreviations

Note: all abbreviations used in the study are included here save those which are document symbols of the United Nations or other international organisations.

ACP	African, Caribbean and Pacific Group of States
Add.	Addendum
APM	anti-personnel mines
ASR	Articles on State Responsibility
AWACS	Airborne Warning and Control System
BVerfG	Bundesverfassungsgericht (German Federal Constitutional Court)
BVerwG	Bundesverwaltungsgericht (German Federal Administrative Court)
CAT	UN Convention Against Torture
CCPR	Covenant on Civil and Political Rights
CFSP	Common Foreign and Security Policy (EU)
col.	column
CPA	Coalition Provisional Authority
CSIS	Canadian Security and Intelligence Service
CTS	Canadian Treaty Series
DARIO	Draft Articles on the Responsibility of International Organizations
DRC	Democratic Republic of the Congo
DSU	Dispute Settlement Understanding
ECHR	European Convention for the Protection of Human Rights and Fundamental Freedoms / *Reports of the European Court of Human Rights* (only in footnotes)
ECOSOC	Economic and Social Council

ECtHR	European Court of Human Rights
ETS	*European Treaty Series*
EuGRZ	*Europäische Grundrechte-Zeitschrift*
EWHC	England and Wales High Court
FAA	Foreign Assistance Act (US)
FCO	Foreign and Commonwealth Office (UK)
GATT	General Agreement on Tariffs and Trade
ICC	International Criminal Court
ICCPR	International Covenant on Civil and Political Rights
ICJ	International Court of Justice
ICRC	International Committee of the Red Cross
ICTR	International Criminal Tribunal for Rwanda
ICTY	International Criminal Tribunal for the former Yugoslavia
ILC	International Law Commission
ILDC	*Oxford Reports on International Law in Domestic Courts*
ILM	*International Legal Materials*
ILR	*International Law Reports*
Inter-AmCtHR	Inter-American Court of Human Rights
ITLOS	International Tribunal for the Law of the Sea
JZ	*Juristen-Zeitung*
MRT	Moldovan Republic of Transdniestria
NATO	North-Atlantic Treaty Organization
NGO	non-governmental organisation
NPT	Non-Proliferation Treaty
OAS	Organization of American States
OAU	Organization of African Unity
OJ	*Official Journal*
OPEC	Organization of Petroleum Exporting Countries
PCIJ	Permanent Court of International Justice
PRC	People's Republic of China
R2P	'responsibility to protect'
Res.	Resolution
RIAA	*Reports of International Arbitral Awards*
SALW	small arms and light weapons
SCC	Supreme Court of Canada
SCR	*Reports of the Decisions of the Supreme Court* (Canada)
sec.	section
SOFA	Status of Forces Agreement

UNCLOS	United Nations Convention on the Law of the Sea
UNESCO	United Nations Educational, Scientific and Cultural Organization
UNTS	*United Nations Treaty Series*
USC	United States Code
Vol.	Volume
WTO	World Trade Organization
YBILC	*Yearbook of the International Law Commission*

1 Introduction

1 The growing role of complicity in international law

This is a book about State responsibility for complicity. It addresses the question whether States which aid or assist other States in the commission of wrongful acts incur responsibility for their support. For a long time, this issue did not receive much attention. This has changed in recent years. The most prominent example of a situation in which complicity played a role is probably the 2003 US-led war on Iraq. While the US and the UK were the main actors in this conflict, they enjoyed support from a 'coalition' of forty-seven States which furnished assistance to varying degrees. In addition, beyond the coalition, there were States such as Germany which officially refused to participate in the attacks, but which nonetheless gave support behind the scenes. How should the contributions of Germany and other European States, which consisted in, for example, the granting of overflight rights or landing and refuelling facilities, be assessed?

Various European States also participated in the programme of so-called 'extraordinary renditions'. This programme involved the transfer of alleged terrorists to third States where they were then subjected to forceful means of interrogation.[1] If two States cooperate directly in the interrogation of a detained individual and violate human rights in so doing, they carry equal responsibility. But is a State that has allowed the transfer of the detainee through its airspace responsible, and, if so, to what extent? And what can be said of a State which more or less regularly receives information from

---

[1] See Georg Nolte, 'With a Little Help from My Friends', *Frankfurter Allgemeine Zeitung*, 17 December 2005, p. 8.

interrogations in which torture or other degrading treatment have occurred?[2]

While the Iraq war and the programme of 'extraordinary renditions' were the most conspicuous cases in which the issue of helping States arose in the last few years, there are further examples from international practice which show that complicity is an issue of general concern for international law. It played a role, for example, in the 2008 war between Russia and Georgia when Russia accused the US of flying 2,000 Georgian soldiers from Iraq to the theatre of conflict in Georgia.[3] In the 2009 conflict in Sri Lanka, India was accused of assisting Sri Lanka's alleged violations of international humanitarian law.[4] In 2008, States were alarmed about possible responsibility arising out of cooperation in the context of multinational military operations when they negotiated a new international agreement on cluster munitions.[5] The matter of complicity also arose in discussions about the Ilisu Dam, a massive infrastructure project in Turkey. Once completed, the dam was expected to contribute to manifold violations of international law (with respect to the rights of neighbouring States, minority rights and environmental law). The European States which Turkey initially approached for support eventually abandoned the project.[6] The list of examples could be extended. These examples demonstrate the truth of what James Crawford has observed: '[I]n practice States hunt in packs but like to be seen as hunting alone.'[7]

---

[2] See, on the one hand, European Commission for Democracy Through Law (Venice Commission), 'Opinion on the International Legal Obligations of Council of Europe Member States in Respect of Secret Detention Facilities and Inter-State Transfer of Detainees', Opinion No. 363/2005 of 17 March 2006, CDL-AD(2006)009, and, on the other hand, UK House of Lords and House of Commons, Joint Committee on Human Rights, 'Allegations of UK Complicity in Torture', Twenty-Third Report of Session 2008–9, HL Paper 152, HC 230, published on 4 August 2009, para. 27.
[3] 'Russians March into Georgia', *The Guardian*, 11 August 2008, p. 1.
[4] 'India Accused of Complicity in Deaths of Sri Lankan Tamils', *The Times*, 1 June 2009, available at www.timesonline.co.uk/tol/news/world/asia/article6401557.ece (last visited 1 November 2010).
[5] 'Collateral Damage', *The Economist*, 13 December 2008, available at lexisnexis.
[6] On the international legal issues in the case, see Georg Nolte and Helmut Philipp Aust, 'Equivocal Helpers – Complicit States, Mixed Messages, and International Law', *International and Comparative Law Quarterly* 58 (2009), pp. 1–30, at pp. 10–12.
[7] James Crawford, 'Responsibility of States and Non-State Actors', Speech at the Biennial Conference of the Japanese Association of International Law, Tokyo, 14 May 2005, manuscript on file with the author, p. 13.

Today, international law provides for the responsibility of States which aid or assist in the commission of internationally wrongful acts. This much is provided for by Article 16 of the International Law Commission's Articles on State Responsibility (ASR):

A State which aids or assists another State in the commission of an internationally wrongful act by the latter is internationally responsible for doing so if:

(a) that State does so with knowledge of the circumstances of the internationally wrongful act; and
(b) the act would be internationally wrongful if committed by that State.[8]

In 2007, the International Court of Justice (ICJ) recognised that this provision reflects customary international law.[9] However, the exact contours of this rule remain unclear. This lack of clarity relates, first of all, to the criteria under which a helping State can be held responsible. What kind of support is required in order to render a State responsible under Article 16 ASR? What need the helping State know? Is it necessary that the helping State somehow wishes to further the ends of the main actor? It is also a difficult matter to determine how responsibility should be divided between the main actor and the complicit State. Furthermore, we need to ask ourselves if the importance of the rule which was violated by the wrongful act to which support was rendered has an influence on the responsibility of the helping State. In other words, is it relevant whether the act for which support is given is a breach of a merely technical norm, for example in international trade law, or is a violation of norms more central to international law such as the prohibition of genocide? We also need to consider how Article 16 ASR relates to other rules within the law of State responsibility. In addition, we will need to consider rules beyond this field of international law. Article 16 ASR is by no means the only rule which addresses conduct in which one State helps another.

---

[8] Responsibility of States for Internationally Wrongful Acts, annexed to UN Doc. A/RES/56/83 of 12 December 2001.
[9] ICJ, *Case Concerning the Application of the Convention on the Prevention and Punishment of the Crime of Genocide*, Judgment, para. 419.

2 The approach of this book

This book aspires to present a coherent and systematic analysis of the problem of State complicity in international law.[10] As a preliminary step, it is necessary to obtain clarity about some conceptual issues. At first sight, Article 16 ASR appears to be a rather technical norm which should lend itself to application without much ado. However, a closer look reveals that Article 16 ASR is a complex provision which sits between various currents of the development of the international legal system. Article 16 ASR is also difficult to reconcile with certain conceptual parameters which underlie the law of State responsibility.

Accordingly, before this book turns to an analysis of customary international law and the interpretation of the rules on complicity, we will need to clear the ground in order to understand better what a major step the recognition of responsibility for complicity is for the international legal system. This conceptual analysis will be effected in two steps.

Following this introductory chapter, Chapter 2 situates complicity within the traditional analytical framework of the contrast between 'bilateralism and community interest'.[11] This framework is initially a tempting conceptualisation for the subject of our study. It offers a narrative which begins with the traditional State-centred positivist international law, characterised pre-eminently by bilateral relationships.[12] Roberto Ago, the most influential international lawyer in the field of

---

[10] For other studies on the issue of complicity, see the two monographs by Maria Luisa Padelletti, *Pluralità di Stati Nel Fatto Illecito Internazionale* (Milan: Giuffrè, 1990); and Andreas Felder, *Die Beihilfe in der völkerrechtlichen Staatenverantwortlichkeit* (Zurich: Schulthess, 2007); as well as the following articles: Eckart Klein, 'Beihilfe zum Völkerrechtsdelikt', in Ingo von Münch (ed.), *Staatsrecht – Völkerrecht – Europarecht. Festschrift für Hans-Jürgen Schlochauer* (Berlin: de Gruyter, 1981), pp. 425–38; John Quigley, 'Complicity in International Law: A New Direction in the Law of State Responsibility', *British Year Book of International Law* 57 (1986), pp. 77–131; Bernhard Graefrath, 'Complicity in the Law of International Responsibility', *Revue Belge de Droit International* 29 (1996), pp. 370–80; Vaughan Lowe, 'Responsibility for the Conduct of Other States', *Kokusaiho Gaiko Zassi* 101 (2002), pp. 1–15; and Georg Nolte and Helmut Philipp Aust, 'Equivocal Helpers', pp. 1–30.

[11] Bruno Simma, 'From Bilateralism to Community Interest in International Law', *Recueil des Cours* 250 (1994-VI), pp. 217–384; Bruno Simma, 'Bilateralism and Community Interest in the Law of State Responsibility', in Yoram Dinstein (ed.), *International Law at a Time of Perplexity – Essays in Honour of Shabtai Rosenne* (Dordrecht: Nijhoff, 1989), pp. 821–44.

[12] On the traditional bilateralism of the law of State responsibility, see James Crawford, *International Law as an Open System* (London: Cameron May, 2002), p. 29; Georg Nolte, 'From Dionisio Anzilotti to Roberto Ago: The Classical International

State responsibility in the twentieth century, stated in 1939 that it was exactly this bilateral structure of international law which made it impossible to think of responsibility for complicity.[13] With the advent of a more community-oriented international law after the Second World War, these constraints appeared to have been pushed aside. We will show, however, that this juxtaposition of the old bilateral and the new community-oriented law goes only part of the way towards illuminating the subject of our study: the allegedly bilateralist old law provided, for example, for rules on the conduct of neutral States in times of war,[14] an issue closely related to questions of complicity. And the theories of the new, community-oriented law fail to provide convincing reasons why complicity is no longer to be tolerated in international law. Nonetheless, the dichotomy between the bilateral and the community-oriented sides of the law provides a useful backdrop against which complicity can be analysed.

We will explore a different theoretical perspective in Chapter 3, which focuses on the international rule of law. This challenging notion[15] is particularly relevant for the problem of complicity for a number of reasons. First, we consider the law of State responsibility to be a *conditio sine qua non* for the international rule of law. State responsibility lies at the heart of the international legal system, as this field of law provides for rules which should generally come to apply once a 'primary' rule of international law has been violated – the primary rules being the substantive obligations in international law.[16] Although the distinction between 'primary' and 'secondary' rules is not undisputed in international law,[17] we hold it to be a useful heuristic device to

---

Law of State Responsibility and the Traditional Primacy of a Bilateral Conception of Inter-State Relations', *European Journal of International Law* 13 (2002), pp. 1083–98.

[13] Roberto Ago, 'Le délit international', *Recueil des Cours* 68 (1939-II), pp. 415–554, at p. 523.

[14] This holds true for both natural law currents as well as the more positivist tendencies of nineteenth-century international law: see Hugo Grotius, *De jure belli ac pacis libri tres*, translated by Francis W. Kelsey, No. 3 of 'The Classics of International Law', Vol. 2 (Oxford: Clarendon Press, 1925), III, XVII, 3 (p. 786), on the one hand, and John Westlake, *International Law*, Part II, *War* (Cambridge: Cambridge University Press, 1907), pp. 179 *et seq.* on the other.

[15] On this notion, see Arthur Watts, 'The International Rule of Law', *German Yearbook of International Law* 36 (1993), pp. 15–45, at p. 16.

[16] Roberto Ago, 'Working Paper on State Responsibility', YBILC 1963, Vol. II, p. 251, at p. 253.

[17] See, e.g., the critique of Alexander Orakhelashvili, *Peremptory Norms in International Law* (Oxford: Oxford University Press, 2006), pp. 80 *et seq.*

understand what the law of State responsibility is, when it intervenes and what it entails.

A second difficult feature of Article 16 ASR is that it does not neatly fit the 'primary'/'secondary' dichotomy. There is general agreement that, before the adoption of the ASR, international law did not provide for a general rule against complicity.[18] Is it then possible to view Article 16 ASR as a secondary rule which does not provide a new international obligation? Without the rule embodied in Article 16 ASR, one might conclude that States would be largely free to help other States violate international law.

Thirdly, even supporters of the 'primary'/'secondary' distinction admit that this distinction has its limits and should not be applied categorically.[19] At this point, the concept of the international rule of law steps in and helps us to understand why a body of secondary rules can include a rule on complicity such as Article 16 ASR. We will develop the notion of the international rule of law in a sense which implies that the law must be capable of solving disputes and providing answers in concrete situations.[20] This relates to the way Hersch Lauterpacht conceived the international legal system to be materially complete.[21] This material completeness need not mean that there are ready-made rules for each and every conceivable factual problem. However, this completeness means that international law should be able to provide answers to the question of the lawfulness of a given conduct. While one way to arrive at this result is to have recourse to the *Lotus* principle, according to which everything which is not expressly forbidden is allowed,[22] it is submitted here that this principle can no longer provide convincing answers in cases where the interests of States clash.[23] It will

---

[18] ILC Commentary to the Articles on State Responsibility, reprinted in 'Report of the International Law Commission of the 53rd Session', UN Doc. A/56/10, at pp. 131 *et seq.*, Article 16, para. 2 (hereinafter 'ILC Commentary'); Christian Dominicé, 'Attribution of Conduct to Multiple States and the Implication of a State in the Act of Another State', in James Crawford, Alain Pellet and Simon Olleson (eds.), *The International Law of Responsibility* (Oxford: Oxford University Press, 2010), pp. 282–9, at p. 287.
[19] This holds true even for Roberto Ago himself, see his Statement at the 1519th Meeting of the ILC, YBILC 1978, Vol. I, p. 240, para. 27.
[20] Joseph Raz, 'The Rule of Law and Its Virtue', in Joseph Raz, *The Authority of Law – Essays on Law and Morality* (Oxford: Clarendon Press, 1979), pp. 210–29, at p. 213.
[21] Hersch Lauterpacht, *The Function of Law in the International Community* (Cambridge: Cambridge University Press, 1933), p. 86.
[22] PCIJ, *Lotus*, Judgment, Series A, No. 10, 18.
[23] ICJ, *Accordance with International Law of the Unilateral Declaration of Independence in Respect of Kosovo*, Advisory Opinion, declaration of Judge Simma, paras. 2 *et seq.*

be shown that, without a general rule on complicity, international law would not be able to strike a balance between two legitimate interests. On the one hand, States affected by wrongful acts have the legitimate interest that third States do not contribute to these wrongful acts and thus render the acts even more damaging. On the other hand, we have the interests of third States in knowing when and under what conditions international co-operation turns into complicity.

This connects, fourthly, with the view that the international rule of law does not exhaust itself in the affirmation that States should apply existing law.[24] If this were to be the sole content of the rule of law, it would be an empty notion and would mean rather 'rule *by* law'.[25] Accordingly, we understand the rule of law to mean that States must do more than merely comply with the law in the narrowest possible sense. The example of complicity makes it particularly clear what this entails: the existence of a rule on complicity in the ASR imposes on States 'more' responsibility than would be the case if the matter were considered only in light of the obligations stemming from 'primary' rules. From these considerations, we will not deduce the existence of a clear-cut rule on complicity. We will find, however, that the analysis of the subject of our study from the viewpoint of the international rule of law suggests that there probably *should* be rules on complicity.

We will then test the presumption just established and conduct an analysis of customary international law in Chapter 4. We will find that there is sufficient practice to speak of a general rule against complicity in the law of State responsibility. We will also be able to establish the necessary *opinio juris*.

Following this exercise, we can turn in Chapter 5 to the doctrinal questions we have already briefly mentioned: under what conditions will a helping State incur responsibility under Article 16 ASR? This will involve looking mainly at three issues: what forms of conduct are eligible to trigger responsibility for complicity? What is the requisite subjective element that the aiding State needs to fulfil? And, finally, what are we to make of the criterion included in Article 16(b) ASR that the assisting State needs to be bound itself by the rule the main actor has violated?

---

[24] See Vaughan Lowe, 'The Iraq Crisis: What Now?', *International and Comparative Law Quarterly* 52 (2003), pp. 859–71, at p. 863.
[25] Brian Z. Tamanaha, *On the Rule of Law – History, Politics, Theory* (Cambridge: Cambridge University Press, 2004), p. 92.

In Chapter 6, we will then discuss the legal consequences of complicity. This involves looking at the division of responsibility between the main actor and the helping State as well as the possibilities for bringing complicit States to court. Here, we are faced with particular problems. It is the established case law of the ICJ that the Court cannot adjudicate disputes in the absence of an 'indispensable third party'. Known as the *Monetary Gold* principle,[26] this principle could prevent many cases involving complicity from ever reaching the Court, as establishment of the responsibility of the complicit State necessarily involves passing judgment, albeit implicitly, on the conduct of the main actor.

In Chapter 7, we will also look at the impact of what is frequently called the regime of 'aggravated responsibility'[27] on issues of complicity. Whereas we are sceptical about any reasoning which deduces the existence of a rule against complicity from the concept of *jus cogens*, it is another matter to see how peremptory norms of international law impact upon the legal qualification of specific situations which involve complicity. Articles 40 and 41 ASR provide a special regime for situations which involve 'serious breaches of peremptory norms' under international law. In this chapter, we will see how Article 16 ASR is connected to the rules in this regime such as the special rule against aid or assistance after the fact which is included in Article 41(2) ASR. We will see how obligations of non-assistance connect with the concept of non-recognition in the same provision and the obligation of cooperation to bring serious breaches of peremptory norms to an end under Article 41(1) ASR. We shall also look at the relationship between complicity and the disputed issue of countermeasures in the collective interest (Article 54 ASR). Through an interconnected reading of these different rules and norms, we will show how international law provides for differentiated responses to State complicity depending on the seriousness of the breach of the law in question. Taken together, the rules of the law of State responsibility could make an important contribution to a further normative clarification of the as yet vague and controversial concept of the 'responsibility to protect'.[28] This is owed to the fact that the rules of

---

[26] ICJ, *Monetary Gold Removed from Rome in 1943*, Judgment, ICJ Rep. 1954, 19, 32; ICJ, *East Timor Case*, Judgment, ICJ Rep. 1995, 90, para. 35.
[27] Antonio Cassese, *International Law*, 2nd edn (Oxford: Oxford University Press, 2005), p. 262.
[28] Report of the International Commission on Intervention and State Sovereignty, 'The Responsibility to Protect', para. 1.22, available at www.iciss.ca/report-en.asp (last visited 1 November 2010).

the law of State responsibility help to define various thresholds for the enforcement of the community interest in international law.

Finally, we need to consider that international law also provides for special rules on complicity in individual subject areas such as the law of collective security, international humanitarian law and human rights law. Not all of these norms, as we will present in Chapter 8, address the issue of complicity directly. But obligations of prevention such as Article I of the 1948 Genocide Convention[29] or the principle of *non-refoulement* in human rights law may be functional equivalents to the rules on complicity. Although they approach the role of helping States in a different way to Article 16 ASR, in terms of substance they allow complicit States to be held responsible, albeit under a different heading. An example of such an approach can be found in the 2007 ruling of the ICJ in the *Genocide Convention* case. There, the Court could find neither direct responsibility of nor complicity by Serbia with the militia of the Republika Srpska which was directly responsible for the genocide in Srebrenica. The ICJ made use, however, of Article I of the Genocide Convention and its obligation to prevent genocide from occurring. In order to establish the responsibility of Serbia in regard to this obligation, the Court emphasised the level of support given by Serbia (i.e. the Federal Republic of Yugoslavia at the time) to the Republika Srpska.[30] Although the Court was not satisfied that the prerequisites for complicity were met in their own right, Serbia's support for the Republika Srpska played a crucial role in establishing responsibility under a different heading.

3 Clarifications

As this book is about State responsibility, it leaves out of consideration the responsibility of international organisations and other types of non-State actors. It should also be mentioned that the term 'complicity' is not meant to refer to criminal law from which the term originally stems. The term was initially used by the ILC for a first draft of the provision which later became Article 16 ASR.[31] The term was then

---

[29] Convention on the Prevention and Punishment of the Crime of Genocide of 9 December 1948, entered into force on 12 January 1951, 78 UNTS 277.
[30] ICJ, *Case Concerning the Application of the Convention on the Prevention and Punishment of the Crime of Genocide*, Judgment, paras. 430, 434.
[31] Roberto Ago, 'Seventh Report on State Responsibility', UN Doc. A/CN.4/307 and Add.1-2, YBILC 1978, Vol. II, Part One, p. 31, at p. 60.

abandoned because several members of the Commission considered it to be too close to criminal law. However, this has not prevented international lawyers from continuing to use the term for the situations covered by Article 16 ASR. We will do the same, if only for reasons of convenience in not having to refer each and every time to 'aid or assistance in the commission of an internationally wrongful act'. A further reason why we continue to use the term is that it allows us to describe situations without the necessity of having to determine whether the support in question fulfils the conditions of Article 16 ASR. To speak of a 'complicit State' will therefore not necessarily mean that the State in question incurs responsibility under Article 16 ASR. According to our concept of a diverse network of rules on complicity, the State may also incur responsibility under a different and more specific rule, for example under the Genocide Convention.

2 Complicity between bilateralism and community interest

Specific international rules do not exist in a vacuum. Rather, they are necessarily connected to the greater whole of the international legal system. This implies that new rules develop in a certain framework. Such a framework is often analysed with respect to the structure of the international legal system which is in place at a given time. A rule on responsibility for complicit States is no exception in this regard. In fact, the law of State responsibility is particularly characteristic of the prevailing general concept of international law because, as Pierre-Marie Dupuy has remarked, every epoch will project therein its concept of the relations between the subjects of international law, their acts and the community to which these actors belong.[1]

As was hinted at in the introduction, two different 'paradigms' are usually considered to be relevant for an analysis of the problem of complicity: the traditional bilateralism of international law and its alleged subsequent turn towards the protection of community interests.[2] The legal status of the rule embodied in Article 16 ASR is not yet conclusively settled. It is therefore important to gain an awareness of the conceptual significance of the provision and to consider how it fits into the current structure of the international legal order. In this chapter, we will be particularly interested in the way the two conflicting views on the structure of international law impact upon our problem: is it really the case that traditional bilateralism stands

---

[1] Pierre-Marie Dupuy, 'Le fait générateur de la responsabilité internationale', *Recueil des Cours* 188 (1984-V), pp. 9-134, at p. 24; see also Martti Koskenniemi, 'Doctrines of State Responsibility', in James Crawford, Alain Pellet and Simon Olleson (eds.), *The Law of International Responsibility* (Oxford: Oxford University Press, 2010), pp. 45-51, at pp. 45-6.
[2] Bruno Simma, 'From Bilateralism to Community Interest', p. 317.

in the way of imposing responsibility for complicity (section 1)? And to what extent has the turn towards community interest contributed to the recognition that complicity is no longer to be tolerated in international law (section 2)?

1 Complicity and the traditional bilateralism of international law

Ce qui paraît ... inconcevable en droit international, c'est toute forme de complicité, de participation, ou de provocation au délit. Le droit des gens, dans sa structure actuelle, ne saurait prévoir ces formes de considération commune de plusieurs sujets par rapport à un seul délit, qui apparaissent comme l'œuvre caractéristique de l'élaboration et de la nature du droit pénal étatique.[3]

With these words, Roberto Ago explained in his 1939 Hague lecture on *Le délit international* why international law could not provide for rules on complicity. This short passage not only underlines that the notion of complicity is of fairly recent origin in international law; it also shows that structural reasons prevented Ago from considering how multiple actors could be involved in the commission of a single wrongful act. This position is interesting as a historical curiosity: Ago was the Special Rapporteur of the ILC who first coined a Draft Article on complicity some forty years after his Hague lecture.[4] In addition, Ago's position has continued to be influential insofar as it has inspired a line of criticism running against the idea of imposing responsibility on complicit States: Eckart Klein, for example, criticised the work of the ILC on complicity in terms very similar to the position Ago held in 1939. In 1981, Klein argued that the imposition of responsibility for complicity would constitute a fundamental change in international law: never before was it necessary, he wrote, for third States to react to violations of international law committed by other States.[5]

---

[3] Roberto Ago, 'Le délit international', p. 523, translation by the author: 'Every form of complicity in, of participation in or instigation to a delict is inconceivable in international law. International law, with its current structure, cannot provide for these forms of the common consideration of a plurality of actors with respect to one individual delict. These forms appear to be characteristic results of the elaboration and nature of domestic criminal law.'

[4] Roberto Ago, 'Seventh Report on State Responsibility', UN Doc. A/CN.4/307 and Add.1-2, YBILC 1978, Vol. II, Part One, p. 31, at p. 60.

[5] Eckart Klein, 'Beihilfe', p. 434.

1.1 Traditional bilateralism

More than any other domain of international law, State responsibility is traditionally characterised by its orientation towards reciprocity and bilateralism.[6] The legal relations between a wrongdoer and an injured State were construed in a way which did not provide room for the inclusion of third actors which may have also impacted upon the given legal relationship. This was owed to the fact that influential authors such as Ago conceived of these relationships as offering a perfect symmetry: one State was violating the obligation it held *vis-à-vis* another State; thus an injury to the latter State materialised.[7] In order to hold a complicit State responsible, it would have been necessary for there to be an explicit obligation incumbent upon the complicit State requiring that no aid or assistance should be given to wrongful conduct. As international law did not provide for such an obligation, it was impossible to provide for the responsibility of the complicit State. At least this was the construction which underlay the remarks Ago made in his 1939 lecture and which inspired commentators such as Klein. This line of thought also continued to dominate the thinking of Special Rapporteur Willem Riphagen in the ILC, the direct successor to Ago. Very much concerned with conceptual and systematic clarity, Riphagen was at pains to show how a secondary rule – which was by definition not meant to impose additional obligations upon States[8] – could be understood in a way which

---

[6] Dionisio Anzilotti, *Lehrbuch des Völkerrechts*, Vol. 1, *Einführung – Allgemeine Lehren* (Berlin/Leipzig: de Gruyter, 1929), p. 361; Franz von Liszt, *Das Völkerrecht systematisch dargestellt*, 3rd edn (Berlin: Haering, 1904), p. 185; Karl Strupp, *Das völkerrechtliche Delikt (= Handbuch des Völkerrechts, Dritter Band, Erste Abteilung a)* (Stuttgart: Kohlhammer, 1920), pp. 14 *et seq.*; Lassa Oppenheim, *International Law – A Treatise*, Vol. I, *Peace*, 2nd edn (London: Longmans, 1912), pp. 206 *et seq.*; for a different position, see Johann Caspar Bluntschli, *Das moderne Völkerrecht der civilisirten Staaten als Rechtsbuch dargestellt* (Nördlingen: C. H. Beck, 1868), § 471; for contemporary assessments, see Georg Nolte, 'From Dionisio Anzilotti', pp. 1083 *et seq.*; Martti Koskenniemi, 'Solidarity Measures: State Responsibility as a New International Order?', *British Year Book of International Law* 72 (2001), pp. 337–56, at p. 340.
[7] Roberto Ago, 'Le délit international', p. 433; Roberto Ago, 'Second Report on State Responsibility', UN Doc. A/CN.4/233, YBILC 1970, Vol. II, Part One, p. 177, at p. 192.
[8] James Crawford, 'Introduction', in James Crawford (ed.), *The International Law Commission's Articles on State Responsibility, Introduction, Text and Commentaries* (Cambridge: Cambridge University Press, 2002), pp. 1–60, at pp. 14–16; Eric David, 'Primary and Secondary Rules', in James Crawford, Alain Pellet and Simon Olleson (eds.), *The Law of International Responsibility* (Oxford: Oxford University Press, 2010), pp. 27–33, at pp. 27–8.

provided for the responsibility of third States aiding or assisting a wrongdoer.[9]

Ago's considerations in his Hague lecture shed further light on this issue. He distinguished between two different forms of legal relationships in international law. Among the first category, he counted the creation of legal obligations. These productive factors of international law would have a systemic effect and would thus exceed the bilateral framework of legal relations between pairs of two States.[10] On the other hand, there would be intersubjective relations between States, amongst which he classified delictual relations. With respect to the latter category, he remarked that wrongful acts (delicts and torts, as he called them) would not have a function with respect to the organisation of the international legal system. Rather, they would have a purely intersubjective character.[11]

Ago further developed this thought: the notion of a 'tort' would be that a legal obligation has been violated. In other words, he said, the subjective right of another legal person has been infringed.[12] Ago did not change his view on this when he became Special Rapporteur on State responsibility for the ILC. In his second report, he held that 'it seems perfectly legitimate in international law to regard the idea of the breach of an obligation as the exact equivalent of the idea of the impairment of the subjective rights of others'.[13]

In this perspective, the problem with respect to complicity becomes apparent: if every legal obligation is a strict mirror image of a subjective right of another legal person, then responsibility for complicity would presuppose a right or some form of legal interest of States not to be harmed by the conduct of complicit States. It is thus this very basic notion of a mirror image between obligations and rights which gives rise to the conceptual problems with complicity in Ago's early works

---

[9] Cf Willem Riphagen, 'Preliminary Report on the Content, Forms and Degrees of International Responsibility', UN Doc. A/CN.4/330, YBILC 1980, Vol. II, Part One, p. 107, paras. 71 et seq.

[10] Cf also Heinrich Triepel, Völkerrecht und Landesrecht (Leipzig: Hirschfeld, 1899), p. 63; Georges Scelle, Précis de droit des gens – Principes et systématique, Vol. I, Introduction – Le milieu intersocial (Paris: Recueil Sirey, 1932), p. 52.

[11] Roberto Ago, 'Le délit international', p. 431.

[12] Ibid., p. 433.

[13] Roberto Ago, 'Second Report on State Responsibility', UN Doc. A/CN.4/233, YBILC 1970, Vol. II, Part One, p. 177, at p. 192.

on State responsibility. His position is representative of the classic approach to this field.[14]

For the purpose of our study, we need not indulge in lengthy discussions of the general structure of the international legal system and how it has changed over time. Structural arguments are always problematic. They are contingent upon the time-frame within which they were originally conceived and therefore have only limited lasting relevance. The structure of international law is always determined by the rules which are in force at a given time. Arguments which rely too heavily on 'the structure' of international law should thus always be assessed cautiously.[15] We should also note that apparently in 2001 the ILC did not consider such structural arguments as standing in the way of a provision on the responsibility of complicit States. Nevertheless, the considerations of Ago, Klein and Riphagen may help us to better understand why the imposition of responsibility for complicity is a relatively recent phenomenon in international law.

1.2 *Third States and the law of neutrality*

At the same time, we should not accept these findings on the bilateral structure in an unconditional manner: is it really the case that the traditional bilateralism of international law stood in the way of imposing responsibility on complicit States? A prominent counter-example could be the law of neutrality as it has developed over the centuries. It is not intended to present the rules on neutrality as direct forerunners to a rule on complicity. However, they touched upon a related issue: by regulating how third parties had to position themselves in an ongoing conflict, they also defined whether or not assistance to one side of the conflict was permitted. We will see in the immediately following passages that the understanding of what constituted permissible forms of participation in war changed over the centuries.

---

[14] See, e.g., PCIJ, *Phosphates in Morocco*, Judgment, Series A/B, No. 74, 10, at 28; Dionisio Anzilotti, *Lehrbuch des Völkerrechts*, p. 362; Karl Strupp, *Das völkerrechtliche Delikt*, pp. 15–16; see, however, Franz von Liszt, *Das Völkerrecht*, p. 185.

[15] Théodore Christakis, 'L'obligation de non-reconnaissance des situations créés par le recours illicite à la force ou d'autres actes enfreignant des règles fondamentales', in Christian Tomuschat and Jean-Marc Thouvenin (eds.), *The Fundamental Rules of the International Legal Order – Jus Cogens and Obligations Erga Omnes* (Leiden: Nijhoff, 2006), pp. 127–66, at p. 131.

If we wish to look for a historical antecedent to a rule on complicity, the law of neutrality comes as close as it gets. For most of the history of international law, there was no separate field of the law of State responsibility.[16] Rather, as Christian Tomuschat has found,

> [I]n former centuries the attention of legal writers was generally focused on the most extreme form of conflict between States, namely war, while significantly less interest was paid to the forms and modes of settlement of conflicts of lower intensity, deriving from non-observance of norms lacking a specific political dimension.[17]

From this perspective, it makes sense to briefly present the traditional rules on neutrality in order to test the alleged incompatibility of responsibility for complicity with the traditional structure of international law.[18]

At the outset, it should be noted that it is problematic to refer to 'the' law of neutrality. Its development has a long history which stretches back across the centuries and, more importantly, was constantly torn between two different politico-legal outlooks. Scholars leaning towards just war theory tended to limit the freedom of third States to choose freely between a status of neutrality and the possibility of siding with one party to a conflict. Positivist writers, on the other hand, were inclined to put more emphasis on State voluntarism. They considered it the natural right of States to decide whether or not they wished to participate in a given conflict. In the following, we can only present some snapshots of the development of the law of neutrality, which are, however, representative for the larger picture of international lawyers grappling with the position of third States in situations of armed conflict.

1.2.1 Just war theory and beyond

The most important contribution of just war theory to the law of neutrality was made by Hugo Grotius.[19] He distinguished between the party with a good cause for war and the one without: 'it is the duty of

---

[16] On early doctrines, see Martti Koskenniemi, 'Doctrines', pp. 47–8.
[17] Christian Tomuschat, 'International Law: Ensuring the Survival of Mankind on the Eve of a New Century: General Course on Public International Law', *Recueil des Cours* 281 (1999), pp. 9–438, at p. 269.
[18] Cf also Vaughan Lowe, 'Responsibility', p. 13.
[19] Cf Hersch Lauterpacht, 'The Grotian Tradition in International Law', *British Year Book of International Law* 23 (1946), pp. 1–53, at p. 38.

those who keep out of a war to do nothing whereby he who supports a wicked cause may be rendered more powerful, or whereby the movements of him who wages a just war may be hampered'.[20] Grotius is thus an example of the continuing relevance of just war doctrine for our subject matter in the seventeenth century. This is so despite the works of writers such as Jean Bodin, Balthazar Ayala and Alberico Gentili. These scholars had all paved the way towards a more formal understanding of war, namely, the understanding that war was to be regarded as just when it was waged between sovereigns with the authority to do so.[21] Nonetheless, in Grotius' position we see that neutrality as a concept, which is based on equal treatment between the different parties to a conflict, was hard to reconcile with just war theory.[22]

In some points similar to Grotius was the position of Emer de Vattel whose work marked a turning point from natural law theories to positivism. In his *Le droit des gens* of 1758, he wrote that it would be permissible to assist in every conceivable manner a nation which waged a just war. In some circumstances, such assistance could be an obligation. However, it was not permissible to help a nation waging an unjust war.[23] Vattel is expanding his understanding of assistance in the context of neutrality to more general lines of thought on the problem of assisting wrongdoers. He continues to note that to aid the 'unjust party' would mean participating in its injustice.[24] Vattel's analysis was very subtle with respect to the different relationships that would ensue from the assistance one State is giving to another. For example, he analysed the relationship between a State and those States assisting the former's enemy in a way which distinguished between those which remained impartial, those which furnished only limited forms of support and those which fully joined the aggressor.[25] The latter States would constitute enemies of the State which was attacked.[26] With respect to the

---

[20] Hugo Grotius, *De jure belli ac pacis*, III, XVII, 3 (p. 786).
[21] On Gentili in particular see Mary Ellen O'Connell, *The Power and Purpose of International Law – Insights from the Theory and Practice of Enforcement* (Oxford: Oxford University Press, 2008), pp. 25–6.
[22] Stefan Oeter, 'Ursprünge der Neutralität. Die Herausbildung des Instituts der Neutralität im Völkerrecht der frühen Neuzeit', *Zeitschrift für ausländisches öffentliches Recht und Völkerrecht* 48 (1988), pp. 447–88, at p. 465.
[23] Emer de Vattel, *Le droit des gens ou principes de la loi naturelle appliqués à la conduite et aux affaires des Nations et de Souverains*, Classics of International Law, ed. by James Brown Scott (Washington, DC: Carnegie Endowment for International Peace, 1916) (originally published in 1758), Vol. III, § 83.
[24] Ibid. [25] Ibid., § 97. [26] Ibid., § 98.

regime of neutrality, Vattel was clear that a State that wished to remain neutral had to be impartial towards both parties to the conflict.[27]

How can this variegated position be reconciled with the above-mentioned position that demanded assistance to the party waging a just war? Vattel construes a right to remain neutral for two reasons. First, the justness of the cause may not be evident.[28] In doubtful cases, a State would be entitled to suspend its judgment and to remain out of the conflict. Secondly, even if a State arrived at a judgment as to which side had the just cause, it could still decide whether or not it wished to become involved in the conflict.[29] This is a somewhat paradoxical position since it very much calls into question the obligation to assist the party to a conflict which wages a just war.[30] In its paradoxical aspects, the position of Emer de Vattel may, however, be proof of the change which occurred in international law at the time.[31] While just war theory was still, at least in a rhetorical way, prevalent, the *jus ad bellum* was about to change significantly, i.e., in the direction of the freedom of States to use armed force in international relations.[32] Vattel's natural law framework 'simply evaporated', as Philip Allott put it.[33]

That this framework was already standing on shaky ground was shown by the work of Cornelius van Bynkershoek whose treatise on international law was published a good twenty years earlier than Vattel's, but whose presentation of the law of neutrality was considered by Lassa Oppenheim to be far superior to Vattel's.[34] Bynkershoek was equally torn between a reaffirmation of just war principles and an acknowledgment that there existed a state of neutrality for States which he called '*non hostes*'.[35] Bynkershoek maintained that the justice or injustice of war does

---

[27] Ibid., § 104.
[28] See also Hugo Grotius, *De jure belli ac pacis libri tres*, II, I (p. 557).
[29] Emer de Vattel, *Le droit des gens*, Vol. III, § 106.
[30] This may be due to the fact that Vattel was not always making a clear distinction between law and morality, Dominique Gaurier, *Histoire du droit international* (Rennes: Presses universitaires de Rennes, 2005), p. 328.
[31] See also Stefan Oeter, 'Neutrality and Alliances', in *Le droit international de Vattel vu du XXIème siècle*, forthcoming, manuscript on file with the author, at p. 2.
[32] Hersch Lauterpacht, 'Grotian Tradition', p. 39.
[33] Philip Allott, *The Health of Nations – Society and Law Beyond the State* (Cambridge: Cambridge University Press, 2002), p. 416.
[34] Lassa Oppenheim, *International Law – A Treatise*, Vol. II, *War and Neutrality*, 2nd edn (London: Longmans, 1912), p. 351.
[35] Cornelius van Bynkershoek, *Quaestionum Juris Publici Libri Duo*, translated by Tenney Frank, No. 14 of 'The Classics of International Law', Vol. 2 (Oxford: Clarendon Press, 1930, originally published 1737), pp. 60 *et seq*.

not concern the neutral,[36] while he was equally determined to stipulate that no aid or assistance should be given to allies which pursue unjust causes by means of war.[37] Essential to his understanding of neutrality was that it could not be expected of States 'to sit in judgment between friends who may be fighting each other'.[38] In this regard, Bynkershoek was already foreshadowing the period which was to follow.[39]

1.2.2 Nineteenth-century positivism and the *liberté à la guerre*

The period following was characterised by a right to use force freely, the so-called *liberté à la guerre*:[40] 'The age of Aquinas had given way to the age of Clausewitz.'[41] In this respect, the 'classic' period of international law reached its apogee in the 'long nineteenth century',[42] which carried on well into the twentieth century and was brought to an end only by the First World War.

Of the freedom to resort to force, the rules on neutrality constitute the supreme example.[43] Hersch Lauterpacht called 'the unrestricted right of war ... the historical foundation of absolute neutrality'.[44] The spirit of the time becomes apparent in the writings of John Westlake, who viewed war essentially as a duel between sovereigns, which would, however, be enlightened by the principles of moral justice. To them, he did not ascribe a legal value. The positive law was largely unaffected by these remnants of just war theory.[45]

---

[36] *Ibid.*, p. 61.   [37] *Ibid.*, p. 63.   [38] *Ibid.*, p. 61.
[39] See further Wilhelm G. Grewe, *Epochen der Völkerrechtsgeschichte* (Baden-Baden: Nomos, 1984), pp. 435 *et seq.*; a further writer who should be mentioned in this regard is the Danish author, Martin Hübner, *ibid.*, pp. 439–40.
[40] Hersch Lauterpacht, 'Grotian Tradition', p. 39; Bardo Fassbender, 'Die Gegenwartskrise des völkerrechtlichen Gewaltverbots vor dem Hintergrund der geschichtlichen Entwicklung', *Europäische Grundrechte-Zeitschrift* 31 (2004), pp. 241–56, at p. 243; Nico Krisch, *Selbstverteidigung und kollektive Sicherheit* (Berlin: Springer, 2001), p. 27.
[41] Stephen C. Neff, *The Rights and Duties of Neutrals – A General History* (Manchester: Manchester University Press, 2000), p. 87.
[42] See Franz J. Bauer, *Das 'lange' 19. Jahrhundert – Profil einer Epoche* (Stuttgart: Reclam, 2004), pp. 24 *et seq.*
[43] Cf Ian Brownlie, *International Law and the Use of Force by States* (Oxford: Clarendon Press, 1963), p. 402.
[44] Hersch Lauterpacht, 'Neutrality and Collective Security', in Elihu Lauterpacht (ed.), *International Law Being the Collected Papers of Hersch Lauterpacht*, Vol. 5, *Disputes, War and Neutrality* (Cambridge: Cambridge University Press, 2005), pp. 611–31, at p. 623.
[45] See John Westlake, *International Law*, pp. 56 *et seq.*; see further Martti Koskenniemi, *The Gentle Civilizer of Nations – The Rise and Fall of International Law 1870–1960* (Cambridge: Cambridge University Press, 2002), pp. 85–6.

While the parties to a war were generally allowed to use all means at their disposal in order to achieve victory, it was recognised that they were barred from directing hostilities against bystanders. Those innocent third parties had obligations, too. They were under an obligation to abstain from the conflict. In addition, the duty of impartiality required them to treat all parties to the conflict even-handedly.[46] These rules are an expression of the understanding of war as a conflict which affected not only the belligerent parties, but the entire world, as Stephen C. Neff has argued.[47] An important change brought about in the period of classic international law was the move from a treaty-based neutrality to the regime of so-called institutional neutrality. This meant that, at the moment a war broke out, the non-participating States found themselves automatically having the status of neutrality.[48] However, neutrality was still considered to be a faculty and not an obligation. In accordance with the free right to wage war, States could decide whether or not to remain neutral in a conflict.[49] Neutrality was understood as the legal situation in which a peaceful State is left, as far as possible, unaffected by the hostilities which take place between the belligerents. The neutral State itself would abstain from any participation in or contribution to the dispute between the belligerent States, which would in turn observe a strict impartiality towards the neutral State.[50]

State practice and authors of this period emphasised this duty of strict impartiality.[51] This understanding of neutrality was also carried forward to the conventions on neutrality adopted at the Second Hague

---

[46] Lassa Oppenheim, *International Law*, Vol. II, *War and Neutrality*, pp. 378 *et seq.*; cf further Ian Brownlie, *Use of Force*, pp. 402–3.

[47] Stephen C. Neff, *War and the Law of Nations – A General History* (Cambridge: Cambridge University Press, 2005), p. 191.

[48] Franz von Liszt, *Das Völkerrecht*, p. 347; Fedor de Martens, *Traité de droit international, tome III*, traduit du russe par Alfred Léo (Paris: Marescqains, 1887), p. 313; Lassa Oppenheim, *International Law*, Vol. II, *War and Neutrality*, p. 362; see further Wilhelm G. Grewe, *Epochen*, p. 629; in practice this was not always easy to determine, cf the discussion on the subjective theories of war which required the intention of States to go to war, Ian Brownlie, *Use of Force*, pp. 26–7.

[49] Lassa Oppenheim, *International Law*, Vol. II, *War and Neutrality*, pp. 361–2; John Westlake, *International Law*, p. 161.

[50] Richard Kleen, *Lois et usages de la neutralité d'après le droit international conventionnel et coutumier des Etats civilisés*, Vol. 1, *Principes fondamentaux – Devoirs des neutres* (Paris: Chevalier-Marescq, 1898), p. 73.

[51] See, e.g., the treatise of the eminent Russian scholar and diplomat Fedor de Martens, *Traité de droit international*, pp. 326–7.

Peace Conference in 1907.[52] These conventions include fairly detailed rules on the rights and duties of neutral powers in respect of warfare on land and at sea.[53] The essence of this classic period of the law of neutrality[54] is its formal understanding of war. Being a duel between States no longer restrained by just war considerations,[55] States could decide whether or not they wished to enter a conflict. It is therefore not surprising that the law of neutrality 'achieved its highest pitch of development' at that time.[56] One should not, however, ridicule this period as the zenith of power politics.[57] While the parties to a conflict were permitted to fight each other with a free rein, they were not permitted to direct hostilities against bystanders. After the uncertainties of the just war period – who is the aggressor, who is the victim? – this was a welcome change and brought about relative stability and security for States which did not wish to be dragged into perilous conflicts.[58] August Wilhelm Heffter held in this regard that nothing would be as important for the existence of a 'moral community of States' than a clear and consistent understanding of neutrality.[59] And Johann Caspar Bluntschli called the institution of neutrality 'one of the most fruitful and useful accomplishments of modern international law'.[60] In this

---

[52] Hague Convention V of 18 October 1907 concerning the Rights and Duties of Neutral Powers and Persons in Case of War on Land, entered into force on 26 January 1910, reprinted in *American Journal of International Law* Supplement No. 2 (1908), pp. 117 *et seq.*; Hague Convention XIII of 18 October 1907 concerning the Rights and Duties of Neutral Powers and Persons in Naval War, entered into force on 26 January 1910, reprinted in *ibid.*, pp. 202 *et seq.*

[53] See Articles 1, 5, 7 and 11 of Hague Convention V and Articles 6, 7 of Hague Convention XIII.

[54] Rudolf L. Bindschedler, 'Neutrality, Concept and General Rules', in Rudolf Bernhardt (ed.), *Encyclopedia of Public International Law*, Vol. III, J–P (Amsterdam: Elsevier, 1997), pp. 549–53, at p. 550.

[55] But see Mary Ellen O'Connell, *Power and Purpose*, p. 39.

[56] Stephen C. Neff, *War and the Law of Nations*, p. 162.

[57] For a discussion of the beneficial effects of nineteenth-century positivism, see Ulrich Scheuner, 'Naturrechtliche Strömungen im heutigen Völkerrecht', *Zeitschrift für ausländisches öffentliches Recht und Völkerrecht* 13 (1950–1), pp. 556–619, at pp. 577 *et seq.*

[58] See also James J. Sheehan, *Kontinent der Gewalt – Europas langer Weg zum Frieden*, translated by Martin Richter (Bonn: Bundeszentrale für politische Bildung, 2008), pp. 18–19 on especially the second half of the nineteenth century as a time of relative peace and stability in Europe.

[59] August Wilhelm Heffter, *Europäisches Völkerrecht der Gegenwart auf den bisherigen Grundlagen*, 8th edn, edited by F. Heinrich Geffcken (Berlin: Schroeder, 1888), p. 315: 'sittliche Staatengemeinschaft'.

[60] Johann Caspar Bluntschli, *Das moderne Völkerrecht*, p. 403: 'eine der fruchtbarsten und nützlichsten Errungenschaften des neuen Völkerrechts'.

respect, he mentioned in particular the function of the law of neutrality as fostering international peace.[61]

1.2.3 Interim conclusions

The relationship between the laws of neutrality and international law's traditional bilateral structure is delicate. Interestingly, both currents – the more positivist one and the one leaning more to the side of just war theory – prescribed legal consequences for States which were not direct parties to a conflict. The latter imposed limits upon third States with respect to legitimate support and at times even envisaged duties to assist the party that is waging war with a just cause. The positivist perspective, with its emphasis on the *liberté à la guerre* and the highly developed 'institutional neutrality', also provided for automatic legal consequences for third parties in the case of war, namely, the loss of status as a neutral power should the State choose to assist either party to the conflict. The development of the rules pertaining to the law of neutrality thus shows that international law has a tradition of extending the reach of a given legal relationship beyond the parties immediately concerned.

Also, during the ascendancy of the so-called 'classic international law' in the nineteenth century, war was considered to trigger the creation of a new legal relationship, which took root not only as between the immediate parties to the conflict, but with respect to all (civilised[62]) States.[63] The content of this new legal relationship was different as between the parties to the conflict and neutral States. In order to retain this position and thus to retain the benefit of not turning into targets for belligerent measures, international law placed certain obligations of impartiality on these third States. If we compare the two forms of legal relationships which develop at the outbreak of war, we find that the relationship between the two belligerent parties is more intense and direct. In comparison, the legal bonds between the belligerents and neutral States are loose in character, at least as long as all sides abide by their respective obligations.

---

[61] Ibid., p. 44.
[62] On the differences between the 'European Public Law' and the state of affairs 'beyond the line', see Carl Schmitt, *Der Nomos der Erde im Völkerrecht des Jus Publicum Europaeum*, 4th edn (Berlin: Duncker & Humblot, 1997) (originally published 1950), p. 62.
[63] See Fedor de Martens, *Traité de droit international*, p. 314.

It is true that, in the structure of the individual obligations set out in the law of neutrality, new symmetries were established. As the law of neutrality was established on the level of what we today call primary rules, for example substantive obligations, new reciprocities came into being, and the perfect symmetry between a legal obligation on the one hand and the subjective right of another State on the other was not disturbed. At a deeper level, it is, however, necessary to realise that these new obligations could be set off by the autonomous decision of two States to go to war (or even of one State to attack another State[64]). As the 'institutional neutrality' commenced automatically at the beginning of hostilities, one bilateral relationship between two States was able to set off the creation of new legal relationships between other States. This process of triggering the development of new legal relationships challenges the idea which is frequently presented as traditional bilateralism. It could of course be objected that the regime of 'institutional neutrality' developed through the processes of customary law-making. Accordingly, State consent as required by voluntarists for the existence of legal norms was always present. However, the decision when the new legal relationships were to be created *in concreto* fell into the hands of 'others'. From the perspective of those States which wished to remain neutral in a given conflict, these were third States. This finding challenges the alleged incompatibility between responsibility for complicity and international law's traditional bilateral structure.

2 Complicity and the move beyond bilateralism

Just as it is frequently assumed that traditional bilateralism would rule out responsibility for complicity, so its introduction is viewed as some sort of by-product of the development of international law beyond its traditional bilateralist mindset.[65] The structural changes to the international legal order – whether they are termed the move 'from a law

---

[64] Cf Stephen C. Neff, *War and the Law of Nations*, pp. 178 *et seq.*
[65] See Astrid Epiney, 'Nachbarrechtliche Pflichten im internationalen Wasserrecht und Implikationen von Drittstaaten', *Archiv des Völkerrechts* 39 (2001), pp. 1–56, at p. 49; Bernhard Graefrath, 'Complicity', pp. 372, 378; Jessica Howard, 'Invoking State Responsibility for Aiding the Commission of International Crimes – Australia, the United States and East Timor', *Melbourne Journal of International Law* 2001, online edition, text accompanying notes 91 *et seq.*

of co-existence to a law of cooperation',[66] 'from bilateralism to community interest'[67] or find expression in theories of the 'constitutionalisation'[68] of the international legal order or the coming into existence of an 'international community'[69] – are well documented elsewhere.[70] The doctrinal phenomena described in these debates could potentially impact on the problem of complicit State behaviour in as much as they have challenged the 'every man for himself' attitude which has for long been ascribed to international law.[71] 'Cooperation', 'community interest', 'constitutionalisation' and the 'international community' – all these expressions appeal to notions of 'international solidarity', a term which is not unknown to international lawyers of previous times.[72] Solidarity strikes an immediate chord with the intuitive notion that

---

[66] Wolfgang Friedmann, *The Changing Structure of International Law* (London: Stevens, 1964), pp. 10–11 and 60 *et seq.*
[67] Bruno Simma, 'From Bilateralism to Community Interest', pp. 217 *et seq.*
[68] For an emphasis on the UN Charter, see Bardo Fassbender, 'The United Nations Charter as Constitution of the International Community', *Columbia Journal of Transnational Law* 36 (1998), pp. 529–619, at pp. 573 *et seq.*; Jochen Abr. Frowein, 'Konstitutionalisierung des Völkerrechts', *Berichte der Deutschen Gesellschaft für Völkerrecht* 39 (2000), pp. 427–45; for an emphasis on the value dimension of international constitutionalism, see Erika de Wet, 'The Emergence of International and Regional Value Systems as Manifestations of the Emerging International Constitutional Order', *Leiden Journal of International Law* 19 (2006), pp. 611–32; for the theory of compensatory constitutionalism, see Anne Peters, 'Compensatory Constitutionalism: The Function and Potential of Fundamental International Norms and Structures', *Leiden Journal of International Law* 19 (2006), pp. 579–610; for a focus on constitutional principles, see Thomas Kleinlein, *Konstitutionalisierung im Völkerrecht: Konstruktion und Elemente einer idealistischen Völkerrechtslehre* (Berlin: Springer, 2011, forthcoming).
[69] Christian Tomuschat, 'Die internationale Gemeinschaft', *Archiv des Völkerrechts* 33 (1995), pp. 1–20; Andreas L. Paulus, *Die internationale Gemeinschaft im Völkerrecht: eine Untersuchung zur Entwicklung des Völkerrechts im Zeitalter der Globalisierung* (Munich: C. H. Beck, 2001); Santiago Villalpando, *L'émergence de la communauté internationale dans la responsabilité des Etats* (Paris: Presses universitaires de France, 2005).
[70] For an overview, see Stefan Kadelbach and Thomas Kleinlein, 'International Law – A Constitution for Mankind? An Attempt at a Re-Appraisal with an Analysis of Constitutional Principles', *German Yearbook of International Law* 50 (2007), pp. 303–47.
[71] From two different perspectives, see Prosper Weil, 'Towards Relative Normativity in International Law?', *American Journal of International Law* 77 (1983), pp. 413–42, at p. 431; and Bruno Simma, 'From Bilateralism to Community Interest', p. 233.
[72] Walther Schücking, *Der Staatenverband der Haager Konferenzen* (Munich: Duncker & Humblot, 1912), p. 17; Nicolas Politis, 'Le problème des limitations de la souveraineté et la théorie de l'abus des droit dans les rapports internationaux', *Recueil des Cours* 6 (1925-I), pp. 1–121, at p. 6; on the 'solidarity school' among French international lawyers, see Martti Koskenniemi, *The Gentle Civilizer of Nations*, pp. 288 *et seq.*

international law should not tolerate complicit State behaviour.[73] In this sense, Bruno Simma commented on the inclusion of an obligation of non-assistance in the commission of 'international crimes'[74] as set out in the Draft Articles the ILC adopted in 1996:

> Obviously, to provide for such duties of 'third' States presupposes a higher degree of solidarity among the members of the international community than in case of the dispensing of rights which may then be exercised or not, according to factual expediency. Thus, the very existence of draft Article 53 is a remarkable victory of community interest over bilateralist reflexes nowhere more profoundly entrenched than in the field of State responsibility.[75]

As a matter of general analysis of the development of international law, Simma's view is certainly right: rules against complicity are an expression of international solidarity. However, we should be as sceptical about this form of structural analysis as we have been with regard to the affirmation of international law's traditional bilateralism as a barrier to responsibility for complicity. After all, the narrative of progress which underlies the affirmation of the move from bilateralism to community interest is inevitably based on the description of international law as bilateral. Now that we have seen that this 'traditional' international law did not necessarily stand in the way of imposing responsibility for complicity, one tenet of this evolutionary saga is called into question.

If we look at the most important normative developments associated with the move beyond bilateralism and scrutinise their impact on complicity, the results are indeed mixed. As we will see, it follows from neither the setting in place of a system of collective security nor the development of 'public interest norms'[76] that complicity is no longer to be tolerated. As will be shown, these developments do have an impact upon the problem of complicity, but not in such a way as to impose ready-made solutions which speak clearly for or against a given rule on complicity.

---

[73] See, e.g., Astrid Epiney, 'Nachbarrechtliche Pflichten', p. 47.
[74] Article 53 of the 1996 Draft Articles, consequences of 'international crimes' (Draft Article 19), YBILC 1996, Vol. I, p. 135.
[75] Bruno Simma, 'From Bilateralism to Community Interest', p. 317.
[76] For the expression, see Jost Delbrück, 'Laws in the Public Interest – Some Observations on the Foundations and Identification of Erga Omnes Norms in International Law', in Volkmar Götz, Günther Jaenicke and Peter Selmer (eds.), *Liber amicorum Günther Jaenicke – zum 85. Geburtstag* (Berlin: Springer, 1998), pp. 17–36.

2.1 Collective security

The concept of collective security could have an impact on the problem of complicity as it has potentially challenged the traditional rules of neutrality. Moreover, collective security may appeal to further-reaching notions of solidarity which could speak against tolerance of complicit State behaviour.

2.1.1 A passing away of the rules of neutrality?

As early as the League of Nations era, it was already a matter of debate whether the law of neutrality was still compatible with the obligations set out in the Covenant of the League.[77] Article 16(1) of the Covenant stipulated that:

> Should any Member of the League resort to war in disregard of its covenants under Articles 12, 13 or 15, it shall ipso facto be deemed to have committed an act of war against all other Members of the League, which hereby undertake immediately to subject it to the severance of all trade or financial relations, the prohibition of all intercourse between their nationals and the nationals of the covenant-breaking State, and the prevention of all financial, commercial or personal intercourse between the nationals of the covenant-breaking State and the nationals of any other State, whether a Member of the League or not.

This provision has been interpreted as abolishing the traditional regime of neutrality altogether.[78] This view was, however, not unchallenged.[79] The League system did not function as originally intended. It was for the individual Member States to determine in most cases who had committed a violation of the obligations set out in Articles 12, 13 or 15 of the Covenant. In addition, the League did not establish a complete ban on the use of force in international relations as there remained the possibility of war being permissible once the dispute settlement mechanism set out in Article 12 was exhausted.[80] In the case

---

[77] Covenant of the League of Nations of 28 June 1919, entered into force on 1 October 1920, 225 Parry 195.
[78] Robert Redslob, *Théorie de la Société des Nations* (Paris: Rousseau, 1927), pp. 96 *et seq.*, the only exception being the privileges accorded to Switzerland, which Redslob finds hard to justify in legal terms as well, *ibid.*, pp. 99 *et seq.*
[79] For a polemical critique, see Carl Schmitt, *Die Wendung zum diskriminierenden Kriegsbegriff*, 3rd edn (Berlin: Duncker & Humblot, 2003) (originally published 1938), pp. 32 *et seq.*; for a more nuanced position, see John Fisher Williams, 'Sanctions under the Covenant', *British Year Book of International Law* 17 (1936), pp. 130–49, at pp. 145 *et seq.*
[80] One should also not forget the possibility of armed interventions and reprisals which were not, at least not expressly, forbidden by the Covenant of the League of

of such a permissible war, the traditional rules of neutrality would apply, as even the most fervent supporters of the League admitted.[81] Hersch Lauterpacht arrived at the conclusion that neutrality 'cannot, as a matter of law and practice, be regarded as banished in a system in which there is no authoritative agency competent and effectively able to determine the fact of aggression'.[82] He further stipulated that:

> in a period when war, insofar as it has been prohibited, is an offence against international law, neutrality stands in the same category as indifference shown by a citizen to a crime committed in his presence. Such an attitude is in some countries, including England, punishable by law.[83]

In this respect, Lauterpacht was able to build on considerations already entertained by his Cambridge predecessor, John Westlake. Westlake, however, clearly marked them as moral considerations and did not deduce legal consequences from them.[84] Lauterpacht, to the contrary, noted the structural changes in international law and predicted:

> It is believed that the more integrated international society will become, the more incompatible will become the rule of law thus established with the continued indifference (called neutrality, qualified or absolute) of States to its violation by unlawful recourse to war ... In this, as in many other matters, progress in international law and relations is conditioned in their approximation to standards prevailing among individuals.[85]

The debate on neutrality resumed after the adoption of the UN Charter[86] along similar lines. The view that neutrality is irreconcilable with the system of collective security put in place by the UN Charter has been advanced by a number of authors.[87] Yet, the majority of authorities come

---

Nations and the Briand–Kellogg Pact, see Stephen C. Neff, *War and the Law of Nations*, pp. 296 *et seq.*
[81] Walther Schücking and Hans Wehberg, *Die Satzung des Völkerbundes*, 2nd edn (Berlin: Vahlen, 1924), p. 513.
[82] Hersch Lauterpacht, 'Neutrality and Collective Security', p. 615.
[83] *Ibid.*, p. 625.
[84] John Westlake, *International Law*, p. 162.
[85] Hersch Lauterpacht, 'Neutrality and Collective Security', pp. 627–8.
[86] Charter of the United Nations of 26 June 1945, entered into force on 24 October 1945, 892 UNTS 119.
[87] C. G. Dehn, in International Law Association (ed.), *Report of the 41st Conference* (Cambridge: International Law Association, 1946), p. 42; Hans Kelsen, 'Théorie du droit international public', *Recueil des Cours* 84 (1953-III), pp. 1–202, at p. 60; Louis Henkin, 'Force, Intervention and Neutrality in Contemporary International Law', *Proceedings of the American Society of International Law* 1963, pp. 147–62, at p. 159;

to a different conclusion.[88] Their analysis is supported both by international practice[89] and by the clear statement in favour of the continued relevance of the law of neutrality by the International Court of Justice in its *Nuclear Weapons* opinion.[90] Lauterpacht himself was ambivalent about the further development of the law when he wrote his article on the 'Grotian tradition' in 1946:

> [I]t is theoretically possible for international law to declare that some wars are illegal and criminal and yet to lay down that the neutral states not involved in the war must act with absolute detachment in relation both to the aggressor and to his victim. The legal consistency of such a system of international law would be questionable; its ethical impropriety would be obvious.[91]

In some respects, the law of neutrality has considerably changed under the impact of the UN Charter rules on the use of force.[92] While States still have a general right to choose whether or not to remain neutral in armed conflicts, this faculty is limited by the condition that aid given to an aggressor is illegal. It is only as between participation on the

---

C. G. Fenwick, 'Is Neutrality Still a Term of Present Law?', *American Journal of International Law* 63 (1969), pp. 100-2, at p. 102.
[88] Ian Brownlie, *Use of Force*, p. 404; Yoram Dinstein, *War, Aggression and Self-Defence*, 4th edn (Cambridge: Cambridge University Press, 2005), p. 163; Alfred Verdross and Bruno Simma, *Universelles Völkerrecht – Theorie und Praxis*, 3rd edn (Berlin: Duncker & Humblot, 1984), § 239; Christopher Greenwood, 'The Concept of War in Modern International Law', *International and Comparative Law Quarterly* 36 (1987), pp. 283-306, at pp. 297 *et seq.*; Elizabeth Chadwick, *Traditional Neutrality Revisited* (The Hague: Kluwer, 2002), p. 181; Christian Dominicé, 'La question du droit de la neutralité', in Laurence Boisson de Chazournes and Philippe Sands (eds.), *International Law, the International Court of Justice and Nuclear Weapons* (Cambridge: Cambridge University Press, 1999), pp. 200-8, at p. 204; Detlev F. Vagts, 'The Traditional Law of Neutrality in a Changing Environment', *American University International Law Review* 14 (1998), pp. 83-102, at p. 91; Natalino Ronzitti, 'Italy's Non-Belligerency During the Iraq-War', in Maurizio Ragazzi (ed.), *International Responsibility Today – Essays in Memory of Oscar Schachter* (Leiden: Nijhoff, 2005), pp. 197-207, at p. 198; Stefan Oeter, *Neutralität und Waffenhandel* (Berlin: Springer, 1992), pp. 69 *et seq.*; Karl Doehring, 'Neutralität und Gewaltverbot', *Archiv des Völkerrechts* 31 (1993), pp. 193-205.
[89] See, e.g., UK Ministry of Defence (ed.), *The Manual of the Law of Armed Conflict* (Oxford: Oxford University Press, 2004), para. 1.43.
[90] ICJ, *Legality of the Threat or Use of Nuclear Weapons*, Advisory Opinion, ICJ Rep. 1996, 226, para. 89.
[91] Hersch Lauterpacht, 'Grotian Tradition', p. 39.
[92] Wolff Heintschel von Heinegg, 'Wider die Mär vom Tod des Neutralitätsrechts', in Horst Fischer, Ulrike Froissart, Wolff Heintschel von Heinegg and Christian Raap (eds.), *Krisensicherung und Humanitärer Schutz/Crisis Management and Humanitarian Protection, Festschrift für Dieter Fleck* (Berlin: Berliner Wissenschafts-Verlag, 2004), pp. 221-41, at p. 232.

side of the victim of aggression and neutrality that States can decide.[93] Even this choice may be further limited when the Security Council has adopted collective security measures under Chapter VII. In such a case, Article 2(5) of the UN Charter would require assistance to the collective security efforts and thus to the State attacked.

In this regard, it has been noted that, at least in theory, the UN Charter envisages a return to just war considerations: support is only allowed to be given to a party to a conflict which is authorised to use force.[94] Article 2(5) of the Charter would require of States, as a minimum, a policy of 'non-belligerency' once the Security Council has decided on enforcement action.[95] Non-belligerency is frequently understood as an intermediate status between neutrality and belligerency.[96] In concrete terms, it would mean that third States are entitled to assist the victim of an aggression while retaining the benefits of neutrality.[97] The most important precedent for such a policy is the US 'Neutrality Act' of 1939 by which the US defined their policy towards the belligerents in the Second World War prior to the attack on Pearl Harbor.[98] The legal justification of this policy was sought by US Attorney General Robert H. Jackson in the right to discriminate between the aggressor and the victim.[99]

Non-belligerency is still invoked in contemporary practice. Italy, for example, relied on it in order to justify its limited support for the US in

---

[93] Hans Kelsen, *Principles of International Law* (New York: Rinehart, 1952), p. 87; Michael Bothe, 'Neutrality', in Dieter Fleck (ed.), *The Handbook of Humanitarian Law in Armed Conflict* (Oxford: Oxford University Press, 1995), pp. 485–515, para. 1104; Ian Brownlie, *Use of Force*, pp. 403–4.
[94] Stephen C. Neff, *War and the Law of Nations*, p. 325.
[95] Stephen C. Neff, *The Rights and Duties of Neutrals*, p. 193.
[96] Natalino Ronzitti, 'Italy's Non-Belligerency', p. 198.
[97] Wolff Heintschel von Heinegg, '"Benevolent" Third States in International Armed Conflicts: The Myth of the Irrelevance of the Law of Neutrality', in Michael N. Schmitt and Jelena Pejic (eds.), *International Law and Armed Conflict: Exploring the Faultlines. Essays in Honour of Yoram Dinstein* (Leiden: Nijhoff, 2007), pp. 543–68, at p. 544.
[98] Neutrality Act of 1939, approved 4 November 1939, reprinted in *American Journal of International Law* 34 (1940), Supplement, pp. 44 *et seq.*; see also Wilhelm G. Grewe, *Epochen*, pp. 743–4.
[99] Robert H. Jackson, 'Address to the Inter-American Bar Association, Havana, Cuba, 27 March 1941', *American Journal of International Law* 35 (1941), pp. 348–59, at pp. 357–8; but for critical contemporary views, see Edwin M. Borchard, 'War, Neutrality and Non-Belligerency', *American Journal of International Law* 35 (1941), pp. 618–25, at pp. 624–5; Herbert W. Briggs, 'Neglected Aspects of the Destroyer Deal', *American Journal of International Law* 34 (1940), pp. 569–87, at p. 569, note 2.

the 2003 war on Iraq.[100] This attack was arguably neither authorised by the UN Security Council nor permitted under other accepted bases for the use of force in international law.[101] Accordingly, Italy's position had limited effects and could not justify its participation in the attacks. However, as Stephen C. Neff has argued, where the Security Council has taken enforcement action, non-belligerency may be seen as the bottom line of what is required by UN Member States in the ensuing conflict.[102] In concrete terms, this means that it may still be justified for States to remain aloof from UN enforcement action (despite Article 48 of the Charter), but there is no option to support the State which was found responsible for the threat to or breach of the peace. The flipside to this right of discrimination between the parties to a conflict is that a 'non-belligerent' UN Member State which does not fully participate in enforcement action but, at the same time, is not completely impartial in the conflict, need not fear countermeasures or other forcible reactions by the State which is targeted by the enforcement action: an aggressor can no longer rely on other States to abide by the obligations of neutrality.[103]

2.1.2 Complicity, solidarity and good faith

Hence, the picture is mixed insofar as the survival of the law of neutrality under the UN Charter is concerned: yes, neutrality still has a role to play in international relations, but only to the extent that it is compatible with the normative imperatives of the UN Charter. Inquiring into the state of health of the law of neutrality alone can thus not fully answer our questions about the role of complicity in an international legal order governed by a system of collective security. More light could be shed on this issue by Article 2(5) of the UN Charter:

All Members shall give the United Nations every assistance in any action it takes in accordance with the present Charter, and *shall refrain from giving assistance to any State against which the United Nations is taking preventive or enforcement action.*[104]

---

[100] See Natalino Ronzitti, 'Italy's Non-Belligerency', pp. 197 *et seq.*
[101] For a concise overview of the possible legal justifications, see Andreas L. Paulus, 'The War Against Iraq and the Future of International Law: Hegemony or Pluralism?', *Michigan Journal of International Law* 25 (2004), pp. 691–733, at pp. 695 *et seq.*
[102] Stephen C. Neff, *The Rights and Duties of Neutrals*, p. 193.
[103] Cf, *mutatis mutandis*, for the League period, John Fisher Williams, 'Sanctions', pp. 145–6.
[104] Emphasis added.

The second half of this provision is sometimes interpreted as dealing with situations of complicity.[105] A crucial argument in this regard would be that Article 2(5) of the UN Charter can be described as an 'accessory' provision.[106] As the ILC Commentary to Article 16 ASR points out, Article 2(5) of the Charter needs to be seen in connection with a general rule concerning aid or assistance to internationally wrongful acts. At the same time, Article 2(5) of the Charter is attributed 'a specific rationale which goes well beyond the scope and purpose of article 16'.[107] This difference in rationale, scope and purpose is, first of all, related to the function of the UN system of collective security. The obligation deriving from Article 2(5) of the Charter is not meant to establish the responsibility of States, but rather is a principle in accordance with which the UN and its Members shall act in the pursuit of the purposes set out in Article 1 of the Charter. It is thus mainly in the interest of the maintenance of international peace and security that Article 2(5) of the Charter is meant to underline the importance of 'closed ranks' of the UN Member States against a State which has become the object of preventive or enforcement action by the UN.[108] The Chairman of the US delegation to the San Francisco Conference interpreted the provision as follows:

It constitutes a general pledge not to strengthen the hand of a state which has violated its obligations under the Charter to the point where preventive or enforcement action has become necessary.[109]

Enforcement action is understood to cover the measures the Security Council can take under Articles 41 and 42 of the Charter[110] whereas

---

[105] John Quigley, 'Complicity', p. 88.
[106] Vera Gowlland-Debbas, *Collective Responses to Illegal Acts in International Law – United Nations Action in the Question of Southern Rhodesia* (Dordrecht: Nijhoff, 1990), p. 380.
[107] ILC Commentary, Article 16, para. 2.
[108] Vera Gowlland-Debbas, *Collective Responses*, p. 380; Mathias Forteau, *Droit de la sécurité collective et droit de la responsabilité internationale de l'Etat* (Paris: Pedone, 2006), p. 201; Andreas F. Bauer, *Effektivität und Legitimität – Die Entwicklung der Friedenssicherung durch Zwang nach Kapitel VII der Charta der Vereinten Nationen unter besonderer Berücksichtigung der neueren Praxis des Sicherheitsrates* (Berlin: Duncker & Humblot, 1996), pp. 34 *et seq*.
[109] Report to the US President, reprinted in Leland M. Goodrich, Edvard Hambro and Anne Patricia Simons, *Charter of the United Nations – Commentary and Documents*, 3rd edn (New York: Columbia University Press, 1969), p. 56.
[110] Jochen Abr. Frowein and Nico Krisch, 'Article 2(5)', in Bruno Simma (ed.), *The Charter of the United Nations – A Commentary*, 2nd edn (Oxford: Oxford University Press, 2002), para. 3.

'preventive measures' is supposed to refer either to Article 40[111] or to enforcement measures taken by the Security Council in order to prevent a breach of the peace from occurring.[112] Notwithstanding this question, there is unanimity that Article 2(5) of the Charter is concerned with Security Council action under Chapter VII of the Charter.[113] In addition to these observations about the purposes of Article 2(5) of the Charter, it has been characterised by Jean Combacau as a secondary rule, meaning that it supplements the principal enforcement action the Security Council has taken.[114] This understanding supports the position of the ILC in viewing Article 2(5) of the Charter in connection with the general rule embodied in Article 16 ASR.

This brings us to the scope of Article 2(5) of the Charter, which is both more far-reaching and more limited than Article 16 ASR. It is more far-reaching insofar as Article 2(5) of the Charter can arguably impose more wide-ranging obligations on UN Member States to dissociate themselves from a State against which preventive or enforcement action is being taken as compared with Article 16 ASR. As will be shown in greater detail later on in this volume, responsibility for complicity under Article 16 ASR requires a relatively close relationship between the support which is furnished and the unlawful conduct assisted thereby.[115] In addition, the supporting State needs to be aware of the circumstances of the internationally wrongful act (see Article 16(a) ASR).[116] In comparison, it does not appear from Article 2(5) of the Charter that similar requirements are to be met in order to trigger its applicability.[117]

It is plausible to relax the relatively onerous preconditions for responsibility as set out in Article 16 ASR when a decision is taken by

---

[111] *Ibid.*
[112] Hans Kelsen, *The Law of the United Nations – A Critical Analysis of its Fundamental Problems* (London: Stevens, 1951), p. 93.
[113] *Ibid.*, p. 92; Jean Combacau, *Le pouvoir de sanction de l'ONU – Etude théorique de la coercition non militaire* (Paris: Pedone, 1974), p. 190; Jochen Abr. Frowein and Nico Krisch, 'Article 2(5)', para. 4; Vera Gowlland-Debbas, *Collective Responses*, p. 380. A group of commentators also notes that it has been attractive for majorities in the General Assembly to marshal support for resolutions which are strictly speaking only recommendations, see Leland M. Goodrich, Edvard Hambro and Anne Patricia Simons, *Charter of the United Nations*, p. 58.
[114] Jean Combacau, *Le pouvoir de sanction*, p. 190.
[115] ILC Commentary, Introduction to Chapter IV of Part One, para. 8.
[116] See the discussion in Chapter 5, text accompanying notes 175 *et seq.*
[117] Cf Jean Combacau, *Le pouvoir de sanction*, p. 191; see also Jochen Abr. Frowein and Nico Krisch, 'Article 2(5)', para. 8.

an institutionalised mechanism such as that of the Security Council. When Special Rapporteur Willem Riphagen considered the legal consequences of international crimes, he discussed the extent to which a 'non-neutral' reaction by third States is required by the law. He departed from the general assumption that 'the basic principle seems to be that a wrongful act does not create a new legal relationship between the guilty State and a State other than the injured State'.[118] He viewed matters differently where a 'collective decision' had intervened and thus clarified the state of the law.[119] In this latter case, States would be aware of which States are subject to those measures and could adapt their practice in international cooperation. The same conditions are not met in the vast majority of cases where responsibility for complicity under Article 16 ASR is at stake. Accordingly, the more wide-ranging scope of Article 2(5) of the Charter is easy to justify.

At the same time, the scope of Article 2(5) of the Charter is more limited than Article 16 ASR. Its benefits in terms of clarity – it can only come into play once preventive and enforcement action has been taken by the Security Council – are at the same time its main weakness: the duty of isolation which is posited by Article 2(5) of the Charter only comes into play once such preventive or enforcement action has actually been taken by the Security Council. In this respect, the provision differs from Article 16, paragraph 1, of the Covenant of the League of Nations,[120] which stipulated that, in case of war started by a Member of the League in disregard of its obligations under Articles 12, 13 or 15 of the Covenant, *ipso facto* this was to be considered as 'an act of war against all other Members of the League, which hereby undertake immediately to subject [the wrongdoing Member] to the severance of all trade or financial relations' and a number of other consequences.[121] It is well known that this prohibition had its limits – in terms of both

---

[118] Willem Riphagen, 'Preliminary Report on the Content, Forms and Degrees of International Responsibility', UN Doc. A/CN.4/330, YBILC 1980, Vol. II, Part One, p. 107, para. 62.

[119] *Ibid.*, paras. 68, 71; see further Kay Hailbronner, 'Sanctions and Third Parties and the Concept of International Public Order', *Archiv des Völkerrechts* 30 (1992), pp. 2–15, at pp. 11–12.

[120] See Alfred Verdross, 'La neutralité dans le cadre de l'ONU particulièrement celle de la République d'Autriche', *Revue générale de droit international public* 61 (1957), pp. 177–92, at p. 182.

[121] See further Hans Kelsen, *The Law of the United Nations*, pp. 725–6; see, however, John Fisher Williams, 'Sanctions', p. 135, on the limits of unilateral action under Article 16 of the Covenant.

what constituted a forbidden war and its practical relevance as well as its workability.[122] It may be asked whether it was due to the limited success this automatic isolation mechanism had that Article 2(5) of the Charter was drafted the way it is.[123]

In comparison to Article 16 ASR, the scope of application of Article 2(5) of the Charter is narrower. The duty of isolation set out in Article 2(5) only applies when the Security Council has taken preventive or enforcement action to secure international peace and security. Furthermore, Article 2(5) provides by implication that the UN Charter does not automatically ban complicity with wrongful acts in an all-encompassing manner. Rather, it provides for an obligation not to render support for certain activities in a narrowly circumscribed area. It may well be the case that the 'spirit' of a system of collective security such as the United Nations requires more of States. This would, however, be related more to the idea of fulfilling the obligations under the Charter in good faith, as is stipulated in Article 2(2) of the Charter (Member States are to 'fulfil in good faith the obligations assumed by them in accordance with the present Charter'). In the words of two commentators, this requires States to adopt an 'objective orientation of their conduct towards the meaning and the spirit of the community objectives agreed upon'.[124] Although Hans Kelsen considered the good faith element in Article 2(2) of the Charter to be superfluous, as 'it is impossible to "fulfil" an obligation in bad faith',[125] the often vague formulations of the relevant provisions of the Charter and the necessarily decentralised implementation of Security Council resolutions make it apparent that States can comply with their obligations under the Charter both narrowly and in a more encompassing fashion.

---

[122] Cf Ian Brownlie, *Use of Force*, p. 58; Jost Delbrück, 'Collective Security', in Rudolf Bernhardt (ed.), *Encyclopedia of Public International Law*, Vol. 1, A–D (Amsterdam: Elsevier, 1992), pp. 646–56, at pp. 650–1.

[123] There is little evidence on the drafting history of Article 2(5) of the UN Charter, see UNCIO III, 1–23 and 282–91, at 284; Jochen Abr. Frowein and Nico Krisch, 'Article 2(5)', para. 1; Ahmed Mahiou, 'Article 2, paragraphe 5', in Jean-Pierre Cot, Alain Pellet and Mathias Forteau (eds.), *La Charte des Nations Unies – Commentaire article par article*, 3rd edn (Paris: Economica, 2005), p. 467.

[124] Jörg P. Müller and Robert Kolb, 'Article 2(2)', in Bruno Simma (ed.), *The Charter of the United Nations – A Commentary*, 2nd edn (Oxford: Oxford University Press, 2002), para. 12.

[125] Hans Kelsen, *The Law of the United Nations*, p. 89; but contrast Alfred Verdross and Bruno Simma, *Universelles Völkerrecht*, § 60: 'Denkt man sich den Grundsatz der bona fides weg, dann bricht das ganze VR [Völkerrecht] in sich zusammen.'

This is especially true for Article 2(5) of the Charter: Stephen Neff has argued that this provision defines a minimum requirement of non-belligerency.[126] But UN Member States are of course free to do more in order to comply with Security Council resolutions authorising enforcement measures. This argument mainly concerns the positive aspect of Article 2(5), that is, the degree of support States must give to enforcement action by the UN. Arguably, this argument will also apply to the negative side of Article 2(5) of the Charter: the requirement not to assist the State targeted by the enforcement action. States will differ in their assessment as to what constitutes forbidden support in this context if the Security Council has not precisely stipulated what constitutes forbidden support for the targeted State.[127] Thus, a certain leeway remains as to what exactly is required by Article 2(5) of the Charter. The difficulties in interpreting Article 2(4) and (5) of the Charter with respect to their meaning for potentially complicit States[128] show that, in the absence of clear and consistent Security Council findings on the requisite obligations, much remains unclear as to what is required of these States.

2.2 Public interest norms

The question whether complicity with wrongful acts can still be legitimate in contemporary international law could also find an answer in the category of 'public interest norms'. Under this heading, peremptory norms (*jus cogens*)[129] and obligations *erga omnes*[130] are frequently grouped together. It is a matter of debate in the literature whether such a merger into a category of public interest norms is justified. Whereas the supporters of such a common category point to the common intellectual

---

[126] Stephen C. Neff, *Rights and Duties*, p. 193.
[127] Cf Mathias Forteau, *Droit de la sécurité collective*, p. 201.
[128] The difficulty with respect to Article 2(4) of the Charter revolves around the reach of the concept of 'indirect aggression'; see, on this problem, Article 3(f) and (g) of the Declaration on the Definition of Aggression, UN Doc. A/RES/3314 (XXIX) of 14 December 1974; Erika de Wet, *The Chapter VII Powers of the United Nations Security Council* (Oxford: Hart, 2004), p. 147; Benedetto Conforti, *The Law and Practice of the United Nations*, 3rd edn (Leiden: Nijhoff, 2005), p. 173.
[129] See Articles 53 and 64 of the Vienna Convention on the Law of Treaties of 23 May 1969, entered into force on 27 January 1980, 1155 UNTS 331.
[130] The concept first appeared in ICJ, *Barcelona Traction, Light and Power Company, Limited*, Second Phase, Judgment, ICJ Rep. 1970, 3, paras. 33–5; on its origins, see further Bruno Simma, 'From Bilateralism to Community Interest', pp. 293 *et seq*.; Santiago Villalpando, *L'émergence*, pp. 96 *et seq*.

origin of the two categories and their ultimate aim – the protection of fundamental norms of the international legal system[131] – sceptics refer to the different functions and legal consequences attached to the two: whereas *jus cogens* norms prevent States from entering into agreements in contravention thereof, obligations *erga omnes* provide for the standing of States not directly injured to bring a claim or initiate court proceedings.[132] We need not disentangle this debate here. We are primarily concerned with a discursive phenomenon which starts precisely with this merger of the two categories. This approach points to the overwhelming importance of the legal interests protected by these norms. There is, of course, nothing inherently wrong with stressing the importance of these legal interests: the values protected by *jus cogens* are indeed of supreme importance. The prohibition of aggression, genocide, torture, slavery and *apartheid* as well as the protection of the most basic human rights and rules of international humanitarian law constitute the *raison d'être* of the international legal order. All these norms also give rise to obligations *erga omnes*. What is problematic is the tendency by some authors[133] and, to a growing extent also by domestic courts,[134] to deduce wide-ranging legal consequences out of these rules and obligations which rely on nothing other than the argument of the inherent importance of the values protected by *jus cogens* and obligations *erga omnes*.

2.2.1 The effects of *jus cogens*

The hierarchical effects of peremptory norms over 'ordinary law' are most forcefully argued with respect to State immunity, which is at times seen as the *bête noire* of contemporary international law. Alexander

---

[131] See Christian Tomuschat, 'International Law', pp. 85–6; Christian Tomuschat, 'Reconceptualizing the Debate on Jus Cogens and Obligations Erga Omnes – Concluding Observations', in Christian Tomuschat and Jean-Marc Thouvenin (eds.), *The Fundamental Rules of the International Legal Order – Jus Cogens and Obligations Erga Omnes* (Leiden: Nijhoff, 2006), pp. 425–36, at p. 425; Andreas L. Paulus, 'Jus Cogens in a Time of Hegemony and Fragmentation', *Nordic Journal of International Law* 74 (2005), pp. 297–334, at p. 317; Ronald St John Macdonald, 'Fundamental Norms in Contemporary International Law', *Canadian Yearbook of International Law* 25 (1987), pp. 115–49, at pp. 138–9; Michael Byers, 'Conceptualising the Relationship Between Jus Cogens and Erga Omnes Rules', *Nordic Journal of International Law* 66 (1997), pp. 211–39, at p. 236.
[132] Cf Stefan Kadelbach and Thomas Kleinlein, 'Constitution for Mankind', pp. 314 et seq.
[133] First and foremost: Alexander Orakhelashvili, *Peremptory Norms*.
[134] See Italian Court of Cassation, *Ferrini* v. *Federal Republic of Germany*, ILR 128, 658.

Orakhelashvili, one of the major voices in this regard, states that '[i]t is the natural effect of peremptory norms as superior norms that they trump the "rules" or principles on the immunity of States and their officials, if and to what extent such rules actually exist'.[135] The alleged superiority of *jus cogens* over the rules of State immunity and the projected clash between them rests on the hypothesis that peremptory norms have the all-encompassing effect of overriding all legal consequences which otherwise attach to a violation of a rule.

This argument relies on an 'international public order' approach. This concept was first fully conceptualised by Hermann Mosler who used it as an analytical tool rather than as a means to deduce new legal consequences from it.[136] Recently, the idea of a public order in international law which demands certain courses of conduct by States has gained momentum. This is reflected in the debate on complicity, where it is at times argued that States are not permitted to assist in violations of this *ordre public*. According to one commentator, States 'cannot be considered as innocent bystanders if they do not fulfil their obligations vis-à-vis the maintenance of the public order of the international community'.[137] However, the same author had to admit that '[t]his obviously leaves room for a wide field of discretion under what conditions a State is to be considered as a third State or as a State assisting in an international delict'.[138] A Greek court had recourse to similar reasoning when the question of German State immunity for atrocities committed in the Second World War was at stake. The court found that:

the recognition of immunity for an act contrary to peremptory international law would amount to complicity of the national court to the promotion of an act strongly condemned by the international public order.[139]

---

[135] Alexander Orakhelashvili, *Peremptory Norms*, p. 341.
[136] Hermann Mosler, 'The International Society as a Legal Community', *Recueil des Cours* 140 (1974-IV), pp. 1–320, at p. 33; Hermann Mosler, *The International Society as a Legal Community* (Alphen aan den Rijn: Kluwer, 1980), p. 17; for earlier emanations of the concept, see ICJ, *Case Concerning the Application of the Convention of 1902 Governing the Guardianship of Infants*, Judgment, separate opinion of Judge Moreno-Quintana, ICJ Rep. 1958, 106; Arnold McNair, *The Law of Treaties* (Oxford: Clarendon Press, 1961), pp. 213–14.
[137] Kay Hailbronner, 'Sanctions', p. 12.   [138] Ibid.
[139] Multi-member Court of Levadia, Case No. 137/1997, Judgment of 30 October 1997, reprinted in *Revue Hellénique de Droit International* 50 (1997), p. 595, at p. 599; for a similar reasoning in the literature, see also Jordan J. Paust, 'Federal Jurisdiction over Extraterritorial Acts of Terrorism and Nonimmunity for Foreign Violators of

However, only seldom is a clear and convincing argument developed *why* public order norms trump others in the case at hand. Can the public order protagonists offer more than a mere recourse to 'hierarchy' and values?[140]

This debate crystallised in the *al-Adsani* case before the European Court of Human Rights and its aftermath: is there really a conflict between the *jus cogens* character of a given norm and the respect for State immunity in a foreign court?[141] This is obviously a matter distinct from complicity, but in no other case have the arguments for and against the wide-ranging effects of *jus cogens* been so clearly developed. As we will see, similar frontlines of the debate can also be conceived with respect to the obligations of complicit States.

In the *al-Adsani* case, a violation of Article 6 of the European Convention on Human Rights[142] by the United Kingdom for not having provided a judicial remedy against the State of Kuwait was alleged.[143] The main reason why the (small) majority of the judges of the Grand Chamber of the European Court of Human Rights did not find a violation of Article 6 of the Convention was that, although the prohibition of torture would have achieved the status of a peremptory norm, this

---

International Law under the FISA and the Act of State Doctrine', *Virginia Journal of International Law* 23 (1983), pp. 191–249, at p. 227; see further Lee M. Caplan, 'State Immunity, Human Rights, and Jus Cogens: A Critique of the Normative Hierarchy Theory', *American Journal of International Law* 97 (2003), pp. 741–81, at pp. 775–6; Thomas Giegerich, 'Do Damage Claims Arising from Jus Cogens Violations Override State Immunity from the Jurisdiction of Foreign Courts?', in Christian Tomuschat and Jean-Marc Thouvenin (eds.), *The Fundamental Rules of the International Legal Order – Jus Cogens and Obligations Erga Omnes* (Leiden: Nijhoff, 2006), pp. 203–38, at p. 226.

[140] For critical remarks, see Robert Kolb, *Théorie du ius cogens international: essai du relecture du concept* (Paris: Presses universitaires de France, 2001), pp. 68 *et seq*. and 172 *et seq*.; Georg Nolte, 'Kosovo und Konstitutionalisierung: Zur humanitären Intervention der NATO-Staaten', *Zeitschrift für ausländisches öffentliches Recht und Völkerrecht* 59 (1999), pp. 941–60, at pp. 942–3; Nathan Lerner, 'Comment: Third States and International Measures Against Terrorism', *Archiv des Völkerrechts* 30 (1992), pp. 55–62, at p. 55, note 1.

[141] Similar considerations apply with respect to the *Ferrini* decision of the Italian Court of Cassation, *Ferrini* v. *Federal Republic of Germany*, ILR 128, 658; for two diverging assessments, see Andrea Bianchi, 'Ferrini v. Federal Republic of Germany', *American Journal of International Law* 99 (2005), pp. 242–8, at pp. 245 *et seq*., and Andrea Gattini, 'War Crimes and State Immunity in the Ferrini Decision', *Journal of International Criminal Justice* 3 (2005), pp. 224–42, at p. 230.

[142] Convention for the Protection of Human Rights and Fundamental Freedoms of 4 November 1950, entered into force on 3 September 1953, ETS No. 5.

[143] ECtHR, *Al-Adsani* v. *United Kingdom*, ECHR 2001-XI, 79.

would not necessarily affect the enjoyment of State immunity.[144] The majority thus implicitly relied on a distinction between substance and process. The minority view emphasised the hierarchical aspects of *jus cogens*, which culminated in the assertion that:

[i]n the event of a conflict between a *jus cogens* rule and any other rule of international law, the former prevails. The consequence of such prevalence is that the conflicting rule is null and void, or, in any event, does not produce legal effects which are in contradiction with the content of the peremptory rule.[145]

Similar lines of debate can be imagined for the problem of complicity: on the one hand, one can argue that support for the unlawful conduct in question is not automatically elevated to a different level merely because the violated norm is of a *jus cogens* character. On the other hand, one could say that the supreme values protected by these norms demand that no forms of conduct which 'hamper the ability of peremptory norms to produce their effects as norms'[146] must be tolerated in international law. In order to maximise the 'public order' effects of peremptory norms, the attitude of third States could prove to be particularly important.[147]

What the minority view in *al-Adsani* left unexplained was where the actual conflict between the peremptory norm against torture and the consideration of State immunity in the context of Article 6 ECHR lies.[148] It is plausible that State immunity, as Hazel Fox has remarked, 'does not contradict a prohibition contained in a *jus cogens* norm but merely diverts any breach of it to a different method of settlement'.[149] Another

---

[144] Ibid., para. 61.
[145] Ibid., dissenting opinion of Judges Rozakis and Caflisch joined by Judges Wildhaber, Costa, Cabral Barreto and Vajic, para. 1; tentative support for this position in Andrew Clapham, 'The Jus Cogens Prohibition of Torture and the Importance of Sovereign State Immunity', in Marcelo G. Kohen (ed.), *Promoting Justice, Human Rights and Conflict Resolution Through International Law – Liber Amicorum Lucius Caflisch* (Leiden: Nijhoff, 2007), pp. 151–69, at p. 169.
[146] Alexander Orakhelashvili, *Peremptory Norms*, p. 578.
[147] Ibid., p. 579.
[148] Christian J. Tams, 'Probleme mit dem Ius Cogens', *Archiv des Völkerrechts* 40 (2002), pp. 331–49, at pp. 341–2; Christian Appelbaum, *Einschränkungen der Staatenimmunität in Fällen schwerer Menschenrechtsverletzungen – Klagen von Bürgern gegen einen fremden Staat oder ausländische staatliche Funktionsträger vor nationalen Gerichten* (Berlin: Duncker & Humblot, 2007), p. 263.
[149] Hazel Fox, *The Law of State Immunity*, 1st edn (Oxford: Oxford University Press, 2002), p. 525; and Hazel Fox, *The Law of State Immunity*, 2nd edn (Oxford: Oxford University Press 2008), p. 156.

commentator has rightly remarked that, for the demonstration of a clash of international law norms, the hierarchy view would need to prove the existence of a *jus cogens* norm that would actually prohibit the granting of immunity for violations of human rights by foreign states – which would not be the case.[150] This debate on the effects of *jus cogens* eventually boils down to a question of methodology: the dividing line has to be drawn between those who argue for wide-ranging consequences of *jus cogens* for the sake of logical clarity and consistency and those who put more emphasis on the traditional methods of international law, i.e., an assessment of international practice and accompanying *opinio juris*.[151]

The protagonists of the former approach argue that there are no fixed boundaries in international law between substantive and procedural norms.[152] At the same time, they view this distinction as being based on a view of the international legal system which emphasises its bilateralism and would not account for the position of individuals.[153] In the view of the present author, it is not convincing to deny the possibility of establishing fixed boundaries between

---

[150] Lee M. Caplan, 'State Immunity', p. 772; see further Andrea Gattini, 'War Crimes', p. 235; Thilo Rensmann, *Wertordnung und Grundgesetz – Das Grundgesetz im Kontext grenzüberschreitender Konstitutionalisierung* (Tübingen: Mohr Siebeck, 2007), p. 395; Hélène Tigroudja, 'La Cour européenne de droits de l'homme et les immunités juridictionelles d'Etats – Observations sous les arrêts McElhinney, Fogarty et al-Adsani', *Revue belge de droit international* 34 (2001), pp. 526–48, at p. 540; for the contrary view, see Alexander Orakhelashvili, 'State Immunity and International Public Order', *German Yearbook of International Law* 45 (2002), pp. 227–67, at pp. 255 and 258; Alexander Orakhelashvili, 'State Immunity and International Public Order Revisited', *German Yearbook of International Law* 49 (2006), pp. 327–65, at p. 355; Alexander Orakhelashvili, 'State Immunity and Hierarchy of Norms: Why the House of Lords Got it Wrong', *European Journal of International Law* 18 (2007), pp. 955–70, at p. 964; more nuanced is Andrea Bianchi, 'Denying State Immunity to Violators of Human Rights', *Austrian Journal of Public and International Law* 46 (1994), pp. 195–229, at p. 206; Andrea Bianchi, 'Ferrini', p. 247; Lorna McGregor, 'State Immunity and Jus Cogens', *International and Comparative Law Quarterly* 55 (2006), pp. 437–46, at p. 444.

[151] This observation has been made by Christian J. Tams, 'Buchbesprechung (Alexander Orakhelashvili, Peremptory Norms, 2006)', *Verfassung und Recht in Übersee* 40 (2007), pp. 380–3, at pp. 382–3.

[152] Alexander Orakhelashvili, 'State Immunity and International Public Order Revisited', p. 360.

[153] Ibid., p. 356; similarly Andrea Bianchi, 'L'immunité des Etats et les violations graves des droits de l'homme: la fonction de l'interpréte dans la détermination du droit international', *Revue générale de droit international public* 108 (2004), pp. 63–101, at p. 67.

substantive and procedural norms while, at the same time, affirming that some rules of international law have to be classified as belonging to the old layers of bilateralism whereas peremptory norms represent the 'new' international law. In comparison to this 'layering' of the various stages of development of international law, the distinction between primary and secondary rules is well settled in international law.[154] The nub of the argument is that, so far, advocates of the far-reaching effects of *jus cogens* on the law of State immunity have failed to demonstrate clearly how such effects derive from the peremptory character of the rules in question. We should be equally critical about tendencies to make too much of *jus cogens* for the problem of complicity.

2.2.2 Obligations *erga omnes* as obligations for third States?

Similar considerations may be entertained with respect to the category of obligations *erga omnes*. In the formulation of the ICJ in the *Barcelona Traction* case, obligations *erga omnes* are 'by their very nature ... the concern of all States'.[155] Traditionally, this is understood to embody a faculty for all States to invoke the responsibility of a State which has violated an obligation *erga omnes*. Third States gain the right to invoke the responsibility of another State even if they are not injured in a traditional sense.[156] At the same time, it appears to be clear that there exists as of now no duty to make use of this right.[157] While there are ongoing discussions with respect to a duty to intervene in particularly grave situations of ongoing or imminent genocide or crimes against

---

[154] With concrete reference to the problem of *jus cogens* and State immunity, see Christian Tomuschat, 'L'immunité des Etats en cas de violations graves des droits de l'homme', *Revue générale de droit international public* 109 (2005), pp. 51–74, at p. 57; see also Pierre-Marie Dupuy, 'L'unité de l'ordre juridique internationale. Cours général de droit international public', *Recueil des Cours* 297 (2002), pp. 9–490, at pp. 361–2; Christian Appelbaum, *Einschränkungen der Staatenimmunität*, p. 269; for a more sceptical assessment, see Ulf Linderfalk, 'State Responsibility and the Primary–Secondary Rules Terminology – The Role of Language for an Understanding of the International Legal System', *Nordic Journal of International Law* 78 (2009), pp. 53–72.
[155] ICJ, *Barcelona Traction, Light and Power Company, Limited*, Second Phase, Judgment, ICJ Rep. 1970, 3, para. 33.
[156] Cf Eckart Klein, 'Beihilfe', p. 437.
[157] Cf Christian J. Tams, *Enforcing Obligations Erga Omnes in International Law* (Cambridge: Cambridge University Press, 2005), p. 11, with further references in note 43; Giorgio Gaja, 'Obligations and Rights Erga Omnes in International Law', *Annuaire de l'Institut de Droit International* 71 (2005), pp. 117–51, at pp. 149–50.

humanity,[158] at least in general no such obligation to react to breaches of obligations *erga omnes* has developed in international law. So much was also made clear in the parallel universe of *jus cogens* when Special Rapporteur John Dugard failed to convince the ILC to include an obligation for States to exercise diplomatic protection if measures were taken by a State 'which constitute the grave breach of a norm of *jus cogens*'.[159]

Stipulating that States have a right to react in some form against violations of obligations *erga omnes*, and have at the same time no duty to do so, does not preclude an intermediate form of obligation to arise which could stipulate, for example, an obligation of non-assistance. This obligation could be seen as a sort of 'mirror image' to the enhanced rights of States to observe compliance with obligations *erga omnes* by other States. In this light, rights would be seen as automatically entailing responsibilities.[160]

The ICJ appears to have given support to such a reading in its 2004 advisory opinion on the Israeli wall in the occupied Palestinian territory.[161] Having determined the violation of various international obligations by Israel, the Court considered the consequences of these violations. It observed that 'the obligations violated by Israel include certain obligations *erga omnes*',[162] among which figured the right of the Palestinian people to self-determination and some of its obligations under international humanitarian law.[163] The Court went on to state that:

> [G]iven the character and the importance of the rights and obligations involved, the Court is of the view that all States are under an obligation not to recognise the illegal situation resulting from the construction of the wall in the Occupied Palestinian Territory, including in and around East Jerusalem. They are also under an obligation not to render aid or assistance in maintaining the situation created by such construction. It is also for all States, while respecting the United Nations Charter and international law, to see to it that

---

[158] Fernando R. Téson, 'The Liberal Case for Humanitarian Intervention', in J. L. Holzgrefe and Robert O. Keohane (eds.), *Humanitarian Intervention – Ethical, Legal and Political Dilemmas* (Cambridge: Cambridge University Press, 2003), pp. 93–129.
[159] John Dugard, 'First Report on Diplomatic Protection', UN Doc. A/CN.4/506, para. 89.
[160] Cf Theodor Meron, *The Humanization of International Law* (Leiden: Nijhoff, 2006), p. 264.
[161] ICJ, *Legal Consequences of the Construction of a Wall in the Occupied Palestinian Territory*, Advisory Opinion, ICJ Rep. 2004, 136.
[162] Ibid., para. 155. [163] Ibid.

any impediment, resulting from the construction of the wall, to the exercise by the Palestinian people of its right to self-determination is brought to an end. In addition, all the States parties to the Geneva Convention relative to the Protection of Civilian Persons in Time of War of 12 August 1949 are under an obligation, while respecting the United Nations Charter and international law, to ensure compliance with international humanitarian law as embodied in that Convention.[164]

This paragraph has given rise to a considerable amount of controversy both within and outside the Court. It was especially the deduction of the obligations of non-recognition and non-assistance from the concept of *erga omnes* which met with criticism. President (then Judge) Higgins remarked that she did

> not think that the specified consequences of the identified violations of international law have anything to do with the concept of *erga omnes* ... The Court's celebrated *dictum* in *Barcelona Traction, Light and Power Company* ... is frequently invoked for more than it can bear ... It has nothing to do with imposing substantive obligations on third parties to a case.[165]

For Judge Higgins, it is self-evident that an illegal situation is not to be recognised or assisted by third parties. These consequences would arguably follow from a finding of an unlawful situation by the UN Security Council or, in this case, from a comparable finding of illegality by the Court itself.[166] Judge Kooijmans supported Higgins' position: he stated that he had 'considerable difficulty in understanding why a violation of an obligation *erga omnes* by one State should necessarily lead to an obligation for third States'.[167]

The finding of these consequences for third States has also puzzled legal commentators. While most of them discussed the obvious similarities in terms of formulation between what the ICJ has found with respect to obligations *erga omnes* and the regime of serious breaches of peremptory norms under general international law (Articles 40 and 41 ASR),[168] one possible way to make sense of the Court's *dictum* is by

---

[164] *Ibid.*, para. 159.
[165] *Ibid.*, separate opinion of Judge Rosalyn Higgins, para. 37.
[166] *Ibid.*, para. 38.
[167] *Ibid.*, separate opinion of Judge Pieter H. Kooijmans, para. 40.
[168] See James Crawford, 'Multilateral Rights and Obligations in International Law', *Recueil des Cours* 319 (2007), pp. 325–482, at p. 475; Ardi Imseis, 'Critical Reflections on the International Humanitarian Law Aspects of the ICJ Wall Advisory Opinion', *American Journal of International Law* 99 (2005), pp. 102–18, at pp. 114 *et seq.*; Daniel-Erasmus Khan, 'Sicherheitszaun oder Apartheidmauer? Das Gutachten des

distinguishing between its findings on the right to self-determination and the international humanitarian law aspects. Christian Tams has remarked that the ICJ 'carefully distinguished between a *duty* to respond based on common article 1 of the Geneva Conventions[169] and *rights* of response based on the *erga omnes* concept'.[170] It can, however, be questioned whether the Court really made this distinction. It is true that the Court included an additional paragraph on the obligation of States to ensure respect for the Geneva Conventions.[171] In the relevant paragraph on the obligations of non-recognition and non-assistance (which has been reproduced above), the Court makes no distinction to this effect. It only stipulates that, in addition to these obligations of non-recognition and non-assistance, States are also under an obligation to ensure compliance with the Geneva Conventions.[172] It is the very source of confusion about the Court's *dictum* that the obligations *erga omnes* which the Court found to be at stake not only were conceptualised as giving States a faculty of reaction, but were meant to establish additional obligations for third States.

It can be speculated whether the grounding of these third States' obligations were owed to the then still prevailing reticence of the Court even to mention the concept of peremptory norms,[173] as it was only in 2006 that the existence of this concept was expressly acknowledged by the Court.[174] The Court pronounced itself on these consequences of obligations *erga omnes* for third parties in a rather equivocal manner. It did not clarify how it arrived at its conclusion. Seen in this perspective,

---

Internationalen Gerichtshofs vom 9. Juli 2004 zu den israelischen Sperranlagen gegenüber dem Westjordanland', *Die Friedenswarte* 79 (2004), pp. 345–70, at p. 368; Alexander Orakhelashvili, 'International Public Order and the International Court's Advisory Opinion on the Legal Consequences of the Construction of a Wall in the Occupied Palestinian Territory', *Archiv des Völkerrechts* 43 (2005), pp. 240–56, at p. 248; Andreas L. Paulus, 'Jus Cogens', p. 315.

[169] The Geneva Conventions I–IV of 12 August 1949, all entered into force on 21 October 1950, (I) 75 UNTS 31; (II) 75 UNTS 85; (III) 75 UNTS 135; (IV) 75 UNTS 287.

[170] Christian J. Tams, *Enforcing Obligations Erga Omnes*, p. 11, footnote 43; similarly Bruno Simma, 'Comment', in Andreas Zimmermann and Rainer Hofmann (eds.), *Unity and Diversity in International Law* (Berlin: Duncker & Humblot, 2006), pp. 467–70, at p. 470.

[171] ICJ, *Legal Consequences of the Construction of a Wall in the Occupied Palestinian Territory*, Advisory Opinion, ICJ Rep. 2004, 136, para. 158.

[172] *Ibid.*, para. 159.

[173] James Crawford, 'Multilateral', p. 475.

[174] Cf ICJ, *Armed Activities on the Territory of the Congo (New Application: 2002)*, Judgment, ICJ Rep. 2006, 5, para. 64.

it is difficult to assume that the Court wanted to present a general concept of obligations for third States flowing from violations of obligations *erga omnes*. As is shown by the criticism by Judges Higgins and Kooijmans,[175] this step would have needed more explanation in order to be seen as a conceptually sound development of international law.

2.2.3 Developments in the law of State responsibility

In its Commentary to the Articles on State Responsibility, the ILC remarks that '[f]rom the first it was recognised that' the developments of *jus cogens* and obligations *erga omnes* 'had implications for the secondary rules of State responsibility which would need to be reflected in some way in the articles'.[176] The ILC first tried to mirror these developments in the field of State responsibility by virtue of the distinction between international crimes and delicts.[177] However, due to resistance on the part of States and a lack of conceptual clarity as to what the criminal responsibility of States would actually mean, the concept

---

[175] See the references in above notes 165 to 167.
[176] ILC Commentary, Introduction to Chapter III of Part Two, para. 5.
[177] See Draft Article 19 as adopted on First Reading:
International crimes and delicts

1. An act of a State which constitutes a breach of an international obligation is an internationally wrongful act, regardless of the subject matter of the obligation breached.
2. An internationally wrongful act which results from the breach by a State of an international obligation so essential for the protection of fundamental rights of the international community that its breach is recognized as a crime by that community as a whole constitutes an international crime.
3. Subject to paragraph 2, and on the basis of the rules of international law in force, an international crime may result, *inter alia*, from:
   a) a serious breach of an international obligation of essential importance for the maintenance of international peace and security, such as that prohibiting aggression.
   b) a serious breach of an international obligation of essential importance for safeguarding the right of self-determination of peoples; such as that prohibiting the establishment or maintenance by force of colonial domination.
   c) a serious breach on a widespread scale of an international obligation of essential importance for safeguarding the human being, such as those prohibiting slavery, genocide or *apartheid*.
   d) a serious breach of an international obligation of essential importance for the safeguarding and preservation of the human environment, such as those prohibiting massive pollution of the atmosphere or the seas.
4. Any internationally wrongful act which is not an international crime in accordance with paragraph 2 constitutes an international delict.

was abandoned and replaced by the category of 'serious breaches of peremptory norms under general international law'.[178] The provisions of this chapter of the Articles, which provide for obligations of third States in the face of such serious breaches, are, however, only one side of the coin of the regime of 'aggravated responsibility'. In addition, the category of obligations *erga omnes* had to be integrated into the law of State responsibility. In the words of the ILC Commentary to the Articles:

Whether or not peremptory norms of general international law and obligations to the international community as a whole are aspects of a single basic idea, there is at the very least substantial overlap between them ... While peremptory norms of general international law focus on the scope and priority to be given to a certain number of fundamental obligations, the focus of obligations to the international community as a whole is essentially on the legal interest of all States in compliance – i.e., in terms of the present articles, in being entitled to invoke the responsibility of any State in breach.[179]

Accordingly, the regime of 'aggravated responsibility' does not exhaust itself in the rules on serious breaches of peremptory norms under general international law, but encompasses the rules on invocation of responsibility by States which are not injured in the sense of Article 42 ASR (see Article 48 ASR), and Article 54, the saving clause on 'measures' (as opposed to countermeasures) taken by States other than an injured State.

As an in-depth examination of the problem of complicity in the regime of aggravated responsibility will be made at a later stage of this study,[180] only some signposts will be mentioned here. First, and most obviously, Article 41(2) ASR itself includes an obligation of non-assistance which supplements Article 16 ASR: 'No State shall recognise as lawful a situation created by a serious breach within the meaning of article 40, nor render aid or assistance in maintaining that situation.'

---

[178] The long and laborious drafting history leading up to these changes need not be recounted here, see instead James Crawford, 'Revising the Draft Articles on State Responsibility', *European Journal of International Law* 10 (1999), pp. 435–60, at 442–3; James Crawford, 'The ILC Articles on State Responsibility: A Retrospect', *American Journal of International Law* 96 (2002), pp. 874–90, at p. 875; Marina Spinedi, 'From One Codification to Another: Bilateralism and Multilateralism in the Genesis of the Codification of the Law of Treaties and the Law of State Responsibility', *European Journal of International Law* 13 (2002), pp. 1099–1125.

[179] ILC Commentary, Introduction to Chapter III of Part Two, para. 7.

[180] See Chapter 7 below.

Accordingly, this provision only comes to apply when a serious breach within the meaning of Article 40 ASR occurs, which is the case when a State has failed to fulfil its obligation under a peremptory norm of general international law in a gross or systematic way (see Article 40(2) ASR). The obligation contained in Article 41(2) ASR is meant to go beyond what is already provided for by Article 16 ASR as it applies to 'conduct after the fact'.[181]

In a broader context, the inclusion of an obligation of non-assistance in the regime of 'aggravated responsibility' underlines the connection between the problem of complicity and international public order. Although the consequences the ILC has attached to serious breaches of peremptory norms appear meagre to some,[182] the range between the duty of cooperation set out in Article 41(1) ASR and the obligations of non-recognition and non-assistance in Article 41(2) ASR potentially encapsulates a whole array of measures which can be set in motion in order to suppress a State's non-compliance with peremptory norms.[183] In the further course of this study, it will be necessary to look in particular at the relationship between the duties of abstention (non-recognition, non-assistance) and the duty to cooperate.

3 Conclusion

For the present stage of our examination, it suffices to point out that the development of the law in this respect is rather unclear. The Commission itself was not sure whether Articles 40 and 41 ASR reflected the state of customary international law. The uncertainty which arose from the ICJ's *Wall* opinion is a further case in point that the law is not settled in this field. This gives us further indications

---

[181] ILC Commentary, Article 41, para. 11.
[182] Andreas L. Paulus, 'Jus Cogens', p. 315; Bardo Fassbender, 'Der Schutz der Menschenrechte als zentraler Inhalt des völkerrechtlichen Gemeinwohls', *Europäische Grundrechte-Zeitschrift* 30 (2003), pp. 1–15, at p. 8; Brigitte Stern, 'La France et le droit de la responsabilité internationale des Etats', in Gérard Cahin, Florence Poirat and Sandra Szurek (eds.), *La France et le droit international*, Vol. I, *Ouverture* (Paris: Pedone, 2007), pp. 169–95, at p. 183.
[183] See also Alain Pellet, 'Les articles de la CDI sur la responsabilité internationale de l'Etat pour fait internationalement illicite suite – et fin?', *Annuaire français de droit international* 43 (2002), pp. 1–23, at p. 18; Andreas Zimmermann and Michael Teichmann, 'State Responsibility for International Crimes', in André Nollkaemper and Harmen van der Wilt (eds.), *System Criminality in International Law* (Cambridge: Cambridge University Press, 2009), pp. 298–313, at p. 312.

that the categories of public order norms do not automatically entail detailed consequences for third States. It would strain the concept of *jus cogens* and obligations *erga omnes* to deduce wide-ranging consequences from them which have no basis in the reality of international law.

It can be observed that the concept of peremptory norms exercises an enormous fascination upon international lawyers and triggers creative doctrinal constructs.[184] Although some of these constructs may not represent the current state of the law, they could nevertheless be interpreted as pointing the direction towards which international law could develop if the protection of community interests takes further roots. They are also a sign that the 'every man for himself' attitude[185] which has prevailed for so long in the international legal realm is receding. For the problem of complicity, this is revealing insofar as a requirement to abstain from support for violations of *jus cogens* norms is, yet again, a much more modest proposal than to disregard the rules of State immunity or immunities of high-ranking State officials due to the impact of *jus cogens*; or to require States to exercise diplomatic protection on behalf of their nations if violations of *jus cogens* norms are at stake. However, it is unclear how such obligations of non-assistance should technically flow from the concept of peremptory norms or obligations *erga omnes*. This preliminary assessment is not meant to prejudge a further issue: at a later stage of the study we will return to the impact of peremptory norms on the concept of complicity as it will be shown to exist in contemporary international law.[186] It is one thing to deduce obligations of non-assistance in an abstract manner out of the concept of peremptory norms, and another to examine whether peremptory norms may impact upon the interpretation of an existing concept of international law. The latter exercise will, however, depend on a more thorough understanding of the general concept of complicity in international law.

On a more general level, the phenomena we have examined contribute to the normative environment of the problem of complicity. They shift the boundaries of tolerable State behaviour and may contribute to

---

[184] Cf Andrea Bianchi, 'Human Rights and the Magic of Jus Cogens', *European Journal of International Law* 19 (2008), pp. 491–508, at pp. 491 *et seq.*; Christian J. Tams, 'Buchbesprechung', pp. 381–2.

[185] Cf again Prosper Weil, 'Relative Normativity', p. 431; Bruno Simma, 'From Bilateralism to Community Interest', p. 233.

[186] See the further our discussion in Chapter 7.

CONCLUSION 49

a development which, step by step, 'encircles' the issue of complicity. In general, however, the repercussions they will have on international practice will be limited: the number of cases which really involve breaches of peremptory norms is not that large. And how many States are willing to react to violations of obligations *erga omnes*?

In light of these considerations, Chapter 3 will reconceptualise the debate on the place complicity assumes in the current structure of international law. At first sight, both the constraints of bilateralism and the promises of the new, community-oriented international law appear to impact heavily on the issue of complicity. After our closer look at those phenomena, it seems to us that they represent nothing more than the usual ascending and descending patterns of legal argument:[187] whereas the bilateral perspective is ascending from voluntarism, the community perspective emphasises law's supremacy over the individual will of the State. As ascending and descending patterns of legal argument tend to be, they are 'exhaustive and mutually exclusive … A middle position seems to be excluded.'[188] This position could be seen as discouraging further examinations on whether a more convincing outlook on the current structure of international law and its relevance for the problem of complicity can be established. But, even if we remain pessimistic about a possible middle ground, we may look for a different paradigm for the discussion on complicity, which may also fall prey to its own inherent contradictions between ascending and descending patterns of argument, but which may carry less ideological baggage than the divide between bilateralism and community interest. It is to this endeavour that we shall turn now in Chapter 3.

---

[187] Cf Martti Koskenniemi, 'Doctrines', p. 49.
[188] Martti Koskenniemi, *From Apology to Utopia – The Structure of International Legal Argument, Reissue with a New Epilogue* (Cambridge: Cambridge University Press, 2005), p. 59.

3 Complicity and the international rule of law

> If a State assists another State which is acting in violation of the law, it participates in an illegal action, and its duty to refrain from illegal actions is implied in the concept of international law.[1]

In the previous chapter, we presented two different perspectives on the problem of complicity in international law: according to the traditional, bilateral outlook, it may appear difficult to accommodate considerations of complicity in the strictly bilateral legal relationships which are brought about by the law of State responsibility. However, we have seen that international law had no difficulties in providing rules for a problem which is very close to that of complicity, namely, to determine what obligations the law of neutrality provides for third States in times of armed conflict. We have also seen that the development of international law beyond its original bilateral constraints, be they real or perceived, is no panacea to hold complicit States responsible. It is very much in the spirit of the move 'from bilateralism to community interest' and the legal developments associated with it to assume that international law will no longer tolerate complicit State behaviour. However, neither the establishment of a system of collective security nor the recognition of peremptory norms and obligations *erga omnes* automatically lead to this result.

We have thus seen that the two conceptual approaches that are usually adopted when the significance of the concept of complicity in international law is considered do not establish conclusive results. In other words, neither is international law as 'backward-oriented' as to

---

[1] Hans Kelsen, 'The Draft Declaration on Rights and Duties of States – Critical Remarks', *American Journal of International Law* 44 (1950), pp. 259–76, at p. 271.

erect structural barriers to hold complicit States responsible (and this applies not only to contemporary international law), nor can one infer wide-ranging consequences from its alleged 'progressiveness'. At the same time, the previous chapter has shown that important conceptual and structural issues are at stake which require us to question how general features of the international legal system impact upon the subject of our study: how does the complicit State fit into the relationship between the wrongdoing State and the injured State? Is it conceptually possible to recognise Article 16 as a secondary rule in the sense of the ASR? These issues are connected with the core question raised by the *Lotus* principle, which affirms one of the fundamentals of positivist twentieth-century international law:

> International law governs relations between independent States. The rules of law binding upon States therefore emanate from their own free will as expressed in conventions or by usages generally accepted as expressing principles of law and established in order to regulate the relations between these co-existing independent communities or with a view to the achievement of common aims. Restrictions upon the independence of States cannot therefore be presumed.[2]

As will be recalled from Chapter 1, the distinction between primary and secondary rules was introduced by the ILC in order to highlight that the codification of the law of State responsibility would not bring about new substantive obligations for States.[3] Rather, this project was meant to be confined to codifying the meta-rules which would apply once the substantive obligations of international law have been violated. While there is some criticism of the conceptual clarity of this approach[4] and as to whether the results of the ILC's codification efforts really conform to this orientation,[5] the case of complicity is especially problematic in this regard: it is a matter of general agreement that there exists no direct and general prohibition of State complicity in international law on the level of *primary* rules.[6] Article 16 ASR is also

---

[2] PCIJ, *Lotus*, Judgment, Series A, No. 10, 18.
[3] Roberto Ago, 'Working Paper on State Responsibility', YBILC 1963, Vol. II, p. 251, at p. 253.
[4] Alexander Orakhelashvili, *Peremptory Norms*, p. 80; Ulf Linderfalk, 'State Responsibility'.
[5] Eric David, 'Primary and Secondary Rules', pp. 29–33.
[6] ILC Commentary, Article 16, para. 2; Christian Dominicé, 'Attribution of Conduct to Multiple States and the Implication of a State in the Act of Another State', in James Crawford, Alain Pellet and Simon Olleson (eds.), *The International Law of Responsibility* (Oxford: Oxford University Press, 2010), pp. 282–9, at p. 287.

not meant to be a rule of attribution. This means that the complicit State does not become responsible *for* the wrongful conduct of another State in which it is implicated.[7] Rather, it is responsible for its own supportive conduct. On this conduct, however, there is, strictly speaking, no primary rule which would establish its wrongfulness. So how can the ASR then establish responsibility for complicity?

In the previous chapter, we have seen how the two traditional models of explanation try to cope with this problem but ultimately fail to produce satisfactory results for the problem of complicity. The main task of this chapter will therefore be to provide an alternative explanation of where the concept of complicity sits in today's international legal order, an explanation which will leave behind the conventionally affirmed dichotomy between an old international law which is bilateral and the new international law which is community-oriented. The alternative explanation will be sought in the concept of an international rule of law and in what will be defined as one of its core constituents, the principle of abuse of rights. The results of this chapter will approach the position Hans Kelsen took in the quotation reproduced at the start of this chapter, but only to a certain extent and admittedly on a different conceptual premise.[8] He argued that the concept of international law itself would rule out the possibility of granting assistance to another State committing an internationally wrongful act. Kelsen's conclusion in this regard was that no special rule on complicity was necessary. In this chapter, we will ultimately reach a different conclusion: although the concept of the international rule of law will establish a strong presumption that complicit behaviour cannot be tolerated, and although this finds further support in the principle of 'abuse of rights', a mature international legal system needs rules which are more refined and which give greater guidance on the question when a State may be held responsible for complicity. In the following, we will first explain what we understand by the international rule of law (section 1), before turning to the principle of abuse of rights (section 2). Finally, the insights we have obtained in these sections will be combined and analysed with respect to their impact on the issue of complicity (section 3).

---

[7] ILC Commentary, Article 16, para. 1.
[8] In particular, it could not have been expected of Kelsen to approve of the concept of abuse of rights which, through its close relation with ideas of good faith, disqualified itself from application in Kelsen's pure theory of law. Good faith, Kelsen argued, is nonsensical, as obligations could only be complied with or not and never in 'bad faith': see Hans Kelsen, *The Law of the United Nations*, p. 89.

1 The international rule of law

The international rule of law is not a concept which lends itself to easy definition. Although elusive in terms of content,[9] the rule of law is beginning to generate more and more interest in academic circles[10] as well as within the United Nations.[11] In trying to define what the 'international rule of law' actually means, some caution is called for. After having surveyed the historical, political and legal origins of the concept throughout the centuries, Brian Tamanaha came to the conclusion that '[a]dding another [definition] in the hope that it would win the day would be redundant and naïve'.[12] Similarly, Arthur Watts remarked that the international rule of law 'is not a concept with any readily identifiable content'.[13]

1.1 Preliminary issues

A study of its own could therefore be written on the precise meaning of the international rule of law. At the moment, a variety of understandings are on offer in academic writings on the matter: they range from reaffirmations of the protection of the individual by human

---

[9] Brian Tamanaha, *Rule of Law*, p. 3.
[10] For doctrinal explorations of the rule of law at the international level see, e.g., Arthur Watts, 'Rule of Law', pp. 15 *et seq.*; Ian Brownlie, *The Rule of Law in International Affairs* (The Hague: Nijhoff, 1998); Nicolas Tsagourias, 'Globalization, Order and the Rule of Law', *Finnish Yearbook of International Law* 11 (2000), pp. 247-64; James Crawford, 'International Law and the Rule of Law', *Adelaide Law Review* 24 (2003), pp. 3-12; Ruti G. Teitel, 'Humanity's Law: Rule of Law for the New Global Politics', *Cornell International Law Journal* 35 (2002), pp. 355-87; Stéphane Beaulac, 'The Rule of Law in International Law Today', in Gianluigi Palombella and Neil Walker (eds.), *Relocating the Rule of Law* (Oxford: Hart, 2009), pp. 197-223; Simon Chesterman, 'An International Rule of Law?', *American Journal of Comparative Law* 56 (2008), pp. 331-61; Terry Nardin, 'International Pluralism and the Rule of Law', *Review of International Studies* 26 (2000), pp. 95-110; Terry Nardin, 'Theorising the International Rule of Law', *Review of International Studies* 34 (2008), pp. 385-401; Sienho Yee, *Towards an International Law of Co-Progressiveness* (Leiden: Nijhoff, 2004), pp. 41 *et seq.*; Brian Tamanaha, *Rule of Law*, pp. 127 *et seq.*; Jeremy Matam Farrall, *United Nations Sanctions and the Rule of Law* (Cambridge: Cambridge University Press, 2007), pp. 24 *et seq.*
[11] On the efforts so far of the United Nations on this matter, see UN Doc. A/RES/62/70 of 8 January 2008; and the Reports of the Secretary General: 'The Rule of Law at the National and International Levels: Comments and Information Received from Governments', UN Doc. A/62/121 of 11 July 2007 and Add.1 of 6 September 2007; 'The Rule of Law at the National and International Levels - Report of the Secretary General', UN Doc. A/63/64 of 12 March 2008.
[12] Brian Z. Tamanaha, *Rule of Law*, p. 114.
[13] Arthur Watts, 'Rule of Law', p. 15.

rights[14] over the rule of law as a benchmark for good governance[15] to understandings which equate the rule of law simply with the idea that there be law in international relations.[16] We wish to follow a different approach, one which identifies the concept of the international rule of law primarily with structural considerations of the international legal system, i.e., with the way its component parts (or legal subjects) interact and how international law is interpreted in light of this ideal.[17] This understanding finds inspiration in rule of law principles which have developed over the centuries in a domestic context, but now seeks further to identify related principles at the international level which are informed by the specificities of the international legal system.[18]

Our approach is thus not so much interested in comparative law aspects. It is of course possible to obtain greater clarity about the content of the international rule of law by means of comparative law.[19] However, different legal systems have developed greatly varying concepts of what they understand as the rule of law. The French and German concepts of *Etat de droit* and *Rechtsstaat* differ greatly from the common law ideal that is the rule of law, if only through their fixation on 'the State' which does not translate easily into common law thinking.[20] As a matter of hermeneutics, it will be impossible to ignore

---

[14] See, e.g., Randall Peerenboom, 'Human Rights and the Rule of Law – What's the Relationship?', *Georgetown Journal of International Law* 36 (2005), pp. 810–945.

[15] See, e.g., the analysis by Daniel Kaufmann, Aart Kray and Massimo Matruzzi, 'Governance Matters VI: Governance Indicators 1996–2006', World Bank Policy Research Paper No. 4280 of July 2007, at pp. 2, 5, 9; see also Urfan Khaliq, *Ethical Dimensions of the Foreign Policy of the European Union – A Legal Appraisal* (Cambridge: Cambridge University Press, 2008), pp. 76 *et seq.*

[16] See, e.g., Matthias Kumm, 'International Law in National Courts: The International Rule of Law and the Limits of the Internationalist Model', *Virginia Journal of International Law* 44 (2003–4), pp. 19–32.

[17] Close to our approach are the following authors: Arthur Watts, 'Rule of Law', pp. 15 *et seq.*; James Crawford, 'Rule of Law'; David Dyzenhaus, *The Constitution of Law – Legality in a Time of Emergency* (Cambridge: Cambridge University Press, 2006), p. 4; Gianluigi Palombella, 'The Rule of Law Beyond the State: Failures, Promises, and Theory', *International Journal of Constitutional Law* 7 (2009), pp. 442–67, at pp. 442–3.

[18] Simon Chesterman, 'Rule of Law', in Rüdiger Wolfrum (ed.), *Max Planck Encyclopedia of Public International Law*, online edition (Oxford: Oxford University Press, 2008), paras. 37–8.

[19] Andreas L. Paulus, 'The International Legal System as a Constitution', in Jeffrey L. Dunoff and Joel P. Trachtman (eds.), *Ruling the World – Constitutionalism, International Law, and Global Government* (Cambridge: Cambridge University Press, 2009), pp. 69–109, at p. 90.

[20] For comparisons of these three different notions, see Luc Heuschling, *Etat de Droit, Rechtsstaat, Rule of Law* (Paris: Dalloz, 2002); Rainer Grote, 'Rule of Law, Rechtsstaat and

the conceptual and ideological baggage which the concept of the rule of law carries with it. At the same time, it does not appear to be a fruitful approach to develop a notion of the international rule of law as a form of the lowest common denominator of the various national conceptions in existence.[21] We can thus agree with Rosalyn Higgins that domestic concepts of the rule of law are not easily transposable to the international level.[22] International law will need to define its own concept of the rule of law.[23]

This study is guided by the assumption that each and every legal system has its own conception of the rule of law, as has been argued by David Dyzenhaus.[24] In this perspective, the rule of law is an ideal immanent in any legal order.[25] This reasoning is partly based on the ethos of the legal community and the possibilities this community conceives of as being at its disposal when making, applying and interpreting the law.[26] Understanding a legal system through the lens of

---

"Etat de Droit"', in Christian Starck (ed.), *Constitutionalism, Universalism and Democracy – A Comparative Analysis* (Baden-Baden: Nomos, 1999), pp. 269–306.

[21] See also André Nollkaemper, 'The Internationalized Rule of Law', *Hague Journal on the Rule of Law* 1 (2009), pp. 74–8, at p. 75.

[22] Rosalyn Higgins, 'The Rule of Law: Some Sceptical Thoughts', in Rosalyn Higgins, *Themes and Theories. Selected Essays, Speeches and Writings in International Law*, Vol. 2 (Oxford: Oxford University Press, 2009), pp. 1330–9, at p. 1334.

[23] Cf, *mutatis mutandis*, with respect to the concept of constitution in international law, Bardo Fassbender, *The Charter of the United Nations as the Constitution of the International Community* (Leiden: Nijhoff, 2009), p. 170.

[24] David Dyzenhaus, *The Constitution of Law*, p. 4; see also Jeffrey Jowell, 'The Rule of Law and Its Underlying Values', in Jeffrey Jowell and Dawn Oliver (eds.), *The Changing Constitution*, 7th edn (Oxford: Oxford University Press, 2007), pp. 5–24, at pp. 5 (summary) and 17; for the international realm, see Andreas L. Paulus, 'International Law After Postmodernism: Towards Renewal or Decline of International Law?', *Leiden Journal of International Law* 14 (2001), pp. 727–55, at p. 753; Andreas L. Paulus, 'The International Legal System', p. 97.

[25] See also Sienho Yee, *Towards*, p. 57.

[26] Hersch Lauterpacht, *The Function of Law in the International Community* (Oxford: Clarendon Press, 1933), p. 437; James Crawford, 'Rule of Law', p. 12; see further Joseph Raz, 'The Politics of the Rule of Law', in Joseph Raz, *Ethics in the Public Domain* (Oxford: Clarendon Press, 1994), pp. 354–62, at p. 362; Martti Koskenniemi, *From Apology to Utopia*, pp. 566 *et seq.*; Martti Koskenniemi, 'The Silence of the Law/the Voice of Justice', in Laurence Boisson de Chazournes and Philippe Sands (eds.), *The International Court of Justice, International Law and Nuclear Weapons* (Cambridge: Cambridge University Press, 1999), pp. 488–510, at pp. 509–10; Anthony Carty, *Philosophy of International Law* (Edinburgh: Edinburgh University Press, 2007), pp. 14 *et seq.*; Ulf Linderfalk, 'State Responsibility', p. 53; Arthur L. Goodhart, 'The Rule of Law and Absolute Sovereignty', *University of Pennsylvania Law Review* 106 (1958), pp. 943–63, at p. 962; these positions all have a certain resemblance to Aristotle's ideal of the rule

the rule of law is one way not to turn into a mere 'managerialist'[27] or technocrat. Relying on the rule of law is here understood as a way to give the law its most effective interpretation and application.[28]

Another question is what the 'rule of law' as a concept can contribute to our understanding of the international legal system.[29] One source of criticism can be found in what authors from the field of critical legal studies have discussed repeatedly: the rule of law would be a misleading concept. Too often, it would suggest a formalisation of 'governance', intending to imply that the politics can be kept out, that decisions on the form of good government could be taken by mere recourse to the law, which would, however, only be a form of politics itself.[30] In this regard, it would take part of the liberal legacy, which aspires to keep the interventions of politics at bay, concentrating rather on the free interplay of the forces of the market.[31] One could counter this criticism by pointing at the various facets the 'rule of law' has adopted over long stretches of time.[32] One can find liberal as well as Marxist, Western as well as Asian conceptions of the rule of law. This diversity is especially reflected in the field of international law.[33]

---

of law as a rule of reason which depended crucially on the character of legal decision-makers, see also Judith N. Shklar, 'Political Theory and the Rule of Law', in Allan C. Hutchinson and Patrick Monahan (eds.), *The Rule of Law – Ideal or Ideology?* (Toronto: Transnational, 1987), pp. 1–16, at p. 3.

[27] Martti Koskenniemi, 'The Politics of International Law – 20 Years Later', *European Journal of International Law* 20 (2009), pp. 7–19, at p. 15.

[28] Cf Alexander Orakhelashvili, *The Interpretation of Acts and Rules in Public International Law* (Oxford: Oxford University Press, 2008), pp. 20 and 393 et seq.

[29] For a sceptical view, see Alexander Somek, 'From the Rule of Law to the Constitutionalist Makeover: Changing European Conceptions of Public International Law', University of Iowa Legal Studies Research Paper No. 09-25, May 2009, at pp. 3 et seq.

[30] Cf David Kennedy, *The Dark Sides of Virtue – Reassessing International Humanitarianism* (Princeton, NJ: Princeton University Press, 2004), p. 155; Martti Koskenniemi, *From Apology to Utopia*, pp. 71, 88–9, 613; for the theoretical underpinnings of this view, see Duncan Kennedy, 'Form and Substance in Private Law Adjudication', *Harvard Law Review* 89 (1976), pp. 1685–1778, especially at pp. 1713–14, with footnote 74, and at p. 1754 with footnote 128; Duncan Kennedy, 'Toward a Critical Phenomenology of Judging', in Allan C. Hutchinson and Patrick Monahan (eds.), *The Rule of Law – Ideal or Ideology?* (Toronto: Transnational, 1987), pp. 141–67.

[31] Martti Koskenniemi, *From Apology to Utopia*, pp. 88 et seq.; see further Martti Koskenniemi, 'The Politics of International Law', *European Journal of International Law* 1 (1990), pp. 4–32.

[32] See Brian Z. Tamanaha, *Rule of Law*, p. 7.

[33] For a recent Chinese exposition in this regard, see Sienho Yee, *Towards*, pp. 41 et seq.

While we thus recognise that it is possible to criticise an international rule of law approach on various grounds, we do not find the alternative approaches more appealing.[34] This does not mean that a concept of the international rule of law will necessarily give rise to well-contoured concrete legal obligations. Rather, deducing such obligations out of a concept as vague and abstract as the international rule of law would most likely smack of *Begriffsjurisprudenz*, i.e., the tendency to deduce legal consequences from words and concepts alone. Also, this does not mean that the choice for the rule of law should be motivated by instrumentalist concerns, i.e., that recourse to law should be had if such fits certain policy objectives.[35]

What our exercise in this concept may do, however, is to help to identify conflicts within the law which may have to be overcome in order to develop a workable international legal order. In this respect, any concept of the rule of law in a given legal system will always have to live off the existing legal norms in that system. However, it will have to go beyond that, as we will now show. By thinking in terms of the rule of law, we suggest a systemic understanding of the international legal system which is based on the conviction that international legal norms and principles do not stand in isolation but feed off each other. They may mutually reinforce themselves. The rule of law perspective which is advocated here aspires to point towards constructive means to develop the law further and to unearth underlying common rationales of rules. Accordingly, thinking in terms of the rule of law is seen here rather as a particular approach to dealing with international law than as a belief that the rule of law comes with any readily identifiable content.

Keeping this in mind, it is not the aim of this chapter to draw up a general 'laundry list' of constituent elements of the rule of law. There is eminent authority for the limited usefulness of such an approach.[36] If we review the predominant elements of the discussion on the international rule of law in recent years, a couple of distinguishing features

---

[34] On the options before today's international lawyer in this regard, see (with a different recommendation than is presented here) Martti Koskenniemi, 'The Fate of Public International Law: Between Technique and Politics', *Modern Law Review* 70 (2007), pp. 1–30, at pp. 27 *et seq.*

[35] For an instrumentalist approach to the rule of law, see Anne-Marie Slaughter, *A New World Order* (Princeton, NJ: Princeton University Press, 2004), pp. 244–5, at p. 261.

[36] Joseph Raz, 'The Rule of Law and Its Virtue', p. 214.

can be identified. First of all, the discussion takes place on two different levels:[37] for some authors, the international rule of law primarily means an international standard which applies to States and which States have to respect in their dealings with their citizens. This understanding of the rule of law finds support in its invocation as a founding principle of several international organisations[38] and in the role it plays in affirmations in the human rights context.[39] In the *Golder* case, the European Court of Human Rights held that the signatory governments to the European Convention on Human Rights 'have a common heritage of political traditions, ideals, freedoms and the rule of law'.[40] Similarly, the work international financial institutions such as the World Bank are putting into development programmes frequently involves an invocation of the 'rule of law', which is here also meant as an international standard the State has to comply with in relation to international investors and its citizens.[41] The debate on rule of law limits to the activities of international organisations – with a particular emphasis on UN Security Council resolutions – follows a similar pattern as it tries to elevate the rule of law standard that was once developed for the domestic context to the international level.[42]

---

[37] See also Andreas L. Paulus, 'The International Legal System', p. 72; for an analysis of the international standards for the rule of law at the domestic level, see also Helmut Philipp Aust and Georg Nolte, 'International Law and the Rule of Law at the National Level', in André Nollkaemper, Randy Peerenboom and Michael Zürn (eds.), *The Dynamics of the Rule of Law*, forthcoming.

[38] See, e.g., Articles 1, 3 and 8 of the Statute of the Council of Europe of 5 May 1949, entered into force on 3 August 1949, ETS No. 1; Article 2 of the Treaty Establishing the European Union of 13 December 2007, entered into force on 1 December 2009, for the latest consolidated version, see OJ C321E/1; Preamble to the Constitutive Act of the African Union of 11 July 2000, entered into force on 26 May 2001, OAU Doc. CAB/LEG/23.15.

[39] See, e.g., the Preamble to the Universal Declaration of Human Rights: 'it is essential … that human rights should be protected by the rule of law', UN Doc. A/RES/217A (III) of 10 December 1948.

[40] ECtHR, *Golder* case, Series A, No. 18, 16.

[41] Alvaro Santos, 'The World Bank's Uses of the "Rule of Law" Promise in Economic Development', in David M. Trubek and Alvaro Santos (eds.), *The New Law and Economic Development* (Cambridge: Cambridge University Press, 2006), pp. 253–302; at the same time, it is interesting to note that legal formalisms have been identified by proponents of the Law and Development Movement of the World Bank as the primary hindrance to the fulfilment of development goals, see David M. Trubek, 'The "Rule of Law" in Development Assistance: Past, Present, and Future', in David M. Trubek and Alvaro Santos (eds.), *The New Law and Economic Development* (Cambridge: Cambridge University Press, 2006), pp. 74–94, at p. 76.

[42] See, e.g., Simon Chesterman, 'An International Rule of Law?', pp. 331 *et seq.*; Gerhard Hafner, 'The Rule of Law and International Organizations', in Klaus Dicke, Stephan

For the present study, however, it is a second level of debate on the international rule of law which is relevant: this level relates to the question whether there is something akin to the rule of law in relations *between* States.[43] For this assessment, the human rights context as just mentioned is arguably not directly relevant.[44] This second meaning of an international rule of law is much harder to grasp than the human-rights-related one. In the words of Arthur Watts:

> While much consideration has been given to the meaning of the 'rule of law' as a characteristic of the relations between a State and those subject to its jurisdiction ... much less attention has been paid to it as a characteristic of relations between States as members of the international community.[45]

1.2 *Individualism or* dédoublement fonctionnel?

Thinking about the international rule of law in the relation between States will require some reformulation of the rule of law doctrine as we know it from the domestic context. We have to account for the legal relationships between States as forms of interaction between sovereign equals.[46] It is thus not a relationship of subordination between various actors but one of coordination. States play a double role in international law: they enact the law to which they are then bound. To this scenario, the idea of the so-called *dédoublement fonctionnel* could apply: Georges Scelle conceptualised this idea with individuals in mind who would fulfil a double role as agents of their home State and of the international community.[47] His considerations have afterwards, *mutatis mutandis*, been applied to States.[48] This transposition of Scelle's concept

---

Hobe, Karl U. Meyn *et al.* (eds.), *Weltinnenrecht – Liber amicorum Jost Delbrück* (Berlin: Duncker & Humblot, 2005), pp. 307–14, at pp. 310 *et seq.*
[43] Terry Nardin, 'Theorising', p. 399; André Nollkaemper, 'Rule of Law', p. 75; Simon Chesterman, 'Rule of Law', paras. 37–8.
[44] Arthur Watts, 'Rule of Law', p. 21.
[45] *Ibid.*, pp. 21–2.
[46] See Article 2(1) of the UN Charter.
[47] Georges Scelle, *Précis de droit des gens*, pp. 42 *et seq.*; Georges Scelle, 'Le phénomène juridique du dédoublement fonctionnel', in Wolfgang Schätzel and Hans-Jürgen Schlochauer (eds.), *Rechtsfragen der internationalen Organisation. Festschrift für Hans Wehberg* (Frankfurt/Main: Klostermann, 1956), pp. 324–42, at pp. 334 *et seq.*
[48] Cf, e.g., Alfred Verdross and Bruno Simma, *Universelles Völkerrecht*, § 46; Antonio Cassese, 'Remarks on Scelle's Theory of "Role-Splitting" (Dédoublement Fonctionnel) in International Law', *European Journal of International Law* 1 (1990), pp. 210–31, at pp. 225 *et seq.*; Stefan Talmon, *La non-reconnaissance collective des Etats illégaux* (Paris: Pedone, 2007), pp. 69–70; for some aspects of what this entails for complicit States, see Georg Nolte and Helmut Philipp Aust, 'Equivocal Helpers', pp. 27 *et seq.*

makes sense insofar as States may at times act as agents for their own interests and may at other times (also) act for the interests of the international community as a whole. Although a lot of his analysis needs adjusting to make it relevant to the current stage of development of the international legal system, characterised as it is by a greater degree of institutionalisation than in Scelle's time,[49] its basic tenets still hold true: international law lacks a general institutional structure which would turn it into a legal system which no longer needs to rely on States for its practical enforcement.[50] Therefore, States may take up different roles on the international level, depending on the circumstances in which they act. In some situations, they are law-makers, whereas in other situations they are subjected to the law they previously enacted. This double role of States has a bearing on the fundamental notions of a legal system. For the rule of law, this is especially true. This concept is ordinarily meant to protect against the exercise of power. In light of the double role of States, it needs to be carefully analysed what the rule of law protects States against.[51]

An all too tempting conceptualisation of the international rule of law is inspired by its domestic counterparts and puts States in the position that individuals and other legal subjects occupy in domestic legal orders.[52] An international rule of law understood in this sense would be nothing more than a more sophisticated expression of the *Lotus* principle: the freedom of individual States to do whatever they please as long as there are no fixed limitations upon their independence.[53] This is, as the legal philosopher Jeremy Waldron argues, not a convincing paradigm for the rule of law at the international level. Waldron's starting point for analysis is rather the fact that State governments do

---

[49] For an argument in this regard, see Bardo Fassbender, *The United Nations Charter*, p. 75; see also Hans Wiebringhaus, *Das Gesetz der funktionellen Verdoppelung: Beitrag zu einer universalistischen Theorie des Internationalprivat- und Völkerrechts*, 2nd edn (Saarbrücken: West-Ost-Verlag, 1955), pp. 30–1.
[50] Antonio Cassese, 'Remarks', pp. 210 *et seq.*; see also Andreas Fischer-Lescano, *Globalverfassung – Die Geltungsbegründung der Menschenrechte* (Weilerswirst: Velbrück, 2005), pp. 102, 160; for a historical account, see Martti Koskenniemi, *The Gentle Civilizer of Nations*, pp. 333 *et seq.*
[51] Cf Terry Nardin, 'Theorising', pp. 398–9.
[52] Cf Jeremy Waldron, 'Are Sovereigns Entitled to the Benefit of the International Rule of Law?', Institute of International Law and Justice Working Paper 2009/3, at p. 13; Jeremy Waldron, 'The Rule of International Law', *Harvard Journal of Law and Public Policy* 30 (2006–7), pp. 15–30.
[53] See above note 2.

not lose their capacity as agencies of public power when they act on the international level.[54] To him, it is crucial to understand the different approaches with which individuals and agencies of public power should define their relation to law as such. The individual citizen enjoys protection by the rule of law in order to safeguard him from the arbitrary exercise of power.[55] In cases of doubt, there is a presumption that the law will not prohibit a certain course of conduct. The rule of law requires, for instance, that no punishment be inflicted upon an individual in the absence of a clear basis in the law.

Waldron asks if this reasoning is transposable to the international level. Does the international rule of law imply that, in the absence of a clear prohibiting rule, States are free to behave as they please?[56] Waldron's concerns about this possible implication of the international rule of law are ultimately rooted in concerns about the various roles States play and thus meet the concept of *dédoublement fonctionnel*: States are not only subjected to the law but are also responsible for its creation and enforcement.[57] No simple exchange of States for individuals will thus be possible for a rule of law turned international.[58]

If we go one step further than Waldron, we can envisage States as not only abstract entities, but as agents of the international community[59] and, hence, trustees for the protection of the individuals who form the respective State and constitute the *raison d'être* of the international community.[60] At the same time, their membership in the international community would require them to respect not only the rights

---

[54] Cf Hans Kelsen, *Principles of International Law*, p. 14; Christian Tomuschat, 'International Law', p. 95; see further Armin von Bogdandy, 'The Telos of International Law', in Pierre-Marie Dupuy, Bardo Fassbender, Malcolm N. Shaw and Karl-Peter Sommermann (eds.), *Völkerrecht als Wertordnung – Festschrift für Christian Tomuschat* (Kehl: N. P. Engel, 2006), pp. 703–21, at pp. 707–8.

[55] Judith N. Shklar, 'Political Theory', p. 2.

[56] Jeremy Waldron, 'Sovereigns', p. 25.

[57] Jeremy Waldron, 'The Rule of International Law', p. 23; see the contributions of Georges Scelle, above note 47.

[58] Cf Anne Peters, 'Humanity as the A and Ω of Sovereignty', *European Journal of International Law* 20 (2009), pp. 513–44, at p. 534.

[59] Hans Kelsen, *Principles of International Law*, p. 14; Christian Tomuschat, 'Die internationale Gemeinschaft', pp. 14–15; Philip Allott, *Eunomia – New Order for a New World* (Oxford: Oxford University Press, 1990), p. 309; Monica Hakimi, 'State Bystander Responsibility', *European Journal of International Law* 21 (2010), pp. 341–85, at p. 347.

[60] Georges Scelle understood the individual to be the only real subject of law, cf *Précis de droit des gens*, p. 42.

of their respective citizens, but also the rights and interests of the international community at large.[61] In this regard, Scelle's concept of the *dédoublement fonctionnel* appears less dated than some may suggest.[62] If States adopt their international role, their role as agents of the international community and trustees of their citizens, different rationales may come into play than when State action has only domestic repercussions.

1.3 The material completeness of the international legal order

Waldron's concerns about the international rule of law are connected to earlier works in international law which inquired into the completeness of the international legal order. The classic piece on the issue was written by Hersch Lauterpacht who devoted the final part of *The Function of Law in the International Community* to the international rule of law.[63] His treatment of the topic was embedded in his critique against the distinction between political and legal disputes, the former not being suitable for judicial dispute settlement or arbitration. In this connection, he emphasised the material completeness of the international legal order, writing that 'the necessary aim of any legal system is … material completeness'.[64] In this regard, he was strongly opposed to the *Lotus* principle (which we discussed above). His emphatic take on the attitude of the Permanent Court deserves to be quoted in greater length:

It is easy to say that as there is no gap in the law, its silence in a particular case must be regarded as having a decisive and negative effect on the claim before the Court. Such reasoning may frequently be correct. But at times, it may be an expression of intellectual inertia or short-sightedness … Thus when we mean to rely on the rule that what is not prohibited is permitted, we may be pursuing only the shadow of a rule. For the actual decision in each case will depend on the question whether we have in mind an express prohibition, specifically and unequivocally laid down – and such prohibitions may be few in an undeveloped system of law labouring under a traditionally exaggerated conception of freedom – or a prohibition deduced from the general body of the law.[65]

---

[61] Similarly, Terry Nardin, 'Theorising', p. 399; Bardo Fassbender, *UN Security Council Reform and the Right of Veto: A Constitutional Perspective* (The Hague: Kluwer, 1998), p. 9.
[62] See above note 49.
[63] Hersch Lauterpacht, *The Function of Law*, pp. 385 *et seq*.
[64] *Ibid*., p. 86.   [65] *Ibid*., pp. 86–7.

Lauterpacht was thus arguing for a decidedly legal outlook on the solution to disputes in international relations. By arguing for the possibility to solve every dispute in terms of law – and not only according to the *Lotus* principle – he wished to expand the 'reign of law', as he put it,[66] in the international sphere. One should not make the mistake of belittling Lauterpacht's views for his involvement in the broadly optimistic 'peace through law' movement of the inter-war period. While it is true that, just as Hans Kelsen was,[67] he was a strong supporter of the idea that the advancement of international peace and the rule of law would ultimately depend on the creation of compulsory legal dispute settlement on the international level,[68] his theoretical ideas about the creation and interpretation of the law cannot be reduced to this context.[69]

It is important to note that Lauterpacht did not make use of the concept of the 'rule of law' in a sense that would have meant mere compliance with existing international obligations by the respective States concerned. A meaningful concept of the international rule of law cannot exhaust itself in the affirmation that the law should be complied with. Whereas one frequently comes across such a reductionist

---

[66] *Ibid.*, p. 437.
[67] See, in retrospect, Hans Kelsen, *Peace Through Law* (Chapel Hill, NC: University of North Carolina Press, 1944), pp. 13–14; on Kelsen's approach in this regard, see Jochen von Bernstorff, *Der Glaube an das universale Recht – Zur Völkerrechtstheorie Hans Kelsens und seiner Schüler* (Baden-Baden: Nomos, 2001), pp. 169 *et seq.*; a divide between Lauterpacht and the Kelsen-dominated Vienna School in international law can, however, be discerned with respect to the question of gaps in the law and interpretation: whereas Lauterpacht saw interpretation as the crucial tool to avoid gaps and to achieve material completeness, this was conspicuously viewed as attempts to reintroduce natural law-thinking into the 'science' of international law by Kelsen and his disciples; see Hans Kelsen, *Principles of International Law*, pp. 304 *et seq.*; Josef L. Kunz, 'The "Vienna School" and International Law', in Josef L. Kunz, *The Changing Law of Nations* (Columbus, OH: Ohio State University Press, 1968), pp. 59–124, at p. 79.
[68] Hersch Lauterpacht, *The Function of Law*, pp. 437–8: 'obligatory arbitration is a *conditio sine qua non* of the normal machinery for the preservation of peace'; on the enthusiasm for the rule of law during the inter-war period, see Martti Koskenniemi, 'History of International Law, World War I to World War II', in Rüdiger Wolfrum (ed.), *Max Planck Encyclopedia of Public International Law*, online edition (Oxford: Oxford University Press, 2008); Antony Anghie, *Imperialism, Sovereignty and the Making of International Law* (Cambridge: Cambridge University Press, 2005), p. 124, with further references.
[69] As Martti Koskenniemi has remarked, Lauterpacht's idealistic commitments were not only addressed to the judge, but also the lawyer and academic in a broader sense, see *The Gentle Civilizer of Nations*, p. 406.

understanding,[70] it appears to be more fruitful to conceive of the 'rule of law' as a concept which encompasses *something more*.[71] But what is this additional value of the rule of law? And how will it manifest itself at the international level? If we first address the former concern, a useful distinction is that between the *rule of law* and *rule by law*. Frequently, authoritarian regimes insist that they comply with the rule of law due to the fact that governmental action is subjected to law in the first place.[72] Tamanaha rightly holds the view that this does not mean very much. In fact, this narrow understanding of the rule of law as *rule by law* means lending legitimacy to the status quo *tout court*.[73] With respect to both the domestic and the international levels, Arthur Watts insisted that the rule of law relates more to 'the underlying characteristics of the community's legal system as a whole than to the content of the rules themselves'.[74] Similarly, Vaughan Lowe has described the rule of law as not being 'simply a set of precepts'. Rather, '[i]t is a way of living; a way of organizing society'.[75] According to another author, it is a meta-concept which tries to 'distinguish one particular kind of social order from the diversity of orders to which the name "law" might be applied'.[76] In this respect, it is part of a twofold theory of international law: on the one hand, there is 'the *actually existing* international legal system', and, on the other hand, there is 'the idea of order regulating the relations of States of which the

---

[70] See, e.g., Antonin Scalia, 'The Rule of Law as a Law of Rules', *University of Chicago Law Review* 56 (1989), pp. 1175–88; Matthew Kramer, 'On the Moral Status of the Rule of Law', *Cambridge Law Journal* 63 (2004), pp. 65–97; Matthias Kumm, 'International Law', pp. 19 *et seq.*; slightly more variegated but eventually along similar lines is Sienho Yee, *Towards*, p. 55.

[71] Cf Joseph Raz, 'The Rule of Law and Its Virtue', p. 212; cf also Robert Kolb, *Interprétation et création du droit international – Esquisse d'une herméneutique juridique moderne pour le droit international public* (Brussels: Bruylant, 2006), p. 138.

[72] Cf Jörg Menzel, 'Domestizierung des Leviathan? Südostasiens Verfassungen und ASEAN's neues Homogenitätskriterium demokratischer Verfassungsstaatlichkeit', *Verfassung und Recht in Übersee* 41 (2008), pp. 534–59, at p. 549.

[73] Brian Z. Tamanaha, *Rule of Law*, p. 92; this view is commonly held by authors as diverse as Joseph Raz, 'The Rule of Law and Its Virtue', p. 212; Jeffrey Jowell, 'The Rule of Law', p. 16; Rudolf Smend, *Staatsrechtliche Abhandlungen und andere Aufsätze*, 3rd edn (Berlin: Duncker & Humblot, 1994), p. 523; and Carl Schmitt, *Verfassungslehre*, 9th edn (Berlin: Duncker & Humblot, 2003) (originally published 1928), pp. 129–30 (for the latter author one needs to take account of his conception of the relationship between law and the political, *ibid.*, pp. 200 *et seq.*).

[74] Arthur Watts, 'Rule of Law', p. 16.

[75] Vaughan Lowe, 'The Iraq Crisis', p. 863.

[76] Terry Nardin, 'International Pluralism', p. 104.

existing international legal order is one (and no doubt an imperfect) instance'.[77] This idea can be traced back to the highly influential work of A. V. Dicey on the rule of law. Arthur Watts was influenced by the idea that the rule of law is about a 'climate of legality' in a given society, an idea attributed to Dicey by E. C. S. Wade who continued Dicey's influential treatise on constitutional law.[78]

1.4 The 'climatic' function of the rule of law

It is to this 'climatic' function of the rule of law that we should turn our attention now. This function is based on the idea that one can distinguish between mere compliance with the laws and the rule of law as a synonym for a 'climate of legality'. In other words, this would imply that the rule of law does not exhaust itself in compliance with the law. This brings us back to a particular aspect of Lauterpacht's discussion on the material completeness of the international legal order. He asked in what way international courts and tribunals would proceed when presented with novel situations in which they cannot make out clear rules speaking in favour of or against a certain interpretation of the law. In this situation, Lauterpacht held, there would be four possible approaches: (1) analogy with specific rules or recourse to general principles of international law; (2) general principles of law, notably of private law; (3) shaping a legal rule through a process of judicial reconciliation of conflicting legal claims; and (4) considerations of the larger needs of the international community and the aim to render legal relations between the parties to a dispute as effective as possible.[79]

On the borderline of categories (1) and (2), Lauterpacht identified the principle of abuse of rights, which he considered to be especially appropriate for the progressive development of the law:

It is consonant with State sovereignty to refuse to recognize any source of liability other than that grounded in consent given by treaty or in a rule of law evidenced as binding by custom. But that limitation of liability to defined categories may not be consistent with justice and with the requirements of law in a progressive society. Conduct which has hitherto been in accordance with the purpose of the law may cease to be so owing to developments which the

---

[77] Terry Nardin, 'Theorising', p. 386.
[78] A. V. Dicey, *An Introduction to the Study of the Law of the Constitution*, 10th edn, ed. by E. C. S. Wade (London: Macmillan, 1961), p. cx.
[79] Hersch Lauterpacht, *The Function of Law*, p. 111.

law has not yet had time to take into account; behaviour which the law is as a rule content to regard as not in contradiction with social needs ceases to be so when the advantage accruing to one party from the exercise of an otherwise legal right results in disproportionately grave injury to others; action which is described as lawful may cease to be so if pursued in an unsocial manner or in a manner contrary to the purpose for which it has been allowed. In all these cases such conduct, while *prima facie* lawful, amounts to an abuse of a right conferred by the law.[80]

It is at this point that the issues of complicity and the international rule of law meet. If a general problem with Article 16 ASR is that it imposes responsibility for conduct which is *prima facie* lawful without being classified as such by a primary rule, the imaginary starting point for this critique is to be seen in the conflict of rights situation Lauterpacht is discussing and which should, according to his view, give rise to the applicability of the abuse of rights principle: if the formal *Lotus* principle is upheld, the State which aids or assists another State in the commission of a wrongful act can claim that it is under no obligation not to render this support. Accordingly, it could claim that no restriction upon its independence will exist in the absence of a specific rule. Likewise, the injured State can claim that it has a legitimate interest not to be injured by another State.[81] As we have discussed in Chapter 2, this scenario is hard to integrate into the traditional bilateral structure of the law of State responsibility as there is no reciprocity between right and obligation. However, especially under the State-centred voluntarist view embodied by the *Lotus* principle, it is readily apparent that a State need not suffer infringements of its sovereignty in the absence of an established obligation to do so: 'Pourquoi devrait-on affirmer le principe individualiste en faveur d'une de ces Parties, le titulaire du droit?'[82]

In these situations of conflict of interests, the *Lotus* principle does not work.[83] Bilateralism defeats itself: the question remains whose

---

[80] Hersch Lauterpacht, 'General Rules of the Law of Peace', in Elihu Lauterpacht (ed.), *International Law Being the Collected Papers of Hersch Lauterpacht*, Vol. 1, *The General Works* (Cambridge: Cambridge University Press, 1970), pp. 179–443, at p. 384.
[81] Cf Martti Koskenniemi, *From Apology to Utopia*, p. 257.
[82] Gabriele Salvioli, 'Les règles générales de la paix', *Recueil des Cours* 46 (1933-IV), pp. 1–164, at p. 69.
[83] Andreas L. Paulus, 'The International Legal System', p. 73; Niels Petersen, 'Der Wandel des ungeschriebenen Völkerrechts im Zuge der Konstitutionalisierung', *Archiv des Völkerrechts* 46 (2008), pp. 502–23, at p. 519.

THE INTERNATIONAL RULE OF LAW   67

sovereignty is to gain the upper hand.[84] The ICJ has not consistently upheld the *Lotus* principle in its jurisprudence.[85] At a very early stage, it had the opportunity of clarifying that the absence of clearly established rules does not always give rise to the results required by the *Lotus* principle. In the *Anglo-Norwegian Fisheries* case, the Court held:

> It does not follow at all that, in the absence of rules having the technically precise character alleged by the United Kingdom Government, the delimitation undertaken by the Norwegian Government in 1935 is not subject to certain principles which make it possible to judge as to its validity under international law. The delimitation of sea areas has always an international aspect; it cannot be dependent merely upon the will of the coastal State as expressed in its municipal law. Although it is true that the act of delimitation is necessarily a unilateral act, because only the coastal State is competent to undertake it, the validity of the delimitation with regard to other States depends upon international law.[86]

The delimitation of sea areas is, obviously, a matter that can be distinguished from situations of State complicity. The case is, however, a substantial reassessment of the *Lotus* principle which calls into question its general thrust as always tilting the balance *pro libertate*.[87] The continuing validity of the *Lotus* principle has been challenged most openly by the advisory opinion of the Court on the legality of the use of nuclear weapons. In its *dispositif*, paragraph 2 E, the Court held that:

> in view of the current state of international law, and of the elements of fact at its disposal, the Court cannot conclude definitively whether the threat or use of nuclear weapons would be lawful or unlawful in an extreme circumstance of self-defence, in which the very survival of a State would be at stake.[88]

This finding of the Court has given rise to differing interpretations both within and outside the Court. Whereas a number of dissenting judges

---

[84] For a discussion of this problem, see Martti Koskenniemi, *From Apology to Utopia*, p. 257; Ulrich Fastenrath, *Lücken im Völkerrecht – Zu Rechtscharakter, Quellen, Systemzusammenhang, Methodenlehre und Funktionen des Völkerrechts* (Berlin: Duncker & Humblot, 1991), pp. 239 *et seq.*; Armin von Bogdandy and Markus Rau, 'The Lotus', in Rüdiger Wolfrum (ed.), *Max Planck Encyclopedia of Public International Law*, online edition (Oxford: Oxford University Press, 2008), para. 18.

[85] For an overview in this regard, see Ole Spiermann, 'Lotus and the Double Structure of International Legal Argument', in Laurence Boisson de Chazournes and Philippe Sands (eds.), *International Law, the International Court of Justice and Nuclear Weapons* (Cambridge: Cambridge University Press, 1999), pp. 131–52.

[86] ICJ, *Fisheries Case*, Judgment, ICJ Rep. 1951, 116, 132.

[87] See further ICJ, *Legality of the Threat or Use of Nuclear Weapons*, Advisory Opinion, ICJ Rep. 1996, 226, para. 97.

[88] *Ibid.*, para. 105.

identified the finding of the Court as a *non liquet*, i.e., a finding which would not confirm the presumption established by the *Lotus* principle,[89] others (for instance, Judges Guillaume[90] and Shahabuddeen[91]) interpreted it in light of the *Lotus* precedent. In his declaration, President Bedjaoui summed up the reasons why the *Lotus* principle may no longer be acceptable:

> The resolutely positivist, voluntarist approach of international law still current at the beginning of the century – and which the Permanent Court did not fail to endorse in the aforementioned Judgment [in the *Lotus* case] – has been replaced by an objective conception of international law, a law more readily seeking to reflect a collective juridical conscience and respond to the social necessities of States organised as a community ... Thus the Court, in this opinion, is far more circumspect than its predecessor in the '*Lotus*' case in asserting today that what is not expressly prohibited by international law is therefore authorized.[92]

We need not clarify here whether the *Lotus* principle has indeed 'withered', as the question is at times so beautifully phrased.[93] The 2010 advisory opinion of the ICJ on the conformity with international law of the Unilateral Declaration of Independence in respect of Kosovo has shown that the view that everything which is not expressly forbidden is allowed, still holds some force in international law.[94] The Court has been heavily criticised for sticking to an outdated *Lotus* approach in this respect.[95] For our purposes, it suffices to note that there is a continuing discussion as to the validity of the maxim of *in dubio pro libertate*, a discussion which relates to the 'philosophical basis of international law itself'.[96]

---

[89] *Ibid.*, dissenting opinion of Judge Schwebel, p. 311, at pp. 322–3; dissenting opinion of Judge Higgins, p. 583, para. 30; dissenting opinion of Judge Koroma, p. 556, at p. 558.

[90] *Ibid.*, separate opinion of Judge Guillaume, p. 287, para. 11.

[91] *Ibid.*, dissenting opinion of Judge Shahabuddeen, p. 375, at pp. 389–90.

[92] *Ibid.*, declaration of President Bedjaoui, p. 268, paras. 13 and 15.

[93] Ole Spiermann, 'Lotus and the Double Structure', p. 131; Nikolaus Schultz, 'Ist Lotus verblüht? Anmerkung zum Urteil des IGH vom 14. Februar 2002 im Fall betreffend den Haftbefehl vom 11. April 2000 (Demokratische Republik Kongo gegen Belgien)', *Zeitschrift für ausländisches öffentliches Recht und Völkerrecht* 62 (2002), pp. 703–58.

[94] ICJ, *Accordance with International Law of the Unilateral Declaration of Independence in Respect of Kosovo*, Advisory Opinion, para. 56.

[95] *Ibid.*, declaration of Judge Simma, paras. 2 *et seq.*; see also Thomas Burri, 'The Kosovo Opinion and Secession: The Sounds of Silence and Missing Links', *German Law Journal* 11 (2010), pp. 881–9.

[96] Dapo Akande, 'Nuclear Weapons, Unclear Law? Deciphering the Nuclear Weapons Advisory Opinion of the International Court of Justice', *British Year Book of International Law* 68 (1997), pp. 165–217, at p. 214.

We should note two things here. First, a rigid understanding of the *Lotus* principle, coupled with a faithful application of the distinction between primary and secondary rules as established by the ILC in its codification project on the law of State responsibility, leads to problems in grasping how the ASR can provide for a rule on complicity. Secondly, however, we should also note the inherent limitations of such a rigid approach: when Max Huber participated in the 1931 Cambridge session of the Institut de Droit International, he explained how he understood the finding of the Court in the *Lotus* decision, in which he participated with a casting vote as President of the Court. He emphasised that the decision had only a limited reach. He was willing to adopt another solution where more acute problems of conflicting sovereignties were at stake:

> L'absence d'une règle qui départagerait les droits des Etats et la liberté qui en résulte pour chaque Etat de faire ce qui n'est pas défendu ne signifie pas un état d'anarchie où chacun aurait le droit de passer outre à la situation créée par un autre Etat. Là où les libertés font une collision *réelle*, le droit *doit* fournir la solution, car le droit international, comme tout droit, repose sur l'idée de la *coexistence* de volontés de la même valeur.[97]

The defence of complicit States that they are not violating clearly established international obligations depends on their freedom to engage in conduct which is not *per se* wrongful. As we have now seen, this situation involves a conflict of two liberties. From an international rule of law perspective, how can this conflict be solved? How can international law arrive at the solution which is, according to President Huber, mandatory?

2 The principle of abuse of rights

One possible technique to solve these conflicts of colliding rights is the application of the principle of abuse of rights.[98]

---

[97] Max Huber, 'Observations (sur le rapport de Louis Le Fur sur Reconnaissance, détermination et signification en droit international du domaine laissé par ce dernier à la compétence exclusive de l'Etat)', *Annuaire de l'Institut de Droit International* 31 (1936-1), pp. 77–81, at p. 79.

[98] Cf Albert Bleckmann, 'Die Handlungsfreiheit der Staaten – System und Struktur der Völkerrechtsordnung', *Österreichische Zeitschrift für öffentliches Recht und Völkerrecht* 29 (1978), pp. 173–96, at p. 193; for a sceptical position in this regard Jean-David Roulet, *Le caractère artificiel de la théorie de l'abus de droit en droit international public* (Neuchâtel: Editions de la Baconnière, 1958), pp. 134 *et seq.*

2.1 General meaning of the concept

This principle implies that individual rights shall be exercised in a manner such that other legal subjects would incur no harm.[99] The prohibition of abuse of rights is frequently considered to be an essential element of the international rule of law. David Dyzenhaus has drawn attention to the fact that abuse of rights is part of the 'background constitution' employed by common law judges.[100] In this regard, he was inspired by Hersch Lauterpacht, who, in the words of one commentator:

> saw 'abuse of rights' as a general means of bringing every action of State sovereignty under international law, though as a matter of policy he was prepared to see some areas of action left untouched. But for him, abuse of rights was more than a general principle of law, it was one of the two prime means of effecting peaceful change in the international community.[101]

Lauterpacht conceived of abuse of rights essentially as a means of balancing interests.[102] As legal rights were conferred upon States by the community, Lauterpacht held, the latter could never allow for an anti-social use of those rights.[103] In the quotation from his 1937 Hague

---

[99] Ian Brownlie, *State Responsibility* (Oxford: Oxford University Press, 1983), p. 51; Bin Cheng, *General Principles of Law as Applied by International Courts and Tribunals* (London: Stevens, 1953), p. 125; Gerald Fitzmaurice, 'The General Principles of International Law Considered from the Standpoint of the Rule of Law', *Recueil des Cours* 92 (1957-II), pp. 1-227, at p. 54; Alexandre Kiss, 'Abuse of Rights', in Rüdiger Wolfrum (ed.), *Max Planck Encyclopedia of Public International Law*, online edition (Oxford: Oxford University Press, 2008), para. 2; Robert Kolb, *La bonne foi en droit international public: contribution à l'étude des principes généraux de droit* (Paris: Presses universitaires de France, 2000), p. 436; Rupert Klaus Neuhaus, *Das Rechtsmißbrauchsverbot im heutigen Völkerrecht – Eine Untersuchung zur Entwicklung und Anwendbarkeit eines Begriffes* (Berlin: Duncker & Humblot, 1984), pp. 78 et seq.; Dietrich Rauschning, 'Allgemeine Völkerrechtsregeln zum Schutz gegen grenzüberschreitende Umweltbeinträchtigungen', in Ingo von Münch (ed.), *Staatsrecht – Völkerrecht – Europarecht: Festschrift für Hans-Jürgen Schlochauer* (Berlin: de Gruyter, 1981), pp. 557-76, at p. 561; see also Alejandro Alvarez, *Le droit international nouveau dans ses rapports avec la vie actuelle des peuples* (Paris: Pedone, 1959), p. 504.
[100] David Dyzenhaus, 'The Rule of (Administrative) Law in International Law', *Law and Contemporary Problems* 68 (2005), Autumn Issue, pp. 127-66, at pp. 139 and 154-5; on the rule of law as part of a background constitution, see also Stefan Kadelbach and Thomas Kleinlein, 'Constitution for Mankind', p. 345.
[101] G. D. S. Taylor, 'The Content of the Rule Against Abuse of Rights in International Law', *British Year Book of International Law* 46 (1972-3), pp. 323-52, at p. 323.
[102] Hersch Lauterpacht, *The Function of Law*, p. 296; see also Robert Kolb, *Interprétation et création*, p. 236; Cedric Ryngaert, *Jurisdiction in International Law* (Oxford: Oxford University Press, 2008), pp. 150-1.
[103] Hersch Lauterpacht, *The Function of Law*, p. 286.

lecture reproduced above, Lauterpacht made it clear that *prima facie* lawful conduct could become wrongful if pursued in an anti-social manner or contrary to the goal accorded to it by international law.[104]

The principle of abuse of rights is a contested notion in international law.[105] This becomes apparent from a basic assumption made by Lauterpacht: he conceives rights as granted by international law. To uphold this position, one needs to assume a solidarist view of the international legal order; i.e., at least one which does not consider the State to precede the existence of international law.[106]

2.2 Abuse of rights as a general principle of international law

Abuse of rights is frequently considered to qualify as a general principle of law[107] under Article 38(1)(c) of the ICJ Statute,[108] whereas others

---

[104] See above note 80.
[105] Andrea Gattini, 'Un regard procédural sur la fragmentation du droit international', *Revue générale de droit international public* 110 (2006), pp. 303-36, at p. 325; see further the careful treatment by Roberto Ago, 'First Report on State Responsibility', UN Doc. A/CN.4/217/Add.2, YBILC 1971, Vol. II, Part One, pp. 193, 221-2, paras. 66-7; Ian Brownlie, *Principles of Public International Law*, 7th edn (Oxford: Oxford University Press, 2008), p. 444; Gerald Fitzmaurice, 'The Law and Procedure of the International Court of Justice: General Principles and Substantive Law', *British Year Book of International Law* 27 (1950), pp. 1-41, at p. 12, and Gerald Fitzmaurice, 'The Law and Procedure of the International Court of Justice, 1951-54: General Principles and Sources of Law', *British Year Book of International Law* 30 (1953), pp. 1-70, at p. 53; as well as Gerald Fitzmaurice, 'Rule of Law', pp. 54-5; for an overview of criticism, see Alexandre Kiss, 'Abuse of Rights', paras. 7 *et seq.*; Robert Kolb, *La bonne foi*, pp. 451 *et seq.*
[106] ICJ, *Conditions of Admission*, Advisory Opinion, ICJ Rep. 1948, 57, individual opinion of Judge Alvarez, p. 69; ICJ, *Corfu Channel Case*, Judgment, ICJ Rep. 1949, 4, individual opinion of Judge Alvarez, pp. 47-8; Alexandre Kiss, 'Abuse of Rights', para. 2; Willem Riphagen, 'General Principles of Law', in Antonio Cassese and Joseph H. H. Weiler (eds.), *Change and Stability in International Law* (Berlin: de Gruyter, 1988), pp. 33-7, at pp. 35-6.
[107] Antonio Cassese, *International Law in a Divided World* (Oxford: Clarendon Press, 1986), p. 157; Bin Cheng, *General Principles of Law*, p. 121; Georg Dahm, Jost Delbrück and Rüdiger Wolfrum, *Völkerrecht*, Vol. I/1, 2nd edn (Berlin: de Gruyter, 1989), p. 64, as well as *Völkerrecht*, Vol. I/3, 2nd edn (Berlin: de Gruyter, 2002), p. 878; Stephan Hobe, *Einführung in das Völkerrecht*, 9th edn (Tübingen: Francke, 2008), p. 197; Robert Kolb, *Interprétation et création*, p. 234; Cedric Ryngaert, *Jurisdiction*, p. 180; Joe Verhoeven, *Droit international public* (Brussels: Larcier, 2000), p. 71; Alfred Verdross and Bruno Simma, *Universelles Völkerrecht*, § 461; Wolfgang Weiß, 'Allgemeine Rechtsgrundsätze des Völkerrechts', *Archiv des Völkerrechts* 39 (2001), pp. 394-431, at p. 398; WTO Appellate Body, *United States – Import Prohibition of Certain Shrimp and Shrimp Products (Complaint by the United States)*, para. 158.
[108] Statute of the International Court of Justice of 26 June 1945, entered into force 24 October 1945, UNCIO Vol. XV, p. 355.

posit that there is no such principle in international law.[109] Some are sceptical with respect to its scope of application[110] and with respect to its ability to provide normative guidance.[111] The question of the legal status of the principle of abuse of rights takes us right into the middle of the doctrinal debate on how such general principles of law can be identified. A variety of positions can be made out in this regard:[112] whereas, traditionally, an emphasis was put on the recognition of these principles in the domestic legal orders of 'civilised nations', more attention has recently been paid to the question whether it is possible to identify general principles of law which are inherent to the *international* legal order. Finally, other authors advocate that both categories exist and that thus a distinction should be drawn between the general principles in the sense of Article 38(1)(c) of the ICJ Statute and the general principles of international law. We need not indulge in this debate here. There is considerable support for the existence of a category of general principles of international law,[113] and it is this category in which we are interested here.

One reason to focus on the international level is that the debate on the existence of abuse of rights as a legal principle in domestic legal orders has proved to be inconclusive so far.[114] Conventional wisdom in

---

[109] Friedrich Berber, *Die Rechtsquellen des internationalen Wassernutzungsrechts* (Munich: Oldenbourg, 1955), pp. 149–50; Jean-David Roulet, *Le caractère artificiel*, p. 150; Knut Ipsen, 'Völkerrechtliche Verantwortlichkeit und Völkerstrafrecht', in Knut Ipsen, *Völkerrecht*, 5th edn (Munich: C. H. Beck, 2004), pp. 615–73, at p. 632; Georg Schwarzenberger, 'Uses and Abuses of the "Abuse of Rights" in International Law', *Transactions of the Grotius Society* 46 (1952), pp. 147–79; Wilhelm Wengler, *Völkerrecht*, Vol. 1 (Berlin: Springer, 1964), pp. 392 *et seq.*

[110] Patricia W. Birnie, Alan E. Boyle and Catherine Redgwell, *International Law and the Environment*, 3rd edn (Oxford: Oxford University Press, 2009), pp. 204–5.

[111] Martti Koskenniemi, *From Apology to Utopia*, p. 269; see also Georg Schwarzenberger, 'Uses and Abuses', pp. 150–1; Georg Schwarzenberger and Edward Duncan Brown, *A Manual of International Law*, 6th edn (Milton: Professional Books, 1976), p. 84.

[112] For an overview of the debate with references to the various positions, see Christian Tomuschat, 'International Law', pp. 335 *et seq.*; Stefan Kadelbach and Thomas Kleinlein, 'Constitution for Mankind', pp. 339 *et seq.*

[113] M. Cherif Bassiouni, 'A Functional Approach to "General Principles of International Law"', *Michigan Journal of International Law* 11 (1990), pp. 768–818, at p. 772; Hermann Mosler, 'General Principles of Law', in Rudolf Bernhardt (ed.), *Encyclopedia of Public International Law*, Vol. II, E–I (Amsterdam: Elsevier, 1999), pp. 511–27, at p. 513; Wolfgang Weiß, 'Allgemeine Rechtsgrundsätze', pp. 409–10.

[114] For an overview of its existence in the domestic legal context, see Michael Byers, 'Abuse of Rights: An Old Principle, A New Age', *McGill Law Review* 47 (2001–2), pp. 389–431, at pp. 391 *et seq.*; and Jean-David Roulet, *Le caractère artificiel*, pp. 13 *et seq.*

this regard posits that abuse of rights is a concept which stems from civil law thinking, more particularly French civil law (*abus de droit*). In contrast, it would be alien to the common lawyer.[115] This dichotomy between common and civil law may however explain less than meets the eye. It is striking that some of the most fervent supporters of the principle of abuse of rights in international law come from or are strongly associated with the common law background.[116] What is more, it seems to be no coincidence that the most influential among them, Hersch Lauterpacht, is a traveller between the two worlds of common law and civil law.[117] In fact, his approach to abuse of rights is a *mélange* of thoughts from both schools of law: whereas it is very much in the common law tradition to accept judicial law-making,[118] civil law systems rely to a larger extent on the codification of principles – such as abuse of rights – which aim to channel the activity the judges in common law systems are more readily able to engage in.

It is possible to identify abuse of rights as a general principle of international law. It is true that some authors call its enduring existence and relevance into question[119] because the principle was initially perceived as an instrument to restrict the harshest consequences of the exercise of sovereign rights.[120] It could be argued that due to today's

---

[115] Alexandre Kiss, 'Abuse of Rights', para. 9.

[116] This holds true for Hersch Lauterpacht, Vaughan Lowe, Michael Byers, G. D. S. Taylor and David Dyzenhaus. Other prominent international lawyers from the common law background also support it, e.g., Gerald Fitzmaurice and Ian Brownlie; cf the references in notes 99–105 above and 140 below.

[117] Cf the half-ironic debate between Martti Koskenniemi and Michael Wood whether Lauterpacht was deliberately hiding his civil law background in England or whether he was successfully assimilated, Keynote Speech and Plenary Session of the 25th Anniversary Conference of the Lauterpacht Centre for International Law, Cambridge, 11 July 2008, audio and video files of the session are available from www.lcil.cam.ac.uk/25th_anniversary/anniversary_audiovisual.php (last visited 1 November 2010).

[118] See Daniel Bodansky, 'Non Liquet and the Incompleteness of International Law', in Laurence Boisson de Chazournes and Philippe Sands (eds.), *The International Court of Justice, International Law and Nuclear Weapons* (Cambridge: Cambridge University Press, 1999), pp. 153–70, at p. 169.

[119] See the references in note 109 above.

[120] This becomes most apparent in the way that Judge Alvarez made use of the concept during his work at the ICJ: see ICJ, *Corfu Channel Case*, Judgment, ICJ Rep. 1949, 4, individual opinion of Judge Alvarez, pp. 47–8; on Alvarez' use of the notion and its relation to Alvarez' understanding of sovereignty and interdependence, see Katharina Zobel, 'Judge Alejandro Álvarez at the International Court of Justice (1946–1955): His Theory of a "New International

virtually omnipresent restrictions upon sovereignty in contemporary international law,[121] this principle would no longer be needed and that it has given way to more special and direct restrictions upon State sovereignty. This argument certainly has its merits although it needs to be put into perspective. It is true that the principle of abuse of rights is fairly broad insofar as it requires States generally to exercise their rights in a way so as not to infringe upon the rights of other States.[122] Especially in international environmental law, more specialised principles of good neighbourliness have been developed, for example with respect to the use of shared natural resources.[123] However, it is difficult to ignore the existence of abuse of rights in international practice. As a matter of treaty law, it has found recognition in Article 300 of the UN Convention on the Law of the Sea (UNCLOS), which provides that: 'States Parties shall fulfil in good faith the obligations assumed under this Convention and shall exercise the rights, jurisdiction and freedom recognised in this Convention in a manner which would not constitute an abuse of right.'[124] It has also featured in the jurisprudence of both the Permanent Court of International Justice and its successor.[125] Recourse to it has also been had in arbitral proceedings[126] and by the

---

Law" and Judicial Law-Making', *Leiden Journal of International Law* 19 (2006), pp. 1017–40, at p. 1031.

[121] Cf Armin von Bogdandy and Markus Rau, 'The Lotus', para. 17; on the contemporary meaning of sovereignty, see James Crawford, *The Creation of States in International Law*, 2nd edn (Oxford: Oxford University Press, 2006), pp. 32–3; Georg Nolte, 'Zum Wandel des Souveränitätsbegriffs', *Frankfurter Allgemeine Zeitung*, 6 April 2005, p. 8; Georg Nolte, 'Sovereignty as Responsibility?', *Proceedings of the American Society of International Law* 99 (2005), pp. 389–93.

[122] On the implied dangers of a broad concept of abuse of rights, see Gianluigi Palombella, 'The Abuse of Rights and the Rule of Law', in András Sajo (ed.), *Abuse – The Dark Side of Fundamental Rights* (Utrecht: Eleven, 2006), pp. 5–28, at p. 9.

[123] Patricia W. Birnie, Alan E. Boyle and Catherine Redgwell, *International Law*, pp. 204–5; Georg Dahm, Jost Delbrück and Rüdiger Wolfrum, *Völkerrecht*, Vol. I/1, pp. 396, 445.

[124] United Nations Convention on the Law of the Sea of 10 December 1982, entered into force on 16 November 1994, 1833 UNTS 3.

[125] PCIJ, *German Interests in Polish Upper Silesia*, Merits, Series A, No. 7, 30; PCIJ, *Free Zones of Upper Savoy and the District of Gex*, Judgment, Series A/B, No. 46, 167; ICJ, *Fisheries Case*, Judgment, ICJ Rep. 1951, 116, 141–2; see also ICJ, *Case Concerning the Gabcikovo-Nagymaros Project*, Judgment, ICJ Rep. 1997, 7, separate opinion of Judge Weeramantry, p. 95; dissenting opinion of Judge Parra-Arranguren, p. 227, para. 22.

[126] *Dispute Concerning Filleting within the Gulf of St Lawrence ('La Bretagne')*, Arbitral Award, ILR 82, 590, para. 28; *Phoenix Action Ltd v. Czech Republic*, ICSID Case No. ARB/06/5, para. 143.

WTO Appellate Body.[127] Furthermore, its existence in international law also finds considerable support in doctrinal writings.[128]

Abuse of rights as a general principle of international law may constitute what has been called a 'norm-source'. This description is meant to express 'that they [the general principles] are not simple rules, where the element of application prevails quite neatly, nor simple "legal ideas", where the legislative element outweighs outrageously, but they are a combination of both'.[129] And, further, they do not deal 'with the *fixed* meaning of rules to be applied, but with the *adaptation* of the rules to some constitutional necessities, to new developments and needs'.[130] Without wanting to subscribe fully to this position – and its implication that some rules could necessarily follow from the finding of a general principle as a 'norm-source', this position is similar to ours insofar as we are interested in the transformative potential of the principle of abuse of rights[131] and not so much how it impacts on concrete cases in, for instance, issues of international environmental law.

Michael Byers has emphasised the role of abuse of rights in contributing to the development of the law in as-of-yet underdeveloped areas where sovereign rights collide.[132] In the early 1930s, Hans-Jürgen Schlochauer developed this line of argument in the following way:

The tighter their multi-meshed international relations are tied, the less free and unchecked are States in exercising their 'rights' according to subjective discretion. It is a necessary consequence of the move from the 'indépendance des états' to 'interdependence', to the construction of the 'communauté internationale', that the originally purely individualistic character of the international legal order changes to a social character and that international law, which is above all trade law and commercial law, constructs its norms from the point of view of social goals. This leads to a progressive widening of state responsibility, whereby it deals above all with the imposition of restrictions on the degree to which a subject of international law has a claim *vis-à-vis*

---

[127] WTO Appellate Body, *United States – Import Prohibition of Certain Shrimp and Shrimp Products*, para. 158.
[128] Robert Kolb, *La bonne foi*, pp. 442 *et seq.*; Wolfgang Weiß, 'Allgemeine Rechtsgrundsätze', p. 398 and all the writings referred to in note 107 above.
[129] Robert Kolb, 'Principles as Sources of International Law (with Special Reference to Good Faith)', *Netherlands International Law Review* 53 (2006), pp. 1–36, at p. 9.
[130] Ibid.
[131] See also Rupert Klaus Neuhaus, *Das Rechtsmißbrauchsverbot*, p. 93.
[132] Michael Byers, 'Abuse of Rights', p. 429.

76   COMPLICITY AND THE INTERNATIONAL RULE OF LAW

another, without the powers of the first state being extended, in other words with certain restrictions on the free discretions of states.[133]

As Schlochauer mentioned, the impact of the principle of abuse of rights would have to be measured in terms of its effects in the law of State responsibility. In this sense, abuse of rights could be a useful 'safeguard in relatively undeveloped or over-inflexible parts of a legal system pending the development of precise and detailed rules'.[134] For the problem of complicity in international law, this could tell us that, even in the absence of a fixed primary rule against participation in the internationally wrongful act of another State, international law could provide for an (albeit imperfect) basis to hold a complicit State responsible.

At the same time, even fervent advocates of the abuse of rights principle point to potential problems with its application. Although it is conceivable that a violation of the principle of abuse of rights gives rise to direct State responsibility,[135] it must be 'wielded with studied restraint'[136] as '[i]ts injudicious or rash application may result in interference with rights conferred by law and meriting its protection', as was noted by Hersch Lauterpacht.[137] It is also a matter of debate whether the general principles of law in the sense of Article 38(1)(c) can 'decide cases' as such.[138] The imprecision of most general principles of law will arguably support the view that most of the time they will only be able to influence the interpretation and application of other rules.

---

[133] Hans-Jürgen Schlochauer, 'Die Theorie des abus de droit im Völkerrecht', *Zeitschrift für Völkerrecht* 17 (1933), pp. 373-94, at pp. 378-9, translation by Michael Byers, 'Abuse of Rights', p. 405.

[134] Robert Jennings and Arthur Watts, *Oppenheim's International Law*, Vol. 1, *The Law of Peace*, 9th edn (London: Longman, 1992), p. 407, note 1; very similarly, Gerald Fitzmaurice, 'Law and Procedure, 1951-54', p. 53; Alfred Bleckmann, 'Handlungsfreiheit', p. 193.

[135] Michael Byers, 'Abuse of Rights', p. 411.

[136] Hersch Lauterpacht, *The Development of International Law by the International Court* (London: Stevens, 1958), p. 164.

[137] Hersch Lauterpacht, 'General Rules', p. 385.

[138] See Michael Akehurst, 'Equity and General Principles of Law', *International and Comparative Law Quarterly* 25 (1976), pp. 801-25, at pp. 814 *et seq.*; Alfred Verdross and Bruno Simma, *Universelles Völkerrecht*, §§ 608 *et seq.*; Robert Kolb, *Interprétation et création*, pp. 233-4; Robert Kolb, *La bonne foi*, p. 463; for a recent overview on general principles of law, see Wolfgang Weiß, 'Allgemeine Rechtsgrundsätze', pp. 394 *et seq.*; with particular emphasis on their constitutional functions and aspects of legal theory, see Stefan Kadelbach and Thomas Kleinlein, 'Constitution for Mankind', pp. 343-4.

The consequences of this view would point the way towards an understanding of abuse of rights as a transformative tool in international law, which exerts an influence on the development of more particular rules or ensures the workability of primary rules, especially in conflict of rights situations.[139] In this respect, Vaughan Lowe has spoken of 'interstitial norms', which 'do not themselves have a normative force of the traditional kind but instead operate by modifying the normative effect of other, primary norms of international law'.[140] One of the examples Lowe gave of these interstitial norms is abuse of rights. According to him, this concept

> is likely to achieve much greater prominence as a check upon exercises of legal power by States. Through the influence of these principles, the whole character of international law and its relation to the most pressing problems of fairness and justice can be materially altered.[141]

2.3 Abuse of rights and the international rule of law

In this respect, the principle of abuse of rights is an important aspect of the international rule of law as it is directed against arbitrariness in the exercise of the sovereign powers of States.[142] As Georges Scelle has

---

[139] Hersch Lauterpacht, *The Function of Law*, p. 298; Gerald Fitzmaurice, 'Rule of Law', p. 55; Wolfgang Friedmann, 'The Uses of "General Principles" in the Development of International Law', *American Journal of International Law* 57 (1963), pp. 279-99, at pp. 288-9; Ian Brownlie, *State Responsibility*, p. 52; Robert Kolb, *La bonne foi*, p. 463; Niels Petersen, 'Der Wandel', pp. 519-20. See also Joe Verhoeven, *La reconnaissance internationale dans la pratique contemporaine – Les relations publiques internationales* (Paris: Pedone, 1973), p. 623 (abuse of rights as a 'technique juridique').

[140] Vaughan Lowe, 'The Politics of Law-Making: Are the Method and Character of Norm Creation Changing?', in Michael Byers (ed.), *The Role of Law in International Politics – Essays in International Relations and International Law* (Oxford: Oxford University Press, 2000), pp. 207-26, at p. 213; on the notion of interstitial changes in international law, see also Josef L. Kunz, 'The Nottebohm Judgment (Second Phase)', *American Journal of International Law* 54 (1960), pp. 536-71, at pp. 562-3.

[141] Vaughan Lowe, 'The Politics of Law-Making', p. 218; see further Robert Kolb, *Interprétation et création*, p. 237.

[142] Cf, in this sense, authors as diverse as Philip Allott, *The Health of Nations*, pp. 65-6; Charles de Boeck, 'L'expulsion et les difficultés internationales qu'en soulève la pratique', *Recueil des Cours* 18 (1927-III), pp. 443-650, at p. 630; Robert Kolb, *La bonne foi*, p. 437; Gerhard Leibholz, 'Das Verbot der Willkür und des Ermessensmißbrauchs im völkerrechtlichen Verkehr der Staaten', *Zeitschrift für ausländisches öffentliches Recht und Völkerrecht* 1 (1929), pp. 77-125, at p. 89; Vaughan Lowe, 'Iraq Crisis', p. 864.

maintained in an *exposé* on behalf of France to the ICJ for the *Admissions* advisory opinion:

> Une décision arbitraire, c'est la négation du droit, c'est le caprice. L'utilisation d'une compétence discrétionnaire, c'est l'application d'un pouvoir juridique. Les deux choses sont essentiellement incompatibles. Faire dégénérer une compétence discrétionnaire en un pouvoir arbitraire revient à commettre ce qu'on appelle dans toutes les langues juridiques un abus de droit.[143]

The bias against arbitrariness is common ground between the various formal and substantive conceptions of the rule of law.[144]

2.3.1 Formal and substantive conceptions of the rule of law

Formal conceptions of the rule of law put an emphasis on the way in which law was promulgated, the clarity of the ensuing norm, as well as its temporal dimension.[145] They are not interested 'to pass judgment upon the actual content of the law itself'.[146] Opposition to substantive concepts of the rule of law is frequently motivated by the fear that any turn towards measuring the virtues of the law through the prism of the rule of law would mean to 'propound a complete social philosophy'.[147] Joseph Raz, for example, emphasised that the rule of law is just 'one of the virtues by which a legal system may be judged and by which it is to be judged'.[148] In other words, Raz tried not to burden the rule of law with the task of upholding social order.[149] Rather, at least in his early writings, Raz concentrated on those aspects of the rule of law which enabled citizens to plan their lives ahead – the reliability of the law being a prime value in this regard. In later works, Raz did not abandon his preferences for a formal conception of the rule of law, but added some additional features to his 'negative' conception of the rule of law, as it has been called by Paul Craig.[150] Here, Raz described the core idea

---

[143] *Conditions of Admission*, ICJ Pleadings 1948, 59, 76.
[144] Cf the differentiated position of Joseph Raz, 'The Rule of Law and Its Virtue', pp. 219–20: 'around the subjective core the notion of arbitrary power has grown a hard objective edge'. See also Bardo Fassbender, *UN Security Council Reform*, p. 9: 'Every community committed to the rule of law must strive to avoid arbitrary acts as much as possible.'
[145] On this and the following, see Paul Craig, 'Formal and Substantive Conceptions of the Rule of Law: An Analytical Framework', *Public Law* (1997), pp. 467–87.
[146] *Ibid.*, p. 467.
[147] Joseph Raz, 'The Rule of Law and Its Virtue', p. 211.   [148] *Ibid*.
[149] See also David Kennedy, *The Dark Sides of Virtue*, pp. 155 and 167.
[150] Paul Craig, 'Formal and Substantive Conceptions', p. 469.

of the rule of law as the 'principled faithful application of the law'.[151] This understanding puts a particular emphasis on the legal culture of a given legal system.[152]

Substantive conceptions of the rule of law are not satisfied with this account. It is not easy to find a common denominator for the substantive approaches to the rule of law. While some are motivated by an allegedly irrefutable connection between the rule of law on the one hand and notions of democracy and human rights on the other, different emanations of the substantive approach focus on aspects of social policy which would need to be pursued by virtue of the rule of law.[153] Ronald Dworkin, the most eminent representative of substantive conceptions of the rule of law, distinguished the 'rule book conception' of the rule of law from the 'rights conception'. The former, argues Dworkin, follows a positivist mindset and excludes all considerations of substantive justice from the purview of the rule of law.[154] The rights conception, which he favours, would 'not distinguish … between the rule of law and substantive justice; on the contrary it requires, as part of an ideal of law, that the rules in the book capture and enforce moral rights.'[155]

2.3.2 The rule of law as an antidote to arbitrariness

However appealing such a substantive conception of the rule of law may be, it has its obvious downsides. Brian Tamanaha has emphasised in the context of domestic societies that, where there are divisions on moral questions, there would be 'little reason for confidence that the collection of legal rules, political principles, or the community moral will be coherent or internally consistent'.[156] It is rather obvious that the same considerations will apply *a fortiori* for the international rule of law where even less coherence is to be found in terms of moral values. As Martti Koskenniemi put it: 'If deformalisation has set the house of international law on fire, to grasp at values is to throw gas on the flames.'[157] From this standpoint, a substantive concept of the international rule of law appears to be ruled out. Simon Chesterman, for

---

[151] Joseph Raz, 'The Politics of the Rule of Law', p. 357.   [152] *Ibid.*, p. 358.
[153] For an overview, see Brian Z. Tamanaha, *Rule of Law*, pp. 102–13.
[154] Ronald Dworkin, *A Matter of Principle* (Cambridge, MA: Harvard University Press, 1985), p. 11.
[155] *Ibid.*, pp. 11–12.   [156] Brian Tamanaha, *Rule of Law*, p. 103.
[157] Martti Koskenniemi, 'Fate', p. 16.

example, argues that '[t]o conceive of the rule of law coherent in a manner across the many contexts in which it is invoked requires a formal, minimalist understanding that does not seek to include substantive political outcomes'.[158]

However, it is another question how useful strict dichotomies between formal and substantive conceptions of the international rule of law can really be.[159] In attempts to theorise the rule of law both domestically and internationally, a tradition exists which tries to establish some common ground between the two different understandings.[160] One can also see Joseph Raz' more recent works on the rule of law in this light: by arguing for a 'principled faithful application of the law' on the basis of his previous formal understanding of the rule of law, he is trying to strike a balance between formal and substantive concepts of the rule of law.[161] In UK constitutional law doctrine, Jeffrey Jowell has attempted to give an expression to these considerations. He insists on a predominantly formal conception of the rule of law. According to him, the rule of law is primarily about the correct promulgation of the law and adequate procedures to provide for an orderly application of it. However, he sees a substantive aspect of the rule of law insofar as it enables judges to strike down government action when it is unreasonable, arbitrary or capricious.[162]

One might object that these inherently vague notions merely reintroduce an overblown substantive conception of the rule of law through the backdoor while pretending to remain within a formalist framework. However, this critique would neglect the common law tradition upon which Jowell's arguments are based. These seemingly vague and imprecise notions have been domesticated through judicial practice. In the framework of common law theory, it is exactly the provenance of the rule of law to give a broader expression to the meaning of these principles.[163] In their daily practice, judges and other legal professionals will not be able to depart from the meaning the legal community has established for these notions. In this sense, the rule of law is a 'background constitution' for the common lawyer, if we use the expression coined by David Dyzenhaus,[164] which is yet again closely modelled on

---

[158] Simon Chesterman, 'An International Rule of Law?', p. 333.
[159] Cf David Dyzenhaus, 'The Rule of (Administrative) Law', p. 130.
[160] See, e.g., Terry Nardin, 'Theorising', p. 396.
[161] Joseph Raz, 'The Politics of the Rule of Law', pp. 357 et seq.
[162] Jeffrey Jowell, 'The Rule of Law', pp. 18 et seq.
[163] Joseph Raz, 'The Politics of the Rule of Law', p. 359.
[164] David Dyzenhaus, 'The Rule of (Administrative) Law', pp. 139 and 154–5.

Hersch Lauterpacht's view that the principle of abuse of rights exists necessarily in the background of every legal order.[165]

2.4 Arbitrariness, the rule of law and the ICJ

In light of these considerations, we can note that the International Court of Justice has used the concept of 'arbitrariness' in precisely that way. In the *Asylum* case, the Court contrasted arbitrary action with the rule of law when it enquired whether the granting of asylum could be in conflict with notions of justice.[166] In the *ELSI* case, a Chamber of the Court had to consider whether a decision of the Prefect of Palermo and the Court of Appeals of Palermo amounted to arbitrary decisions under a treaty of commerce, friendship and navigation between the United States and Italy.[167] Not having found an arbitrary decision, the Court made the following remark: 'Arbitrariness is not so much something opposed to *a* rule of law, as something opposed to *the* rule of law.'[168] One has to be cautious not to make too much of these two pronouncements. Both deal with rule of law requirements a State has to respect in the relationship with its citizens and/or foreigners. However, they do point to an international understanding of the rule of law which is of relevance for the present study. The two remarks underline that the rule of law cannot be reduced to mere observance of the law, but that the rule of law is a larger concept than that. They also underline that international law knows the concept of the rule of law[169] and that it is thus not a futile exercise to explore its meaning and its relevance for a specific problem of international law such as that of complicity.

3 Abuse of rights and complicity

Three arguments militate for a close relationship between the principle of abuse of rights and the problem of complicity in international law. The first argument is connected to what Joseph Raz has identified as a key element of any concept of the rule of law: the law 'must

---

[165] Hersch Lauterpacht, *The Development of International Law*, p. 165.
[166] ICJ, *Asylum Case*, Judgment, ICJ Rep. 1950, 266, at p. 287.
[167] Treaty of Friendship, Commerce and Navigation between the United States of America and the Italian Republic of 2 March 1948, 79 UNTS 171.
[168] ICJ, *Elettronica Sicula SpA (ELSI)*, Judgment, ICJ Rep. 1989, 15, para. 128, emphasis added.
[169] See also with respect to the two decisions of the ICJ James Crawford, 'Rule of Law', p. 8.

be capable of being obeyed'.[170] In the absence of a rule on complicity, international law would frequently give rise to situations in which two interests collide: the liberty of the complicit State to pursue its formally not forbidden conduct and the interest of the injured State not to suffer injury. The preceding discussion has shown that this is a situation which can be understood as one in which the principle of 'abuse of rights' may come to the rescue and show the way for an application of the law which does not lead to such a collision of rights. In the words of Joseph Raz: the rule of law has to assure that the law's 'different parts do not fight each other.'[171]

The second argument relates to the fact that there is some support in the literature for the application of abuse of rights doctrine to situations in which a State allows another State to make use of its territory to the detriment of a third State – an authorisation by which the first State may become complicit in the second State's violation of the law. In his 1931 treatise on international law, Ellery C. Stowell wrote that, 'since the object of international law is the preservation and prosperity of the society of states, it follows that the rights which it has recognised for the protection of each state are subject always to the restriction or proviso that they be not used to the detriment of others'.[172] Hersch Lauterpacht wrote similarly that '[i]t is particularly the use of a State's territory in a manner prejudicial to the interests of other States which may give rise to the application of the prohibition of abuse of rights'.[173] The concept of abuse of rights is thus considered to be very similar to the basic rule against one of the most important forms of complicity: that a State is not permitted to allow another State to use its territory to the detriment of another State. It is also noteworthy that the first cases in which the issue of complicity was raised in international protests concerned the use of territory for the unlawful use of force against another State. In the 1950s, the Soviet Union repeatedly protested against certain European States which had granted the United States permission to make use of their territory as a launching pad.[174]

---

[170] Joseph Raz, 'The Rule of Law and Its Virtue', p. 213.
[171] Joseph Raz, 'The Politics of the Rule of Law', p. 359.
[172] Ellery C. Stowell, *International Law* (New York: Henry Holt, 1931), p. 123; see further Jean Combacau and Serge Sur, *Droit international public*, 7th edn (Paris: Montchrestien, 2006), p. 429.
[173] Hersch Lauterpacht, *The Function of Law*, p. 303.
[174] On the role these Soviet protests had for the genesis of a norm on complicity, see John Quigley, *Soviet Legal Innovation and the Western World* (Cambridge: Cambridge

Thirdly and finally, an interesting parallel can be drawn between the principle of abuse of rights and the way we understand responsibility for complicity in contemporary international law through the requirement of a subjective element on the side of the State respectively abusing its rights and becoming complicit. The conduct under consideration in both instances is *prima facie* lawful. Accordingly, it will be necessary to establish intent on the part of the State in question to infringe upon the rights of another State.[175] Without wanting to anticipate our discussion on the requisite subjective element for Article 16 ASR,[176] we shall mention here that there is a presumption that mere objective responsibility will not yield to satisfactory results with respect either to abuse of rights or to complicity. The underlying problem is the same for the two categories: how might it be possible to distinguish between a State which is pursuing its normal course of business and a State which is about to abuse its rights or to render aid or assistance with a view to furthering the commission of an internationally wrongful act by another State?

It is well understood that practical problems will arise in order to establish such a subjective element. As Martti Koskenniemi put it, 'we cannot assume to know these states better than those organs themselves'.[177] However, practical difficulties alone will not allow us to dispense with a necessary criterion to distinguish between various forms of State conduct. Be that as it may – and we will return to the issue in Chapter 5 – the important point here is the similarity between abuse of rights and complicity. In consequence, we shall now look more closely at how the law of State responsibility could accommodate the problem of complicity. In this respect, we will first consider how this field of international law relates to the notion of the international rule of law we have developed so far and then how this relationship impacts upon the problem of complicity.

3.1 State responsibility and the rule of law

The law of State responsibility is connected to the idea of an international rule of law in two different ways.

University Press, 2007), at pp. 162 *et seq.* On these protests, see below Chapter 4, section 3.1.3.

[175] For abuse of rights, see Hans-Jürgen Schlochauer, 'Abus de droit', p. 375; Joe Verhoeven, *La reconnaissance internationale*, p. 622.

[176] See Chapter 5, section 2, text accompanying notes 175 *et seq.*

[177] Martti Koskenniemi, *From Apology to Utopia*, p. 269.

3.1.1 The rule of law and the enforcement of the laws

First, the law of State responsibility could be said to constitute an important part of an international rule of law as it potentially furthers the compliance with and enforcement of international law.[178] In this respect, we can refer to *dicta* of the ICJ and of its predecessor which held that responsibility is the necessary corollary to a right and that reparation must as far as possible wipe out all the consequences of the illegal act.[179] Accordingly, the law of State responsibility fulfils the function of upholding *this* narrow version of the international rule of law insofar as it provides the rules, procedures and remedies by which a State can vindicate its rights and, at least as a side effect, international legality.[180] This statement needs to be qualified to a certain extent. As we have discussed, a meaningful understanding of the international rule of law cannot exhaust itself in the postulate that law should be observed. At the same time, violations of the law do not necessarily call into question the existence of a specific rule of international law,[181] let alone the international rule of law. However, the idea of the rule of law is frequently associated with the expectation not only that the law should be universally applicable among the subjects of a legal order, but also that its enforcement should be of similarly universal character.[182] It would demand too much of the law of State responsibility to guarantee the universal application and enforcement of international law.[183] Despite this caveat, it can be observed that the law of State

---

[178] Cf Ian Brownlie, *Rule of Law*, p. 79.
[179] PCIJ, *Factory at Chorzów*, Jurisdiction, Series A, No. 9, 21; ICJ, *Barcelona Traction, Light and Power Company, Limited*, Second Phase, Judgment, ICJ Rep. 1970, 3, para. 36.
[180] See Hans Kelsen, *Principles of International Law*, p. 25; Ian Brownlie, *Rule of Law*, pp. 79, 94; Andrea Gattini, 'Post 1945 German International Law and State Responsibility', *German Yearbook of International Law* 50 (2007), pp. 407–14; Helmut Philipp Aust, 'Through the Prism of Diversity – The Articles on State Responsibility in the Light of the ILC Fragmentation Report', *German Yearbook of International Law* 49 (2006), pp. 165–200, at p. 167.
[181] Cf the position of the ICJ that violations of a rule do not automatically betray the wish of States to see the rule modified, ICJ, *Military and Paramilitary Activities In and Against Nicaragua*, Merits, ICJ Rep. 1986, 14, para. 207; see also H. L. A. Hart, *The Concept of Law*, 2nd edn (Oxford: Oxford University Press, 1994), p. 220.
[182] Ian Brownlie, *Rule of Law*, p. 94; Arthur Watts, 'Rule of Law', p. 39; Andreas L. Paulus, 'The International Legal System', p. 99.
[183] On the limited usefulness to conceive of the law of State responsibility in instrumental terms, see Helmut Philipp Aust, 'The Normative Environment for Peace – On the Contribution of the ILC's Articles on State Responsibility', in Georg Nolte (ed.), *Peace Through International Law – The Role of the International Law Commission* (Berlin: Springer, 2009), pp. 13–46, at pp. 43 *et seq.*

responsibility as we know it today – as a collection of secondary rules which come to apply once primary rules have been violated[184] – is at least potentially in the position to enable States to raise the responsibility of another State in every conceivable situation, i.e., every time an internationally wrongful act has been committed. As a set of general rules which apply across the whole spectrum of international law if there has been no derogation in the form of *lex specialis*, they provide a language which is susceptible to increasing the rationality of the settlement of international disputes.[185]

There exists a generalised expectation that the commission of internationally wrongful acts may lead to a claim for cessation, reparation or satisfaction. This expectation may be qualified in some instances, especially due to factual inequalities, and may be wholly unrealistic in situations such as the 2003 Iraq war.[186] But these factual inequalities do not call into question the general ambit of the law of State responsibility. That its rules are not invoked in a particular situation does not mean that there exists no State responsibility.[187] In addition, the functions of the law of State responsibility can no longer be reduced to its traditional emphasis on reparation: the rules of responsibility also fulfil 'systemic' functions insofar as they help to establish and form a discourse on international legality.[188] This is an important difference to the state of affairs at the time Roberto Ago was developing his general theory of international responsibility in his 1939 Hague lecture. As we have already seen in Chapter 2, Ago did not accord systemic functions to the law of responsibility. It was purely bilateral, insofar as its only function was to help the injured State vindicate the damage incurred.[189] This state of affairs has considerably changed.

---

[184] On the distinction between primary and secondary rules and the drafting history of the ASR in this regard, see James Crawford, 'Introduction', pp. 14 *et seq*.

[185] A similar argument with respect to the law of diplomatic protection is made by Annemarieke Vermeer-Künzli, 'Exercising Diplomatic Protection – The Fine Line Between Litigation, Demarches and Consular Assistance', *Zeitschrift für ausländisches öffentliches Recht und Völkerrecht* 66 (2006), pp. 321–50, at p. 350.

[186] Cf Christine Chinkin, 'The Continuing Occupation? Issues of Joint and Several Liability and Effective Control', in Phil Shiner and Andrew Williams (eds.), *The Iraq War and International Law* (Oxford: Hart, 2008), pp. 161–83, at p. 182.

[187] ILC Commentary, Introduction to Part Three.

[188] On the systemic functions of the law of State responsibility, see André Nollkaemper, 'Concurrence Between Individual Responsibility and State Responsibility in International Law', *International and Comparative Law Quarterly* 52 (2003), pp. 615–40, at p. 622; see also Pierre-Marie Dupuy, 'Le fait générateur', p. 79.

[189] Roberto Ago, 'Le délit international', p. 431.

In sum, the rules of the law of State responsibility contribute to a 'climate of legality' in international law. In fact, the image of the international legal system as being a unity depends to a large degree on the existence of uniform secondary rules on the enforcement of responsibility.[190] Even though the uniformity of these rules may be challenged by the development of specialised sub-systems of international law,[191] these regimes are typically not wholly self-contained and allow for a 'fall-back' onto the general rules of State responsibility once their own dispute settlement and enforcement mechanisms have failed.[192]

3.1.2 The rule of law and the community interest

The second reason why the law of State responsibility is intimately connected to the idea of an international rule of law goes beyond its availability as a 'meta-language'[193] of international law and focuses upon the community-related aspects of the law of State responsibility. The establishment of a form of graded responsibility, the possibility for non-injured States to invoke the responsibility of other States for violations of obligations *erga omnes* and ultimately the faculty to resort to countermeasures in the collective interest point to the transformation of the law of State responsibility into a regime in which States have an

---

[190] Ian Brownlie, *Rule of Law*, p. 79; Pierre-Marie Dupuy, 'L'unité', pp. 359–60; as well as Pierre-Marie Dupuy, 'Quarante ans de codification du droit de la responsabilité internationale des Etats. Un bilan', *Revue générale de droit international public* 107 (2003), pp. 305–47, at p. 345; see also the statement of Mexico in 'The Rule of Law at the National and International Levels: Comments and Information Received from Governments, Report of the Secretary General', UN Doc. A/62/121, at p. 24.

[191] See, e.g., Andreas Fischer-Lescano and Gunther Teubner, 'Regime-Collisions: The Vain Search for Legal Unity in the Fragmentation of Global Law', *Michigan Journal of International Law* 25 (2003–4), pp. 999–1046, at p. 1015 and Andreas Fischer-Lescano and Gunther Teubner, *Regime-Kollisionen: Zur Fragmentierung des globalen Rechts* (Frankfurt/Main: Suhrkamp, 2006); for a comprehensive overview on this issue, see Bruno Simma, 'Self-Contained Regimes', *Netherlands Yearbook of International Law* 16 (1985), pp. 111–36; Bruno Simma and Dirk Pulkowski, 'Of Planets and the Universe: Self-Contained Regimes in International Law', *European Journal of International Law* 17 (2006), pp. 483–530; 'Fragmentation of International Law: Difficulties Arising from the Diversification and Expansion of International Law', Report of the Study Group of the International Law Commission, finalized by Martti Koskenniemi, UN Doc. A/CN.4/L.682 (2006).

[192] Bruno Simma and Dirk Pulkowski, 'Planets and the Universe', pp. 516–17 and 519–20.

[193] Cf Thomas Kleinlein, 'The Language of Public International Law', in Société Française pour le droit international (ed.), *Droit international et diversité des cultures juridiques* (Paris: Pedone, 2008), pp. 199–208, at p. 201.

interest in the observance of law *per se*.[194] Whether this development has yet reached its climax is hard to judge. In general, what Karl Strupp remarked in his monograph on the law of State responsibility in 1920 still holds true in terms of the *lex lata*:

> It is a completely different problem, for all international agreements and accords – as every violation of the law touches upon the cardinal sentence of the sanctity of treaties – whether the violation, be it of a bilateral, pluri- or multilateral agreement, constitutes an internationally wrongful act against all States of the community of international law (for which the sentence *pacta sunt servanda* is universally valid).[195]

Strupp answered in the negative: although from the viewpoint of morality and world justice it would be desirable that every State would be injured by such a violation, even more so as every State had an interest in the observance of the principle of *pacta sunt servanda*, this would not enable all States to adopt countermeasures (reprisals in the terminology of the time) against the culprit.[196] Rather, these other States could only resort to measures of retorsion.[197] However, in today's international law these findings are qualified to the extent that they no longer apply to all fields of international law. As we have seen in the preceding chapter, this traditional bilateralism of the law has been effectively abandoned in a number of areas.

These community-oriented developments have concentrated on the aspect of the rights of third States.[198] They have provided States which are not injured in a traditional sense with the opportunity to enforce what they conceive of as the international rule of law. In this respect, this development bears some resemblance to the notion of the international rule of law we have developed in this chapter. If conditions under which one could speak of the existence of an international rule of law would require more of States than mere compliance with their own obligations, the faculty to adopt countermeasures in the collective interest could be one expression of such a concept. In invoking the responsibility of another State in the interest of the international

---

[194] On this and the following, see also Georg Nolte, 'From Dionisio Anzilotti', pp. 1089 *et seq.*; Santiago Villalpando, 'The Legal Dimension of the International Community: How Community Interests Are Protected in International Law', *European Journal of International Law* 21 (2010), pp. 387–419, at pp. 389, 395.
[195] Karl Strupp, *Das völkerrechtliche Delikt*, pp. 13–14, translation by the author.
[196] *Ibid.*, p. 14.   [197] *Ibid.*, p. 16.
[198] Cf Eckart Klein, 'Beihilfe', p. 427.

community and in, possibly, also adopting countermeasures in the collective interest, States take it upon themselves to enforce the international rule of law.

While it is in principle desirable to enhance the capacity of States to make a stand against egregious violations of international law which run counter to the most important community interests, it goes almost without saying that this also bears the potential for abuse.[199] There is an inherent dialectic to these attempts for a better enforcement of the international rule of law, as Arthur Watts has reminded us:

> It is evident that it is in this general area of enforcement of international law, particularly where questions of peace and security are in issue, that the international rule of law is at its weakest. Paradoxically, it is this weakness which, when coupled with the growing concern of States that international law should be properly applied and enforced, can lead to action which while intended to strengthen the international rule of law in practice may weaken it even further.[200]

This is further corroborated by the fact that affirming the right of third States to adopt countermeasures in the collective interest eventually means creating new discretionary powers. A world police is created, but one which does not operate according to any 'principle of legality' – to borrow from German terminology – but on the basis of the *Opportunitätsprinzip*, i.e., the principle that the enforcer of the law may decide whether or not she deems it fit to intervene.[201] We need only remember the intervention of Georges Scelle on the relationship between arbitrariness, discretion and abuse of rights[202] to grasp the dialectical relationship between beneficial and adverse effects of this development for the international rule of law.

Seen in this perspective, we are faced with good reasons to inquire into alternative models for a more efficient enforcement of international

---

[199] Among the vast literature, see the differing assessments by Michael Akehurst, 'Reprisals by Third States', *British Year Book of International Law* 44 (1970), pp. 1–18, at pp. 15 *et seq.*; Jochen Abr. Frowein, 'Reactions by Not Directly Affected States to Breaches of Public International Law', *Recueil des Cours* 248 (1994-IV), pp. 345–438, at p. 423; Martti Koskenniemi, 'Solidarity Measures', pp. 344 *et seq.*; Alexander Orakhelashvili, *Peremptory Norms*, pp. 270 *et seq.*; Christian J. Tams, *Enforcing Obligations Erga Omnes*, pp. 249 *et seq.*; Elena Katselli, *The Problem of Enforcement in International Law – Countermeasures, the Non-Injured State and the Idea of International Community* (London: Routledge, 2010), p. 9.

[200] Arthur Watts, 'Rule of Law', p. 44.

[201] Martti Koskenniemi, 'Solidarity Measures', p. 347.

[202] See above note 143.

law.[203] Given the central role played by the law of State responsibility for the concept of the international rule of law, it is important to look for alternatives within this field.

3.2 Complicity and the international rule of law

Putting more emphasis on the responsibility of complicit States may be such an alternative. There are, again, two reasons why the international rule of law has a particular bearing on this issue.

3.2.1 Complicity and the enforcement of international law

The first reason is a somewhat logical extension of the importance of the law of State responsibility for the international rule of law. If State responsibility is a tool for the enforcement of international law which, in turn, is a crucial aspect of the international rule of law, then, as a matter of logic, it could only be positive to draw a wider circle of responsible actors which have to answer for their unlawful activities. Although initially compelling, this position has some weaknesses to it and is, to a certain extent, a bit circular. For one, it lacks conceptual clarity and is not likely to provide us with sufficient reasons to inquire into the relationship between complicity and the international rule of law. Complicity is, in this perspective, just an annex to the general question of how the law of State responsibility and the international rule of law relate to each other. In addition, one should be aware that a greater number of responsible actors is not necessarily conducive to a stronger entrenchment of the international rule of law.[204] Spreading responsibility may also divert it. If, due to a wide interpretation of rules on State complicity, too large a number of States becomes implicated in internationally wrongful acts, participation in such illegality is likely to become the norm rather than the exception. Such a development is

---

[203] Cf Jochen Abr. Frowein, 'Die Verpflichtungen erga omnes im Völkerrecht und ihre Durchsetzung', in Rudolf Bernhardt et al. (eds.), *Völkerrecht als Rechtsordnung – Internationale Gerichtsbarkeit – Menschenrechte. Festschrift für Hermann Mosler* (Berlin: Springer, 1984), pp. 241–62, at p. 260 (for an emphasis on duties of non-recognition of not directly injured States and thus a more cautious position than in his later Hague lecture, see above note 199).

[204] Cf Eckart Klein, 'Beihilfe', p. 435; Georg Nolte, 'Zusammenarbeit der Staaten bei der Friedenssicherung – Steuerung durch Haftungsrecht', in Marten Breuer, Astrid Epiney, Andreas Haratsch, Stefanie Schmahl and Norman Weiß (eds.), *Im Dienste des Menschen: Recht, Staat und Staatengemeinschaft. Forschungskolloquium anlässlich der Emeritierung von Eckart Klein* (Berlin: Duncker & Humblot, 2009), pp. 19–35, at p. 34.

not likely to be conducive to more respect for international law as it would give the impression to States that it is unavoidable to become caught up in relations of State responsibility for even remote aid or assistance to another State. In this context, one should remember that responsibility for complicity as set out by Article 16 ASR is based on the assumption that the aid or assistance which is furnished to the main actor is not in itself wrongful in character.[205] Responsibility for the complicit State is only generated through its connection with the wrongful act of another State.

Still, carefully worked out rules on complicity may have the potential to create greater awareness of the implications of State behaviour on the part of the States concerned. Vaughan Lowe has pointed to these potential implications in the field of foreign (development) aid:

> The bonds that tie us most effectively are those of which we are least aware, those with which we comply out of sheer habit ... [I]t is likely that before very long it will become a matter of routine in donor States to review the legality of conduct of the recipient State that is materially facilitated by that aid. Such a bureaucratisation of the monitoring of compliance with international law, partial as it might be, would make a significant contribution to the entrenchment of the rule of law in the international community.[206]

If considerations of international law are introduced into these policy-making and planning decisions, much would indeed be gained for a more systematic observance of international law.[207] In addition, two arguments militate for the importance of the issue of complicity for the rule of law. These arguments need to be seen in connection with the criticism on the taking of countermeasures in the collective interest and the inherent potential of abuse. First, it needs to be taken into account that the impact of these countermeasures on the enforcement of the international rule of law is limited to some particularly important legal values, that is, obligations *erga omnes*. While there are good reasons for this restriction, it should be noted that only very few international obligations enjoy this status and that, hence, the potential

---

[205] Cf Roberto Ago, 'Seventh Report on State Responsibility', UN Doc. A/CN.4/307 and Add.1-2, YBILC 1978, Vol. II, Part One, pp. 31, 58, at para. 72; Bernhard Graefrath, 'Complicity', p. 374.
[206] Vaughan Lowe, 'Responsibility', p. 14.
[207] Cf also Christine Chinkin, 'Continuing Occupation?', pp. 182-3, on the 'soft factors' which should also guide potentially complicit States; see further Sigrun I. Skogly, *Beyond National Borders: States' Human Rights Obligations in International Cooperation* (Antwerp: Intersentia, 2006), pp. 37 *et seq.*

impact of countermeasures in the collective interest is indeed limited. A prohibition of complicity could, however, be applied across the whole spectrum of international law, thus turning into a more effective tool of requiring all States to do more for the enforcement of international law, if and only if this 'more' consists of doing less, i.e., abstaining from rendering aid or assistance to wrongful conduct. Secondly, such a rule on complicity would arguably operate on the basis of a 'principle of legality' and not on the basis of the *Opportunitätsprinzip*. This description is of course at odds with the traditional field of application for these maxims, as they envisage decisions about taking positive action. That is, however, exactly the point: establishing new bases for responsibility does not open up new discretionary options for States. Rather, it requires a certain conduct by them. In terms of the stability and predictability of the law – key features of any concept of the rule of law – rules on State complicity are thus an appealing alternative to other modes of enforcement of the community interest.

3.2.2 Complicity and the material completeness of the legal order

The second meeting point between the problem of complicity and the international rule of law is of a conceptual nature and relates to the more intricate aspects of the international rule of law. We have highlighted in the previous subsections on the international rule of law that, among other features, the invocation of the rule of law generates an expectation towards the material completeness of a legal system and also towards it fulfilling basic notions of fairness. It has also been mentioned before that a general uncertainty relating to the problem of complicity is whether international law actually includes a rule against it. In the structural perspective of the early Roberto Ago, the main reason why international law would not allow for a rule on complicity was as follows: in the system of perfect reciprocity between rights and obligations, a 'delictual' relation was only conceivable between a pair of States where the right inherent to one of them equalled an obligation on the part of the other.[208] Here, if the complicit State action in itself does not constitute a wrongful act, we are left in this model with the situation that the complicit behaviour cannot be integrated into

---

[208] Roberto Ago, 'Le délit international', p. 433; Roberto Ago, 'Second Report on State Responsibility', UN Doc. A/CN.4/233, YBILC 1970, Vol. II, Part One, p. 177, at p. 192.

these relations. This model perfectly represents the positivist outlook on the international legal system which found its epitome in the *dictum* of the Permanent Court of International Justice in the *Lotus* case.[209] This *dictum* is representative of an understanding of the international legal system which focuses on the formal completeness of the legal order: State behaviour which is not expressly forbidden is permitted. The connection with the problem of complicity now lies in the above-mentioned lack of clarity as to whether Article 16 ASR integrates well into the ILC Articles in terms of it being a secondary rule.[210] It has been criticised for being a primary rule which sets up a new obligation in international law, namely, not to aid or assist another State in the commission of an internationally wrongful act.[211] It has been defended against this charge, *inter alia*, by Special Rapporteur James Crawford who pointed out its similarity to the rules on attribution set out in the ILC Articles, rules which would undoubtedly belong to the category of secondary rules.[212]

How far can this analogy with the rules of attribution be carried? The discussion on the attribution of the acts of private actors has gone through various phases. In the beginning, international law conceptualised the impact of a State upon certain wrongs by private actors through a theory of complicity.[213] Through its *patientia* or *receptus* – in the terminology of Grotius[214] – a State turned into an 'accomplice' of the wrongful act committed by the private actor. To a growing extent, this theory of State complicity with private actors was seen to be in contradiction to international law's limited reach, namely, its regulating only relations between sovereign States.[215] Accordingly, arbitral

---

[209] PCIJ, *Lotus*, Judgment, Series A, No. 10, 18, reproduced in the text accompanying note 2 above.

[210] Pierre d'Argent, *Les réparations de guerre en droit international public. La responsabilité internationale des Etats à l'épreuve de la guerre* (Brussels: Bruylant, 2002), p. 550.

[211] See, e.g., Robert Q. Quentin-Baxter, Statement at the 1518th Meeting of the ILC, YBILC 1978, Vol. I, p. 236, para. 32.

[212] James Crawford, 'Second Report on State Responsibility', UN Doc. A/CN.4/498/Add.1, para. 165.

[213] Cf J. L. Brierly, 'The Theory of Implied State Complicity in International Claims', *British Year Book of International Law* 9 (1928), pp. 42–9.

[214] Hugo Grotius, *De Jure Belli ac Pacis*, pp. 523–6; for an overview of Grotius' position, see Friedrich Klein, *Die mittelbare Haftung im Völkerrecht* (Frankfurt/Main: Klostermann, 1941), pp. 47–8.

[215] Dionisio Anzilotti, 'La responsabilité internationale des Etats à raison des dommages soufferts par des étrangers', *Revue générale de droit international public* 13

practice and legal doctrine developed notions of agency and established the view which is still held today, that States are only responsible for the acts of private actors if they exercise direction or control over these acts.[216] This remains, broadly speaking, the state of the law today.[217] Besides that, States only incur responsibility when they violate obligations of due diligence or of vigilance which would require them to prevent certain wrongs from happening, such as infringements upon the immunity of diplomatic premises.[218]

These developments are significant to our problem because they refer to a similar point of departure for the existence of these rules and those which concern the problem of complicity: in the case of attribution of private conduct, it is also the case that generally States will not have such conduct attributed to them in the absence of a special relation to it.[219] There is no objective responsibility of the State for all conduct committed by its citizens and other individuals present on its territory.[220] At the same time, neighbouring States have the legitimate expectation not to suffer undue harm emanating from that State's territory, as is also expressed in the rationale that no State shall allow

---

(1906), pp. 5-29, at pp. 14-15; Paul Schoen, *Die völkerrechtliche Haftung der Staaten aus unerlaubten Handlungen* (Breslau: Kern, 1917), pp. 35 *et seq.*; Friedrich Klein, *Die mittelbare Haftung*, pp. 50 *et seq.*; for a recent overview and discussion, see Tal Becker, *Terrorism and the State – Rethinking the Rules of State Responsibility* (Oxford: Hart, 2006), pp. 19 *et seq.*

[216] Dionisio Anzilotti, 'La responsabilité internationale', pp. 14-15; see also the *Alabama Arbitration*, reprinted in John Bassett Moore (ed.), *History and Digest of the International Arbitrations to Which the United States Has Been a Party* (Washington DC: Government Printing Office, 1898), Vol. I, pp. 653 *et seq.*; see further Heinrich Triepel, *Völkerrecht und Landesrecht*, p. 340; Karl Strupp, *Das völkerrechtliche Delikt*, pp. 56 *et seq.*; for a contemporary account of *due diligence*, see Riccardo Pisillo Mazzeschi, 'The Due Diligence Rule and the Nature of International Responsibility of States', *German Yearbook of International Law* 35 (1992), pp. 9-51.

[217] Although the details remain subject to debate: compare ICJ, *Case Concerning the Application of the Convention on the Prevention and Punishment of the Crime of Genocide*, para. 124, with ICTY, *Prosecutor v. Dusko Tadic*, para. 120; see further Antonio Cassese, 'The Nicaragua and Tadic Tests Revisited in Light of the ICJ Judgment on Genocide in Bosnia', *European Journal of International Law* 18 (2007), pp. 649-68.

[218] ICJ, *United States Diplomatic and Consular Staff in Tehran*, Judgment, ICJ Rep. 1980, 3, paras. 58, 67.

[219] Cf the observations of Eduardo Savarese who views the ICJ judgment in the *Genocide Convention* case as an affirmation that the notion of effective control is only a particularly intense form of complicity: 'Complicité de l'Etat dans la perpétration d'actes de génocide: Les notions contiguës et la nature de la norme', *Annuaire français de droit international* 53 (2007), pp. 280-90, at p. 285.

[220] ICJ, *Corfu Channel Case*, Judgment, ICJ Rep. 1949, 4, 18.

a use of its territory to the detriment of another State.[221] As we have seen in our previous discussion, this rule finds some inspiration in the concept of abuse of rights.[222] Seen from this perspective, the issue of attribution of private conduct and the problem of complicity are both connected to abuse of rights situations. In the absence of concretely established obligations, a balancing of interests between the freedoms of two States has to be made. Hence, the analogy to which Special Rapporteur James Crawford has referred is a meaningful one, although its conceptual underpinnings were not fully revealed in the ILC Report.[223]

One should of course be cautious not to read too much into the principle of abuse of rights. Over-enthusiastic recourse to it could see it mutating into *the* norm of international law underlying all other rules and principles: after all, all legal rules aspire in some manner to solve conflicts between colliding rights.[224] This objection is, however, only partially legitimate. It is legitimate insofar as it points to the possible dangers of too ready a recourse to the principle of abuse of rights. The strengths of this principle, in Lauterpachtian terms its potential to transform the international legal system as a whole,[225] are also its main weaknesses. Its already limited coherence would become completely unbundled if it were to be referred to without the 'studied restraint' for which Lauterpacht also called.[226] The generality of its scope, i.e., its ability to balance conflicting sovereignties, makes it theoretically conceivable to reduce a great number of international rights and obligations to this maxim. Ultimately, however, such an approach would miss the point. Abuse of rights is a principle which intervenes precisely

---

[221] *Island of Palmas Case*, RIAA II, 829, 839; ICJ, *Corfu Channel Case*, Judgment, ICJ Rep. 1949, 4, 22.
[222] Ellery C. Stowell, *International Law*, p. 123; Hersch Lauterpacht, *The Function of Law*, p. 303; see further Jean Combacau and Serge Sur, *Droit international public*, p. 429.
[223] See further on this aspect Jean d'Aspremont, 'Rebellion and State Responsibility: Wrongdoing by Democratically Elected Insurgents', *International and Comparative Law Quarterly* 58 (2009), pp. 427–42, at pp. 430 *et seq.*; Eduardo Savarese, 'Complicité', p. 285.
[224] An approach which was, in fact, suggested by Gerhard Leibholz, 'Verbot der Willkür', pp. 124–5; see also, *mutatis mutandis*, for sceptical remarks on such an approach, Christian Tomuschat, 'Völkerrechtlicher Vertrag und Drittstaaten', *Berichte der Deutschen Gesellschaft für Völkerrecht* 28 (1988), pp. 9–49, at pp. 28 and 35.
[225] Hersch Lauterpacht, *The Function of Law*, p. 286; on Lauterpacht's position in this regard, see G. D. S. Taylor, 'Abuse of Rights', p. 323.
[226] Hersch Lauterpacht, *The Development of International Law*, p. 164.

in the 'grey areas' of international law. These grey areas, however, are contingent upon the respective development of the international legal system. Due to the growth of the system, new norms will create new conflicts between different 'sovereignties'. In this situation, the principle of abuse of rights may come to intervene. Subsequently, the international legal system may bring about new rules which are directly applicable to this conflict of sovereignties. These new rules will replace the vague notion of abuse of rights with respect to this precise conflict of rights.[227] This does not mean that the principle of abuse of rights becomes redundant and useless. Rather, it will reappear in other situations in which new conflicts materialise. In addition, it may still exist in the background of specialised rules and may contribute to explain why these specific rules exist.[228]

4 Conclusion

Considering the problem of complicity from the viewpoint of the international rule of law and the doctrine of abuse of rights may thus show that we are ultimately concerned with the material completeness of the legal order. This finding does not prejudice the outcome of further study. It should not be understood in a way which would require the international legal system to include a certain rule on State complicity which is characterised by features A, B and C which all flow naturally from considerations of fairness, justice and the greater good. Such an approach would deduce too much from the concept of abuse of rights and of the larger image behind it, the international rule of law.

Our assessment may, however, show that, from the perspective of the international rule of law, a plausible case can be made that it will be necessary to find an answer in international law which responds to the problem of complicity. This goes beyond the policy concerns that it would be welcome to have rules on this matter. *How* international law responds to this expectation is a matter of further examination in terms of the positive law. A strong presumption exists, of course, for the solution the ILC has adopted in Article 16 ASR. We will turn our attention to this provision in the following chapter and examine whether this provision has a basis in customary international law. In

---

[227] Hersch Lauterpacht, *The Function of Law*, p. 298; Vaughan Lowe, 'The Politics of Law-Making', p. 213.
[228] Cf Martti Koskenniemi, 'The Silence of the Law', p. 499.

the meantime, alternative suggestions would be possible, too. In the absence of a specific rule on the matter, much can indeed be said for an application of the principle of abuse of rights – along the lines Hersch Lauterpacht has suggested for filling existing gaps in the law. Others, such as Hans Kelsen, would have objected to such an approach and would have turned rather to the question what the normativity of individual international rules would entail for States participating in wrongful acts of other States. Kelsen might also have suggested that, as a default solution, more credit should be given to the *Lotus* principle and that eventually the freedoms of two States will clash.[229] At the present stage of our examination, we need not and cannot take a position on these suggestions. Rather, we will turn to an assessment of international practice and see whether positive international law provides for an answer in this regard.

---

[229] Cf Hans Kelsen, *Principles of International Law*, p. 306.

4 Complicity in customary international law

In the previous chapter, we saw that there is a strong presumption for the existence of rules on complicity in international law. This presumption is based on systematic considerations, i.e., the situation of conflict of rights which would otherwise ensue. If the international legal system aspires to material completeness, it can thus be expected that rules will have come into existence that would remedy this conflictual situation. At the same time, we have held that, although the concept of an international rule of law speaks in favour of this line of reasoning, it cannot be expected that concrete rules can be deduced from these considerations. Rather, an assessment of international practice will have to show whether customary rules on the matter exist. It goes without saying that the work of the ILC in the field of State responsibility cannot but strengthen the presumption we have already expressed. Hence, there is a great likelihood that Article 16 ASR will be an adequate expression of the customary international law on the matter. However, it is not advisable to accept this finding without question: the ILC is not beyond reproach and, as we will see, especially with respect to Article 16 ASR there exist good reasons to enquire into the basis of this provision in customary international law.

In its final commentaries to the ASR, the ILC appears to uphold the customary character of Article 16 ASR. Although the Commentary does not mention this directly, it can be inferred from formulations such as 'State practice supports assigning international responsibility to a State which deliberately participates in the internationally wrongful conduct of another through the provision of aid or assistance'[1] or '[i]n any event, wrongful assistance given to another State has frequently

---

[1] ILC Commentary, Article 16, para. 7.

led to diplomatic protests. States are entitled to assert complicity in the wrongful conduct of another State.'[2] This confirmation of the character of Article 16 ASR as a rule of customary international law stands in marked contrast to what Special Rapporteur Roberto Ago still held when he presented his initial Draft Article on complicity, namely, that the provision would be part of the progressive development of international law,[3] and also to remarks of Special Rapporteur James Crawford after the completion of the Draft Articles.[4] Academic writings on this question are divided: while the vast majority of authors hold that Article 16 ASR represents customary international law,[5]

---

[2] *Ibid.*, para. 11.
[3] Roberto Ago, 'Seventh Report on State Responsibility', UN Doc. A/CN.4/307 and Add.1-2, YBILC 1978, Vol. 1, Part One, p. 59, para. 74.
[4] James Crawford, 'Responsibility of States', p. 13.
[5] See, e.g., Michael Bothe, 'Der Irak-Krieg und das völkerrechtliche Gewaltverbot', *Archiv des Völkerrechts* 41 (2003), pp. 255–71, at p. 266; Andrew Clapham, 'Symbiosis in International Human Rights Law: The Öcalan Case and the Evolving Law on the Death Penalty', *Journal of International Criminal Justice* 1 (2003), pp. 475–89, at p. 479; Olivier Corten, 'Quels droits et quels devoirs pour les Etats tiers? Les effets juridiques d'une assistance à un acte d'aggression', in Karine Bannelier, Théodore Christakis, Olivier Corten and Pierre Klein (eds.), *L'intervention en Irak et le droit international* (Paris: Pedone, 2004), pp. 105–28, at p. 110; Olivier Corten, 'L'arrêt rendu par la CIJ dans l'affaire du crime de génocide (Bosnie-Herzégovine c. Serbie): Vers un assouplissement des conditions permettant d'engager la responsabilité d'un Etat pour génocide?', *Annuaire français de droit international* 53 (2007), pp. 249–79, at p. 277; Georg Dahm, Jost Delbrück and Rüdiger Wolfrum, *Völkerrecht*, Vol. I/3, p. 879; Oliver Dörr, 'Staats- und völkerrechtliche Aspekte des Irak-Krieges 2003', *Informationsschriften zum Humanitären Völkerrecht* 16 (2003), pp. 181–8, at pp. 184–5; Astrid Epiney, 'Nachbarrechtliche Pflichten', pp. 46–7; Astrid Epiney, 'Umweltvölkerrechtliche Rahmenbedingungen für Entwicklungsprojekte', *Berichte der Deutschen Gesellschaft für Völkerrecht* 41 (2005), pp. 329–77, at pp. 360–1; Peter Hilpold, *Der Osttimor-Fall* (Frankfurt/Main: Peter Lang, 1996), p. 38; Walter Kälin and Erika Schläppi, *Schweizerische Wirtschaftshilfe und internationale Menschenrechte: Konflikte und Konvergenzen aus völkerrechtlicher Sicht, Studie im Rahmen des NFP 'Außenpolitik', Synthesebericht vom 3. März 2000* (Bern: Sekretariat Nationalfonds, 2000), p. 8; Claus Kress, 'Anmerkung zu Generalbundesanwalt, Entschließung v. 21.3.2003 zu § 80 StGB', *Juristenzeitung* (2003), pp. 911–16, at p. 913; Claus Kress, 'The German Chief Federal Prosecutor's Decision Not to Investigate the Alleged Crime of Preparing Aggression Against Iraq', *Journal of International Criminal Justice* 2 (2004), pp. 245–64, at pp. 251–2; John Quigley, 'Complicity', pp. 103, 131; Steven R. Ratner, 'Corporations and Human Rights: A Theory of Legal Responsibility', *Yale Law Journal* 111 (2003), pp. 443–545, at pp. 500–1; Steven R. Ratner, 'Predator and Prey: Seizing and Killing Suspected Terrorists Abroad', *Journal of Political Philosophy* 15 (2007), pp. 251–75, at p. 265; Matthias Ruffert, 'Zusammenarbeit der Staaten bei der Friedenssicherung: Kommentar', in Marten Breuer, Astrid Epiney, Andreas Haratsch, Stefanie Schmahl and Norman Weiß (eds.), *Im Dienste des Menschen: Recht, Staat und Staatengemeinschaft.*

others discuss this issue,[6] while some are outrightly sceptical in this regard.[7]

In the meantime, the International Court of Justice has stated that Article 16 ASR represents customary international law.[8] Earlier in the jurisprudence of the Court, Judge Stephen M. Schwebel had already reached this conclusion, albeit in a dissenting opinion.[9] Although the ICJ is, just as the ILC, not beyond reproach when it comes to determinations that a given rule has a customary character,[10] in general there is little likelihood of 'de-customising' a rule once it has been blessed

Forschungskolloquium anlässlich der Emeritierung von Eckart Klein (Berlin: Duncker & Humblot, 2009), pp. 37–42, at p. 40; Theodor Schweisfurth, 'Aggression', *Frankfurter Allgemeine Zeitung*, 28 April 2003, p. 10; Stefan Talmon, 'A Plurality of Responsible Actors: International Responsibility for Acts of the Coalition Provisional Authority in Iraq', in Phil Shiner and Andrew Williams (eds.), *The Iraq War and International Law* (Oxford: Hart, 2008), pp. 185–230, at p. 218; see also the declaration of more than 300 international lawyers on the implications of the Iraq war, reprinted (including the list of signatories) in *Revue belge de droit international* 36 (2001), pp. 271–85: 'All forms of participation in such a war on the part of the United States, including all forms of assistance to the United States by third States or a regional organization, also constitute a violation of the prohibition of the use of force.'

[6] See, e.g., Andreas Felder, *Die Beihilfe*, pp. 239–40; Vaughan Lowe, *International Law* (Oxford: Oxford University Press, 2007), p. 121; Christian J. Tams, 'All's Well That Ends Well – Comments on the ILC Articles on State Responsibility', *Zeitschrift für ausländisches öffentliches Recht und Völkerrecht* 62 (2002), pp. 759–96, at pp. 793–4; Georg Nolte and Helmut Philipp Aust, 'Equivocal Helpers', pp. 7 *et seq.*; see also the nuanced position of Jean d'Aspremont, 'Rebellion', p. 430, note 19, arguing that Article 16 lacked the quality of a customary rule in 2001 but has since acquired it.

[7] Eckart Klein, 'Beihilfe', pp. 425 *et seq.*; Wolff Heintschel von Heinegg, 'Wider die Mär', p. 222, note 4; see also Bruno Simma, 'Grundfragen der Staatenverantwortlichkeit in der Arbeit der International Law Commission', *Archiv des Völkerrechts* 24 (1985), pp. 357–407, at p. 380 (but see also Alfred Verdross and Bruno Simma, *Universelles Völkerrecht*, § 1285); Knut Ipsen, 'Völkerrechtliche Verantwortlichkeit', p. 648; Birgit Kessler, *Die Durchsetzung der Genfer Abkommen von 1949 in nicht-internationalen bewaffneten Konflikten auf Grundlage ihres gemeinsamen Art. 1* (Berlin: Duncker & Humblot, 2001), p. 107.

[8] ICJ, *Case Concerning the Application of the Convention on the Prevention and Punishment of the Crime of Genocide*, Judgment, para. 420.

[9] ICJ, *Military and Paramilitary Activities In and Against Nicaragua*, Jurisdiction, dissenting opinion of Stephen M. Schwebel, ICJ Rep. 1984, 558, para. 74. This position is not surprising as Judge Schwebel chaired the ILC Drafting Committee which gave (then) Draft Article 27 its final form, see below, at note 17.

[10] In this regard, reference can be made to the enormous amount of criticism the Court was faced with after its judgment on the merits in the *Nicaragua* case: see Anthony D'Amato, 'Trashing Customary International Law', *American Journal of International Law* 81 (1987), pp. 101–5; and Fred L. Morrison, 'Legal Issues in the Nicaragua Opinion', *American Journal of International Law* 81 (1987), pp. 160–6, at pp. 160–1.

with this hallmark of approval by the Court.[11] This does not mean that the assumption of the Court that a certain rule represents customary international law should be followed uncritically. Yet, a pronouncement by the Court on such a matter is impossible to ignore.[12] What the very short statement of the Court does not, however, elucidate are the exact contours of a rule on complicity in customary international law. This is a view which is also held in international practice.[13] As the Court only posited the customary character of Article 16 ASR and assessed neither State practice nor the underlying *opinio juris*, it is also not possible to infer from the judgment what the Court had in mind as the exact content of the rule. Therefore, it is worthwhile attempting to shed more light on Article 16 ASR as an expression of customary international law. Accordingly, this chapter will offer an overview of the relevant international practice on complicity.[14] In doing so, it will also provide the backdrop to the following chapters which will analyse the rules on complicity in greater detail.

1 The evolution of the Article on complicity in the ILC

The development or evolution of a putative customary rule on complicity needs to be seen against the background of the parallel work of the ILC in the field of State responsibility. The provision which eventually turned into Article 16 ASR underwent a number of changes over the twenty-five years of its gestation. It is therefore necessary briefly to present its various emanations as the comments of States on this provision necessarily relate to a specific version of the provision.

The first draft of the provision was presented by Special Rapporteur Roberto Ago in his Seventh Report on State Responsibility in 1978. It read:

---

[11] For general support for the ICJ's findings with respect to customary international law, see Alain Pellet, 'Article 38', in Andreas Zimmermann, Christian Tomuschat and Karin Oellers-Frahm (eds.), *The Statute of the International Court of Justice – A Commentary* (Oxford: Oxford University Press, 2006), para. 235.
[12] Cf Hermann Mosler, *The International Society*, p. 149.
[13] See the statement of the UK representative in the UN General Assembly's Sixth Committee on 19 October 2010, Agenda Item 75, indicating that, although the principle embodied in Article 16 ASR would be representative of customary international law, its text 'has gaps of some significance': manuscript on file with the author.
[14] The most complete surveys of international practice so far have been conducted by John Quigley, 'Complicity', pp. 77 *et seq.*; and Andreas Felder, *Die Beihilfe*.

Article 25 Complicity of a State in the internationally wrongful act of another State
The fact that a State renders assistance to another State by its conduct in order to enable or help that State to commit an international offence against a third State constitutes an internationally wrongful act of the State, which thus becomes an accessory to the commission of the offence and incurs international responsibility thereby, even if the conduct in question would not otherwise be internationally wrongful.[15]

Following the discussion in the Commission, the Drafting Committee made a number of changes. Under the chairmanship of Stephen M. Schwebel, the Committee proposed the following title and text of what would turn into Draft Article 27:

Article 27 Aid or assistance by a State to another State for the commission of an internationally wrongful act
Aid or assistance by a State to another State, if it is established that it is rendered for the commission of an internationally wrongful act, carried out by the latter, itself constitutes an internationally wrongful act, even if, taken alone, such aid or assistance would not constitute a breach of an international obligation.[16]

Schwebel explained that it had been the aim of the Drafting Committee to retain the 'essence of the original text in terms as simple and balanced as possible, while removing any source of ambiguity or misunderstanding'.[17] To achieve this, the Commission had discarded terms such as 'complicity', 'accessory' and 'international offence' as well as the criticised reference to a third State against whom the internationally wrongful act would have to be committed.[18] The Chairman of the Committee also made it clear that it was the opinion of its members that the crucial element of intent should be brought out more clearly in the provision. This was accordingly meant to be secured through the wording 'if it is established that it is rendered for the commission'.[19] Through the inclusion of the words 'carried out by the latter', the Drafting Committee wished to emphasise that the internationally wrongful act of the assisted State needed to have been actually committed.[20] As there was no disapproval voiced among the

---

[15] Roberto Ago, 'Seventh Report on State Responsibility', UN Doc. A/CN.4/307 and Add.1-2, YBILC 1978, Vol. II, Part One, p. 31, at p. 60.
[16] YBILC 1978, Vol. I, p. 269, para. 2.
[17] Stephen M. Schwebel, Statement at the 1524th Meeting of the ILC, YBILC 1978, Vol. I, p. 269, para. 3.
[18] *Ibid.*   [19] *Ibid.*, pp. 269-70, para. 5.   [20] *Ibid.*

members of the Commission, the title and text of Draft Article 27 were therefore agreed upon by the Commission.[21]

This was the provision as it stood for almost twenty years, and which formed part of the Draft Articles adopted on First Reading in 1996. When Special Rapporteur James Crawford reviewed the Articles in the course of the Second Reading, he made several changes to the Article, in particular to accommodate the provision to criticism which was voiced by States in the Sixth Committee of the UN General Assembly and directed at the ILC. The Draft Article then read:

Article 27 Assistance or direction to another State to commit an internationally wrongful act
A State which aids or assists, or directs or controls, another State in the commission of an internationally wrongful act is internationally responsible for doing so if:

(a) That State does so with knowledge of the circumstances of the internationally wrongful act; and
(b) The act would be internationally wrongful if committed by that State.[22]

The major change reflected in the new Draft Article was paragraph (b). This requirement was included to ensure that States would only incur responsibility for aid or assistance when they were also bound by the obligation the main actor was violating. Otherwise, the Draft Article would venture too far into the realm of primary rules. Another change in the Draft Article was the inclusion of the element of direction or control, which was previously included in a separate Article. As this latter change did not persuade the Commission, it was not retained.

After further discussion in the Commission and in the Drafting Committee, the Commission finally adopted the following provision:

Article 16 Aid or assistance in the commission of an internationally wrongful act
A State which aids or assists another State in the commission of an internationally wrongful act by the latter is internationally responsible for doing so if:

(a) that State does so with knowledge of the circumstances of the internationally wrongful act; and

---

[21] *Ibid.*, para. 6.
[22] James Crawford, 'Second Report on State Responsibility', UN Doc. A/CN.4/488/Add.1, p. 21.

(b) the act would be internationally wrongful if committed by that State.

Thus, there were only minor changes effected from Draft Article 27 to Article 16. The 'direction or control' element was removed and inserted into Article 17. In addition, it was set out more clearly that it would need to have been an internationally wrongful act of the assisted State ('by the latter') to which the support was rendered and that it was the support for which responsibility would thus be incurred.

2 Preliminary remarks on customary international law

According to Article 38(1)(b) of the ICJ Statute and the established jurisprudence of the Court, customary international law presupposes 'a general practice accepted as law'.[23] It is not necessary to engage in abstract debates on the relationship between the two elements, State practice and *opinio juris*, at this point of the study.[24] The same holds true for the various theories on the ultimate foundation of customary international law.[25] Where our evaluation of the relevant international practice calls for discussion of such factors, this will be done.

As to the selection of cases and statements which are presented, it is virtually impossible to consider all instances in which the complicity of a State has been invoked. This is so for a variety of reasons: with respect to diplomatic protests, not all of them are documented.[26] Some

---

[23] For the classic definition of these elements, see ICJ, *North Sea Continental Shelf Cases*, Judgment, ICJ Rep. 1969, 3, para. 77.
[24] But cf Michael Akehurst, 'Custom as a Source in International Law', *British Year Book of International Law* 47 (1974-5), pp. 1-53; Wolff Heintschel von Heinegg, 'Die weiteren Quellen des Völkerrechts', in Knut Ipsen, *Völkerrecht*, 5th edn (Munich: C. H. Beck, 2004), pp. 210-56, at pp. 214 *et seq.*; Martti Koskenniemi, *From Apology to Utopia*, pp. 410 *et seq.*; Maurice H. Mendelson, 'The Formation of Customary International Law', *Recueil des Cours* 272 (1998), pp. 155-410; Robert Kolb, 'Selected Problems in the Theory of Customary International Law', *Netherlands International Law Review* 50 (2003), pp. 119-50; Vaughan Lowe, *International Law*, pp. 38 *et seq.*
[25] But see the overview by Alfred Verdross and Bruno Simma, *Universelles Völkerrecht*, §§ 549 *et seq.*; and, in greater detail, Alfred Verdross, 'Entstehungsweisen und Geltungsgrund des universellen völkerrechtlichen Gewohnheitsrechts', *Zeitschrift für ausländisches öffentliches Recht und Völkerrecht* 29 (1969), pp. 635-53.
[26] Cf Michael Akehurst, 'Custom as a Source', p. 13, on the general problems of documentation of State practice; see also Dionisio Anzilotti, *Lehrbuch des Völkerrechts*, p. 56.

may have gone unnoticed and may not have been published in surveys of the respective States' practice.[27]

With respect to the other categories of conceivable practice, for example, more general statements which refer to complicity and State conduct, from which reliance on a complicity provision can be inferred, only the most pertinent instances can be presented here. Without a doubt, the notion of complicity plays an important role in international political discourse. However, it is not the case that every situation in which a governmental representative comments on a situation using the word 'complicity' indicates a reference to complicity in a legally relevant manner. An example of a situation in which it appears that the word 'complicity' was used to ascribe political blameworthiness but which lacks legal relevance is the accusation levelled at the US by the Russian Prime Minister, Vladimir Putin, of US complicity in Georgia's 'war of aggression' in the summer of 2008.[28]

At the other end of the spectrum, one can find apologies made by States for misconduct and, quite frequently, for participation in such misconduct by other States. For example, US President Bill Clinton apologised for cooperation in and failure to prevent the gross human rights violations committed in Guatemala,[29] Rwanda[30] and Greece.[31] However,

---

[27] Protests which have gone unnoticed need to be differentiated from secret practice which does not count for the establishment of State practice: see Yoram Dinstein, 'Customary International Law and Treaties', *Recueil des Cours* 322 (2006), pp. 243–427, at p. 275.

[28] See note 3 in Chapter 1.

[29] President Clinton said, on 10 March 1999, in Guatemala City: 'For the United States it is important that I state clearly that support for military forces and intelligence units which engaged in violence and widespread repression was wrong, and the United States must not repeat that mistake. We must, and we will, instead, continue to support the peace and reconciliation process in Guatemala.' Reprinted in Mark Gibney and Erik Roxstrom, 'The Status of State Apologies', *Human Rights Quarterly* 23 (2001), pp. 911–39, at p. 916.

[30] President Clinton said, on 25 March 1998: 'The international community, together with nations in Africa, must bear its share of responsibility for this tragedy, as well. We did not act quickly enough after the killing began. We should not have allowed the refugee camps to become safe havens for killers. We did not immediately call these crimes by their rightful name: genocide.' Reprinted in Andreas Felder, *Die Beihilfe*, p. 196.

[31] President Clinton said, on 19 November 1999, in Athens: 'When the junta took over in 1967 … the United States allowed its interests in prosecuting the Cold War to prevail over its interests – I should say its obligation – to support democracy, which was, after all, the cause for which we fought the Cold War. It is important that we acknowledge that.' Reprinted in Mark Gibney and Erik Roxstrom, 'State Apologies', p. 916.

these apologies were framed in such terms as to make it apparent that no legal responsibility was admitted. It is another question whether such a distinction will always be convincing and whether courts – be they domestic or international – would accept that such wrongdoing triggered only moral and not legal responsibility. For our purposes, such apologies – which obviously restrict themselves to moral considerations – are not relevant, as they do not betray the requisite *opinio juris*, i.e., the conviction of the apologising State that through its participation it acted contrary to international law. At the same time, it is hard to judge whether States always have to be fully aware of the legal intricacies of their protests, statements and actions. Although this question already borders on the issue of how the requisite *opinio juris* of States is to be evidenced, we can note here with Dionisio Anzilotti that quite frequently States will not fully grasp what legal consequences in terms of State practice their actions could entail.[32] Accordingly, for international practice to count it is not strictly necessary that States expressly characterise their actions as contributions to the development of international law.

There is no shortage of 'international incidents'[33] in which States have become complicit. For a great number of internationally wrongful acts it will be possible to identify another State which has furnished some kind of support to this action. It would be of limited usefulness to compile all those instances in order to get an overall impression of the behaviour of complicit States. This would amount to an exercise of sociology which might be interesting in its own right but would not help to shed light on the contours of the pertinent international rules.[34] One could object to this position by raising the issue that such an overview could be said to reflect 'negative practice' with respect to complicity in international law. This argument would have to rest on the assumption that sufficiently frequent violations of a prohibition of complicity could call its customary status into question as the practice of States would not be characterised by the requisite degree of consistency. Olivier Corten has conducted such an exercise with respect to the widespread support that the US-led coalition of States has enjoyed in its 2003 attack on Iraq. Corten was not able to identify States which

---

[32] Dionisio Anzilotti, *Lehrbuch des Völkerrechts*, p. 53.
[33] This expression was coined by W. Michael Reisman and Andrew R. Willard (eds.), *International Incidents* (Princeton, NJ: Princeton University Press, 1988).
[34] On sociological approaches, see Josef L. Kunz, 'The Vienna School', p. 65.

claimed that they had a right to assist in the commission of wrongful attacks.[35] In this respect, one can hold with the ICJ and authors such as Hans Kelsen and H. L. A. Hart that violations of a rule do not necessarily call its normative value into question: quite to the contrary, such violations may strengthen the binding force of a rule if law-breaking States attempt to justify their conduct with well-accepted grounds for precluding wrongfulness.[36]

Violations of the law themselves thus do not constitute relevant practice for our purposes. Where no State or other relevant actor of international law protested against or at least commented on the complicity issue, there is no basis for ascribing importance to the situation in terms of State practice for the establishment of a customary rule. Relevant actors in this sense include international organisations as subjects of international law which may contribute to the development of new customary law. In contrast, statements of non-governmental organisations cannot be included in this survey except within narrow confines. NGOs do not enjoy the status of subjects of public international law which would enable them to participate in international law-making processes. However, it is acknowledged that the work of NGOs may play a role in the articulation of a 'global legal consciousness' and may thus help to trigger developments in the law.[37] Under certain circumstances, statements of NGOs may therefore be considered to play a role in the establishment of new customary rules. This may especially be the case where they provoked reactions on the part of States.[38]

Another type of situation in which no diplomatic protest or comment by another State intervened and which may still be relevant for the formation of customary international law concerns decision-making procedures of the most diverse kind on the domestic level. Here, States may establish legislation or may act in a certain way due to restrictions imposed upon their behaviour by international law. Where relevant

---

[35] Olivier Corten, *Le droit contre la guerre* (Paris: Pedone, 2008), pp. 287 et seq.

[36] Cf ICJ, *Military and Paramilitary Activities In and Against Nicaragua*, Merits, ICJ Rep. 1986, 14, para. 207; Hans Kelsen, 'Unrecht und Unrechtsfolge im Völkerrecht', *Zeitschrift für öffentliches Recht* 12 (1932), pp. 481–608, at p. 581; H. L. A. Hart, *The Concept of Law*, p. 220.

[37] Cf ICJ, *Arrest Warrant of 11 April 2000*, Judgment, ICJ Rep. 2002, 3, dissenting opinion of Judge van den Wyngaert, para. 27; see further Andreas Fischer-Lescano, *Globalverfassung*, pp. 96–7.

[38] On the various roles of NGOs cf Christian Tomuschat, *Human Rights – Between Idealism and Realism*, 2nd edn (Oxford: Oxford University Press, 2008), pp. 281 et seq.

domestic actors clearly state that their course of action is motivated by concerns of international law, their actions may constitute practice for the development of new customary rules.[39]

One final remark is called for before we present the situations and cases in which complicity played a role. Reliance by international actors on the concept of complicity may be erroneous but may nevertheless play a role for the establishment of customary rules in this regard. States may allege complicity in acts which were perfectly lawful. States and other international actors may also have recourse to the concept of complicity in situations which do not fit the concept as it has been developed by the ILC. Such deficiencies in reasoning do not, however, permit us to disregard such practice. In trying to establish the customary character of Article 16 ASR, it does not matter whether there really was a violation of the law or whether the use of a legal concept is based on an erroneous assessment of facts or the law. In the present stage of development of the international legal system, it is inevitable that States are still self-judging their legal positions.[40] In the absence of a centralised and omni-competent mechanism of dispute settlement, States present their claims and have to reach agreement with each other sooner or later. For our purposes, it should therefore be understood that the inclusion of a situation or case in this list of practice does not mean that there has necessarily been a violation of international law to which aid or assistance has been furnished. We are interested in *assertions* that States have aided or assisted an allegedly wrongful act as well as in the mechanisms and rules with which States wish to prevent complicity from occurring.

3 International practice on complicity

The cases and situations which are reported are grouped into thematic categories in order to identify situations in which complicity has so far played a role in international law. Following this collection of practice, governmental statements will be analysed which have been presented in the Sixth Committee of the UN General Assembly and directly to the ILC. These statements will help to clarify whether and to what

---

[39] Cf Wolff Heintschel von Heinegg, 'Die weiteren Quellen', p. 219.
[40] See Robert Kolb, *Interprétation et création*, p. 287.

extent States see themselves bound to a secondary rule on complicity, and what views they have as to its interpretation. In general, the relevance of the assembled practice will only be discussed once the governmental comments have been presented. However, some cases will call for more explanation at the time.

With these observations in mind, the international practice on complicity is presented in the following order:

1. Assistance in the unlawful use of force.
2. The 2003 Iraq war as an example of assistance in the unlawful use of force.
3. Implication of third States in the context of the US programme of 'extraordinary renditions' and unlawful detention in the fight against terrorism.
4. Support for unlawful activities through the provision of shelter and safe haven.
5. Military support and violations of international law.
6. Foreign aid and violations of international law.
7. Economic cooperation.
8. International cooperation as a consolidation of unlawful events.
9. UN Security Council practice: establishing obligations of non-assistance.
10. UN Security Council practice: exonerating resolutions.
11. Extradition.
12. Legal assistance.
13. Other cases: protests and comments over unspecified forms of support.

3.1 Assistance in the unlawful use of force

The issue of complicity has frequently arisen with respect to situations which involve either the unlawful use of force or other forcible or at least physical infringements upon the territorial integrity or sovereignty of States.

3.1.1 United Kingdom claims in the Corfu Channel case

In the *Corfu Channel* case, the United Kingdom alleged Albanian responsibility for the explosion of mines in the Corfu Channel in 1946. Several warships of the UK were destroyed and forty-four men were killed and forty-two injured. The question who actually laid the mines in the Channel was unresolved. Albania was apparently not capable of doing so itself, as it lacked a navy. The absent third party from the ICJ case – who was never named, but whose implication in the case appears to have been widely assumed – was Yugoslavia.[41] In its written memorial, the United Kingdom alleged Albanian complicity in the laying of the mines: 'The responsibility of Albania rests, firstly, upon a direct complicity in the existence of the minefield which is created by her knowledge of it, whether or not she laid it or connived in its actual laying.'[42] Regardless of whether the United Kingdom thus wished to base its legal position on a notion of complicity which comes close to our contemporary understanding, it is relevant insofar as it sought to establish that Albania was acting together with another State and thus incurred responsibility for being complicit in the resulting explosion of the mines.

3.1.2 UN resolutions on the Korean crisis

During the Korean crisis of 1950/1, UN organs repeatedly called on States not to assist either the North Korean authorities or the People's Republic of China which intervened in support of the former. The Security Council called upon UN Member States to refrain from giving assistance to the North Korean authorities.[43] The UN General Assembly also expressed itself on issues of complicity in the context of the Korean crisis, acting under the Uniting for Peace Resolution.[44] It first stated that: '[T]he Central People's Government of the People's Republic of China, by giving direct aid and assistance to those who were already engaged in committing aggression in Korea and by engaging in hostilities against United Nations forces there, has itself engaged in aggression in Korea.'[45] Furthermore, it called upon 'all States and authorities to refrain from giving any assistance to the aggressors in Korea'.[46]

3.1.3 Various protests by the Soviet Union in the 1950s

The Soviet Union filed a number of diplomatic protests in the 1950s concerning the granting of overflight rights and the permission to use airbases for military aircraft in the context of air strikes.[47] First, the

---

[41] See Christine Chinkin, *Third Parties in International Law* (Oxford: Clarendon Press, 1993), p. 319.
[42] ICJ, *Corfu Channel Case (United Kingdom v. Albania)*, Memorial submitted by the United Kingdom, ICJ Pleadings 1949, Vol. I, p. 19, para. 94.
[43] UN Doc. S/RES/82 (1950), III.
[44] UN Doc. A/RES/377 (V) of 3 November 1950.
[45] UN Doc. A/RES/498 (V) of 1 February 1951, operative para. 1.
[46] *Ibid.*, operative para. 5.
[47] On the lasting influence of this Soviet practice, see John Quigley, *Soviet Legal Innovation*, pp. 162 *et seq.*

Soviet Union protested against the Federal Republic of Germany in 1958 for having allowed the US to use airbases in Frankfurt and near Munich for aircraft which took part in the US attacks on Lebanon in the same year.[48] Similar protests were raised against Italy[49] and Israel[50] in the same year. The Federal Republic and Italy responded to these protests in a similar fashion. They replied that the US conduct in question was lawful and that therefore no responsibility on their part came into being.[51]

In a similar context, protests have been raised with respect to violations of territorial integrity and sovereignty. Again, it was the Soviet Union which protested against the Federal Republic of Germany in 1955[52] and against Turkey in 1956[53] over the launching by the United States of observation balloons from their territory. Turkey replied to this protest by asserting that the balloons were only meant for meteorological use and also flew at high altitudes.[54]

3.1.4 Stanleyville, 1964

The issue of complicity arose in the rescue operation Belgium undertook in 1964 in the Democratic Republic of Congo (DRC). In the town of Stanleyville, a rebel group took 1,600 Europeans hostage. The government of the DRC was not able to deal with the situation and thus invited Belgium and the United States to carry out a rescue mission.[55] The legality of this intervention was disputed by several African States, which saw the intervention in the context of an ensuing offensive by

---

[48] Reprinted in Helmut Alexy, 'Völkerrechtliche Praxis der Bundesrepublik Deutschland im Jahre 1958', *Zeitschrift für ausländisches öffentliches Recht und Völkerrecht* 20 (1960), pp. 636–82, at pp. 663–4.
[49] Cf John Quigley, 'Complicity', p. 84.
[50] Notes of 1 August 1958, reprinted in *Archiv der Gegenwart* 28 (1958), 7223 D, 1.
[51] The German response is reprinted in Helmut Alexy, 'Völkerrechtliche Praxis', pp. 663–4; for the Italian reaction, see *Neue Zürcher Zeitung*, 28 August 1958, pp. 1–2 (Fernausgabe).
[52] Note to Germany of 13 September 1955, reprinted in *Archiv der Gegenwart* 25 (1955), 5332 C, 16; and Note to Germany of 4 February 1956, reprinted in *Archiv der Gegenwart* 26 (1956), 5613 B, 2.
[53] Note to Turkey of 20 February 1956, reprinted in *Archiv der Gegenwart* 26 (1956), 5613 B, 2.
[54] Cf John Quigley, 'Complicity', p. 85.
[55] See the Letter of 24 November 1964 by Prime Minister Moïse Tshombé, addressed to the Secretary General, UN Doc. S/6060; for a more detailed description of the background to and further development of the case, see Georg Nolte, *Eingreifen auf Einladung – Zur Zulässigkeit des Einsatzes fremder Truppen im internen Konflikt auf Einladung der Regierung* (Berlin: Springer, 1999), pp. 261 *et seq.*

the government of the DRC against the rebels which also resulted in massacres of the civilian population. They also considered the rescue mission to be an unlawful intervention into African affairs by the former colonial powers.

In a Security Council debate, Guinea and Mali criticised the United Kingdom for complicity in the intervention in the DRC. The UK had allowed the use of Ascension Island, a dependent territory of the UK, for the landing and taking off of Belgian and US aircraft.[56] Guinea considered the intervention to be an aggression and referred to the 'complicity of the United Kingdom' in this intervention.[57] The representative of Mali stated:

> Another aspect of the aggression launched against the people of Stanleyville is the question of the existence of foreign bases in other countries. We ... should like here to pin-point the share of responsibility in the tragic events at Stanleyville which the United Kingdom assumed by making its colonial bases on Ascension Island available to the troops engaging in the United States and Belgium intervention.[58]

3.1.5 United Kingdom protest against Yemen

The United Kingdom protested – through the United States – against Yemen in 1965 when an aircraft of the United Arab Republic attacked a village and a guard post at Beihan in South Arabia and apparently made use of Yemeni airspace. In the House of Commons, the Secretary of State for the Colonies was asked to explain the situation. He stated:

> I am informed that a village and a guard post in the State of Beihan in South Arabia were attacked with rockets and machine guns yesterday morning by two MiG fighters which subsequently flew off into the Yemen ... Her Majesty's Ambassador in Cairo has been instructed to make a strong protest to the Government of the United Arab Republic about these attacks and to call for payment of compensation to those affected ... We are asking the United States Government to convey on our behalf a similar protest and warning to the Republican authorities in the Yemen and are also reporting the circumstances to the President of the Security Council.[59]

---

[56] For the British position, see Letter of 23 November 1964 addressed to the Secretary General, UN Doc. S/6059 of 24 November 1964.
[57] UN Doc. S/PV.1171 of 10 December 1964, p. 3, para. 8.
[58] *Ibid.*, p. 15, para. 53.
[59] Reprinted in Elihu Lauterpacht (ed.), *British Practice in International Law in 1965* (London: British Institute for International and Comparative Law, 1967), p. 84.

3.1.6 The Osirak incident

In 1981, Israel destroyed the nuclear site of Osirak in Iraq in what was widely considered to be a violation of Article 2(4) of the UN Charter.[60] In this context, the Movement of Non-Aligned States urged States not to render aid or assistance to Israel in the context and aftermath of the Osirak crisis:

> The non-aligned countries called upon all States, and especially the United States of America, to refrain from giving Israel any assistance, whether military, political or economic, that might encourage it to pursue its aggressive policies against the Arab countries and the Palestinian people.[61]

Subsequently, the UN General Assembly also condemned the attack and reiterated 'its call to all States to cease forthwith any provision to Israel of arms and related material of all types which enable it to commit acts of aggression against other States'.[62]

3.1.7 US attacks Against Libya in 1986

Libya issued protests against the United Kingdom in 1986 over alleged UK complicity in US air strikes in Libya. The United Kingdom had allowed US aircraft to take off from a base in the United Kingdom which subsequently attacked targets in Libya. Libya asserted that the UK 'would be held partly responsible' for 'having supported and contributed in a direct way' to the attack.[63] The UK responded that, in its view, the US attacks on Libya were justified on the ground of self-defence against Libyan terrorist attacks.[64] In the context of the same conflict, France refused to grant overflight rights to the US aircraft[65] but did not state clearly that international law considerations were its

---

[60] UN Doc. S/RES/487 (1981), para. 1: The Security Council '[s]*trongly condemns* the military attack by Israel in clear violation of the Charter of the United Nations and the norms of international conduct'; see also Horst Fischer, 'Friedenssicherung und friedliche Streitbeilegung', in Knut Ipsen, *Völkerrecht*, 5th edn (Munich: C. H. Beck, 2004), pp. 1065–1194, at p. 1088.

[61] See Note Verbale dated 16 June 1981 from the Permanent Mission of Cuba to the United Nations addressed to the President of the Security Council, presented on behalf of the Non-Aligned Movement, UN Doc. S/14544.

[62] UN Doc. A/RES/36/27 of 11 November 1981, operative para. 3.

[63] Statement of Ambassador Hamed Houdeiry, Libyan People's Bureau, Paris, reprinted in *The Times*, 16 April 1986: 'Airspace denial confirmed', available at lexisnexis.

[64] *New York Times*, 16 April 1986, sec. A, p. 14.

[65] The French statement is reprinted in *Annuaire français de droit international* 31 (1986), p. 1026 and *Revue générale de droit international public* 90 (1986), p. 981.

motivation.[66] Subsequently, the French President, François Mitterand, stated that no political divisions had appeared in the alliance between France and the US, and affirmed that 'he supported the attacks on Libya'.[67] The UN General Assembly called 'upon all States to refrain from extending any assistance or facilities for perpetrating acts of aggression against the Libyan Arab Jamahiriya'.[68]

3.1.8 Iranian claims in the *Oil Platforms* case

Article 16 ASR was invoked by Iran in the *Oil Platforms* case against the United States. In this case, some aspects of the so-called 'tanker war' in the Persian Gulf were at issue.[69] In particular, Iran accused the United States of having violated its duties as a neutral State by actively supporting Iraq in a political, economic, diplomatic and military way. In a response to the United States' Counter Claims issued in September 2001, Iran expressly relied on Article 16 ASR to attribute responsibility to the United States. It called Article 16 ASR a 'general principle of law that participation in a violation of the law committed by a different actor itself constitutes a violation'.[70] The memorial then cited Article 16 ASR. It further explained that:

[t]he activities of the United States described above were not only violations of the law of neutrality; they also constituted unlawful assistance to an aggression, i.e., a violation of the prohibition of the use of force. This violation engages the international responsibility of the United States. This means that the United States is liable to make compensation for any damage sustained by the victim of that aggression. At the very least, as already explained above, the existence of this legal duty must be a bar to any claim for compensation raised by the United States in this case.[71]

---

[66] But see Olivier Corten, *Le droit contre la guerre*, p. 277, for an interpretation which sees a stronger connection to the problem of complicity.
[67] *New York Times*, 18 April 1986, sec. A, p. 8.
[68] UN Doc. A/RES/41/38 of 20 November 1986, operative para. 3 (79 in favour, 28 against, 33 abstentions).
[69] On the legal aspects of the 'tanker war' and its effects on neutral and other States not directly participating in the hostilities, see Francis V. Russo, 'Neutrality at Sea in Transition: State Practice in the Gulf War as Emerging International Customary Law', *Ocean Development and International Law* 19 (1988), pp. 381–99; Farhang Mehr, 'Neutrality in the Gulf War', *Ocean Development and International Law* 20 (1989), pp. 105–6; Michael Bothe, 'Der Irak-Krieg', p. 268.
[70] ICJ, *Oil Platforms Case (Islamic Republic of Iran v. United States of America)*, Further Response to the United States of America Counter-Claim submitted by the Islamic Republic of Iran, 24 September 2001, para. 7.50.
[71] *Ibid.*, para. 7.51.

3.1.9 The United States, Israel and Iran

The granting of overflight rights was at issue when Israel allegedly asked for United States approval to use Iraqi airspace for a targeted operation against nuclear facilities in Iran in July 2008. The United States did not approve but, according to a newspaper source, reasoned that it would be against United States interests to have Israel attack Iran at this point in time. There was no reporting of international law considerations which motivated the denial of overflight rights over Iraqi territory.[72] Such concerns were, however, mentioned in an investigatory press article by the *New York Times* in January 2009.[73] The article relied heavily on off-the-record interviews with US government officials. The credibility of the article is strengthened by its authors' claim to have omitted a number of details 'at the request of senior United States intelligence and administration officials, to avoid harming continuing operations'. The article reveals how senior White House officials said 'hell, no' to the Israeli request for overflight rights over Iraq. It is reported that 'White House officials discussed the possibility that the Israelis would fly over Iraq without American permission. In that case, would the American military be ordered to shoot them down? If the United States did not interfere to stop an Israeli attack, would the Bush administration be accused of being complicit in it?'[74]

In this context, one should take note of the Status of Forces Agreement Iraq concluded with the US in 2008. According to Article 27(4) of this agreement, '[i]t is not permitted to use Iraqi land, water and airspace as a route or launching pad for attacks against other countries'.[75] Given the degree of *de facto* control that the US was at the time still exercising over Iraqi territory and airspace, one could assume that this agreement

---

[72] See 'US Puts Brakes on Israeli Plan for Attack on Iran Nuclear Facilities', *Haaretz*, 13 August 2008, available at www.haaretz.com/hasen/objects/pages/PrintArticleEn.jhtml?itemNo=1010938 (last visited 1 November 2010).
[73] 'US Rejected Aid for Israeli Raid on Iranian Nuclear Site', *New York Times*, 11 January 2009, p. A1.
[74] This scenario raises several issues with respect to possible US complicity in its own right. These will be discussed in greater detail in Chapter 5, text accompanying notes 80 *et seq.*
[75] Agreement on the withdrawal of United States Forces from Iraq and the organization of their activities during their temporary presence in Iraq of 17 November 2008, entered into force on 1 January 2009, available from the website of the *New York Times*, http://graphics8.nytimes.com/packages/pdf/world/20081119_SOFA_FINAL_AGREED_TEXT.pdf (last visited 1 November 2010).

would speak in favour of an obligation of the US to at least attempt to prevent an attack on Iran which makes use of Iraqi airspace.

3.2 The 2003 Iraq war

Among other forms of support for the 2003 attacks on Iraq, the granting and refusing of overflight rights as well as the use of airbases played a prominent role in the public debate on the conflict.[76]

3.2.1 Austria and Switzerland

As far as can be gathered from information which is publicly available, Austria and Switzerland consistently denied the granting of overflight rights to US and UK aircraft involved in the attacks on Iraq. However, both relied on their traditional status of neutrality, so this refusal cannot be counted as State practice with respect to complicity *per se*.[77] In the case of Switzerland, there are important nuances to its position. For example, the President of Switzerland argued that the attacks on Iraq were illegal under international law.[78] In addition, it was affirmed in another context that Switzerland would have decided on a case-by-case basis whether or not to grant overflight rights if the attacks had been authorised by a UN Security Council resolution.[79] This could be said to imply that the Swiss position on this issue may have been motivated by more than its traditional status of neutrality.[80] However, it seems more persuasive to explain the Swiss conduct primarily through its status as a neutral power. So much was affirmed in an official study by the Swiss Federal Council on the Iraq conflict.[81]

---

[76] For an overview of the position of States with respect to this conflict, see Olivier Corten, 'Quels droits', pp. 117 *et seq.*; Georg Nolte and Helmut Philipp Aust, 'Equivocal Helpers', pp. 2 *et seq.*
[77] Olivier Corten, *Le droit contre la guerre*, p. 279; for Austria, see also the *New York Times*, 14 February 2003, sec. A, p. 14, col. 6.
[78] Olivier Corten, 'Quels droits', pp. 125–6.
[79] *Ibid.*, p. 126.
[80] In fact, the Austrian government made similar remarks to decisions on a case-by-case basis which would take into consideration 'action by the United Nations', *New York Times*, 14 February 2003, sec. A, p. 14, col. 6.
[81] 'La neutralité à l'épreuve du conflit en Irak', étude préparée par le Conseil fédéral en reponse à un postulat de M. Reimann, député au Conseil des Etats, et à une motion déposée au Conseil national par le Groupe parlementaire de l'Union démocratique du centre (UDC), reprinted in Lucius Caflisch, 'La pratique suisse en matière de droit international public 2005', *Schweizerische Zeitschrift für Internationales und Europäisches Recht* 16 (2006), pp. 605–57, at pp. 645 *et seq.*, especially at pp. 651 *et seq.*

3.2.2 Ireland

In comparison, Ireland, despite its traditional status of neutrality, did not refuse to grant overflight rights to US aircraft. The issue of Irish complicity formed the subject matter of High Court proceedings in which the constitutionality of the Irish participation in the war was at stake. The plaintiffs raised the issue of Article 16 ASR. The court refused to take a position on the granting of overflight rights. It did, however, note:

> The issue of 'participation' is not a black and white issue. It may well ultimately be, as stated by the Taoiseach, a matter of 'substance and degree'. However, that is quintessentially a matter for the Government and the elected public representatives in Dáil Eireann to determine and resolve. In even an extreme case, the court would be still obliged to extend a considerable margin of appreciation to those organs of State when exercising their functions and responsibilities under Article 28 [of the Irish Constitution].[82]

3.2.3 Kyrgyzstan

Kyrgyzstan refused to allow an airbase on its territory to be used in connection with the Iraq war. The airbase was frequently employed as a base for US flights into Afghanistan. However, in its explanation of this move, Kyrgyzstan made no reference to its otherwise aiding or assisting in the commission of an internationally wrongful act.[83]

3.2.4 Turkey

Similarly, the temporary refusal of Turkey to allow the use of its territory and airspace for the purpose of the attacks on Iraq cannot necessarily be counted as practice which is informed by the concept of complicity. Rather, this refusal appears to have been owed to political concerns of a new majority in the Turkish parliament which decided not to help the US in these attacks.[84] As far as can be gathered from the information available, international law played no particular role in this decision-making process. In addition, the decision was quickly amended by the Turkish government which wished to secure its

---

[82] See the decision of the Irish High Court, *Edward Horgan v. An Taoiseach and others*, para. 174.
[83] UN Doc. S/PV.4726 of 26 March 2003, Resumption 1, 17.
[84] *New York Times*, 4 March 2003, sec. A, p. 11, col. 1; *New York Times*, 5 March 2003, sec. A, p. 11, col. 5.

influence over the future of northern Iraq and the issue of the Kurds.[85] Subsequently, the Turkish armed forces entered the north of Iraq and Turkish airspace was also used by US paratrooper units which were brought to the theatre of operations in Iraq.[86]

3.2.5 Germany

The German position on the 2003 Iraq war can be called ambiguous at best. While the Federal Government publicly claimed that Germany would not participate in the war, it never denied that more technical assistance would be furnished which was, in the view of the Federal Government, owed to the United States and other allies due to commitments under the NATO Treaty.[87] Whatever the merits of this argument,[88] it does not shed particular light on the German position as to possible responsibility for complicity through its participation in the attacks on Iraq. The exact amount of German participation has been a matter of discussion in an investigatory committee of the German Federal Parliament. In its final report, which was released in the spring of 2009, the committee was not able to reach a common position on the German participation in the war.[89] Some members of the committee have reached the conclusion that Germany indirectly participated in the 2003 war through the furnishing of intelligence information by two agents of the German secret service. These two agents were present

---

[85] *New York Times*, 19 March 2003, sec. A, p. 15, col. 1; for a different assessment of the Turkish conduct, see Theodor Schweisfurth, 'Aggression', who holds the view that Turkey has thus prevented responsibility for complicity. However, he leaves it open whether this was intended or merely a side-effect; this issue also has implications for the other States which helped to protect Turkey against possible attacks emanating from Iraq, on this issue, see Helmut Philipp Aust and Mindia Vashakmadze, 'Parliamentary Consent to the Use of the German Armed Forces Abroad: The 2008 AWACS Decision of the Federal Constitutional Court', *German Law Journal* 9 (2008), pp. 2223–36, at pp. 2229 *et seq.*; Michael Bothe, 'Der Irak-Krieg', p. 268.

[86] See *The Guardian*, 22 March 2003, p. 2: 'War in the Gulf: Turkish Troops Enter Northern Iraq'; see further Helmut Philipp Aust and Mindia Vashakmadze, 'Parliamentary Consent', pp. 2231–2.

[87] See the speech of *Bundeskanzler* Gerhard Schröder at the *Bundestag* on 19 March 2003, reprinted in Matthias Hartwig, 'Völkerrechtliche Praxis der Bundesrepublik Deutschland im Jahr 2003', *Zeitschrift für ausländisches öffentliches Recht und Völkerrecht* 65 (2005), pp. 741–88, at p. 775.

[88] See Georg Nolte and Helmut Philipp Aust, 'Equivocal Helpers', p. 4.

[89] 'Bericht des 1. Untersuchungsausschuss', *Bundestags-Drucksache* 16/13400 of 18 June 2009.

in Baghdad during the US attacks. It is a matter of debate whether the information that they furnished to US agents were relevant for targeting. According to some sources close to the government, the two agents only helped to avoid attacks on protected sites.[90]

3.2.5.1 The decision of the Chief Federal Prosecutor

The Chief Federal Prosecutor was faced with several applications to prosecute members of the German Federal Government by reason of Germany's participation in the war on Iraq. These applications, initiated by citizens and NGOs, were based on section 80 of the German Criminal Code, according to which the preparation of an aggressive war is, under certain circumstances, a criminal act.[91] The Chief Federal Prosecutor did not consider the requirements of this provision to be met. For the purposes of our study, it is relevant that he found the German participation in the conflict to consist of mere tolerance of or acquiescence in US acts. Such forms of non-prevention of aggressive acts could not be understood to constitute a form of participation in the war.[92]

3.2.5.2 The decision of the German Federal Administrative Court

The issues of overflight rights and the use of airbases for the 2003 attacks on Iraq were directly addressed in a judgment of the German Federal Administrative Court. The case involved a major of the German armed forces, the *Bundeswehr*, who refused to obey certain orders for fear of contributing to Germany's illegal participation in the Iraq war. The Court held that the granting of overflight rights and the permission to use airbases situated in German territory to the US gave rise to grave concerns under international law. In the underlying analysis, the

---

[90] *Süddeutsche Zeitung*, 6 June 2009, p. 7: 'Am Krieg indirekt beteiligt'.
[91] The provision reads: 'Anyone who prepares an aggressive war (Article 26, para. 1 of the Basic Law), in which the Federal Republic of Germany is said to participate, and thus increases the danger of a war for the Federal Republic of Germany, will be punished by imprisonment for life or not less than ten years.' Translation by the author. Article 26, para. 1, of the Basic Law reads: 'Acts tending to and undertaken with intent to disturb the peaceful relations between nations, especially to prepare for a war of aggression, shall be unconstitutional. They shall be made a criminal offence.' Translation by Christian Tomuschat and David P. Currie and revised by Christian Tomuschat and Donald P. Kommers, available at www.bundestag.de (last visited 1 November 2010).
[92] 'Entschließung des Generalbundesanwalts' of 21 March 2003, reprinted in *JZ* 2003, pp. 908 *et seq.*, especially at p. 911; for a critical analysis, see Claus Kress, 'Anmerkung', pp. 912–13.

Court made express reference to Article 16 ASR, alongside Article 3(f) of the Definition of Aggression and the traditional rules of neutrality.[93] It concluded:

> As emerges from the foregoing explanations ... serious concerns in international law exist about several acts of assistance of the Federal Republic of Germany in favour of the USA and the UK in connection with the war against Iraq begun on 20th March 2003 ...
> This applies in any case for the granting of overflight rights for military aircraft of the USA and the UK, flying over federal territory on the way to or returning from the war zone in the Gulf region in the framework of the Iraq war. This also applies to the permission for the sending of troops and the transport of weapons and military supplies to the war zone from German soil and for all undertakings which could lead to German state territory serving as starting point or 'hub' for military operations directed against Iraq ... the objective sense and purpose of these measures was to facilitate or even promote the military action of the USA and the UK. Because of these objectives grave concerns in international law exist about the conduct of the federal government in this respect, as regards the prohibition of the use of force in international law and the said provisions of the Fifth Hague Convention.[94]

3.2.6 Norway

Finally, the position of Norway merits consideration as it is a good example of the dichotomy between legal and political considerations with respect to the Iraq war of 2003. Two days after the start of the military operations, on 21 March 2003, the Norwegian Prime Minister, Kjell Magne Bondevik, addressed the Norwegian parliament on the situation in Iraq. His very detailed statement included a close analysis of the international legal issues. The Prime Minister states at the beginning that 'Norway's position is clear. We cannot lend our support to this war.'[95] A legal assessment of the various conceivable justifications for the attacks follows, which finds them to be unpersuasive. The statement culminates in the following finding:

> This is our assessment, but we fully realise that others will argue different points of view. Nevertheless the Norwegian Government's position is not

---

[93] German Federal Administrative Court, 2 WD 12.04 = ILDC 483 (DE 2005), with an English translation of the relevant parts of the judgment by ILDC and commentary by this author.
[94] *Ibid.*, translation of ILDC, para. 4.1.4.1.4.
[95] Reprinted in Rolf Einar Fife, 'Elements of Nordic Practice 2001/2003: Norway', *Nordic Journal of International Law* 73 (2004), pp. 551-7, at p. 563.

primarily based on consideration of international law and legal opinions. The Government has made an overall assessment of the situation and reached a political conclusion. And that political conclusion is clear. We cannot give our support to the present military operations. This is a political rather than a legal assessment.[96]

Although the decision not to participate in the war on Iraq can thus not be attributed exclusively to legal considerations – and thus possibly to considerations of responsibility for complicity – the statement leaves the door open insofar as it only affirms that it was a decision which was not *primarily* based on international law. Accordingly, considerations of international law may still have played a role in the decision-making process and we can therefore cautiously infer some relevance for the problem of complicity from this statement.

3.3 Rendition and detention

The issue of complicity was raised in various contexts in the debate on so-called 'extraordinary renditions'.[97] This term is understood to mean a process by which a detainee is transferred to another State's custody outside regular legal proceedings and with the prospect of being subjected to torture or at least cruel, inhuman or degrading treatment.[98] European States were confronted with the allegation that they were, to varying degrees, facilitating this practice. European support would have consisted in the granting of overflight rights, the provision of secret detention facilities (an allegation which was made with particular reference to Poland and Romania), and cooperation in the exchange of intelligence material.[99]

3.3.1 Investigations by international organisations

The issue was investigated by both the Parliamentary Assembly of the Council of Europe and the European Parliament of the European Union. A resolution of the Parliamentary Assembly of the Council of

---

[96] Ibid., p. 567.
[97] See Philippe Sands, 'International Rule of Law: Extraordinary Rendition, Complicity and Its Consequences', *European Human Rights Law Review* 2006, 411–21.
[98] Cf European Commission for Democracy through Law (Venice Commission), 'Opinion on the International Legal Obligations of Council of Europe Member States in Respect of Secret Detention Facilities and Inter-State Transport of Prisoners', Opinion No. 363/2005 of 17 March 2006, CDL-AD(2006)009.
[99] On this latter issue, see Jack L. Goldsmith, *The Terror Presidency: Law and Judgment Inside the Bush Administration* (New York: Norton, 2007), pp. 127–8.

Europe held that States need to ensure that 'all international cooperation and mutual legal assistance is carried out only in circumstances that respect human rights and international conventions in the field'.[100] Furthermore, the Council of Europe Member States were urged to undertake investigations into the practices of extraordinary renditions which 'should examine thoroughly any action taken by state or foreign agents linked to acts of rendition as well as laws or practices which may facilitate such acts'.[101] The Secretary General of the Council of Europe put it this way:

> The activities of foreign agencies cannot be attributed directly to States. Their responsibility may nevertheless be engaged on account of either their duty to refrain from aid or assistance in the commission of wrongful conduct, acquiescence or connivance in such conduct, or, more generally, their positive obligations under the Convention. In accordance with the generally recognised rules on State responsibility, States may be held responsible for aiding or assisting another State in the commission of an internationally wrongful act. There can be little doubt that aid or assistance by agents of a State party in the commission of human rights abuses by agents of another State acting within the former's jurisdiction would constitute a violation of the Convention. Even acquiescence and connivance of the authorities in the acts of foreign agents affecting Convention rights might engage the State party's responsibility under the Convention.[102]

In its opinion on the legal obligations of Council of Europe Member States, the European Commission for Democracy through Law ('Venice Commission') held that knowingly providing 'transit facilities to another State could amount to providing assistance to the latter in committing a wrongful act, if the former State is aware of the wrongful character of the act concerned', and made reference to Article 16 ASR.[103]

The European Parliament took note of the fact that 'a Council of Europe member state's responsibility is also engaged where its agents (police, security forces, etc.) cooperate with foreign authorities or do

---

[100] Parliamentary Assembly of the Council of Europe, Resolution 1507 (2006), para. 19.4.
[101] *Ibid.*, para. 19.8.
[102] Council of Europe, 'Report of the Secretary General on the Use of His Powers under Article 52 of the European Convention on Human Rights', SG/Inf (2006) 5, para. 23.
[103] European Commission for Democracy through Law (Venice Commission), 'Opinion on the International Legal Obligations of Council of Europe Member States in Respect of Secret Detention Facilities and Inter-State Transport of Prisoners', Opinion No. 363/2005 of 17 March 2006, CDL-AD(2006)009, para. 45.

not prevent an arrest or unacknowledged detention without government knowledge, acting ultra vires'.[104]

3.3.2 United Kingdom

The issue of complicity has also been considered on the part of States which were confronted with allegations of their support for extraordinary renditions. The United Kingdom issued the following statement:

> UK policy on rendition of detainees to third countries is very clear. Where we are requested to assist another State and our assistance would be lawful, we will decide whether or not to assist taking into account all the circumstances. We would not assist in any case if to do so would put us in breach of UK law or our international obligations, including the UN Convention Against Torture. In particular, we would not facilitate the transfer of an individual from or through the UK to another State where there were grounds to believe that the person would face a real risk of torture.[105]

That the UK government considers it to be illegal to assist in an extraordinary rendition is also confirmed by a confidential memo from the Foreign and Commonwealth Office to 10 Downing Street which was leaked to the public.[106] The introduction to the memo states:

> Armed with Rice's statement and the Foreign Secretary's Response, we should try to situate the debate not on whether the US practices torture (and whether the UK is complicit in it): they have made clear they do not – but onto the strong US statements in Rice's text to their commitment to domestic and international instruments.[107]

And, further on, the question whether UK cooperation in the practice of extraordinary rendition could be lawful is discussed:

---

[104] European Parliament, 'Resolution on the alleged use of European countries by the CIA for the transportation and illegal detention of prisoners', adopted midway through the work of the Temporary Committee, 2006/2027 (INI), para. 2.

[105] House of Commons Debates, 20 December 2005, col. 2840W, reprinted in House of Commons, 'Extraordinary Rendition', Standard Note: SN/IA/3816, last updated 23 March 2006. See also the similar response of an FCO Minister in the House of Commons reprinted in *British Year Book of International Law* 77 (2006), p. 659.

[106] Its authoritativeness may be inferred from the fact that it is cited in the House of Commons Standard Note SN/IA/3816 and that there have been no protests about its provenance.

[107] The memo of Irfan Siddiq (FCO) to Grace Cassey (10 Downing Street) is available at www.newstatesman.com/pdf/rendition/rendition.pdf (last visited 1 November 2010).

If the US were to act contrary to its international legal obligations, then cooperation with such an act would also be illegal if we knew of the circumstances ... Where we have no knowledge of illegality but allegations are brought to our attention, we ought to make reasonable enquiries.[108]

Particularly striking is the close similarity between this statement and the language of Article 16 ASR ('knew of the circumstances'). Foreign Minister David Miliband has reaffirmed this as the legal position of the UK when he admitted that the British airbase in Diego Garcia in the Indian Ocean had twice been used by the United States for stopovers.[109]

The possible implication of the UK in secret detentions and torture have also been subject to the scrutiny of the Joint Committee on Human Rights of the UK House of Lords and House of Commons. In this report, Article 16 ASR is expressly referred to as part of the normative framework for an assessment of this participation.[110] The Committee also highlighted what would amount to complicity in torture in this respect. It held:

> [T]he following situations would all amount to complicity in torture, for which the State would be responsible, if the relevant facts were proved:
>
> > A request to a foreign intelligence service, known for its systematic use of torture, to detain and question a terrorist suspect.
> > The provision of information to such a foreign intelligence service enabling them to apprehend a terrorism suspect.
> > The provision of the questions to such a foreign intelligence service to be put to a detainee who has been, is being, or is likely to be tortured.
> > The sending of interrogators to question a detainee who is known to have been tortured by those detaining and interrogating them.
> > The presence of intelligence personnel at an interview with a detainee being held in a place where he is, or might be, being tortured.
> > The systematic receipt of information known or thought likely to have been obtained from detainees subjected to torture.[111]

Finally, in November 2010, the UK government agreed to pay allegedly millions of British pounds of compensation to a number of former

---

[108] *Ibid.*
[109] The statement of 21 February 2008 is available at http://news.bbc.co.uk/1/hi/uk_politics/7257500.stm (last visited 1 November 2010); for a thorough documentation of the events at Diego Garcia, see Peter H. Sand, *United States and Britain in Diego Garcia* (New York: Palgrave Macmillan, 2009), pp. 45–9.
[110] UK House of Lords/House of Commons, Joint Committee on Human Rights, 'Allegations of UK Complicity in Torture', Twenty-Third Report of Session 2008–9, HL Paper 152, HC 230, published on 4 August 2009, para. 25.
[111] *Ibid.*, para. 43.

Guantanamo detainees in the context of an out-of-court settlement over the role of UK security services in the programme of 'extraordinary renditions'. The UK government was adamant that these payments would not constitute any form of acknowledgment of wrongdoing on the part of the UK. Rather, they would be effected in order to defend the national interest from being infringed in court proceedings where evidence would have to be produced on the exact role of the UK in the treatment of the terrorist suspects.[112]

3.3.3 The Netherlands

In its response to a questionnaire drawn up by the Council of Europe on CIA detention centres in Europe, the Dutch government made it clear that it had not participated in abductions by foreign secret services on its national territory or in another State. The relevant response to the questionnaire reads: 'The Dutch government has no knowledge of such abductions and has not been involved in such abductions either actively or passively.'[113] Furthermore, the Minister of Foreign Affairs affirmed during a parliamentary session that 'the Dutch Government has no knowledge of transports by the CIA of illegally detained terrorist subjects via the Netherlands. Accordingly, the Netherlands has not cooperated in, does not know of and has no concrete indications regarding extraordinary rendition of terrorist suspects by US authorities via the Netherlands.'[114]

3.3.4 Other States

In the context of the investigation of the Council of Europe's Secretary General under Article 52 of the European Convention on Human Rights, Council of Europe Member States were asked whether 'any public officials [have] been involved in the unacknowledged deprivation of liberty of any individual, or transport of any individual while so deprived of their liberty'.[115] According to the Secretary General, most States gave a clear and complete answer, indicating that there was, at least to the

---

[112] 'Guantanamo Bay Detainees To Be Paid Compensation by UK Government', *The Guardian*, 16 November 2010, p. 1.
[113] Reprinted in P. C. Tange, 'Netherlands State Practice for the Parliamentary Year 2005–2006', *Netherlands Yearbook of International Law* 38 (2007), pp. 263–366, at p. 289.
[114] *Ibid.*
[115] 'Secretary General's report under Article 52 ECHR on the question of secret detention and transport of detainees suspected of terrorist acts, notably by or at the instigation of foreign agencies', SG/Inf (2006) 5, p. 17.

knowledge of the authorities, no involvement of the kind mentioned.[116] Other States did not conclusively reply[117] or did not reply at all.[118]

Other States have admitted their participation in the programme of extraordinary renditions. This is the case for Bosnia and Herzegovina as well as for Canada.[119] In the latter case, the Canadian Prime Minister, Stephen Harper, apologised to Maher Arar, a Canadian citizen who was intercepted at John F. Kennedy Airport in New York and subsequently tortured in Syria. Canadian authorities helped insofar as they provided intelligence information on Mr Arar which in the end did not prove to be viable. After being released from prison in Syria, Arar filed a lawsuit against the Canadian government in order to obtain compensation. Together with the apology of Prime Minister Harper, the Canadian government offered him compensation amounting to US$8.9 million. Subsequently, Arar did not pursue his lawsuit any further.[120]

3.3.5 Canada's participation in the 'Guantanamo Bay process'

In *Canada (Justice)* v. *Khadr*,[121] the Canadian Supreme Court addressed the question whether the Canadian Charter of Rights and Freedoms would apply to the extraterritorial conduct of Canadian State authorities. The case dealt with Canadian officials, including agents of the Canadian Security and Intelligence Service (CSIS), questioning a Canadian citizen at Guantanamo Bay and sharing the products of these interviews with US authorities.

The Court found several violations of international law by the United States by having recourse to the jurisprudence of the US Supreme Court. It said that '[t]he violations of human rights identified by the

---

[116] Armenia, Azerbaijan, Belgium, Bulgaria, Cyprus, Czech Republic, Denmark, Finland, France, Germany, Hungary, Iceland, Ireland, Liechtenstein, Luxembourg, Malta, Moldova, Netherlands, Portugal, Romania, San Marino, Sweden, Turkey and the United Kingdom, see *ibid*.
[117] Russian Federation, Andorra, Austria, Croatia, Estonia, Greece, Italy, Latvia, Monaco, Norway, Poland, Serbia and Montenegro, Slovakia, Slovenia, Spain, Switzerland, Ukraine, see *ibid*., p. 18.
[118] Bosnia and Herzegovina, Georgia, Lithuania, Macedonia, see *ibid*.
[119] This was noted by European Parliament 'Resolution on the alleged use of European countries by the CIA for the transportation and illegal detention of prisoners', adopted midway through the work of the Temporary Committee, 2006/2027 (INI), para. 143.
[120] The statement of apology by Canadian Prime Minister Stephen Harper can be accessed at: www.pm.gc.ca/eng/media.asp?category=1&id=1509 (last visited 1 November 2010).
[121] Supreme Court of Canada, *Canada (Justice)* v. *Khadr*, 2008 SCC 28.

United States Supreme Court are sufficient to permit us to conclude that the regime providing for the detention and trial of Mr Khadr at the time of the CSIS interviews constituted a clear violation of fundamental human rights protected by international law.'[122] The Court inferred from this that participation 'in the Guantanamo Bay process' would be contrary to Canada's international obligations. As for the applicability of the Canadian Charter of Rights and Freedoms, the Court stated:

> We conclude that the principles of international law and comity that might otherwise preclude application of the *Charter* to Canadian officials acting abroad do not apply to assistance they gave to US authorities at Guantanamo Bay ... By making the product of its interviews of Mr Khadr available to US authorities, Canada participated in a process that was contrary to Canada's international human rights obligations.[123]

3.3.6 Canada's role in transferring detainees in Afghanistan

The issue of potential complicity of a State transferring detainees has also been discussed with respect to Canadian policy in Afghanistan.[124] Two NGOs, the British Columbia Civil Liberties Association (BCCLA)[125] and Amnesty International Canada,[126] initiated litigation against the Chief of the Defence Staff for the Canadian Forces, the Minister of National Defence and the Attorney General of Canada. The litigation aimed at ensuring the applicability of international human rights standards and those set out in the Canadian Charter of Rights and Freedoms for individuals transferred to the Afghan authorities.

Under an initial arrangement of 18 December 2005, no specific guarantees were provided which would have allowed for Canadian oversight of the fate of the detainees. After news of mistreatment emerged, Canada and Afghanistan concluded a new arrangement on 3 May 2007 which specifically set out that the 'Afghan authorities will be responsible for treating such individuals in accordance

---

[122] *Ibid.*, para. 24.   [123] *Ibid.*, paras. 26–7.
[124] Cf Michael Byers, 'Afghanistan: We Cannot Risk Complicity in Torture', *Globe and Mail*, 27 September 2005, p. A17.
[125] For an overview of their activities in this regard, see www.bccla.org/antiterrorissue/afghan_detainee_litigation.html (last visited 1 November 2010).
[126] See especially the report 'Afghanistan – Detainees Transferred to Torture: ISAF Complicity?' of 2007, available at www.amnesty.ca/amnestynews/upload/ASA110112007.pdf (last visited 1 November 2010).

with Afghanistan's international human rights obligations including prohibiting torture and cruel, inhuman or degrading treatment, protection against torture and using only such force as is reasonable to guard against escape'. Furthermore, the arrangement required Afghanistan not to transfer to another State a detainee handed over by Canada without the prior written agreement of the government of Canada.[127]

In the course of the litigation on this issue, the Canadian government relied on a report of Christopher Greenwood in which Article 16 ASR was considered. Greenwood held that the conditions for responsibility under Article 16 ASR would not be met due to an absence of the subjective element of the provision, namely, Canada's lack of intent or knowledge with respect to the alleged torture.[128] In 2008, it emerged that Canada had quietly halted all transfers of detainees to Afghan authorities in November 2007.[129] In February 2008, the transfer of detainees resumed, however.[130]

With respect to the litigation initiated by the two NGOs, the Canadian Federal Court of Appeal denied the applicability of the Canadian Charter of Rights and Freedoms in Afghanistan when non-Canadian citizens were held in detention by Canadian forces. The reasons for this decision was a lack of effective control on the part of the Canadian forces over the detention centre and an alleged agreement between the Canadian and Afghan governments that Afghan law and international humanitarian law should apply to the conduct of the Canadian forces.[131]

---

[127] Arrangement for the Transfer of Detainees between the Government of Canada and the Government of the Islamic Republic of Afghanistan of 3 May 2007, reproduced as Exhibit A referred to in the affidavit of Scott Proudfoot in the Canadian Federal Court Case *Amnesty International Canada and British Columbia Civil Liberties Association v. Chief of the Defence Staff for the Canadian Forces, Minister of National Defence and the Attorney General of Canada*, Court File No. T-324-07, available at www.bccla.org/antiterrorissue/afghan_detainee_litigation.html (last visited 1 November 2010).

[128] Christopher Greenwood, 'Report on the International Law Framework for the Treatment of Persons Detained in Afghanistan by Canadian Forces', para. 66, available at *ibid*.

[129] 'Canadian Military Has Quit Turning Detainees over to Afghans', *New York Times*, 24 January 2008, p. A7.

[130] See www.amnesty.ca/take_action/actions/canada_afghan_detainee_transfers.php (last visited 1 November 2010).

[131] Federal Court of Appeal, *Amnesty International Canada and British Columbia Civil Liberties Association v. Chief of the Defence Staff for the Canadian Forces, Minister of National Defence and the Attorney General of Canada*, paras. 24 *et seq*.

3.4 Provision of shelter and safe haven

Allowing another State to carry out unlawful activities on one's own territory could amount to complicity through the provision of shelter or safe haven. Although accusations in this regard are mostly raised in the context of support for private actors (for example, terrorists), similar considerations apply with respect to the inter-State level.

3.4.1 US protest against Sudan

In 1998, the United States protested against Sudan for allegedly allowing Iraq to manufacture chemical weapons on its territory.[132] The allegation was denied by Iraq's representative to the United Nations.[133]

3.4.2 The US position in the fight against terrorism

Obligations of non-assistance have also been affirmed in various contexts of the fight against terrorism since 11 September 2001. In his address to the United States Congress on 20 September 2001, President Bush said: 'we will pursue nations that provide aid or safe haven to terrorism. Either you are with us, or you are with the terrorists. From this day forward, any nation that continues to harbor or support terrorism will be regarded by the United States as a hostile regime.'[134] This view is not dissimilar to the UK legal position after the attacks of 11 September 2001. A Downing Street memo on international law apparently held that the ASR 'make responsible those states that allow their territory to be used for terrorist attacks'.[135]

3.4.3 Security Council Resolution 1373

The obligation not to support terrorism was also embodied in various UN Security Council resolutions adopted after the attacks of 11 September 2001. In Resolution 1373, it is set out that all States shall refrain from 'providing any form of support, active or passive, to entities or persons involved in terrorist acts'[136] and shall 'deny safe haven

---

[132] *New York Times*, 26 August 1998, sec. A, col. 1, p. 8.
[133] ILC Commentary, Article 16, para. 7.
[134] Available at www.washingtonpost.com/wp-srv/nation/specials/attacked/transcripts/bushaddress_092001.html (last visited 1 November 2010).
[135] This is reported in Gerry Simpson, *Great Powers and Outlaw States: Unequal Sovereigns in the International Legal Order* (Cambridge: Cambridge University Press, 2004), p. 329, note 25.
[136] UN Doc. S/RES/1373 (2001), operative para. 2(a).

to those who finance, plan, support or commit terrorist acts, or provide safe havens'.[137]

The main purpose of the statements by the US and UK governments as well as by UN Security Council Resolution 1373 was not to provide for an obligation of non-assistance on the inter-State level. The focus was instead on the responsibility of States not to support terrorist acts by non-State actors. Nonetheless, the legal significance of these statements for the issue of inter-State complicity cannot be ruled out as the notion of terrorism does not exclude *per se* State terrorism.[138] One could also assume that the expectation not to harbour actors committing unlawful acts *vis-à-vis* third States applies *a fortiori* with respect to State actors.

3.5 Military support and violations of international law

The category of military support is broad. Granting military support to another State may comprise different levels of State involvement. It can consist of security assistance in the sense that a government has decided to furnish military supplies or services to another government free of charge. It can also involve the furnishing of supplies in exchange for other goods or money. Finally, mention has to be made of private arms sales and supplies of military goods and services which, in the vast majority of States, need to be licensed by the home State's government.[139] Supplying military support to another State which uses this support to violate international law could potentially lead to responsibility of the complicit State in whichever form this support takes.[140]

These different degrees of State involvement would arguably play a role in an ultimate determination as to whether or not a given State incurs responsibility for complicity due to military support it

---

[137] *Ibid.*, operative para. 2(c).
[138] The issue of State terrorism is hotly contested and forms one of the main obstacles to arriving at a universally recognised definition of terrorism: see on this issue Christian Tomuschat, 'Internationale Terrorismusbekämpfung als Herausforderung für das Völkerrecht', *Die Öffentliche Verwaltung* (2006), pp. 357–69, at pp. 360–1; Ben Saul, 'Attempts to Define Terrorism in International Law', *Netherlands International Law Review* 52 (2003), pp. 57–83.
[139] See Stefan Oeter, *Neutralität und Waffenhandel*, pp. 216 *et seq.*; Patricia Egli, 'Rechtliche Schranken des Handels mit Kriegsmaterial', *Schweizerische Zeitschrift für Internationales und Europäisches Recht* 15 (2005), pp. 665–83, at p. 673.
[140] Cf Stefan Oeter, *Neutralität und Waffenhandel*, p. 240.

furnished to another State. The European Commission on Human Rights made it clear that the export of weapons to a country violating provisions of international law does not automatically generate State responsibility under the ECHR. In the case, the complaint was based on the absence, under Italian law, of legislation which would have barred the export of mines to Iraq. The plaintiff argued that Italy would have been obligated not to export mines to a country with such an abysmal human rights record. The Commission held in this regard that the applicant's injury

> can not be seen as a direct consequence of the failure of the Italian authorities to legislate on arms transfers. There is no immediate relationship between the mere supply, even if not properly regulated, of weapons and the possible 'indiscriminate' use thereof in a third country, the latter's action constituting the direct and decisive cause of the accident which the applicant suffered. It follows that the 'adverse consequences' of the failure of Italy to regulate arms transfers to Iraq are 'too remote' to attract the Italian responsibility.[141]

Hence, different degrees of proximity and factual influence upon the commission of an internationally wrongful act will need to be taken into account. However, at the stage of assembling international practice, this is not the primary issue. Rather, it will need to be determined whether or not considerations of State complicity actually play a role in the way States make decisions on the granting of military support to another State.

3.5.1 International practice

3.5.1.1 *Tripartite Declaration, 1950*

The governments of the United Kingdom, France and the United States adopted a tripartite declaration regarding security in the Near East in 1950. In relevant parts it read: 'The three Governments declare that assurances have been received from all states in question, to which they permit arms to be supplied from their countries, that the purchasing state does not intend to undertake any act of aggression against any other State. Similar assurances will be requested from any other State in the area to which they permit arms to be supplied in the future.'[142]

---

[141] See European Commission on Human Rights, *Rasheed Haje Tugar* v. *Italy*, unpublished.

[142] US Department of State Bulletin, Vol. XXII, No. 570, 5 June 1950, p. 886.

3.5.1.2 United Kingdom

The issue of arms supplies was discussed in a 1958 statement of the British Secretary of State. The underlying scenario involved 'substantial shipments of arms from the Soviet *bloc* ... to the Yemen and some of this equipment, including mortars and heavy machine guns, has been used on the frontier' to (then British) Aden.[143] The Secretary of State was asked in parliament about the position of the British government towards the question of the arms trade. According to him,

> the policy of her Majesty's Government has always been to urge restraint in arms deliveries to the Middle East while arms deliveries in themselves would not constitute grounds for protest. Her Majesty's government have of course reported to the United Nations acts of Yemeni aggression on the frontier and have protested to the Yemeni government.[144]

This statement was discussed in a survey of British practice by Elihu Lauterpacht. He argued that:

> the Answer suggests that the responsibility for the use of those arms [e.g., those supplied by one State to another] ... must rest primarily upon the State which receives them. There is, however, nothing in the Answer to support the view that a State which knowingly supplies arms to another for the purpose of assisting the latter to act in a manner inconsistent with its international obligations can thereby escape legal responsibility for complicity in such illegal conduct.[145]

The United Kingdom reaffirmed in 2004 that no military assistance would be granted 'to individuals or units known, or suspected to have been, implicated in human rights abuses or in collusion with paramilitary forces'.[146] This statement is, however, ambiguous as to whether it also has delivery of weapons to States in mind, as the Under Parliamentary Secretary of State for the Foreign and Commonwealth Office spoke of 'individuals or units' and not of States. However, one could assume that the same rationale should apply to States which engage in human rights abuses. Support for this interpretation can be derived from the fact that, in March 2009, the UK government 'quietly ended nearly a decade of military aid to Colombia's armed forces', as one

---

[143] House of Commons Debates, Vol. 589, col. 891, 17 June 1958.
[144] Elihu Lauterpacht, 'The Contemporary Practice of the United Kingdom in the Field of International Law – Survey and Comment', *International and Comparative Law Quarterly* 7 (1958), pp. 514–76, at p. 551.
[145] Ibid.
[146] See the statement reprinted in *British Year Book of International Law* 75 (2004), p. 706.

newspaper source reported.[147] It has been mentioned that accusations of gross violations of human rights have been the motive for this decision. In a previous statement to the parliament, the Foreign Secretary had announced that the UK government 'shares the concern ... that there are officers and soldiers of the Colombian armed forces who have been involved in, or allowed, abuses'.[148] The actual termination of the military aid was not commented on by UK government sources. The Colombian deputy defence minister acknowledged, however, the termination, and said his government was 'extremely surprised'.[149]

3.5.1.3 The Netherlands

The Netherlands stopped financial support for the maintenance of the Surinam military after a new military government was blamed for massive human rights violations in 1982. Under agreements concluded in 1975, the Netherlands had agreed to deliver economic subsidies and financial assistance for the maintenance of the military. In 1982, the Dutch government suspended the 1975 treaties and protested against the human rights violations.[150] Although the Netherlands government did not motivate its move entirely on the basis of considerations of complicity but primarily on the basis of the *clausula rebus sic stantibus*, it is noteworthy that in a diplomatic note of 14 December 1982 presented to Surinam it made reference to its position that the granting of development assistance shall not entail co-responsibility for serious human rights violations.[151] In this perspective, considerations of complicity could constitute the very change of circumstances which prompts a State to terminate its treaty relationship with another State engaged in violations of international law.[152]

---

[147] 'UK Ends Bilateral Military Aid to Colombia', *The Guardian*, 29 April 2009, available at www.guardian.co.uk/world/2009/apr/29/colombia-uk-military-aid (last visited 1 November 2010).
[148] Statement of Foreign Secretary David Miliband of 31 March 2009, available at www.fco.gov.uk/en/newsroom/latest-news/?view=PressS&id=15660494 (last visited 8 June 2009).
[149] See *The Guardian*, 29 April 2009, above note 147.
[150] This is reported in Christian J. Tams, *Enforcing Obligations Erga Omnes*, p. 227.
[151] A translation of the note into German is provided by Hans-Heinrich Lindemann, 'Die Auswirkungen der Menschenrechtsverletzungen in Surinam auf die Vertragsbeziehungen zwischen den Niederlanden und Surinam', *Zeitschrift für ausländisches öffentliches Recht und Völkerrecht* 44 (1984), pp. 64–93, at pp. 67–8, note 17.
[152] See generally Frank Hoffmeister, *Menschenrechts- und Demokratieklauseln in den vertraglichen Außenbeziehungen der Europäischen Gemeinschaft* (Berlin: Springer, 1998), p. 205.

3.5.1.4 Switzerland

In 2004, the Commission on Foreign Affairs of the Swiss *Bundesrat* appealed to the Swiss government to stop arms deliveries to Israel as long as Israel did not comply with its obligation under international law, most notably its obligations under the Geneva Conventions.[153]

3.5.1.5 Angola, Cuba and the Soviet Union

There have also been official protests by Angola, Cuba and the Soviet Union in March 1986 against the United States allegedly granting military and financial support to South Africa in its aggression against and partial occupation of the territory of Angola.[154]

3.5.1.6 Czechoslovakia

In the context of Iraq's unlawful invasion of Kuwait in the summer of 1990, Czechoslovakia suspended all military support for Iraq. In a statement of 3 August 1990 – and thus prior to the adoption of the first Security Council resolution adopting measures against Iraq under Chapter VII of the Charter[155] – the government of the Czech and Slovak Federal Republic stipulated:

> In the context of the military intervention in Kuwait, the Government of the Czech and Slovak Federal Republic has decided to suspend all supplies of a military character to the Republic of Iraq. At the same time, the Czech and Slovak Federal Republic stops delivering also all other items that could be used by Iraq for military purposes.[156]

3.5.1.7 Germany

After the occupation of the Falkland Islands in 1982, the Federal Republic of Germany refused to allow further exports of weapons and war materials to Argentina. The German Federal Government posited in a statement that it would prevent the delivery of arms to a State

---

[153] Reported in Patricia Egli, 'Rechtliche Schranken', p. 666.
[154] These protests are referred to – without further references – in Gaetano Arangio-Ruiz, 'Fifth Report on State Responsibility', UN Doc. A/CN.4/454 and Add.1–3, YBILC 1993, Vol. II, Part One, p. 1, at p. 54, para. 246.
[155] UN Doc. S/RES/661 (1990).
[156] Letter of 3 August 1990 from the Permanent Representative of the Czech and Slovak Federal Republic to the United Nations, S/21488 of 10 August 1990, also reprinted in Daniel Bethlehem (ed.), *The Kuwait Crisis: Sanctions and Their Economic Consequences*, Part I (Cambridge: Cambridge University Press, 1991), p. 101.

responsible for a violent act contrary to international law and in non-compliance with UN Security Council resolutions.[157]

In 1995, the Federal Government stated that it was in close contact with the Turkish government to survey whether the limitations attached to German arms deliveries to Turkey were respected. These limitations provided that the arms delivered could only be used in a situation in which Article 5 of the NATO Treaty[158] would be applicable (self-defence against an armed attack). The Federal Government would constantly monitor Turkey's compliance with this requirement.[159]

3.5.1.8 Iran

Iran protested against the United Kingdom and France over the alleged supply of chemical weapons to Iraq which were subsequently used against Iranian troops in the First Gulf War. Both the United Kingdom[160] and France[161] denied having furnished such weapons to Iraq.

3.5.1.9 Rwanda

In 2006, Rwanda broke off diplomatic relations with France and set up a commission to investigate the role of France in the 1994 genocide against the Tutsi and Hutu moderates. France was a traditional supporter of the Rwandan government at the time, delivered arms and other military supplies and also had military advisers in the country about whom opinion is divided as to whether they were in any way involved in the planning of military operations which had an impact on the genocide.[162] Credible sources testify that the delivery of ammunition and communication technology for the military continued

---

[157] Documented in Hans-Heinrich Lindemann, 'Völkerrechtliche Praxis der Bundesrepublik Deutschland im Jahre 1982', *Zeitschrift für ausländisches öffentliches Recht und Völkerrecht* 44 (1984), pp. 495–584, at p. 557.

[158] North Atlantic Treaty of 4 April 1949, entered into force on 24 August 1949, 34 UNTS 243.

[159] Reported in Rainer Grote, 'Völkerrechtspraxis der Bundesrepublik Deutschland im Jahre 1995', *Zeitschrift für ausländisches öffentliches Recht und Völkerrecht* 57 (1997), pp. 923–1164, at p. 1128.

[160] *New York Times*, 5 March 1984, p. A3.

[161] *Neue Zürcher Zeitung*, 9 March 1984, p. 4 (Fernausgabe).

[162] On the role of France and other external powers, see Romeo Dallaire, Kishan Manocha and Nishan Degnarain, 'The Major Powers on Trial', *Journal of International Criminal Justice* 3 (2005), pp. 861–78, at pp. 863 *et seq.*; Andrew Wallis, *Silent Accomplice – The Untold Story of France's Role in Rwandan Genocide* (London: I. B. Tauris, 2006), pp. 102 *et seq.*

while the genocide was already progressing.[163] Rwanda has announced its intention to bring a case before the ICJ if the Commission's results were to show that France was complicit in the genocide.[164] In 2007, Rwanda has reiterated this position.[165] In 2008, it finally published the Commission's report which held, *inter alia*, that '[a]t all times during the genocide, France diplomatically and militarily assisted the interim government which planned and implemented the genocide'.[166] The French government has denied all of the charges presented by the Rwandan government and held them to contain 'unacceptable accusations'.[167] At the end of 2009, the two countries re-established diplomatic relations and there is no longer talk of judicial action against France.[168]

3.5.1.10 Russia
In 2008, Russia protested against alleged arms deliveries by Ukraine to Georgia during the summer conflict of 2008. Russia considered Georgia's use of military force in the breakaway province of South Ossetia as a violation of international law. In the context of a meeting concerning bulk gas supplies in October 2008, Prime Minister Putin told his Ukrainian counterpart, Yulia Tymoshenko, that 'a more serious crime than arms deliveries in a conflict cannot be imagined'.[169] Russian President Dmitri A. Medvedev remarked in this regard that '[u]nfortunately, several countries close to us participated in this', meaning the Georgian conduct in the summer of 2008.[170] The

---

[163] Romeo Dallaire, Kishan Manocha and Nishan Degnarain, 'The Major Powers', pp. 865–6; see also Fred Grünfeld and Anke Huijboom, *The Failure to Prevent Genocide in Rwanda: The Role of Bystanders* (Leiden: Nijhoff, 2007), pp. 233 et seq.
[164] *Le Monde*, 2 November 2006, p. 6; *Neue Zürcher Zeitung*, 27 November 2006, p. 5.
[165] *Libération*, 19 April 2007, p. 9.
[166] Republic of Rwanda, Ministry of Justice: 'Report of the Independent National Commission responsible for collection of evidence indicating the role of the French State in the genocide against the Tutsi that was perpetrated in Rwanda in 1994'; the report was available at www.gov.rw/government/Rapport%20France_Genocide/RAPPORT%20COMPLET%20Version%20definitive%2015-11-07.pdf (last visited 8 June 2009).
[167] 'Point de presse du porte-parole du Ministère des affaires étrangères du 06.08.2008', available at https://pastel.diplomatie.gouv.fr/editorial/actual/ael2/print_pp.asp?liste=20080806.html (last visited 1 November 2010).
[168] See 'Rwanda and France Restore Diplomatic Relations', *BBC World News*, 30 November 2009, available at http://news.bbc.co.uk/2/hi/africa/8385887.stm (last visited 1 November 2010).
[169] 'Pipe Down', *The Economist*, 10 January 2009, p. 26.
[170] 'Claims of Secret Arms Sales Rattle Ukraine's Leaders', *New York Times*, 30 November 2008, p. A24.

Ukrainian response to this allegation is evasive. Ukrainian President Yushchenko has affirmed that 'Ukraine has every right to sell weapons to any country, including Georgia, that is not under international sanctions'.[171]

3.5.1.11 UN practice

Calls to stop the supply of arms and military assistance can also be found in the practice of various UN organs. Arms embargos have been the most frequently applied form of particular sanctions by the UN Security Council, with nearly every sanction regime incorporating prohibitions against arms deliveries at some stage.[172] However, an order not to deliver arms to a specific country or a given group within that State will in most of the cases not necessarily be inspired by considerations of State complicity. First, it needs to be taken into account that the UN Security Council is not primarily engaged in upholding respect for international law, but is fulfilling its main task of preserving international peace and security when acting under Chapter VII of the Charter.[173] Secondly, the imposition of an arms embargo is frequently not considered as a supplementary measure to prevent potential State complicity in a given situation, but rather as the most immediate and effective measure conceivable to induce a change of behaviour among an unruly State government. Some examples from UN Security Council practice may be exceptional in this regard: the calls not to assist Southern Rhodesia, South Africa and Israel. These sanctions regimes were based on considerations of illegality, i.e., unlawful behaviour on the part of the respective States. Therefore, they will be discussed in section 3.9 below, in the context of the establishment of obligations of non-assistance by the UN Security Council.

---

[171] Ibid.
[172] Jeremy Matam Farrall, *United Nations Sanctions*, p. 110.
[173] For a linkage between the rules of State responsibility and UN Charter mechanisms, see Vera Gowlland-Debbas, 'Security Council Enforcement Action and Issues of State Responsibility', *International and Comparative Law Quarterly* 43 (1994), pp. 55-98; for sceptical positions in this regard, see Josef L. Kunz, 'Sanctions in International Law', in Josef L. Kunz, *The Changing Law of Nations* (Columbus, OH: Ohio State University Press, 1968), pp. 621-60, at pp. 628 *et seq.*; Giorgio Gaja, 'Réflexions sur le rôle du Conseil de Sécurité dans le nouvel ordre mondial', *Revue générale de droit international public* 97 (1993), pp. 297-319, at p. 300; Georg Nolte, 'The Limits of the Security Council's Powers and Its Functions in the International Legal System', in Michael Byers (ed.), *The Role of Law in International Politics* (Oxford: Oxford University Press, 2000), pp. 315-26, at pp. 322-3.

3.5.1.12 Preparatory conference on an Arms Trade Treaty

In July 2010, UN Member States met in New York for a preparatory conference on an Arms Trade Treaty (ATT). The treaty *in statu nascendi* is meant to regulate the transfer of conventional weapons among States, a major source of international conflict.[174] A diplomatic conference to negotiate the final treaty is expected to take place in 2012. While there is no general evidence that States in general view such a potential treaty as directly related to the issue of complicity, there are some indications to this effect in individual statements of States which attended the 2010 conference.[175]

The representative of Norway remarked on 12 July 2010 that any licence application procedure should assess 'whether the specific transfer is likely [to] contribute to or be used for violations of international *humanitarian* or *human rights* law'.[176] The Swiss representative remarked on 12 July 2010 that the arms exports regime in place in Switzerland would assure 'qu'un commerce des armes ne contribue pas à une violation du droit international'.[177] On 13 July 2010, the representative of Mexico affirmed that among the aims of the ATT should be the prevention of 'arms transfers that could translate into human rights or humanitarian law violations'. In this sense, he affirmed, 'the co-responsibility' as well as 'shared responsibility' of exporting and importing States would need to be upheld.[178] The delegate of Trinidad and Tobago underlined that 'a critical element should be the enforcement of the principle of state responsibility. States which supply weapons must be accountable to the international community for their sale.'[179] The representative of New Zealand counted among the goals and objectives of the ATT the prevention of 'international transfers of conventional arms that contribute to armed conflict, violations of international human rights law and humanitarian law'.[180] The representative of the International Committee of the Red Cross remarked on 14 July 2010 that an ATT 'should include a requirement to a) assess the likelihood that serious violations of IHL [international humanitarian law] will be committed with the weapons being transferred and b) not

---

[174] See UN Doc. A/RES/64/48 of 12 January 2010.
[175] The following statements are all available from www.un.org/disarmament/convarms/ATTPrepCom/Statements.html (last visited 1 November 2010).
[176] *Ibid.*, emphasis in the original.
[177] *Ibid.*   [178] *Ibid.*   [179] *Ibid.*   [180] *Ibid.*

authorize transfers if there is a clear risk that the arms will be used to commit serious violations of IHL'.[181]

3.5.2 Domestic legislation

Domestic legislation establishing limits on the supply of military support to foreign countries could also constitute relevant international practice.[182] Two concrete examples of domestic legislation will be presented in greater detail before an overview of mechanisms in other States is given.

3.5.2.1 United States

In the United States, various restrictions apply to programmes of security assistance. In the Arms Export Control Act (AECA), the purpose for which defence articles and services may be sold is limited to 'international security, for legitimate self-defence, ... to permit recipient countries to participate in regional or collective agreements or *measures consistent with the Charter of the United Nations*'.[183] The Foreign Assistance Act of 1961 (FAA) provides that:

[T]he President is directed to formulate and conduct international security assistance programs of the United States of America in a manner which will promote and advance human rights and avoid identification of the United States, through such programs, with governments which deny to their people internationally recognized human rights and fundamental freedoms, in violation of international law or in contravention of the policy of the United States as expressed in this section or otherwise.[184]

In addition, section 116(a) states:

No assistance may be provided under [the development assistance authorities of the FAA] to the government of any country which engages in a consistent pattern of gross violations of internationally recognized human rights, including torture or cruel, inhuman, or degrading treatment or punishment, prolonged detention without charges, causing the disappearance of persons by the abduction and clandestine detention of those persons,

---

[181] Ibid.
[182] For an analysis of the domestic legislation of the United States, France, the United Kingdom, Germany, Italy, Sweden, Switzerland, Austria, Brazil and Israel with special emphasis on the law of neutrality, see Stefan Oeter, *Neutralität und Waffenhandel*, pp. 174 et seq.
[183] International Security Assistance and Arms Export Control Act, Pub. L. No. 94-329, § 201, 90 Stat. 729 (1976), section 4, emphasis added.
[184] Foreign Assistance Act of 1961, 22 USC § 2151 (2004), section 502B(a)(3).

or other flagrant denial of the right of life, liberty and security of the person, unless such assistance will directly benefit the needy people in such a country.

Accordingly, domestic legislation provides for limits to security assistance which are derived from international law.[185] These limits are based, however, only on the UN Charter and respect for human rights law. No general restriction not to engage in unlawful behaviour through the granting of security assistance can be inferred from these provisions. In addition, it can be noted that there has never been a formal determination or decision that a particular government is engaging in a 'consistent pattern of gross violations of internationally recognized human rights' in the sense of these provisions – a striking contrast to frequent determinations of States which support terrorism and which are therefore to be excluded from US security assistance programmes.[186]

Mention should furthermore be made of a congressional initiative, the so-called 'McKinney Rohrbacher Code of Conduct'[187] which was passed into law by the US Congress.[188] This statute ordered the President to 'attempt to achieve the foreign policy goal of an international arms sales code of conduct'. The act further laid down criteria which the President was required to consider during the negotiations which would ensue. These included general respect for human rights – the government of the country to which weapons were to be exported was required not to engage persistently in gross violations of internationally recognised human rights. Furthermore, the act required the recipient country also to refrain from grave breaches of international

---

[185] See also Stephen B. Cohen, 'Conditioning US Security Assistance on Human Rights Practices', *American Journal of International Law* 76 (1982), pp. 246–79, at p. 247.

[186] See section 620A of the FAA of 1961: 'The United States shall not provide any assistance under [the FAA] ... to any country if the Secretary of State determines that the government of that country has repeatedly provided support for acts of international terrorism.' Determinations have been made with respect to Iran, Iraq, Libya, North Korea, Syria, Cuba and Sudan. See Todd F. Buchwald and Michael J. Matheson, 'US Security Assistance and Related Programs', in John Norton Moore and Robert F. Turner (eds.), *National Security Law* (Durham, NC: Carolina Academic Press, 2005), pp. 1179–1206, at pp. 1199–1200.

[187] See further Zeray Yihdego, *The Arms Trade and International Law* (Oxford: Hart, 2007), p. 127.

[188] International Arms Sales Code of Conduct of 1999, Part of HR 3194, Consolidated Appropriations Act, 106th Congress, 1st Session.

humanitarian law and acts of aggression. The act appears not to have had significant practical effects.

3.5.2.2 Germany

Article 26(2) of the Basic Law provides that '[w]eapons designed for warfare may be manufactured, transported, or marketed only with the permission of the Federal Government. Details shall be regulated by a federal law.' This provision is *lex specialis* to Article 26(1) of the Basic Law, according to which the preparation and carrying out of aggressive wars is forbidden.[189] To comply with this constitutional requirement, the War Weapons Control Act (*Kriegswaffenkontrollgesetz*)[190] establishes limits to the export of weapons by the Federal Republic. According to section 6, paragraph 3, of this statute, no permission to export weapons can be obtained when there is a danger that the weapons will be used for a war of aggression or that there would be reason to believe that the licensing of the export could violate Germany's obligations under international law or *endanger* compliance with them. Outside of the domain of arms exports, restrictions are less stringent. The Foreign Commerce Act (*Außenwirtschaftsgesetz*)[191] only allows for optional limitation of commercial relations if German security interests are impaired or a disruption of the peaceful coexistence of peoples is to be expected.[192] This cannot, however, deflect from the fact that the regulations of the

---

[189] Rudolf Streinz, 'Artikel 26', in Michael Sachs (ed.), *Grundgesetz – Kommentar*, 5th edn (Munich: C. H. Beck, 2009), para. 35; Udo Fink, 'Artikel 26', in Hermann von Mangoldt, Friedrich Klein and Christian Starck (eds.), *Das Bonner Grundgesetz – Kommentar*, Vol. 2, *Artikel 20 bis 78*, 5th edn (Munich: Vahlen, 2005), para. 57.

[190] Kriegswaffenkontrollgesetz of 22 November 1990 as amended by Article 24 of the Regulation of 31 October 2006, *Federal Law Gazette* I 1990, 2506; *Federal Law Gazette* I 2006, 2407.

[191] Außenwirtschaftsgesetz in the version of 26 June 2006, *Federal Law Gazette* I 2006, 1386.

[192] For an analysis of the relevant provisions of this statute, see Bruno Simma and Daniel-Erasmus Khan, 'Verwaltungshandeln im Außenwirtschaftsrecht – Die Berücksichtigung menschenrechtlicher Gesichtspunkte bei der Auslegung und Anwendung nationaler Vorschriften zur Steuerung der grenzüberschreitenden Wirtschaftstätigkeit', in B. Großfeld, R. Sack and Th J. Möllers (eds.), *Festschrift für Wolfgang Fikentscher zum 70. Geburtstag* (Tübingen: Mohr Siebeck, 1998), pp. 1009–29, at pp. 1016 *et seq.*; see also the motivation for the introduction of this law which is reproduced in Werner Morvay, 'Völkerrechtliche Praxis der Bundesrepublik Deutschland im Jahre 1959', *Zeitschrift für ausländisches öffentliches Recht und Völkerrecht* 21 (1961), pp. 259–300, at p. 285, which highlights the political motivation to restrict the export of some goods which can disrupt friendly relations between States.

Kriegswaffenkontrollgesetz are uncompromising insofar as they do not allow the export of arms and military supplies which may contribute to the violation of international law.[193]

3.5.2.3 Other countries

The state of the law in the United States of America and in Germany is fairly representative for the way most States lay down criteria for the granting of export licences for weapons and other military material. One comes across stipulations in statutory law which require the government to take into consideration international commitments (for example, South Africa[194] and Kazakhstan[195]), public international law as such (Switzerland[196]), the non-commission of acts of aggression, general accordance with peace, security and stability (for example, China[197]) or UN embargos (Israel[198]). Frequently, these requirements are framed as non-binding obligations ('should take into consideration'). Such is the case, for example, with South Korea, where respect for 'generally accepted international rules' figures among the criteria for arms exports, but only insofar as 'the Minister of Commerce, Industry and Energy *may* restrict or prohibit the export and import of goods'.[199] Similar formulations can be found in the Austrian *Kriegsmaterialgesetz* ('it is to be taken into consideration').[200] In other States, restrictions figure only in policy guidelines (see, for example,

---

[193] For criticism on Germany's compliance with these norms, see Herbert Wulf, 'The Federal Republic of Germany', in Ian Anthony (ed.), *Arms Export Regulations* (Oxford: Oxford University Press, 1991), pp. 72–85, at pp. 81–2.

[194] Regulation of Foreign Military Assistance Act, 1998, section 7, para. 1, Government Gazette, Vol. 395 of 20 May 1998, No. 18912.

[195] Law of the Republic of Kazakhstan on the Export Control of Weapons, Military Technology, and Dual-Use Goods of 18 June 1996, Article 2.

[196] *Bundesgesetz über das Kriegsmaterial* (KMG) of 13 December 1996 (SR.514.51), Article 22, *Systematische Sammlung* 514.51.

[197] People's Republic of China Regulations on Control of Military Products Export (promulgated on 22 October 1997 by the PRC State Council and the PRC Central Military Commission under Order No. 234; revised according to the 'Decision of the State Council and the Central Military Commission on Amending the PRC Regulations on Control of Military Products Export' on 15 October 2002), Article 5(2), available at www.nti.org/db/China/engdocs/milexcon.htm (last visited 1 November 2010).

[198] Defence Export Controls Act of 2007, 5766-2007.

[199] Foreign Trade Act, Article 5(4), emphasis added; the text was available at http://unpan1.un.org/intradoc/groups/public/documents/APCITY/UNPAN011483.pdf (last visited 1 November 2010).

[200] *Kriegsmaterialgesetz*, section 3, *Federal Law Gazette* I 540/1977 in the version of the *Federal Law Gazette* I 50/2005.

Australia[201]). Other States (for example, Mexico[202]) do not provide for material limits for the export of weapons but only stipulate that it is for the Minister of Defence to give permission. Finally, other States acknowledge that – from the viewpoint of their domestic law – it is only a political question whether or not arms exports will be permitted (France, the United Kingdom).[203] Canada, for example, emphasises that security interests are the primary consideration in deciding whether or not to grant export licences.[204]

3.5.2.4 Preliminary assessment
With respect to arms exports controls, the picture thus appears to be too varied to infer from it a general practice of States which limits the granting of export licences of weapons out of considerations of international law. For some States, it may be possible to deduce such a motivation out of their statutory regulations (see, for example, Germany, Switzerland, South Korea), but, in most cases, the language appears to be too weak to put too much emphasis on considerations of international law in this regard. An absolute rarity is the statement of Switzerland in the context of the ATT preparatory conference where the Swiss delegate expressly held that the Swiss laws are meant to ensure that no violations of international law occur due to Swiss arms exports.[205] This absence of concrete references to international legal obligations not to export arms in domestic legislation does not, however, mean that international restrictions do not apply.

3.5.3 Voluntary codes and soft-law instruments

Voluntary codes and soft-law instruments are legal texts which do not purport to be binding. No legal obligation is infringed when a State does not comply with them.[206] Nonetheless, such texts may be indicative of States' expectations with regard to their behaviour. They cannot

---

[201] Export Control Policy Criteria, available at www.defence.gov.au/strategy/deco/applications.htm#3 (last visited 1 November 2010).
[202] Federal Law on Firearms and Explosives, Articles 37, 40 and 56, available at http://info4.juridicas.unam.mx/ijure/tcfed/114.htm?s (last visited 8 June 2009).
[203] Cf with further references Zeray Yihdego, *The Arms Trade*, p. 128.
[204] Section 3, para. 1(a), of the National Policy Statement, available at www.sipri.org/contents/expcon/canada.html (last visited 3 February 2009).
[205] See above at text following note 175.
[206] See generally Dinah Shelton, 'International Law and "Normative Relativity"', in Malcolm D. Evans (ed.), *International Law*, 2nd edn (Oxford: Oxford University Press, 2006), pp. 159–85, at pp. 180 *et seq.*

automatically be counted as instances of international practice, but may contribute to an emerging *opinio juris*.[207]

3.5.3.1 EU Code of Conduct for Arms Exports
One of the most comprehensive documents on the international transfer of arms is the EU Code of Conduct for Arms Exports, adopted in 1998.[208] The Code establishes eight criteria for the issuance of export licences of which four are considered to be mandatory (albeit in a non-legally binding fashion). Of relevance for the issue of State complicity are criteria 2 and 4 of the Code, according to which export licences are to be refused when there are clear risks that the exported material will be used for violations of human rights law or be used 'aggressively against another country or to assert by force a territorial claim'. Some authors have interpreted these criteria to be more far-reaching than Article 16 ASR, as a 'clear risk' is sufficient to warrant the non-granting of an export licence.[209] The general respect of the buyer country for international law, however, figures only among the criteria which are considered to be non-mandatory. In addition, it is ambiguously formulated. Although its heading refers to 'international law', its individual sections establish a distinction between 'compliance with ... international obligations, in particular on the non-use of force' which is, in turn, said to include 'international humanitarian law applicable to international and non-international armed conflicts'. Furthermore, it makes reference to obligations in the field of non-proliferation. This distinction between international law and international obligations may not be completely irrelevant, more so as it can also be found in the texts of another group of States which is concerned with arms exports.

3.5.3.2 Wassenaar Arrangement
The so-called Wassenaar Arrangement is a group of forty arms-exporting States[210] that has set itself the mission 'to contribute to

---

[207] *Ibid.*, p. 181.
[208] Available at www.consilium.europa.eu/uedocs/cmsUpload/08675r2en8.pdf (last visited 1 November 2010).
[209] Alexandra Boivin, 'Complicity and Beyond: International Law and the Transfer of Small Arms and Light Weapons', *International Review of the Red Cross* 87 (2005), No. 887, pp. 467–96, at p. 488.
[210] These States are: Argentina, Australia, Austria, Belgium, Bulgaria, Canada, Croatia, Czech Republic, Denmark, Estonia, Finland, France, Germany, Greece,

regional and international security and stability, by promoting transparency and greater responsibility in transfers of conventional arms and dual-use goods and technologies, thus preventing destabilising accumulations'.[211] The Wassenaar Arrangement is not organised in the form of a traditional international organisation, and its participating States do not intend to set out legal obligations by codes of conduct they establish within this arrangement. In 2002, it agreed a Best Practice Guide on the export of small arms and light weapons (SALW).[212] In section 3 of this guide, it is stipulated that each participating State will, when contemplating proposed exports of SALW, take into consideration '[t]he record of compliance of the recipient country with regard to international obligations and commitments, in particular on the suppression of terrorism, and on the non-use of force, and in the field of non-proliferation, or in other areas of arms control and disarmament, and the record of respect for international law governing the conduct of armed conflict'.

This requirement is noteworthy in several regards. Apart from the fact that it is of course non-binding and only stipulates a requirement to 'take into consideration', the distinction in the wording between 'international obligations and commitments' on the one hand and 'international law' on the other hand is noteworthy.[213] Although one should not read too much into the wording of non-binding best practice guides, it cannot be assumed that it was a mere coincidence that led the participating States to draft section 3 and also criterion 6 of the EU Code of Conduct in this way. If we take it at face value, this discrepancy could mean that international obligations and commitments can be of a political nature and should be taken into account comprehensively. International legal considerations are, however,

---

Hungary, Ireland, Italy, Japan, Latvia, Lithuania, Luxembourg, Malta, Netherlands, New Zealand, Norway, Poland, Portugal, Republic of Korea, Romania, Russian Federation, Slovakia, Slovenia, South Africa, Spain, Sweden, Switzerland, Turkey, Ukraine, the United Kingdom and the United States; see www.wassenaar.org/participants/index.html (last visited 1 November 2010).

[211] Wassenaar Arrangement, Initial Elements of 11–12 July 1996, available at www.wassenaar.org (last visited 1 November 2010).

[212] As amended in 2007, available at www.wassenaar.org/publicdocuments/2007/docs/SALW_Guidelines.pdf (last visited 1 November 2010).

[213] Eyal Benvenisti has noted, in a different context, that policy-makers at times deliberately employ 'international commitments' instead of 'international law': 'The Conception of International Law as a Legal System', *German Yearbook of International Law* 50 (2007), pp. 393–405, at pp. 403–4.

mandatory only for the decision-making process where international humanitarian law is concerned. This is telling insofar as the 'political cost' to include a general requirement to take the compliance of the recipient State with international law into account would have been fairly low. From the viewpoint of the participating States of the Wassenaar Arrangement and the EU Member States, it thus appears as if they do not ascribe particular relevance to the issue of responsibility for complicity through arms exports. The instruments they have created do not reveal a particular emphasis on questions of international law. Hence, it is not possible to interpret these instruments as mechanisms to prevent the States which back them from incurring responsibility for complicity in violations of international law committed by the recipient States.

3.6 Foreign aid and violations of international law

Foreign aid in general may also contribute to violations of international law. As Antonio Cassese has remarked:

> The question whether foreign economic assistance to states grossly disregarding human rights has an impact on the enjoyment of civil and political rights in those states is undoubtedly very complex. The nexus between economic assistance and human rights is often indirect and subtle.[214]

Although it may thus in practice be difficult to find State responsibility for complicity through the provision of foreign aid, it may nonetheless be possible to shed further light on States' attitudes to the granting of foreign aid to States which could be said to violate international law.

3.6.1 Positions towards Chile after 1973

A number of exemplary statements on this issue were made in the context of an examination by a UN Sub-Committee of ECOSOC after the military coup in Chile in 1973. The Sub-Committee questioned States on their conduct towards the military government in Chile. Belgium stated that, 'since the coup d'état of 11 September 1973, Belgium has refrained from supplying military or financial aid to Chile', and 'that the position of the Belgian Department of Foreign Affairs will remain unchanged until the rule of law is restored and human rights are fully

---

[214] Antonio Cassese, 'Foreign Economic Assistance and Respect for Civil and Political Rights: Chile – A Case Study', *Texas International Law Journal* 14 (1979), pp. 251–63, at p. 251.

re-established in Chile'.[215] The United Kingdom asserted that it had 'taken a series of measures aimed at exerting pressure on the military regime in Chile over human rights', including 'a ban on all arms supplies', 'suspension of British aid' and 'denial of debt re-scheduling facilities'.[216] The Federal Republic of Germany stated that it had not provided Chile with any more development aid and had also discontinued supplies of weapons and other military equipment.[217] Italy stated that it had 'suspended the privileges enjoyed by Chile under the Insurance and Export Credit Law' and that 'official aid by Italy to the Chilean government is virtually non-existent'.[218] The Netherlands[219] and Norway[220] also stated that they had suspended their aid to Chile.

3.6.2 EC and EU practice

One should also note the position that the European Community adopted towards the regime of Idi Amin in Uganda. The EC owed development assistance to Uganda under the Lomé I Convention.[221] At the insistence of the United Kingdom, the EC Council adopted 'Uganda Guidelines' in 1977 stipulating that development assistance under the Lomé Convention should not contribute to the serious and continuing human rights violations in Uganda.[222] In this respect, one can note that these EC actions were the very first step towards EC and later EU policy in requiring the inclusion of conditionality clauses in external agreements with third States and organisations.[223] An agreement amending

---

[215] Study of the Impact of Foreign Economic Aid and Assistance on Respect for Human Rights in Chile, Sub-Committee on the Prevention of Discrimination and the Protection of Minorities, UN Doc. E/CN.4/Sub.2/412 (1978), para. 414.
[216] 'Report of the Economic and Social Council: Protection of Human Rights in Chile, Report of the Secretary General', UN Doc. A/32/234 (1977), pp. 17–18.
[217] Ibid., p. 9.
[218] UN Doc. E/CN.4/Sub.2/412 (1978), para. 407.
[219] UN Doc. A/32/234 (1977), pp. 12–13.
[220] UN Doc. E/CN.4/Sub.2/412 (1978), para. 410.
[221] Lomé I Agreement between the African, Caribbean and Pacific Group of States and the European Economic Community of 28 February 1975, entered into force on 1 April 1976, OJ 1976 L25/1, reprinted in ILM 14 (1975), p. 606.
[222] EC Bulletin 1977, No. 6, para. 2.2.59; see further Martin Dawidowicz, 'Public Law Enforcement without Public Law Safeguards? An Analysis of State Practice on Third-Party Countermeasures and Their Relationship to the UN Security Council', British Year Book of International Law 77 (2006), pp. 333–418, at p. 358.
[223] For a description of the development of these clauses, see Lorand Bartels, Human Rights Conditionality in the EU's International Agreements (Oxford: Oxford University Press, 2005), pp. 7–31; Frank Hoffmeister, Menschenrechts- und Demokratieklauseln, pp. 7 et seq.

the Fourth Lomé Convention first included a so-called 'essential elements' clause which allowed for the suspension of the provisions of the Convention in the case of fundamental and systematic abuses of those values covered by the clause.[224] The subsequent Cotonou agreement includes such a clause in its Article 9, according to which respect for internationally defined human rights constitutes an essential element of the agreement.[225] The inclusion of such clauses enables the EC to invoke violations of its terms in order legitimately to suspend or terminate the agreement under international law according to Articles 60-62 of the Vienna Convention on the Law of Treaties.[226]

On a more general level, an EC regulation is illustrative of the restrictions which need to be respected when foreign aid is at issue. Regulation EC 1638/2006 establishes the general provisions for a European neighbourhood and partnership programme. The regulation provides that: 'It is important that Community assistance under this Regulation be provided in compliance with the international agreements and conventions to which the Community, the Member States and the partner countries are parties and that it will be delivered taking into account the general principles of international law commonly accepted by the parties.'[227]

3.7 Economic cooperation

Considerations of complicity may also play a role in the context of economic cooperation. Two areas are particularly pertinent in this regard: the rules pertaining to foreign investment and WTO law.

3.7.1 Export credit guarantees: the Ilisu Dam project

An example for the impact complicity issues have on economic cooperation is the Ilisu Dam project in Turkey. It consists of the construction of a huge dam on the River Tigris for the purposes of irrigation and hydroelectricity. It was seen by critics as giving rise to possible

---

[224] See Article 366a of the Fourth ACP–EEC Convention (Lomé IV) of 15 December 1989, entered into force on 1 March 1990, OJ L229/3 of 17 August 1991.
[225] Article 9 of the Partnership Agreement between the members of the African, Caribbean and Pacific Group of States of the one part, and the European Community and its Member States of the other part, signed in Cotonou on 23 June 2000, entered into force on 1 April 2003, OJ L317/3.
[226] Cf further Urfan Khaliq, *Ethical Dimension*, pp. 112–13; Christian Tomuschat, *Human Rights*, pp. 162–3 and 275–6.
[227] Regulation (EC) No. 1368/2006 of 24 October 2006, OJ L310/1.

violations of international law in three respects. First, it would entail the internal displacement of a large number of Kurds, which could raise issues of the protection of minorities under international law. According to some estimates, up to 70,000 Kurds would have to be relocated. Secondly, UNESCO-protected cultural heritage in the form of the 10,000-year-old town of Hasankeyf would be flooded. And, thirdly, the construction of the dam could reduce the amount of water available to the downstream States of Syria and Iraq.[228]

Syria issued a protest against the United Kingdom with respect to the granting of an export credit guarantee for the construction of the dam.[229] The Arab League also lodged a formal protest with the UK in this connection.[230] The UK denied all responsibility in this context,[231] but nevertheless subsequently withdrew from the project. Prior to the withdrawal, a UK government official acknowledged the disagreements over the case in the House of Commons:

> [T]he Secretary of State for Trade and Industry has had no discussions with the governments of Turkey, Syria or Iraq on the Ilisu Dam. We are of course aware that the Syrian and Iraqi governments have made representations to the Foreign and Commonwealth Office regarding the project, and the issue of waterflow to downstream states is one of the four conditions outlined by [the Secretary of State for Trade and Industry] in his statement to the press last December.[232]

After the withdrawal of the United Kingdom from the project, Germany, Austria and Switzerland stepped in and decided to grant the export credit guarantee subject to a series of conditions obliging Turkey to abide by international law as well as soft-law standards.[233] One of the conditions set out in the decisions of the respective governments was that the neighbouring States will be adequately consulted throughout

---

[228] For an overview, see Astrid Epiney, 'Nachbarrechtliche Pflichten'; Georg Nolte and Helmut Philipp Aust, 'Equivocal Helpers', pp. 10–12.
[229] *The Independent*, 16 July 2000, p. 10; Hilal Elver, 'World Commission on Dams Report Challenges Financing for Ilisu Dam', *Turkish Daily News*, 20 March 2001.
[230] 'Turkey Dam Violates Law Says Arab League', *Gulf Daily News*, 18 July 2000, available at lexisnexis.
[231] *The Independent*, 16 July 2000, p. 10.
[232] *Hansard*, House of Commons, Written Answers for 30 November 2000, col. 748W.
[233] 'Bedingte Zustimmung zu Ilisu-Staudamm – Bundesrat gewährt Exportrisikogarantie unter Auflagen', *Neue Zürcher Zeitung*, 16 December 2006, available at www.nzz.ch (last visited 1 November 2010); Press Release of the German Ministry for Economic Affairs of 26 March 2007, available at www.bmwi.de (last visited 1 November 2010).

the construction of the dam, an issue which had previously been raised by Syria and the Arab League with the UK.[234] This conditionality, however, neither ensures that the three States do not violate international law by granting the guarantee nor that the project is now actually in conformity with international law. In the meantime, Switzerland has abandoned the project and Germany and Austria had threatened to pull out too. In late 2008, it appeared as if Germany and Austria would have made the decision to withdraw from the project in the face of recurring Turkish violations of the conditions.[235] In July 2009, Germany and Austria finally withdrew from the project.[236] In December 2009, it has emerged that China would consider granting the necessary export credit guarantees.[237]

3.7.2 Foreign (dis-)investment: Norway's Wealth Fund

Another example where considerations of possible State complicity in violations of human rights may play a role is the practice of the Norwegian Wealth Fund to disinvest from companies which are potentially engaged in human rights violations in other States.[238] The Fund's mandate is to invest a significant share of the country's oil revenues in order to generate wealth for the time when this source of income has run dry. As it is a government fund, its implication in violations of international law could potentially give rise to State responsibility.[239] The Fund has a practice to blacklist companies which do not conform to its ethical guidelines. It does not limit itself to ethical questions, however. A sensitivity to legal questions can be inferred from the documents

---

[234] See the statement of the Iraqi Minister for Water Affairs, 'Türkei – Lässt Damm den Irak austrocknen?', *Die Presse*, 4 May 2007, available at lexisnexis.
[235] See 'Abschied vom Mega-Staudamm', *Frankfurter Rundschau*, 21 December 2008, p. 4.
[236] See the Press Release of the German Ministry for Economic Cooperation and Development of 7 July 2009, available at www.bmz.de/de/presse/ aktuelleMeldungen/archiv/2009 (last visited 1 November 2010).
[237] See 'Damm-Bruch', *Süddeutsche Zeitung*, 4 December 2009, p. 1.
[238] For a general overview on the practice of the Fund and the international law issues connected to it, see Simon Chesterman, 'The Turn to Ethics: Disinvestment from Multinational Corporations for Human Rights Violations – The Case of Norway's Sovereign Wealth Fund', *American University International Law Review* 23 (2008), pp. 577–615.
[239] See further Robert McCorquodale and Penelope Simons, 'Responsibility Beyond Borders: State Responsibility for Extraterritorial Violations by Corporations of International Human Rights Law', *Modern Law Review* 70 (2007), pp. 598–625, at pp. 606 *et seq*.

establishing an Advisory Commission on International Law in the early years of the Fund's existence. In its *Singapore Technologies Engineering* case, the Advisory Commission identified a possible risk of a violation of Norway's obligations under Article 1 of the Ottawa Convention on Anti-Personnel Land Mines[240] through assistance in the production of land-mines.[241] The Advisory Commission was replaced by a Council on Ethics in 2004. This Council still considers questions of potential relevance for international law. However, its broader mandate makes it difficult to clearly establish practice which is motivated by international law considerations. Its mandate reads in relevant parts:

The Council is to issue recommendations on negative screening of one or several companies on the basis of the production of weapons whose normal use is in violation of fundamental humanitarian principles. The Council is to issue recommendations on the exclusion of one or more companies from the investment universe where there is deemed to exist a considerable risk of contributing to actions or omissions that involve:

- Gross or systematic violation of human rights, such as murder, torture, deprivation of liberty, forced labour, the worst forms of child labour and other forms of child exploitation
- Gross violations of individual rights in war or conflict situations
- Severe environmental degradation
- Gross corruption
- Other particularly serious violations of fundamental ethical norms.[242]

Accordingly, concerns over Norway's indirect participation in human rights violations still play a pivotal role which is also reflected in the practice of the Council.[243] Any Norwegian responsibility through the form of an investment would be indirect and would thus be difficult

---

[240] Convention on the Prohibition of the Use, Stockpiling, Production and Transfer of Anti-Personnel Land Mines and on Their Destruction of 18 September 1997, entered into force on 1 March 1999, Article 1(c), 2056 UNTS 211.

[241] The Petroleum Fund Advisory Commission on International Law, Question of whether investments in Singapore Technologies Engineering can imply a violation of Norway's international obligations, Memorandum of 22 March 2002, available at www.regjeringen.no/en/dep/fin/Selected-topics/andre/Ethical-Guidelines-for-the-Government-Pension-Fund-Global-/Advisory-Commission-Documents/Advisory-Commission.html?id=413581 (last visited 1 November 2010).

[242] Available at www.regjeringen.no/en/dep/fin/Selected-topics/andre/Ethical-Guidelines-for-the-Government-Pension-Fund-Global-/The-Council-on-Ethics-for-the-Government-Pension-Fund -Global.html?id=447010 (last visited 1 November 2010).

[243] Cf Simon Chesterman, 'Turn to Ethics', pp. 591 *et seq.* and 606.

to conceptualise in terms of the law of State responsibility. However, the underlying reasoning is similar to that in the Ilisu Dam case just described: through the backing of an investment, a State could potentially be seen as contributing to violations of international law.

3.7.3 WTO law

Considerations of complicity may also play a role in the way States justify non-compliance with obligations under WTO law. An obligation not to contribute to internationally wrongful acts could play a role with respect to the notion of public morals in Article XX of the GATT[244] concerning general exceptions to GATT obligations.[245] In this field, complex legal relations can arise which involve various actors at first sight only remotely connected to possible violations of international law. An example of such an array of legal relations are the trade sanctions that the European Union adopted towards Burma in 2007. In a Common Position under the Common Foreign and Security Policy (CFSP), the Council of the European Union required EU Member States to prohibit intentional and knowing 'participation' in activities that 'directly or indirectly' have the 'object or effect' of circumventing the ban.[246]

The decisive question then is whether Article XX(a) GATT and its concept of 'public morals' allows non-compliance with the substantive obligations under the GATT, such as the Most Favoured Nations Clause and National Treatment, for the reason that participation in human rights violations is to be prevented.[247] Some authors have argued that this is possible, especially due to the consideration that 'the act of trading with an abusive regime raises the more specific concern of complicity: exchanging money for goods that are produced even indirectly with the support of forced labor perpetuates this practice'.[248]

---

[244] General Agreement on Tariffs and Trade of 30 October 1947, provisionally entered into force on 1 January 1948, 55 UNTS 187.
[245] See generally Matthias Herdegen, *Internationales Wirtschaftsrecht*, 7th edn (Munich: C. H. Beck, 2008), § 9, paras. 65 *et seq.*
[246] Council Common Position (EC) No. 2007/750/CFSP of 19 November 2007 amending Common Position 2006/318/CFSP renewing restrictive measures against Burma/Myanmar, Article 2(b), OJ 2007 L308/1.
[247] Cf generally Nicola Wenzel, 'Article XX lit a GATT', in Rüdiger Wolfrum, Peter-Tobias Stoll and Anja Seibert-Fohr (eds.), *Max Planck Commentaries on World Trade Law*, Vol. 3, *WTO – Technical Barriers and SPS Measures* (Leiden: Nijhoff, 2007), paras. 22 *et seq.*
[248] Robert L. Howse and Jared M. Genser, 'Are EU Trade Sanctions on Burma Compatible with WTO Law?', *Michigan Journal of International Law* 29 (2008), pp. 165–96, at p. 186.

Another aspect which needs to be taken into account in this connection is the relation between Article XX(a) GATT and Article XX(d) GATT which allows for general exceptions from the GATT obligations when it is 'necessary to secure compliance with laws and obligations not inconsistent with this agreement'. Mexico tried to justify an additional tax on soft drinks imported from the US which included a certain sweetener by making reference to the need to induce US compliance with its obligations under the North American Free Trade Agreement (NAFTA). The Appellate Body did not consider this as a valid ground for invoking Article XX(d) GATT. It was held that the term 'laws or regulations' in Article XX(d) did not include 'obligations of another WTO Member under an international agreement'.[249] *A contrario*, one can infer from this *dictum* that the obligations of the WTO Member who imposes the general exceptions to its obligations under the GATT may very well be covered by Article XX(d) GATT.[250] It could thus be seen as legitimate not to comply with obligations under the GATT in order not to incur responsibility for having aided or assisted another State in the commission of an internationally wrongful act.

That considerations of State complicity can generally play a role under WTO law has been made clear by a 1999 WTO Panel report which pointed out that Turkey could incur responsibility for measures taken by the Turkey–EC customs union on the basis of the principle reflected in (then draft) Article 27 ASR.[251] Although the precise impact of this provision on the Turkey–EC customs union is not made clear (and may be hard to establish), this reference shows that complicit State action could potentially also lead to findings of non-compliance with GATT obligations by the WTO dispute settlement mechanism.

3.8 *Cooperation as consolidation of unlawful events*

Complicity may also play a role with respect to the consolidation of the effects of unlawful events. *Prima facie*, these situations imply that something wrongful has already occurred. They are thus close to what

---

[249] WTO Appellate Body, *Mexico – Tax Measures on Soft Drinks and Other Beverages*, para. 69.
[250] Susanne Reyes-Knoche and Katrin Arend, 'Article XX lit d GATT', in Rüdiger Wolfrum, Peter-Tobias Stoll and Anja Seibert-Fohr (eds.), *Max Planck Commentaries on World Trade Law*, Vol. 3, *WTO – Technical Barriers and SPS Measures* (Leiden: Nijhoff, 2007), para. 9.
[251] WTO Panel, *Turkey – Restrictions on Imports of Textile and Clothing Products*, para. 9.42.

common law systems would include within the category of 'conduct after the fact'.[252] However, in international law the boundary between complicity which occurs prior to and during the violation of an international legal obligation on the one hand and aid or assistance which intervenes afterwards on the other is not easily defined. In its final ASR, the ILC did not retain the distinction between breaches of international obligations by an act of the State not extending in time and those having a continuing character.[253] Violations of international law can, however, be of an ongoing character. Assistance which is given only after the initial breach of international law by another State could therefore also fall within the scope of Article 16 ASR.

3.8.1 Sweden

In this sense, one can interpret a written statement of Sweden which was presented to the International Court of Justice in the context of the *Wall* opinion. Sweden considered the legal consequences of the construction of the wall in the occupied Palestinian territory by Israel – which it held to be in violation of international law – and stated:

> Another consequence of the illegality of the construction of the barrier is that, under international customary law as codified by Article 16 of the Articles on Responsibility of States for Internationally Wrongful Acts, third states must not aid or assist Israel in its measures. Further, serious breaches of obligations under peremptory norms entail additional legal consequences for third states, as set out in Article 41 of the said Articles.[254]

3.8.2 Saudi Arabia and the League of Arab States

A similar statement was issued by Saudi Arabia. The statement refers to the obligation of 'all States to cooperate to bring to an end, not to recognise as lawful the situation created, and not to render any assistance to the occupying Power' with regard to Israel's alleged violation of the right of the Palestinian people to self-determination, an obligation which it considered to arise under a peremptory norm of general

---

[252] See also ILC Commentary, Article 41, para. 11; Andreas Felder, *Die Beihilfe*, pp. 139 et seq.
[253] See Draft Articles 24 and 25 of the Draft Articles on State Responsibility adopted on First Reading. These provisions suffered from 'over-complexity' and 'over-refinement': James Crawford, 'Introduction', p. 20.
[254] Written Statement of Björn Skala, Swedish Ambassador to the Netherlands, of 30 January 2004, available at www.icj-cij.org (last visited 1 November 2010).

international law.[255] Finally, the League of Arab States filed a statement nearly identical to that of Saudi Arabia.[256]

3.8.3 Germany

Similar considerations can furthermore be found in domestic court proceedings which deal with the application of foreign laws considered to be contrary to public international law. The German Federal Constitutional Court examined this issue in a case in which the respect of a foreign statute for the principle of *ne bis in idem* was at stake. In the case, the Court's reasoning departed from Article 25 of the German Basic Law, according to which '[t]he general rules of international law shall be an integral part of federal law. They shall take precedence over the laws and directly create rights and duties for the inhabitants of the federal territory.' The Court stated that this Article prevented German authorities from applying and interpreting German law in a way which would violate these general rules of international law which are generally understood to embody customary international law. In addition, the Court held, this Article would also require German authorities and courts not to give effect to acts of foreign authorities which were contrary to international law; and especially not to contribute significantly to such an act by a foreign authority contrary to international law.[257]

This consideration was further developed by the Court in a 2004 decision on expropriations effected under the authority of the occupying power of the Soviet Union, prior to the coming into existence of the German Democratic Republic in 1949.[258] The question underlying this case was whether the German Basic Law required the Federal Republic to provide for a compensation for these expropriations. This issue was intertwined with complicated aspects of the German reunification process and the question whether the Federal Republic was, in 1989/90, under an obligation not to recognise the expropriations effected by the Soviet Union in the immediate aftermath of the Second World War.

---

[255] Statement of the Kingdom of Saudi Arabia of 30 January 2004, *ibid.*
[256] Written Statement of the League of Arab States on the Legal Consequences of the Construction of a Wall in the Occupied Palestinian Territory, January 2004, *ibid.*
[257] German Federal Constitutional Court, BVerfGE 75, 1, 18-19; see on this decision Rainer Hofmann, 'Art. 25 GG und die Anwendung völkerrechtswidrigen ausländischen Rechts', *Zeitschrift für ausländisches öffentliches Recht und Völkerrecht* 49 (1989), pp. 41-60, at p. 51.
[258] German Federal Constitutional Court, BVerfGE 112, 1; for a more detailed summary of the case, see Helmut Philipp Aust, 'German Constitutional Law Cases 2004-2006', *European Public Law* 13 (2007), pp. 205-21, at pp. 217 *et seq.*

The Court again dealt with Article 25 of the Basic Law and found that under certain circumstances there was an obligation on German State bodies to 'enforce public international law in their own areas of responsibility if third-party states violate it'.[259] In this respect, the Court reaffirmed its finding from the *ne bis in idem* case: the German authorities are 'prevented from cooperation in a decisive way in an act by non-German public authorities in violation of general rules of international law'.[260] The Court was, however, rather ambiguous about the concrete meaning of this. It stated that:

> There may ... be a tense relationship between this outwardly directed duty and the international cooperation between the states and other subjects of public international law, which is also intended by the constitution, in particular if a violation of law may be terminated only by cooperation.[261]

Here, the Court made reference to the constitutionally mandated imperative for German reunification, which could justify a balancing between the obligation to abstain from participation in unlawful acts and a different and supervening constitutional goal.[262] Interestingly, the Court then made reference to the ASR, but limited itself to noting Articles 40 and 41. Only in cases which involve serious breaches of peremptory norms under general international law would a duty to act arise. Here, the Court also made reference to Article 41(2) and its obligation of non-assistance.[263]

3.8.4 Greece

A Greek lower court in a case involving German atrocities committed during the Second World War commented on the issue of complicity with respect to the recognition of State immunity. The case concerned a claim for injury suffered as the result of acts carried out by the German armed forces during the military occupation of Greece, more precisely in the context of the massacre at Distomo on 10 June 1944. The Court of Levadia found that 'the recognition of immunity for an act contrary to peremptory international law would amount to complicity by the national court in the promotion of an act strongly condemned by the

---

[259] German Federal Constitutional Court, BVerfGE 112, 1, 24 (para. 88).
[260] *Ibid.*, p. 27 (para. 95).
[261] *Ibid.* (para. 96 of the English translation). [262] *Ibid.*
[263] *Ibid.*, p. 35 (para. 121 of the English translation). The Court's findings have been heavily criticised in a dissenting opinion by Judge Lübbe-Wolff, *ibid.*, pp. 47 *et seq.* (paras. 157 *et seq.*).

international public order'.[264] The invocation of complicity appears to be rather untechnical, as one would have to conceive the German war crime committed in Distomo as an ongoing violation of international law in order to ascribe any relevance to considerations of complicity.

3.8.5 Italy

In this respect, reference can also be made to the jurisprudence of the Italian Court of Cassation. In its *Ferrini* decision of 2004[265] and later decisions[266] – which form the subject matter of ICJ proceedings instituted by Germany against Italy in December 2008 – several issues concerning Italian military internees in the Second World War were in issue. In its 2004 *Ferrini* decision, the Court of Cassation quoted Article 41 ASR approvingly, making reference to the fact that States are not allowed to assist in the maintenance of situations brought about by a serious breach of a peremptory norm under general international law.[267] As is the case with the Greek decision just mentioned, it is difficult to identify the exact impact considerations of complicity may have played in this case. As the Court of Cassation expressly referred to Article 41(2) ASR, it is more likely that it wanted to put an emphasis on the obligation of non-recognition contained in the same provision.

3.8.6 United Kingdom

Similarly, Lord Bingham of Cornhill made reference to Article 41(2) ASR and the obligation of non-assistance therein when he considered the question whether evidence obtained under torture could be admissible in UK court proceedings. He concluded:

There is reason to regard it as a duty of states, save perhaps in limited and exceptional circumstances, as where immediately necessary to protect a person from unlawful violence or property from destruction, to reject the fruits of torture inflicted in breach of international law.[268]

---

[264] Multi-member Court of Levadia, Case No. 137/1997, Judgment of 30 October 1997, reprinted in *Revue Hellénique de Droit International* 50 (1997), pp. 595, 599.
[265] Italian Court of Cassation, *Ferrini* v. *Germany*, ILR 128, 658.
[266] Italian Court of Cassation, *Federal Republic of Germany* v. *Giovanni Mantelli and Others*. For an analysis, see Carlo Focarelli, 'Case Note (Federal Republic of Germany v. Giovanni Mantelli and Others)', *American Journal of International Law* 103 (2009), pp. 122–31.
[267] Italian Court of Cassation, *Ferrini* v. *Germany*, ILR 128, 658, para. 9.
[268] UK House of Lords, *A (FC) and others (FC)* v. *Secretary of State for the Home Department and others*, opinion of Lord Bingham, para. 34.

Our remarks on the Greek and Italian cases apply *mutatis mutandis*, although a stronger impact of considerations of complicity appears conceivable: despite their limitations to the concrete case at hand, Lord Bingham's observations may well have been motivated in erecting a general barrier against the use of such 'forbidden fruits'. As other scenarios may very well include those in which a person is still detained and may still be subjected to torture, it is easier to conceive the use of evidence obtained under torture as some form of moral participation or encouragement which could amount to complicity if these acts are conducted by a third State.[269] This position was also held by the Eminent Jurists' Panel of the International Commission of Jurists in their 2009 report on terrorism and human rights. The Panel found that by relying on information obtained by other States through means of torture, States become 'consumers' and thus create a 'market' for torture.[270]

Finally, similar considerations can be found in the report of the Joint Committee on Human Rights of the UK House of Lords and House of Commons. The Committee noted:

> We have found it more difficult to decide whether the passive receipt of information which has or may have been obtained under torture amounts to complicity in torture ... The passive receipt of information is ... not obviously a form of 'assistance' or facilitation, because it seems likely that the torture will continue to take place anyway whether the information is received or not by the other State. This would not apply, however, to circumstances where the receipt of such information ... is so regular that it becomes an expectation, or where it is part of a reciprocal arrangement (regardless of whether the arrangement is formal or explicit), or where the information is received over a long period with no apparent concern being raised about its provenance.[271]

The Committee assessed this scenario further in terms of the legal consequences:

> We therefore consider that, if the UK is demonstrated to have a general practice of passively receiving intelligence information which has or may have

---

[269] A similar scenario was considered in UK High Court of Justice, *R. (on the Application of Binyan Mohammed) v. Secretary of State for Foreign and Commonwealth Affairs*, see especially at paras. 86 *et seq.*

[270] International Commission of Jurists' Eminent Panel, 'Assessing Damage – Urging Action: Report on Terrorism, Counter-Terrorism and Human Rights' of February 2009, 85, available at http://ejp.icj.org/IMG/EJP-Report.pdf (last visited 1 November 2010).

[271] UK House of Lords/House of Commons, Joint Committee on Human Rights, 'Allegations of UK Complicity in Torture', Twenty-Third Report of Session 2008–9, HL Paper 152, HC 230, published on 4 August 2009, para. 38.

been obtained under torture, that practice is likely to be in breach of the UK's international law obligation not to render aid or assistance to other States which are in serious breach of their obligation not to torture.[272]

In a footnote to this passage, the Committee referred expressly to Article 41(2) ASR.[273]

3.9 UN resolutions and non-assistance

Another source of international practice which is frequently mentioned in studies on complicity in the law of State responsibility is United Nations practice.[274] This is not surprising, as every UN Security Council-imposed sanctions regime has included an arms embargo against the targeted State except the Resolution 1054 sanctions regime against Sudan[275] and the measures adopted in the context of the Hariri murder in Lebanon in 2005.[276, 277] Just as with domestic legislation banning the export of arms and weapons, UN Security Council resolutions banning the granting of military support could be considered as having been adopted with a view to prevent support for unlawful activities. Hence, they could be considered as forming part of international practice for a rule against State complicity. However, this reasoning would presuppose that UN Security Council resolutions impose sanctions in response to unlawful behaviour of the targeted State. That is, however, not necessarily the case. The UN Security Council, being a political organ, has a duty to ensure international peace and security according to Article 24(1) of the UN Charter. For this reason, not every sanctions regime which calls for some form of non-assistance to a State should be considered as contributing international practice relevant for this study. Things are, however, different with respect to sanctions regimes and other resolutions where notions of lawfulness have clearly played a role.

---

[272] *Ibid.*, para. 42.   [273] *Ibid.*, note 59.
[274] See, e.g., Andreas Felder, *Die Beihilfe*, pp. 206 *et seq.*; John Quigley, 'Complicity', pp. 92–3.
[275] UN Doc. S/RES/1054 (1996).
[276] UN Doc. S/RES/1636 (2005).
[277] Jeremy Matam Farrall, *United Nations Sanctions*, p. 110, names seven sanctions regimes which have consisted entirely of arms sanctions: the measures adopted against South Africa (UN Doc. S/RES/418 (1977)), Yugoslavia (UN Doc. S/RES/713 (1991)), Somalia (UN Doc. S/RES/733 (1992)), Liberia (UN Doc. S/RES/788 (1992)), Rwanda (UN Doc. S/RES/918 (1994)), the Federal Republic of Yugoslavia (UN Doc. S/RES/1160 (1998)) and Eritrea and Ethiopia (UN Doc. S/RES/1298 (2000)).

3.9.1 Southern Rhodesia

In this regard, the sanctions against the racist regime of Southern Rhodesia were based on considerations of legality. The minority rule of the regime under Ian Smith was considered to be in violation of the right to self-determination of the majority of Rhodesians.[278] In Resolution 217, the Council called upon States to undertake a range of voluntary measures against the minority regime. These measures included not recognising the illegal regime's claim to power or entertaining diplomatic relations with it, refraining from providing arms to the illegal regime, and breaking all economic relations with the illegal regime.[279] These obligations were further strengthened in successive resolutions which called on all States not to provide financial or economic aid to the racist regime[280] and 'to refrain from recognising the illegal regime or rendering any assistance to it'.[281] In contrast to other sanctions regimes, this connection between the determination that the regime in Southern Rhodesia was 'illegal' and the adoption of sanctions may warrant the assumption that the idea of complicity had some role to play in the considerations leading up to this sanctions regime.

3.9.2 South Africa

Considerations of illegality and the attitude of third States towards it also played a role in the way UN organs dealt with South Africa's continued presence in Namibia. Formerly under a South African mandate granted by the League of Nations, it was at issue after the Second World War and the founding of the United Nations whether the territory of Namibia was to be introduced into the United Nations' trusteeship system or whether, as was claimed by South Africa, it was to form part of the latter's territory. After protracted institutional developments,[282] the mandate of the League of Nations was terminated by the UN General Assembly.[283] In Resolution 276 (1970), the Security Council recognised this termination and further defined the legal status of Namibia and the ensuing obligations of South Africa and other UN Member States. In paragraph 2 of the resolution, it declared 'that the continued presence of the South African authorities in Namibia is illegal and that

---

[278] UN Doc. S/RES/217 (1965). [279] Ibid.
[280] UN Doc. S/RES/232 (1966). [281] UN Doc. S/RES/277 (1970).
[282] For a concise summary, see Andreas Felder, *Die Beihilfe*, pp. 209–10.
[283] UN Doc. A/RES/2145 (XXI) of 27 October 1966, para. 4.

160   COMPLICITY IN CUSTOMARY INTERNATIONAL LAW

consequently all acts taken by the Government of South Africa on behalf of or concerning Namibia after the termination of the Mandate are illegal and invalid'.[284] Furthermore, it called upon 'all States, particularly those which have economic and other interests in Namibia, to refrain from any dealings with the Government of South Africa which are inconsistent with paragraph 2 of the present resolution'.[285] To further clarify the situation, an advisory opinion was secured by the UN General Assembly from the ICJ.

3.9.3 The legal basis for the obligation of non-assistance

In both situations, concerning Southern Rhodesia and South Africa's continued presence in Namibia, the crucial question was on which legal basis the obligation of non-assistance rested: did the UN Security Council have a general concept of complicity in mind? Or did it only impose an obligation of non-assistance in order to provide for an effective application of the sanctions? In this respect, the Court held in its advisory opinion on Namibia that '[a] binding declaration made by a competent organ of the United Nations to the effect that a situation is illegal cannot remain without consequence'.[286] As to the immediate effects for third States, the Court held that:

> The Member States of the United Nations are, for the reasons given in paragraph 115 above, under an obligation to recognize the illegality and invalidity of South Africa's continued presence in Namibia. They are also under an obligation to refrain from lending any support or any form of assistance to South Africa with reference to its occupation of Namibia, subject to paragraph 125 below.[287]

In this context, it is important to note that paragraph 115 of the opinion sets out that the Security Council decisions in question were binding upon UN Member States due to Articles 24 and 25 of the UN Charter.[288] This could give rise to the interpretation that the obligation of non-assistance the Court mentioned was only derived from UN law. Accordingly, no general obligation of non-assistance would have

---

[284] UN Doc. S/RES/276 (1970), operative para. 2.
[285] *Ibid.*, operative para. 5; see also UN Doc. S/RES/301 (1971), operative para. 11, on the further concretisations obtained through the ICJ advisory opinion.
[286] ICJ, *Legal Consequences for States of the Continued Presence of South Africa in Namibia (South West Africa) Notwithstanding Security Council Resolution 276 (1970)*, Advisory Opinion, ICJ Rep. 1971, 16, para. 117.
[287] *Ibid.*, para. 119.   [288] *Ibid.*, para. 115.

been mentioned by the Court. However, this interpretation is called into question by another paragraph of the opinion in which the Court stipulates that it will

> confine itself to giving advice on those dealings with the Government of South Africa which, under the Charter of the United Nations and general international law, should be considered as inconsistent with the declaration of illegality and invalidity made in paragraph 2 of resolution 276 (1970), because they may imply a recognition that South Africa's presence in Namibia is legal.[289]

While this paragraph may be read so as to confirm the impact of general international law on the legal consequences to be derived from the declaration of illegality and invalidity, one should note that the Court was careful to limit these considerations to the issue of non-recognition. While it is indeed easier to identify obligations resulting from general international law in this respect,[290] it cannot be ruled out that the Court *also* wanted to refer to a general international law obligation not to render assistance to wrongful conduct, which has thus been recognised by a competent UN organ.

3.9.4 Israel

Beginning in 1980, various UN organs called on Member States not to assist Israel in the illegal occupation of the West Bank. The Security Council called upon States 'not to provide Israel with any assistance to be used specifically in connexion with settlements in the occupied territory'.[291] The General Assembly repeatedly called on States not to assist Israel in its occupation and annexation of the occupied Palestinian territory.[292] In one of these resolutions, the General Assembly expressly mentioned 'the international responsibility of any parties that supply Israel with arms or economic aid that augment its war potential'.[293] The Human Rights Commission called on States not to aid or assist in annexing and colonising territory under its military occupation. The Commission

---

[289] *Ibid.*, para. 122.
[290] Cf Stefan Talmon, *Kollektive Nichtanerkennung illegaler Staaten* (Tübingen: Mohr Siebeck, 2006), pp. 360–1.
[291] UN Doc. S/RES/465 (1980), para. 7; S/RES/471 (1980), para. 5.
[292] UN Doc. A/ES-7/4 (1982), para. 9b; A/RES/38/180 (1983), paras. A9, A13, A14, D11, E2, E3; A/RES/39/146 (1984), paras. A11, B9, B13–14; A/RES/40/168 (1985), paras. A11, B9, B13–14; A/RES/41/162 (1986), paras. A11, B9, B13–14.
[293] UN Doc. A/RES/38/180 (1983), para. E1.

reiterate[d] its call to all States, in particular the States parties to the Geneva Conventions relative to the Protection of Civilian Persons in Time of War, in accordance with article 1 of that Convention ... to avoid ... extending any aid which might be used by Israel in its pursuit of the policies of annexation and colonization or any other policies and practices referred to in the present resolution.[294]

3.10 UN Security Council practice: exonerating practice

Just as the UN Security Council can establish obligations of non-assistance, it may dispense with them due its power to adopt binding resolutions under Chapter VII of the Charter. Even though Article 103 of the Charter only mentions other international agreements of States over which obligations under the Charter will prevail, it is widely held that this provision also applies with respect to customary international law.[295] Given that the main role of the Security Council is not to enforce international law, but the maintenance of international peace and security (Article 24(1) of the Charter), the Council may arrive at the decision that, although international law would require States not to assist a given State or a group of States in a certain situation, the interests of peace and security may require it to effect changes in this regard.

A case in point is Security Council Resolution 1483,[296] which ended the sanctions regime against Iraq.[297] The resolution also established a framework under which States were allowed to cooperate with the 'authority', meaning the States which were occupying powers at the time.[298] Although the resolution does not indicate directly that considerations of complicity played a role, careful remarks to that effect were made in the accompanying Security Council debate. Jeremy Greenstock, Ambassador of the United Kingdom to the United Nations, noted that 'the resolution gives a sound basis for the international community, to come together, in the interests of the Iraqi people, consistent with international law'.[299] This statement could be interpreted as making

---

[294] UN Human Rights Commission, Res. 1984/1 of 20 February 1984, para. 12.
[295] See Rudolf Bernhardt, 'Article 103', in Bruno Simma (ed.), *The Charter of the United Nations – A Commentary*, 2nd edn (Oxford: Oxford University Press, 2002), para. 21; Bardo Fassbender, *The Charter of the United Nations*, p. 120.
[296] UN Doc. A/RES/1483 (2003).
[297] See further Gregory H. Fox, *Humanitarian Occupation* (Cambridge: Cambridge University Press, 2008), pp. 263–70.
[298] For a detailed and thorough overview of the responsibility issues concerning the occupying powers and the Coalition Provisional Authority (CPA), see Stefan Talmon, 'Plurality', pp. 185 *et seq.*
[299] Statement of Jeremy Greenstock, UN Doc. S/PV.4761 (2003), p. 5.

reference to the fact that other States may have found themselves to be inhibited in contributing to the reconstruction of Iraq for fear of becoming responsible for complicity in the potentially unlawful occupation of Iraq.[300] The Security Council resolution effectively changed the application of the rules of State responsibility with respect to the situation in Iraq.[301] The Security Council authorisation to cooperate with the occupying powers in Iraq may therefore be seen as providing a ground for precluding the wrongfulness of the States which would otherwise face responsibility for complicity.[302]

The legal position of a number of States which were engaged in the post-conflict reconstruction of Iraq testifies that considerations of complicity may have played a role. The Dutch Minister for Foreign Affairs, for instance, emphasised in a letter of 6 June 2003 that the Security Council resolution established the legal basis for sending Dutch troops to Iraq. In addition, he was adamant that:

[t]he preamble of the resolution indicates that a distinction should be made between the United States and the United Kingdom, which are operating in Iraq in the capacity as occupying powers, and States not operating in this capacity. This conclusion of the Security Council in a resolution adopted under Chapter VII of the UN Charter should be interpreted as an authoritative opinion concerning the status of the participating States, an opinion that is binding on the UN Member States.[303]

---

[300] Cf Christine Gray, *International Law and the Use of Force*, 3rd edn (Oxford: Oxford University Press, 2008), p. 365; for the implications of complicity on the post-war administration of Iraq, see further Frédéric Dopagne and Pierre Klein, 'L'attitude des Etats tiers et de l'ONU à l'égard de l'occupation de l'Irak', in Karine Bannelier, Théodore Christakis, Olivier Corten and Pierre Klein (eds.), *L'intervention en Irak et le droit international* (Paris: Pedone, 2004), pp. 325–41, at pp. 329 *et seq*.

[301] *Ibid.*, pp. 330 and 338-9; Hélène Tigroudja, 'Le régime d'occupation en Iraq', *Annuaire français de droit international* 50 (2004), pp. 77–101, at p. 96. See also Alain Pellet, 'Conclusions', in Christian Tomuschat and Jean-Marc Thouvenin (eds.), *The Fundamental Rules of the International Legal Order – Jus Cogens and Obligations Erga Omnes* (Leiden: Nijhoff, 2006), pp. 417–24, at p. 424, on Security Council Resolutions 1244 and 1546 as effectively limiting the reach of the principle of non-recognition.

[302] This could also follow, by way of implication, from the analysis of Gregory Fox, who denies both a change of the international law on occupation towards the recognition of transformative ideals and an overruling of the pertinent provisions of international humanitarian law by the Council. This, effectively, leaves only the possibility of the Council having derogated from the pertinent rules of responsibility. See Gregory Fox, *Humanitarian Occupation*, p. 270.

[303] Reprinted in P. C. Tange, 'Netherlands State Practice for the Parliamentary Year 2002–2003', *Netherlands Yearbook of International Law* 35 (2004), pp. 317–94, at pp. 378–9.

Also, in later years, the Dutch government emphasised the limited amount of responsibility the Netherlands would incur through their participation in the reconstruction of Iraq. The Dutch Foreign Minister was asked in Parliament on 7 June 2006 how he would 'view the fact that President Bush has admitted these mistakes [concerning weapons of mass destruction] for the first time? Does the Dutch Government, which gave political support to the war, agree with this criticism?' The Minister answered that 'these decisions were taken by the United States and the United Kingdom and that they accordingly fell under their responsibility. Dutch responsibility in Iraq was limited to its contribution to the stabilisation of southern Iraq.'[304] Closely resembling the Dutch position, Norway also emphasised that it was a Security Council resolution which allowed it to participate in the reconstruction of Iraq.[305]

3.11 Extradition

The issue of complicity has been raised in court decisions on the lawfulness of extraditing a person who was previously lured out of a third State.

3.11.1 Switzerland

A 1982 decision by the Swiss Federal Court (*Bundesgericht*) dealt with a Belgian citizen who was lured out of Belgium into Switzerland for the purpose of then being extradited to the Federal Republic of Germany. A direct extradition from Belgium to the Federal Republic would not have been possible as Belgium was prohibited by its constitution from extraditing its own citizens. The Swiss Federal Court did not allow the extradition as this would have turned Switzerland into an accomplice to a violation of Belgian sovereignty.[306]

3.11.2 Germany

In a 2003 decision, the German Federal Constitutional Court had to consider the extradition of two Yemeni citizens to the United States

---

[304] Reprinted in P. C. Tange, 'Netherlands State Practice for the Parliamentary Year 2005–2006', *Netherlands Yearbook of International Law* 38 (2007), pp. 263–366, at pp. 350–1.
[305] Memorandum of the Norwegian Foreign Ministry of 15 December 2003, reprinted in Rolf Einar Fife, 'Elements', p. 570.
[306] Swiss Federal Court of Justice, P1201/81/fs, reprinted in *EuGRZ* 10 (1983), pp. 435 *et seq*. This decision is not overruled by Swiss Federal Court of Justice, 1B_87/2007, reprinted in *EuGRZ* 34 (2007), p. 571, which rests on a different factual scenario.

who were lured out of Yemen to Frankfurt under the pretext of negotiations about the funding of terrorist activities. They were then arrested with a view to extradition to the United States. After initial court proceedings in the ordinary courts, the two Yemenis filed a constitutional complaint against their extradition. The German Federal Constitutional Court did not hold an extradition to be contrary to international law. The Court explained that, if the act of luring the two Yemenis out of Yemen by a US agent was a wrongful act, the responsibility of the United States *vis-à-vis* Yemen would be established. In such a case, the danger would arise that Germany could also incur responsibility through the extradition of the plaintiffs to the United States. In this respect, the Court referred to Article 16 ASR which it held to be an expression of customary international law.[307] The Court was ultimately of the opinion that there would exist no prohibition against the extradition of someone who was lured out of his or her home State.[308] In this respect, the Court reviewed recent developments in international practice and was willing to admit that the validity of the maxim of *male captus, bene detentus* may very well be challenged in those cases in which serious human rights violations underlie the apprehension of the person. However, the Court was able to distinguish the case under deliberation from such situations as no violence was exercised with respect to the complainants. Furthermore, it noted that there was no apparent collusion between the German and the US authorities to lure the two Yemenis specifically to Germany.[309]

3.12 Legal assistance and cooperation

3.12.1 Switzerland

The Swiss *Bundesgericht* has affirmed limits to judicial cooperation in another context. In a decision of 2007, it refused to grant legal assistance to the Russian Federation in the context of proceedings against former Yukos owner, Michail Chodorkowskij.[310] The Court did not clearly state the legal basis upon which it pronounced itself on the limits of cooperation with the Russian authorities. The case is further

---

[307] German Federal Constitutional Court, BVerfGE 109, 13, 26–7 = ILDC 10 (DE 2003) with an English translation and commentary by Matthias Hartwig.
[308] *Ibid.*, p. 27. [309] *Ibid.*, p. 29.
[310] For the political context and further details of the case, see 'Zweifel an russischer Justiz – Schweiz lehnt Rechtshilfe im Fall Chodorkowskij ab', *Süddeutsche Zeitung*, 25/26 August 2007, p. 11.

complicated by the enormously complex factual assessment as the Russian authorities put forward a number of diverging requests for judicial assistance which concerned various persons, alleged crimes and legal motives. This was acknowledged by the Swiss Court which found the Swiss Law on Judicial Assistance in Matters of Penal Law to be technically not directly applicable.[311] Instead, it turned towards international norms which would impact upon the case and made reference to the procedural guarantees enshrined in the ECHR and the ICCPR.[312] These rules were part of an 'international public order' which meant that Switzerland would contravene its international obligations if it 'collaborated' with legal proceedings which were potentially contrary to these guarantees, notably in the form of discriminatory treatment.[313]

3.12.2 Canada

3.12.2.1 General principles

In the context of international judicial cooperation, the Canadian Supreme Court has found that usually aspects of comity speak against the application of Canadian law to situations which take place abroad. The Court stated: 'Where our laws – statutory or constitutional – could have an impact on the sovereignty of other states, the principle of comity will bear on their interpretation.'[314] This would extend to the admissibility of evidence for court proceedings obtained through cooperation between Canadian and foreign authorities. The Court maintained that '[c]ooperation between states is imperative if transnational crimes are not to be committed with impunity because they fall through jurisdictional cracks along national borders'.[315] This would entail that '[i]n order to foster such cooperation, and in the spirit of comity, Canada cannot either insist that the Charter [of Rights and Freedoms] be applied in other countries or refuse to participate. When Canadian authorities are guests of another state whose assistance they seek in a criminal investigation, the rules of that state govern.' However, comity could

---

[311] Loi fédérale sur l'entraide internationale en matières penales du 20 mars 1981, Recueil systématique 351.1.
[312] International Covenant on Civil and Political Rights of 12 December 1966, entered into force on 23 March 1976, 999 UNTS 171.
[313] Swiss Federal Court of Justice, *Mikhail Khodorkovski v. Ministère public de la Confédération*, para. 2.3.
[314] Supreme Court of Canada, *R v. Hape*, 2007 SCC 26, para. 48.
[315] *Ibid.*, para. 99.

not cover all conceivable situations. Moreover, the limits for such cooperation would be defined by international law:

> Acts of comity are justified on the basis that they facilitate interstate relations and global cooperation; however, comity ceases to be appropriate where it would undermine peaceable interstate relations and the international order ... The principle of comity does not offer a rationale for condoning another state's breach of international law.[316]

With respect to the application of the Canadian Charter of Rights and Freedoms this entails, according to the Court, the following: 'comity cannot be invoked to allow Canadian authorities to participate in activities that violate Canada's international obligations.'[317] In R v. Hape, the Court was still cautious about the legal consequences of this finding. It merely affirmed that remedies under the Canadian Charter of Rights and Freedoms might be available in the case of such participation. In the more recent Khadr case, discussed above,[318] it was more willing to affirm the applicability of the Charter in a straightforward manner.

3.12.2.2 The Schreiber case
Considerations of complicity also played a role in the long and complicated story of the extradition of lobbyist and arms dealer Karl-Heinz Schreiber from Canada to Germany. Schreiber, a dual citizen of Canada and Germany, awaited prosecution in Germany for various counts of tax fraud, dating back to his involvement in the sale of Airbus jets to Canada and Thailand and his role in a scandal concerning the financing of a major German political party. A peculiar aspect of the case was that for some time Switzerland accused Germany of having misused information it obtained through forms of legal assistance. Allegedly, Germany was about to prosecute Schreiber not only for tax fraud, but also for tax evasion, a conduct which is not a crime in Switzerland (only an offence). According to the treaty between Germany and Switzerland on mutual legal assistance, information obtained under the treaty may not be used in proceedings which involve offences.[319] At the end of 2007, Schreiber's lawyers tried unsuccessfully to persuade the Canadian authorities

---

[316] Ibid., paras. 50-1.   [317] Ibid., para. 101.   [318] See above at note 121.
[319] For a description of the facts of the case and a brief legal assessment (*nota bene*, from a lawyer who wrote a file for Mr Schreiber), see Michael Byers, 'Extraditing Schreiber Now Violates International Law', *Globe and Mail*, 30 January 2008.

not to extradite Schreiber under these conditions as the extradition would amount to Canadian complicity in Germany's violations of international law. After his extradition was suspended in March 2008 due to an ongoing investigation in a political affair involving former Canadian Prime Minister Mulroney, the Canadian Supreme Court finally decided in December 2008 against granting Schreiber leave to appeal.[320] Schreiber's arguments were further weakened by the fact that Germany and Switzerland have settled their dispute on the use of the information provided by the latter.[321] Schreiber was extradited to Germany in August 2009.

3.13 Other cases: unspecified support

Finally, some cases can be identified in which the forms of assistance have not been clearly specified.

3.13.1 US claim against Hungary and the Soviet Union

In the *Treatment in Hungary of Aircraft and Crew of United States of America* case,[322] the United States stated the following:

> The claim of the Government of the United States of America is briefly that the Government of the Hungarian People's Republic *in concert with and aided and abetted by* the Government of the Union of the Soviet Socialist Republics on November 19, 1951, wilfully and unlawfully caused to be seized a United States Air Force C-47 type aircraft together with its crew of four American nationals and its contents, driven over Hungary by winds unknown to the crew; that thereafter both Governments engaged in unlawful actions against the crew and against the United States with respect to the incident, constituting both serious violations of existing treaties as well as manifest denials of justice and other international wrongs.[323]

As the cases were removed from the list in 1954, there was no further exchange on these claims (none at least which has been made public).[324]

---

[320] Supreme Court of Canada, *Karlheinz Schreiber* v. *Minister of Justice*, Decision of 11 December 2008, leave to appeal denied.
[321] See 'Schweizer Gefälligkeiten', *Süddeutsche Zeitung*, 1 April 2008, p. 7.
[322] *Treatment in Hungary of Aircraft and Crew of United States of America (United States of America* v. *Hungarian People's Republic; United States of America* v. *Union of Soviet Socialist Republics)*, Application Instituting Proceedings Against the Hungarian People's Republic, ICJ Pleadings 1954, 9 and 43.
[323] *Ibid.* (emphasis added).
[324] ICJ, *Treatment in Hungary of Aircraft and Crew of United States of America*, Order, ICJ Rep. 1954, 99; ICJ, *Treatment in Hungary of Aircraft and Crew of United States of America*, Order, ICJ Rep. 1954, 103.

However, the reference to Hungary having been aided can be understood as a reference to the complicity of the Soviet Union.

3.13.2 Non-assistance in controversial rescue operations

In the context of controversial rescue operations of nationals abroad, third States have from time to time asserted that they did not assist in these operations. This was the case, for example, when Kenya denied any involvement in the Israeli operation in 1976 to free hostages held at Entebbe Airport in Uganda, as well as with the US operation to rescue its hostages in Tehran in 1980 where a number of Arab States denied any involvement.[325]

4 Governmental statements

From 1978 to 2008, more than forty States commented on the complicity provision in the Draft Articles either directly to the ILC or in the Sixth Committee of the UN General Assembly. So far in our discussion, no distinction has been made between State practice and *opinio juris* for the establishment of customary international law. We have dealt with instances of international practice without entering into a debate on whether specific incidents in which the issue of complicity was at stake also betray an accompanying *opinio juris* of States, i.e., the conviction that they were required not to render aid or assistance or that they believed that other States were under an obligation not to do so. This evaluation will take place in the next section. It will, however, be greatly facilitated by an evaluation of governmental statements on the issue of complicity. It is not necessary here to re-enter the debate whether statements constitute practice or expressions of *opinio juris*.[326] It is submitted that the kind of statements referred to in this section will arguably not constitute State practice as they concern expressions in the abstract. States have not made these statements with respect to concrete situations. In the latter case, a statement could very well constitute State practice as it may be viewed as a protest.[327] In the context of the Sixth Committee and also when States are addressing

---

[325] References in Olivier Corten, *Le droit contre la guerre*, p. 277.
[326] For the two diverging positions, see, on the one hand, Michael Akehurst, 'Custom as a Source', p. 47, and, on the other hand, Antony D'Amato, *The Concept of Custom in International Law* (Ithaca, NY: Cornell University Press, 1971), p. 98.
[327] Cf Vaughan Lowe, *International Law*, p. 46.

their comments directly to the ILC, however, they express their legal views without having specific incidents in mind. Therefore, these statements should be conceived rather as expressions of *opinio juris*.[328] To take them into account at this point of the analysis will help to shed light on whether the instances of practice discussed so far match the *opinio juris* States have expressed by means of these governmental statements.

In order to obtain a better overview of the discussion, the governmental statements are grouped into three categories: States which have objected to the idea of a provision on complicity in the Articles on State Responsibility; States which have generally recognised the concept but saw possibilities to improve the drafting or content of the provision; and finally States which have expressed their support for the work of the ILC on this matter. Some States will appear in more than one group, having changed their views over the course of time. This will be noted whenever necessary. In addition, the comments of some States have been inconclusive and do not yield to a clear picture of that State's position on the matter.[329] Yet other States have commented on the topic of State responsibility in general or only in relation to other particular rules. This survey does not construe general support for the Articles as necessarily being support for the complicity provision in the Articles. The only instances taken into account are those in which a State has made express reference to complicity, or at least specifically to Chapter IV of Part One of the Articles.

4.1 Objection

Five States have objected expressly to a provision on aid or assistance in the ILC Articles. Yet, on closer inspection, this number needs to be qualified. The German Democratic Republic was opposed to Draft Article 27 in a 1988 comment which emphasised that the scope of application of the provision would already be regulated by the then still existing draft Articles on international crimes.[330] This criticism partly

---

[328] Jonathan I. Charney, 'Universal International Law', *American Journal of International Law* 87 (1993), pp. 529-51, at p. 545.
[329] See the statements of Bangladesh (UN Doc. A/C.6/33/SR.42, para. 25); Guatemala (UN Doc. A/C.6/56/SR.16, para. 29, and UN Doc. A/C.6/59/SR.15, paras. 104-5); Poland (UN Doc. A/C.6/33/SR.28, para. 5, UN Doc. A/C.6/54/SR.21, para. 56, UN Doc. A/CN.4/515/Add.2, p. 7); Slovakia (UN Doc. A/C.6/54/SR.22, para. 50); Thailand (UN Doc. A/C.6/33/SR.38, para. 14).
[330] UN Doc. A/CN.4/414, YBILC 1988, Vol. II, Part One, p. 4.

echoed the initially sceptical position of the Netherlands. In 1982, the Netherlands had argued in a similar way while having already,[331] in 1978, commented on a possible contradiction between draft Article 27 and the *pacta tertiis nec nocent nec prosunt* principle.[332] The objections of these two States can, however, be put to one side, as the former had its basis in the distinction between international delicts and crimes which has not survived the further drafting process, while the latter has changed its position in the course of the Second Reading (see subsections 2.4.2 and 2.4.3 below).

The comment made by France in 1978 is not self-explanatory. While the French delegate to the Sixth Committee expressed the view of the French government that draft Article 27 represents customary international law, France nevertheless objected to its inclusion in the Draft Articles as it considered the provision to belong to the realm of primary rules.[333] This, however, also means that France accepts the general proposition that aid or assistance to wrongful acts is unlawful.

Finally, two States objected rather strongly. The first is the Federal Republic of Germany, which twice argued that the draft Article would lack a basis in customary international law.[334] The interesting aspect of this opposition is that it stands in marked contrast to the attitudes that the German Federal Constitutional Court and the German Federal Administrative Court have taken.[335] This inconsistency will need to be addressed in the further assessment of the international practice but merits a mention at this point.

The second State which objected very strongly to the draft Article on complicity was Switzerland. It did so in a 1998 comment in which it argued, similarly to Germany's position, that the Article had no basis in customary international law.[336] The straightforward message of this statement is, however, blurred by a 1999 comment in the Sixth Committee where the Swiss delegate particularly welcomed the fact that Chapter IV of Part One of the Articles (in which the provision of complicity figures) was retained and also welcomed the modifications the ILC had effected with respect to then draft Article 27.[337]

---

[331] UN Doc. A/CN.4/351, YBILC 1982, Vol. II, Part One, p. 18.
[332] UN Doc. A/C.6/33/SR.31, paras. 9–10.
[333] UN Doc. A/C.6/33/SR.42, para. 17.
[334] UN Doc. A/CN.4/488, 74–5; UN Doc. A/C.6/54/SR.23, para. 3.
[335] See above notes 93, 257, 258 and 307 respectively.
[336] UN Doc. A/CN.4/488, 75.   [337] UN Doc. A/C.6/54/SR.22, paras. 70 *et seq.*

4.2 Constructive criticism

A considerably larger number of States have made criticism *en détail* while neither approving nor rejecting the draft Article on complicity in general. Some States have expressed their views on the question whether the aiding or assisting State needs to have intent or whether knowledge should be sufficient. The Czech Republic,[338] the Republic of Korea,[339] the United Kingdom[340] and the United States[341] have argued that the subjective element should be strengthened. Argentina[342] and Mexico[343] on the other hand have wondered whether the conditions laid down by the ILC would not be too restrictive. In their 2001 statement, the Netherlands even argued for changing the draft Article to the effect that it would be sufficient that a State should have known about the circumstances of the internationally wrongful act in order to incur responsibility for its aid or assistance thereto.[344]

Some States were generally favourable to the draft Article on complicity, but viewed it as a component of the progressive development of the law. However, these statements – by Canada,[345] Iran,[346] Italy in 1978[347] and Swaziland[348] – did not object in any way to the inclusion of the provision in the Articles.

Yet another group of States has expressed rather unspecific criticism with respect to the drafting of the provision while not appearing to be hostile towards the inclusion of the draft Article in the project. These States include China,[349] Japan in 1999,[350] Sweden in 1981[351] and Yugoslavia.[352]

---

[338] UN Doc. A/C.6/54/SR.22, para. 80.   [339] UN Doc. A/CN.4/515, 27.
[340] UN Doc. A/C.6/33/SR.37, para. 18; UN Doc. A/CN.4/488, 75–6; UN Doc. A/CN.4/515, 27–8.
[341] UN Doc. A/CN.4/488, 76; UN Doc. A/CN.4/515, 28; UN Doc. A/C.6/56/SR.14, para. 76.
[342] UN Doc. A/CN.4/515/Add.3, 4.
[343] UN Doc. A/C.6/55/SR.20, para. 42; the Mexican Statement is of 2000 and is situated between two statements from 1999 and 2001 in both of which Mexico expressed general support for the rule.
[344] UN Doc. A/CN.4/515, 28.
[345] UN Doc. A/C.6/33/SR.37, para. 53.   [346] UN Doc. A/C.6/33/SR.45, para. 17.
[347] UN Doc. A/C.6/33/SR.31, para. 35; but compare with the Italian statement of 1999, below in section 4.3.
[348] UN Doc. A/C.6/33/SR.45, para. 33.   [349] UN Doc. A/C.6/54/SR.22, para. 64.
[350] UN Doc. A/CN.4/492, p. 11; in the same year, however, Japan commented very favourably on then draft Article 27 in the Sixth Committee, see below in section 4.3.
[351] UN Doc. A/CN.4/342, YBILC 1981, Vol. II, Part One, p. 77; Sweden's statement is, however, eclipsed by the ones issued by Denmark 'on behalf of the Nordic Countries' in 1999 and 2001, see below in section 4.3.
[352] UN Doc. A/C.6/33/SR.35, para. 9.

4.3 Support

The largest group of States includes those which have expressed their support for the draft Article on complicity. The delegate of the Russian Federation said that 'Chapter IV of the draft articles ... was of fundamental importance. His delegation did not agree that the articles in that chapter would rarely be applied in practice, but in fact held a diametrically opposite view.'[353] The Mexican delegate to the Sixth Committee reiterated Mexico's position on the question of complicity by saying that 'it has long been accepted that States incur responsibility for aiding in the commission of internationally wrongful acts'.[354] Some States viewed the final version of the provision as not going far enough. New Zealand, for example, considered it to be conceivable to expand the Article so as also to include interference with the contractual rights of other States.[355] This would mean *a fortiori* that there is at least responsibility for aid and assistance under the premises the ILC envisaged. Other States which have expressed support for the provision are Bulgaria,[356] Cyprus,[357] Czechoslovakia,[358] Denmark (on behalf of the Nordic Countries),[359] Ethiopia,[360] Finland,[361] Greece,[362] Italy in 1999,[363] Jamaica,[364] Japan,[365] Mali,[366] Nigeria,[367] Romania,[368] Slovenia,[369] the Netherlands in 2001,[370] Trinidad and Tobago,[371] Tunisia,[372] the Ukrainian Socialist Soviet Republic[373] and Venezuela.[374] In the 2007 discussion on the future of the ILC Articles, the representative of the People's Republic of China also strongly pronounced himself in favour

---

[353] UN Doc. A/C.6/54/SR.23, paras. 75–6.
[354] UN Doc. A/C.6/54/SR.23, para. 15; UN Doc. A/C.6/55/SR.20, para. 42; UN Doc. A/CN.4/515/Add.1, 4.
[355] UN Doc. A/C.6/54/SR.23, para. 30.   [356] UN Doc. A/C.6/33/SR.40, para. 28.
[357] UN Doc. A/C.6/54/SR.26, para. 80.
[358] UN Doc. A/CN.4/362, YBILC 1983, Vol. II, Part One, p. 3.
[359] UN Doc. A/C.6/54/SR.22, para. 3; UN Doc. A/CN.4/515, 27.
[360] UN Doc. A/C.6/33/SR.35, para. 16.   [361] UN Doc. A/C.6/33/SR.39, para. 4.
[362] UN Doc. A/C.6/54/SR.28, para. 1.   [363] UN Doc. A/C.6/54/SR.24, para. 23.
[364] UN Doc. A/C.6/33/SR.32, para. 22.
[365] UN Doc. A/C.6/54/SR.22, para. 8, but contrast the more sceptical comment on the quality of drafting mentioned in section 4.2 above.
[366] UN Doc. A/CN.4/328, YBILC 1980, Vol. II, Part One, 101.
[367] UN Doc. A/C.6/33/SR.42, para. 41.   [368] UN Doc. A/C.6/33/SR.38, para. 37.
[369] UN Doc. A/C.6/54/SR.22, para. 34.   [370] UN Doc. A/CN.4/515, 28.
[371] UN Doc. A/C.6/33/SR.42, para. 2.   [372] UN Doc. A/C.6/54/SR.25, para. 26.
[373] UN Doc. A/C.6/33/SR.37, para. 31.
[374] UN Doc. A/CN.4/351, YBILC 1982, Vol. II, Part One, p. 19; UN Doc. A/C.6/54/SR.23, para. 52.

of a general rule on non-assistance in international law. When discussing the regime of aggravated responsibility in Articles 40 and 41 ASR, he made the point that it would not be necessary to include an obligation of non-assistance there, as '[a]ll international wrongful acts should not be recognized or rendered assistance to'.[375]

5 Evaluation

5.1 Standards for establishing customary international law

In order to represent customary international law, practice should be general, which is understood to mean that it is 'extensive and virtually uniform'.[376] There is a far-reaching consensus that not all States need to have participated in the formation of general customary international law.[377] However, a representative number of States, ideally from different legal cultures and traditions, should have participated in the process.[378] These States should also include those specifically affected.[379] Still, there is no unanimity as to how many instances of practice are required to create new customary law.[380] It is apparent that this process of customary norm creation cannot be measured using quantitative criteria. Rather, a number of variables need to be taken into account.[381] A particularly important question is whether an existent rule of customary international law needs to be overturned for the new custom to emerge.[382] If this is the case, the number of cases will

---

[375] Statement by Mr Ma Xinmin, 23 October 2007, available at www.fmprc.gov.cn/ce/ceun/eng/xw/t375208.htm (last visited 1 November 2010); this part of the statement is not reproduced in the verbatim records of the meeting of the UN General Assembly, see UN Doc. A/C.6/62/SR.12, para. 88.
[376] ICJ, *North Sea Continental Shelf Cases*, Judgment, ICJ Rep. 1969, 3, para. 74.
[377] Michael Akehurst, 'Custom as a Source', p. 17; Alfred Verdross and Bruno Simma, *Universelles Völkerrecht*, § 557; Vaughan Lowe, *International Law*, p. 37; Robert Kolb, 'Selected Problems', p. 135.
[378] Wolff Heintschel von Heinegg, 'Die weiteren Quellen', pp. 216–17; Alfred Verdross and Bruno Simma, *Universelles Völkerrecht*, § 557.
[379] ICJ, *North Sea Continental Shelf Cases*, Judgment, ICJ Rep. 1969, 3, para. 74; Wolff Heintschel von Heinegg, 'Die weiteren Quellen', pp. 216–17; Vaughan Lowe, *International Law*, p. 37.
[380] Cf Robert Kolb, 'Selected Problems', p. 134.
[381] Cf also Bruno Simma, *Das Reziprozitätselement in der Entstehung des Völkergewohnheitsrechts* (Munich: Fink, 1970), p. 30, on the eclecticism necessarily inherent in the analysis of customary international law.
[382] Josef L. Kunz, 'The Nature of Customary International Law', in Josef L. Kunz, *The Changing Law of Nations* (Columbus, OH: Ohio State University Press, 1968), pp. 335–46, at p. 342.

need to be significantly higher than in a case where no pre-existing custom exists on the matter.[383]

The same holds true with respect to the time requirement and the number of States which participate in the creation of new customary international law.[384] It is possible that only a small group of States formulates a new customary rule through their practice and *opinio juris* which then does not meet with opposition from many remaining States.[385] Some form of opposition to a newly emerging rule does not prevent it evolving into customary international law.[386] The notion of persistent objection is said to allow for some States to opt out of the formation of customary international law without being able to effectively hinder the coming into existence of the new rule,[387] if one is willing to still acknowledge the practical relevance of this concept.[388] While thus not all States need to participate in the formation of customary international law, it must be the case, however, that the practice is not confined to isolated incidents but amounts to a settled practice.[389] When assessing this uniformity and generality of practice, the requirements must not be exaggerated. A uniformity of practice does not require that the rule in question should necessarily have been invoked in each and every instance in which it would have been technically applicable.[390] There is as yet no duty in international law to respond to internationally wrongful acts, and States are therefore not obliged to invoke the responsibility of complicit States.[391]

---

[383] Cf Michael Akehurst, 'Custom as a Source', pp. 16 *et seq.*
[384] ICJ, *North Sea Continental Shelf Cases*, Judgment, ICJ Rep. 1969, 3, 42: the Court held that the provisions in question could be transformed into customary law 'even without the passage of any considerable period of time'.
[385] Michael Akehurst, 'Custom as a Source', p. 14; Alfred Verdross and Bruno Simma, *Universelles Völkerrecht*, § 557.
[386] Vaughan Lowe, *International Law*, pp. 55 *et seq.*
[387] ICJ, *Fisheries Case*, Judgment, ICJ Rep. 1951, 116, 131; for analysis of this doctrinal figure, see Jonathan I. Charney, 'The Persistent Objector Rule and the Development of Customary International Law', *British Year Book of International Law* 56 (1985), pp. 1–24; Michael Byers, *Custom, Power and the Power of Rules – International Relations and Customary International Law* (Cambridge: Cambridge University Press, 1999), pp. 180 *et seq.*
[388] Sceptical of its remaining relevance is Christian Tomuschat, 'International Law', p. 330.
[389] Christian J. Tams, *Enforcing Obligations Erga Omnes*, p. 234; Tullio Treves, 'Customary International Law', in Rüdiger Wolfrum (ed.), *Max Planck Encyclopedia of Public International Law*, online edition (Oxford: Oxford University Press, 2008), para. 35.
[390] Cf Hans Kelsen, 'Unrecht und Unrechtsfolge', p. 581.
[391] Roger S. Clark, 'Obligations of Third States in the Face of Illegality – Ruminations Inspired by the Weeramantry Dissent in the Case Concerning East Timor', in

Normally, the most difficult part of the exercise of establishing the customary status of a rule pertains to the problem of establishing the *opinio juris* of States. There are various theories about the importance of this element. While some authors are willing to neglect it altogether,[392] the majority of writers[393] as well as the jurisprudence of the International Court of Justice[394] supports the view that this second element of customary international law cannot be dispensed with. It is, however, striking that the Court engages only very rarely in a separate assessment of whether the practice underlying a given norm is supported by *opinio juris*. This approach is shared by those authors who take the position that the *opinio juris* can in most cases be inferred from the practice of States.[395] When the practice is unequivocal and not contradicted by contrasting statements, it is safe to assume that States engaged in this practice out of the feeling of a legal obligation. This approach has, however, some limits when a prohibitive rule such as one on complicity is sought. Here, one has no positive conduct from which reliance upon a legal right can be inferred. Rather, an abstention on the part of States is to be identified or the expectation by States that other States do not engage in such behaviour. This expectation is difficult to grasp in terms of reciprocity, an element which is normally

Antony Anghie (ed.), *Legal Visions of the 21st Century – Essays in Honour of Judge Christopher Weeramantry* (The Hague: Kluwer, 1998), pp. 631–51, at p. 651, who nonetheless sees a tendency towards growing obligations of States to react towards internationally wrongful acts of a particularly serious nature; see also John Dugard, 'First Report on Diplomatic Protection', UN Doc. A/CN.4/506, 27, for a Draft Article 4 which would have required States to exercise diplomatic protection in cases of grave breaches of *jus cogens* norms. The proposal failed to convince the Commission.

[392] For a discussion of *opinio juris*, with further references, see Robert Kolb, 'Selected Problems', p. 123; Hans Kelsen was probably the most prominent author to generally neglect the importance of *opinio juris* for the establishment of customary law: see 'Théorie du droit coutumier', reprinted in Nicoletta Bersier Ladavac, *Hans Kelsen à Genève (1933–1940)* (Geneva: Thémis, 1996), pp. 33–64, at pp. 47 *et seq.* Kelsen, however, changed his mind: see his 1952 treatise, *Principles of International Law*, p. 307; on Kelsen's approach in this regard, see Jochen von Bernstorff, *Der Glaube an das universale Recht*, pp. 149–50.

[393] Michael Akehurst, 'Custom as a Source', p. 31; Ian Brownlie, *Principles*, pp. 8 *et seq.*; Malcolm N. Shaw, *International Law*, 6th edn (Cambridge: Cambridge University Press, 2008), pp. 84 *et seq.*; for further references, see Sienho Yee, 'The News That Opinio Juris "Is Not a Necessary Element of Customary [International] Law" Is Greatly Exaggerated', *German Yearbook of International Law* 43 (2000), pp. 227–38.

[394] ICJ, *North Sea Continental Shelf Cases*, Judgment, ICJ Rep. 1969, 3, para. 77.

[395] Maurice H. Mendelson, 'Formation', p. 290; Christian J. Tams, *Enforcing Obligations Erga Omnes*, p. 238; John Quigley, 'Complicity', p. 100.

considered to be of defining importance for the formation of customary international law.[396] Rather, one needs to look for some form of 'objective' reciprocity, i.e., a general expectation that, if a State does not itself aid or assist the wrongful conduct of other States, it can expect other States to do the same.[397]

With these general observations in mind, we will now proceed to an evaluation of the elements of practice assembled so far. First, we will discuss three aspects relating to the representativeness of the practice, i.e., whether the number of States participating, the range of subject matters touched upon and the time span in which this practice has developed allow us to posit the existence of a customary rule establishing responsibility for complicity and thus to support the findings of the ILC and the ICJ. Following that, some further remarks will be made on the relationship between the consistency of the practice and the degree of compliance with the rule whose establishment is sought, before we finally turn to a discussion of whether the established practice is also equipped with an underlying *opinio juris* of States.

5.2 *Representativeness of the practice*

5.2.1 Representativeness *ratione personae*

A first category of representativeness of the assembled practice concerns the number of States which have contributed to this practice. At the same time, this exercise requires us to establish how widespread this practice is among the members of the international community and to see whether the origins of the practice are sufficiently diverse in geographical and cultural terms. A variety of States which represent different legal cultures of the world have issued diplomatic protests against complicit States, have commented on situations invoking a rule prohibiting complicity or have applied a presumably customary rule on complicity in their domestic law. These States cannot be reduced to a particular geographical or cultural region. They include European States (United Kingdom, France, Germany, Switzerland, Sweden, Belgium, the Netherlands, Italy, Norway, the Soviet Union/Russia and Czechoslovakia), African States (Angola, Guinea, Kenya, Libya, Mali and Rwanda), Middle Eastern States (Iraq, Syria, Iran and Saudi Arabia), Latin American States (Cuba) and the United States. With

---

[396] See Bruno Simma, *Das Reziprozitätselement*, pp. 45 *et seq.*   [397] *Ibid.*, p. 47.

respect to other States, it is possible to point at least to statements and declarations which show some awareness of the problem of complicity (for example, Canada and the United Kingdom). Furthermore, domestic courts have entertained considerations involving responsibility for complicity, for instance in Germany, Switzerland, Greece, Italy and the United Kingdom. The issue of complicity has also played a role in a number of authoritative statements emanating from international organisations such as the Council of Europe, the European Union, the League of Arab States and the Movement of Non-Aligned States. One can therefore say that practice is not limited to a particular geographical or cultural region. Although the sheer number of States which have participated in the creation of practice is not the decisive criterion for the establishment of customary international law, it can be observed that a fairly large number of States is implicated in this process.

5.2.2 Representativeness *ratione materiae*

One objection to the putative customary status of a rule establishing responsibility for complicity could, however, consist in the very diverse array of situations which have been described so far. This could prompt the question whether the practice is dense enough. In this respect, we are faced with a dilemma which relates to the character of the rules of State responsibility as secondary rules. The way they have been conceived of by the ILC implies that they apply across the whole spectrum of international law, regardless of the kind of breach of international law to which they are applied.[398] A lack of density with respect to one subject matter thus does not necessarily imply that a general rule on the matter would not be applicable in this field of the law. It is of course another matter whether a thin empirical basis allows us to consider the existence of a general rule in the first place. In this respect, judgment must be reserved until we have reviewed the further conditions for the coming into existence of customary international law. A lack with respect to one necessary factor may potentially be set off by others which are more clearly represented.[399] One remark, however, may be made here. A comparative look at the empirical basis upon which the

---

[398] On the downsides of the necessary generalisations inherent in this approach, see Philip Allott, 'State Responsibility and the Unmaking of International Law', *Harvard International Law Journal* 29 (1988), pp. 1–26, at p. 7.

[399] Frederic L. Kirgis, 'Custom on a Sliding Scale', *American Journal of International Law* 81 (1987), pp. 146–51, at p. 149.

ILC has recognised the customary status of most of the other provisions in the ASR reveals that most provisions do not rest on a more generous bed of practice which covers more substantive fields of international law. It could thus very well be the case that the concept of general rules in the field of international responsibility almost by definition leads to a 'thinning' of the available practice in individual fields.

5.2.3 Representativeness *ratione temporis*

Finally, the representativeness of the practice needs to be assessed with respect to its extension *ratione temporis*. Here, it appears to be unproblematic to find this criterion satisfied as the practice we have assembled stretches from the beginning of the 1950s well into the present day. Regardless of whether one requires a certain period of time to lapse before one can speak of customary law or whether one accepts the possibility of instant custom,[400] a time-frame of sixty years is enough to allow for the maturing of a norm into customary international law.

5.3 Consistency and compliance

One potential objection is the weak record of compliance with a supposed norm positing responsibility for complicity. There are two grounds to support this objection. First, it is apparent that States quite frequently become complicit in the violations of international law by other States. Secondly, a look at the practice we have assembled in this chapter may allow us to speak of a consistent pattern insofar as States quite frequently appear to take responsibility for complicity into consideration. Nevertheless, the number of 'real' diplomatic protests, countermeasures or international court proceedings in which complicity plays a central role may be said to be comparatively small. The first argument has already briefly been dealt with in the opening passages of this chapter and is easier to dismiss than the second one. Violations of the law do not necessarily call its normative character into question. It is precisely the task of the law to erect an order which is based on a difference between the 'is' and the 'ought' (*Sein und Sollen*).[401] In

---

[400] On the time factor, see ICJ, *North Sea Continental Shelf Cases*, Judgment, ICJ Rep. 1969, 3, para. 73; see further René-Jean Dupuy, 'Coutume sage et coutume sauvage', in *Mélanges offerts à Charles Rousseau* (Paris: Pedone, 1974), pp. 75–87, at pp. 76–7.

[401] With respect to customary international law, this dichotomy between the 'is' and the 'ought' is, however, especially peculiar: see Prosper Weil, 'Cours général de droit international public: le droit international en quête de son identité', *Recueil des Cours* 237 (1992-VI), pp. 9–370, at pp. 164–5; Vaughan Lowe, *International Law*,

addition, it is important to note that, although States may be complicit in such and such violation of the law, it is not apparent that States have in any circumstance raised the argument that they would be allowed to render aid or assistance to the commission of internationally wrongful acts.[402] In this regard, one can also note that there was no anterior rule in customary international law which would have expressly condoned the granting of aid or assistance to the wrongful conduct of other States. Rather, the point of comparison is the 'initial' situation represented by the *Lotus* principle.[403]

With respect to the second argument, it has to be admitted that it would be easier to establish the customary status of a rule providing for responsibility for complicity if there were more 'hard facts' in the guise of concrete diplomatic protests and court proceedings. However, one needs to take into account that a change of perspective on the law of State responsibility has taken place in the last few years. In addition to its classic, reparation-oriented function, the systemic functions of this field of the law have attracted more attention.[404] This development is part of the movement which sees the law of State responsibility as an essential element of the international rule of law[405] and which puts an emphasis on the 'internalization'[406] of those rules.[407] Seen from this perspective, it is just as relevant when domestic actors invoke complicity as a factor in decision-making processes or in domestic court

---

p. 19; Niels Petersen, 'Der Wandel', p. 504. On the same problem for the closely related issue of non-recognition, see Théodore Christakis, 'Non-Reconnaissance', p. 133.

[402] With respect to the use of force this was noted by Olivier Corten, *Le droit contre la guerre*, pp. 284 *et seq.*

[403] See our discussion in Chapter 3, text accompanying notes 98 *et seq.*

[404] See Pierre-Marie Dupuy, 'A General Stocktaking of the Connections between the Multilateral Dimension of Obligations and Codification of the Law of State Responsibility', *European Journal of International Law* 13 (2002), pp. 1053–81, at p. 1057; André Nollkaemper, 'Concurrence', p. 622; Eyal Benvenisti, 'Conception', p. 394; see also Christian J. Tams, 'Unity and Diversity in the Law of State Responsibility', in Andreas Zimmermann and Rainer Hofmann (eds.), *Unity and Diversity in International Law* (Berlin: Duncker & Humblot, 2006), pp. 437–60, at pp. 444 *et seq.*; Helmut Philipp Aust, 'Normative Environment', pp. 32 *et seq.*

[405] On the relationship between State responsibility and the rule of law, see above Chapter 3, section 3, text accompanying notes 178 *et seq.*

[406] Cf Harold H. Koh, 'Why Do Nations Obey International Law?', *Yale Law Journal* 106 (1997), pp. 2598–2659.

[407] Cf André Nollkaemper, 'Internationally Wrongful Acts in Domestic Courts', *American Journal of International Law* 101 (2007), pp. 760–99, on the uses to which the rules of State responsibility are put by domestic courts.

proceedings, as when a formal diplomatic claim is brought by State A against State B.

5.4 *Opinio juris*

In order to generate customary international law, the existence of practice alone is not sufficient. Rather, it needs to be supplemented by the accompanying *opinio juris*, the belief that the form of conduct represented by the practice is required by law.

5.4.1 Unclear motivation?

One could argue that the motivation behind the practice we have assembled is far from clear. It is not self-evident that States have refrained from complicit behaviour or have challenged the complicit conduct of other States on the basis of a belief that there exists a rule which establishes responsibility for complicity. Other conceivable factors which could have impacted upon their assessment range from political motives, domestic constitutional imperatives or moral considerations to sheer coincidence. This difficulty in digesting the exact motivation for feeling bound by a certain rule is, as was already briefly mentioned, particularly acute if the rule in question is imposing a duty on States or is limiting their freedom. Whereas in the case of new rights one can safely presume that States will wish to act lawfully and thus assume that a given form of conduct is meant to rest on this legal conviction, the same certainty only rarely applies with respect to new limitations of State freedom.[408] We have already made reference to the fact that sometimes States may not even know why they act in a given way, notwithstanding that there are legal consequences to such actions. The problem we have already discussed with respect to the consistency of the practice arises here once again: the situations covered by a general rule in the field of State responsibility are so diverse that it is wellnigh impossible to deduce a particular belief on the part of States from a field of practical examples which covers matters as diverse as the use of force and the granting of export credit guarantees. The secondary rules on State responsibility are characterised by a high degree of abstraction. The same applies with respect to their underpinnings in customary international law.

---

[408] Vaughan Lowe, *International Law*, p. 51.

Not all the examples referred to in this chapter will have been accompanied by the requisite *opinio juris*. So much will be clear, for example, for the vast field of domestic legislation on arms exports. Similarly, one can always question the legal motivation behind protests over the cases involving the use of force. The Norwegian explanation of its position towards the Iraq war is also a case in point: in public, governments tend to comment on political rather than legal aspects.[409] A certain ambiguity is also apparent with respect to the UN practice to which we have made reference. The crucial issue for us is, however, whether the differing motives behind the conduct of States can ultimately deflect from their consideration for the establishment of customary international law. Even if explained on a narrow rationale or based on different considerations, such conduct may become entangled in a greater normative development. Ascribing legal relevance to State conduct *a posteriori* will always be artificial to a certain extent. If such conduct is itself in line with a broad legal development, it may very well be counted as practice supporting this development. This finding could of course raise concerns about an arbitrary scholarly extrapolation of facts. This anxiety may, however, be remedied by the existence of express statements by States concerning their view on the issue of responsibility for complicity. If the States themselves affirm their general belief in the existence of a given rule in international law, it is possible to identify their practice more liberally. Affirmations by States in the abstract which confirm the existence of a rule establishing responsibility for complicity hence allows us to view certain elements of practice in a different light.

5.4.2 The governmental statements analysed

The list of governmental comments on the complicity provision shows that only very few States were strictly opposed to the inclusion of such a rule in the codification project. In addition, the position of some of these States has changed over the years. As far as one can tell, France has not changed its opinion that the draft Article 27 on which it commented rather represented a primary than a secondary rule. It thus did not call into question, however, that international law would recognise a rule according to which responsibility for aid and assistance would be incurred.

---

[409] See above note 95.

(The Federal Republic of) Germany has opposed the draft Article on several occasions and has reaffirmed that it sees no basis for it in customary international law.[410] This position was once shared by Switzerland which, however, seems to have changed its position, at least according to the overwhelmingly positive comment its representative made in the 6th Committee in 1999 about Chapter IV of Part One of the Draft Articles in general. This comment was however about the whole of that chapter of the Draft Articles; the comment did not deal specifically with the Article on complicity, and so its position remains ambiguous.

The Netherlands is another example of a State which has changed its position in this regard. In its earlier comments, it focused on the *pacta tertiis nec nocent nec prosunt* rule which it saw endangered by draft Article 27. Special Rapporteur James Crawford took into consideration this critique and introduced the new subparagraph (b) in the course of the Second Reading. Subsequently, the Netherlands withdrew its criticism of the provision and even wished to see it strengthened by proposing, as not many States have done, to loosen the subjective requirement set out in the Article by including within the Article's ambit those cases in which a State should have known that its assistance was used to further an internationally wrongful act.

A few other States have remarked that the draft Article forms part of the progressive development of international law. It is interesting to note, however, that no State has made such a comment in the second phase of deliberations from 1998 onwards.

5.4.3 The special case of Germany

This survey of comments therefore shows that only one State, the Federal Republic of Germany, has consistently denied the customary basis of Article 16 ASR. The case of Germany is especially interesting because the position of the Federal Government is in conflict with the jurisprudence of the German Federal Constitutional Court and the German Federal Administrative Court which have both affirmed

---

[410] One can wonder, however, about the scope of a statement of the German representative in the Sixth Committee in 2005 when he commented on Draft Article 12 on the Responsibility of International Organizations (DARIO) which includes a parallel provision for aid or assistance furnished by international organisations. There he 'commended' the Commission for Articles 12–16 DARIO without, however, addressing the scope of Germany's support for the idea of complicity any further. See UN Doc. A/C.6/60/SR.13, para. 33.

the character of Article 16 ASR as a rule of customary international law. This leads us to the question which position should take the upper hand. Scholars from the beginning of the twentieth century were still reluctant to consider anything other than the practice of the executive of a State as being capable of contributing to State practice.[411] Karl Strupp, for example, held the view that only the State organs which are able to bind the State internationally can contribute to its State practice.[412] This view has, however, long since been seen as too narrow, and it is now accepted that the legislative and the judicial branches may also contribute to the formation of State practice.[413] But what happens if the practice of domestic courts is in contradiction with the position of the executive? It has been suggested in scholarly writings that, 'if, by any chance, there is a contradiction between the positions of the Government and the courts, it seems … that this goes more to the *weight* of the evidence of State practice than to its *admissibility*'.[414]

However, this quotation does not deal with the exact same situation as we are faced with in the case of Germany. Here, we have State practice in the form of a number of recent and very authoritative court decisions and we have conflicting *opinio juris*, in the form of governmental statements in the Sixth Committee of the UN General Assembly and to the ILC. Therefore, one might be inclined to say that, while court decisions reflect State practice, they lack the necessary *opinio juris* which would need to be expressed by the executive. However, there appears to be no rule in international law which would limit the ability of the judiciary to contribute to State practice without having at the same time the capacity to express the correlating *opinio juris*. It would also be counter-intuitive to assume that the courts would satisfy themselves with considering mere State practice. This would amount to reproaching the courts with the application of non-law, i.e., mere

---

[411] Dionisio Anzilotti, *Lehrbuch des Völkerrechts*, p. 54; but see Hans Kelsen, 'Unrecht und Unrechtsfolge', pp. 510–11.

[412] Karl Strupp, 'Les règles générales du droit de la paix', *Recueil des Cours* 47 (1934), pp. 259–595, at pp. 313 *et seq*.

[413] Yoram Dinstein, 'Customary International Law', pp. 272–3; see also Alain Pellet, 'Article 38', para. 312, on the issue of whether domestic court decisions fall under Article 38(1)(d), i.e., subsidiary means for the determination of rules of law. Pellet holds that domestic court decisions should rather be seen as elements of domestic practice.

[414] Maurice H. Mendelson, 'Formation', p. 200.

facts.[415] In the case of the German court decisions, reference has been made to Article 16 ASR constituting customary international law. This statement not only refers to State practice but, necessarily, also to the subjective element of *opinio juris*. Thus we are faced with two conflicting views on *opinio juris*. As it is the case with conflicting State practice, there is no argument available to short-circuit either the position of the government or the position of the courts.[416] Instead, the inconsistent German practice needs to be taken into account as it stands. Its inconsistency is, however, likely to weaken its impact on the assessment of the customary character of Article 16 ASR.

5.4.4 Preliminary assessment

We are thus faced with a situation in which nearly forty States have commented in a largely favourable manner on the existence of a rule in international law which establishes responsibility for complicity.[417] This group of States is also characterised by a considerable diversity in terms of geographical location and cultural origin. One should not discount this broad support in the Sixth Committee of the UN General Assembly and in the statements provided to the ILC as merely expressions of the usual diplomatic politeness.[418] After all, States have been fairly outspoken with respect to other problems in the field of State responsibility where they saw their interests endangered. For example, the inclusion of a right to countermeasures in the collective interest met with fierce opposition among States before the conclusion of the Second Reading.[419] This opposition partly led Special Rapporteur James Crawford and the Commission to the adoption of the vague compromise solution that is Article 54 ASR which avoids expressly stipulating that third States may take countermeasures in the collective interest.[420] Also, in other respects, States were

---

[415] On the distinction between legal acts and legal facts, see Jean d'Aspremont, 'Softness in International Law: A Self-Serving Quest for New Legal Materials', *European Journal of International Law* 19 (2008), pp. 1075–93, at pp. 1077 *et seq*.
[416] Cf Michael Akehurst, 'Custom as a Source', p. 22, who argues against any 'overgeneralizations about the greater expertise of the Foreign Office and the greater impartiality of the Courts'.
[417] See above notes 338–75.
[418] See further Alan Boyle and Christine Chinkin, *The Making of International Law* (Oxford: Oxford University Press, 2007), p. 179.
[419] See, e.g., James Crawford, 'Introduction', p. 56.
[420] For a slightly different position, see Christian J. Tams, *Enforcing Obligations Erga Omnes*, pp. 246–7.

engaged in a critical dialogue with the Commission and commented openly on those parts of the ASR which they viewed as inconsistent with the present state of international law or potentially dangerous as regards their 'own best interests'. After all, one should not forget that the field of State responsibility is one in which States are most reluctant to accept new ties that bind them, as Bruno Simma has remarked.[421]

If States thus express a view in this field that leads potentially to new bases of responsibility, one should take their statements at face value.[422] Although the element of *opinio juris* should generally not be reduced to State consent,[423] one can observe with Maurice Mendelson that, if a State has consented, 'so much the better': consent would be a sufficient condition for being bound although it has never been required as the necessary condition for the formation of customary law.[424] The number of positive statements available allows us to ascribe the necessary *opinio juris* to the elements of practice we have assembled to a degree that is seldom found in international law. Whereas usually authors have to take refuge in the assertion that the *opinio juris* will have to be inferred from the relevant conduct, not only can we point towards a significant amount of practice here, but we can underline its legal significance with the amount of support Article 16 ASR has found in the deliberations of States in the United Nations.

5.5 Remaining uncertainties

Nevertheless, two uncertainties remain which are of a cross-cutting nature.

---

[421] Bruno Simma, 'Grundfragen', p. 358; see also Christian Dominicé, 'Responsabilité des Etats et responsabilité internationale: commentaires sur l'approche de la Commission; exposé', in United Nations (ed.), *The International Law Commission Fifty Years After: An Evaluation* (New York: United Nations, 2000), pp. 30–42, at p. 31.

[422] Antonio Cassese, 'Statement', in Antonio Cassese and Joseph H. H. Weiler (eds.), *Change and Stability in International Law-Making* (Berlin: de Gruyter, 1988), pp. 112–13, at p. 113; Olufemi Elias, 'The Nature of the Subjective Element in Customary International Law', *International and Comparative Law Quarterly* 44 (1995), pp. 501–20, at p. 515; Rein Müllerson, 'The Interplay of Objective and Subjective Elements in Customary International Law', in Karel Wellens (ed.), *International Law: Theory and Practice. Essays in Honour of Eric Suy* (The Hague: Nijhoff, 1998), pp. 161–78, at p. 167.

[423] Alain Pellet, 'Article 38', paras. 219–20.

[424] Maurice H. Mendelson, 'Formation', p. 260; see further Pierre-Marie Dupuy, 'L'unité', p. 171; see also Olufemi Elias, 'Nature', pp. 509 *et seq.*, for a view which puts more emphasis on the equation of *opinio juris* with consent.

5.5.1 Practice with respect to primary or secondary rules?

A number of instances in which diplomatic protests have been raised and in which States commented on the complicit behaviour of other States can be explained on a different rationale: they could be said to refer to situations in which 'primary' rules on complicity are at stake.[425] This is the case, for example, in almost all situations which involve the use of force. Here, it needs to be taken into account that Article 3(f) of the Definition of Aggression stipulates that the 'action of a State in allowing its territory, which it has placed at the disposal of another State, to be used by that other State for perpetrating an act of aggression against another State' qualifies as an act of aggression.[426] Similarly, the arbitral award of Judge Huber in the *Island of Palmas* case made reference to the obligation of each State not to allow its territory to be used for wrongful acts against another State.[427] In other instances, the laws of neutrality could potentially provide further guidance on conduct during an armed conflict which would not be compatible with the status of a neutral State.[428]

Whether State practice, which can also be counted as appertaining to a primary rule, can count for the establishment of the more general, secondary rule is a matter which resembles the controversy over whether treaty law (and especially bilateral treaties) may be counted as instances of State practice. The arguments are interchangeable: treaties may be an expression of a general tendency and may thus foster the coming into being of customary rules. Treaties may, however, also be an expression of the express wish of States not to contribute to the formation of customary law.[429] If the same subject matter could be regulated by customary law, why then bother with the formulation of treaty law?[430] The situation is similar with respect to practice underlying primary and/or secondary rules on complicity: primary rules may be seen as part of the general trend towards establishing responsibility for complicity. Practice which invokes primary rules on complicity could therefore

---

[425] Andreas Felder, *Die Beihilfe*, p. 162.   [426] Cf John Quigley, 'Complicity', p. 86.
[427] *Island of Palmas Case*, RIAA II, 829, 839.
[428] See Wolff Heintschel von Heinegg, 'Wider die Mär', pp. 221 *et seq.*
[429] Cf Hanspeter Neuhold, 'Völkerrechtlicher Vertrag und "Drittstaaten"', *Berichte der Deutschen Gesellschaft für Völkerrecht* 29 (1988), pp. 51–103, at p. 59; Alain Pellet, 'Article 38', paras. 212-13.
[430] On this issue, see ICJ, *North Sea Continental Shelf Cases*, Judgment, ICJ Rep. 1969, 3, paras. 70-1; Theodor Meron, *Humanization*, pp. 376 *et seq.*; Vaughan Lowe, *International Law*, pp. 83 *et seq.*

also be seen as practice counting towards the secondary rule on complicity. This practice can, however, also be interpreted as an affirmation that States mostly raise diplomatic protests and change their behaviour when there is a specific primary rule on the issue of complicity. How can this array be disentangled when practice could count as practice with respect to the primary as well as to a secondary rule?

A solution to this dilemma could be seen in a functional understanding of the relationship between primary and secondary rules on complicity.[431] The key to this functional understanding lies in the insight that with respect to complicity the boundaries between primary and secondary rules are blurred. This was already conceded by Special Rapporteur Roberto Ago. When asked whether or not Draft Article 27 would leave behind the strict distinction between primary and secondary rules, Ago remarked that 'in his opinion the Commission should not hesitate to leap that barrier whenever necessary'.[432] Primary rules on complicity are difficult to grasp as solely primary in character because they do not set forth a particular, clear-cut obligation. Instead, they inform their addressees that assistance to a given violation of another obligation is prohibited. Accordingly, they provide for a derivative obligation which differs from other primary obligations which just set forth a rather clear command in the form of 'do not violate the right x of State y'.[433] Likewise, the secondary rule on complicity is peculiar as it has some features of a primary rule.[434] It does not merely address the consequences of a wrongful act, but extends them to a State which would otherwise not incur responsibility.[435] In light of these considerations, it may be artificial to uphold too strict a distinction between practice which is motivated by a primary rule and practice which is owed to the existence of a secondary rule.[436] Frequently, States will not determine

---

[431] James Crawford, Statement at the 2578th Meeting of the ILC, YBILC 1999, Vol. I, p. 78, para. 39.
[432] Roberto Ago, Statement at the 1519th Meeting of the ILC, YBILC 1978, Vol. I, p. 240, para. 27.
[433] See also John Quigley, 'Complicity', p. 86.
[434] Cf Robert Q. Quentin-Baxter, Statement at the 1518th Meeting of the ILC, YBILC 1978, Vol. I, p. 236, para. 32.
[435] Bruno Simma, Statement at the 2578th Meeting of the ILC, YBILC 1999, Vol. I, p. 79, para. 41: Draft Article 27 'tackled primary rules head on, and that was a positive development'.
[436] See the statement by Constantin Economides at the 2578th meeting of the ILC, YBILC 1999, Vol. I, p. 77, para. 30: 'The question of primary and secondary rules should ... not be taken too far.'

their behaviour in such a legalistic manner, even if they behave in a certain way out of the conviction that it is international law that requires them to adopt a certain behaviour. Legal advisors will not be asked by their respective governments whether there is a secondary rule which speaks against cooperation with another State in a given situation but simply whether international law speaks against such cooperation.

The key to resolving this problem thus lies in an understanding of the relationship between primary and secondary rules on complicity which does not overestimate the possibility of erecting clear-cut barriers between these two bodies of law.[437] Rather, 'primary rules' on complicity should more aptly be termed *special* rules on complicity. The 'secondary rule' on complicity would in this perspective represent the *general* rule on complicity. The special rules on complicity share certain characteristics of the general rule insofar as they attach responsibility to conduct which is 'accessory', which is only wrongful through its connection to the wrongful conduct of another State. The general rule on complicity shares characteristics of the category of primary rules in general as it establishes responsibility for conduct which is otherwise not wrongful.

This re-partition between the general and the special rules on complicity follows the patterns which the ILC has generally laid down in Article 55 ASR on the issue of *lex specialis*.[438] In this respect, special rules on complicity will most likely erect stricter standards for complicit States.[439] In this regard, James Crawford asserted that it would 'suffice to ensure that the rule embodied in article 27 did not establish a more extensive form of responsibility' than the existing primary

---

[437] See, in different contexts, Ulf Linderfalk, 'State Responsibility', p. 72; André Nollkaemper, 'Domestic Courts', p. 763; Malcolm D. Evans, 'State Responsibility and the European Convention on Human Rights: Role and Realm', in Malgosia Fitzmaurice and Dan Sarooshi (eds.), *Issues of State Responsibility before International Judicial Institutions* (Oxford: Hart, 2004), pp. 139–60, at p. 140; Alexander Orakhelashvili, *Peremptory Norms*, p. 80. Note that this is not meant to call into question the methodological and theoretical benefits of the established distinction between primary and secondary rules. In fact, they appear to be a crucial step towards the further maturing of the international legal order: see on this issue, with further references, Helmut Philipp Aust, 'Normative Environment', pp. 21 *et seq*.

[438] Note that, in contrast to the Draft Article 37 as adopted on First Reading, Article 55 ASR applies with respect to the whole set of provisions embodied in the ASR. This is expressly stated in the ILC Commentary, Article 55, para. 6.

[439] Georg Nolte and Helmut Philipp Aust, 'Equivocal Helpers', p. 17.

ones.[440] The special rules on complicity are an expression of the consent of States to reinforce the prohibition of complicity in a given field or of the anterior insight that even in the absence of a general rule this form of wrongful conduct was not to be assisted.[441] As States will not necessarily distinguish in their practical dealings whether or not they wish to avoid responsibility for complicity on the basis of a primary or a secondary rule, these considerations do not speak against the inclusion of these cases for our present survey.

5.5.2 Practice only with respect to qualified norms?

Another issue concerns the interpretation of the practice we have assembled. Other authors have come to the conclusion that most instances of practice on complicity primarily relate to peremptory norms or obligations *erga omnes*.[442] This finding is correct insofar as many of the norms and obligations concerned in the cases we have assembled potentially relate to *jus cogens* or obligations *erga omnes*.

However, it needs to be assessed carefully whether it is really *jus cogens* which is at stake in most of these issues. It is frequently noted that the category of *jus cogens* plays no prominent role in international practice.[443] We can remark that the category of *jus cogens* was mostly absent from the way States communicated about the cases presented.[444] It rather appears to be the case that States are inclined not to have careless recourse to the category of peremptory norms in their practice. The same applies to the category of obligations *erga omnes*. In the cases we have assembled, it was not necessary for the concerned States to rely on this doctrinal figure. In most cases it was the directly injured State which protested against the complicity of a third State. One cannot therefore reduce this reaction to an epiphenomenon of the *erga*

---

[440] James Crawford, Statement at the 2578th Meeting of 28 May 1999, YBILC 1999, Vol. I, p. 78, para. 39.
[441] Cf Andreas Felder, *Die Beihilfe*, p. 163; Georg Nolte and Helmut Philipp Aust, 'Equivocal Helpers', p. 17.
[442] Maria Luisa Padelletti, *Pluralità di stati*, p. 221; Andreas Felder, *Die Beihilfe*, pp. 232–3.
[443] Ian Brownlie, 'Discussion Statement', in Antonio Cassese and Joseph H. H. Weiler (eds.), *Change and Stability in International Law-Making* (Berlin: de Gruyter, 1988), pp. 108–10, at p. 110; Andreas L. Paulus, 'Jus Cogens', p. 330; Oliver Dörr, 'Codifying and Developing Meta-Rules: The ILC and the Law of Treaties', *German Yearbook of International Law* 49 (2006), pp. 129–64, at pp. 147 *et seq*.
[444] Save for a few exceptions: see notably the statement of Saudi Arabia concerning the Israeli wall and the prominence that considerations of *jus cogens* and obligations *erga omnes* enjoy in domestic court proceedings (Greece, Italy, United Kingdom).

omnes effect of the norm concerned. Where third States have commented against complicit State behaviour one can equally hold that it is not necessary to refer to the category of obligations *erga omnes* because it is widely held that all States have a right to comment on violations of international law. This is not a distinct feature of obligations *erga omnes*.[445] Accordingly, there is no apparent reason to restrict the finding with respect to the customary character of a rule establishing responsibility for complicity to the domain of peremptory norms or obligations *erga omnes*.

6 Conclusion

In light of these findings, the affirmation that customary international law includes a general rule on responsibility for complicity can be upheld. The survey of practice has shown that there is a sufficient number of cases to which reference can be made. States have expressed their *opinio juris* that a rule on complicity exists within the framework of the law of State responsibility. It can thus be concluded that a general rule on complicity has entered the corpus of customary international law. This was rightly affirmed by the ICJ in its *Genocide Convention* case.

---

[445] See Jochen Abr. Frowein, 'Reactions', p. 416; Christian Hillgruber, 'The Right of Third States to Take Countermeasures', in Christian Tomuschat and Jean-Marc Thouvenin (eds.), *The Fundamental Rules of the International Legal Order – Jus Cogens and Obligations Erga Omnes* (Leiden: Nijhoff, 2006), pp. 265–94, at p. 266.

5 The concept of complicity in Article 16 ASR

During the 2003 attacks on Iraq, Ireland, a traditionally neutral State, allowed US military aircraft to stop over at Irish airbases. A citizen initiated High Court proceedings on the constitutionality of what he viewed as Irish participation in the Iraq war. In order to substantiate his claim, the plaintiff relied on Article 16 ASR: he intended to show that Irish participation in the attacks would be wrongful under international law. The Irish High Court was not willing to rule on the matter, but, nonetheless, made the following remark:

> The issue of 'participation' is not a black and white issue. It may well ultimately be, as stated by the Taoiseach, a matter of 'substance and degree'. However, that is quintessentially a matter for the Government and the elected public representatives in Dáil Eireann to determine and resolve. In even an extreme case, the court would be still obliged to extend a considerable margin of appreciation to those organs of State when exercising their functions and responsibilities under Article 28 [of the Irish Constitution,].[1]

Although the Court thus did not want to pass a judgment on the issue, it highlighted one of the crucial issues concerning complicity in international law: what actually counts as aid or assistance triggering responsibility of the supporting State? In order to identify what form of conduct is eligible in this regard, a further issue needs to be dealt with: the requisite degree of knowledge or intent on the part of the complicit State. This subjective element is also likely to cause greater problems. As Philippe Sands has remarked, it is exactly 'the crux of the issue on complicity: What is the extent of the Government's obligation to satisfy

---

[1] Irish High Court, *Edward Horgan* v. *An Taoiseach and others*, Application for declaratory relief, para. 174.

itself that no internationally illegal acts are occurring?'[2] Article 16 ASR and its commentary do not necessarily provide answers to these questions. What is more, the solution the ILC has adopted in Article 16 ASR has been criticised by some authors for being unduly monolithic. It was mentioned that there would be different levels of facilitating the commission of internationally wrongful acts of other States: 'International law should recognise this, and it should also differentiate between varying degrees of complicity.'[3] Criticism in this regard is connected to developments in other fields of international law: with respect to what is frequently called 'corporate complicity', international lawyers have learned to distinguish between differing degrees of complicity, i.e., direct, beneficial and silent complicity.[4] Whereas usually it is assumed that the debate on corporate responsibility in international law will have something to learn from the principles of State responsibility,[5] it cannot be ruled out that conversely the debate on State responsibility for complicity could benefit from the import of conceptual distinctions developed with respect to the international responsibility of corporations.[6] Any analogies with this debate would, however, need to be effected cautiously. The same applies with respect to domestic law. The concept of complicity will remind many of related criminal law concepts.[7] Others might see parallels with accomplice liability in tort law or the law of non-contractual obligations.[8] Still others would look at the field of international criminal law.[9]

---

[2] Philippe Sands, 'International Rule of Law', p. 419.
[3] Mark Gibney, Katarina Tomasevski and Jens Vedsted-Hansen, 'Transnational State Responsibility for Violations of Human Rights', *Harvard Human Rights Law Journal* 12 (1999), pp. 267–95, at p. 295.
[4] Andrew Clapham and Scott Jerbi, 'Categories of Corporate Complicity in Human Rights Abuses', *Hastings International and Comparative Law Review* 24 (2001), pp. 339–49, at pp. 342 *et seq.*
[5] See, e.g., Steven R. Ratner, 'Corporations and Human Rights', pp. 495 *et seq.*
[6] See also the cryptic remark of the ILC in its Commentary to the ASR, that 'it is not excluded that developments may occur in the field of [international] individual civil responsibility', see ILC Commentary, Article 58, para. 2.
[7] See, e.g., John Cerone, 'Re-examining International Responsibility: "Complicity" in the Context of Human Rights Violations', *ILSA Journal of International and Comparative Law* 14 (2008), pp. 525–34, at p. 526.
[8] Cf John Quigley, 'Complicity', p. 117.
[9] See Erik Kok, 'The Principle of Complicity in the Law of State Responsibility and in International Criminal Law', in Larissa van den Herik and Carsten Stahn (eds.), *The Diversification and Fragmentation of International Law* (T. M. C. Asser Press: Cambridge, 2011), forthcoming.

It is submitted here that these intra-disciplinary comparisons will not provide for ready-made answers to our problem. Arguments for the limited usefulness of such approaches abound: recently, the International Commission of Jurists analysed domestic tort law in order to find common principles for the field of corporate complicity. Its result in this regard was that it is not possible to find a common standard with respect to accomplice liability in domestic civil law. Most common law jurisdictions do not even know this concept.[10] In international criminal law, controversies reign over the relationship between aiding and abetting in international crimes and complicity in genocide.[11] These debates show that there is no common ground on which these matters rest in domestic, let alone international law.[12] Accordingly, we find it more promising to engage in a systematic analysis of the 'normative environment' of Article 16 ASR in order to obtain greater clarity about its precise content and scope. This is not to say that comparative insights from domestic or international criminal law may not be useful in one regard or another. The same applies for legal philosophy and legal theory which have at times dealt with the problem of complicity and, more generally, responsibility for joint conduct.

In the following, we will discuss first what actually qualifies as 'aid or assistance' within the meaning of Article 16 (section 1). Secondly, we will ask what the aiding or assisting State needs to know or possibly even 'wish' for with respect to the commission of the internationally wrongful act by the State to which it is granting aid or assistance (section 2). Finally, we will address Article 16(b) which requires that the act to which aid or assistance is provided would need to be also internationally wrongful if committed by the complicit State. In simpler terms: the complicit State needs to be bound by the rule which is violated by the main actor (section 3). Our analysis will support the assumption of the Irish High Court: it is indeed less a matter of black

---

[10] 'Corporate Complicity and Legal Accountability, Volume 3 – Civil Remedies', Report of the International Commission of Jurists of 28 October 2008, Expert Legal Panel on Corporate Complicity in International Crimes, available at www.icj.org/IMG/Volume_3.pdf (last visited 1 November 2010).

[11] Chile Eboe-Osuji, '"Complicity in Genocide" Versus "Aiding and Abetting in Genocide"', *Journal of International Criminal Justice* 3 (2005), pp. 56–81.

[12] Markus D. Dubber, 'Criminalizing Complicity – A Comparative Analysis', *Journal of International Criminal Justice* 5 (2007), pp. 977–1001; see, however, Kai Ambos, *Der Allgemeine Teil des Völkerstrafrechts – Ansätze einer Dogmatisierung* (Berlin: Duncker & Humblot, 2002), pp. 619 *et seq.*

1 Significant, yet incidental?: the scope of 'aid or assistance'

The ILC has not defined what constitutes relevant 'aid or assistance'. It is theoretically conceivable that 'aid or assistance' comprises every act (or omission) which facilitates the commission of an internationally wrongful act by another State. The ILC has explained in its Commentary that no particular kind or level of assistance is needed as long as the aid or assistance materially facilitates or contributes significantly to the performance of the wrongful act.[13]

1.1 The discussion in the ILC

The basic consideration underlying the discussion has been a dispute on whether the original draft Article 25[14] should be construed narrowly or widely. This debate had two components. One was the question of intent, the other was the problem of whether some qualifications would apply for the necessary material element to establish complicity.

Nikolai Ushakov described the general problem as follows: while participation must necessarily be of an active and direct character, it must not be too direct, because then 'the participant ... became a co-author of the offence, and that went beyond complicity. If, on the other hand, participation were too indirect, there might be no real complicity.'[15] Other members of the Commission pointed to the danger of responsibility for complicity in too remote cases,[16] while still others tended to shift the problem to the level of intent. According to Willem Riphagen, assistance would need to be of an 'abnormal' character in order to qualify as complicity. In order not to circumvent the traditional rule that relations between State A and State B do not concern State C, he suggested that the interests affected by the assistance should be 'the interests of the international community in general'.[17] Thereby, Riphagen

---

[13] ILC Commentary, Article 16, para. 5.
[14] For the text of Draft Article 25 ASR (1978), see the text accompanying note 15 in Chapter 4.
[15] Nikolai A. Ushakov, Statement at the 1519th Meeting of the ILC, YBILC 1978, Vol. I, p. 239, para. 11.
[16] Paul Reuter, Statement at the 1517th Meeting of the ILC, YBILC 1978, Vol. I, p. 229, para. 4.
[17] Willem A. Riphagen, Statement at the 1518th Meeting of the ILC, YBILC 1978, Vol. I, p. 233, para. 8.

seems to have opted for a restrictive construction of the material element of draft Article 25. This was in turn rejected by Roberto Ago, who pointed out that the effect of Riphagen's proposal would be to limit the scope of application for draft Article 25 to the case of international crimes as envisaged by (then) draft Article 19.[18]

In the course of the Second Reading, the question of what would constitute aid or assistance within the meaning of the provision was again not given much attention. In his Second Report, Special Rapporteur James Crawford discussed the issue under the rubric of the necessary nexus between assistance and the wrongful act. He made reference to the Commentary that the ILC adopted to the First Reading provision which provided that 'the aid or assistance must have the effect of making it *materially* easier for the State receiving the aid or assistance in question to commit an internationally wrongful act'.[19] While this would be correct in principle, Crawford was of the view that the term 'materially' should not be retained as it was likely to cause confusion with the notion of 'material breach' in Article 60 of the Vienna Convention on the Law of Treaties.[20] It should not be used because the draft Article would not require the aid or assistance to be indispensable to the wrongdoing. 'Aids or assists' would suffice as a formulation and could be explained further in the Commentary.[21] In the discussion in the ILC plenary, the issue of the quality of the aid or assistance was not discussed with much eagerness either.[22] It was Bruno Simma who pointed to the importance of this topic. In his view, 'the substantial or essential element was virtually absent'. This, he said,

was a real problem, namely, how to be more precise and specific about the interrelationship between the aid provided to the State and the wrongful act it committed. To do so, it was important either to restrict the notion of complicity to the most serious breaches of international law and, in particular, the violation of obligations *erga omnes*, and then to be less restrictive on the link between aid and the wrongful act, or to confine oneself to forms of aid which

---

[18] Roberto Ago, Statement at the 1519th Meeting of the ILC, YBILC 1978, Vol. I, p. 240, para. 22.
[19] Commentary to Draft Article 27, para. 17, reprinted in YBILC 1978, Vol. II, Part Two, pp. 99 *et seq.*
[20] James Crawford, 'Second Report on State Responsibility', UN Doc. A/CN.4/498/Add.1, para. 180.
[21] *Ibid.*
[22] But see the Statement of Emmanuel Akwei Addo at the 2578th Meeting of the ILC, YBILC 1999, Vol. I, p. 76, para. 23.

were essential and then require a causal link between the aid and the wrongful act or, lastly, to emphasize the positive and active nature of the link, i.e., the existence of a specific link between the aid and the wrongful act.[23]

While this proposal was rejected by Ian Brownlie 'on pragmatic grounds',[24] it struck a certain chord with James Crawford who nevertheless warned 'not to reintroduce the "delicts/crimes" dichotomy through the backdoor'.[25] He reacted favourably to the idea of including 'a greater element of materiality' in the Article.[26] This did not, however, lead to any changes in the wording of the provision. Nor was it emphasised in the Commentary where it is merely stipulated that 'the aid or assistance must be given with a view to facilitating the commission of the wrongful act, *and must actually do so*'.[27] Quite to the contrary, according to the Commentary, there is no requirement that the aid or assistance should have been essential to the performance of the wrongful act. It would be sufficient to have it contribute significantly to it.[28] To complete confusion on this matter, the ILC comments differently on this issue at another point, when it says that 'the assistance may have been only an incidental factor in the commission of the primary act, and may have contributed only to a minor degree, if at all, to the injury suffered'.[29]

1.2 *Interpretation of the provision*

The picture of what actually constitutes aid or assistance within the meaning of Article 16 ASR is thus rather unclear. A first issue which merits attention is the wording of the provision. Article 16 ASR speaks of 'aid or assistance'. This does not necessarily mean that the two terms have different meanings. No explanation has been given in this respect by the Commission. Nor is the distinction apparent from previous international practice or systematic considerations. Whatever the reasons behind this unclear terminology, Article 16 ASR needs to be examined with respect to the meaning of 'aid or assistance'. One

---

[23] Bruno Simma, Statement at the 2578th Meeting of the ILC, YBILC 1999, Vol. I, p. 79, para. 41.
[24] Ian Brownlie, Statement at the 2578th Meeting of the ILC, YBILC 1999, Vol. I, p. 79, para. 43.
[25] James Crawford, Statement at the 2578th Meeting of the ILC, YBILC 1999, Vol. I, p. 79, para. 44.
[26] *Ibid.*, para. 45.   [27] ILC Commentary, Article 16, para. 5, emphasis added.
[28] *Ibid.*   [29] *Ibid.*, para. 10.

possibility would be to refer back to the typology of cases and situations which were surveyed for the determination of Article 16 ASR as a customary rule (section 1.2.1). Another approach would be to draw inspiration from primary/special rules on complicity (section 1.2.2). However useful these two approaches might be, they are arguably not capable of providing definite normative guidance. The ILC has given some guidance as to what qualifies as aid or assistance insofar as it has stated that the support rendered must have facilitated the commission of the internationally wrongful act. This implies a notion of causality, which will be examined in turn (section 1.2.3). As it will emerge that causality in itself cannot provide the basis for responsibility in the case of complicity, we are left with the remaining possibility of inquiring into negative categories which could shed some light on the matter of what does not qualify as aid or assistance (section 1.2.4).

1.2.1 Problems with an abstract definition

A first approach in determining what constitutes aid or assistance within the meaning of Article 16 ASR is to look at instances of international practice. The examples which have thus far been assembled make it possible to assume, for example, that the granting of overflight and landing rights for the unlawful use of force[30] or for the commission of human rights violations[31] may constitute aid or assistance within the meaning of Article 16 ASR. The same applies to a State allowing its territory to be used by another State which assembles its troops and then conducts its attack from the first State's territory.[32] It could also qualify as aid or assistance when a State furnishes logistic support to the unlawful conduct of another State.[33] Support to be characterised as aid or assistance might also consist in the provision of valuable intelligence.[34] To furnish weapons, military technology or other kinds of military assistance to oppressive regimes could also qualify as aid or

---

[30] Cf the various protests of the Soviet Union against the Federal Republic of Germany, Italy and Israel on the granting of overflight rights for the attacks on Lebanon in 1958 and the refusal of France to grant overflight rights for the US to attack Libya in 1986; see Chapter 4 above, notes 48, 49, 50, 52, 53 and 65.
[31] Cf the debates on the European support for the so-called 'CIA flights': see Chapter 4 above, the text accompanying notes 97 et seq.
[32] See Olivier Corten, 'Quels droits', pp. 123 et seq. on the position of Kuwait during the 2003 attacks on Iraq.
[33] German Federal Administrative Court, 2 WD 12.04 = ILDC 483 (DE 2005).
[34] Cf *Süddeutsche Zeitung*, 25 March 2008, p. 8, on US support to the Colombian attack on FARC rebels in Ecuador.

assistance.[35] Support which allows a State to circumvent the requirements of binding UN Security Council resolutions (for example, allowing a targeted State to produce weapons of mass destruction on one's territory[36]) may also count as aid or assistance under Article 16 ASR. In addition to these relatively clear cases, we have also seen how other conduct could, rather surprisingly, be counted as aid or assistance, an example being the provision of an export credit guarantee for large infrastructure projects which violate international legal obligations.[37] It is also conceivable that the provision of funds pure and simple may constitute aid or assistance.[38] While it is most certainly difficult to establish any form of specific causality between the granting of a certain amount of money and a specific internationally wrongful act,[39] it would provide States with a very tempting loophole if they could avoid responsibility for complicity simply by resorting to cash flows instead of providing material aid in the traditional sense. An example is the substitution of 'traditional military support' by financial support in the form of the donor State paying for the use of a 'private military firm' (PMF). This course of action was adopted by moderate Arab States which wished to support the Bosnian government after the Yugoslav war in 1995 without sending their own military personnel. At the same time, they wanted to counter the influence of more radicalising Iranian military aid.[40]

The compiling of a list of typical forms of aid or assistance will, however, not lead to satisfactory results. The nature of Article 16 ASR as a general rule speaks against the authoritativeness of a list thus assembled. It is illuminating only insofar as it informs legal advisors and other practitioners about the most likely repercussions that responsibility for complicity will have in international practice. If we wish to

---

[35] See the various statements of States on their position with regard to the military regime in Chile after the coup d'état in 1973, text accompanying notes 215 *et seq.* in Chapter 4 above.
[36] Cf the alleged support of Sudan for Iraq in manufacturing weapons of mass destruction, see the text accompanying note 132 in Chapter 4 above.
[37] Cf the example of the Ilisu Dam project, see the text accompanying note 228 in Chapter 4 above.
[38] Andreas Felder, *Die Beihilfe*, p. 253; but see Monica Hakimi, 'State Bystander Responsibility', p. 367, note 160.
[39] Astrid Epiney, 'Umweltvölkerrechtliche Rahmenbedingungen', p. 363.
[40] Cf P. W. Singer 'Corporate Warriors: The Rise of the Privatized Military Industry and Its Ramifications for International Security', *International Security* 26, No. 3 (2001-2), pp. 186–220, at p. 212.

uphold our finding that the list of international practice we have been able to assemble gives rise to a general rule on complicity, it would leave the job half done to stop there and declare these forms of aid or assistance to be the content the ILC had in mind when it was drafting Article 16 ASR. Rather, Article 16's relation to the diverse subject matters of international law will always be dynamic. Through its generality, Article 16 ASR may be applied across the whole spectrum of international law. A list of typical cases will thus not be able to provide us with normative guidance on the contours of the concept of 'aid or assistance'.

1.2.2 Conceptions of 'assistance' in special ('primary') rules

Alternatively, one could inquire into the meaning of aid or assistance within the realm of 'primary rules'. Keeping in mind the conclusion reached above, that the rules on complicity will in most cases be neither clearly primary nor clearly secondary in character, it is through the concept of *lex specialis* that their relationship can be operationalised.[41] Arguably, this implies that the general rule set out in Article 16 ASR will not exceed what is required by the primary (i.e., special) rules. Thus, insight derived from the interpretation of what assistance means in the context of special rules may shed some light on the interpretation of Article 16 ASR. Such a transfer cannot be carried out in a mechanical way. Rather, the interpretation of primary rules contributes to an understanding of the 'normative environment' in which Article 16 ASR needs to be seen. In this respect, we can draw on statements by governmental representatives which have been made in the context of specific obligations of non-assistance with respect to the production, stockpiling and use of certain types of weapons.

1.2.2.1 *The Convention on Anti-Personnel Land Mines*
An example of the difficulties States have agreeing on the meaning of assistance even where the subject matter is fairly precise can be seen in the interpretation of Article 1(1)(c) of the Convention on the Prohibition of the Use, Stockpiling, Production and Transfer of Anti-Personnel Land Mines and on Their Destruction of 1997 ('Ottawa Convention'). Article 1(1)(c) of the Convention provides:

---

[41] See above in Chapter 4, section 5, text accompanying notes 425 *et seq.*

Each State Party undertakes never under any circumstances:

...

(c) To assist, encourage or induce, in any way, anyone to engage in any activity prohibited to a State party under this Convention.[42]

The meaning of assistance within the scope of this Convention was not discussed in depth during the drafting process of the provision.[43] Subsequent to the adoption of the treaty, practical issues arose which led States to inquire into the meaning of the wording 'to assist'.[44] Some States adopted rather restrictive views on what 'to assist' would actually mean in the context of Article 1(1)(c) of the Ottawa Convention. Australia, for example, issued the following interpretative declaration when it ratified the Convention:

> Australia will interpret the word 'assist' to mean the actual and direct physical participation in any activity prohibited by the Convention but does not include indirect support such as the provision of security for the personnel of a State not party to the Convention engaging in such activities.[45]

The Czech Republic issued the following declaration concerning the meaning of assistance in the context of the Convention:

> It is the understanding of the Government of the Czech Republic that the mere participation in the planning or execution of operations, exercises or other military activities by the Armed Forces of the Czech Republic, or individual Czech Republic nationals, conducted in combination with the armed forces of States not party to the [Convention], which engage in activities prohibited

---

[42] Similar provisions are included in the Convention on the Prohibition of the Development, Production, Stockpiling and Use of Chemical Weapons and on Their Destruction of 3 September 1992, entered into force on 29 April 1997, Article 1(d), 1974 UNTS 45; the Convention on the Prohibition of the Development, Production and Stockpiling of Bacteriological (Biological) and Toxin Weapons and on Their Destruction of 10 April 1972, entered into force on 26 March 1975, Article III, 1015 UNTS 163; and the Treaty on the Non-Proliferation of Nuclear Weapons of 1 July 1968, entered into force on 5 March 1970, Article I, 729 UNTS 161.

[43] Which may partly be explained by the fact that it was adapted almost verbatim from the Chemical Weapons Convention of 1993; see Stuart Maslen, *Commentaries on Arms Control Treaties*, Vol. I, *The Convention on the Stockpiling, Production, and Transfer of Anti-Personnel Mines and on Their Destruction*, 2nd edn (Oxford: Oxford University Press, 2005), p. 94.

[44] For an overview, see *ibid.*, pp. 93 *et seq.*

[45] Declaration of Australia, available at www.icrc.org/ihl.nsf/NORM/C94AC352BD44A2 494125658500442880?OpenDocument (last visited 1 November 2010).

under the Convention, is not, by itself, assistance, encouragement or inducement for the purposes of Article 1, paragraph 1(c) of the Convention.[46]

Zimbabwe made the following comment in the Standing Committee:

We therefore, in our view, believe that the term assist should be interpreted, relating directly to the activity in question and should not be applied liberally or given too wide a definition ... *Active participation* in Zimbabwe's context is when reference is made to a prohibited activity and includes providing finance to such activities with full knowledge that such finance is to be used to procure, manufacture, training in the use of, and or distribution of APMs. Active participation also means actively participating in the carrying, laying and training in the use, manufacture, distribution, encouraging and or inducing someone in the use of APMs. It is therefore our humble submission that the term assist and active participation in the context of Article 1 means *knowingly and intentionally* participating directly and or rendering assistance on the use, transfer or production of APMs.[47]

Other State parties to the Ottawa Convention took a more liberal approach to the interpretation of assistance in Article I of the Convention. Brazil, for example, adopted a position according to which

[a]ll States Parties should commit strictly to observe the provisions of Article I, which would include giving the term 'assist' as broad an interpretation as possible.[48]

The United Kingdom also opted for a broad interpretation of the term 'to assist'. It would cover:

[the] planning with others for the use of anti-personnel mines (APM); training others for the use of APM; agreeing Rules of Engagement permitting the use of APM; agreeing operational plans permitting the use of APM in combined operations; requests to non-State Parties to use APM; and providing security

---

[46] Declaration of the Czech Republic, available at www.icrc.org/ihl.nsf/NORM/11EE1 B6FEAE7F92A41256585004BB306?OpenDocument (last visited 1 November 2010); a very similar declaration was made by Serbia, available at www.icrc.org/ihl.nsf/ NORM/6A7BBED120E461ECC1256DAE004C3BE2?OpenDocument (last visited 1 November 2010) and the United Kingdom, available at www.icrc.org/ihl.nsf/NORM /8E616974F39078BC41256586004AB729?OpenDocument (last visited 1 November 2010).

[47] Statement of Zimbabwe in the Standing Committee of the Ottawa Convention of 31 May 2002, available at www.apminebanconvention.org/fileadmin/pdf/mbc/IWP/ SC_may02/speeches_gs/Statement_Zimbabwe.pdf (last visited 1 November 2010).

[48] Statement of Brazil in the Standing Committee of 1 February 2002, available at www.apminebanconvention.org/fileadmin/pdf/mbc/IWP/SC_jan02/speeches_gs/ Brazil_article_1.pdf (last visited 1 November 2010).

or transport for APM. Furthermore, it is not acceptable for UK forces to accept orders that amount to assistance in the use of APM.[49]

The States Parties to the Ottawa Convention did not agree on any definition of assistance within the scope of Article I. However, some guidance may be obtained from a 'non-paper' (i.e., a summary of views of the States parties without formal validity) of the Chairs of the Standing Committee on the General Status and Operations of the Convention which was presented in June 2004. The non-paper holds that States Parties engaging in military operations with other States or groups of States should, *inter alia*, not participate in planning for the use of anti-personnel mines, participate in operations wherein direct military benefit is known to be derived from the use of anti-personnel mines in the area of those operations, provide protection, maintenance or transport for identified storage or use of anti-personnel mines and should not consent to the transit of anti-personnel mines over territory under their jurisdiction or control.[50] These conclusions are of limited impact, however, as they are not generally supported by the States Parties to the Ottawa Convention. Hence, the interpretation of Article 1(1)(c) of that Convention shows that, while it is potentially easier to clarify the scope of 'assistance' with respect to a particular subject matter in international law, a consensus on the matter for even this rather limited context is still not readily apparent.

1.2.2.2 The Cluster Munitions Convention

As the practical problems of what 'to assist' would mean in this context arose in the aftermath of the adoption of the Ottawa Convention, it is not surprising that States were more alert to this problem when the Convention on Cluster Munitions was negotiated and adopted at a diplomatic conference in Dublin in May 2008.[51] The big question in this

---

[49] United Kingdom Intervention on Article 1, Statement in the Standing Committee of 16 May 2003, available at www.apminebanconvention.org/fileadmin/pdf/mbc/IWP/SC_may03/speeches_gs/UK_Art_1.pdf (last visited 1 November 2010).

[50] Non-Paper, available at www.apminebanconvention.org/fileadmin/pdf/mbc/IWP/SC_june04/speeches_GS/Co_chairs_nonpaper_art123_21June04.pdf (last visited 1 November 2010).

[51] Convention on Cluster Munitions, Diplomatic Conference for the Adoption of a Convention on Cluster Munitions, CCM/77 of 30 May 2008, entered into force on 1 August 2010, available at www.clusterconvention.org/downloadablefiles/ccm77_english.pdf (last visited 1 November 2010).

regard was the 'interoperability' between the armed forces of a plurality of States. As the agreement would also include an obligation of non-assistance, the concern of a number of States focused on how this requirement would impact upon joint operations with allies which so far have refused to join the Oslo Process on cluster munitions.[52] Article 1 of the Convention stipulates in terms very similar to the Ottawa Convention:

Each State Party undertakes never under any circumstances to:
...
(c) Assist, encourage or induce anyone to engage in any activity prohibited to a State Party under this Convention.

However, the provision needs to be seen in context with Article 21 ('Relations with States not party to this Convention') of the Convention which provides:

1. Each State Party shall encourage States not party to this Convention to ratify, accept, approve or accede to this Convention, with the goal of attracting the adherence of all States to this Convention.
2. Each State Party shall notify the governments of all States not party to this Convention, referred to in paragraph 3 of this Article, of its obligations under this Convention, shall promote the norms it establishes and shall make its best efforts to discourage States not party to this Convention from using cluster munitions.
3. Notwithstanding the provisions of Article 1 of this Convention and in accordance with international law, States Party, their military personnel or nationals, may engage in military cooperation and operations with States not party to this Convention that might engage in activities prohibited to a State Party.
4. Nothing in paragraph 3 of this Article shall authorise a State Party:
   (a) To develop, produce or otherwise acquire cluster munitions;
   (b) To itself stockpile or transfer cluster munitions;
   (c) To itself use cluster munitions; or
   (d) To expressly request the use of cluster munitions in cases where the choice of munitions is within its exclusive control.

This provision strikes a delicate compromise between the wish to outlaw most effectively the use of cluster munitions and the desire of

---

[52] See generally on the Cluster Munitions Convention Karen Hulme, 'The 2008 Cluster Munitions Convention: Stepping Outside the CCW Framework (Again)', *International and Comparative Law Quarterly* 58 (2009), pp. 219–27; Detlev Justen, *Der Oslo-Prozess zum Verbot von Streumunition* (Berlin: Stiftung Wissenschaft und Politik, 2008).

some States to retain 'interoperability'. So much becomes clear from the diplomatic negotiations in Dublin. At the outset of the deliberations – when Article 21 of the Convention did not yet figure in the draft – Germany, supported by a number of EU Member States, proposed an amendment to Article 1(c) in order to clarify that the obligation not to 'assist' would

not preclude the mere participation in the planning or the execution of operations, exercises or other military activities by the Armed Forces or by an individual national of a State Party to this Convention, conducted in combination with Armed Forces of States not Parties to this Convention which engage in activity prohibited under this Convention.[53]

In parallel, the United Kingdom even submitted a proposal which would have deleted paragraph (c) with its obligation of non-assistance.[54] France opted for an additional Article which would have provided that:

Nothing in this Convention shall be interpreted as in any way preventing military interoperability between States parties and non-States parties to the Convention.[55]

In response to the German proposal, Morocco, supported by Senegal and Mauritania, made a further suggestion for amendment. In order to clarify the meaning of the German proposal, its suggested Article 1(c) would have included the passage that

the States not party explain to the States Parties participating in the planning or the execution of operations, the military necessity for engaging in such activities and taking into account the humanitarian concerns addressed by the Convention. The States Parties shall refrain from engaging in activities prohibited under this Convention in any joint military operations with States not parties.[56]

---

[53] Proposal by Germany, supported by Denmark, France, Italy, Slovakia, Spain, the Czech Republic and the United Kingdom for the amendment of Article 1, 19 May 2008, CCM/13, available at www.clustermunitionsdublin.ie/documents.asp (last visited 1 November 2010).
[54] Proposal by the United Kingdom for the amendment of Article 1, 19 May 2008, CCM/14, *ibid*.
[55] Proposal by France for the amendment of Article 1, 19 May 2008, CCM/16, *ibid*.
[56] Proposal by Morocco, supported by Senegal and Mauritania, for the amendment of the Proposal by Germany, supported by Denmark, France, Italy, Slovakia, Spain, the Czech Republic and the United Kingdom for the amendment of Article 1, 20 May 2008, CCM/69, *ibid*.

In the plenary discussions, this conflict between an affirmation of the obligation not to assist other States in the use of cluster munitions and the desire to retain interoperability continued. The dividing line in this debate can be largely drawn between the so-called 'core group' of States which comprised Norway, Austria, New Zealand, Ireland, Peru and Mexico and an informal group of mostly European States, the so-called 'Group of 20'. While the core group was the driving force behind the negotiations and wished to adopt a wide-ranging prohibition of cluster munitions, the 'Group of 20' was also motivated by concerns of military practicality.[57] In the latter sense, the United Kingdom emphasised that 'a clear understanding of the meaning of "assist" in Article 1 of the Convention was required'.[58] The UK then referred to its domestic criminal law in order to further elucidate the meaning of 'assist' and pleaded for a 'realistic legal position'.[59] In contrast, Central and South American States were reluctant to accept any compromise which would have included a rule on interoperability.[60] In the final days of the conference, the compromise solution that is Article 21 was, however, accepted.

What inferences can we draw from this provision? The gist of the relationship between Article 1(c) and Article 21 of the Convention is that cooperation with another State which uses unlawful methods is not sufficient to trigger responsibility under Article 1. Thus, a State cannot be reproached for merely joining an alliance with another State. It might now be asked whether Article 21(3) of the Convention speaks for or against the existence of a general rule in this regard. One could argue that the desire by some States to have a provision on interoperability included in the Convention reflects an assumption that generally the notion of assistance could cover a mere association with a wrongdoer. However, such an inference is probably far-fetched. The wish to have Article 21 of the Convention included appears to stem rather from the need for certainty and clarification. The reasoning of Article 21 is also confirmed in other fields of international law. The ECtHR, for instance, did not hold several members of the 'coalition

---

[57] On the general climate of negotiations and the diverging policy agendas of the actors involved, see Detlev Justen, *Der Oslo-Prozess*, pp. 14 *et seq.*

[58] Summary Record of the Tenth Session of the Committee of the Whole, held at Croke Park, Dublin, on Monday, 26 May 2008, CCM/CW/SR/10 of 18 June 2008, available at www.clustermunitionsdublin.ie/summary-records.asp (last visited 1 November 2010).

[59] *Ibid.*   [60] See the statements of Argentina, Mexico and Honduras, *ibid.*

of States' which had attacked Iraq in 2003 responsible for the capture and detention of Saddam Hussein on the mere basis that they formed this coalition.[61] Given the fact that we have confirmed the statement of Special Rapporteur James Crawford that the general rule on complicity will not go beyond what the primary rules stipulate,[62] this interpretation of Article 21 of the Convention as speaking against complicity by mere association should also be valid for the interpretation of Article 16 ASR.[63]

At the same time, Article 21 of the Convention makes a case for 'best efforts' obligations in such alliances. Also, its reference to 'exclusive control' in paragraph 4 highlights that, whenever it is in the power of the potentially complicit State so to do, it should try to prevent violations of the law from occurring. In this regard, non-compliance with such a requirement to encourage allied States to abstain from the use of prohibited munitions, borders closely on complicity. This is shown by the concern of, for example, the United Kingdom.[64] The diplomatic proceedings also show that States are increasingly aware of the potential legal risk to which they are exposed in military cooperation. The urgency with which the 'Group of 20' wished to clarify that mere participation in joint military efforts would not trigger responsibility under Article 1(c) of the Convention shows that States take the risk of responsibility for complicity more and more seriously.

1.2.2.3 The Nuclear Non-Proliferation Treaty
Finally, mention should be made of Article I of the Nuclear Non-Proliferation Treaty (NPT). Here, for obvious reasons, discussions cannot centre publicly on issues of 'interoperability' as the whole rationale underlying the treaty is a different one. It does not aim to outlaw the use of a certain weapon in armed conflicts but aims at non-proliferation of weapons and technology, at nuclear disarmament (Article VI NPT)

---

[61] ECtHR, *Saddam Hussein v. Albania, Bulgaria, Croatia, Czech Republic, Denmark, Estonia, Hungary, Iceland, Ireland, Italy, Latvia, Lithuania, the Netherlands, Poland, Portugal, Romania, Slovakia, Slovenia, Turkey, Ukraine and the United Kingdom*, unpublished.
[62] See in Chapter 4 the text accompanying notes 437 *et seq.*
[63] This interpretation is also adopted by commentators on the Ottawa Convention, see Stuart Maslen, *Commentaries*, p. 101.
[64] The position of the United Kingdom is also noteworthy as it is diametrically opposed to its broad understanding of 'assistance' with respect to the Ottawa Convention. One explanation is the differing assessment about the strategic value of land mines and cluster bombs; see further Karen Hulme, 'Cluster Munitions Convention', p. 222.

and at the possibility for non-nuclear-weapon States to develop civil nuclear technology (Article IV NPT).[65] Article I NPT provides in its relevant part:

> Each nuclear-weapon State Party to the Treaty undertakes ... not in any way to assist, encourage, or induce any non-nuclear-weapon State to manufacture or otherwise acquire nuclear weapons or other nuclear explosive devices, or control over such weapons or explosive devices.[66]

It has been noted that this provision is problematic insofar as potentially any kind of international nuclear assistance may be useful to a nuclear-weapons programme.[67] It was perceived as a problem that most nuclear assistance would be neutral in character. It could also be used for both civil and military purposes. Accordingly, emphasis is laid on safeguards agreements pursuant to Article III NPT to ensure that nuclear assistance is not derailed for non-peaceful purposes.[68] The duty of non-assistance under Article I NPT seems to have played a role in late 2007 when the United States administration considered whether it was entitled to provide Pakistan with a security system for its nuclear weapons, Pakistan not being a party to the NPT.[69] Intense discussions took place within the administration whether this would really qualify as unlawful assistance under international law or whether it was rather a legitimate effort to mitigate the adverse consequences of Pakistan's possession of nuclear weapons.

The question what constitutes forbidden assistance under Article I NPT arose with even greater urgency on the occasion of the signing of the US–India Agreement Concerning Peaceful Uses of Nuclear Energy.[70]

---

[65] These are the three pillars of the NPT; cf Jörn Müller, 'The Signing of the US–India Agreement Concerning Peaceful Uses of Nuclear Energy', *Goettingen Journal of International Law* 1 (2009), pp. 179–98, at pp. 183 and 185–6.

[66] Cf also Article II NPT, which provides for a corresponding duty of non-nuclear-weapon States not to seek or receive assistance for the manufacturing of nuclear weapons.

[67] Mason Willrich, *Non-Proliferation Treaty: Framework for Nuclear Arms Control* (Charlottesville, VA: Michie Company, 1969), pp. 93–4; Mohamed I. Shaker, 'The Evolving International Regime of Nuclear Non-Proliferation', *Recueil des Cours* 321 (2006), pp. 9–202, at p. 30.

[68] Mason Willrich, *Non-Proliferation Treaty*, p. 94.

[69] 'US Secretly Aids Pakistan in Guarding Nuclear Arms', *New York Times*, 18 November 2007, p. A1.

[70] Agreement for Cooperation concerning the Peaceful Uses of Nuclear Energy, with agreed minute of 10 October 2008, entered into force on 6 December 2008, available at www.state.gov/documents/treaties/122068.pdf (last visited 10 June 2009).

For present purposes, the question need not be discussed whether the agreement undermines the object and purpose of the NPT or whether it is a legitimate attempt to move India closer to the regime of the NPT through its requirement that India conclude a safeguards agreement with the International Atomic Energy Agency (IAEA).[71] The crucial issue here is what amounts to 'assistance' under Article I NPT. A partial answer to this question derives from Article III(2) NPT which requires safeguards if certain material is transferred to a non-nuclear-weapon State for peaceful purposes. In the concrete case at hand, it is, however, subject to debate how stringently the criteria provided for by the NPT are respected by the US–India agreement, especially since the agreement can be interpreted in a way which would allow India to withdraw from the safeguards system without an automatically ensuing termination of US–Indian cooperation.[72] However interesting this problem is, the possible repercussions of the interpretation of Articles I and III NPT on the understanding of Article 16 ASR are limited. The institutional setting of the NPT and the possibility of scrutinising compliance with the imposed limits of the use of the furnished material through the means of safeguards is too peculiar to allow us to draw conclusions for the general problem of complicity.

1.2.2.4 Interim conclusions
While there are limitations to the value of insights derived from an interpretation of special rules on the interpretation of Article 16 ASR, our analysis suggests that it will not be possible to establish a list of abstract criteria for the determination of what constitutes aid or assistance within the meaning of Article 16 ASR. However, it does show that the majority of States are eager to limit the concept of assistance to cases in which active participation is given. It is furthermore of interest that intent has been said to be necessary in this regard. Particularly noteworthy is the position of the United Kingdom. Whereas it advocated a very broad interpretation of 'assistance' in the context of the Ottawa Convention on anti-personnel land mines, it adamantly argued

---

[71] For the various positions, see Kate Heinzelmann, 'Towards Common Interests and Responsibilities: The US-India Civil Nuclear Deal and the International Nonproliferation Regime', *Yale Journal of International Law* 33 (2008), pp. 447–78; Jörn Müller, 'US–India Agreement', pp. 191–2; Leonard Weiss, 'US–India Nuclear Cooperation – Better Later Than Sooner', *Nonproliferation Review* 14 (2007), pp. 429–57.

[72] Jörn Müller, 'US–India Agreement', p. 195.

for a more restrictive interpretation of the same term in the Cluster Munitions Convention. This change of position may be explained by two factors. First, it is important to take into account that, in conflicts such as in Afghanistan or Iraq, cluster munitions were widely used whereas anti-personnel land mines have been abandoned long ago by the UK and also – most importantly – by practically all relevant allies of the UK.[73] A second explanation – which is more hypothetical in character – could consist in the growing awareness of States of the problem of complicity over the course of recent years. In particular, the public scrutiny of the conduct of a number of European States in both the Iraq war in 2003 and the so-called 'extraordinary renditions' put more pressure on third States. It cannot be ruled out that this public scrutiny spills over into other thematic fields and thus that governments will be more cautious to create 'safety nets' for what they perceive to be legitimate cooperation.

All in all, it does not appear to be possible to provide abstract and normative criteria of what could constitute complicity in each and every conceivable situation. Rather, the assessment whether the support a State is rendering to another State constitutes aid or assistance within the meaning of Article 16 ASR needs to be established with respect to the facts of the specific case.

1.2.3 Complicity and causality

One such factor which can only be assessed in the specific case at hand is causality.[74] The ILC has made it clear in its Commentary that 'the assisting State will only be responsible to the extent that its own conduct has caused or contributed to the internationally wrongful act'.[75] At another point in its Commentary, it has clarified this by stating that '[t]here is no requirement that the aid or assistance should have been essential to the performance of the internationally wrongful act; it is sufficient if it contributed significantly to that act'.[76] Hence, the determination of what constitutes aid or assistance within the meaning of Article 16 ASR needs to take into account issues of causality.[77] This

---

[73] Karen Hulme, 'Cluster Munitions Convention', p. 222.
[74] Cf Brigitte Bollecker-Stern, *Le préjudice dans la théorie de la responsabilité internationale* (Paris: Pedone, 1973), p. 189; see also, *mutatis mutandis*, Kai Ambos, 'Article 25', in Otto Triffterer (ed.), *Commentary on the Rome Statute of the International Criminal Court – Observers' Notes, Article by Article*, 2nd edn (Munich/Oxford: C. H. Beck and Hart, 2008), para. 21.
[75] ILC Commentary, Article 16, para. 1.   [76] *Ibid.*, para. 5.
[77] Cf Tal Becker, *Terrorism and the State*, p. 326.

does not necessarily clarify things, however, as it has been noted that causality is, 'as an aspect of State responsibility ... an undeveloped area of international law'.[78]

Causality leads a peculiar existence in the law of State responsibility: if things run according to the normal course of events, it will hardly ever be mentioned. In most of the cases where there is a straightforward finding of a breach of international law which involves only one State as the possible perpetrator, the link of causality between its conduct, the commission of the wrongful act and the eventual injury will simply be assumed. In this respect, the law follows pretty much the theory of Dionisio Anzilotti whose objective conception of the law of State responsibility conceptualised the rules of attribution as a translation of principles of causation.[79] Only in the few cases where there is uncertainty as to 'who has caused precisely what' will issues of causality arise. Of these cases, complicity is one of the most pressing.[80] Other instances in which the issue of causality has been raised in the last few years concern its potential as an alternative to the rules of attribution laid down in the ASR which are deemed by some to be too strict in the face of new challenges, especially in the field of non-State terrorist actors.[81] Tal Becker has argued for a reconceptualisation of the law of State responsibility which replaces the, in his view, too rigid rules of agency and attribution with a more flexible and case-specific test of causality.[82] Things lie differently with respect to inter-State complicity: here, it is not the substitution of an unwelcome test but the construction of the provision by the ILC which requires us to explore issues of causality in greater depth. This is somewhat paradoxical as general legal theory which deals with issues of complicity or assistance is practically unanimous in its finding that ordinary conceptions of causality will not work in these situations.[83] Hence, we will have to look for a

---

[78] Donald D. Caron, 'The Basis of Responsibility: Attribution and Other Transsubstantive Rules', in Richard B. Lillich and Daniel Barstow Magraw (eds.), *The Iran–United States Claims Tribunal: Its Contribution to the Law of State Responsibility* (Irvington-on-Hudson, NY: Transnational, 1998), pp. 109–84, at p. 153.
[79] Cf Dionisio Anzilotti, 'La responsabilité internationale', p. 291; on Anzilotti's approach in this regard, see Roberto Ago, 'Das Verschulden im völkerrechtlichen Unrecht', *Zeitschrift für öffentliches Recht* 20 (1940), pp. 449–84, at p. 453.
[80] See also Maria Luisa Padelletti, *Pluralità di stati*, pp. 74–5.
[81] Tal Becker, *Terrorism and the State*, pp. 239 et seq.
[82] Ibid., pp. 285 et seq.
[83] H. L. A. Hart and Tony Honoré, *Causation in the Law*, 2nd edn (Oxford: Clarendon Press, 1985, reprint 2002), p. 388; Christopher Kutz, *Complicity – Ethics and Law for a Collective Age* (Cambridge: Cambridge University Press, 2000), pp. 217–18; Christopher

specific emanation of the concept of causality which is suitable for the elucidation of the nexus between the aid or assistance furnished to the commission of the wrongful act by the main actor.

1.2.3.1 Explanations by the ILC

An analysis of the issue of causality needs to start with the meagre indications the ILC has left in its Commentary. The two statements which have been reproduced from the Commentary at the beginning of this subsection make it plain that on the one hand some form of causality is required, as the assisting State will only be held responsible to the extent that its assistance caused and contributed to the internationally wrongful act.[84] On the other hand, the Commission is also quite clear that the support need not have been an essential contribution to the commission of the wrongful act. Rather, it would be enough for the aid or assistance to contribute significantly to it. This two-pronged approach suggests that the Commission finds itself in line with considerations of general legal theory, namely, that, in the case of assistance to a wrongful act, the participant would neither cause the principal to act nor would the latter act in consequence of this assistance.[85] It is thus clear that the relationship between complicity and causality cannot be found in any form of 'but for' test or of a *conditio sine qua non* test.[86] Both tests assume[87] that, in the absence of a cause, the result of the action would not have been a conceivable outcome. It is apparent that this would be too strict a test for complicity.[88] Rather, if the

---

Kutz, 'Responsibility', in Jules Coleman and Scott Shapiro (eds.), *The Oxford Handbook of Jurisprudence and Philosophy of Law* (Oxford: Oxford University Press, 2002), pp. 548–87, at p. 563; see also Sanford H. Kadish, 'Complicity, Cause and Blame: A Study in the Interpretation of Doctrine', *California Law Review* 73 (1985), pp. 323–410, at pp. 356 *et seq.*, who holds causality and complicity to be cognate concepts; for a different assessment, however, see Michael S. Moore, *Causation and Responsibility – An Essay in Law, Morals and Metaphysics* (Oxford: Oxford University Press, 2009), p. 300.

[84] Tal Becker, *Terrorism and the State*, p. 326.
[85] H. L. A. Hart and A. M. Honoré, *Causation in the Law*, p. 347.
[86] Similarly Andreas Felder, *Die Beihilfe*, p. 249; see further Sanford H. Kadish, 'Complicity', p. 367.
[87] There is some confusion whether the two can be equated and what this means: contrast Tal Becker, *Terrorism and the State*, p. 292, who emphasises the potential limitlessness of the two, with James D. Fry, 'Coercion, Causation and the Fictional Elements of Indirect State Responsibility', *Vanderbilt Journal of Transnational Law* 40 (2007), pp. 611–41, at p. 633, who holds the 'but for' test to be the strictest test of liability. In criminal law scholarship, the two tests are held to be identical: see Kai Ambos, *Der Allgemeine Teil des Völkerstrafrechts*, p. 625.
[88] Pierre d'Argent, *Les réparations de guerre*, p. 552; cf further H. L. A. Hart and Tony Honoré, *Causation in the Law*, p. 388.

support could be qualified as a *conditio sine qua non*, it is more likely to assume that an independent responsibility of the assisting State would arise in the form of the main authorship of the wrongful act.[89]

1.2.3.2 Causality in domestic and international criminal law
It has already been mentioned that it is difficult to import solutions from domestic legal orders into the interpretation of Article 16 ASR if only because of the widely diverging views on 'accomplice liability' in criminal and civil matters across the various jurisdictions. What we can be sure of is that standards for causality in cases of complicity do not presuppose that the complicit action was a *conditio sine qua non*. Nonetheless, domestic criminal law systems typically require some form of nexus between the support rendered and the commission of the criminal act: otherwise, complicity would collapse into responsibility for attempted complicity or the widest conceivable forms of moral support for the commission of crimes.[90]

Parallel problems play a role in international criminal law where they have been at issue in several decisions of international tribunals. The Trial Chamber of the ICTY has developed a rather liberal understanding of what would constitute 'aiding and abetting' under its statute.[91] On the basis of an evaluation of the case law of US and UK military commissions and courts after the Second World War, it found that the 'assistance given by an accomplice need not be tangible and can consist of moral support in certain circumstances'.[92] None of the cases available would have suggested that 'the acts of the accomplice need bear a causal relationship to, or be a *conditio sine qua non* for, those of the principal'.[93] Instead, the Trial Chamber held that 'the assistance must have a substantial effect on the commission of the crime'.[94]

---

[89] Andreas Felder, *Die Beihilfe*, p. 249, note 643.
[90] See, e.g., Karl Lackner and Kristian Kühl, *Strafgesetzbuch mit Erläuterungen*, 26th edn (Munich: C. H. Beck, 2007), § 27, para. 2; K. J. M. Smith, *A Modern Treatise on the Law of Criminal Complicity* (Oxford: Clarendon Press, 1991), p. 87.
[91] See Article 6(1) of the ICTY Statute: 'A person who planned, instigated, ordered, committed or otherwise aided or abetted in the planning, preparation or execution of a crime referred to in Articles 2 to 4 of the present Statute, shall be individually responsible for the crime.' Annex to the Report of the Secretary General pursuant to para. 2 of SC Res. 808 (1993), UN Doc. S/25704 of 3 May 1993. See also Article 7(1) of the ICTR Statute, Annex to UN Doc. S/RES/955 (1994).
[92] ICTY, *Prosecutor v. Anto Furundzija*, IT-95-17/1-T, para. 232.
[93] *Ibid.*, para. 233.
[94] *Ibid.*, para. 234; see also ICTY, *Prosecutor v. Tihomir Blaskic*, Judgment of 3 March 2000, IT-95-14-T, para. 285.

Hence, the Trial Chamber differentiated between the nature of the support rendered and its effect upon the act of the main perpetrator.[95] The Appeals Chamber followed this line of argument in its *Tadic* decision.[96] In the literature on international criminal law, it is widely held that this requirement neither clarifies much nor sets a very high standard.[97] We should also note that differing sources from this field of law envisage differing standards. The 1996 Draft Code of Crimes against the Peace and Security of Mankind, which was established by the ILC, required in its Article 2(3)(d) for accomplice liability assistance which 'contributes directly and substantially to the commission of the crime' as well as a facilitation of the commission of the crime in a significant way.[98] However, Article 25(3)(c) of the Rome Statute of 1998 does not mention these criteria.[99] At the same time, the Rome Statute requires a purposive intent which was, in turn, not required by the jurisprudence of the *ad hoc* tribunals.[100]

Nevertheless, in comparison to the law of State responsibility, the field of international criminal law is characterised by the availability of more doctrinal material on the issue of causality in contexts of aiding, abetting or complicity. Given the widely held view that issues of causality have less to do with the individual legal field or system than with the idea of law itself,[101] it thus appears possible to transfer some insights into our field which allow us to lend some doctrinal coherence to the issue of causality with respect to complicit States. This is less problematic than, for instance, a transfer of the requirements of the *mens rea* from international criminal law would be.

---

[95] Kai Ambos, 'Article 25', para. 18.
[96] ICTY, *Prosecutor* v. *Dusko Tadic*, Case No. IT-94-1-A, para. 229; see also ICTY, *Prosecutor* v. *Tihomir Blaskic*, Judgment of 29 July 2004, IT-95-14-A, para. 45.
[97] Kai Ambos, 'Article 25', para. 21; Robert Cryer, Hakan Friman, Darryl Robinson and Elizabeth Wilmshurst, *An Introduction to International Criminal Law and Procedure* (Cambridge: Cambridge University Press, 2007), p. 311; Chia Lehnardt, 'Individual Liability of Private Military Personnel under International Criminal Law', *European Journal of International Law* 19 (2008), pp. 1015–34, at pp. 1023–4.
[98] Draft Code of Crimes against the Peace and Security of Mankind with Commentary, reprinted in 'Report of the International Law Commission on the Work of Its Forty-Eighth Session', YBILC 1996, Vol. II, Part Two, pp. 19 *et seq.*
[99] See further William A. Schabas, *An Introduction to the International Criminal Court*, 3rd edn (Cambridge: Cambridge University Press, 2007), pp. 213–14.
[100] See Robert Cryer, Hakan Friman, Darryl Robinson and Elizabeth Wilmshurst, *International Criminal Law*, p. 312.
[101] H. L. A. Hart and Tony Honoré, *Causation in the Law*, p. 9; François Rigaux, 'International Responsibility and the Principle of Causality', in Maurizio Ragazzi

1.2.3.3 Reasonable distinctions

A useful distinction we can import from the field of international criminal law is that between causality with respect to the effects of assistance on the main actor and the ultimate wrongful act. It is indeed problematic to project a requirement of causality onto the legal effects of the support rendered as it would then be difficult to distinguish complicit acts from co-perpetration or even solitary perpetration.[102] If the complicit actor has caused a given event, why does she only incur liability for complicity? It has been remarked in works of general legal theory that 'complicitous accountability puts pressure on consequence-oriented models'.[103] The challenge is, in the words of Christopher Kutz, 'how responsibility can outrun both causation and control, without becoming simply a free-form virtual guilt shared by all'.[104] It has been a concern for criminal lawyers for a long time how causality can nevertheless be a meaningful criterion with respect to the effect of the assistance upon the eventual commission of the criminal act.[105] If a common denominator from the existing jurisprudence of the tribunals and the positions in scholarly works can be identified, it is the requirement that the support must have made some difference for the main actor in carrying out its deed.[106] Similar considerations will have to apply for complicity in the law of State responsibility. In order to find responsibility of a complicit State, its support should have changed the situation for the main actor. It must have made it 'substantially' easier to commit the internationally wrongful act. In international criminal law, different standards exist in this regard. It is noteworthy that the ILC required a very similar degree of causal impact in its commentaries to Article 2(3)(d) of the

---

(ed.), *International Responsibility Today: Essays in Memory of Oscar Schachter* (Leiden: Nijhoff, 2005), pp. 81–92, at p. 81; Tal Becker, *Terrorism and the State*, p. 288.

[102] Cf, *mutatis mutandis*, Albin Eser, 'Individual Criminal Responsibility', in Antonio Cassese, Paola Gaeta and John R. W. D. Jones (eds.), *The Rome Statute of the International Criminal Court, A Commentary*, Vol. I (Oxford: Oxford University Press, 2002), pp. 767–822, at p. 799.

[103] Christopher Kutz, 'Responsibility', p. 563. [104] *Ibid*.

[105] See the treatment by K. J. M. Smith, *A Modern Treatise*, pp. 55 *et seq*.; Sanford H. Kadish, 'Complicity', pp. 323 *et seq*.; see also H. L. A. Hart and Tony Honoré, *Causation in the Law*, p. 43.

[106] Antonio Cassese, *International Criminal Law*, 3rd edn (Oxford: Oxford University Press, 2008), p. 214; Gerhard Werle, *Völkerstrafrecht*, 2nd edn (Tübingen: Mohr Siebeck, 2007), para. 444.

Draft Code of Crimes against the Peace and Security of Mankind and to Article 16 ASR. Whereas the former elucidated that the commission of a crime must have been 'facilitated in some significant way',[107] the latter refers to the requirement that the aid or assistance in question 'contributed significantly' to the wrongful act,[108] which has to be read in conjunction with the previously stated requirement that 'the aid or assistance must be given with a view to facilitating the commission of that act; and must actually do so'.[109]

How can these requirements be understood in more practical terms? When we think of the granting of overflight rights to the United States by Germany in the context of the 2003 attacks on Iraq, it would be unpersuasive to argue that the granting of these rights were a *conditio sine qua non* for the attacks on Iraq. They cannot realistically be characterised as such with respect to the attacks as a whole and not even with respect to individual attacks. Nevertheless, they greatly facilitated the carrying out of the attacks. If no State had provided stopover and overflight rights in a zone reasonably close to Iraq (and Germany may well count in this regard), the US would have had to limit itself to using its aircraft carriers which would have greatly diminished its potential to carry out widespread attacks in a timely manner. Hence, in this case one can hold that the granting of the overflight and stopover rights made a significant difference to the conduct of operations.

1.2.3.4 Variables

The notion of causality has to be normative and case-specific.[110] As Brigitte Stern has argued, operations of causality are always intellectually based and do not correspond to natural or scientific understandings of causality.[111] In the case of complicity, this implies that an understanding of causality is required which, on the one hand, emphasises that

---

[107] Draft Code of Crimes against the Peace and Security of Mankind with Commentary, reprinted in 'Report of the International Law Commission on the Work of Its Forty-Eighth Session', YBILC 1996, Vol. II, Part Two, p. 21, para. 11.
[108] ILC Commentary, Article 16, para. 5.
[109] *Ibid.*, para. 4.
[110] Cf Mindia Ugrekhelidze, 'Causation: Reflection in the Mirror of the European Convention on Human Rights (A Sketch)', in L. Caflisch, J. Callewaert, R. Liddell, P. Mahoney and M. Villiger (eds.), *Liber Amicorum Luzius Wildhaber: Human Rights – Strasbourg Views* (Kehl: N. P. Engel, 2007), pp. 469–81, at p. 478; see also, *mutatis mutandis*, Kai Ambos, 'Article 25', para. 21; Kai Ambos, *Der Allgemeine Teil des Völkerstrafrechts*, p. 631.
[111] Brigitte Bollecker-Stern, *Le prejudice*, p. 189.

the aid or assistance must have made a difference[112] but, on the other hand, does not require this difference to be of such a substantial character that the threshold for a joint commission of the wrongful act is overstepped.[113] In considering the causal impact of the complicit State's action, one necessarily has to take into account the legal evaluation of the position of the main actor: requiring too much causal impact of the complicit State might eventually absolve the main actor from part of its responsibility. If the support was a *sine qua non* for the commission of the wrongful act, would it then be conceivable at all to hold the main actor responsible for its conduct? The *sine qua non* test generally lacks the potential to distinguish between significant and less significant causes.[114] This is also the reason why it is universally supplemented with additional criteria which are meant to regulate what action is considered to be causal with respect to a given outcome. In trying to flesh out these criteria for our purposes, only limited usefulness can be ascribed to traditional notions such as 'adequacy', 'immediacy', 'proximity' or 'remoteness'.[115] There is nothing inherently wrong with such theories[116] and they give expression to the normativity of the intellectual, causal operation. However, it is not to be expected that judicial practice will settle on such notions. Instead, the specificities of the individual case at hand will have to be considered. In addition, the general theories of causation are challenged by the complicating factor of a third State entering the picture.[117] Thus, any application of the general theories of causation would arguably have to be attenuated. Given the scarcity of available international practice on the issue of causality with respect to complicit States, it is to be expected that a highly casuistic approach will be resorted to if a court or tribunal is to deal with the matter.

---

[112] Pierre d'Argent, *Les réparations de guerre*, p. 552; cf further H. L. A. Hart and Tony Honoré, *Causation in the Law*, p. 29.

[113] For a position which requires a 'but for' test for complicity, see Franceso Capotorti, 'Cours général de droit international public', *Recueil des Cours* 248 (1994-IV), pp. 9–344, at pp. 254–5.

[114] Tal Becker, *Terrorism and the State*, p. 292.

[115] See, with respect to the ECHR, Mindia Ugrekhelidze, 'Causation', pp. 477 *et seq.*; cf further H. L. A. Hart and Tony Honoré, *Causation in the Law*, p. 4.

[116] Stefan Kadelbach, 'Staatenverantwortlichkeit für Angriffskriege und Verbrechen gegen die Menschlichkeit', *Berichte der Deutschen Gesellschaft für Völkerrecht* 40 (2001), pp. 63–102, at pp. 72–3.

[117] On issues of causality when this third party is a non-State actor, see Brigitte Bollecker-Stern, *Le préjudice*, pp. 196 *et seq.*

What doctrine can do in this situation is to point towards the requirement of some causal notion within the contours we have sketched so far. Different cases will involve different primary rules which have been violated. Again, these rules will call for different standards in terms of causality.[118] If, for instance, positive obligations or requirements to invest 'best efforts' (such as in the Cluster Munitions Convention) mingle with the issue of complicity, it will be reasonable to require a lesser degree of causal influence upon the commission of the wrongful act. If, however, the normative environment in which the complicity took place is bereft of any such additional factors, stricter standards should apply in terms of the causal impact of the complicit action.

These considerations are, once again, owed to the general nature of Article 16 ASR. With respect to more precise obligations of non-assistance, it will be easier to identify rules on causality. The discussion we have presented on the meaning of Article 1(c) of the Cluster Munitions Convention and the subsequent adoption of Article 21 of this agreement underline that States parties are apparently unwilling to accept an understanding of assistance which would consider an 'enabling' environment in a joint operation as a form of assistance which triggers responsibility under this agreement. Things may lie differently when, for example, established and longstanding jurisprudence in the field of human rights law imposes additional obligations upon States for individuals in their custody.[119] If assistance is rendered in a form which involves such custody over an individual, it will also be possible to be satisfied with a contribution to, for instance, an inhuman or degrading form of treatment, which consists in the provision of such an enabling environment as may be seen in the presence of intelligence, police or military personnel during an interrogation by a third party or the signalling of a general willingness to turn a blind eye to a particular form of treatment.

1.2.3.5 Interim conclusions on complicity and causality

Finally, one should see the issue of causality in a broader perspective. In abstraction from concrete domestic jurisdictions, legal theorists have

---

[118] Cf Mindia Ugrekhelidze, 'Causation', p. 471.
[119] See, e.g., ECtHR, *Tomasi v. France*, Series A, No. 241-A, paras. 107 *et seq.*; ECtHR, *Ribitsch v. Austria*, Series A No. 336, paras. 34 *et seq.*; see further Christoph Grabenwarter, *Europäische Menschenrechtskonvention*, 3rd edn (Munich: C. H. Beck, 2008), § 20, para. 33.

argued that responsibility for complicity is imposed precisely because it covers action which could not be understood within the confines of traditional doctrine on causality.[120] Christopher Kutz has suggested an alternative model which substitutes the requirement of causality with the criterion of participatory intentions.[121] As joint conduct usually implies shared benefits, it would be a legitimate consideration to distribute risks among the potential beneficiaries as well.[122] We will see in the course of this chapter that this poses its own problems in international law but it is important nevertheless to keep this suggestion in mind. At the same time, it is apparent that only very few if any legal systems and legal theorists are willing to entirely discard the requirements of some form of causality when issues of complicity are at stake.[123] The somewhat unclear and unsatisfying state of the law with respect to the requirement of causality in Article 16 ASR may thus reflect the intermediate state of development of the international legal system.

1.2.4 Defining 'aid or assistance' by negative criteria

So far, we have seen that it is difficult to identify concrete criteria which help to shed further light on what 'aid or assistance' means in the sense of Article 16 ASR. At the same time, we have been able to identify some negatives: States do not accept the idea of responsibility for complicity through mere association, and notions of causality have to be deployed with great care when complicity is at stake. In addition, further negative criteria may be identified by delimiting complicity from other grounds of responsibility in international law which also involve the conduct of a plurality of States.

1.2.4.1 Related bases for responsibility
The collaboration of a plurality of States can take various forms which are accommodated in different ways in the law of State responsibility. With regard to their relation to complicity, we can distinguish the following scenarios:

(1) A State may have contributed to such an extent to the wrongful act of another State that it is no longer sufficient to attribute to it the

---

[120] Sanford H. Kadish, 'Complicity', pp. 359 *et seq.*
[121] Christopher Kutz, 'Responsibility', p. 563.
[122] Christopher Kutz, *Complicity*, p. 223.
[123] H. L. A. Hart and Tony Honoré, *Causation in the Law*, p. 48; Sanford H. Kadish, 'Complicity', p. 334.

role of a complicit State. Rather, a joint commission of the wrongful act has to be assumed.[124] With respect to the case of aggression, Ian Brownlie has exemplified this distinction:

[T]he supply of weapons, military aircraft, radar equipment, and so forth, would in certain situations amount to 'aid or assistance' in the commission of an act of aggression but would not give rise to joint responsibility. However, the supply of combat units, vehicles, equipment and personnel, for the specific purpose of assisting an aggressor, would constitute a joint responsibility.[125]

An example may be the case of the respective roles of the United States and the United Kingdom in the attacks on Iraq in 2003. It is not convincing to see the UK as a mere 'accomplice' to the acts of the United States. In such a case, the ordinary form of individual responsibility according to Article 1 ASR will be the correct category. When assessing the role helping States have played in a particular enterprise, one should, however, make an important distinction. Frequently, the main actor will be interested in assembling as much support as possible for its violation of the law. In the case of the 2003 attacks on Iraq, it was important to note the US insistence on having established a coalition of forty-seven States which would jointly enforce the will of the international community *vis-à-vis* Iraq. On closer inspection, the contribution of some of these States was rather insignificant.[126] One should thus not treat such political rhetoric as a realistic assessment of the partition of responsibility in a group of States engaged in a collective enterprise. Things are different when the 'junior partner' itself assumes responsibility. Stefan Talmon has conducted an investigation into the US and UK responsibility for the acts of the Coalition Provisional Authority (CPA) in Iraq in 2003-4.[127] On the face of it, the CPA constituted an organ of the United States. The significant decisions were all made in Washington and the influence of London on the work of the CPA was minimal. However, the UK itself emphasised the 'jointness' of this enterprise. It thus assumed responsibility for the acts of the CPA, regardless of the fact that it did not have much say in the actual running of affairs.[128] Where a State

---

[124] See also Peter C. R. Kabatsi, Statement at the 2578th Meeting of the ILC, YBILC 1999, Vol. I, Part One, p. 76, para. 17.
[125] Ian Brownlie, *State Responsibility*, p. 191.
[126] On the practices by which this 'coalition was assembled', see Anne Peters, 'The Growth of International Law between Globalization and the Great Power', *Austrian Review of International and European Law* 8 (2003), pp. 109-40, at pp. 116-17.
[127] Stefan Talmon, 'Plurality', pp. 185 *et seq.*   [128] *Ibid.*, p. 229.

ascribes such a role to itself, it must be held to its words. This scenario is to be distinguished from Article 11 ASR which deals with *ex post* assumption of responsibility.

(2) Article 11 ASR provides that '[c]onduct which is not attributable to a State under the preceding articles shall nevertheless be considered an act of that State under international law if and to the extent that the State acknowledges and adopts the conduct in question as its own'. Although this provision primarily addresses the issue of the attribution of private acts,[129] the ILC has made it clear that it conceivably also covers responsibility for the conduct of another State.[130] This possibility is interesting insofar as it covers the only relevant exception to the general rule that psychological support will not count as aid or assistance within the meaning of Article 16 ASR. International law knows no responsibility for incitement.[131] A mere psychological relation to the commission of a given wrongful act will not suffice to establish responsibility for complicity either.[132] Only if this subjective position towards the commission of the act in question amounts to an acknowledgment and adoption of the conduct does it become conceivable that a shift of attribution intervenes. As Article 11 ASR generally applies with respect to the conduct of private actors, further uncertainties ensue. In this respect, it is unclear whether the State whose conduct has been at the origin of the wrongful act has to give its consent to the acknowledgment and adoption by another State. With respect to the interpretation of Article 16 ASR, it is, however, sufficient to note that this possibility under Article 11 ASR provides

---

[129] ILC Commentary, Article 11, para. 3; for the most prominent example from practice, see ICJ, *United States Diplomatic and Consular Staff in Tehran*, Judgment, ICJ Rep. 1980, 3, paras. 69 *et seq.*
[130] ILC Commentary, Introduction to Chapter IV of Part One, para. 9.
[131] Roberto Ago, 'Seventh Report on State Responsibility', YBILC 1978, Vol. II, Part One, pp. 30, 55, para. 63; ICJ, *Military and Paramilitary Activities In and Against Nicaragua*, Merits, ICJ Rep. 1986, 14, dissenting opinion of Judge Schwebel, pp. 388–9; Christian Dominicé, 'Attribution of Conduct', p. 285; Paolo Palchetti, 'State Responsibility for Complicity in Genocide', in Paola Gaeta (ed.), *The UN Genocide Convention – A Commentary* (Oxford: Oxford University Press, 2009), pp. 381–93, at p. 387; see now also Article 16 DARIO as provisionally adopted by the ILC, UN Doc. A/64/10, on the responsibility of international organisations for recommendations to their Member States.
[132] Cf Bernhard Graefrath, 'Complicity', p. 373; Jörg Künzli, *Vom Umgang des Rechtsstaats mit Unrechtsregimes – Völker- und landesrechtliche Grenzen des Verhaltensspielraums der schweizerischen Außenpolitik gegenüber Völkerrecht missachtenden Staaten* (Bern: Stämpfli, 2008), p. 407; Georg Nolte and Helmut Philipp Aust, 'Equivocal Helpers', p. 13.

for an exception to the general rule that moral support will not suffice to trigger responsibility for complicity. Similarly, assistance 'after the fact' needs to be distinguished from 'aid or assistance' in the sense of Article 16 ASR. The latter presupposes some form of effect upon the commission of the wrongful act. Accordingly, support which is rendered *ex post* will in most situations not count as aid or assistance. Our survey of international practice has shown that not all participants in the international legal discourse ascribe identical importance to this distinction. In addition, a wrongful act of a continuing character may call for a different assessment (and thus may exclude the notion of complicity after the fact).

(3) The contribution of a State may further exceed the scope of complicity insofar as its influence upon the conduct of another State has to be described in terms either of direction and control or of coercion. These facets of collaboration between States are addressed in Articles 17 and 18 ASR. As the ILC notes in its Commentary, the most significant examples for such relationships are historical ones.[133] Relationships such as 'suzerainty' or the exercise of a protectorate over another State no longer figure prominently in international practice.[134] Article 17, which addresses such forms of direction or control, was nonetheless retained in the ASR as the general feeling prevailed that otherwise a loophole for responsibility could be created. Article 18, on the other hand, addresses more factual forms of control, for example real coercion concerning individual wrongful acts. It is also striking here that no contemporary practice was cited by the ILC. However, the reason for retaining this provision is largely the same as with respect to Article 17.[135] For our present purposes, it should not be too difficult to distinguish the situations covered by Articles 17 and 18 from those envisaged by Article 16: whereas the role of the complicit State is relatively minor insofar as it is only supporting the main actor, Articles 17 and 18 ASR address the relationship between what has also been called the 'puppet master' and the 'puppet'.[136]

---

[133] ILC Commentary, Article 17, para. 2.
[134] But see Ralph Wilde, *International Territorial Administration: How Trusteeship and the Civilizing Mission Never Went Away* (Oxford: Oxford University Press, 2008), pp. 289 *et seq.*
[135] See the criticism by James D. Fry, 'Coercion', pp. 621 *et seq.*
[136] Vaughan Lowe, 'Responsibility', p. 4; see further Maria Luisa Padelletti, *Pluralità di stati*, pp. 87–8.

(4) More intricate is a rule of attribution that the ILC has set out in Article 6 ASR. According to this provision, '[t]he conduct of an organ placed at the disposal of a State by another State shall be considered an act of the former State under international law if the organ is acting in the exercise of elements of the governmental authority of the State at whose disposal it is placed'. In its Commentary, the ILC makes it clear that 'mere aid or assistance offered by organs of one State to another on the territory of the latter is not covered by article 6'.[137] Furthermore, it is stipulated that 'the organ must ... act in conjunction with the machinery of that State and under its exclusive direction or control, rather than on instructions from the sending State'.[138] While it is clear that individually committed wrongful acts under such exclusive direction or control will be attributed to the State at the disposal of which these organs have been placed, uncertainties remain with respect to the 'borrowing' State.[139] Does the fact that the other State incurs responsibility absolve it from its responsibility? In theory, this is the construction Article 6 ASR envisages. It is, however, a different matter whether one can conceivably distinguish between the transfer of responsibility with respect to the individual wrongful acts and the contribution to a larger situation in which the mere placing at the disposal of another State of an organ may be counted as aid or assistance.[140] The ILC does not give any indications on how this puzzle is to be solved. A related issue has, however, been discussed in the context of the responsibility of international organisations. In its *Behrami* and *Saramati* decision, the European Court of Human Rights relied on Draft Article 5 on the Responsibility of International Organizations which mirrors Article 6 ASR.[141] Accordingly, acts of a State organ placed at the disposal of an international organisation are attributable to the latter if the organisation exercises exclusive direction or control over it.[142] It is far from being undisputed whether the Court made correct use of the Draft Article of the ILC and whether the latter actually represents customary international law or provides an adequate solution for the partition of responsibility between a State and an international

---

[137] ILC Commentary, Article 6, para. 3.   [138] *Ibid.*, para. 2.
[139] See also the discussion by Maria Luisa Padelletti, *Pluralità di stati*, pp. 67 *et seq.*
[140] Cf Stefan Talmon, 'Plurality', p. 218.
[141] ECtHR, *Agim Behrami and Bekir Behrami* v. *France* and *Ruzhdi Saramati* v. *France, Germany and Norway*, 133 ILR 1, 50, para. 151.
[142] Cf 'Report of the ILC on Its Fifty-Ninth Session', UN Doc. A/62/10, paras. 325 *et seq.*

organisation.[143] The important point here is that the European Court of Human Rights conceived the responsibility of the United Nations to be exclusive.[144] Several authors have pointed out that the ILC did not presuppose this to be the case.[145] Parallel responsibility of a State and an international organisation is conceivable.[146] *Mutatis mutandis*, similar considerations will apply with respect to the interpretation of Article 6 ASR. Here, however, one has to discount a driving force behind the criticism of the *Behrami* decision, namely, its creation of an 'accountability gap'. This problem is less marked in the case when responsibility is shifted from one State to another. Still, practical reasons here may also militate for a finding of parallel responsibility, and it is far from clear whether the application of Article 6 ASR automatically excludes the responsibility of the 'borrowing' State under Article 16 ASR.[147]

(5) Another type of situation which is to be distinguished from the one covered by Article 16 ASR is the classic *Soering* scenario.[148] Here, a State incurs direct responsibility for having created a risk of a given treatment. At issue is the prohibition of *non-refoulement* in its various emanations, on the basis of either human rights[149] or refugee

---

[143] For further discussion, see Philippe Lagrange, 'Responsabilité des Etats pour actes accomplis en application du Chapitre VII de la Charte des Nations Unies', *Revue générale de droit international public* 112 (2008), pp. 85–109, at pp. 93 *et seq.*; Kjetil Mujezinovic Larsen, 'Attribution of Conduct in Peace Operations: The "Ultimate Authority and Control" Test', *European Journal of International Law* 19 (2008), pp. 509–31; Aurel Sari, 'Jurisdiction and International Responsibility in Peace Support Operations: The *Behrami* and *Saramati* Cases', *Human Rights Law Review* 8 (2008), pp. 151–70, at pp. 164 *et seq.*; for a more positive assessment of the decision, see Christian Tomuschat, 'Case Note: R (on the Application of al-Jedda) v. Secretary of State for Defence – Human Rights in a Multi-Level System of Governance and the Internment of Suspected Terrorists', *Melbourne Journal of International Law* 10 (2008), at p. 5 (online version).

[144] ECtHR, *Agim Behrami and Bekir Behrami v. France* and *Ruzhdi Saramati v. France, Germany and Norway*, 133 ILR 1, 51, para. 152.

[145] Kjetil Mujezinovic Larsen, 'Attribution', p. 517; Pierre Bodeau-Livinec, Gionata P. Buzzini and Santiago Villalpando, 'Case Note (on Behrami and Behrami v. France, Samarati v. France, Germany and Norway)', *American Journal of International Law* 102 (2008), pp. 323–31, at p. 328.

[146] See Giorgio Gaja, 'First Report on the Responsibility of International Organizations', UN Doc. A/CN.4/532 (2003), p. 20, para. 38; see also his 'Second Report', UN Doc. A/CN.4/541 (2004), p. 4, para. 7; and the 'Seventh Report', UN Doc. A/CN.4/610 (2009), para. 25.

[147] In this sense also Stefan Talmon, 'Plurality', p. 218.

[148] ECtHR, *Soering v. United Kingdom*, Series A, No. 161.

[149] *Ibid.*; see further Erika de Wet, 'The Prohibition of Torture as an International Norm of Jus Cogens and Its Implications for National and Customary Law', *European Journal of International Law* 15 (2004), pp. 97–121, at p. 101.

law.¹⁵⁰ In practice, as regards the actual conduct, the situation is hard to distinguish from what Article 16 ASR covers. The extradition of a person to another State where he/she faces the risk of mistreatment can readily be seen as aid or assistance to the incriminated conduct. What is missing, however, is the special relationship between the rendering of the person and the eventual mistreatment.¹⁵¹ This conduct does not so much rest on the issue of causality that we have already discussed – the rendering does have an impact on the way the mistreatment intervenes; it may even constitute a *conditio sine qua non* – but rather on the subjective requirement. The person is not necessarily rendered *for* the purpose of the commission of the intervening mistreatment but 'merely' exposed to this risk. On the issue of the substantive contribution, the situation is thus not distinguishable from Article 16 ASR.¹⁵²

1.2.4.2 Complicity through omission
In its *Genocide Convention* case, the ICJ delimited responsibility for complicity in genocide from the question of responsibility for having violated the obligation to prevent genocide in the following way:

[C]omplicity always requires that some positive action has been taken to furnish aid or assistance to the perpetrators of the genocide, while a violation of the obligation to prevent results from mere failure to adopt and implement suitable measures to prevent genocide from being committed. In other words, while complicity results from commission, violation of the obligation to prevent results from omission; this is merely the reflection of the notion that the ban on genocide and the other acts listed in Article III, including complicity, places States under a negative obligation, the obligation not to commit the

---

[150] See Article 33 of the 1951 Convention Relating to the Status of Refugees of 28 July 1951, entered into force 22 April 1954, 189 UNTS 137; see further Elihu Lauterpacht and Daniel Bethlehem, 'The Scope and Content of the Principle of Non-Refoulement: Opinion', in Erika Feller, Volker Türk and Frances Nicholson (eds.), *Refugee Protection in International Law – UNHCR's Global Consultations on International Protection* (Cambridge: Cambridge University Press, 2003), pp. 87–177, at p. 89.
[151] Andreas Felder, *Die Beihilfe*, p. 133; Monica Hakimi, 'State Bystander Responsibility', p. 366.
[152] See also Christian J. Tams, 'The Abuse of Executive Powers: What Remedies?', in Andrea Bianchi and Alexis Keller (eds.), *Counterterrorism: Democracy's Challenge* (Oxford: Hart, 2008), pp. 313–34, at p. 318, who argues for a close relationship between Article 16 ASR and obligations of *non-refoulement*; see also UK House of Lords/House of Commons, Joint Committee on Human Rights, 'Allegations of UK Complicity in Torture', Twenty-Third Report of Session 2008–9, HL Paper 152, HC 230, published on 4 August 2009, para. 23; see further our discussion in Chapter 8, text accompanying notes 74 *et seq*.

prohibited acts, while the duty to prevent places States under positive obligations, to do their best to ensure that such acts do not occur.[153]

Accordingly, omissions might be ruled out as a relevant form of aid or assistance. One might be tempted to reduce the importance of this statement for our analysis by placing it within the framework of international criminal law.[154] Article III of the Genocide Convention was originally meant to establish grounds for the criminal liability of individuals.[155] In contemporary international criminal law, a distinction is frequently made between 'complicity in genocide' and 'aiding and abetting genocide'.[156] The International Criminal Tribunal for Rwanda has found one of the differences between the two counts to be that complicity requires a positive act whereas aiding and abetting could also consist of an omission.[157] However, this distinction is far from being established conclusively. Rather, it has been said that the state of the law presents itself as a 'complete and total conceptual mess' in this regard.[158] In addition, it is not apparent that the Court wished to see its comment anchored in some comparative notion of criminal law in this regard as it saw no reason to make any substantive distinction between 'complicity in genocide' (Article III(e)) and 'aid or assistance' by a State in the commission of an internationally wrongful act.[159] Accordingly, the Court's *dictum* may have a bearing on the interpretation of Article 16 ASR.[160]

The ILC Commentary to Article 16 ASR contains no reference to an example where responsibility for complicity is incurred on the basis of an omission. However, the Commentary is generally silent on the issue. This means that either the question escaped the attention of the ILC

---

[153] ICJ, *Case Concerning the Application of the Convention on the Prevention and Punishment of the Crime of Genocide*, Judgment, para. 432.
[154] See Antonio Cassese, 'On the Use of Criminal Law Notions in Determining State Responsibility for Genocide', *Journal of International Criminal Justice* 5 (2007), pp. 875–87, at p. 879.
[155] Cf William A. Schabas, *Genocide in International Law* (Cambridge: Cambridge University Press, 2000), pp. 257 *et seq.* and 285 *et seq.*
[156] Chile Eboe-Osuji, 'Complicity in Genocide', pp. 56 *et seq.*; see further Antonio Cassese, 'Criminal Law Notions', pp. 883 *et seq.*
[157] ICTR, *Prosecutor v. Akayesu*, ICTR-96-4T, para. 548.
[158] Marko Milanovic, 'State Responsibility for Genocide: A Follow-Up', *European Journal of International Law* 18 (2007), pp. 669–94, at p. 681.
[159] ICJ, *Case Concerning the Application of the Convention on the Prevention and Punishment of the Crime of Genocide*, Judgment, para. 420.
[160] See also Paolo Palchetti, 'Complicity in Genocide', p. 384.

or the ILC saw no reason to deviate from its general rule, namely, that State conduct can consist of an action or an omission (Article 2 ASR). In its commentary to this latter provision, the ILC has held that cases in which international responsibility has been invoked for omissions are at least as frequent as are those which are based on actions.[161] A prominent example in case is the *Corfu Channel* case, which is also particularly instructive for the present study as it concerns a situation which borders on complicity.[162] Albania incurred responsibility for not having warned third States of the presence of the mines in its territorial waters, a presence it knew about or at least should have known about as the Court found.[163] It is fairly easy to construe the *Corfu Channel* case in a way which would replace Albania's direct responsibility with complicity-based responsibility.[164] Not warning third States of the presence of the mines is then the quintessential aid or assistance to the State which laid the mines. Now it could be argued that this is an unconvincing example as Albania could only be held responsible for not warning third States when there was a duty incumbent on it to take action with regard to the mines.[165] However, a separate responsibility for complicity would not then be needed as the complicit State would already be obliged to warn third States on the basis of an independent primary obligation. No additional basis for responsibility for complicity would therefore be required.

Regardless of whether the *Corfu Channel* case can be reconceived as a potential example of complicity through omission, there are scenarios in which the aid or assistance could consist of a mere omission.[166] This

---

[161] ILC Commentary, Article 2, para. 4.
[162] Another prominent example of a case in which responsibility for an omission is at stake is: ICJ, *United States Diplomatic and Consular Staff in Tehran*, Judgment, ICJ Rep. 1980, 3, paras. 63, 67.
[163] ICJ, *Corfu Channel Case*, Judgment, ICJ Rep. 1949, 4, at pp. 22–3.
[164] Alexander Orakhelashvili, 'Division of Reparation Between Responsible Entities', in James Crawford, Alain Pellet and Simon Olleson (eds.), *The Law of International Responsibility* (Oxford: Oxford University Press, 2010), pp. 647–65, at p. 658; see also François Rigaux, 'International Responsibility', p. 85.
[165] Andreas Felder, *Die Beihilfe*, pp. 254–5.
[166] Vaughan Lowe, 'Responsibility', p. 6; Marko Milanovic, 'Follow-Up', p. 687; Andrea Gattini, 'Breach of the Obligation to Prevent and Reparation Thereof in the ICJ's Genocide Convention Judgment', *European Journal of International Law* 18 (2007), pp. 695–713, at pp. 702–3; Philippe Weckel, 'L'arrêt sur le génocide: Le souffle de l'avis de 1951 n'a pas transporté la Cour', *Revue générale de droit international public* 111 (2007), pp. 305–31, at p. 327; see also Georg Nolte and Helmut Philipp Aust, 'Equivocal Helpers', p. 10.

would be the case, for example, when a State is using the airspace of another State to overfly in order to attack a third State. How is the situation to be characterised when the territorial State is simply not protesting or taking any other measures against the use of its airspace? Given that it could at any time at least protest against this use of its airspace, it is conceivable to categorise this omission as 'aid or assistance' in accordance with Article 16 ASR.[167]

As we have seen in the preceding chapter, this is the scenario which has allegedly confronted US government officials when they were faced with a request by Israel to permit the use of Iraqi airspace for an attack on Iran.[168] First of all, it may be recalled that, as a matter of general international law, responsibility for complicity through omission appears to be conceivable only if there is a duty upon the complicit State to act.[169] This, however, calls very much into question whether there could be a sensible scope of application for complicity through omission. If there is a specific duty to act, this duty would need to be established on the level of primary rules.[170] If the State in question fails to act, then it would incur responsibility for not having complied with this positive obligation. However, this syllogistic reasoning falls short of fully explaining the potential relevance of complicity through omission. In our hypothetical example of the US helping Israel through a non-interference with the latter's use of Iraqi airspace, we could point to an independent obligation of the US to prevent such incursions into Iraqi airspace. If we take the 2008 Status of Forces Agreement (SOFA) between the US and Iraq into consideration, the US was to coordinate its military efforts with the Iraqi government. Article 27(2) of the SOFA stipulates that:

In the event of any external or internal threat or aggression against Iraq that would violate its sovereignty, political independence, or territorial integrity,

---

[167] A different position was held by the German Federal Prosecutor, 'Entschließung des Generalbundesanwalts' of 21 March 2003, reprinted in JZ 2003, pp. 908 *et seq.*

[168] 'US Rejected Aid for Israeli Raid on Iranian Nuclear Site', *New York Times*, 11 January 2009, p. A1; see also the description of the situation in Chapter 4, text accompanying notes 72 *et seq.*

[169] This requirement mirrors the general state of the law that States will only incur responsibility for omissions if an obligation to act was incumbent upon them: see ICJ, *United States Diplomatic and Consular Staff in Tehran*, Judgment, ICJ Rep. 1980, 3, paras. 63, 66; see also Georg Dahm, Jost Delbrück and Rüdiger Wolfrum, *Völkerrecht*, Vol. I/3, p. 876.

[170] This follows from the general conception of the ASR as secondary rules: see James Crawford, 'Introduction', pp. 14–15.

waters, airspace, its democratic system or its elected institutions, and upon request by the Government of Iraq, the Parties shall immediately initiate strategic deliberations and, as may be mutually agreed, the United States shall take appropriate measures, including diplomatic, economic, or military measures, or any other measure, to deter such a threat.[171]

This provision makes it clear that – on the face of it – it is neither the obligation nor the right of the United States to take unilateral measures such as the shooting down of an Israeli aircraft without further consultation with the Iraqi government. Given that Article 27(4) of the SOFA also states that 'Iraqi land, sea, and air shall not be used as a launching pad or transit point for attacks against other countries', and given also the factual preponderance of US military strength in Iraq in late 2008/early 2009, we can, however, also hold that much speaks against granting the US too much leeway in condoning a possible Israeli attack which would make use of Iraqi airspace. This is underscored by the fact that Israel has asked the US for permission. Here, we can distinguish between, on the one hand, the different scope of the positive obligation incumbent upon the US which would possibly be violated if they did not refuse to grant permission for Israeli aircraft to enter Iraqi airspace and, on the other hand, the much more burdensome responsibility which would be incumbent upon the US were it to become complicit – through its omission to intervene – if Israel attacked Iran. In other words, US responsibility for complicity with a violation of the prohibition of the use of force weighs much heavier than a mere violation of the US obligations under the SOFA with Iraq. As the US omission would, however, be closely connected with any eventual attack, it is justifiable to consider its omission as a form of aid or assistance in this regard. Accordingly, the existing positive obligation upon the US to coordinate with the Iraqi government in order to protect Iraq's integrity can be said to trigger the obligation to intervene without fully exhausting the scope of application of Article 16 ASR. Hence, complicity through omission may also become relevant if there is already a duty to act incumbent upon the potentially complicit State.

---

[171] Agreement on the withdrawal of United States Forces from Iraq and the organization of their activities during their temporary presence in Iraq of 17 November 2008, entered into force on 1 January 2009, available at http://graphics8.nytimes.com/packages/pdf/world/20081119_SOFA_FINAL_AGREED_TEXT.pdf (last visited 1 November 2010).

In light of these considerations, it does not appear as clear-cut as the ICJ put it in the *Genocide Convention* case that complicity through omission is inconceivable.[172] It is conceivable that aid or assistance may also consist of an omission.[173] The example we have just discussed once again points towards the conclusion that any assessment in this regard will be highly case-specific. Whereas it is generally plausible to affirm that responsibility for complicity through omission will be a rare phenomenon, the example shows that the gravity of the situation may very well impact upon the legal assessment and that an omission may be as relevant as any form of active support.

1.2.5 Interim conclusion

The generality of Article 16 ASR speaks against the compiling of a concrete list which clearly indicates which forms of conduct would amount to aid or assistance and which would not. Such a list would not only be of limited practical relevance, it would also run counter to the idea of a general rule on complicity anchored in the domain of the secondary rules on State responsibility. It would rather amount to drawing up primary rules of conduct. Instead, 'aid or assistance' is a normative and case-specific concept, meaning that its content will always have to be determined in the specific situation, with a view to the relation between supportive conduct to the neighbouring normative environment and the enabling function it played in the case at hand.[174] The normativity of this intellectual operation will have to be supplemented by a further criterion: the 'mental' relationship between the complicit State, its support and the supported activity.

2 The subjective element

As already mentioned, the question of intent is intimately linked to the previous one concerning the material element. If one wishes to restrict the applicability of a provision on complicity, one can either do so through narrowing down the number of cases in which the assistance

---

[172] See above note 153.
[173] Vaughan Lowe, 'Responsibility', p. 6; Brian D. Smith, *State Responsibility and the Marine Environment – The Rules of Decision* (Oxford: Oxford University Press, 1988), p. 12; Paolo Palchetti, 'Complicity in Genocide', p. 385.
[174] See similarly for the parallel provision of Article 13 DARIO, Giorgio Gaja, 'Seventh Report on the Responsibility of International Organizations', UN Doc. A/CN.4/610, para. 75.

itself 'counts', or one can put an emphasis on the necessary subjective or psychological element. Although there is disagreement over its precise scope and content, there is near unanimity in the literature that responsibility under Article 16 ASR requires some subjective relationship between the assisting State and the commission of the wrongful act by the main actor.[175]

2.1 Preliminary remarks

It is a longstanding debate in the field of State responsibility whether some form of wrongful intent or fault is required for a State to be responsible for a given conduct. Traditional theory – inspired by Hugo Grotius – was of the opinion that fault was an indispensable element of responsibility. This view prevailed until the 1920s.[176] Since then, one can broadly distinguish between three possible views on the general character of the rules of State responsibility. First, they could require some form of subjective element.[177] Secondly, they could rest on an objective basis.[178] A third possibility would be a further enhanced notion of objective responsibility which is then labelled *absolute* objective responsibility.[179] There are variants to these theories, for instance the view which distinguishes between internal acts of States – legislative, executive or judicial – for which the standard of responsibility is objective and external acts of States where there is supposed to exist a due diligence obligation which is in this case conceived of as being subjective in character.[180] The nature of due diligence is, however, subject to intense debate.[181] Other authorities see it as an objective concept in contrast to *diligentia in qua suam*.[182] Over the course of time, most

---

[175] For the various positions in the literature, see Andreas Felder, *Die Beihilfe*, pp. 256 *et seq.*; John Quigley, 'Complicity', pp. 109 *et seq.*; Eckart Klein, 'Beihilfe', pp. 431-2 and 435-6; Georg Nolte and Helmut Philipp Aust, 'Equivocal Helpers', pp. 13 *et seq.*; Monica Hakimi, 'State Bystander Responsibility', p. 365.

[176] See Roberto Ago, 'Das Verschulden', pp. 449 *et seq.*; Prosper Weil, 'Cours général', pp. 347 *et seq.*

[177] Bin Cheng, *General Principles of Law*, pp. 218 *et seq.*

[178] Ian Brownlie, *State Responsibility*, p. 38.

[179] See Benedetto Conforti, 'Cours général de droit international public', *Recueil des Cours* 212 (1988-V), pp. 9–210, at p. 174.

[180] Max Sørensen, 'Principes de droit international public', *Recueil des Cours* 101 (1960-III), pp. 5–254, at pp. 228–9.

[181] See Andrea Gattini, *Zufall und force majeure im System der Staatenverantwortlichkeit anhand der ILC-Kodifikationsarbeit* (Berlin: Duncker & Humblot, 1991), pp. 197 *et seq.*

[182] Eduardo Jimenez de Arechaga, 'International Law in the Past Third of a Century', *Recueil des Cours* 159 (1978-I), pp. 1–344, at p. 270.

authors seem to have adopted the position that responsibility is generally objective with possible exceptions.[183]

The ILC has opted for a pragmatic conception of international responsibility.[184] It has not excluded the issue of fault from the Articles altogether. Rather, it has emphasised that 'different primary rules of international law impose different standards ranging from "due diligence" to strict liability'.[185] This will also be the case for Article 16 ASR: due to its generality it covers aid or assistance furnished to violations of the most diverse kind of rules. It can therefore not be expected that a clear-cut general rule on 'the' intent standard with respect to complicity in international law will be deducible.[186] However, the work of the ILC and the existing international practice give us some indications about the necessary requirements. In addition, a systematic interpretation of Article 16 ASR with respect to its relation to other bases of responsibility and international law in general may prove helpful to gain further insights into this *problématique*.

2.2 The discussion in the ILC

In his Seventh Report on State Responsibility, Special Rapporteur Roberto Ago devoted a small but important part to the question of intent. He discussed this issue in connection with the one pertaining to breaches of independent obligations which would render a complicit State responsible. After having affirmed that such independent obligations exist, for example when a State supplies arms to the government of South Africa in breach of its obligations set down by the UN Security Council, he said that, in most situations covered by the draft Article, 'the conduct in question, taken in isolation, will be an act which is not, as such, of a wrongful character'.[187] In these cases, it was crucial to know 'whether or not the conduct adopted by the State was *intended* to enable another State to commit an international offence or to make it easier for it to do so'.[188] Furthermore:

---

[183] For a nuanced position, see Alfred Verdross and Bruno Simma, *Universelles Völkerrecht*, § 1266.
[184] James Crawford, 'Introduction', pp. 12 *et seq.*
[185] *Ibid.*, p. 13; in this sense, see Roberto Ago, 'Das Verschulden', p. 477.
[186] Cf, *mutatis mutandis*, Andrea Gattini, *Zufall und force majeure*, p. 203.
[187] Roberto Ago, 'Seventh Report on State Responsibility', YBILC 1978, Vol. II, Part One, p. 58, para. 72.
[188] *Ibid.*, emphasis added.

The very idea of 'complicity' in the internationally wrongful act of another necessarily presupposes an *intent* to collaborate in the commission of an act of this kind, and hence, in the cases considered, knowledge of the specific purpose for which the State receiving certain supplies *intends* to use them. Without this condition, there can be no question of complicity.[189]

The issue of intent caused some controversy among the members of the Commission, which was basically divided into two groups. A first group of ILC members contended that 'too narrow a definition [of intent] would nullify the scope of the article. No State would admit that it was helping another State to commit a wrongful act.'[190] Nikolai Ushakov put the problem in a larger perspective when he noted that the Commission 'had never so far taken intent into consideration'.[191] In his view, States would take their decisions knowingly by definition. Therefore, no need would arise to emphasise an intent requirement.[192]

This view was, however, disputed by the second group. At the forefront of this group, Paul Reuter said that he saw no reason why intent should not be included in the draft Article.[193] He found support among a great variety of other members of the Commission who either emphasised that the intent requirement appeared as the solution to the most difficult problems of the provision on complicity[194] or urged it to be retained and clarified.[195] Other members of the Commission confined themselves to pointing to the difficulties in establishing the intent of a State.[196] Yet another proposal was made by Doudou Thiam, who was of the view that there should be a presumption of intent or at least knowledge on the

---

[189] *Ibid.*, emphasis added.
[190] Frank X. J. C. Njenga, Statement at the 1518th Meeting of the ILC, YBILC 1978, Vol. I, p. 236, para. 28. This was vehemently contested by Stephen M. Schwebel, who gave the example that 'Hitler's plans of aggression had been published in explicit detail', Statement at the 1519th Meeting of the ILC, YBILC 1978, Vol. I, p. 237, para. 37.
[191] Nikolai A. Ushakov, Statement at the 1518th Meeting of the ILC, YBILC 1978, Vol. I, p. 233, para. 4.
[192] *Ibid.*
[193] Paul Reuter, Statement at the 1519th Meeting of the ILC, YBILC 1978, Vol. I, p. 235, para. 23.
[194] Stephen M. Schwebel, Statement at the 1519th meeting of the ILC, YBILC 1978, Vol. I, p. 237, para. 36; Alexander Yankov, Statement at the 1519th meeting of the ILC, YBILC 1978, Vol. I, p. 238, para. 3.
[195] C. W. Pinto, Statement at the 1518th Meeting of the ILC, YBILC 1978, Vol. I, p. 234, para. 13; Doudou Tabibi, Statement at the 1518th Meeting of the ILC, YBILC 1978, Vol. I, p. 235, para. 17.
[196] Jorge Castañeda, Statement at the 1517th Meeting of the ILC, YBILC 1978, Vol. I, p. 230, para. 12.

part of the complicit State which would then have the burden of proof of showing that it did not fulfil the necessary subjective requirements.[197] Roberto Ago summarised the discussion in a rather solomonic way. He considered that, 'if intent should not, perhaps, be overemphasized, it was impossible to pass it over in silence, since a State could not be accused of complicity if it had acted in all innocence'.[198]

While the Commission thus glossed over the differences with respect to the question of intent, the problem had not gone unnoticed by States. Our survey of governmental statements has shown that the question of intent or knowledge was a common and central concern to States.[199] It was thus only natural that in the course of the Second Reading, Special Rapporteur James Crawford again accorded quite some attention to the problem. Departing from the standpoint that it would be too harsh to impose a standard of strict liability on assisting States, he held that, '[g]iven the nature of inter-State relations and the great diversity of situations which may be involved, article 27 should cover only those cases where the assistance is clearly and unequivocally connected to the subsequent wrongful act'.[200] In the ensuing discussion among the members of the Commission, widespread support for the Special Rapporteur's position was expressed. Bruno Simma 'heartily welcomed' the incorporation of the subjective element into the provision although it was a departure from the Commission's usual practice.[201] Still others found subparagraph (a) of the draft Article to be 'pleonastic', as Ian Brownlie put it, 'as the elements of aiding, assisting' would already encompass the element of knowledge.[202]

The Commission was also confronted with an array of widely differing governmental comments. While some States urged the Commission to strengthen the element of intent,[203] others, such as the Netherlands,

---

[197] Doudou Thiam, Statement at the 1519th Meeting of the ILC, YBILC 1978, Vol. I, p. 238, para. 8.
[198] Roberto Ago, Statement at the 1519th Meeting of the ILC, YBILC 1978, Vol. I, p. 240, para. 25.
[199] See above in Chapter 4, text accompanying notes 338 et seq.
[200] James Crawford, 'Second Report on State Responsibility', UN Doc. A/CN.4/488/Add.1, para. 178.
[201] Bruno Simma, Statement at the 2577th Meeting of the ILC, YBILC 1999, Vol. I, p. 70, para. 26.
[202] Ian Brownlie, Statement at the 2577th Meeting of the ILC, YBILC 1999, Vol. I, p. 70, para. 27.
[203] See, e.g., the statement of the United Kingdom, UN Doc. A/CN.4/488 (1998), pp. 75–6.

asked the Commission to provide for responsibility for aiding and assisting not only when there was knowledge of the circumstances of the internationally wrongful act but also when there *should* have been knowledge.[204] In the view of these conflicting demands, it was not surprising that no further clarification on the subjective part of the provision was introduced into the provision. Rather, it was the Commentary which was supposed to elucidate these questions.[205]

2.3 Interpretation of the provision

2.3.1 Various interpretations of the subjective element

It is a matter of debate whether this can be considered a convincing solution. In a comparison between draft Article 27 as adopted on First Reading and Article 16 ASR, it is notable that the requirement that the aid or assistance given to another State must be 'rendered *for* the commission of an internationally wrongful act'[206] no longer figures in Article 16. Rather, Article 16 includes only a reference to the 'knowledge of the circumstances of the internationally wrongful act'. According to the Commentary, this is supposed to mean that 'the aid or assistance must be given *with a view to* facilitate the commission of the act and must actually do so'.[207]

The Commentary thus narrows the textual meaning of Article 16 and runs counter to the general thrust of the ILC Articles, which, *in general*, presuppose no distinct or separate requirement of fault or wrongful intent for an internationally wrongful act. However, again according to the Commentary, a requirement of fault or wrongful intent may be found in specific Articles of the Draft or may be derived from primary norms which impose different standards of liability.[208] It thus appears that the ILC wants Article 16 to be interpreted narrowly so that the 'knowledge' element turns into something more akin to a requirement of wrongful intent.[209] Likewise, the International Court of Justice has, *mutatis mutandis*, adopted this approach in its *Genocide Convention* case. Here, the Court was faced with the special intent requirement from the Genocide Convention, namely, the *dolus specialis* which is directed towards the elimination of a

---

[204] UN Doc. A/CN.4/515 (2001), p. 28.
[205] This was the conclusion drawn by James Crawford in light of the comments the ILC had received, see UN Doc. A/CN.4/517/Add.1, 3.
[206] Emphasis added.   [207] ILC Commentary, Art. 16, para. 3.
[208] See James Crawford, 'Introduction', p. 12.
[209] See similarly Alexandra Boivin, 'Complicity and Beyond', p. 471.

group protected under Article II of the Convention. Applying Article 16 ASR by means of analogy, the Court held that:

> [T]here is no doubt that the conduct of an organ or a person furnishing aid or assistance to a perpetrator of the crime of genocide cannot be treated as complicity in genocide unless *at the least* that organ or person acted knowingly, that is to say, in particular, was aware of the specific intent (*dolus specialis*) of the principal perpetrator.[210]

If the analogy to Article 16 ASR is supposed to be meaningful, this entails that knowledge of the circumstances of the wrongful act is required *at the least* (as the Court has put it) also with respect to Article 16. Moreover, the words 'at the least' suggest that, as a general rule, more than mere knowledge is required.[211] Most authors who have expressed views on the issue of complicity have, however, been sceptical towards the intent or knowledge requirements provided for by the ILC.[212] A variety of authors have criticised the intent requirement for making 'the whole construction of complicity unworkable'.[213] It would be especially difficult to prove the intent of the assisting State of actually wishing to further the commission of the wrongful act.[214] Some authors would therefore require only that the State has the possibility of obtaining the knowledge,[215] whether in terms of due diligence[216] or foreseeability.[217] In addition, it is also debated whether the assisting

---

[210] ICJ, *Case Concerning the Application of the Convention on the Prevention and Punishment of the Crime of Genocide*, Judgment, para. 421, emphasis on 'at the least' added.
[211] Georg Nolte and Helmut Philipp Aust, 'Equivocal Helpers', p. 14; see also Christian Dominicé, 'Attribution of Conduct', p. 286.
[212] See, e.g., Andreas Felder, *Die Beihilfe*, pp. 261 *et seq.*; Eckart Klein, 'Beihilfe', pp. 435–6; Kate Nahapetian, 'Confronting State Complicity in International Law', UCLA Journal of International Law and Foreign Affairs 7 (2002), pp. 99–127, at pp. 108 *et seq.*
[213] Bernhard Graefrath, 'Complicity', p. 375; John Quigley, 'Complicity', p. 111; Alexander Orakhelashvili, 'Division', pp. 650–1.
[214] Alexandra Boivin, 'Complicity and Beyond', p. 471; Andreas Felder, *Die Beihilfe*, p. 261; Mark Gibney, Katarina Tomasevski and Jens Vedsted-Hansen, 'Transnational State Responsibility', p. 294; André de Hoogh, 'Australia and East Timor – Rights Erga Omnes, Complicity and Non-Recognition', *Australian International Law Journal* 1999, pp. 63–90, at p. 79; Jessica Howard, 'Invoking State Responsibility', text accompanying note 186; Bruno Simma, 'Grundfragen', p. 380.
[215] Olivier Corten, 'Quels droits', p. 113; John Quigley, 'State Responsibility for Ethnic Cleansing', *UC Davis Law Review* 32 (1999), pp. 341–85, at p. 361.
[216] For a due diligence requirement *de lege ferenda*, see Stefan Talmon, 'Plurality', p. 219.
[217] Vaughan Lowe, 'Responsibility', p. 8; Brian D. Smith, *State Responsibility*, p. 12.

State must actually share the purpose of the primary law-breaker or whether it is sufficient to wish to further the concrete conduct to which assistance is furnished.[218] It has furthermore been argued that the intent requirement is exclusively a concern of Western States.[219] Some authors, however, have expressed support for the intent requirement as conceived by the ILC.[220]

2.3.2 Taking intent seriously

It is submitted here that the popular criticism of an intent requirement in Article 16 ASR fails to account for a number of important aspects. *Prima facie*, it appears indeed as if the intent requirement is taking away what the ILC has introduced itself, namely, responsibility for a great many cases in which States support others in the commission of internationally wrongful acts. It can be admitted that the way the ILC has introduced the intent requirement only into the Commentary and not into the text of the Articles has not been helpful. However, as the rules set out in the ILC Articles aspire to be customary in nature, an analysis of what the law prescribes cannot stop at the wording of the provisions.[221] Thus, to point to the wording of a provision which does not establish the intent requirement[222] is certainly not the end of the matter. Taking into consideration that it is a rule of customary international law which is being analysed, one should pay due attention to the governmental statements on the subjective element of Article 16 ASR. As was shown in the analysis of these comments, more States wished

---

[218] Roger S. Clark, 'Obligations', p. 648, note 60; Vaughan Lowe, 'Responsibility', pp. 8–9; Paolo Palchetti, 'Complicity in Genocide', p. 389; tentatively Monica Hakimi, 'State Bystander Responsibility', p. 365.

[219] Christine Chinkin, *Third Parties*, p. 298.

[220] See Maya Brehm, 'The Arms Trade and States' Duty to Ensure Respect for Humanitarian and Human Rights Law', *Journal of Conflict and Security Law* 12 (2008), pp. 359–87, at p. 385; Christian Dominicé, 'Attribution of Conduct', p. 286; Jörg Künzli, *Unrechtsregimes*, p. 408; Georg Nolte and Helmut Philipp Aust, 'Equivocal Helpers', pp. 13 et seq.; Maria Luisa Padelletti, *Pluralità di Stati*, p. 76 (but see also ibid., p. 97, for some critical remarks); Paolo Palchetti, 'Complicity in Genocide', p. 389; Thorsten Stein, 'International Measures Against Terrorism and Sanctions By and Against Third States', *Archiv des Völkerrechts* 30 (1992), pp. 38–54, at p. 49; Birgit Kessler, *Durchsetzung*, p. 109. That it was indeed intent and not knowledge which was 'intended' by the ILC is made clear by James Crawford, 'Responsibility of States', p. 13.

[221] Cf David D. Caron, 'The ILC Articles on State Responsibility: The Paradoxical Relationship Between Authority and Form', *American Journal of International Law* 96 (2002), pp. 857–73, at p. 869.

[222] See, e.g., Alexandra Boivin, 'Complicity and Beyond', p. 471.

to have the intent requirement strengthened[223] than weakened.[224] It is of course possible to assume that this reluctance on the part of States needs to be attributed to the fact that States are always cautious about more far-reaching restrictions of their sovereignty.[225] While this may certainly be true, it is no argument *per se* to construe a rule of customary international law against the expressed will of the States who are the law-makers in this regard. This is even more so as Article 16 ASR does not rest on an entirely settled international practice. A provision which is still described by some authors as belonging to the progressive development of international law[226] should not be interpreted in the broadest possible form.[227] Such an interpretation would be detached from international practice and would give rise to expectations on the establishment of responsibility for complicity which are not warranted.

Emphasising the importance of the intent element is, however, not just a matter of accommodating State interests and reflecting the bleak picture of international relations. It is also consistent with a systematic interpretation of the complicity provision in light of its underlying theoretical assumptions. In order to understand what responsibility for complicity actually means, it is necessary to refer back once more to the fundamental assumption underlying the construction of Article 16 ASR: responsibility is ascribed for behaviour which is *per se* not unlawful. This was evinced more clearly in the original draft Article 25, in which it was stated that 'the conduct in question would not otherwise be internationally wrongful' – one (if not the only) advantage of the original draft over the final provision of Article 16 ASR.[228] Although no

---

[223] See the statements of the Czech Republic (UN Doc. A/C.6/54/SR.22, para. 80), the Republic of Korea (UN Doc. A/CN.4/515, 27), the United Kingdom (UN Doc. A/C.6/33/SR.37, para. 18; UN Doc. A/CN.4/488, 75–6; UN Doc. A/CN.4/515, 27–8) and the United States (UN Doc. A/CN.4/488, 76; UN Doc. A/CN.4/515, 28; UN Doc. A/C.6/56/SR.14, para. 76).

[224] See the statements of Argentina (UN Doc. A/CN.4/515/Add.3, 4), Mexico (UN Doc. A/C.6/55/SR.20, para. 42) and the Netherlands (UN Doc. A/CN.4/515, 28).

[225] Which holds especially true for the field of State responsibility: see Bruno Simma, 'Grundfragen', p. 358.

[226] See, e.g., James Crawford, 'Responsibility of States', p. 13; Wolff Heintschel von Heinegg, 'Wider die Mär', p. 222, note 4; see also Bruno Simma, Statement at the 2578th Meeting of the ILC, YBILC 1999, Vol. I, Part One, p. 78, para. 40.

[227] Cf, *mutatis mutandis*, the traditional *'in dubio mitius'* rule: PCIJ, *Article 3, paragraph 2 of the Treaty of Lausanne (Frontier between Turkey and Iraq)*, Advisory Opinion, Series B, No. 12, 25.

[228] See similarly Constantin Economides, Statement at the 2577th Meeting of the ILC, YBILC 1999, Vol. I, Part One, p. 68, para. 4.

longer included in the text of the Article, this underlying assumption was never abandoned.[229] After all, the very rationale for having a provision on complicity in the ASR is to ascribe responsibility for conduct which would not otherwise trigger responsibility. As the ICJ has found in its *Genocide Convention* case, it would not make much sense to provide for responsibility for complicity if the State in question had already incurred responsibility for having committed the principal act.[230] At the same time, Article 16 ASR has a vast field of potential application as it covers all kinds of internationally wrongful acts and is not limited to breaches of a particular gravity or to violations of obligations of a *jus cogens* character or giving rise to obligations *erga omnes*.[231] A complicity provision without an intent requirement would arguably move the provision very close to responsibility for lawful behaviour. In the preceding section, we have also seen that notions of causality will in most cases not effectively limit the scope of application of Article 16 ASR.

In this context, we may refer back to the impact of the principle of abuse of rights on the problem of complicity.[232] As we discussed in Chapter 3 of this study, the imposition of responsibility for complicity somewhat mirrors the rationale of the prohibition of abuse of rights in international law.[233] Abuse of rights also presupposes a subjective element, i.e., the wish to harm another State through an otherwise lawful exercise of rights. A requirement of intent is also the only possible conceptual means to distinguish the situation of complicity in the sense of Article 16 ASR from the typical situation of *non-refoulement* (the *Soering* scenario[234]).

It is difficult to see how one could sensibly distinguish between ordinary forms of cooperation and aid or assistance in the commission of a wrongful act if the intent element is discarded.[235] In such

---

[229] Cf Bernhard Graefrath, 'Complicity', pp. 374–5.
[230] ICJ, *Case Concerning the Application of the Convention on the Prevention and Punishment of the Crime of Genocide*, Judgment, para. 380.
[231] Bernhard Graefrath, 'Complicity', p. 377.
[232] See our discussion in Chapter 3, text accompanying notes 98 *et seq*.
[233] As is shown especially by those cases in which the principle of abuse of rights is introduced to emphasise the obligation of a State not to allow its territory to be used to the detriment of another State; cf Hersch Lauterpacht, *The Function of Law*, p. 303; Ellery C. Stowell, *International Law*, p. 123; see further Jean Combacau and Serge Sur, *Droit international public*, p. 429.
[234] See above note 148.
[235] Maria Luisa Padelletti, *Pluralità di Stati*, p. 79; Christian Dominicé, 'Attribution of Conduct', p. 286.

a case, cooperation would turn into a particularly hazardous form of conduct – in fact, Article 16 ASR would introduce a risk-based form of responsibility through the back door. Risk-based responsibility for complicity may be justified where particularly important legal values are at stake. For example, we can imagine the rule against *refoulement* as such an emanation.[236] In the face of imminent torture by another State, such a risk-based form of responsibility is the only possible means to safeguard the human dignity of the person to be extradited. If it were otherwise, there would be no means to remedy this situation. For the vast majority of cases, however, we need to keep in mind that cooperation is vital for the realisation of important community goals.[237] International law should be an enabling factor in this regard, not a suffocating one. The European Court of Human Rights has made this clear when it considered the limits of inter-State cooperation.[238] Christine Chinkin has also reminded us that

[g]overnments have an obligation to exercise due diligence in ensuring the safety of their citizens. Assisting other states in these tasks is part of the duty of cooperation and of fostering good relations between states. Similarly, in the context of post-conflict administration 'burden sharing and unity of command are the twin pillars of successful nation-building'.[239]

In other words, the widest possible interpretation of Article 16 ASR would not only stand in contravention of the international practice of States but could thus also lead to other negative results. The interdependence of States in today's world has become proverbial, if not a cliché. However, there is substance to the point about the scale and intricacy of the existing interconnections such that a broadly defined provision on complicity – such as Article 16 ASR without an intent requirement – would multiply the bases of responsibility beyond sensible reach.[240] It is in the interest of the international community not just to develop a morally satisfactory provision on complicity but also one which is 'workable'.[241] At this point, we should remember what

---

[236] Cf Christian J. Tams, 'Abuse', p. 318; see further our discussion of *non-refoulement* in Chapter 8, text accompanying notes 74 *et seq.*
[237] Georg Nolte and Helmut Philipp Aust, 'Equivocal Helpers', p. 12.
[238] ECtHR, *Drozd and Janousek v. France and Spain*, Series A, No. 240, para. 110.
[239] Christine Chinkin, 'Continuing Occupation?', p. 182, footnote omitted.
[240] Eckart Klein, 'Beihilfe', p. 437.
[241] Bernhard Graefrath, 'Complicity', pp. 377 *et seq.*

Joseph Raz has identified as an important element of the rule of law: the law 'must be capable of being obeyed'.[242]

2.3.3 Practical issues

One should of course not neglect the problems associated with the requirement of intent. It is well known and need not be repeated here at great lengths that psychological requirements with respect to States are problematic insofar as the State cannot have a certain will.[243] It has also been observed that 'we cannot assume to know these states better than those [State] organs themselves'.[244] David Enoch expressed this dilemma in the following way when he wrote about the intentions of States:

> But now think about the nature of such mental states: they are determined by the intention of individuals, by facts about decision-making mechanisms, by matters of institutional design, by internal power struggles. They are, in other words, highly complex and, in a sense, also artificial things.[245]

It is, however, doubtful whether discarding the notion of intent in Article 16 ASR would make a great difference for the field of non-judicial dispute settlement between States. Just because one would no longer require intent, it is not to be expected that injured States would face fewer hurdles to holding complicit States responsible. Most certainly, the latter would use other arguments to defend their conduct. How abstract notions and criteria such as intent will be applied in diplomatic settlements is another question again. In diplomatic contexts, deviations from the standards set out in the ASR occur frequently.[246] In other words, rewriting the requirements of a provision in the law of State responsibility in order to accommodate diplomatic negotiations not only is questionable in terms of doctrinal clarity but also potentially useless, as the settlement of individual disputes can always lead to a modification of the general principles.

---

[242] Joseph Raz, 'The Rule of Law and Its Virtue', p. 213.
[243] Cf Dionisio Anzilotti, 'La responsabilité internationale', p. 287; Hans Kelsen, 'Unrecht und Unrechsfolge', p. 539.
[244] Martti Koskenniemi, *From Apology to Utopia*, p. 269.
[245] David Enoch, 'Intending, Foreseeing, and the State', *Legal Theory* 13 (2007), pp. 69–99, at p. 86.
[246] Kazuhiro Nakatani, 'Diplomacy and State Responsibility', in Maurizio Ragazzi (ed.), *International Responsibility Today – Essays in Memory of Oscar Schachter* (Leiden: Nijhoff, 2005), pp. 37–47, at p. 38.

For our purposes, this raises the question on which type of situation we should base our considerations. Should we interpret the law of State responsibility with a view to its application in the situation where concerned States judge their behaviour for themselves? Or should we interpret its rules in light of their possible application in the increasingly rich landscape of international courts and tribunals?[247] While it is not possible to answer this question in the abstract, we should consider what inferences we should draw from this multiplicity of different situations and fora in which rules on complicity may play a role. In our opinion, it cannot be the goal to construct a rule on complicity which is based on considerations of the least favourable environment for its application, namely, the bilateral dispute situation in which one State flatly rejects its responsibility. Article 16 ASR will need to be applied in a variety of scenarios in which the situation is more favourable, i.e., in which international courts and tribunals can pronounce themselves on the issue, or when domestic courts (which are in an even better position to judge the attitude of their forum State) do the same.

Nevertheless, this should not deflect our attention from practical problems with the finding of intent by a State which impact upon the work of international courts and tribunals.[248] The alleged difficulty of proving the intent of the assisting State (to actually render the aid or assistance with a view to the furtherance of the commission of the internationally wrongful act) is one of the focal points of criticism with respect to the mental element. In this respect, we will have to take into account that the issues of intent and knowledge have a considerable overlap with standards concerning evidence and proof.

As a preliminary remark, it appears as if the authors who have made critical remarks on the difficulties of establishing the intent of States have an over-idealised view of establishing the intent of individual persons.[249] It is apparent that domestic legal systems have no ready-made rules or procedures at hand which would help them to determine whether a person acted intentionally or not. It is a judicial exercise in which very often the intent of a person is inferred from his actual demeanour. This does not, however, mean that the subjective element

---

[247] On these two scenarios for the application of international law, see Robert Kolb, *Interprétation et création*, pp. 286 et seq.
[248] Cf Andrea Gattini, *Zufall und force majeure*, p. 221.
[249] Proof of intent of complicit individuals is similarly difficult to prove, see, e.g., Christopher Kutz, *Complicity*, p. 234.

is discarded altogether.[250] Rather, it is treated as a separate criterion for civil or criminal liability. In fact, this is not dissimilar to the way international law deals with a psychological element in another context: the establishment of customary international law. Here, it is also the case that very often *opinio juris* will be inferred from State practice,[251] but, very importantly, this is not done in all cases and according to the majority of authorities it should also not lead to an abandonment of the psychological element of custom.[252] Bin Cheng has pointed out that, just as in other areas of law, the intention of States may be ascertained and are deducible from what a State has said or done. Psychological elements in law would not necessarily correspond to reality; instead, the establishment of a psychological element in international law would almost always be an intellectual construct.[253]

If we accept that the establishment of intent will not be possible along the lines of ready-made and clear-cut formulae, we need to turn to the question of how international courts and tribunals take and assess evidence. This assessment needs to depart from the general principle that it is the party alleging a fact which bears the burden of proof (*actori incumbit probatio*).[254] The parties to a dispute before an international court are, however, also under an obligation to cooperate with the court or tribunal and to supply it with all the evidence they have on all conceivable matters of fact and law in the case.[255]

---

[250] Cf Andrea Gattini, *Zufall und force majeure*, p. 221.
[251] Maurice H. Mendelson, 'Formation', p. 290; Christian J. Tams, *Enforcing Obligations Erga Omnes*, p. 238; John Quigley, 'Complicity', p. 100; Alfred Verdross and Bruno Simma, *Universelles Völkerrecht*, § 562.
[252] Mark E. Villiger, *Customary International Law and Treaties – A Manual on the Theory and Practice of the Interrelation of Sources*, 2nd edn (The Hague: Kluwer, 1997), p. 50; Alain Pellet, 'Article 38', paras. 231 *et seq.*
[253] Bin Cheng, 'Custom: The Future of General State Practice in a Divided World', in Ronald St John Macdonald and Douglas M. Johnston (eds.), *The Structure and Process of International Law*, (Dordrecht: Nijhoff, 1986), pp. 513–54, at pp. 530–1.
[254] Chittharanjan F. Amerasinghe, *Evidence in International Litigation* (Leiden: Nijhoff, 2005), pp. 61–2; Shabtai Rosenne, *The Law and Practice of the International Court of Justice 1920–2005*, Vol. III, 4th edn (Leiden: Nijhoff, 2006), p. 1040; Tobias Thienel, 'The Burden and Standard of Proof in the European Court of Human Rights', *German Yearbook of International Law* 50 (2007), pp. 543–88, at pp. 550–1.
[255] Chittharanjan F. Amerasinghe, *Evidence*, p. 97. If a party refuses to produce evidence, the court in question may draw adverse inferences from this behaviour. Such a refusal may even be considered as an admission, cf Gérard Niyungeko, *La preuve devant les juridictions internationales* (Brussels: Bruylant, 2005), pp. 184 *et seq.*; Rüdiger Wolfrum, 'Taking and Assessing Evidence in International Adjudication', in Tafsir Malick Ndiaye and Rüdiger Wolfrum (eds.), *Law of the Sea, Environmental Law*

Some authors argue that the intent or knowledge of the aiding or assisting State should, as a matter of principle, be inferred from its conduct.[256] The onus would then be upon that State to exonerate itself from the assumption that it has furnished its support with a view to facilitating the commission of the internationally wrongful act. Two considerations speak against this position. First, this would run counter to the general principle just mentioned, i.e., that the party which brings a claim carries the burden of proof. However, this rule can of course be reversed in specific instances.[257] The second and stronger consideration is that it would then be upon the allegedly complicit State to prove that it did not have the intent to furnish aid or assistance to the internationally wrongful act. It would thus need to prove 'a negative'.[258] In its *Nicaragua* case, the ICJ recognised that this is a particularly difficult exercise when it stated that '[t]he evidence or material offered by Nicaragua in connection with the allegation of arms supply has to be assessed bearing in mind the fact that, in responding to the allegation, Nicaragua has to prove a negative'.[259] Likewise, for a State which faces the allegation that it was complicit in a violation of international law, it would be particularly difficult to prove that it did not intend to do so. It thus seems more appropriate to retain the traditional model insofar as it requires the claimant to prove its cause, given that the procedural law of international courts and tribunals provides mechanisms to assist the State which brings the claim in this regard.

2.3.4 Necessary modifications of the intent requirement

Nevertheless, a caveat is appropriate here. The requirement of wrongful intent should not allow States to deny their responsibility

---

and *Settlement of Disputes – Liber Amicorum Judge Thomas A. Mensah* (Leiden: Nijhoff, 2007), pp. 341–56, at p. 353. This consequence will, however, not automatically be drawn from the non-compliance with a request by the Court under Article 49 of its Statute, cf Christian J. Tams, 'Article 49', in Andreas Zimmermann, Christian Tomuschat and Karin Oellers-Frahm (eds.), *The Statute of the International Court of Justice – A Commentary* (Oxford: Oxford University Press, 2006), para. 19; see further ICJ, *Corfu Channel Case*, Judgment, ICJ Rep. 1949, 4, 32; as well as the report on a procedural decision in the *Diversion of Waters from the Meuse Case* in PCIJ, Series E, No. 14, 149.

[256] Cf, e.g., Eckart Klein, 'Beihilfe', p. 436; Doudou Thiam, Statement at the 1519th Meeting of the ILC, YBILC 1978, Vol. I, p. 238, para. 8.
[257] Chittharanjan F. Amerasinghe, *Evidence*, p. 89.
[258] Rüdiger Wolfrum, 'Taking and Assessing Evidence', p. 353.
[259] ICJ, *Military and Paramilitary Activities In and Against Nicaragua*, Merits, ICJ Rep. 1986, 14, para. 147.

for complicity in situations where internationally wrongful acts are manifestly being committed. The intent standard of Article 16 ASR could be subject to modifications under certain conditions. As James Crawford has pointed out, it was the assumption of the ILC Articles that different primary rules could provide for different standards of knowledge and intent which need to be fulfilled for a State to incur responsibility.[260] A less rigorous requirement of knowledge and intent may be found in the regime of serious breaches of peremptory rules under general international law, an issue that will be looked at more closely when that regime is analysed.[261] However, there may also be other situations in which the standard of intent may be modified.[262] One such example may be a State permitting its territory to be used by other States. In the *Corfu Channel* case, Albania incurred responsibility *vis-à-vis* the United Kingdom for the explosion of several mines in the Corfu Channel.[263] As Albania did not have the technical means to lay the mines, they must have been laid by a third State. While most of the evidence pointed towards Yugoslavia, this could not be formally established due to a lack of evidence and, above all, because Yugoslavia was not a party to the dispute before the Court.[264] Nevertheless, the Court held Albania responsible for not having warned the United Kingdom of the presence of the mines in its territorial waters. How could Albania have been supposed to know about the mines? The judgment stipulated that Albania must have known about the laying of the mines as the explosions occurred very close to the Albanian coast. A test which was carried out by a fact-finding mission established that even under the most unfavourable conditions, it would have been impossible not to notice a ship laying the mines given the very close proximity of the mines to the Albanian coast. Albania was thus presumed to know about the activities occurring in its territorial waters and thus within its territorial sovereignty. In particular – and here the question of intent mingled with the issue of evidence and proof[265] – the United Kingdom was

---

[260] James Crawford, 'Introduction', p. 13.   [261] See below Chapter 7.
[262] Cf Rosalyn Higgins, *Of Problems and Process* (Oxford: Clarendon Press, 1994), p. 156.
[263] ICJ, *Corfu Channel Case*, Judgment, ICJ Rep. 1949, 4.
[264] The *Monetary Gold* rule was formally developed only after the *Corfu Channel Case*: see ICJ, *Monetary Gold Removed from Rome in 1943*, Judgment, ICJ Rep. 1954, 19 and further in Chapter 6 of this study, section 2, text accompanying notes 133 et seq.
[265] Ian Brownlie, *State Responsibility*, p. 47.

allowed to have recourse to more flexible means in order to substantiate its claim.

Furthermore, a modification of the intent standard may be called for due to differing standards in human rights law.[266] The Inter-American Court of Human Rights has interpreted Article 1(1) of the American Convention on Human Rights[267] so as to require the State 'to organise the government in such a way as to guarantee rights recognised in the Convention' and to protect individuals against violations of the Convention committed by non-State actors with the acquiescence of the host State.[268] The Court made use of a due diligence standard in order to arrive at this conclusion.[269] It is true that State obligations towards the conduct of non-State actors and towards other States are two different things. Yet, it is questionable whether a distinction between the standards of care to be employed by a host State in ensuring the fulfilment of its human rights obligations is adequate for the aim of the human rights obligations: the most effective protection of the human rights of the persons within a State's jurisdiction. From the perspective of the victim of a forcible abduction, it does not make much difference whether the host State acquiesces in and maybe even supports an abduction by non-State actors or by the security personnel of another State. The effect on the abducted person is, at least *prima facie*, the same. The common denominator of the two situations is that a State is acquiescing in or even contributing to conduct on its territory which leads to serious human rights violations.

However, the question remains whether other reasons could militate against such heightened duties of vigilance towards other States. For example, this could be the case when a Status of Forces Agreement between a host State and a foreign State has established such a degree of control by the foreign State over a military base in the host State's territory that the latter cannot be expected to be able to scrutinise

---

[266] Cf Giorgio Gaja, Statement at the 2577th Meeting of the ILC, YBILC 1999, Vol. I, Part One, p. 73, para. 54. The issue how human rights law impacts upon situations in which complicity is at stake will be addressed in greater detail in Chapter 8, section 2, text accompanying notes 63 *et seq.*

[267] Article 1(1) reads in relevant parts: 'The State Parties to this Convention undertake to respect the rights and freedoms recognized herein and to ensure to all persons subject to their jurisdiction the free and full exercise of those rights and freedoms.' American Convention on Human Rights of 22 November 1969, entered into force on 18 July 1978, OAS Treaty Series No. 36.

[268] Inter-AmCtHR, *Velásquez Rodríguez v. Honduras*, Series C, No. 4, paras. 166 *et seq.*

[269] *Ibid.*, para. 174.

the foreign State's conduct in an effective manner.[270] Similar considerations apply when diplomatic immunities are used as a shield for unlawful behaviour by the foreign State.[271] While it is clear that these diplomatic immunities do not absolve the authorities of the foreign State from respect for the host State's laws and public order, they present themselves as a serious obstacle to a more rigorous scrutiny of the activities of the foreign State on the host State's territory. Another comparable situation is the use of the host State's airspace and airbases for the transportation of detainees. If this transportation is carried out by State aircraft, these presumably also enjoy immunity.[272] In all three cases, however, the situation is likely to change once the host State has viable information at its hands that the foreign State is abusing its privileges in order to carry out human rights violations. All immunities accorded to the foreign State have only a functional character.[273] This means that they are not to be construed in such a way as to allow the foreign State to shield itself behind these immunities. Technically speaking, the host State will always be warranted to conduct a search in the premises of the embassy or in a State aircraft if it believes, for example, that a person unlawfully abducted and being transported to another country in order to be subjected to torture or inhuman and degrading treatment will be found in the premises or the aircraft. From a factual perspective, however, this is unlikely to occur. If the abuse of the immunities cannot be proven, then the host State would itself have committed a serious violation of international law. Therefore, it is highly unlikely that such searches will be conducted unless the host State can be reasonably sure that the immunities it has accorded to the foreign State are being abused.

---

[270] Cf European Commission for Democracy through Law (Venice Commission), 'Opinion on the International Legal Obligations of Council of Europe Member States in Respect of Secret Detention Facilities and Inter-State Transport of Prisoners', Opinion No. 363/2005 of 17 March 2006, CDL-AD(2006)009, paras. 105 et seq.

[271] See further J. Craig Barker, *The Abuse of Diplomatic Privileges and Immunities – A Necessary Evil?* (Aldershot: Ashgate, 1996), pp. 94 et seq.

[272] See, again, European Commission for Democracy through Law (Venice Commission), 'Opinion on the International Legal Obligations of Council of Europe Member States in Respect of Secret Detention Facilities and Inter-State Transport of Prisoners', Opinion No. 363/2005 of 17 March 2006, CDL-AD(2006)009, para. 95.

[273] That other State conduct is not shielded by any kind of immunity is also underlined by the *dictum* of the PCIJ in the *Lotus* case, where it held that first and foremost States are not entitled to exercise jurisdiction in another State's territory; see PCIJ, *Lotus*, Judgment, Series A, No. 10, at p. 18.

These considerations are not based solely on pragmatic grounds. Immunities of foreign States and their officials have a longstanding basis in international law and thus contribute to the 'normative environment' which is to be taken into account when Article 16 ASR is interpreted.[274] While this principle originally derives from Article 31(3)(c) of the Vienna Convention on the Law of Treaties and thus relates to treaty interpretation, it also represents the 'general principle of "systemic integration" whereby international obligations are interpreted by reference to their normative environment'.[275] The question of which degree of vigilance is required of potentially complicit States can thus not always be determined in the abstract but needs to be assessed with reference both to the factual situation and to other normative factors which impact on the case at hand.

Given the frequently unreliable degree of information, it is therefore questionable whether a host State can be expected to exert a degree of scrutiny towards another State comparable to the degree of scrutiny it may exert over non-State actors. This is also a question of international comity. In the ordinary course of events, States are entitled to presume that the actions of other States are lawful.[276] However, there is no room for such comity when the wrongfulness of a given conduct is clearly established.[277] If, for example, there is reliable information that a foreign State is using the host State's territory for serious human rights violations, the host State would at the very least be required to initiate investigations.[278] Therefore, it is also warranted to assume a due diligence standard with respect to the conduct of foreign States on the host State's territory. In such a situation, it needs to be determined what kind of diligence is due in the specific case. The assessment of this standard may vary from case to case, taking into consideration factors such as the reliability of the foreign State, its general human rights record, information about human rights

---

[274] Cf, *mutatis mutandis*, ECtHR, *Al-Adsani* v. *United Kingdom*, ECHR 2001-XI, 79, para. 55.
[275] 'Fragmentation of International Law: Difficulties Arising from the Diversification and Expansion of International Law', Report of the Study Group of the International Law Commission, finalized by Martti Koskenniemi, UN Doc. A/CN.4/L.682, para. 413.
[276] Cf Vaughan Lowe, 'Responsibility', p. 10.
[277] This consideration also emerges from Supreme Court of Canada, *Canada (Justice)* v. *Khadr*, 2008 SCC 28, paras. 24 *et seq.*; see further Georg Nolte and Helmut Philipp Aust, 'Equivocal Helpers', p. 16.
[278] On investigatory duties stemming from the ECHR, see Christoph Grabenwarter, *Europäische Menschenrechtskonvention*, § 20, para. 18, with further references to the case law of the ECtHR.

violations committed abroad and the willingness of the foreign State to cooperate in such investigations.

2.4 Conclusion

The intent requirement is thus to be taken seriously. Unlike the majority of authors who have dealt with the problem, our position is that it is indispensable for two major reasons: first of all because of the structure of the provision and its systematic place in the international legal order; and, secondly, because of otherwise overbroad ascriptions of responsibility. It is a different matter how intent will be established and whether in special cases less imposing standards may apply. In judicial proceedings, international courts and tribunals have a variety of procedural means at their hands in order to assess the intent of a State in the sense of whether or not it wished to aid or assist in the commission of an internationally wrongful act. Outside of court proceedings, it is not legal interpretation pure and simple anyway: the question whether a State will be able to obtain reparation from a complicit State will most likely be determined by other factors and not by the difficulties of proving its adversary's intent.

3 Complicity and the pacta tertiis rule: Article 16(b) ASR

The third element of Article 16 which calls for interpretation is its subparagraph (b), which requires that 'the act would be internationally wrongful if committed by that State', meaning that the aiding or assisting State needs to be bound by the rule that the main actor is violating. As the ILC sets out in its Commentary, 'a State is not bound by obligations of another State *vis-à-vis* third States. This basic principle is also embodied in articles 34 and 35 of the Vienna Convention on the Law of Treaties.'[279] These provisions state:

Article 34 General rule regarding third States

A treaty does not create either obligations or rights for a third State without its consent.

Article 35 Treaties providing for obligations for third States

An obligation arises for a third State from a provision of a treaty if the parties to the treaty intend the provision to be the means of establishing the obligation and the third State expressly accepts that obligation in writing.

---

[279] ILC Commentary, Article 16, para. 6.

In short, these rules spell out the age-old maxim of *pacta tertiis nec nocent nec prosunt*.[280] On the face of it, this part of Article 16 ASR does not seem to pose particular problems. At a closer look, however, two questions merit further attention. The first issue is whether the inclusion of Article 16(b) is warranted in general terms (section 3.1). Secondly, it has to be asked whether in some cases it is difficult to establish if the assisting State is really bound by the rule that the main actor has violated (section 3.2).

3.1 Complicity and the pacta tertiis rule

At first sight, the introduction of sub-paragraph (b) into the provision on complicity appears to be reasonable. It is indeed problematic to hold States responsible for having aided another State in the commission of an act which would not be wrongful if committed by the supporting State. One of the arguments raised in the discussion of the ILC was that in the absence of such a requirement the provision on complicity would stray too far into the realm of primary rules, as it would effectively establish new obligations of the complicit State.[281] While the introduction of this requirement was generally welcomed by the majority of the members of the ILC who commented on it,[282] some also voiced criticism. Constantin Economides, for example, maintained:

> That provision considerably reduced, without good reason, the scope of application of article 27. It did not exclude bilateral obligations alone. It also excluded multilateral obligations by which the aiding or assisting State was not bound. The condition was not necessary, since it was most unlikely that a State would knowingly and deliberately help another State to breach its bilateral or multilateral treaty obligations. Neither the commentary to the draft articles adopted on First Reading nor the second report of the Special Rapporteur contained any examples drawn from international practice.[283]

---

[280] Cf Christos L. Rozakis, 'Treaties and Third States: A Study in the Reinforcement of the Consensual Standards in International Law', *Zeitschrift für ausländisches öffentliches Recht und Völkerrecht* 35 (1975), pp. 1–40, at p. 4; Christian Tomuschat, 'Völkerrechtlicher Vertrag', pp. 9 *et seq.*; Eric David, 'Article 34', in Olivier Corten and Pierre Klein (eds.), *Les Conventions de Vienne sur le droit des traités – Commentaire article par article*, Vols. I–III (Brussels: Bruylant, 2006), para. 1.

[281] James Crawford, Statement at the 2577th Meeting of the ILC, YBILC 1999, Vol. I, Part One, p. 68, para. 11.

[282] Bruno Simma, Statement at the 2577th Meeting of the ILC, YBILC 1999, Vol. I, Part One, p. 70, para. 25; Ian Brownlie, *ibid.*, para. 27; Robert Rosenstock, *ibid.*, p. 71, para. 31; Gerhard Hafner, Statement at the 2578th Meeting of the ILC, YBILC 1999, Vol. I, Part One, p. 74, para. 1, and p. 75, para. 9.

[283] Statement of Constantin Economides at the 2577th Meeting of the ILC, YBILC 1999, Vol. I, Part One, p. 68, para. 5.

Economides thereby attacked the critical point in the construction of sub-paragraph (b). The condition for holding complicit States responsible only if they are bound to the rule violated by the main actor is difficult to deduce from international practice. One can of course point out that the cases assembled both by the ILC and by other surveys of international practice – as in Chapter 4 of this study – show that responsibility has indeed only been raised in cases which fulfil this criterion.[284] However, it has to be admitted that it is problematic to deduce this criterion from the absence of practice indicating the contrary.[285] Is 'negative practice' in this regard crucial? Or is it rather the case that this issue has so far escaped the attention of States? It is indeed difficult if not impossible to establish what has been the determining factor in this regard.

The ILC, and especially its Special Rapporteur James Crawford, therefore took refuge in structural considerations, and imported the *pacta tertiis* rule from the law of treaties into the law of State responsibility. While nothing speaks against the continued validity of this rule in the field of the law of treaties,[286] it has been questioned whether the principle necessarily applies to situations of complicity.[287] In order to further substantiate his position on the matter, Special Rapporteur James Crawford conducted a comparative law survey of whether domestic legal systems would generally impose liability upon a private party inducing a breach of contract by another party owed to a third party.[288] Whereas he found considerable support for this position in British,

---

[284] See Andreas Felder, *Die Beihilfe*, p. 246.
[285] For a discussion of this problem, see in general Max Sørensen, *Les sources du droit international – Etude sur la jurisprudence de la Cour permanente de la Justice internationale* (Copenhagen: Munskgaard, 1946), pp. 98 *et seq.*; Vaughan Lowe, *International Law*, pp. 45–6; Wolff Heintschel von Heinegg, 'Die weiteren Quellen', p. 219.
[286] Anthony Aust, *Modern Treaty Law and Practice*, 2nd edn (Cambridge: Cambridge University Press, 2007), pp. 256–7; Eric David, 'Article 34', paras. 1 *et seq.*; Alfred Verdross and Bruno Simma, *Universelles Völkerrecht*, § 771; Bruno Simma, 'From Bilateralism to Community Interest', pp. 375–6; Wolff Heintschel von Heinegg, 'Die völkerrechtlichen Verträge als Hauptrechtsquelle des Völkerrechts', in Knut Ipsen, *Völkerrecht*, 5th edn (Munich: C. H. Beck, 2004), pp. 112–209, at pp. 157 *et seq.*; but see Hans Kelsen, *Principles of International Law*, p. 348: 'It is … a characteristic tendency of modern international law to restrict this principle. Treaties imposing obligations upon third states have been generally recognized in a steadily increasing measure.'
[287] Vaughan Lowe, 'Responsibility', p. 7; Alexander Orakhelashvili, 'Division', p. 652.
[288] James Crawford, 'Second Report on State Responsibility', UN Doc. A/CN.4/498/Add.3.

French and German law – although differing in degree and under different doctrinal premises – this result was called into question by greater uncertainties pertaining to both Russian and Islamic law. Even if one were to admit the existence of a general principle along the lines of the Western law of civil obligations, Crawford concluded that the picture was too heterogeneous to establish a general principle of law in the sense of Article 38(1)(c) of the ICJ Statute.[289]

Indeed, the question will need to be answered on a different level, the level of international law itself. Crawford's Cambridge predecessor, Hersch Lauterpacht, devoted a small note to the problem in 1936. According to him, it would be wrongful for a State to enter into a treaty by which the agreement between two other States would be broken. However, Lauterpacht's position is contingent upon the time in which he was writing. Among other considerations, he remarked that there are relatively few treaties in international law and that they would be a matter of general knowledge.[290] This may have held true in 1936 but certainly cannot be said of today's international legal system with its myriad of bilateral agreements. In addition, Lauterpacht was interested in a question of treaty law – the question of which agreement would prevail in such circumstances – and not in the question of whether a third State would incur responsibility for having aided in the commission of a breach of an obligation to which it was itself not bound.

The crucial issue is thus whether the *pacta tertiis* rule really stands in the way of imposing responsibility for complicity in the breach of an obligation to which the supporting State is not bound. It should be borne in mind that this scenario does not apply only to bilateral treaties. It also extends to situations in which an assisting State is not bound to a multilateral treaty to which the assisted State is a party.[291]

For the moment, it is, however, useful to concentrate on the situation in which State A is aiding State B to breach a bilateral agreement with State C. In this situation, the solution of the ILC is indeed plausible for the situation in which there is no agreement in the form of a treaty between A and B. It has been discussed in the Commission whether or not the requirement of sub-paragraph (b) could not be deleted as

---

[289] *Ibid.*, para. 15.
[290] Hersch Lauterpacht, 'Contract to Breach a Contract', in Elihu Lauterpacht (ed.), *International Law Being the Collected Papers of Hersch Lauterpacht*, Vol. 4, *The Law of Peace, Parts VII–VIII* (Cambridge: Cambridge University Press, 1978), pp. 340–75, at p. 374.
[291] Cf Giorgio Gaja, Statement at the 2577th Meeting of the ILC, YBILC 1999, Vol. I, Part One, p. 73, para. 54.

the assisting State would hardly ever know of the bilateral agreement between State B and State C and could not therefore incur responsibility under Article 16 anyway.[292] Special Rapporteur James Crawford rightly remarked in this regard that this would not prevent well-publicised bilateral agreements imposing obligations upon States not party to an agreement.[293] In order to illustrate his case, he made reference to some examples, of which the following scenario most forcefully captures the problem: if State B and State C enter into an agreement which prohibits the export of certain IT technology to third States and then State A obtains this technology from State B, would State A be responsible for having aided and assisted State B in the breach of its agreement with State C?[294] This would indeed appear to be too far-reaching. Another example Special Rapporteur Crawford gave was a hypothetical agreement between OPEC Member States prohibiting the export of oil below a given retail price to non-OPEC States. Would a State which bought oil from an OPEC Member State below this price then incur responsibility for having aided or assisted this Member State in violating the intra-OPEC agreement?[295] In this scenario, the solution adopted by Article 16(b) ASR appears to provide for a reasonable solution.

In a different hypothetical situation, the assessment may, however, change. Here, we would be faced with the situation of a conflict of obligations for State B as it has entered into two bilateral agreements it cannot satisfy at the same time: State A owes assistance to State B and State B has an agreement with State C not to engage in a certain conduct; all obligations arise from bilateral agreements between the respective parties. A natural reaction to this situation would be to turn to the law of treaties in order to obtain guidance on which of the two agreements should prevail. However, Article 30(4) of the Vienna Convention on the Law of Treaties does not clarify this situation. It expressly excludes the *lex prior* principle,[296] and provides that:

When the parties to the later treaty do not include all the parties to the earlier one ... (b) as between a State Party to both treaties and a State Party to only

---

[292] For this suggestion, see Constantin Economides, Statement at the 2577th Meeting of the ILC, YBILC 1999, Vol. I, Part One, p. 68, para. 5.
[293] James Crawford, Statement at the 2577th Meeting of the ILC, YBILC 1999, Vol. I, Part One, p. 69, para. 12.
[294] Ibid.   [295] Ibid., para. 17.
[296] See Joost Pauwelyn, *Conflict of Norms in Public International Law – How WTO Law Relates to Other Rules of International Law* (Cambridge: Cambridge University Press, 2003),

one of the treaties, the treaty to which both States are parties governs their mutual rights and obligations.

The solution in the law of treaties is thus a non-solution and refers to the law of State responsibility:[297] the State which finds itself in a conflict of rights situation has to make a decision which of the two conflicting norms it wishes to comply with and which it wishes to breach.[298] In light of this situation, one could ask whether the reliance by the ILC on the *pacta tertiis* rule could be said to show a bias towards the application of international law's traditional bilateralism. The way the ILC restricted Article 16 ASR could be seen as unduly favouring the complicit State's interests over the interests of the injured State. In this scenario, it could even be possible to think of the *pacta tertiis* rule in both ways. The construction of Article 16(b) ASR cements the *pacta tertiis* rule with respect to State A. However, State C could also claim that it should not be affected by the agreement between States A and B. The question is, however, whether it is for the law of State responsibility to provide a solution in this regard. One possible way out of this dilemma would be a recourse to the principle of abuse of rights.[299] Under certain conditions, one could argue that State A, if it knew about the other agreement, could not rely on the *pacta tertiis* rule without committing an abuse of rights and potentially incurring responsibility for complicity.

As the law of treaties itself does not solve this conflict but rather ascribes to the rules of responsibility the task of 'compensating' the one State whose bilateral agreement has not been honoured, it would go beyond the original scope of the law of State responsibility to propose a different solution. In any case, the question is what Article 16 ASR could contribute in this regard. The original dilemma, that is, the question of which bilateral treaty should be complied with and

---

pp. 424 *et seq.*; see further Anthony Aust, *Modern Treaty Law*, p. 216; an application of the *lex posterior* principle appears not to be warranted here as the parties to the two agreements differ: see 'Fragmentation of International Law: Difficulties Arising from the Diversification and Expansion of International Law', Report of the Study Group of the ILC, finalized by Martti Koskenniemi, UN Doc. A/CN./L.682, para. 243.

[297] See Article 30(5) of the Vienna Convention on the Law of Treaties; see further Felipe Paollilo, 'Article 30 – Convention de 1969', in Olivier Corten and Pierre Klein (eds.), *Les Conventions de Vienne sur le droit des traités – Commentaire article par article*, Vols. I–III (Brussels: Bruylant, 2006), paras. 55 *et seq.*

[298] Joost Pauwelyn, *Conflict of Norms*, p. 427.

[299] See our discussion in Chapter 3, text accompanying note 98.

which disregarded, will remain the same. Traditionally, the *pacta tertiis* rule was only considered to be valid in connection with another principle of treaty law: that a treaty between two States may not infringe upon the rights of other States. Were this the case, the treaty would be illegal and a *delictual* relationship would enter into being.[300] The Vienna Convention on the Law of Treaties did not integrate these considerations into the regulation it has effected in Article 30(4). Although, on the face of it, the rationale that the *pacta tertiis* rule works both ways is still correct, it is not supplemented by principles according to which conflicts between bilateral agreements could be resolved. Although the way Article 16(b) is formulated thus appears to be an unsatisfactory solution, it may, however, be an inevitable one, taking into account the present state of development of the international legal system.

3.2 Difficult cases

Despite this somewhat disconcerting conceptual landscape, Article 16(b) raises practical issues which need to be addressed. These relate to conceivable scenarios in which it is not entirely clear whether a State is bound by a rule to the violation of which it is furnishing aid or assistance. Two categories will be presented before we discuss an interpretation of sub-paragraph (b) which could help to avoid the conundrums presented by these scenarios.

3.2.1 Objective regimes

A first category of problematic cases concerns so-called 'objective regimes'. These regimes mostly relate to the regulation of territorial situations and are understood to impose obligations upon third States.[301] Would a complicit State incur responsibility under Article 16(b) for having assisted in the commission of a breach of such an objective regime to which it is not directly party? In order to answer this question it is first necessary to briefly define what constitutes an objective regime (if indeed there is such a phenomenon in international law).

Frequently mentioned examples of objective regimes include the creation of servitudes and treaties by which territorial changes are

---

[300] Cf Walther Schücking, *Internationale Rechtsgarantien – Ausbau und Sicherung der zwischenstaatlichen Beziehungen* (Hamburg: Broschek, 1918), p. 82.

[301] Hans Ballreich, 'Treaties, Effects on Third States', in Rudolf Bernhardt (ed.), *Encyclopedia of Public International Law*, Vol. 4 (Amsterdam: Elsevier, 2000), pp. 945–9, at p. 947.

established or new States created.[302] In these situations, it would be established that a situation was regulated by a number of States which had effects *erga omnes*, meant here in the sense that the regulation was opposable to third States which had to accept this regulation although they were not parties to the agreement.[303] Examples which are frequently mentioned in this regard are the Act of the Congress of Vienna of 1815[304] establishing the Republic of Krakow, the Versailles Peace Treaty creating the Free City of Danzig[305] or the Peace Treaty with Italy[306] establishing Trieste.[307]

The issue of objective regimes was discussed in the ILC during the work on the law of treaties.[308] Eventually, the Commission decided not to include this doctrinal figure in its Draft Articles.[309] As Christian Tomuschat has found,

> it was obviously felt by the members of the ILC that to permit the establishment of objective regimes binding upon non-participating States would amount to a retroactive rehabilitation and perhaps even revival of such institutions of the past as the European Concert.[310]

That this assessment is not too far-fetched can be seen in the position of Judge McNair as expressed in an individual opinion. He wrote that:

> From time to time it happens that a group of great Powers, or a large number of States both great and small, assume a power to create by multipartite treaty

---

[302] Hans Kelsen, *Principles of International Law*, pp. 345 *et seq.*; see also Maurizio Ragazzi, *The Concept of International Obligations 'Erga Omnes'* (Oxford: Oxford University Press, 1997), pp. 18 *et seq.*

[303] Anne Peters, 'Compensatory Constitutionalism', p. 587; Nele Matz, *Wege zur Koordinierung völkerrechtlicher Verträge – Völkervertragsrechtliche und institutionelle Ansätze* (Berlin: Springer, 2005), p. 255.

[304] Final Act of the Congress of Vienna of 9 June 1815, 2 Martens Nouveau Recueil 427.

[305] Versailles Peace Treaty of 28 June 1919, entered into force on 10 January 1920, 225 Parry 118.

[306] Treaty of Peace with Italy of 10 February 1947, entered into force on 15 September 1947, 49 UNTS 125.

[307] See the references and further examples given by Wolff Heintschel von Heinegg, 'Die völkerrechtlichen Verträge', p. 159.

[308] See the Draft Article on objective regimes proposed by Special Rapporteur Humphrey Waldock, 'Third Report on the Law of Treaties', YBILC 1964, Vol. II, p. 5.

[309] On the discussions in the ILC, see Christos L. Rozakis, 'Treaties and Third States', pp. 9–10; Malgosia Fitzmaurice, 'Third Parties and the Law of Treaties', *Max Planck Yearbook of United Nations Law* 6 (2002), pp. 37–137, at pp. 74 *et seq.*; Maurizio Ragazzi, *The Concept*, pp. 37 *et seq.*

[310] Christian Tomuschat, 'Obligations Arising for States Without or Against Their Will', *Recueil des Cours* 241 (1993-IV), pp. 195–374, at p. 245.

some new international regime or status, which soon acquires a degree of acceptance and durability extending beyond the limits of the actual contracting parties and giving it an objective existence. This power is used when some public interest is involved.[311]

The notion of objective regimes thus has a very close connection to what Bruno Simma has called the self-appointment of 'guardians of community interest'.[312]

Today, the issue of objective regimes is most prominently discussed with respect to the Antarctic Treaty System, which claims regulatory power *vis-à-vis* States not party to the Antarctic Treaty.[313] The crucial issue is always in what way third States actually become bound to an objective regime.[314] As Eckart Klein has noted in his comprehensive analysis of the phenomenon, the regulatory power is usually only claimed by the parties to the objective regime (*Ordnungsbehauptung*) and then needs to be accepted by other States in order to create legal effects beyond the circle of parties to the agreement.[315] Similarly, Alfred Verdross and Bruno Simma have concluded that the principle of consent is only seemingly called into question in these cases: in reality, the consent of third party States to such an objective regime will always be required.[316] It may therefore be intellectually appealing to reflect on the impact of Article 16(b) ASR on situations in which objective regimes are involved. In addition to the fact that the practical relevance of such considerations will not be very high as it is not to be expected that cases will arise which involve this factual situation, the majority of authorities appear to support the suggestion that it will also be possible to determine by traditional means, including State consent, whether or not the complicit State was actually bound

---

[311] ICJ, *International Status of South West Africa*, Advisory Opinion, ICJ Rep. 1950, 128, individual opinion of Judge McNair, p. 153.

[312] Bruno Simma, 'From Bilateralism to Community Interest', p. 364.

[313] See Christian Tomuschat, 'Obligations', p. 245; Bruno Simma, 'The Antarctic Treaty as a Treaty Providing for an "Objective Régime"', *Cornell International Law Journal* 19 (1986), pp. 189–209.

[314] Cf Nele Matz, *Koordinierung völkerrechtlicher Verträge*, pp. 257 et seq.

[315] Eckart Klein, *Statusverträge im Völkerrecht – Rechtsfragen territorialer Sonderregime* (Berlin: Springer, 1980), p. 345; for a different assessment, see Suzanne Bastid, *Les traités dans la vie internationale – Conclusion et effets* (Paris: Economica, 1985), p. 153.

[316] Alfred Verdross and Bruno Simma, *Universelles Völkerrecht*, § 770; see also Alfred Verdross, *Die Quellen des universellen Völkerrechts – Eine Einführung* (Freiburg: Rombach, 1973), p. 67; Wolff Heintschel von Heinegg, 'Die weiteren Quellen', p. 159.

by the regime in question.[317] Although the concept of objective regimes is thus not really challenging the requirement of Article 16(b) ASR, it is a useful illustration of the fact that States and international lawyers have always tried to find ways around the traditional consent requirement[318] – an insight that may be useful for other aspects of the interpretation of Article 16(b) ASR.

3.2.2 Overlapping obligations

More relevant in practical terms is the overlap of obligations in respect of the same subject matter which stem from different sources. State A may assist in the commission of a wrongful act by State B which is contrary to a regional human rights treaty entered into by the latter. Now let us assume that State A is party to a different regional human rights treaty which grants, substance-wise, the same human right as the regional human rights treaty entered into by State B. At the same time, the human right in question does not enjoy the status of customary international law. In the context of the 'extraordinary rendition' programme of the United States, the issue arose whether it mattered for the human rights obligations of Council of Europe Member States that the United States is obviously not bound by the European Convention on Human Rights. If we assume, for the sake of the argument, that the US is bound to the American Convention on Human Rights, there would be a partial overlap with the rights set out in the European convention.[319] Technically speaking, a European State would, however, not be bound to the same obligation the US would have violated if close attention is devoted to the requirement of Article 16(b) ASR (always assuming that the human right in question does not enjoy customary status).

The same technical issue is at stake with respect to different bilateral treaties in force for the respective States. This scenario may be best

---

[317] Cf Hans Ballreich, 'Treaties', p. 947; Malgosia Fitzmaurice, 'Third Parties', pp. 136–7; Maurizio Ragazzi, *The Concept*, p. 41; Hanspeter Neuhold, 'Völkerrechtlicher Vertrag', p. 61; Nele Matz, *Koordinierung völkerrechtlicher Verträge*, p. 259, who points to the *de facto* effects of so-called objective regimes which need to be distinguished from their legal effects.

[318] Bruno Simma, 'Antarctic Treaty', p. 189.

[319] On the relationship between the two Conventions Antônio Augusto Cançado Trindade, 'The Development of International Human Rights Law by the Operation and Case-Law of the European and the Inter-American Courts of Human Rights', *Human Rights Law Journal* 25 (2004), pp. 157–60.

illustrated by an example we already mentioned briefly in Chapter 4.[320] In 2007, Germany sought the extradition of Karl-Heinz Schreiber from Canada. Schreiber, a German-Canadian dual citizen, was implicated in a major political scandal in Germany involving alleged tax frauds, violations against rules on party funding and potentially corruption. Parts of the German evidence were obtained from Switzerland which had furnished the evidence to Germany on the understanding that these tax records would only be used in criminal law proceedings but not with respect to tax frauds (which is not a crime in Switzerland, but a mere administrative offence). This condition is enshrined in a multilateral agreement to which Switzerland and Germany are parties and which is further supplemented by a bilateral agreement laying down the conditions under which legal assistance in criminal matters will be granted between the two States.[321] From this factual situation, it is at first sight not conceivable that Canada could, through the extradition of Schreiber, aid or assist in a breach by Germany of the Swiss–German treaty on judicial assistance. It is exactly the situation the ILC wished to exclude from Article 16 ASR through the inclusion of sub-paragraph (b). On a closer look, however, this assessment is less clear. The detail which calls this assessment into question is that Canada is party to an agreement with Switzerland providing for the substantively identical obligations in the context of judicial assistance.[322]

Does this affect the interpretation of Article 16(b)? From a technical perspective, this does not appear to be the case. After all, Canada is *technically* not bound to the treaty Germany would be violating. It is an agreement in force between these two countries and in that regard is *res inter alios acta* for Canada. But can Canada in good faith rely on Article 16(b) when it owes an essentially identical obligation to Switzerland? Would this not amount to an abuse of rights? After all, States are required to comply with their treaty obligations in good faith and

---

[320] See the text accompanying notes 319 *et seq.* in Chapter 4 above.
[321] European Convention on Mutual Assistance in Criminal Matters of 20 April 1959, entered into force on 12 June 1962, ETS No. 30, Article 1, in combination with a bilateral agreement between Germany and Switzerland: Vertrag zwischen der Bundesrepublik Deutschland und der Schweizerischen Eidgenossenschaft über die Ergänzung des Europäischen Übereinkommens über die Rechtshilfe in Strafsachen vom 20. April 1959 und die Erleichterung seiner Anwendung of 13 November 1969, *Federal Law Gazette* II 1975, 1169, Article I(a).
[322] Treaty between Canada and the Swiss Confederation on Mutual Assistance in Criminal Matters of 7 October 1993, E 101631 – CTS 1995 No. 24, Article 1(1) and (2).

not to frustrate their object and purpose.[323] Seen in this perspective, it could very well be argued that Article 16(b) should be interpreted differently when such parallel bilateral treaties are at stake. But how could such a reading be reconciled both with the structural analysis of the ILC and with the legitimate concern that States cannot always know what treaty obligations other States have? Here, one could potentially distinguish between, on the one hand, subject matters which are routinely dealt with in bilateral treaties and where an expectation therefore exists that a similar treaty will be in force between two other States, and, on the other hand, subject matters where this is not the case. As well as judicial assistance treaties, bilateral investment treaties also spring to mind. Today, more than 2,000 bilateral treaties of this kind exist. Although overlapping to a considerable degree, there is no unanimity as to whether these treaties have led to the establishment of customary law rules.[324]

In this context, Eyal Benvenisti and George Downs have drawn attention to the phenomenon of 'serial bilateralism'. By this term, they understand 'the negotiation of separate bilateral agreements with different states all dealing with the same issue'.[325] The impact of 'serial bilateralism', a tool 'used by powerful states to shape the evolution of norms', would be especially significant in the sphere of the protection of foreign investment.[326] One can see this phenomenon from two perspectives: Benvenisti and Downs highlight its potential to circumvent traditional law-making processes by channelling State consent into parallel bilateral treaties where the bargaining power of powerful States is sufficiently strong to pressure smaller States into consensus. Over time, it is thus to be expected that customary international law will develop. Apart from this meta-perspective, practical issues arise

---

[323] Cf Article 26 of the Vienna Convention on the Law of Treaties, see further on good faith Alfred Verdross and Bruno Simma, *Universelles Völkerrecht*, § 60; Jörg P. Müller and Robert Kolb, 'Article 2(2)', para. 12.

[324] See Eyal Benvenisti and George W. Downs, 'The Emperor's New Clothes: Political Economy and the Fragmentation of International Law', *Stanford Law Review* 60 (2007), pp. 595–631, at p. 611; Gabriella Blum, 'Bilateralism, Multilateralism, and the Architecture of International Law', *Harvard International Law Journal* 49 (2008), pp. 323–79, at pp. 334 *et seq.*; Vaughan Lowe, *International Law*, p. 86; Jeswald W. Salacuse and Nicolas P. Sullivan, 'Do BITs Really Work? An Evaluation of Bilateral Investment Treaties and Their Grand Bargain', *Harvard International Law Journal* 46 (2005), pp. 67–130, at p. 89.

[325] Eyal Benvenisti and George W. Downs, 'Emperor's New Clothes', pp. 610–11.

[326] *Ibid.*, p. 611.

such as the one concerning the scope of Article 16(b) ASR. One may enrich this perspective with another insight of Benvenisti and Downs: serial bilateralism is conceived by them as means to foster fragmentation.[327] Although greater unity is not in itself a virtue and thus does not impose itself as a *topos* of interpretation of international law,[328] it is legitimate to ask how this phenomenon of 'serial bilateralism' could also weaken the generally beneficial aspects of the law of State responsibility, i.e., to provide for a general framework for reparation and the enforcement of the law which corresponds to existing international obligations.

A rather traditional and formalist interpretation of the law is faced with a paradox here. On the one hand, an interpretation of Article 16(b) ASR which would evade its direct wording and instead focus on the phenomenon of 'serial bilateralism' could be said to contribute to this very process. This would bestow further normative consequences upon the hegemonic efforts to change the law in a different form than traditional law-making processes. On the other hand, one need not necessarily share the focus of Benvenisti and Downs. It is also conceivable that 'serial bilateralism' is employed to avoid more encompassing normative bounds and to constrain consent to the narrow and individual aspect of each bilateral agreement. Those States participating in such a development should, however, be held to their commitments. In this perspective, an interpretation of Article 16(b) ASR which would allow the ascription of responsibility in such cases could reinforce respect for international law and make States aware of the broader normative implications of their behaviour. However, this issue borders upon considerations of policy and may thus not lend itself to a clear and unequivocal answer in terms of international law.

3.2.3 Norms, sources and obligations

The examples of objective regimes and overlapping obligations we have discussed eventually converge on one question, namely, to what extent it is possible to distinguish between the concrete obligations which are imposed by rules X and Y and the underlying common norm Z. Would this mean for the interpretation of Article 16(b) ASR that the

---

[327] *Ibid.*, p. 625.
[328] Cf Martti Koskenniemi and Päivi Leino, 'Fragmentation of International Law? Postmodern Anxieties', *Leiden Journal of International Law* 15 (2002), pp. 553–79, at p. 560.

assisting State and the main actor both need to be bound by rule X? Or is it sufficient that they are both bound by the same norm Z, the same standard so to speak, which can be derived independently from rules X and Y? Is it possible to hold that different rules may represent the same norm?[329]

This question takes us into very uncertain territory – discussions about the theory of sources usually answer less questions than they raise.[330] Nevertheless, the issue we have evoked will briefly be discussed here. It pertains to the distinction between formal and material sources of the law.[331] Wolfgang Friedmann distinguished between the two in the following way:

> The term 'formal' source of law indicates the repository of authority, or in Hart's words, 'the criteria of legal validity accepted in the legal system in question'. The 'material' sources are the sum of the substantive rules, principles or other materials from which a particular legal norm is nourished.[332]

For the international lawyer primarily interested in practical matters, the relevant question is whether there can be binding law apart from an emanation in a formal source of international law.[333] This question boils down to the point whether the formal source is something distinct which precisely identifies the obligation in question or whether the formal source is 'only' a technicality which tells us where we can find 'evidence' of international law. Almost poetically, Oppenheim characterised the problem as such:

> When we see a stream of water and want to know whence it comes, we follow the stream upwards until we come to the spot where it rises naturally from

---

[329] Cf Kelsen's distinction between *Rechtssatz* and *Rechtsnorm*: Hans Kelsen, *Reine Rechtslehre*, 2nd edn (Vienna: Franz Deuticke, 1960), pp. 73–4.

[330] Anthony D'Amato, *The Concept of Custom*, p. 264; Martti Koskenniemi, *From Apology to Utopia*, pp. 303 *et seq.*; Christian Tomuschat, 'Völkerrechtlicher Vertrag', p. 43.

[331] Cf Gionata P. Buzzini, 'La théorie des sources face au droit international général: réflexions sur l'émergence du droit objectif dans l'ordre juridique internationale', *Revue générale de droit international public* 106 (2002), pp. 581–617, at p. 586.

[332] Wolfgang Friedmann, 'General Principles', p. 279, note 2; see further Clive Parry, *The Sources and Evidence of International Law* (Manchester: Manchester University Press, 1965), pp. 1 *et seq.*; Gerald Fitzmaurice, 'Some Problems Regarding the Formal Sources of International Law', in Frederik Mari van Asbeck (ed.), *Symbolae Verzijl: présentées au professeur J. H. W. Verzijl à l'occasion de son LXX-ième anniversaire* (The Hague: Nijhoff, 1958), pp. 153–76, at pp. 153–4.

[333] Cf Martti Koskenniemi, 'Introduction', in Martti Koskenniemi (ed.), *Sources of International Law* (Aldershot: Ashgate, 2000), pp. xi–xxviii, at p. xii.

the ground. On that spot, we say, is the source of the stream of water. We know very well that this source is not the cause of the existence of the stream of water.[334]

By this passage, Oppenheim is alluding to *the* cause behind the law and not to *a rule* which finds expression in several sources. His considerations thus appear to relate more to the issue of a *Grundnorm* (fundamental norm) of the international legal system than to our current problem.[335] Instead, we may find guidance in some – admittedly pragmatic and less principled – considerations of the ICJ in the *Nicaragua* case.[336]

In *Nicaragua*, the Court was barred from considering the prohibition of the use of force under Article 2(4) of the UN Charter due to a reservation that the US had filed with their declaration according to Article 36(2) of the ICJ Statute. The Court therefore felt inclined to consider the customary law prohibition of the same content.[337] After having remarked that the Court had in no way ruled out the possibility of identical norms in treaty and customary law in its *North Sea Continental Shelf* cases,[338] it turned to the prohibition of the use of force. In this regard, it held that '[t]here are a number of reasons for considering that, even if two norms belonging to two sources of international law appear identical in content, and even if the States in question are bound by these rules both on the level of treaty law and on that of customary law, these norms retain a separate existence'.[339] The Court thus made it clear that identical content of norms does not turn these norms into one. It also emphasised that its considerations apply in cases where both States are bound by both norms. For the interpretation of Article 16(b), these findings point towards an interpretation which would not allow holding a State responsible in the problematic scenarios we have just discussed. For one, it is not technically bound by the norm that the

---

[334] Lassa Oppenheim, *International Law – A Treatise*, Vol. I, *Peace* (ed. by Hersch Lauterpacht) (London: Longmans, 1955), p. 24.
[335] Whether this understanding corresponds to Kelsen's theory of the *Grundnorm* is an entirely different matter: see Hans Kelsen, *Reine Rechtslehre*, pp. 196 *et seq.*, and especially at pp. 238–9 on his critique of the idea of sources.
[336] ICJ, *Military and Paramilitary Activities In and Against Nicaragua*, Merits, ICJ Rep. 1986, 14.
[337] See further Fred L. Morrison, 'Legal Issues', pp. 160–1.
[338] ICJ, *North Sea Continental Shelf Cases*, Judgment, ICJ Rep. 1969, 3, para. 63.
[339] ICJ, *Military and Paramilitary Activities In and Against Nicaragua*, Merits, ICJ Rep. 1986, 14, para. 178.

main actor is violating and, secondly, although identical in content, the two norms retain their individual existence. But is this not too formalistic an interpretation? Is it not also the case that the Court expressly stipulated that '[t]he essential consideration is that both the Charter and the customary international law flow from a common fundamental principle outlawing the use of force in international relations'?[340] And is this not expressly the scenario we are considering, i.e., different rules representing the same norm?

One has to be cautious not to infer too much from this last quotation. The prohibition of the use of force occupies a special place in the international legal order[341] and it will not be possible to directly translate these findings into the more technical field of application of the average bilateral treaty. In those cases, it will be much harder to identify a 'common fundamental principle' underlying the scenarios than it was for the ICJ. However, this reference to an underlying principle may also point the way for a constructive interpretation which could alleviate the consequences of an overly formalistic reading of Article 16(b) ASR.

Whereas, as has just been mentioned, such an underlying principle will not be identifiable in most instances involving bilateral treaties, it is conceivable to rely on this argument *per analogiam* in the case of overlapping multilateral obligations, and especially in the field of human rights law. It speaks very much against the object and purpose of the human rights obligation entered into to justify aid or assistance in the commission of violations of virtually identical obligations by another State which is, however, responsible only under a different human rights regime. Here, it appears to be a reasonable solution to hold the complicit State responsible. This solution also finds support in our understanding of the principle of abuse of rights.[342] Although the aiding and assisting State would not be technically barred from granting such support, it is reasonably clear that through its conduct

---

[340] *Ibid.*, para. 181.
[341] Cf on Article 2(4) of the Charter as a 'cornerstone' of the international legal order Humphrey Waldock, 'The Regulation of the Use of Force by Individual States in International Law', *Recueil des Cours* 81 (1952-II), pp. 451–517, at p. 492; Christine Gray, *International Law*, p. 30; Albrecht Randelzhofer, 'Article 2(4)', in Bruno Simma (ed.), *The Charter of the United Nations – A Commentary*, 2nd edn (Oxford: Oxford University Press, 2002), para. 12; ICJ, *Armed Activities on the Territory of the Congo (Democratic Republic of Congo v. Uganda)*, Judgment, ICJ Rep. 2005, 168, para. 148.
[342] See above Chapter 3, text accompanying notes 98 *et seq.*

it will harm a third State (or more precisely in this case an individual protected by the given human rights treaty). Moreover, the State would have to rely on the purely formal argument that, although it is contributing to a violation of a rule to which it is bound, it could avoid responsibility due to the rule in question being laid down in differing sources.

Similar considerations may even apply in cases of 'serial bilateralism' in the sense of Benvenisti and Downs.[343] However, the solution discussed here is less imposing in this respect as it is in the field of human rights law. The analysis of 'serial bilateralism' is still subject to debate and one may draw different policy conclusions from their findings. However, it should not be ruled out that a reasonable case can also be made to attenuate the interpretation of Article 16(b) in such cases.

An objection that could be raised to this construction with its emphasis on the underlying common fundamental principle is that in most cases the same result could be attained by a more liberal recourse to customary international law.[344] However, this is exactly the crux of the matter: especially in the field of human rights law, the positing of the customary nature of a given rule quite frequently strains the traditional categories for establishing customary rules.[345] Similarly, the issue whether the 'leap to the level of customary law'[346] is to be taken in the presence of a plurality of bilateral treaties with identical content remains hotly contested.[347] It is submitted here that this emphasis on common principles underlying technically different rules is a preferable solution over the expansion of concepts of customary international law which lose all resemblance to what is traditionally accepted as such.

3.3 Concluding observations on Article 16(b) ASR

We have seen that Article 16(b) ASR poses more problems than may appear at first sight. Its existence is directly owed to structural considerations, i.e., the *pacta tertiis* rule which is thereby translated into

---

[343] See above note 324.
[344] Cf Christian Tomuschat, 'Völkerrechtlicher Vertrag', p. 35.
[345] Bruno Simma and Philip Alston, 'The Sources of Human Rights Law: Custom, Jus Cogens, and General Principles', *Australian Yearbook of International Law* 12 (1992), pp. 82–108, at p. 84.
[346] Hanspeter Neuhold, 'Völkerrechtlicher Vertrag', p. 59: 'gewohnheitsrechtlicher Qualitätssprung'.
[347] Gabriella Blum, 'Bilateralism', pp. 369 *et seq.*

the law of State responsibility. Apart from the fact that such structural linkages are always problematic – as we have already discussed in Chapter 2 – the rule in question here is not so unequivocal as to allow for convincing solutions to the interpretation of Article 16 ASR. Accordingly, an unsatisfactory state of the law is created which cannot be remedied by the interpretation of Article 16 ASR alone. Furthermore, practically relevant cases challenge the clear-cut rule Article 16 ASR wishes to establish. It is thus a mixed picture which emerges. In the absence of concrete international practice on this precise matter, we have to await the further development of the law. For this development, considerations of 'overlap' may provide sensible criteria to decide cases which may arise and require a reinterpretation of Article 16(b) ASR.

4 Conclusion

If we pick up the theme of the international rule of law which we have developed in Chapter 3, one could object to the findings of this chapter that they are too sceptical, too timid to provide for the further promotion of the international rule of law. Why insist on a narrow interpretation of Article 16 if, generally speaking, providing rules on complicity is conducive to respect for the international rule of law? Here, one can hold with Leslie Green that, paradoxical as it may seem, 'from the perspective of the rule of law there can be not only too little compliance, but also too much'. The rule of law may well be endangered if the law is over-enforced: 'Obedience is part of the rule of law, but not the whole, and not always the most important part.'[348]

In other words, more responsibility for complicity is not necessarily better. We have already made reference to factors which also speak for a narrow interpretation of Article 16: for instance, the obligation to cooperate in the international fight against terrorism.[349] If norms against complicity become too imposing, the willingness for cooperation could potentially shrink. Generally, cooperation among States is a positive virtue[350] and one should take this factor into account, even

---

[348] Leslie Green, 'Law and Obligations', in Jules Coleman and Scott Shapiro (eds.), *The Oxford Handbook of Jurisprudence and Philosophy of Law* (Oxford: Oxford University Press, 2002), pp. 514–47, at p. 545.
[349] Cf Christine Chinkin, 'Continuing Occupation?', p. 182.
[350] See already Georg Nolte and Helmut Philipp Aust, 'Equivocal Helpers', p. 12.

as part of the 'normative environment'[351] of Article 16 ASR, when expounding the latter's outer limits. This interpretation is also connected to the results of our treatment of the principle of abuse of rights in Chapter 3 and the discussion of the impact of the *pacta tertiis* rule in the present chapter: in imposing responsibility for complicity, a cure for a certain deficiency of international law's traditional bilateralism is provided. However, responsibility for complicity relies on a balance. As important as it is that the traditional equation of bilateralism does not always disadvantage the injured State, one has to be careful not to provide for an interpretation of Article 16 ASR which turns this situation on its head and provides for the responsibility of States in the most unlikely instances. We need to refer again to one of the fundamentals of Article 16 ASR: it refers to conduct which is, if assessed on its own, lawful. Confining situations which trigger responsibility for complicity to those in which it is clearly established that aid or assistance was furnished with the requisite intent is thus not detrimental to the international rule of law, but on the contrary a necessary emanation of it, especially in light of the potentially harsh consequences of State responsibility.[352] To take up the theme of the judgment of the Irish High Court, the matter of what constitutes 'aid or assistance' is rather an issue of 'substance and degree' and not necessarily of 'black or white'.

One can of course be sceptical towards this assessment and decry it as apologist in character. However, in interpreting Article 16 ASR one should also not overburden this provision. It is useful to take a comparative look at domestic legal systems where more far-reaching possibilities exist to hold accomplices and joint actors liable. There, procedural mechanisms are in existence which channel demands for reparation and which also provide for the requisite defences of potentially responsible actors.[353] In the 'free market place' which is the international legal system, this is not necessarily the case. Overbroad bases of responsibility may very well only favour the powerful which have at their disposal the necessary means to enforce their rights.

---

[351] Cf 'Fragmentation of International Law: Difficulties Arising from the Diversification and Expansion of International Law', Report of the Study Group of the International Law Commission, finalized by Martti Koskenniemi, UN Doc. A/CN.4/L.682, para. 413.

[352] Cf Arthur Watts, 'Rule of Law', p. 44.

[353] Cf James Crawford, Statement at the 2577th Meeting of the ILC, YBILC 1999, Vol. I, Part One, p. 69, para. 15.

Generally, responsibility for complicity should be a potentiality of which States need to be aware. Its most important function is as a signpost against collaboration with wrongdoers. That States take such matters seriously is shown most forcefully by the United Kingdom's insistence on further clarifications of what the term 'assistance' would mean in the 2008 Cluster Munitions Convention. As a matter of policy, Article 16 ASR should be interpreted in a way which makes it 'frightening' enough to deter States from engaging in wrongful conduct without erecting barriers to generally beneficial forms of international cooperation. It is not necessarily helpful when, as one member of the ILC did, the issue of complicity is seen in the context of the 'means deployed by the cold-blooded monsters ... becoming more and more complex in technical terms', such as to require 'safeguards that would check the natural urge of States to take whatever steps were required to further their dark designs'.[354] One may adopt this position as a matter of policy. However, the workability of a provision on complicity rests on the acceptance by States – those 'cold-blooded monsters' – to introduce it into their legal and political rhetoric and practice. This may be deplorable but in the absence of further integration of the international community it remains an incontestable fact.

---

[354] Statement of Guillaume Pambou-Tchivounda at the 2578th Meeting of the ILC, YBILC 1999, Vol. I, Part One, p. 80, para. 53.

6 The consequences of complicity

At least as pressing as the determination of when a State incurs responsibility for aid or assistance to an internationally wrongful act of another State is the question of what consequences flow from this assessment. In this respect, two distinct but interrelated issues can be identified. First of all, it needs to be clarified what the consequences of complicity are in terms of the law of State responsibility. This involves an examination of the content as well as the implementation of responsibility in a situation where there are multiple responsible actors (section 1). Secondly, uncertainties as to the consequences of complicity exist with respect to judicial dispute settlement. To hold a complicit State responsible necessarily implies a finding on the conduct of another State, i.e. the State to which aid or assistance has been rendered. Due to some procedural peculiarities before international courts and tribunals, it could prove to be difficult to hold a complicit State responsible in international judicial forums (section 2).

1 The content and implementation of responsibility for complicity

On the face of it, the usual consequences in terms of content and implementation for responsibility apply for complicit States. That means that content-wise Articles 28–41 ASR apply as well as Articles 42–54 implementation-wise. However, it needs to be borne in mind that these consequences have been largely modelled on the bilateral relation between one wrongdoing State and one injured State.[1]

---

[1] Samantha Besson, 'La pluralité d'Etats responsable – Vers une solidarité internationale?', *Schweizerische Zeitschrift für Internationales und Europäisches Recht* 17

The additional presence of a third State is thus likely to complicate the situation. Accordingly, this section will assess whether and to what extent the rules laid down in Articles 28–41 and 42–54 are fit to determine the consequences of complicity. When the content and implementation of responsibility is at stake, it should be understood that these general rules address a large array of fairly diverse cases. Breaches of international law may involve anything from the trivial to the serious breach of peremptory norms. Accordingly, the application of the rules on content and implementation of responsibility may be adapted due to the seriousness of the breach. In general, however, the consequences which the ILC has codified in the ASR apply without modification. As the Commission has put it in its commentaries, 'over and above the gravity or effects of individual cases, the rules and institutions of State responsibility are significant for the maintenance of respect for international law and for the achievement of the goals which States advance through law-making at the international level'.[2] Hence, the presumption is that in general the ordinary consequences of responsibility shall apply. No regard is to be given *a priori* to the seriousness of a breach of international law save for the determination of the specific consequences such as the form and dimension reparation is to take in a specific case. Nevertheless, some special questions may arise: Special Rapporteur Willem Riphagen noted that Draft Article 27, as adopted on First Reading, would raise the issue how the responsibility of the complicit State could be distinguished from the responsibility of the main actor.[3] ILC member Chusei Yamada mentioned during the Second Reading of the Articles that Article 27 raised the problem 'how to determine the distribution of responsibility between the assisting State, and the assisted State'. He 'saw no reference to that question in the draft articles of part two adopted on First Reading. The Commission should give some thought to that aspect when it considered part two.'[4] In scholarly writings, it is only infrequently considered

---

(2007), pp. 13–38, at p. 18; Phoebe N. Okowa, *State Responsibility for Transboundary Air Pollution in International Law* (Oxford: Oxford University Press, 2000), p. 195.

[2] ILC Commentary, Introduction to Part Two, Chapter I, para. 1; see also Robert P. Barnidge, 'Questioning the Legitimacy of Jus Cogens in the Global Legal Order', *Israel Yearbook of Human Rights* 38 (2008), pp. 199–225, at p. 215.

[3] Willem Riphagen, 'Preliminary Report on the Content, Forms and Degrees of International Responsibility', UN Doc. A/CN.4/330, YBILC 1980, Vol. II, Part One, p. 111, para. 14.

[4] Chusei Yamada, Statement at the 2576th Meeting of the ILC, YBILC 1999, Vol. I, p. 66, para. 46.

whether, and if so how, the consequences of the law of State responsibility need to be modified for cases of complicity.[5]

1.1 Content of responsibility for complicity

1.1.1 The general consequences of responsibility

In general, the ASR provide for three different consequences of responsibility in terms of content:[6] first of all, Article 29 ASR holds that 'the legal consequences of an internationally wrongful act under this Part do not affect the continued duty of the responsible State to perform the obligation breached'. Secondly, according to Article 30(a) ASR, that responsible State is under an obligation to cease that act, if it is continuing and, according to Article 30(b), 'to offer appropriate assurances and guarantees of non-repetition, if circumstances so require'. Finally, Article 31(1) ASR provides that '[t]he responsible State is under an obligation to make full reparation for the injury caused by the internationally wrongful act'. Two further provisions in this chapter of the ASR set out that a responsible State may not rely on its internal law in order not to comply with the consequences of responsibility (Article 32) and that the consequences set out in this part of the ASR are 'without prejudice to any right, arising from the international responsibility of a State, which may accrue directly to any person or entity other than a State' (Article 33(2)).

1.1.2 Complicity and the 'new legal relationship'

Before the issue is addressed which of these provisions can be applied without further amendments to complicit States and which provisions would need further refinement, a preliminary question needs to be dealt with. It has been argued by Felder that, technically speaking, the legal consequences of State responsibility as set out in the provisions just mentioned cannot apply *telle quelle*.[7] The reason for this scepticism lies in the construction by the ILC of these consequences as the 'new legal relationship which arises upon the commission by a State of an internationally wrongful act'.[8] This construction of responsibility as the

---

[5] Notable exceptions include Andreas Felder, *Die Beihilfe*, pp. 273-9; John Quigley, 'Complicity', pp. 125 *et seq.*; Dietrich Rauschning, 'Verantwortlichkeit der Staaten für völkerrechtswidriges Verhalten', *Berichte der Deutschen Gesellschaft für Völkerrecht* 24 (1984), pp. 7-34, at p. 27; Pierre d'Argent, *Les réparations de guerre*, pp. 554, 746 *et seq.*; Alexander Orakhelashvili, 'Division'.
[6] For a similar classification, see Ian Brownlie, *State Responsibility*, p. 199.
[7] Andreas Felder, *Die Beihilfe*, p. 275.
[8] ILC Commentary, Introduction to Part Two, para. 1.

new legal relationships brought about by an internationally wrongful act is at the very centre of the codification project of the ILC, being already set out by Article 1 ASR which provides that '[e]very internationally wrongful act of a State entails the international responsibility of that State'.[9] The heart of this construction can be described as a legal fiction: the situation is treated as if, automatically, the new legal relationship has replaced the old one. The wrongful act is in this perspective the *'fait générateur'* of the new legal relationship.[10]

As the prime characteristic of responsibility for complicity would be the fact that the complicit State did not commit a wrongful act save through the association with the wrongful conduct of another State, it would not be possible to apply the consequences the ILC has considered straight away.[11] This problem was, as far as can be seen, not considered by the ILC in the drafting history of the ASR, except for the very general remarks in the line of the quotations reproduced by Riphagen and Yamada.[12] From what flows from the ILC commentary to Article 16, however, the principles laid down in Part Two of the ASR are considered to be applicable to responsibility which has arisen under Article 16 ASR. In its relevant part, the Commentary states that:

[b]y assisting another State to commit an internationally wrongful act, a State should not necessarily be held to indemnify the victim for all the consequences of the act, but only for those which, in accordance with the principles stated in Part Two of the articles, flow from its own conduct.[13]

This pragmatic stance towards the consequences of responsibility for complicity is consequential as otherwise the practical relevance of Article 16 ASR would be greatly diminished. It would be futile to include a provision on responsibility for aid or assistance in the ASR only to exclude the applicability of the legal consequences attached to it.

In this regard, Felder suggests that, although there is, originally, no legal relationship between the complicit State and the injured State (due to the absence of an original wrongful act), a 'quasi-legal relationship' (*rechtsähnliche Beziehung*) exists between the two States.[14] This

---

[9] For different conceptualisations, see Dionisio Anzilotti, *Lehrbuch des Völkerrechts*, pp. 362 *et seq.*; Hans Kelsen, *Principles of International Law*, pp. 20 *et seq.*; Roberto Ago, 'Le délit international', p. 430.
[10] Cf Pierre-Marie Dupuy, 'Le fait générateur', pp. 25–6.
[11] Andreas Felder, *Die Beihilfe*, p. 275.   [12] See notes 3 and 4 above.
[13] ILC Commentary, Article 16, para. 10.   [14] Andreas Felder, *Die Beihilfe*, p. 275.

quasi-legal relationship, Felder argues, is brought about by the characteristic features of responsibility for complicity: on the one hand, the complicit State is bound by the obligation that the main actor is violating; on the other hand, there is a close relationship between its support and the commission of the internationally wrongful act. Accordingly, the complicit State would enter *indirectly* into the legal relationship between the main actor and the injured State. This construction would justify applying the consequences which the ILC has set out in Part Two of the ASR.[15] Felder's position certainly takes into account the subtleties of Article 16 ASR. It touches upon the very difficult issue of how responsibility for complicity can be classified under Article 16 ASR: is it responsibility for wrongful behaviour? Or is the solution of the ILC closer to imposing responsibility upon lawful behaviour which is triggering responsibility through its relation with the unlawful conduct of another State?

To defend the inclusion of Article 16 in the ASR, it is necessary to find that an element of wrongfulness attaches to the aid or assistance furnished to another State for the commission of the internationally wrongful act in question. Felder is right in pointing to the fact that, judged on its own merits, the aid or assistance is not wrongful in character. Through the close connection between, *prima facie*, lawful support and the wrongful act, wrongfulness is established. This wrongfulness is, however, only brought about on the level of secondary rules. In this regard lies the parallelism between Article 16 ASR and the rules of attribution of the acts of non-State actors: in both cases, it is only at the level of secondary rules that the breach of an international obligation by the State in question is ultimately established.[16] Expectations for lawful behaviour and against deviations from it may exist beyond the individual primary rules: the concept of an international rule of law and constituent principles of it, such as the one on abuse of rights, may give expression to those expectations.[17] Article 16 ASR is then a transformative provision in the realm of secondary rules: it gives expression

---

[15] *Ibid.*
[16] This parallelism was also highlighted by Special Rapporteur James Crawford as one of the reasons why it was possible to retain (at the time) Draft Article 27 as a secondary rule: see 'Second Report on State Responsibility', UN Doc. A/CN.4/498/Add.1, 6, para. 165.
[17] On this whole complex, see our discussion in Chapter 3; see also *mutatis mutandis* ICJ, *Accordance with International Law of the Unilateral Declaration of Independence in Respect of Kosovo*, Advisory Opinion, declaration of Judge Simma, para. 9.

to the requirement that States do not become complicit in violations of international law by other States.

1.1.3 A first survey on the consequences of complicity

Some of the provisions on the content of responsibility can be applied to a responsible complicit State without any special problems. Accordingly, a complicit State is under a continuing duty to perform the obligation it has breached (Article 29 ASR; although some theoretical problems are conceivable as the complicit State has not exactly breached a primary obligation). According to Article 30(a) ASR, the complicit State is under an obligation to cease the complicit act if it is continuing. It is also conceivable to require of a complicit State to offer appropriate assurances and guarantees of non-repetition, if circumstances so require, under Article 30(b) ASR.[18] In addition, it is not apparent in what respect Articles 32 and 33 ASR could pose particular problems, as a complicit State plainly may not rely on its internal law as a justification for its failure to comply with its obligations under this part (Article 32). Article 33 ASR finally sets out the scope of obligations set out in this part, which does not pose specific problems for complicit States.

1.2 Reparation

Problems begin, however, with Article 31 ASR and its further concretisations in Chapter Two of Part Two of the ASR. Article 31 ASR provides:

1. The responsible State is under an obligation to make full reparation for the injury caused by the internationally wrongful act.

2. Injury includes any damage, whether material or moral, caused by the internationally wrongful act of that State.

With respect to reparation, one needs to distinguish between the various forms that Chapter Two of Part Two of the ASR sets out.[19] The forms of reparation are restitution (Article 35), compensation (Article 36) and satisfaction (Article 37). It is apparent that in the case of complicity, at least two States have 'caused' the injury to be remedied. Put more

---

[18] Doctrinal suggestions that assurances and guarantees of non-repetition should only apply with respect to aggravated responsibility have not been successful: see Alain Pellet, 'Can a State Commit a Crime? Definitely, Yes!', *European Journal of International Law* 10 (1999), pp. 425–34.

[19] Which were identified as the relevant forms of reparation by earlier scholarly writings: see Ian Brownlie, *State Responsibility*, pp. 199 *et seq.*; Christine D. Gray, *Judicial Remedies in International Law* (Oxford: Clarendon Press, 1988), pp. 11 *et seq.*

precisely, through its aid or assistance, the complicit State has contributed to the injury caused by the main actor. Although two separate wrongful acts exist, the injury is one and the same.[20] One approach to this issue would be simply to reaffirm what the ILC has held: as it is an independent internationally wrongful act,[21] one could argue that no problems arise with respect to the division of shares of responsibility. The complicit State would simply be responsible for the part of responsibility it has caused and the same applies for the main actor.

Although this reasoning may indeed be the formally correct answer, it is at odds with what Judge Simma has described as 'factually "indivisible" acts'.[22] Simma's treatment of the issue was related to the so-called 'generic counter-claim' of the United States in the *Oil Platforms* case. The United States reproached Iran for having violated the Treaty of Amity of 1955 between the two States.[23] In concrete terms, the US argued that Iran had contributed to the general deterioration of conditions for maritime shipping in the Persian Gulf by laying mines and staging other attacks on neutral shipping during the so-called 'tanker war' between 1980 and 1988. The problem with this counter-claim was that Iran's involvement in individual incidents where ships had hit mines was not possible to prove. Both Iran and Iraq had resorted to mine-laying in the Gulf. For the purposes of the generic counter-claim (as opposed to specific counter-claims having individual incidents in mind), Judge Simma argued that it was immaterial to establish the particular extent of Iran's responsibility:

It is sufficient to establish that Iran, because of the Iran–Iraq war, was responsible for a significant portion of those actions, and that such actions impaired the freedom of commerce between the United States and Iran guaranteed by the 1955 Treaty in ways not justifiable simply because of the existence of a state of war.[24]

The situation of complicity is different from what Judge Simma was considering when he wrote about factually indivisible acts. However, similar considerations apply with respect to complicity: although

---

[20] Brian D. Smith, *State Responsibility*, p. 45.
[21] ILC Commentary, Article 16, para. 10.
[22] ICJ, *Oil Platforms*, Judgment, ICJ Rep. 2003, 161, separate opinion of Judge Simma, para. 78.
[23] Treaty of Amity, Economic Relations, and Consular Rights of 15 August 1955, entered into force on 16 June 1957, 284 UNTS 93.
[24] *Ibid.*, para. 60.

there exist two distinct 'new legal relationships' – one between the main actor and the injured State; the other between the complicit State and the injured State – it will in most cases be difficult to distinguish between the injury the two internationally wrongful acts have caused.[25]

The general problem thus lies in the apportioning of the shares of responsibility: how much responsibility has the main actor to bear and how much can the injured State recover from the complicit State? This question evidently needs to be assessed in light of the individual case and cannot be answered by an abstract formula.[26] However, criteria need to be determined which can give guidance for these individual cases, more so as the law of State responsibility is rather underdeveloped in this regard.[27] If the law provides no criteria in this regard, the effects of a provision on complicity would be considerably reduced. International law would then fail to provide policy-makers with the means to calculate the 'costs' for engaging in complicit behaviour. As desirable as application of the law 'as law' is, this additional factor needs to be taken into account. At the very least, clearly discernible rules on the apportioning of shares of responsibility which highlight the 'liability risks' for States in this regard can contribute to a more effective enforcement of international law against complicit behaviour[28] and thus exert a 'pull towards compliance'.[29]

1.2.1 Restitution

Restitution is the first form of reparation provided for in the ILC Articles (Article 35). It involves the 'reestablishment as far as possible of the situation which existed prior to the commission of the internationally wrongful act, to the extent that any changes that have occurred in that situation may be traced to that act'.[30] This is the very

---

[25] Pierre d'Argent, *Les réparations de guerre*, p. 553.
[26] Gaetano Arangio-Ruiz, 'Second Report on State Responsibility', UN Doc. A/CN.4/425 and Add.1, YBILC 1989, Vol. II, Part One, p. 15, para. 46; Andreas Felder, *Die Beihilfe*, p. 274.
[27] John E. Noyes and Brian D. Smith, 'State Responsibility and the Principle of Joint and Severable Liability', *Yale Journal of International Law* 13 (1988), pp. 225–67, at p. 225; Alexander Orakhelashvili, 'Division', p. 664.
[28] With respect to a plurality of responsible States in general, see Samantha Besson, 'La pluralité', p. 38.
[29] Thomas M. Franck, *Fairness in International Law and Institutions* (Oxford: Clarendon Press, 1995), p. 30.
[30] ILC Commentary, Article 35, para. 1.

core of the law of State responsibility as formulated by the PCIJ in the *Chorzów Factory* case:

The essential principle contained in the actual notion of an illegal act – a principle which seems to be established by international practice and in particular by the decisions of arbitral tribunals – is that reparation must, as far as possible, wipe out all the consequences of the illegal act and re-establish the situation which would, in all probability, have existed if that act had not been committed.[31]

While it is theoretically possible that a complicit State may provide for restitution, it is hard to imagine practical cases where this possibility will materialise: as the State which provided aid or assistance to the internationally wrongful act is only responsible for doing so through the connection of its support to the latter act, it will arguably not be in a position to re-establish the situation as it existed before the commission of the wrongful act. It would only be possible to do so within very narrow confines, for example demanding the main wrongdoing State to return military supplies provided earlier.[32] Such a measure would, however, arguably not constitute restitution in the full meaning of the term, as it would not re-establish a situation which had existed earlier in terms of the injury which has been inflicted on the victim. This becomes apparent from the typical examples the ILC has given for cases of restitution: they include the release of detained individuals, the handing over to a State of an individual arrested in its territory, the restitution of shops or of other types of property.[33] If we imagine the involvement of a complicit State in the wrongful acts giving rise to the need for these forms of restitution, it will only be the main actor who exercises control over the requisite persons or objects to comply with this requirement. Accordingly, what holds true generally – that 'there are often situations where restitution is not available' so 'that other forms of reparation take priority'[34] – is all the more fitting for situations which involve complicity.

In exceptional cases, restitution may, however, be an adequate form of reparation even in the case of complicity. From the survey of international practice on complicity conducted earlier in this study,[35] some forms of potential State complicity could be remedied by means of

---

[31] PCIJ, *Chorzów Factory Case*, Merits, Series A, No. 17, 47.
[32] See Andreas Felder, *Die Beihilfe*, pp. 276–7.
[33] ILC Commentary, Article 35, para. 5.   [34] *Ibid.*, para. 4.
[35] See Chapter 4 above.

restitution. These include the situations where responsibility for complicity is brought about by virtue of the recognition of foreign laws and judgments which are contrary to international law. As we have seen, some commentators and courts alike treat these issues as forms of complicity.[36] Here, one could argue that, as the application or recognition of the foreign law by virtue of statute or a court decision is the only form of bolstering its effects, a mere correction of the law or its application in the courts could constitute restitution. These will, however, be marginal cases. It is not entirely clear whether these issues should be discussed under the heading of complicity or whether they do not belong to situations which involve obligations of non-recognition in international law. Given that one is willing to see in such situations instances of complicity, restitution may thus have a role to play as an adequate form of reparation.

1.2.2 Compensation

Compensation poses significant problems with respect to complicit States.[37] At the same time, it is the most relevant form of reparation in practical terms. Article 36 ASR provides:

1. The State responsible for an internationally wrongful act is under an obligation to compensate for the damage caused thereby, insofar as such damage is not made good by restitution.

2. The compensation shall cover any financially assessable damage including loss of profits insofar as it is established.

As the ILC itself notes in its Commentary, restitution, 'despite its primacy as a matter of legal principle, is frequently unavailable or inadequate … Even where restitution is effected, it may be insufficient to ensure full reparation. The role of compensation is to fill in any gaps so as to ensure full reparation for damage suffered.'[38] This, again, closely follows the conception of the PCIJ in the *Chorzów Factory* case:

Restitution in kind, or, if this is not possible, payment of a sum corresponding to the value which a restitution in kind would bear; the award, if need be, of damages for loss sustained which would not be covered by restitution in kind of payment in place of it – such are the principles which should serve

---

[36] See, e.g., German Federal Constitutional Court, BVerfGE 75, 1, 18–19; see further Rainer Hofmann, 'Art. 25 GG', p. 51.
[37] Samantha Besson, 'La pluralité', p. 23.
[38] ILC Commentary, Article 36, para. 3; see also Ian Brownlie, *State Responsibility*, p. 211.

to determine the amount of compensation due for an act contrary to international law.[39]

The difficulty with complicity lies in measuring the exact 'share' of responsibility to be attributed to the complicit State. In this respect, the problem of causality needs to be taken into account again.[40] The general principle on reparation set out in Article 31(2) ASR is that the '[i]njury includes any damage, whether material or moral *caused* by the internationally wrongful act of a State' (emphasis added). According to the ILC, this is meant to 'make clear that the subject matter of reparation is, globally, the injury resulting from and ascribable to the wrongful act, *rather than any and all consequences flowing from an internationally wrongful act*'.[41] To identify the importance of causality for the determination of compensation does not, however, necessarily clarify things. As we have already seen in Chapter 5 and as numerous commentators have remarked, there is no single test of causality in international law and the state of the law on this matter is currently underdeveloped.[42] The ILC itself stated in its Commentary that 'the requirement of a causal link is not necessarily the same in relation to every breach of an international obligation'.[43] The situation is even more complex with respect to complicity, as has been already discussed in Chapter 5: ascribing responsibility for complicity can be at odds with notions of causality. The important aspect of causality that may thus be retained is the significant difference the aid or assistance has had on the carrying out of the main act. A difference lies, however, in the importance of the causal factor with respect to the establishment that there has been aid or assistance which triggers responsibility under Article 16 ASR and its influence on the determination of compensation due to the injured State (in German legal terminology, *haftungsbegründende* and *haftungsausfüllende Kausalität*). Whereas the general importance of causality in the first category may be questioned – and the ILC Commentary gives some

---

[39] PCIJ, *Chorzów Factory Case*, Merits, PCIJ Series A, No. 17, 47; for later affirmations of that principle, see ICJ, *Gabcikovo-Nagymaros Case*, Judgment, ICJ Rep. 1997, 7, para. 152; ICJ, *Legal Consequences of the Construction of a Wall in the Occupied Palestinian Territory*, Advisory Opinion, ICJ Rep. 2004, 136, paras. 152–3.
[40] See our discussion in Chapter 5, text accompanying notes 74 *et seq.*
[41] ILC Commentary, Article 31, para. 9, emphasis added.
[42] See, e.g., Gaetano Arangio-Ruiz, 'Second Report on State Responsibility', UN Doc. A/CN.4/425 and Add.1, YBILC 1989, Vol. II, Part One, p. 15, para. 46; Tal Becker, *Terrorism and the State*, pp. 287 *et seq.*; Andrea Gattini, 'Breach', p. 708.
[43] ILC Commentary, Article 31, para. 10.

indications to that effect[44] – there is no way around it in the second category. If it is already a general principle applicable to compensation in traditional bilateral settings that 'remote' damages or 'indirect' damages are not susceptible to compensation, this must apply *a fortiori* for the case of complicity where the attribution of remote consequences to the complicit State would be especially unfair and would go against the general structure of the law in that regard.[45]

Generally speaking, the factor of causality will thus have to limit the amount of compensation which can be demanded from the complicit State. This already flows, at least in principle, from the conception of Article 16 ASR as an independent internationally wrongful act.[46] It is, however, important to reaffirm this with respect to the consequences of complicity. It is all too easy to assume otherwise and to introduce a regime of compensation which would require complicit States to compensate for a larger part of the injury than their actual share of contribution.[47] Part of this tendency is owed to a confusion between complicity, joint conduct and joint parallel conduct. Graefrath argues that in terms of the 'legal consequence of responsibility any distinction between an accomplice and a co-author disappears because complicity too, is treated as a separate wrongful act'.[48] By contrast, Vaughan Lowe has rightly emphasised the essential difference between complicity and joint responsibility.[49] If this barrier is not to break down, international law will have to acknowledge the fundamentally different character of these two categories: the peculiar element of responsibility for complicity is the lawful character of the support rendered which only becomes unlawful by virtue of its connection to the wrongful act of another State, whereas joint responsibility presupposes wrongful conduct on

---

[44] The ILC Commentary spells out that 'the aid or assistance must be given with a view to facilitate the commission of that act, and must actually do so' (Article 16, para. 4), whereas it is also possible that it 'may have contributed only to a minor degree' (Article 16, para. 10).

[45] See also Chittharanjan F. Amerasinghe, *Diplomatic Protection* (Oxford: Oxford University Press, 2008), p. 275.

[46] ILC Commentary, Article 16, para. 10; see also Christine D. Gray, *Judicial Remedies*, p. 23.

[47] See, e.g., John Quigley, 'Complicity', p. 128; Bernhard Graefrath, 'Complicity', p. 379; more tentative in that regard are Andreas Felder, *Die Beihilfe*, p. 277; Alexander Orakhelashvili, 'Division', p. 658.

[48] Bernhard Graefrath, 'Complicity', p. 379.

[49] Vaughan Lowe, 'Responsibility', p. 11; see also Olivier De Schutter, 'Globalization and Jurisdiction: Lessons from the European Convention on Human Rights', *Baltic Yearbook of International Law* 6 (2006), pp. 185–247, at p. 239.

the part of both (or all) wrongdoing States. If this distinction ought to have any meaning, it is necessary to affirm that complicit States will only have to award compensation insofar as they have, by virtue of their support, contributed to the 'factually indivisible' damage the injured State suffered.

A relevant point of comparison in that regard is the *Corfu Channel* case.[50] It has to be remembered that this was a case in which complicity was not the main issue, although the United Kingdom included references to Albanian complicity in the mine-laying in its written submissions.[51] According to the ICJ, the destruction of the British ships and the loss of lives of British sailors was caused by the action of a third State in laying the mines *and* by the Albanian failure to warn of the presence of the mines in the Corfu Channel. A similar line of reasoning was adopted by the United States when it initiated proceedings against Hungary and the Soviet Union in the *Treatment of Aircraft and Crew* case in 1954. As has been mentioned earlier in the chapter on international practice,[52] the United States wanted to hold the two States jointly responsible and made reference to both joint responsibility and the Soviet Union having aided and abetted Hungary in the allegedly unlawful arrest of the aircraft and crew.[53] In another case, the *Aerial Incident* case which was brought against Bulgaria by the United States, the United Kingdom and Israel (in separate applications), the United States held the view that 'in all civilised countries the rule is substantially the same. An aggrieved plaintiff may sue any or all joint tortfeasors, jointly or severally, although he may collect from them, or any one or more of them, only the full amount of his damage.'[54]

The conclusion the ILC drew from these cases is that,

[a]lthough ... the injury in question was caused by a combination of factors, only one of which is to be ascribed to the responsible State, international practice and the decisions of international tribunals do not support the reduction

---

[50] ICJ, *Corfu Channel Case*, Judgment, ICJ Rep. 1949, 4.
[51] *Ibid.*, British Memorial, ICJ Pleadings 1949, Vol. I, p. 19, paras. 77 and 94.
[52] See Chapter 4, text accompanying notes 322 *et seq.*
[53] *Treatment in Hungary of Aircraft and Crew of United States of America (United States of America v. Hungarian People's Republic; United States of America v. Union of Soviet Socialist Republics)*, Application Instituting Proceedings Against the Hungarian People's Republic, ICJ Pleadings 1954, 10.
[54] *Aerial Incident Cases (United States of America v. Bulgaria)*, Memorial of 2 December 1958, ICJ Pleadings 1958, 229.

or attenuation of reparation for concurrent causes, except in cases of contributory fault.[55]

This position is, however, not uncontested.[56] Special Rapporteur Gaetano Arangio-Ruiz considered that, whenever concurrent causes have contributed to an internationally wrongful act and the injury it has brought about, the shares of compensation ought to be reduced according to the causal contribution of each wrongful act.[57] He wrote:

Consideration must be given to cases in which the injuries are not caused exclusively by an unlawful act but have been produced also by concomitant causes among which the unlawful act plays a decisive but not exclusive role. In such cases, to hold the author State liable for full compensation would be neither equitable nor in conformity with a proper application of the causal link criterion. The solution should be the payment of partial damages, in proportion to the amount of injury presumably to be attributed to the wrongful act and its effects, the amount to be awarded on the basis of the criteria of normality and predictability ... Economic, political and natural factors and actions by third parties are just a few of the innumerable elements which may contribute to a damage as concomitant causes.[58]

It is difficult to say what inferences are to be drawn from this position for the problem of complicity. The emphasis on the separateness of responsibility of the complicit State and the principal wrongdoing State will not by itself lead to convincing results in all cases. *Corfu Channel* shows that courts and tribunals may be willing to redefine situations of complicity in order to hold States which are only indirectly responsible liable for a greater share of damage.[59] The more recent *Genocide Convention* case points, however, in the opposite direction and shows greater reluctance on the part of the Court to order compensation to be paid by a State which has indirectly influenced the commission of an internationally wrongful act.[60] Having found a violation of Article I of the Genocide Convention, the obligation to prevent and punish

---

[55] ILC Commentary, Article 31, para. 12; on concurrent causes in general legal theory, see H. L. A. Hart and Tony Honoré, *Causation in the Law*, p. 205.
[56] See also Pierre d'Argent, *Les réparations de guerre*, p. 747.
[57] Gaetano Arangio-Ruiz, 'Second Report on State Responsibility', UN Doc. A/CN.4/425 and Add.1, YBILC 1989, Vol. II, Part One, p. 14, para. 44.
[58] *Ibid.*, paras. 44–5.
[59] See Ian Brownlie, *State Responsibility*, p. 189.
[60] ICJ, *Case Concerning the Application of the Convention on the Prevention and Punishment of Genocide*, Judgment, para. 462.

genocide, the Court explored whether it could award compensation to Bosnia and Herzegovina.[61] It held that it

> must ascertain whether, and to what extent, the injury asserted by the Applicant is the consequence of the wrongful conduct by the Respondent with the consequence that the Respondent should be required to make reparation for it, in accordance with the principle of customary international law stated above. In this context, the question just mentioned, whether the genocide at Srebrenica would have taken place even if the Respondent had attempted to prevent it by employing all means in its possession, becomes directly relevant, for the definition of the extent of the obligation of reparation borne by the Respondent as a result of its wrongful conduct. The question is whether there is a *sufficiently direct and certain causal nexus* between the wrongful act ... and the injury suffered by the Applicant, consisting of all damage of any type, material or moral, caused by the acts of genocide. Such a nexus could be considered established only if the Court were able to conclude from the case as a whole and with a sufficient degree of certainty that the genocide at Srebrenica would in fact have been averted if the Respondent had acted in compliance with its legal obligations. However, the Court cannot clearly do so.[62]

For the present purpose, it needs to be remembered that the Court was dealing with an omission. Issues of causality are especially tricky when omissions are involved.[63] The Court had to face the difficulty of assessing whether the omitted action by the Federal Republic of Yugoslavia would have made any difference at all. It is thus not possible to apply the findings of the Court directly to the issue of complicity which will, in most cases,[64] involve active conduct. In addition, the reasoning of the Court on the finding whether there can be compensation for the breach of the obligation to prevent, is open to criticism for a number of reasons, among them that the Court is greatly reducing the practical value of its enhanced interpretation of Article I of the Genocide Convention through its restrictive position on the issue of reparation.[65] However, the underlying rationale of the Court's reasoning emphasises

---

[61] *Ibid.*, para. 460. [62] *Ibid.*, para. 462, emphasis added.
[63] Andrea Gattini, 'Breach', p. 709; see further Gordon A. Christenson, 'Attributing Acts of Omission to the State', *Michigan Journal of International Law* 12 (1991), pp. 312–70.
[64] Whether complicity is conceivable in situations of omission is another problematic matter; see our discussion in Chapter 5, text accompanying notes 153 *et seq.*
[65] Cf Christian Tomuschat, 'Reparation in Cases of Genocide', *Journal of International Criminal Justice* 5 (2007), pp. 905–12, at pp. 907 *et seq.*; Marko Milanovic, 'Follow-Up', p. 691; for a more positive assessment, see Pierre-Marie Dupuy, 'Crime sans châtiment ou mission accomplie', *Revue générale de droit international public* 111 (2007), pp. 243–57, at pp. 255–6.

the limits of imposing compensation for wrongful acts if different wrongful acts have contributed to the eventual injury. If we imagine a continuous line of wrongful acts, one could place the commission of a solitary wrongful act by a main actor at one end of the line while the breach of an obligation to prevent the act would sit at the other end of the line. Arguably, the complicity situation sits somewhere in between these two extremes. This would imply that the attribution of compensation to be paid will not have to surmount hurdles as high as those established by the ICJ in the *Genocide Convention* case. Compensation in cases of complicity does not have to rest on the assumption that the wrongful act would not have occurred but for the aid or assistance furnished in its support.[66] At the same time, the situation of complicity is arguably not that different from the way the ICJ interpreted the obligation to prevent in Article I of the Genocide Convention which would support the argument that compensation has to be strictly limited to the effects the aid or assistance caused. This degree of causation can only be determined in a normative way: it will have to rest, to some degree, on a judicial decision which applies certain standards in order to delimit the shares of responsibility. An example of such an approach is given by the ECtHR in its *Ilascu* case where the Court found both Moldova and the Russian Federation responsible for certain acts committed in Transdniestria.[67] The Court divided the 'just satisfaction' under Article 41 ECHR between the two respondent States without giving further reasons as to the balance (two-thirds to one-third) it struck.[68]

1.2.3 Satisfaction

Of the three forms of reparation, satisfaction poses the least significant problems for situations of complicity. Satisfaction is only considered an adequate form of reparation if 'the act cannot be made good by restitution or compensation' (Article 37(1) ASR). It can then consist 'in an acknowledgement of the breach, an expression of regret, a formal apology or another appropriate modality' (Article 37(2) ASR). In this regard, satisfaction 'shall not be out of proportion to the injury and may not take a form humiliating to the responsible State' (Article 37(3) ASR).

---

[66] It is questionable whether this was really required with respect to the obligation to prevent: see Andrea Gattini, 'Breach', p. 710.
[67] ECtHR, *Ilascu and Others* v. *Moldova and Russia*, ECHR 2004-VII, 179, paras. 484 *et seq.*
[68] See also Stefan Talmon, 'Plurality', p. 210, note 156.

Satisfaction may also consist of a declaratory judgment of an international court or tribunal.[69]

Although the degree of satisfaction a wrongdoing State has to offer to the injured State will therefore vary, it is easier to adjust the measure of satisfaction than it is to reach agreement on the amount of monetary compensation a complicit State owes to an injured State as compared to the main actor. Hence, satisfaction is a form of reparation which could be rather easily obtained in the case of complicity. A similar reasoning underlies the ICJ's finding that Bosnia and Herzegovina was entitled to satisfaction from Serbia and Montenegro for the violation of Article I of the Genocide Convention.[70] Only the general obstacles to reaching agreement on the issue of whether satisfaction is due have to be overcome, which are, however, in the case of complicity no greater than in any other form of international responsibility. In other words, there exist no structural reasons why reparation in the form of satisfaction is harder to determine in the case of complicity than 'in ordinary situations'.

An acknowledgment of responsibility, or a formal apology, can take account of the secondary role the complicit State played. This factor can be reflected in the statement that is issued by the complicit State. In fact, satisfaction may turn out to be the most appropriate form of remedy for a large number of situations involving complicity. As has been shown with respect to compensation, it will in most situations be difficult to calculate the actual share of responsibility for which a complicit State can be held accountable.[71] One danger which has to be taken into account is the possibility that satisfaction is automatically awarded following a finding of responsibility for complicity. As Andrea Gattini has remarked in a different context, awarding satisfaction instead of compensation may give rise to an impression of 'half-heartedness' on the part of a court.[72] Although satisfaction may be the most appropriate remedy in a good number of situations which involve complicity, the potentiality needs to be preserved that *restitution ad integrum* or compensation may also be awarded in judicial or arbitral proceedings as

---

[69] ICJ, *Corfu Channel Case*, Judgment, ICJ Rep. 1949, 4, 35–6; ICJ, *Case Concerning the Application of the Convention on the Prevention and Punishment of Genocide*, Judgment, para. 463; Ian Brownlie, *State Responsibility*, pp. 200–1; ILC Commentary, Article 37, para. 6.
[70] ICJ, *Case Concerning the Application of the Convention on the Prevention and Punishment of Genocide*, Judgment, para. 463.
[71] John E. Noyes and Brian D. Smith, 'State Responsibility', p. 241.
[72] Andrea Gattini, 'Breach', p. 711.

well as in diplomatic settings in order to underline the risks of liability complicit States will face.

A constructive solution to this problem lies in the granting of satisfaction in the form of a monetary payment.[73] Although the ILC did not include monetary forms of satisfaction in its Commentary, the wording of the provision ('Satisfaction may consist in … or another appropriate modality' (Article 37(2) ASR)) indicates that the forms mentioned (acknowledgment of the breach, expression of regret, formal apology) are not exclusive of other forms of satisfaction. Tomuschat mentions that the possibility of awarding a symbolic monetary compensation under the guise of satisfaction was considered by the tribunal in the *Rainbow Warrior* case.[74] There, the tribunal held the view that 'an order for the payment of monetary compensation can be made in respect of the breach of international obligations involving, as here, serious moral and legal damage, even though there is no material damage'.[75] Although the tribunal considered this form of monetary compensation for immaterial damage under the heading of compensation, moral damage would need to be taken into account as part of satisfaction. This follows from the approach of the ILC, which requests that damages to be considered for compensation need to be financially assessable.[76] Accordingly, Tomuschat's suggestion to award satisfaction in monetary terms may be a way out of the dilemma of how to determine shares of responsibility in terms of compensation. Obviously, this process would involve approximation, equity and policy considerations on the part of judges and arbitrators to determine what amount of money would be appropriate as a form of satisfaction.[77] However, once States have submitted a dispute to judicial or arbitral dispute settlement, they will have conferred jurisdiction upon the body in question to decide on the legal consequences of unlawful acts.[78]

1.3 *Implementation of responsibility*

Implementation is the logical consequence of the determination of the content of responsibility. Generally, a State must of course only

---

[73] Ian Brownlie, *State Responsibility*, pp. 208–9; Brian D. Smith, *State Responsibility*, p. 49; Christian Tomuschat, 'Reparation', p. 909.
[74] *Ibid.*
[75] *Rainbow Warrior*, Arbitral Award, 82 ILR 499, para. 118.
[76] See Article 36, para. 2, ASR; and ILC Commentary, Article 36, para. 1.
[77] Christian Tomuschat, 'Reparation', p. 909.
[78] PCIJ, *Chorzów Factory Case*, Jurisdiction, Series A, No. 9, 21.

face implementation within the limits established under the respective rules on the content of its responsibility. Implementation of State responsibility is concerned with the means at the disposal of States faced with a breach of an international obligation. The rules on implementation govern what action may be taken 'in order to secure the performance of the obligations of cessation and reparation on the part of the responsible State'.[79] However, at the same time, situations are conceivable wherein a State may face measures of implementation which go beyond the content of its own responsibility. So much was made clear by the ICJ in the *Nauru* case. There, Australia raised the preliminary objection that its responsibility could only be brought before the Court as part of a claim directed against the totality of the three States making up the Administering Authority under the Trusteeship Agreement. In this regard, the Court held:

Australia has raised the question whether the liability of the three States would be 'joint and several' (*solidaire*), so that any one of the three would be liable to make full reparation for damage flowing from any breach of the obligations of the Administering Authority, and not merely a one-third or some other proportionate share. This is a question which the Court must reserve for the merits; but it is independent of the question whether Australia can be sued alone.[80]

The ILC has subdivided the topic of implementation into the invocation of responsibility and the taking of countermeasures. Both parts of this field of law are relevant for the implementation of responsibility of complicit States and are generally applicable to these situations. As is the case with the content of responsibility, however, certain problems may exist which could call for deviation from the general standards as set out in the ASR. This applies for the invocation of responsibility to a greater extent than it does with respect to countermeasures.

Countermeasures are unlawful measures directed against a State responsible for the commission of an internationally wrongful act in order to induce the responsible State to comply with its obligations.[81]

---

[79] ILC Commentary, Introduction to Part Three, para. 1.
[80] ICJ, *Certain Phosphate Lands in Nauru*, Preliminary Objections, ICJ Rep. 1992, 240, para. 48; see also *ibid.*, separate opinion of Judge Shahabuddeen, p. 286.
[81] *Air Service Agreement of 27 March 1946 Between the United States of America and France*, Arbitral Award, RIAA XVIII, 417, paras. 80 *et seq.*; ICJ, *Gabcikovo-Nagymaros Case*, Judgment, ICJ Rep. 1997, 7, paras. 82 *et seq.*; ILC Commentary, Introduction to Part Three, Chapter Two, paras. 1 *et seq.*

The taking of countermeasures is controversial in general. As the modern denomination of the traditional forms of self-help which were called 'reprisals',[82] this instrument has been criticised for its inherent potential to contribute to the escalation of international disputes.[83] As States are generally self-judging whether or not they wish to resort to countermeasures, a risk exists that different parties to a legal relationship all resort to countermeasures, all of them holding the view that they are entitled to do so.[84] There are, however, no structural reasons which exacerbate the problem of countermeasures in the case of complicit States beyond the policy argument that a multiplication of countermeasures may not necessarily be conducive to cooperation and peace between States.[85] The taking of countermeasures against States responsible under Article 16 ASR also does not infringe upon the principle that third States shall not be affected by countermeasures.[86] In the literature on obligations *erga omnes*, it has been noted that countermeasures have always been directed against the States directly responsible and not against a State merely condoning the situation. This is explained by a general rule according to which countermeasures cannot affect the rights of third States.[87] While this is, in principle, correct, it does not concern countermeasures against complicit States as these can no longer be classified as 'third States'.

The picture is different with respect to the invocation of responsibility. The pertinent question is whether a complicit State may be sued for the whole injury suffered by an injured State. If answered in the affirmative, the subsequent question would then be whether the complicit State has a right of recourse against the main actor State.

Article 47 ASR may be pertinent in this regard. The ILC has not been very clear on the question whether this Article applies to responsibility for complicity under Article 16. Article 47 provides:

---

[82] See *Naulilaa Incident Arbitration*, Arbitral Award, RIAA II, 1012, at pp. 1025 *et seq.*
[83] For a discussion, with further references, see Mary Ellen O'Connell, *Power and Purpose*, pp. 229 *et seq.*
[84] It was a matter of long and protracted debate whether the ASR should include a dispute settlement mechanism which would have been mandatory before the taking of countermeasures; see on this issue Christian J. Tams, 'All's Well', pp. 786 *et seq.*
[85] For this policy argument, see Eckart Klein, 'Gegenmaßnahmen', *Berichte der Deutschen Gesellschaft für Völkerrecht* 37 (1997), pp. 39–71, at p. 52.
[86] ILC Commentary, Article 49, para. 5.
[87] Christian J. Tams, *Enforcing Obligations Erga Omnes*, p. 230.

1. Where several States are responsible for the same internationally wrongful act, the responsibility of each State may be invoked in relation to that act.
2. Paragraph 1:
   (a) does not permit any injured State to recover, by way of compensation, more than the damage it has suffered;
   (b) is without prejudice to any right of recourse against the other responsible States.

The wording of this provision speaks against the assumption that it would apply to situations covered by Article 16 ASR. It deals with situations where a plurality of States are responsible for the *same* wrongful act. This is arguably not the case with respect to Article 16 ASR, where the Commission has been fairly clear in stating that 'the assisting State is responsible for its own act in deliberately assisting another State ... It is not responsible, as such, for the act of the assisted State.'[88] However, the Commentary is not very succinct insofar as it distinguishes between situations in which 'the assistance is a necessary element in the wrongful act in absence of which it could not have occurred' and the case in which 'the assistance may have been only an incidental factor'.[89] In the former situation, the Commission points out that 'the injury suffered can be concurrently attributed to the assisting and the acting State'.[90] With respect to consequences, the Commission refers to Article 47 ASR.[91] In general, the Commission appears to hold the view that the liability of the complicit State is limited to the consequences which flow from its own conduct, for example the assistance furnished to the principal actor.[92] To hold otherwise would also challenge the very construction of Article 16 ASR: if the contribution to a wrongful act and the ensuing injury is so great as to warrant a finding that the complicit State is responsible for the whole injury, that would raise the assumption of no longer classifying the State in question as complicit but rather as a (or even the) main actor.

The reason for the confusion as to the applicability of Article 47 ASR appears to lie in a conflation of the wrongful act with the injury caused by a wrongful act. The relevant passage of the ILC Commentary speaks about the situation in which an injury is to be attributed to several States, whereas the wording of Article 47 ASR

---

[88] ILC Commentary, Article 16, para. 10.   [89] *Ibid.*
[90] *Ibid.*   [91] *Ibid.*, note 301.   [92] *Ibid.*, Article 16, para. 10.

clearly presupposes not an injury caused by several States, but an identical wrongful act, i.e., two (or more) States having acted jointly. Situations which are covered by Article 16 ASR are therefore not mentioned in the commentary to Article 47 ASR, unlike situations where one State directs or controls another State which are governed by Article 17 ASR.[93]

Although Article 47 ASR thus appears to be not directly applicable to situations of complicity,[94] it could provide guidance for the implementation of responsibility in situations covered by Article 16 ASR. Article 47 ASR allows an injured State to hold each responsible State liable for the conduct attributable to it, without having to reduce its claim due to the mere fact that another State contributed to the *same* internationally wrongful act. In this regard, the Article reaffirms the position of the ICJ in the *Corfu Channel* case.[95] Article 47(2) ASR makes it clear, however, that its scope is limited to the implementation stage: according to sub-paragraph (b), the provision is without prejudice to any right of recourse against the other responsible States.

Is it conceivable that a similar regime of joint and several responsibility in terms of implementation applies to complicit States? After all, the situation of 'factually indivisible wrongful acts', as identified by Judge Simma in the *Oil Platforms* case,[96] could call for this solution. Authors who have dealt with this issue with respect to complicity have underlined that it is in the interest of the best protection of injured States that they could hold a complicit State responsible for the whole of the injury caused.[97] However, it should be borne in mind what Vaughan Lowe has underlined: if the boundary between joint perpetratorship of wrongful acts and complicity is not to be blurred, certain distinctions have to apply in terms of the consequences attached to the different forms of States acting together.[98]

One reason for caution regarding a solution of joint and several responsibility with respect to complicity is the unclear status this

---

[93] *Ibid.*, Article 47, para. 2.
[94] Contra: Alexander Orakhelashvili, 'Division', p. 658.
[95] ICJ, *Corfu Channel Case*, Judgment, ICJ Rep. 1949, 4, 22–3.
[96] ICJ, *Oil Platforms*, Judgment, ICJ Rep. 2003, 161, separate opinion of Judge Simma, para. 78.
[97] Bernhard Graefrath, 'Complicity', p. 379; Andreas Felder, *Die Beihilfe*, p. 277.
[98] Vaughan Lowe, 'Responsibility', p. 10; see also Linos-Alexandre Sicilianos, *Les réactions décentralisées à l'illicite – Des contremesures à la légitime défense* (Paris: LGDJ, 1990), p. 78; Olivier De Schutter, 'Globalization and Jurisdiction', p. 239.

doctrine enjoys even in cases of joint conduct by States.[99] Article 47 ASR does not give clear guidance in this regard and has been considered to be generally of limited authority.[100] There was considerable criticism of joint and several responsibility in the dissenting opinions of Judges Ago and Schwebel in the *Nauru* case.[101] Although Judge Simma was more willing to acknowledge the existence of a principle of joint and several responsibility in international law,[102] authority on this matter is otherwise sparse.[103] Scholarly treatments of the issue usually set out to develop such a regime, but do so in a prospective style.[104] In arbitral practice, caution prevails even in situations where the responsibility of joint organs of States has been at stake.[105] In the *Eurotunnel* arbitration, for instance, the tribunal held that, although cooperation was required by joint organs of France and the United Kingdom, the issue '[w]hether particular breaches of the Concession Agreement result from the fault of one or the other or both States will depend on the particular obligation violated and on all the circumstances'.[106] The position of the ILC in its Article 47 and the accompanying commentary is not very clear either. The careful wording of both Article and the commentary speak against the assumption that the ILC wanted to make a clear statement for the

---

[99] Christine Chinkin, *Third Parties*, pp. 208–9; Pierre d'Argent, *Les réparations de guerre*, p. 748.
[100] Samantha Besson, 'La pluralité', p. 15; Pierre d'Argent, *Les réparations de guerre*, p. 751; see also *Eurotunnel Arbitration*, Partial Award, 132 ILR 1, paras. 162 *et seq.*
[101] ICJ, *Certain Phosphate Lands in Nauru*, Preliminary Objections, ICJ Rep. 1992, 240, dissenting opinion of Judge Ago, p. 328; dissenting opinion of Judge Schwebel, p. 342.
[102] ICJ, *Oil Platforms*, Judgment, ICJ Rep. 2003, 161, separate opinion of Judge Simma, para. 78.
[103] Phoebe N. Okowa, *State Responsibility*, pp. 200–1; see also US Court of Claims, *Anglo-Chinese Shipping Company Ltd v. United States*, 22 ILR 982, 986: This issue 'has never been decided'. See also the opinion of the Swiss federal political bureau: 'Responsabilité internationale pour des dommages causé dans la zone de Tanger' of 30 April 1952, reprinted in Paul Guggenheim, 'Documentation – Droit international public', *Schweizerisches Jahrbuch für Internationales Recht* 10 (1953), pp. 191–254, at pp. 238 and 247–8.
[104] Samantha Besson, 'La pluralité', pp. 15 *et seq.*; John E. Noyes and Brian D. Smith, 'State Responsibility', pp. 225 *et seq.*; Brian D. Smith, *State Responsibility*, pp. 59 *et seq.*; but see Alexander Orakhelashvili, 'Division', p. 657, who holds the concept to be well established in international law.
[105] For a similar assessment, see Stephan Wittich, 'Joint Tortfeasors in Investment Law', in Christina Binder, Ursula Kriebaum, August Reinisch and Stephan Wittich (eds.), *International Investment Law for the 21st Century – Essays in Honour of Christoph Schreuer* (Oxford: Oxford University Press, 2009), pp. 708–23, at p. 716.
[106] *Eurotunnel Arbitration*, Partial Award, ILR 132, 1, para. 187.

recognition of the concept of joint and several responsibility in international law.[107] In contrast, a clearly established rule in this regard can be found in the Convention on the International Liability for Damage Caused by Space Objects.[108] Article IV of the Convention provides:

1. In the event of damage being caused elsewhere than on the surface of the earth to a space object of one launching State or to persons or property on board such a space object by a space object of another launching State, and of damage thereby being caused to a third State or to its natural or juridical persons, the first two States shall be jointly and severally liable to the third State, to the extent indicated by the following:

(a) If the damage has been caused to the third State on the surface of the earth or to aircraft in flight, their liability to the third State shall be absolute;

(b) If the damage has been caused to a space object of the third State or to persons or property on board that space object elsewhere than on the surface of the earth, their liability to the third State shall be based on the fault of either of the first two States or on the fault of persons for whom either is responsible.

2. In all cases of joint and several liability referred to in paragraph 1 of this article, the burden of compensation for the damage shall be apportioned between the first two States in accordance with the extent to which they were at fault; if the extent of the fault of each of these States cannot be established, the burden of compensation shall be apportioned equally between them. Such apportionment shall be without prejudice to the right of the third State to seek the entire compensation due under this Convention from any or all of the launching States which are jointly and severally liable.

These formulations leave no doubt as to the establishment of a system of joint and several liability where the injured State can recover the entire compensation from only one of the liable States. Article V of the Convention establishes also joint and several liability for the case of two or more States launching space objects which leads to damage.[109] These provisions are, however, not expressive of a general principle. They are *leges speciales* and they are also concerned with issues of liability instead of breach-based responsibility as is the case with the

---

[107] Stephan Wittich, 'Joint Tortfeasors', p. 717.
[108] Convention on the International Liability for Damage Caused by Space Objects of 29 March 1972, entered into force on 1 September 1972, 961 UNTS 187.
[109] On the regime of the Convention, see further Peter Malanczuk, 'Haftung', in Karl-Heinz Böckstiegel (ed.), *Handbuch des Weltraumrechts* (Cologne: Heymanns, 1991), pp. 755–803, at pp. 785 *et seq.*

ASR.[110] One thing that can be inferred from them is, however, that their formulation is much more explicit than Article 47 ASR where the ILC leaves the impression that ultimately Article 47 ASR can be interpreted as being both favourable for and cautious about affirming joint and several liability.[111] For the case of complicity, this would suggest that caution should apply *a fortiori* with respect to this weaker form of participation in the commission of a wrongful act.

Another argument against joint and several responsibility between the complicit State and the main actor lies in the fact that the international legal system is lacking a general infrastructure to adjudicate the claims of internal recourse in an appropriate manner.[112] It also lacks mechanisms to order third States to enter judicial proceedings.[113] Phoebe N. Okowa has observed that the harshness of a rule of solidary responsibility which exists in most domestic legal systems 'has been mitigated by a statutory right of contribution as between tortfeasors in both Civil and Common law systems. The apportionment of responsibility in any subsequent action for contribution is determined either on the basis of relative causation or blameworthiness (or both).'[114] However, an effective judicial administration of joint and several responsibility is not conceivable at the international level, at least for the time being. To a certain extent, the choice of against which State to bring a claim of solidary responsibility is arbitrary. The injured State could focus on the 'weakest link in the chain', i.e., a rather remote complicit State, which would then have to redress the whole of the injury suffered by the injured State. Whether this State subsequently has an effective remedy at its disposal to redress its losses against the other responsible States is open to doubt. While one could see this uncertainty and arbitrariness as a welcome step in the direction of a more effective enforcement of responsibility for complicity (as it would highlight the liability risks for complicit States), it is more representative of the German adage '*mitgegangen, mitgefangen, mitgehangen*'[115] than of the development of a

---

[110] See also ILC Commentary, Article 47, para. 5; Stephan Wittich, 'Joint Tortfeasors', p. 719.
[111] Cf Pierre d'Argent, *Les réparations de guerre*, p. 751.
[112] Cf Brian D. Smith, *State Responsibility*, p. 59.
[113] ICJ, *Certain Phosphate Lands in Nauru*, Preliminary Objections, ICJ Rep. 1992, 240, para. 53.
[114] Phoebe N. Okowa, *State Responsibility*, p. 198.
[115] This adage is not easily translated. It literally means 'gone with the gang, captured and hung with it'.

progressive regime for the apportionment of international claims in the face of multiple responsible actors.

Finally, a right to internal recourse would need to be considered if there was joint and several liability between the complicit State and the main actor. Here, we would need to differentiate between the situation where the complicit State has been held responsible and was obligated to satisfy the full demands of the injured State and the situation where the main actor has effected full compensation to the injured State. In the first case, it would appear to be unjustifiable not to give the complicit State a right of internal recourse against the main actor if the former has been held responsible beyond the share of responsibility it has actually caused. In the second case, however, it would appear to be doubtful whether it is justified to give a main actor a right of recourse against complicit States. Such a right would effectively condone an 'unlawful relationship' between the main actor and the complicit State. It would mean that international law would sanction the entering into of a 'pact of unlawfulness' between two States. It would create a legitimate expectation on the side of wrongdoing States that a share of the responsibility for internationally wrongful acts can be recovered. From a policy perspective, this could encourage wrongdoing States to assemble as many allies as possible. However, it needs to be assessed critically whether such a policy perspective is helpful here. It may be counter-intuitive to give the main actor a right of redress against its accomplices. However, one needs to take into account other rules and principles of international law. One which springs to mind in this regard is the principle of unjust enrichment.[116] If the complicit State is absolved from any claims against it by virtue of the main actor having compensated the injured State, it is warranted to give the main actor a right of internal recourse against the complicit State. This would presuppose that the complicit State is still unjustifiably enriched by its complicit behaviour. The unjust enrichment may lie in the fact that it would no longer have to satisfy a claim which could otherwise have been brought against it. Arguably, this will first and foremost concern cases of compensation as measures of restitution and satisfaction demanded of the main actor will already take into account the specificity of its conduct. Compensation is more likely to cover the exact

---

[116] Cf Christoph Schreuer, 'Unjust Enrichment', in Rudolf Bernhardt (ed.), *Encyclopedia of Public International Law*, Vol. IV, Q–Z (Amsterdam: Elsevier, 2000), pp. 1243–6.

amount of financially assessable injury which will then often include the shares of injury which would have to be attributed to the participation of more remote actors.

1.4 Policy considerations for a prospective regime

After having reviewed this unsatisfactory state of the law, it can safely be stated that there is a need for further development of the law with respect to the content and invocation of responsibility for complicity in international law. Thinking about these prospective rules involves the making of policy decisions. The first of them revolves around the issue whether there should be a presumption for a reduced share of responsibility for the complicit State. As we have seen, the complicit State is technically not responsible for the internationally wrongful act of the State to which it granted aid or assistance. However, on a practical level, the two different internationally wrongful acts are hard to distinguish as they will, in most cases, have led to a single damage or injury on the part of the injured State ('factual indivisibility'[117]). One solution is, as has been discussed, to hold the complicit State responsible for the whole damage suffered by the injured State, as was done in the *Corfu Channel* case, albeit not on the basis of responsibility for complicity, but with respect to a violation of an individual international obligation by Albania.[118]

However, this solution appears unwarranted. Effectively, it holds the complicit State responsible in the very same way as international law would hold a main actor responsible. It would diminish the importance of developing rules on complicity if the complicit State ultimately faced the same consequences as a State which has acted jointly together with another State.[119] One policy choice would thus be to provide for a reduced form of responsibility for the complicit State, at least in comparison to the amount of responsibility of the main actor. This solution is, strictly speaking, not only a policy decision: it follows the position of the ILC that the complicit State is only responsible for its own actions, i.e. the amount of aid or assistance it has provided to the State committing the internationally wrongful act. It would find confirmation in the general position of the ILC that compensation should not be payable

---

[117] ICJ, *Oil Platforms*, Judgment, ICJ Rep. 2003, 161, separate opinion of Judge Simma, para. 78.
[118] ICJ, *Corfu Channel Case*, Judgment, ICJ Rep. 1949, 4.
[119] Similarly, Vaughan Lowe, 'Responsibility', p. 10.

for 'any and all consequences flowing from an internationally wrongful act'.[120]

The second policy choice to be made concerns the issue whether, implementation-wise, a complicit State can be held responsible for the whole damage suffered by the injured State (and could then have recourse against the main actor). To give injured States such a right would possibly strengthen the prohibition of complicity in international law as complicit States would face considerable liability risks under this model. However, this model might effectively let powerful States who commit wrongful acts off the hook too easily. Such States would also be given the incentive to 'assemble a posse'[121] of complicit States. These allies, which would typically be less powerful States,[122] would be easier targets from whom to obtain reparation for damages caused primarily by the conduct of the main actor. In turn, it could be difficult for the complicit State to gain redress from the main actor. In this perspective, it does not appear as a legitimate solution to hold complicit States and the main actor 'jointly and severally' responsible.

2 Complicit States before international courts and tribunals

Holding States responsible before international courts and tribunals is a different issue from the question whether a State is responsible for the commission of an internationally wrongful act. The mere fact that no judicial avenue exists to hold a State responsible does not change the fact that there exists international responsibility. This is also true for the case of complicity.[123] However, there is a further reason to inquire into the means available to hold complicit States responsible: it is necessary to establish the responsibility of another State, i.e., the main actor, before responsibility for complicity can be established. Although situations may occur where all relevant States involved in a dispute have consented to the exercise of jurisdiction by

---

[120] ILC Commentary, Article 31, para. 9.
[121] On this rhetorical figure and its origins in international legal and political discourse, see Alejandro Rodiles, 'Coalitions of the Willing: Coyuntura, Contexto y Propriedades. Un primer esbozo', *Anuario Mexicano de Derecho Internacional* 7 (2007), pp. 675–702, at p. 679.
[122] See Mary Ellen O'Connell, 'Who Helps the Hegemon?', *Austrian Review of International and European Law* 8 (2003), pp. 91–100, at p. 99.
[123] ILC Commentary, Article 16, para. 11.

a given court or tribunal, in the majority of cases this will not be the case. In order to understand more fully the implications of complicity in contemporary international law, it is desirable to inquire briefly into its potential role in international judicial dispute settlement. As Christine Gray has written, awareness of existing judicial remedies should be a prerequisite before one calls for a more effective enforcement of international law.[124]

2.1 The indispensable third party

Adjudicating a situation which involves a complicit State will require an international court or tribunal to consider a triangular situation, which involves: the injured State which will have brought the claim, the complicit State and – in order to find that aid or assistance has been furnished to an internationally wrongful act – the main actor to which the support has been granted. The structure of international dispute settlement is largely bilateral.[125] Usually, only two States will be involved in judicial dispute settlement. In the case of the ICJ, for example, a State which has an interest of a legal nature which may be affected by a decision may submit a request to the Court to be permitted to intervene in the proceedings (Article 62(1) of the ICJ Statute). If the State is given permission to intervene, the judgment will be equally binding upon it (Article 62(2) of the ICJ Statute), which distinguishes this situation from the usual case that decisions of the Court have, according to Article 59 of the ICJ Statute, 'no binding force except between the parties and in respect of the particular case'. The flipside to this right of intervention in proceedings is the lack of a procedure to compulsorily join parties to a dispute if they are implicated in wrongful conduct.[126]

An innocent interpretation of these provisions could be that the adjudication of a case between an injured State and a complicit State would not give rise to particular problems: after all, Article 59 of the ICJ Statute protects the absent third State, the main actor, from the consequences

---

[124] Christine D. Gray, *Judicial Remedies*, pp. 1–2.
[125] Phoebe N. Okowa, *State Responsibility*, p. 197; Shabtai Rosenne, *The Law and Practice*, Vol. II, p. 539; Peter Hilpold, *Der Osttimor-Fall*, pp. 31 et seq.; Brian D. Smith, *State Responsibility*, pp. 46–7.
[126] As affirmed several times by the ICJ: see ICJ, *Continental Shelf*, Judgment, ICJ Rep. 1984, 3, para. 40; ICJ, *Military and Paramilitary Activities In and Against Nicaragua*, Jurisdiction, ICJ Rep. 1984, 392, para. 88; ICJ, *Land, Island and Maritime Frontier Dispute*, Judgment, ICJ Rep. 1990, 92, para. 99; ICJ, *Certain Phosphate Lands in Nauru*, Preliminary Objections, ICJ Rep. 1992, 240, para. 53.

of a binding judgment passed in its absence.[127] Furthermore, if a legal interest of the third State is at stake, it could always join the proceedings under Article 62(1) of the ICJ Statute. However, this is not the prevailing interpretation of the law.[128] The ICJ[129] and a large number of doctrinal authorities[130] point to Article 36 of the ICJ Statute which defines the Court's competence to decide disputes between States. The underlying principle of Article 36 is that of State consent to the exercise of jurisdiction by the Court.[131] In order to determine the extent to which the principle of consent to the exercise of jurisdiction of the ICJ impacts on complicity cases, it will be necessary to present briefly the Court's jurisprudence on the indispensable third party.

2.2 The case law of the ICJ

2.2.1 The Monetary Gold case

The background to the *Monetary Gold* case is a complex factual scenario which involves issues of the settlement of reparations after the Second World War, the confiscation of monetary gold by the Allied Powers which

---

[127] Cf Santiago Torres Bernárdez, 'The New Theory of "Indispensable Parties" under the Statute of the International Court of Justice', in Karel Wellens (ed.), *International Law: Theory and Practice. Essays in Honour of Eric Suy* (The Hague: Kluwer, 1998), pp. 737–50, at pp. 747 *et seq.*; Rudolf Bernhardt, 'Article 59', in Andreas Zimmermann, Christian Tomuschat and Karin Oellers-Frahm (eds.), *The Statute of the International Court of Justice – A Commentary* (Oxford: Oxford University Press, 2006), para. 68.

[128] *Ibid.*

[129] ICJ, *Monetary Gold Removed from Rome in 1943*, Judgment, ICJ Rep. 1954, 19, 32.

[130] See Rudolf Bernhardt, 'Article 59', para. 67; Christian Tomuschat, 'Article 36', in Andreas Zimmermann, Christian Tomuschat and Karin Oellers-Frahm (eds.), *The Statute of the International Court of Justice – A Commentary* (Oxford: Oxford University Press, 2006), paras. 20 *et seq.*; Emmanuelle Jouannet, 'Le principe de l'or monétaire à propos de l'arrêt de la Cour du 30 juin 1995 dans l'affaire du Timor Oriental (Portugal c. Australie)', *Revue générale de droit international public* 100 (1996), pp. 673–714, at p. 676; Hugh Thirlway, 'Injured and Non-Injured States Before the International Court of Justice', in Maurizio Ragazzi (ed.), *International Responsibility Today – Essays in Memory of Oscar Schachter* (Leiden: Nijhoff, 2005), pp. 311–28, at pp. 317 *et seq.*; Andreas Zimmermann, 'Die Zuständigkeit des Internationalen Gerichtshofs zur Entscheidung über Ansprüche gegen am Verfahren nicht beteiligte Staaten', *Zeitschrift für ausländisches öffentliches Recht und Völkerrecht* 55 (1995), pp. 1051–76, at p. 1052.

[131] Shabtai Rosenne, *The Law and Practice*, Vol. II, p. 539; Hugh Thirlway, 'The Law and Procedure of the International Court of Justice, Part Nine', *British Year Book of International Law* 69 (1998), pp. 1–83, at p. 4; Sabine Schorer, *Das Konsensprinzip in der internationalen Gerichtsbarkeit* (Frankfurt/Main: Peter Lang, 2003), pp. 32 *et seq.*; Peter Hilpold, *Der Osttimor-Fall*, p. 31; more critical of the role of consent in this regard is D. H. N. Johnson, 'The Case of the Monetary Gold Removed from Rome in 1943', *International and Comparative Law Quarterly* 4 (1955), pp. 98–115, at p. 109.

was previously removed from Rome in 1943 by Nazi Germany and the aftermath of the *Corfu Channel* case. Part III of the Paris Agreement on Reparation[132] provided that all monetary gold which had been found in Germany was to be distributed to the countries which had suffered from losses due to German seizures since 1938.[133] This distribution was to be effected by France, the United Kingdom and the United States as occupying powers. Both Albania and Italy made representations to claim that they had a right to recover the confiscated monetary gold in question. The case before the ICJ was brought against the three Allied Powers by Italy and was filed in response to an arbitral award of 20 February 1953 by Arbitrator Sauser-Hall to the effect that the gold belonged to Albania.[134] Italy claimed, however, that the gold should be delivered to it as a matter of satisfaction for Italian claims against Albania which related to the confiscation of assets of the National Bank of Albania by Albania in 1945, the bank being 88.5 per cent owned by Italian shareholders at the time.[135] Italy's decision to bring the case before the ICJ was, however, not entirely voluntary. It was rather forced upon Italy by the Paris Agreement, which provided that the monetary gold would fall to the United Kingdom unless within ninety days of the arbitral award either Albania or Italy contested the transfer of the gold to the UK before the ICJ. Italy had to hasten to become a party to the Paris Agreement and to bring the case against France, the UK and the US to the ICJ. Subsequently, it raised the issue of the ICJ's lack of competence due to Albania's non-participation in the case.[136] The ICJ did eventually decline to exercise its jurisdiction due to the absence of Albania which was considered to be an indispensable third party to the case:

> Italy believes she possesses a right against Albania for the redress of an international wrong which, according to Italy, Albania has committed against her. In order, therefore, to determine whether Italy is entitled to receive the gold, it is necessary to determine whether Albania has committed any international wrong against Italy, and whether she is due under an obligation to pay

---

[132] Agreement on Reparation from Germany, on the Establishment of an Inter-Allied Reparation Agency and on the Restitution of Monetary Gold of 14 January 1946, entered into force on 24 January 1946, 555 UNTS 69.

[133] On the factual background to the case, see Norbert Wühler, 'Monetary Gold Case', in Rudolf Bernhardt (ed.), *Encyclopedia of Public International Law*, Vol. III, J-P (Amsterdam: Elsevier, 1997), pp. 445–7; Peter Hilpold, *Der Osttimor-Fall*, pp. 33–4.

[134] *Gold Looted by Germany from Rome in 1943*, Arbitral Advice, 20 ILR 441, 479.

[135] Norbert Wühler, 'Monetary Gold', p. 446.

[136] On this procedural particularity, see Covey T. Oliver, 'The Monetary Gold Decision in Perspective', *American Journal of International Law* 49 (1955), pp. 216–21, at pp. 219–21.

compensation to her; and, if so, to determine also the amount of compensation. In order to decide such questions, it is necessary to determine whether the Albanian law of January 13th, 1945, was contrary to international law. In the determination of these questions – questions which relate to the lawful or unlawful character of certain actions of Albania vis-à-vis Italy – only two States, Italy and Albania, are directly interested. To go into the merits of such questions would be to decide a dispute between Italy and Albania.

The Court cannot decide such a dispute without the consent of Albania ... To adjudicate upon the international responsibility of Albania without her consent would run counter to a well-established principle of international law embodied in the Court's Statute, namely, that the Court can only exercise jurisdiction over a State with its consent.[137]

The Court also addressed the issue whether this lack of consent to the exercise of its jurisdiction on the part of Albania was not effectively remedied by the possibility of intervening under Article 62 of the ICJ Statute or that Albania's interests were at least protected by the *inter partes* rule of Article 59 of the Statute. The Court replied to both issues in the negative. With respect to Article 62, it held that, '[i]n the present case, Albania's legal interests would not only be affected by a decision, but would form the very subject-matter of the decision'.[138] On the issue of the effect of a decision, the Court identified Albania's responsibility as 'the vital issue' in the case and argued it was thus not in a position as to give a judgment.[139]

2.2.2 Monetary Gold attenuated: the Nauru case

Despite various affirmations of this principle in the case law of the Court[140] and separate opinions of some of its judges alike,[141] the

---

[137] ICJ, *Monetary Gold Removed from Rome in 1943*, Judgment, ICJ Rep. 1954, 19, 32.
[138] *Ibid.*
[139] *Ibid.*, p. 33; it should be noted that, in this case, the Court also seemed to advocate the position that the indispensable third party could join the proceedings under Article 62 of the Statute. This position was later renounced in ICJ, *Land, Island and Maritime Frontier Dispute Case*, Judgment, ICJ Rep. 1990, 92, para. 56, where the Court drew a distinction between intervention under Article 62 and joining a case as a party, on that development, see Christine Chinkin, 'Article 62', in Andreas Zimmermann, Christian Tomuschat and Karin Oellers-Frahm (eds.), *The Statute of the International Court of Justice – A Commentary* (Oxford: Oxford University Press, 2006), para. 16; Christine Chinkin, *Third Parties in International Law*, pp. 175 *et seq.*
[140] See, e.g., ICJ, *Continental Shelf*, Judgment, ICJ Rep. 1984, 3, para. 40; ICJ, *Military and Paramilitary Activities In and Against Nicaragua*, Jurisdiction, ICJ Rep. 1984, 392, para. 88; ICJ, *Land, Island and Maritime Frontier Dispute*, Judgment, ICJ Rep. 1990, 92, para. 99; ICJ, *Certain Phosphate Lands in Nauru*, Preliminary Objections, ICJ Rep. 1992, 240, para. 53.
[141] See *ibid.*, dissenting opinion of Judge Schwebel, p. 330.

Monetary Gold principle remained a fairly isolated precedent until the *East Timor* case of 1995.[142] However, before the Court decided that case and declined to exercise jurisdiction due to the *Monetary Gold* principle, it had adopted a seemingly more relaxed position on the issue in its 1992 decision in the *Nauru* case.[143] In this case, Nauru wanted to obtain compensation from Australia for the exploitation of certain phosphate mines in Nauru which had occurred during the administration of Nauru under UN trusteeship.[144] Before its independence on 31 January 1968, Nauru was administered by the joint trustees, Australia, the United Kingdom and New Zealand. Before that, Nauru was administered under the Mandates System of the League of Nations, being a British mandate.[145] For the UN period, a Trusteeship Agreement existed between Australia, the United Kingdom and New Zealand.[146] Nauru alleged a breach of certain obligations under this agreement and violations of the principle of self-determination as well as the right of the Nauruan people to permanent sovereignty over their natural resources.[147] As Nauru only brought a case against Australia and not against the United Kingdom or New Zealand, the issue arose whether a judgment by the Court on Australia's responsibility would also, quasi-automatically, establish the responsibility of the other trustee powers on whose behalf Australia had acted.[148] Australia argued that the claim

[142] Andreas Zimmermann, 'Zuständigkeit', p. 1052.
[143] ICJ, *Certain Phosphate Lands in Nauru*, Preliminary Objections, ICJ Rep. 1992, 240.
[144] Cf Article 76 of the UN Charter.
[145] Cf Article 22 of the Covenant of the League of Nations.
[146] Article 2 of which provided that: 'The Governments of Australia, New Zealand and the United Kingdom (hereinafter called "the Administering Authority") are hereby designated as the joint Authority which will exercise the administration of the Territory.' The agreement was approved by the UN General Assembly on 1 November 1947; see ICJ, *Certain Phosphate Lands in Nauru*, Preliminary Objections, ICJ Rep. 1992, 240, para. 9; the text of Article 2 is reprinted *ibid.*, para. 45.
[147] For a concise summary of the background to the case, see Karin Oellers-Frahm, 'Phosphate Lands in Nauru Case (Nauru v. Australia)', in Rüdiger Bernhardt (ed.), *Encyclopedia of Public International Law*, Vol. III, J-P (Amsterdam: Elsevier, 1997), pp. 1025-7, at p. 1025.
[148] See Article 4 of the Trusteeship Agreement: 'The Administering Authority will be responsible for the peace, order, good government and defence of the Territory, and for this purpose, in pursuance of an Agreement made by the Governments of Australia, New Zealand and the United Kingdom, the Government of Australia will, on behalf of the Administering Authority and except and until otherwise agreed by the Governments of Australia, New Zealand and the United Kingdom, continue to exercise full powers of legislation, administration and jurisdiction in and over the Territory.' Reprinted in ICJ, *Certain Phosphate Lands in Nauru*, Preliminary Objections, ICJ Rep. 1992, 240, para. 45.

of Nauru would, in substance, not be a claim against Australia itself but against the Administering Authority. The Court would therefore not be in a position to pass judgment without adjudicating also upon the responsibility of New Zealand and the United Kingdom.[149]

In order to address this Australian objection, the Court referred to its case law and especially to the *Monetary Gold* principle. The crucial question was, according to the Court, whether the interests of the third States which are not party to the case and which may be affected by a decision form the very subject matter of the decision that was sought for by Nauru.[150] The Court analysed the difference between *Monetary Gold* and *Nauru* in the following way:

> In the present case, the interests of New Zealand and the United Kingdom do not form the very subject-matter of the judgment to be rendered on the merits of Nauru's Application and the situation is in that respect different from that with which the Court had to deal in the *Monetary Gold* case. In the latter case, the determination of Albania's responsibility was a prerequisite for a decision to be taken on Italy's claims. In the present case, the determination of the responsibility of the responsibility of New Zealand or the United Kingdom is not a prerequisite for the determination of the responsibility of Australia, the only object of Nauru's claim.[151]

Australia had further argued that there would nonetheless be a *simultaneous* determination of the responsibility of the United Kingdom and New Zealand. To that claim the Court responded that, contrary to the *Monetary Gold* case, no findings in respect of the legal situation of New Zealand or the United Kingdom would be needed as a logical basis for the Court's decision on Nauru's claims against Australia. A decision might well have implications for the States not party to the dispute but that alone would not suffice to trigger the applicability of the *Monetary Gold* principle.[152]

2.2.3 Monetary Gold reaffirmed: the East Timor case

In the *East Timor* case, Portugal alleged that Australia violated, *inter alia*, the East Timorese right to self-determination through its negotiation, conclusion and initial performance of the so-called 'Gap Treaty' of 11 December 1989 with Indonesia on the delimitation of

---

[149] *Ibid.*, para. 39. [150] *Ibid.*, para. 54. [151] *Ibid.*, para. 55.
[152] *Ibid.*; but see *ibid.*, dissenting opinion of President Jennings, p. 301; dissenting opinion of Judge Ago, p. 328; and dissenting opinion of Judge Schwebel, p. 342.

the continental shelf in the area of the Timor Gap.[153] Portugal relied on the *erga omnes* character of obligations entailed by the right of self-determination. This concept, as Christian Tams has highlighted, came into effect at two different levels of the case: first, in order to justify the standing of Portugal, and, secondly, in order to serve as a potential bar against a strict interpretation of the *Monetary Gold* principle.[154] The Court, however, was not convinced by these points. Although it upheld Portugal's claim that the right to self-determination gave rise to obligations *erga omnes*,[155] it emphasised that issues of standing were not to be conflated with that point.[156] In addition, it reaffirmed the importance of the *Monetary Gold* principle.[157] Accordingly, a lack of consent to the exercise of jurisdiction by the Court is not automatically remedied by the mere involvement of obligations *erga omnes*.[158]

Portugal had advanced another argument to defend its cause of action. It alleged that the illegality of the Indonesian occupation of East Timor had been recognised several times by both the UN Security Council and the UN General Assembly.[159] Accordingly, the illegality of Australian recognition of and cooperation with the Indonesian occupation could be treated as a given and a pronouncement of the Court on this issue would add no additional legal obligations for Indonesia. In this respect, the Court noted that this position presupposed that the United Nations resolutions and in particular those by the Security Council could be read as imposing an obligation on States not to recognise any authority on the part of Indonesia over the territory; a fact of which the Court was not convinced.[160]

---

[153] Treaty between Australia and the Republic of Indonesia on the Zone of Cooperation in an Area between the Indonesian Province of East Timor and Northern Australia of 11 December 1989, entered into force on 9 February 1991, in relevant parts reprinted in ICJ, *East Timor*, Judgment, ICJ Rep. 1995, 90, para. 10.
[154] Christian J. Tams, *Enforcing Obligations Erga Omnes*, p. 183.
[155] ICJ, *East Timor*, Judgment, ICJ Rep. 1995, 90, para. 29.
[156] Ibid.   [157] Ibid.
[158] Sandesh Sivakumaran, 'Impact on the Structure of International Obligations', in Menno T. Kamminga and Martin Scheinin (eds.), *The Impact of Human Rights Law on General International Law* (Oxford: Oxford University Press, 2009), pp. 133–50, at p. 140.
[159] For the UN Security Council, see UN Doc. S/RES/384 (1975); S/RES/389 (1976); for the UN General Assembly, see UN Doc. A/RES/34/85 (XXX) (1975); A/RES/31/53 (1976); A/RES/32/34 (1977); A/RES/33/79 (1978); A/RES/34/40 (1979); A/RES/35/27 (1980); A/RES/36/50 (1981); A/RES/37/30 (1982).
[160] ICJ, *East Timor*, Judgment, ICJ Rep. 1995, 90, para. 31.

As it has been observed, the Court thus put the concept of obligations *erga omnes* back into the 'procedural straitjacket' of the *Monetary Gold* principle.[161] The Court's application of the *Monetary Gold* principle was also criticised by members of the Court in separate and dissenting opinions.[162] Some of their arguments may pave the way to an application of the *Monetary Gold* principle which does not stand in the way of bringing complicity-type situations before the ICJ. Judge Oda, for example, pointed to the difference in factual circumstances between the *Monetary Gold* and *East Timor* cases. In particular, he emphasised that the Court in 1954 was not in a position to exercise its jurisdiction because it would have had to decide a dispute between Italy and Albania, whereas, in 1995, the whole case would have related

> solely to the question *whether Portugal or Indonesia*, as a State lying opposite to Australia, was entitled to the continental shelf in the 'Timor Gap'. This could have been the subject of a dispute between Portugal and Indonesia, but cannot be a matter in which Portugal and Australia can be seen to be in dispute with Indonesia as a State with an 'interest of a legal nature which may be affected'.[163]

Similarly, Judge Weeramantry in his dissent distinguished the *Monetary Gold* precedent on the basis that Albanian property and wrongdoing were the very subject matter on which the Italian claim was based.[164] Judge Weeramantry was the most fervent critic of the Court's restrictive approach in *East Timor*. The Court's reasoning would entail, he argued, that whenever

> a claim by State A against State B cannot be made good without demonstrating, as a prerequisite, some wrongful conduct on the part of State C, State B can avoid an enquiry into its own conduct, however wrongful, by pointing to C's wrongdoing as a precondition to its own liability.[165]

---

[161] Bruno Simma, 'From Bilateralism to Community Interest', p. 298; see also Iain Scobbie and Catriona Drew, 'Self-Determination Undetermined: The Case of East Timor', *Leiden Journal of International Law* 9 (1996), pp. 185–211, at p. 197; Christine Chinkin, 'The East Timor Case', *International and Comparative Law Quarterly* 45 (1996), pp. 712–25, at p. 721; for a less sceptical treatment of this issue Emmanuelle Jouannet, 'L'or monétaire', pp. 694–5; Christian J. Tams, *Enforcing Obligations Erga Omnes*, p. 184; Andreas Zimmermann, 'Zuständigkeit', p. 1074.

[162] ICJ, *East Timor*, Judgment, ICJ Rep. 1995, 90, separate opinion of Judge Ranjeva, p. 129, especially at pp. 131–2.

[163] *Ibid.*, separate opinion of Judge Oda, p. 107, para. 8.

[164] *Ibid.*, dissenting opinion of Judge Weeramantry, pp. 139, 156.

[165] *Ibid.*, p. 161.

2.3 Complicity and the indispensable third party

Given that the last time the ICJ pronounced on the indispensable third party rule was in *East Timor* and that it did so in a fairly restrictive way, one could arrive at the conclusion that the prospects are bleak for holding complicit States responsible before the ICJ. However, several reasons could militate for a restrictive application of the *Monetary Gold* principle in cases where complicity is at stake.

2.3.1 Monetary Gold as an outer limit

The issue whether the *Monetary Gold* rule will bar cases involving complicity has not been afforded a great deal of attention so far. States appear to take this issue seriously, however: when the Federal Republic of Germany filed its declaration under Article 36(2) of the ICJ Statute in 2008, it expressly excluded the use of the German military armed forces abroad as well as the use of the German territory and other areas under German jurisdiction for military purposes by other States from the jurisdiction of the ICJ.[166] A certain anxiety about becoming entangled in legal disputes in which Germany has participated only remotely emerges from these exceptions.[167]

The ILC has contented itself with noting that the principle may well apply to cases under Article 16 ASR, 'since it is of the essence of the responsibility of the aiding or assisting State that the aided or assisted State itself committed an internationally wrongful act'.[168] At the same time, it has noted that 'that principle is not all-embracing and ... may not be a barrier to judicial proceedings in every case'.[169] In more general contexts, authors keep mentioning that the ICJ has been prepared to settle disputes, even if theoretically the dispute would also involve rights and obligations of third States not party to the case before it.[170] In light of what the ICJ determined in the *Monetary Gold* case and reaffirmed in its *East Timor* case, the wrongfulness of the act committed by the aided or assisted State would need to form the 'very subject

---

[166] See further Christophe Eick, 'Die Anerkennung der obligatorischen Gerichtsbarkeit des Internationalen Gerichtshofs durch Deutschland', *Zeitschrift für ausländisches öffentliches Recht und Völkerrecht* 68 (2008), pp. 763–77, at pp. 771–2.
[167] Christian J. Tams and Andreas Zimmermann, '"The Federation Shall Accede to Agreements Providing for General and Compulsory International Arbitration" – The German Optional Clause Declaration of 1 May 2008', *German Yearbook of International Law* 51 (2008), pp. 391–416, at pp. 413–14.
[168] ILC Commentary, Article 16, para. 11.   [169] *Ibid.*
[170] Phoebe N. Okowa, *State Responsibility*, p. 196.

matter' of the case at issue in order to trigger the *Monetary Gold* principle. Arguably, it will not be possible to develop a clear-cut rule for *all* situations involving complicity. Whether or not the wrongful act of the main actor will form the very subject matter of the case or whether a determination of its wrongfulness would only affect the legal interests of the third State not present in the proceedings has to be determined in light of the individual case. The ICJ itself has affirmed that its approach in the *Monetary Gold* case represents the outer limit of its ability to decline jurisdiction:

> There is no doubt that in appropriate circumstances the Court will decline, as it did in the case concerning *Monetary Gold Removed from Rome in 1943*, to exercise the jurisdiction conferred upon it where the legal interests of a State not party to the proceedings 'would not only be affected by decision, but would form the very subject-matter of the decision'. The circumstances of the *Monetary Gold* case probably represent the limit to the power of the Court to refuse to exercise its jurisdiction; and none of the States referred to can be regarded as in the same position as Albania in that case, so as to be truly indispensable to the pursuance of the proceedings.[171]

In another case, the Court has affirmed that, in the absence of any compulsory mechanism whereby a third State could be cited by the Court to appear in a case before the Court, it would indeed be its duty to give the fullest decision possible in the circumstances of each case.[172] Judge Weeramantry has held the view that the *Monetary Gold* principle is frequently cited as authority for more ground than it could cover. In his dissent to the *East Timor* case, he was mindful of what he called the 'extremely limited circumstances' of the case, namely, the fact that 'Albanian property could not be appropriated on the basis of Albanian wrongdoing in the absence of Albania'.[173] In this light, there is in fact an apparent difference between the *Monetary Gold* situation and the typical complicity situation: the 1954 judgment concerned a direct apportionment of property. The very State whose property was to be apportioned did not partake in the proceedings before the Court. It was also eventually the lawfulness of a domestic Albanian statute which would have been at issue. This is indeed a different scenario than one in which

---

[171] ICJ, *Military and Paramilitary Activities In and Against Nicaragua*, Jurisdiction, ICJ Rep. 1984, 431, para. 88.
[172] ICJ, *Continental Shelf*, Judgment, ICJ Rep. 1984, 3, para. 40.
[173] ICJ, *East Timor*, Judgment, ICJ Rep. 1995, 90, dissenting opinion of Judge Weeramantry, pp. 139, 156.

the Court would have to pass an incidental judgment on the wrongfulness of the actions of another State as would be the case in a dispute between an injured State and a complicit State.[174] However, this interpretation of the *Monetary Gold* principle could find itself at odds with the Court's findings in the *East Timor* case.

The guidance we can obtain from the development of the case law of the ICJ is thus limited.[175] Its more relaxed position in the *Nauru* case could be seen as having been overturned by the more restrictive outlook of the *East Timor* case.

2.3.2 The procedural imbroglio of the East Timor case

A different explanation for the Court's refuge to the *Monetary Gold* principle in the *East Timor* case could be seen in its unease towards the construction of the Portuguese claim against Australia. Although the Court was heavily criticised for negating the essence of what has been its *Barcelona Traction obiter dictum* on obligations *erga omnes* in this case,[176] it needs to be borne in mind that the adversarial position of the parties in *East Timor* was a highly unusual one: not only was Australia the addressee of the claim albeit its role amounted to not more than being an 'accomplice after the fact'.[177] With Portugal it was also a non-injured State which took upon itself the enforcement of an obligation *erga omnes*. It is imaginable that the combination of two unusual elements of judicial dispute settlement had a role to play in the Court's careful and conservative treatment of the issue of the lack of consent by what it conceived as the indispensable third party in the case, namely, Indonesia. Christian Tams has described this attitude of the Court as a form of 'canalisation of *erga omnes* enforcement action'.[178]

---

[174] See also ICJ, *Certain Phosphate Lands in Nauru*, Preliminary Objections, ICJ Rep. 1992, 240, separate opinion of Judge Shahabuddeen, p. 270, at p. 297, who distinguishes *Nauru* from *Monetary Gold* by pointing to the fact that a judgment on the merits in the *Nauru* case would 'not affect the rights of New Zealand or the United Kingdom in the sense in which a judgment deploys its effects, as would have been the case with Albania. *New Zealand and the United Kingdom will not be deprived of any rights in the subject-matter of the case*, or at all. Certainly, *no property or property rights* belonging to them *will be transferred or otherwise affected* by that decision.' Emphasis added.

[175] See also Christian J. Tams and Andreas Zimmermann, 'Federation', p. 414: 'the Court's rather unpredictable application of the *Monetary Gold* principle.'

[176] See the references in note 161 above.

[177] Christian J. Tams, *Enforcing Obligations Erga Omnes*, p. 184.   [178] *Ibid.*

Although it is not possible to prove that this concern was indeed a rationale which explained the Court's declining to exercise its jurisdiction under Article 36(2) of its Statute, these considerations show that, in future cases, the Court would have enough leeway to depart from its rigid understanding of its jurisdiction without having expressly to renounce its previous position in *East Timor*. In this light, it would be possible for the Court to establish a difference between the highly specific procedural situation that was *East Timor* and the more ordinary case in which a directly injured State wishes to recover damages from a complicit State.

2.3.3 Other factors

Other factors are conceivable which would allow the Court to find a basis upon which it could exercise jurisdiction in a dispute between an injured State and the complicit State without having to determine the responsibility of the State not party to a dispute. One such solution was advocated by Portugal in the *East Timor* case. Portugal argued that the wrongfulness of the Indonesian occupation of East Timor was already established by relevant UN Security Council and General Assembly resolutions.[179] The Court did not accept this argument. But it did not, however, generally rule out the possibility that the illegality of a given situation can be established by resolutions of the political UN organs. This can be inferred from the Court's reference to the resolutions in question and its examination of the implications of the UN General Assembly continuously referring to Portugal as the 'administering power'. The Court concluded that, '[w]ithout prejudice to the question whether the resolutions under discussion could be binding in nature, the Court considers as a result that they cannot be regarded as "givens" which constitute a sufficient basis for determining the dispute between the Parties'.[180] Accordingly, other situations could be conceivable in which such a determination could be affirmed easier. An example of such a determination can be found in the Court's advisory opinion on Namibia in 1971 where the Court put more emphasis on repeated declarations of the unlawfulness of South Africa's continued presence in its former mandate territory. In this opinion, the Court held that 'a binding determination made by a competent organ of the United Nations to the effect that a situation is illegal cannot remain

---

[179] See note 159 above.   [180] ICJ, *East Timor*, Judgment, ICJ Rep. 1995, 90, para. 31.

without consequences'.[181] This passage insinuates that, in the presence of a clear determination of unlawfulness by the UN Security Council, the Court could well pass over its restrictive jurisprudence on the indispensable third party. This finding is further corroborated by the immediately following sentence in the *Namibia* opinion: 'Once the Court is faced with such a situation, it would be failing in the discharge of its judicial functions if it did not declare that there is an obligation, especially upon Members of the United Nations, to bring that situation to an end.'[182] From this finding it is a short step to a subtle reinterpretation of the Court's findings in the *East Timor* case.

A more delicate question would be whether the same considerations apply in a case in which the ICJ itself has already declared the illegality of a certain conduct, for example in an advisory opinion. Is it conceivable for State A to initiate proceedings against State B for aid or assistance rendered to Israel in the maintenance of the situation created by the construction of the wall in the Occupied Palestinian Territory? After all, State A could argue that the wrongfulness of Israel's conduct has already been established by the Court[183] and that thus a finding on State B's complicity in that regard would not involve a new and additional determination of wrongfulness with respect to Israel. Such an approach would, however, amount to a circumvention *ex post* of the so-called *Eastern Carelia* principle,[184] i.e., that advisory proceedings shall not be instituted to replace the missing consent for contentious proceedings.[185] Although the scope of this principle is disputed,[186] an approach such as the one canvassed here would put considerable strain on the concept of advisory proceedings before the ICJ and could considerably reduce the willingness among competent UN organs to have recourse to the instrument of advisory opinions.[187]

---

[181] ICJ, *Legal Consequences for States of the Continued Presence of South Africa in Namibia (South West Africa) Notwithstanding Security Council Resolution 276 (1970)*, Advisory Opinion, ICJ Rep. 1971, 16, para. 117.
[182] *Ibid.*
[183] ICJ, *Legal Consequences of the Construction of a Wall in the Occupied Palestinian Territory*, Advisory Opinion, ICJ Rep. 2004, 136.
[184] PCIJ, *Status of Eastern Carelia*, Advisory Opinion, Series B, No. 5, 27.
[185] See further Shabtai Rosenne, *The Law and Practice*, Vol. II, p. 976.
[186] Cf ICJ, *Western Sahara*, Advisory Opinion, ICJ Rep. 1975, 12, para. 31; cf also ICJ, *Legality of the Threat or Use of Nuclear Weapons*, Advisory Opinion, ICJ Rep. 1996, 226, para. 14.
[187] But cf ICJ, *Legal Consequences of the Construction of a Wall in the Occupied Palestinian Territory*, Advisory Opinion, ICJ Rep. 2004, 136, separate opinion of Judge Higgins, *ibid.*, para. 38.

Another situation under which the effects of the *Monetary Gold* principle could be reduced would be given when the main actor has expressed its general consent to the jurisdiction of the Court by means of a declaration under Article 36(2) of the ICJ Statute. In this regard, one has to note that the concept of the indispensable third party is applicable regardless of the fact whether the absence of the third State is due to its voluntary decision or whether it has not been properly impleaded.[188] The existence of general consent to the jurisdiction of the Court under Article 36(2) of the ICJ Statute thus does not render the *Monetary Gold* principle inapplicable. However, in such a case, its effects are greatly mitigated as the State which wishes to bring a claim against the complicit State could likewise file a case against the main actor, given that all other criteria are met.

2.3.4 Concluding remarks

In discussing the impact of the *Monetary Gold* principle on cases in which complicity is to be adjudicated, one should not forget the fundamental rationale of this principle: it is an expression of 'elemental due process'[189] insofar as it prevents the Court from adjudicating disputes in the absence of a State.[190] It also works the other way around: without its consent, a complicit State cannot be dragged into ongoing proceedings between the main actor and the injured State.[191] In this perspective, the *Monetary Gold* principle may also appear as a safeguard against arbitrary courses of action which are directed only against a remote actor while the 'main culprit' is left unaffected. Although deplorable from a viewpoint of legal policy, the option to remain absent from dispute settlement proceedings still exists in the contemporary international legal order.[192] Against the background of the not very succinct case law of the ICJ it has to remain the task of the Court to

find the appropriate balance between preventing parties submitting as bilateral disputes claims to the Court which discount third party interests, and not

---

[188] Shabtai Rosenne, *The Law and Practice*, Vol. II, p. 539.
[189] Covey T. Oliver, 'Monetary Gold', p. 221; approvingly quoted by Christine Chinkin, *Third Parties*, p. 200.
[190] This argument finds no favour with Alexander Orakhelashvili, 'Division', p. 664.
[191] Cf Christian J. Tams and Andreas Zimmermann, 'Federation', p. 414.
[192] Phoebe N. Okowa, *State Responsibility*, p. 197; Andreas Zimmermann, 'Zuständigkeit', p. 1074.

allowing the absence of third parties to deprive the Court of jurisdiction legitimately bestowed upon it by the parties.[193]

In this respect, the 'multilateralisation' of international disputes should be taken into account.[194] In the words of Michael Reisman: 'Among any group of individuals, the acts of one or several will have peripheral effects on all the others. The likelihood and intensity of third-party effects increases as the level of interaction rises.'[195] Of this tendency Article 16 ASR is but one expression.

It cannot remain insignificant to the development of the Court's case law on its jurisdiction when international law provides new bases to hold States responsible. The Court has made it clear in *East Timor* that new developments such as obligations *erga omnes* and the question of consent to its jurisdiction remain two distinct issues. In the abstract this is true. However, in the long-term perspective, a credibility gap is likely to develop if international law provides for more and more bases on which States can be held responsible without, at the same time, developing related procedural means. This concern not only mirrors general worries about the ineffectiveness of the enforcement of international law. The responsibility of States exists independently of procedural means to implement it. However, if structural reasons stand in the way of effectively implementing new bases of the responsibility of States, it is a legitimate question to inquire into these structural weaknesses and to seek change in that regard.[196]

2.4 Essential parties before other courts and tribunals

The ICJ is the principal judicial organ of the UN.[197] In this respect, it must occupy a central place in considerations about the role which complicity may play in judicial dispute settlement. In a time of 'proliferation' of international courts and tribunals,[198] it is, however,

---

[193] Christine Chinkin, *Third Parties*, p. 202; see also ICJ, *Certain Phosphate Lands in Nauru*, Preliminary Objections, ICJ Rep. 1992, 240, dissenting opinion of Judge Schwebel, p. 335.
[194] See also Peter Hilpold, *Der Osttimor-Fall*, p. 32; Santiago Torres Bernárdez, 'The New Theory', pp. 749–50.
[195] W. Michael Reisman, *Nullity and Revision – The Review and Enforcement of International Judgments and Awards* (New Haven, CT: Yale University Press, 1971), p. 329.
[196] Cf also Bruno Simma, 'From Bilateralism to Community Interest', p. 298.
[197] Article 92 of the UN Charter.
[198] On this phenomenon, see Pierre-Marie Dupuy, 'The Danger of Fragmentation or Unification of the International Legal System and the International Court of Justice',

important to consider alternative avenues in which complicit States could be held judicially responsible. In this respect, the prospects are more promising: in no other international judicial forum is the protection of absent third parties as imposing as it is in the case law of the ICJ. We cannot present the other various forms of dispute settlement in great depth. Some signposts will have to suffice in order to indicate the alternative possibilities for finding State responsibility for complicity in international courts and tribunals. Not all of the systems briefly mentioned have already seen cases involving complicity. However, in none of them can it be ruled out that this will happen in the future. Some general remarks can be made at the outset: the problem of an 'indispensable' or 'essential' third party will arguably not arise within a legal system in which there is compulsory judicial dispute settlement. This is confirmed, for instance, by the provisions of the United Nations Convention on the Law of the Sea (UNCLOS), the European Convention on Human Rights and the WTO Dispute Settlement Understanding. In all three cases, recourse to judicial means of dispute settlement is open to all parties to the respective agreement. Therefore, general consent has been expressed by the parties to these agreements that disputes under these treaties can be dealt with by a court, tribunal or other form of judicial dispute settlement. These mechanisms and some others will be briefly presented here in order to sound out alternatives for judicial and quasi-judicial dispute settlement involving complicit States.

2.4.1 WTO dispute settlement

That the WTO dispute settlement system knows no concept of essential parties was most clearly stated by a WTO Panel in *Turkey – Textiles*, where Turkey, the respondent State, claimed that the Panel should dismiss the applicant's claims (India) as they were aimed at measures taken pursuant to a regional trade agreement between Turkey and the European Communities. Accordingly, Turkey argued, the EC should also have been a party to the dispute. The Panel did not follow this argument. Quite to the contrary, it affirmed:

It should be noted that there is no WTO concept of 'essential parties'. The European Communities, had it so wished, could have availed itself of the

New York University Journal of International Law and Politics 31 (1999), pp. 791–807; Karin Oellers-Frahm, 'Multiplication of International Courts and Tribunals and Conflicting Jurisdictions – Problems and Possible Solutions', *Max Planck Yearbook of United Nations Law* 5 (2001), pp. 67–104.

provisions of the DSU ... in order to represent its interests. We recall in this context that Panel and Appellate Body reports are binding on the parties only.[199]

This view follows closely the architecture of the DSU,[200] wherein the participation of third parties is regulated in Article 10. According to Article 10(4), a third party which considers that a measure which is already the subject of a panel proceeding nullifies or impairs benefits accruing to it under any covered agreement may have recourse to 'normal dispute settlement procedures under this Understanding'.[201]

2.4.2 Dispute settlement under UNCLOS

With respect to UNCLOS, the broadly formulated rule on intervention of third parties in proceedings before the International Tribunal for the Law of the Sea (ITLOS) does not support a concept of 'essential parties' which could bar ITLOS from taking jurisdiction. Article 31(1) of the Statute of ITLOS provides that, '[s]hould a State Party consider that it has an interest of a legal nature which may be affected by the decision in any dispute, it may submit a request to the Tribunal to be permitted to intervene'.[202] Article 31(3) provides that, if such intervention is granted, the decision of ITLOS shall also be binding upon the third party insofar as it relates to matters in respect of which this party intervened. Although generally modelled upon the rules of the ICJ Statute with regard to intervention, this latter aspect[203] and the generalised grant of consent to the exercise of jurisdiction[204] lead to a markedly different picture of the role of third States in ITLOS proceedings as compared to those before the ICJ.

---

[199] WTO Panel, *Turkey – Restrictions on Imports of Textile and Clothing Products*, para. 9.11.
[200] Dispute Settlement Understanding, Annex 2 to the Marrakesh Agreement Establishing the World Trade Organization of 15 April 1994, entered into force on 1 January 1995, 1869 UNTS 401.
[201] See further Katrin Arend, 'Article 10 DSU', in Rüdiger Wolfrum, Peter-Tobias Stoll and Karen Kaiser (eds.), *Max Planck Commentaries on World Trade Law*, Vol. 2, *WTO – Institutions and Dispute Settlement* (Leiden: Nijhoff, 2006), para. 16.
[202] Statute of the International Tribunal for the Law of the Sea, Annex VI to the United Nations Convention on the Law of the Sea of 10 December 1982, entered into force on 16 November 1994, 1833 UNTS 3.
[203] See Rüdiger Wolfrum, 'Intervention in the Proceedings before the International Court of Justice and the International Tribunal for the Law of the Sea', in Volkmar Götz, Günther Jaenicke and Peter Selmer (eds.), *Liber amicorum Günther Jaenicke – Zum 85. Geburtstag* (Berlin: Springer, 1998), pp. 427–42, at p. 440.
[204] Rüdiger Wolfrum, 'Das Streitbeilegungssystem des VN-Seerechtsübereinkommens', in Wolfgang Graf Vitzthum (ed.), *Handbuch des Seerechts* (Munich: C. H. Beck, 2006), pp. 463–97, para. 18.

2.4.3 The European Court of Human Rights

The position is similar with respect to the European Convention on Human Rights and the possibility of individual complaints under Article 34. If more than one Member State of the ECHR is to be found responsible for violations of the Convention, it is unproblematic to file the complaint against a plurality of States, a practice which frequently occurs.[205] Moreover, third party interventions are possible under Article 36 of the Convention and Rule 44 of the Rules of the Court. More problematic from the viewpoint of an 'essential parties' concept would be a complaint which implicates a State not party to the ECHR. This problem was squarely addressed in the *Soering* case, where the extradition of an individual from the United Kingdom to the United States was at issue. In this respect, the Court remarked that 'the Convention does not govern the actions of States not Parties to it, nor does it purport to be a means of requiring the Contracting States to impose Convention standards on other States'.[206] This did not, however, prevent the Court from dealing with the situation and determining whether the United Kingdom incurred responsibility for 'foreseeable consequences of extradition suffered outside' its jurisdiction.[207] The key element of the Court's findings in this regard is that the Convention itself does not aim to regulate the conduct of non-parties to the Convention.[208] A finding which implicitly passes judgment on the conduct of a non-party State is thus, at least technically, devoid of any legal meaning for the latter State.

2.4.4 Arbitration

With respect to international arbitration, the picture is necessarily complex. There are no procedural rules which govern arbitrations in general.[209] The diversity of situations is too great: arbitrations may involve two States, a State and a private actor (for example, an investor) or, in

---

[205] See, e.g., ECtHR, *Ilascu and Others v. Moldova and Russia*, ECHR 2004-VII, 179; ECtHR, *Saddam Hussein v. Albania, Bulgaria, Croatia, Czech Republic, Denmark, Estonia, Hungary, Iceland, Ireland, Italy, Latvia, Lithuania, the Netherlands, Poland, Portugal, Romania, Slovakia, Slovenia, Turkey, Ukraine and the United Kingdom*.
[206] ECtHR, *Soering v. United Kingdom*, Series A, No. 161, para. 86; see also ECtHR, *Medvedyev and others v. France*, para. 63.
[207] ECtHR, *Soering v. United Kingdom*, Series A, No. 161, para. 86; see also ECtHR, *Al-Saadoon and Mufdhi v. United Kingdom*, Merits and Just Satisfaction, para. 124.
[208] See also ECtHR, *Mamatkulov and Askarov v. Turkey*, ECHR 2005-II, 293, para. 67.
[209] Cf W. Michael Reisman, *Nullity and Revision*, p. 330.

the field of international commercial arbitration, two private actors. For our purposes, the first two scenarios are more relevant than the last. Christine Chinkin has argued that, by analogy with *Monetary Gold*, an arbitral tribunal should refuse to hear a case which could conceivably impact upon third party rights.[210] However, at the same time, she had to admit that no general protective devices would exist in international arbitration.[211] At least in theory, she conceded, concerns about third party effects of awards would be redundant since no arbitral award could ever be binding upon a non-party.[212] However, factually, an arbitral award may very well impact heavily upon the position of third parties: due to the secrecy of proceedings, a third State may not even know about a situation being dealt with by an arbitral tribunal which could later negatively affect its position.[213] Conversely, a publicly held arbitration, possibly with arbitrators of high standing and a published decision, may contribute to the development of the law as a precedent and may thus impact negatively upon a third party.[214] To determine whether an arbitral tribunal is legally bound to decline hearing a case on the ground that third party rights are implicated, the relevant arbitral agreement will have to be consulted. That said, there have always been international agreements which expressly exclude arbitration between the parties if the rights or interests of third States were to be affected.[215] In sum, it will depend upon the arbitrators in question whether they consider the third party effects of an award to be so dramatic as to deny their jurisdiction.

2.4.5 The International Criminal Court

In a conceptually different manner, the issue of third party rights may also play a role in proceedings before the International Criminal Court. It is of course the case that in such proceedings individual responsibility will be at issue. As is clearly provided for in Article 25(4) of the Rome Statute, '[n]o provision of this Statute relating to individual

---

[210] Christine Chinkin, *Third Parties*, p. 273.
[211] *Ibid.*, p. 249.   [212] *Ibid.*, p. 250.
[213] Cf Loukas A. Mistelis, 'Confidentiality and Third Party Participation – UPS v. Canada and Methanex Corporation v. United States of America', *Arbitration International* 21 (2005), pp. 211–32; W. Michael Reisman, *Nullity and Revision*, p. 330.
[214] Christine Chinkin, *Third Parties*, p. 250.
[215] See, e.g., Convention concernant le règlement pacifique des conflits internationaux; signée à Londres, le 14 octobre 1903 entre le Royaume-Uni et la France, Martens, *Nouveau Recueil Général de Traités* (2e), XXXII, 479, Article I.

criminal responsibility shall affect the responsibility of States under international law'. However, it is also apparent that determinations of individual responsibility may very well affect, albeit implicitly, State responsibility: especially in the case of so-called 'leadership crimes'[216] a finding of individual responsibility of a high-ranking State official will at the very least establish a strong presumption for concurrent State responsibility.[217] These considerations may also underlie the concerns of non-parties to the Rome Statute about the exercise of criminal jurisdiction over their nationals. In general, the ICC may exercise jurisdiction in three situations: if a crime has been committed on the territory of a party to the Rome Statute, if the perpetrator is a national of a State party or if the Security Council has referred a situation to the ICC.[218] It is the first of these situations which has triggered concerns about the Statute's consistency with the *pacta tertiis* rule.[219] Whatever the merits of this argument,[220] it is relevant for our study to see that through the territoriality principle embodied in the Rome Statute, the conduct of third States may come under scrutiny and that there is no procedural rule built into the Rome Statute which would prevent the exercise of jurisdiction in such a case.[221] It is thus conceivable that, implicitly, the conduct of a complicit State may come under scrutiny in ICC proceedings.

2.4.6 Human rights bodies

In the practice of human rights bodies, one finds no direct provision for an 'essential parties' concept in their rules and procedures. An example of how such a body might consider human rights violations in the absence of the alleged main actor is the *Agiza* case before the UN Committee Against Torture.[222] In the case, a removal by the complainant

---

[216] Cf Kevin Jon Heller, 'Retreat from Nuremberg: The Leadership Requirement in the Crime of Aggression', *European Journal of International Law* 18 (2007), pp. 477–97, at p. 478.
[217] On the relationship between State and individual responsibility in international law, see André Nollkaemper, 'Concurrence', pp. 615 *et seq.*, especially at pp. 627 *et seq.*
[218] See Articles 12 and 13 of the Rome Statute of the International Criminal Court, UN Doc. A/CONF.183/9 of 17 July 1998, entered into force on 1 July 2002.
[219] See, e.g., Ruth Wedgwood, 'The International Criminal Court: An American View', *European Journal of International Law* 10 (1999), pp. 93–107, at pp. 99 *et seq.*
[220] Cf Frédéric Mégret, 'Epilogue to an Endless Debate: The International Criminal Court's Third Party Jurisdiction and the Looming Revolution of International Law', *European Journal of International Law* 12 (2001), pp. 247–68, at p. 249.
[221] See further Ruth Wedgwood, 'American View', p. 102.
[222] UN Committee Against Torture, Individual Complaint of Mr Ahmed Hussein Mustafa Kamil Agiza, Decision of 24 May 2005, UN Doc. CAT/C/34/D/233/2003.

from Sweden to Egypt (where Mr Agiza was most likely subjected to torture) was under consideration. He was deported to Egypt after Sweden received a diplomatic assurance that he would not be subjected to torture. *Inter alia*, the Committee found that 'it was known, or should have been known, to the State party's authorities at the time of the complainant's removal, that Egypt resorted to consistent and widespread use of torture against detainees, and that the risk of such treatment was particularly high in the case of detainees held for political and security reasons'.[223]

2.4.7 Domestic courts

Finally, a brief mention should be made of domestic courts, which increasingly apply international law and also the secondary rules of State responsibility.[224] Principles of State immunity (*par in parem non habet imperium*) will, in most cases, prevent the exercise of direct jurisdiction over foreign States. It is, however, conceivable, and has already occurred, that domestic courts may consider the complicity of their own State, thus implicating the wrongfulness of the conduct of another State.[225]

2.4.8 Concluding remarks

This brief survey of other procedural possibilities for holding complicit States responsible may show that the *Monetary Gold* principle may prevent the ICJ from entertaining cases on complicity – although the Court may have leeway to abandon its jurisprudence – but that, with respect to other judicial and quasi-judicial avenues, the prospects are more promising. State consent plays a different role in these fora: in some situations, it is no obstacle, as all members to a treaty regime have automatically consented to the exercise of jurisdiction by a court or tribunal. In other situations, third States are not legally affected by a decision of a court or tribunal established under such a regime as they are not members of the regime. In this perspective, it is the peculiar

---

[223] *Ibid.*, para. 13.3.
[224] On the latter phenomenon, see André Nollkaemper, 'Domestic Courts'.
[225] See, e.g., the Canadian Supreme Court, *R* v. *Hape*, 2007 SCC 26; *Canada (Justice)* v. *Khadr*, 2008 SCC 28; the UK High Court of Justice, *R. (on the Application of Binyan Mohammed)* v. *Secretary of State for Foreign and Commonwealth Affairs*; the Swiss Federal Court of Justice, EuGRZ 10 (1983), pp. 435 *et seq.*; the German Federal Constitutional Court, BVerfGE 109, 13, 26–7 = ILDC 10 (DE 2003) as well as the German Federal Administrative Court, 2 WD 12.04, Judgment of 21 June 2005 = ILDC 483 (DE 2005).

position of the ICJ which makes its reliance on consent so important: the effects of its jurisprudence are so readily apparent that the bindingness *inter partes* of a judgment is not a sufficient means of protection for third parties. This is arguably a less acute problem with respect to other courts and tribunals which are not blessed with the hallmark of being 'the principal judicial organ of the United Nations'. Although the *Monetary Gold* principle is sometimes presented as a general principle of law applicable beyond ICJ proceedings,[226] its effects will have to be carefully established with respect to the features of the judicial dispute settlement at hand.

---

[226] Shabtai Rosenne, 'International Courts and Tribunals, Jurisdiction and Admissibility of Inter-State Applications', in Rüdiger Wolfrum (ed.), *Max Planck Encyclopedia of Public International Law*, online edition (Oxford: Oxford University Press, 2008), para. 7.

7 Complicity and aggravated responsibility

1 Introductory remarks

Ever since its inception in Articles 53 and 64 of the Vienna Convention on the Law of Treaties, the concept of *jus cogens* has puzzled legal commentators with respect to its possible ramifications beyond the law of treaties.[1] Together with its conceptual sibling, obligations *erga omnes*,[2] its existence has pointed to the need for coining forms of graded responsibility. The expectation was that the coming into existence of these forms of international public order could not leave unaffected what, through the work of the ILC, turned into a central element for

---

[1] Christos L. Rozakis, *The Concept of Jus Cogens in the Law of Treaties* (Amsterdam: North-Holland Publishing Company, 1976), p. 22; Giorgio Gaja, 'Jus Cogens Beyond the Vienna Convention', *Recueil des Cours* 172 (1981-III), pp. 271–316, at p. 290; Bruno Simma, 'From Bilateralism to Community Interest', p. 288; Theodor Meron, 'International Law in the Age of Human Rights – General Course on Public International Law', *Recueil des Cours* 301 (2003), pp. 9–490, at p. 420; Andreas L. Paulus, 'Jus Cogens', pp. 308 *et seq.*; Antônio Augusto Cançado Trindade, 'International Law for Humankind: Towards a New Jus Gentium (I), General Course on Public International Law', *Recueil des Cours* 316 (2006), pp. 9–440, at p. 339; Alexander Orakhelashvili, *Peremptory Norms*, p. 205; Dinah Shelton, 'Normative Hierarchy in International Law', *American Journal of International Law* 100 (2006), pp. 291–323, at pp. 304–5; Andrea Bianchi, 'Magic of Jus Cogens', pp. 496 and 501.

[2] Christian Tomuschat, 'International Law', pp. 85–6; Stefan Kadelbach, 'Jus Cogens, Obligations Erga Omnes and Other Rules: The Identification of Fundamental Rules', in Christian Tomuschat and Jean-Marc Thouvenin (eds.), *The Fundamental Rules of the International Legal Order: Jus Cogens and Obligations Erga Omnes* (Leiden: Nijhoff, 2006), pp. 21–40, at p. 27; Michael Byers, 'Conceptualising', pp. 211 *et seq.*; André de Hoogh, *Obligations Erga Omnes and International Crimes – A Theoretical Inquiry into the Implementation and Enforcement of the International Responsibility of States* (The Hague: Kluwer, 1996), pp. 53 *et seq.*; Christian J. Tams, *Enforcing Obligations Erga Omnes*, pp. 139 *et seq.*

the enforcement of international law.[3] As is the case with respect to other elements of the law of State responsibility,[4] the question arises how the problem of complicity is affected by the categories of peremptory norms and obligations *erga omnes*. In Chapter 2, we discussed the extent to which these categories have helped to overcome the bilateral mindset which used to pervade the law of State responsibility. However, we have also found that it would strain this analysis to deduce straight consequences for the issue of complicity from these findings. Accordingly, a more detailed analysis is called for as it is not only the case that these important elements of international public order may have played a role in paving the way towards the recognition that complicity in the commission of internationally wrongful acts is no longer acceptable; they may also call for different consequences in the cases in which complicity in the violation of peremptory norms is at stake.

Given that the regime of 'aggravated responsibility'[5] has been described in detail in manifold ways,[6] only a short overview of its development will be given in the next section (section 2). Following that, the impact of the rules on aggravated responsibility on the problem of complicity will be considered, which will involve a discussion of Articles 40 and 41 ASR (section 3), the relationship between complicity and obligations of cooperation in the law of State responsibility (section 4) as well as their relation to countermeasures in the collective interest (section 5).

2 The community interest in the law of State responsibility

One of the cornerstones of Roberto Ago's work as Special Rapporteur on State responsibility was his determination to make visible in the law

---

[3] See ILC Commentary on Draft Article 19, paras. 15 *et seq.*, YBILC 1976, Vol. II, Part Two, p. 101.
[4] See, e.g., Stefan Kadelbach, *Zwingendes Völkerrecht* (Berlin: Duncker & Humblot, 1992), pp. 50 *et seq.*; Alexander Orakhelashvili, *Peremptory Norms*, pp. 241 *et seq.*
[5] Santiago Villalpando, *L'émergence*, p. 379; Antonio Cassese, *International Law*, p. 262.
[6] Marina Spinedi, 'International Crimes of State: The Legislative History', in Joseph H. H. Weiler, Antonio Cassese and Marina Spinedi (eds.), *International Crimes of State: A Critical Analysis of the ILC's Draft Article 19 on State Responsibility* (Berlin: de Gruyter, 1989), pp. 7–138; Marina Spinedi, 'From One Codification to Another', pp. 1099–1100; Stefan Kadelbach, *Zwingendes Völkerrecht*, pp. 52 *et seq.*; Andreas L. Paulus, *Die internationale Gemeinschaft*, pp. 386 *et seq.*; Eric Wyler, 'From "State Crime" to "Serious Breaches of Obligations under Peremptory Norms of General International Law"', *European Journal of International Law* 13 (2002), pp. 1147–60, at pp. 1148 *et seq.*

of State responsibility the changes the international legal order had witnessed since the end of the Second World War.[7] The development of rules which were deemed so important to the international community that they could no longer be analysed along the lines of the traditional bilateral paradigm of international law had already materialised in the adoption of the concept of *jus cogens* in Articles 53 and 64 of the Vienna Convention on the Law of Treaties.[8] The International Court of Justice recognised in its *Barcelona Traction* case the existence of some international obligations which were owed not only to the individual right-holders, but to the international community of States as a whole – thus the concept of obligations *erga omnes*[9] was, if not introduced, then pushed to the forefront of international law.[10] The ILC tried to accommodate these developments in the concept of international crimes, which were to be distinguished from the ordinary form of international responsibility, namely, 'delicts'. Article 19(2) of the 1996 Draft Articles stipulated:

An internationally wrongful act which results from the breach by a State of an international obligation so essential for the protection of fundamental interests of the international community that its breach is recognized as a crime by that community as a whole constitutes an international crime.[11]

Article 19(3) included a non-exhaustive list of examples which referred to situations the Commission had in mind when speaking about international crimes. The list was composed of serious breaches relating to the maintenance of international peace and security (especially concerning the prohibition of aggression), the self-determination of peoples, fundamental norms on the protection of the human being (expressly spelled out were genocide, slavery and *apartheid*) as well as

---

[7] Roberto Ago, 'Fifth Report on State Responsibility', UN Doc. A/CN.4/291 and Add.1-2, YBILC 1976, Vol. II, Part One, p. 3.
[8] For comprehensive treatments of *jus cogens*, see Stefan Kadelbach, *Zwingendes Völkerrecht*; Alexander Orakhelashvili, *Peremptory Norms*; for what is frequently viewed as the first conceptualisation of peremptory norms, see Alfred Verdross, 'Forbidden Treaties in International Law', *American Journal of International Law* 31 (1937), pp. 571-7; but see also August Freiherr von der Heydte, 'Die Erscheinungsformen des zwischenstaatlichen Rechts: jus cogens und jus dispositivum im Völkerrecht', *Zeitschrift für Völkerrecht* 16 (1932), pp. 461-78.
[9] ICJ, *Barcelona Traction, Light and Power Company, Limited*, Second Phase, Judgment, ICJ Rep. 1970, 4, para. 33.
[10] On the historical development of this concept, see Christian J. Tams, *Enforcing Obligations Erga Omnes*, pp. 48 et seq.; Maurizio Ragazzi, *The Concept*, pp. 18 et seq.
[11] For the initial draft, see YBILC 1976, Vol. II, Part Two, p. 95.

serious breaches of international obligations of essential importance for the safeguarding and preservation of the human environment.

The concept of international crimes was controversial for a number of reasons.[12] While it was already subject to debate whether international law really knew such a concept,[13] the more important dispute related to the consequences of international crimes.[14] This was owed to the fact that Roberto Ago left open the question of what consequences would be attached to the commission of crimes. He remarked only that the distinction between delicts and crimes 'will necessarily be reflected in the legal consequences attached ... and in the determination of the subject or subjects of international law authorized to implement those consequences'.[15] In subsequent years, more or less all successors to Roberto Ago struggled with the 'implementation' of this legacy in their respective reports.[16]

While the concept of international crimes proved to be controversial, it nonetheless enjoyed some support in the Commission and among writers. For Alain Pellet, for example, the concept of crimes was indispensable to the international legal system: in his view, it would be absurd to consider that genocide would trigger the applicability of the same regime as does the breach of a bilateral trade agreement between States.[17] However, the uncertainty over the legal consequences of international crimes overshadowed the benefits of this category for many members of the Commission when the Draft Articles were adopted in First Reading in 1996.[18] As Part One of the Articles was already adopted in 1980 and remained unchanged until 1996, the Commission included a footnote to Article 40(3) of the 1996 Draft Articles[19] stipulating that:

---

[12] For an overview, see André de Hoogh, *Obligations Erga Omnes*, pp. 56 *et seq.*
[13] Cf Stefan Kadelbach, *Zwingendes Völkerrecht*, p. 56.
[14] For a summary of the discussion and critique, see Andreas L. Paulus, *Die internationale Gemeinschaft*, pp. 390 *et seq.*
[15] Roberto Ago, Commentary to draft Article 19, YBILC 1976, Vol. II, Part Two, p. 97, para. 7.
[16] With respect to the solutions proposed by Willem Riphagen and Gaetano Arangio-Ruiz, see Mathias Forteau, *Droit de la sécurité collective*, pp. 526 *et seq.*; Helmut Philipp Aust, 'Prism of Diversity', pp. 195–6.
[17] Alain Pellet, 'Can a State', pp. 425–6; see also Georges Abi-Saab, 'Que reste-t-il du "crime international"', in *Droit du pouvoir – Pouvoir du droit: Mélanges offerts à Jean Salmon* (Brussels: Bruylant, 2007), pp. 69–91, pp. 79 *et seq.*
[18] For a contemporary analysis, see Bruno Simma, 'From Bilateralism to Community Interest', pp. 304 *et seq.*
[19] Providing that: 'In addition, "injured State" means, if the internationally wrongful act constitutes an international crime, all other States.' Cf YBILC 1996, Vol. II, Part Two, p. 63.

[t]he term 'crime' is used for consistency with article 19 of Part One of the articles. It was, however, noted that alternative phrases such as 'international wrongful act of a serious nature' or 'an exceptionally serious wrongful act' could be substituted for the term 'crime', thus, *inter alia*, avoiding the penal implication of the term.

Through these compromise formulations, one can sense the amount of disagreement over the question whether or not to retain the concept of crimes in the Articles. Eventually, as we know, the Commission decided against it and replaced the category of 'international crimes' with the one of 'serious breaches of peremptory norms under general international law' (Articles 40 and 41 ASR). As numerous commentators have noted, this was a bold move in itself, as there was, prior to the ILC's conclusion of the work on State responsibility, no indication that *jus cogens* norms would produce obligations for third States along the lines of what the ILC eventually decided on.[20]

Special Rapporteur James Crawford has explained the reasons for this development: apparently, there was agreement to a certain extent that, in order to be labelled as 'crimes', more consequences would have to follow than just an expanded notion of standing or the right to react to breaches of the law. In addition, in order to deal with crimes, international law would presumably require a special regime which was non-existent and also did not figure in the Draft Articles the Commission had adopted in 1996. Crawford identified five components of such a regime: (1) a proper definition of the crimes following the maxim of *nullum crimen sine lege*; (2) an adequate procedure to determine the existence of crimes on behalf of the international community; (3) a system of due process with respect to the adjudication of crimes; (4) appropriate sanctions to follow international crimes; and (5) 'some system by which the wrongdoing entity could purge its guilt, i.e., could work its way out of the condemnation of criminality'.[21] These conditions were not met in the drafts of the ILC.[22] At the same time, Crawford argued, there was a need not to simply abandon the concept of crimes altogether. For the reason to retain some of its substance but without the problematic label of 'crimes' attached to it, the Commission finally

---

[20] Andreas L. Paulus, 'Jus Cogens', p. 316; Alexander Orakhelashvili, *Peremptory Norms*, p. 287.
[21] James Crawford, 'Introduction', pp. 18–19; see also his 'First Report on State Responsibility', UN Doc, A/CN.4/490/Add.3, paras. 52 *et seq.*
[22] This perspective met with criticism for being overly formalistic: see Alexander Orakhelashvili, *Peremptory Norms*, p. 280; Alain Pellet, 'Les articles', p. 12.

decided to opt for the 'serious breaches' model instead. Under this scheme, which is embodied in Articles 40 and 41 ASR, the additional consequences for *third States* were included which were originally spelt out in Draft Article 53 of the 1996 Draft.[23] Other aspects of the international crimes which related to the standing of States to invoke the responsibility in cases in which they were not directly injured were salvaged by adding them into the rules on the invocation and implementation of responsibility and can now be found in Articles 42 and 48 ASR. The hotly contested issue whether or not States could have recourse to countermeasures in the collective interest was largely left open in Article 54 ASR – an issue to which we will have to return in due course.[24]

The main reason for deleting 'crimes' and inserting a more 'neutral' category was to free the ASR from any misconceived analogies with domestic systems of criminal law.[25] Whether the concept of 'international crimes' really ever envisaged a criminalisation of the law of State responsibility in the true sense is a matter open to dispute.[26] Although Roberto Ago admitted some role for punishment in his early treatment of the international law on 'delicts',[27] punishment was not what he intended the concept of international crimes to be.[28] Some authors have argued that, despite the deletion of the concept of international crimes, the substance has remained alive and well in the law of State responsibility.[29] Whether they mean by that the law of State

---

[23] On the question whether the State responsible for the serious breach incurs additional consequences, see Christian J. Tams, 'Do Serious Breaches Give Rise to Any Specific Obligations of the Responsible State?', *European Journal of International Law* 13 (2002), pp. 1161–80.

[24] For now, see David J. Bederman, 'Counterintuiting Countermeasures', *American Journal of International Law* 96 (2002), pp. 817–32.

[25] Eric Wyler, 'State Crime', p. 1148.

[26] Stefan Kadelbach, *Zwingendes Völkerrecht*, p. 53; Alain Pellet, 'Les articles', pp. 11–13.

[27] Roberto Ago, 'Le délit international', pp. 427 *et seq.*

[28] Eric Wyler, 'State Crime', p. 1050; but see also Martti Koskenniemi, 'Solidarity Measures', p. 338, on Hersch Lauterpacht and his interpretation of the law of State responsibility as '*ersatz* criminal law'.

[29] Alexander Orakhelashvili, *Peremptory Norms*, p. 281; Eric Wyler, 'State Crime', p. 1159; Alain Pellet, 'Les articles', pp. 15–16; slightly different Georges Abi-Saab, 'Que reste-t-il', p. 91; in this regard, reference should also be made to several separate opinions of Judge Cançado Trindade in decisions of the Inter-American Court of Human Rights, in which he maintained the continuing validity of the category of State crimes and criticised the ILC for having abandoned that concept: see Inter-AmCtHR, *Myrna Mack Chang v. Guatemala*, Merits, Reparations and Costs,

responsibility in general or its emanation in the ASR is not entirely clear, however.

3 Complicity and serious breaches of peremptory norms

An obligation of non-assistance figures among the legal consequences the ASR attach to the commission of a serious breach of a peremptory norm under general international law. Articles 40 and 41 ASR provide:

Article 40 Application of this Chapter
1. This Chapter applies to the international responsibility which is entailed by a serious breach by a State of an obligation arising under a peremptory norm of general international law.
2. A breach of such an obligation is serious if it involves a gross or systematic failure by the responsible State to fulfil the obligation.

Article 41 Particular consequences of a serious breach of an obligation under this Chapter
1. States shall cooperate to bring to an end through lawful means any serious breach within the meaning of article 40.
2. No State shall recognize as lawful a situation created by a serious breach within the meaning of article 40, nor render aid or assistance in maintaining that situation.
3. This article is without prejudice to the other consequences referred to in this Part and to such further consequences that a breach to which this Chapter applies may entail under international law.

Article 41(2) ASR thus sets out an additional obligation of non-assistance in addition to that embodied in Article 16 ASR. This entails two initial questions. What is the relationship of this special provision to Article 16 ASR? How does non-assistance under Article 41(2) relate to the obligation of non-recognition? These two obligations are grouped together in one paragraph and are seen by some as representing a close unity.[30] These two questions shall be addressed first, before we turn our attention to the relationship between these 'duties of isolation'[31] and the obligation of cooperation embodied in Article 41(1)

Series C, No. 101, separate opinion of Judge Cançado Trindade, paras. 5 *et seq.*; Inter-AmCtHR, *Miguel Castro Castro Prison (Peru)*, Merits, Series C, No. 160, separate opinion of Judge Cançado Trindade, paras. 41 *et seq.*

[30] Santiago Villalpando, *L'émergence*, p. 389.
[31] Andrea Gattini, 'A Return Ticket to "Communitarisme", Please', *European Journal of International Law* 13 (2002), pp. 1181–99, at p. 1188.

(section 4) as well as the notion of countermeasures in the collective interest (section 5).

Before we turn to these issues, some brief remarks on the concept of 'serious breaches' itself are in order. As Article 40(2) ASR provides, a breach is serious if it is 'a gross or systematic failure by the responsible State to fulfil the obligation' in question. In other words, the ILC can imagine non-serious breaches of peremptory norms which lack this gross or systematic character. In particular with respect to the *jus cogens* norm of the prohibition of genocide, this has earned the Commission some criticism: is it conceivable that genocide can be committed non-systematically and, even more unlikely, in a manner which is not 'gross'?[32] The ILC was of course well aware of this problem but nonetheless decided to retain this limiting factor as 'relatively less serious cases of breach of peremptory norms can be envisaged'.[33] While judgment may be reserved whether this is a sensible distinction and whether the – not too far-reaching – consequences of Article 41 should not apply in general when there are violations of *jus cogens* norms, any interpretation of Articles 40 and 41 ASR will have to be effected with this limiting condition in mind.[34]

3.1 Non-recognition and non-assistance

The understanding that the obligations of non-recognition and non-assistance must be viewed together is encouraged by the ILC Commentary, which speaks of 'a duty of abstention' covering both obligations.[35]

3.1.1 Preliminary remarks on non-recognition

Traditionally, the doctrine of non-recognition has been applied with respect to the effects of illegal acquisition of territory and denials of the right to self-determination of peoples.[36] Its origins lie in the

---

[32] Cf the discussion on the seriousness test embodied in Draft Article 19 by Nina Jørgensen, *The Responsibility of States for International Crimes* (Oxford: Oxford University Press, 2000), pp. 114–15; Beatrice I. Bonafè, *The Relationship Between State and Individual Responsibility for International Crimes* (Leiden: Nijhoff, 2009), pp. 75 *et seq.*; Sandra Szurek, 'Responsabilité de protéger, nature de l'obligation et responsabilité internationale', in Société française pour le droit international (ed.), *La responsabilité de protéger* (Paris: Pedone, 2008), pp. 91–134, at p. 112.
[33] ILC Commentary, Article 40, para. 7.
[34] Cf Alain Pellet, 'Les articles', p. 15.   [35] ILC Commentary, Article 41, para. 4.
[36] Jochen Abr. Frowein, 'Collective Enforcement of International Obligations', *Zeitschrift für ausländisches öffentliches Recht und Völkerrecht* 47 (1987), pp. 67–79, at p. 77; Andrea Gattini, 'Return Ticket', p. 1189; Jörg Künzli, *Unrechtsregimes*, p. 353;

so-called 'Stimson Doctrine' by which US Secretary of State Henry Lewis Stimson declared in 1932 that the US would not recognise any territorial acquisition of Japan in Manchurian China. The argument for this decision rested on the Briand–Kellogg Pact of 1928.[37] After 1945, the most important examples for the application of the doctrine of non-recognition have been resolutions by UN bodies, notably by the Security Council, on the unilateral declaration of independence by the racist minority regime in Southern Rhodesia, on South Africa's claim over Namibia as well as on its Homelands policy.[38] The functions of non-recognition have been described most cogently by Hersch Lauterpacht:

> The principle of non-recognition fulfils in the present stage of international organization an important function in the maintenance of the authority of the law. From the jurisprudential point of view the acceptance of the policy or of the obligation of non-recognition amounts to a vindication of the legal character of international law as against the 'law-creating effects of facts'. It is the minimum of resistance which an insufficiently organized but law-abiding community offers to illegality; it is a continuous challenge to a legal wrong.[39]

Non-recognition as expressed in Article 41(2) ASR goes beyond the traditional scope of the principle insofar as it applies not only to 'status'-related questions[40] such as territorial titles or the right of self-determination, but also to the effects of serious breaches of peremptory norms in general. In light of this expansion, concerns have been voiced in the literature that the obligation of non-recognition, as it figures in Article 41(2) ASR, would be devoid of a concrete legal content. It would be hard to imagine how non-recognition could operate in, for instance,

---

David Turns, 'The Stimson Doctrine of Non-Recognition: Its Historical Genesis and Influence on Contemporary International Law', *Chinese Journal of International Law* 2 (2003), pp. 105–44, at p. 135; in greater detail on the various forms and functions of non-recognition, see Vera Gowlland-Debbas, *Collective Responses*, pp. 273 et seq.

[37] See further Hersch Lauterpacht, *Recognition in International Law* (Cambridge: Cambridge University Press, 1948), pp. 412 et seq. (also with an overview of earlier practice); Heiko Meiertöns, *Die Doktrinen US-amerikanischer Sicherheitspolitik – Völkerrechtliche Bewertung und ihr Einfluss auf das Völkerrecht* (Baden-Baden: Nomos, 2006), pp. 96–7; Stefan Talmon, *Kollektive Nichtanerkennung*, pp. 90 et seq.

[38] See Jochen Abr. Frowein, 'Non-Recognition', in Rudolf Bernhardt (ed.), *Encyclopedia of Public International Law*, Vol. III (Amsterdam: Elsevier, 1995), pp. 627–9, at p. 628.

[39] Hersch Lauterpacht, *Recognition in International Law*, pp. 430–1.

[40] Willem A. Riphagen, 'State Responsibility: New Theories of Obligation in Interstate Relations', in Ronald St John Macdonald and Douglas M. Johnston (eds.), *The Structure and Process of International Law: Essays in Legal Philosophy, Doctrine and Theory* (The Hague: Nijhoff, 1983), pp. 581–625, at p. 619, note 63.

situations involving a breach of the *jus cogens* norms of the prohibition of torture, slavery or racial discrimination.[41] The importance and pertinence of the principle has also been called into question in a more general way: an obligation of non-recognition would have no basis in international law. Other authors, however, have maintained that there is even a general obligation of non-recognition in international law which would relate not only to the effects of serious breaches of peremptory norms, but more generally to all violations of international law.[42] Non-recognition has also been singled out by some authors as 'the most important consequence forming part of the special regime of violations of fundamental rules of the international legal order'.[43]

Yet others have affirmed that non-recognition can only be properly understood in light of the category of *jus cogens*. Otherwise, as argued notably by John Dugard, the UN Security Council could 'invoke any violation of international law, however minor, as a ground for non-recognition', which would mean 'that political whim rather than legal principles guide the Council on such matters'.[44] In opposition to this view, it has also been argued that non-recognition cannot fulfil a useful function especially in those cases where violations of *jus cogens* are at stake: as the means of 'subsequent validation' such as acquiescence or consent cannot produce legal effects in such cases, non-recognition would no longer be necessary.[45]

---

[41] For criticism with respect to the predecessor of Article 41(2) ASR, namely, Draft Article 53(a) as adopted in 1996, see Christian Tomuschat, 'International Crimes by States: An Endangered Species?', in Karel Wellens (ed.), *International Law: Theory and Practice. Essays in Honour of Eric Suy* (The Hague: Kluwer, 1998), pp. 253-74, at pp. 258-9; on Article 41(2), see Stefan Talmon, 'The Duty Not to "Recognize as Lawful" a Situation Created by the Illegal Use of Force or Other Serious Breaches of a Jus Cogens Obligation: An Obligation without Real Substance?', in Christian Tomuschat and Jean-Marc Thouvenin (eds.), *The Fundamental Rules of the International Legal Order: Jus Cogens and Obligations Erga Omnes* (Leiden: Nijhoff, 2006), pp. 99-125, at p. 104; Martin Dawidowicz, 'The Obligation of Non-Recognition of an Unlawful Situation', in James Crawford, Alain Pellet and Simon Olleson (eds.), *The Law of International Responsibility* (Oxford: Oxford University Press, 2010), pp. 677-86, at p. 683.

[42] See, e.g., Bardo Fassbender, 'Schutz der Menschenrechte', p. 8; Andreas L. Paulus, 'Jus Cogens', p. 315; Christian J. Tams, 'All's Well', p. 774; Enrico Milano, *Unlawful Territorial Situations in International Law – Reconciling Effectiveness, Legality and Legitimacy* (Leiden: Nijhoff, 2006), p. 141, note 22.

[43] Andreas Zimmermann and Michael Teichmann, 'State Responsibility', p. 307.

[44] John Dugard, *Recognition and the United Nations* (Cambridge: Grotius, 1987), p. 163; a similar position is held by Alexander Orakhelashvili, *Peremptory Norms*, pp. 378-9.

[45] Cf Stefan Talmon, 'Duty', p. 107.

Despite this uncertain state of affairs, the principle of non-recognition has figured in important resolutions of the UN General Assembly,[46] in the jurisprudence of the ICJ,[47] in the work of the ILC and in State practice.[48] The way the ILC conceived of non-recognition in Article 41(2) ASR occupies the middle ground between the various doctrinal propositions: neither is it limited to the traditional field of application of non-recognition nor does it expand the concept to the effects of any conceivable breach of international law. What an obligation of non-recognition may entail beyond its traditional field of application remains to be seen.[49] As Ian Brownlie noted, the potential application of non-recognition need not be limited to its traditional functions. Rather, the concept could fruitfully be deployed with respect to

> legal titles, liabilities and immunities ... The failure to protest, the pattern of conduct generally described as acquiescence, and admissions against interest (for example, in the form of maps), are all juridical fellows with the group of questions referred to loosely as 'the problem of recognition'.[50]

So far, it appears that the doctrine is most forcefully applied with respect to the effects of granting immunity to States and their officials in the context of serious international crimes.[51] The jurisprudence of domestic courts, for instance of the UK House of Lords,[52] has shown that a more broadly formulated doctrine of non-recognition may also

---

[46] See Declaration on Principles of International Law concerning Friendly Relations and Co-operation among States in Accordance with the Charter of the United Nations, UN Doc. A/RES/2625 (XXV) of 24 October 1970: 'No territorial acquisition resulting from the threat or use of force shall be recognized as legal.' See also Declaration on the Definition of Aggression, UN Doc. A/RES/3314 (XXIX) of 14 December 1974, Article 5(3): 'No territorial acquisition or special advantage from aggression is or shall be recognized as lawful.'

[47] ICJ, *Legal Consequences for States of the Continued Presence of South Africa in Namibia (South West Africa) Notwithstanding Security Council Resolution 276 (1970)*, Advisory Opinion, ICJ Rep. 1971, 16, para. 121.

[48] For an overview of State practice, see Théodore Christakis, 'Non-Reconnaissance', pp. 146 *et seq.*; Martin Dawidowicz, 'Non-Recognition', pp. 679 *et seq.*

[49] See also Willem A. Riphagen, 'Third Report on the Content, Forms and Degrees of International Responsibility (Part 2 of the Draft Articles)', UN Doc. A/CN.4/354 and Add.1-2, YBILC 1982, Vol. II, Part One, pp. 22, 49 (para. 7 of commentary on Draft Article 6).

[50] Ian Brownlie, 'Recognition in Theory and Practice', *British Year Book of International Law* 53 (1982), pp. 197–211, at p. 201.

[51] Italian Court of Cassation, *Ferrini* v. *Germany*, 128 ILR 658, para. 9.

[52] UK House of Lords, *A (FC) and others (FC)* v. *Secretary of State for the Home Department and others*, opinion of Lord Bingham, para. 34.

be deployed to negate the legality of the use of evidence obtained through torture. Whatever the merits of the arguments in the concrete cases at hand,[53] they show that a doctrine of non-recognition may have stretched out into new fields of application, a development reinforced or potentially even triggered by the work of the ILC.[54]

Various facets of non-recognition have to be distinguished.[55] Recognition of States and governments in general is a matter of discretion and has to be distinguished from non-recognition on legal grounds, i.e., non-recognition which is rendered mandatory by international law.[56] The core idea of an obligation of non-recognition as traditionally understood is that certain dealings with an illegal regime will condone its exercise of jurisdiction and will thus help to consolidate its title over a given territory. In this respect, the obligation could be of a differing intensity. Whereas a mere declaration not to recognise a claim to a given title is considered to be sufficient by some,[57] others demand more exacting measures of isolation such as the suspension of diplomatic relations[58] or the cessation of economic cooperation by which the unlawful exercise of authority would become further entrenched.[59] It is even imaginable to conceive of a general duty of isolation which comprises roughly all channels of communication and interaction between the non-recognising States and the wrongdoer.[60]

---

[53] For a sceptical position with regard to the applicability of Article 41 ASR in the House of Lords case, see Tobias Thienel, 'The Admissibility of Evidence Obtained by Torture under International Law', *European Journal of International Law* 17 (2006), pp. 349–67, at p. 364, note 115; for a similar assessment of the Italian decision, see Andrea Gattini, 'War Crimes', p. 236; for a doctrinal development of the effects of non-recognition in such cases, see Andrea Bianchi, 'L'immunité des Etats', p. 92; Andrea Bianchi, 'Ferrini', p. 247; Alexander Orakhelashvili, *Peremptory Norms*, pp. 283–4.

[54] Cf Ian Brownlie, 'Recognition', p. 201; Alexander Orakhelashvili, *Peremptory Norms*, p. 282.

[55] Cf Heike Krieger, *Das Effektivitätsprinzip im Völkerrecht* (Berlin: Duncker & Humblot, 2000), pp. 194 *et seq.*

[56] James Crawford, *Creation of States*, pp. 157–8; Eckart Klein, 'Die Nichtanerkennungspolitik der Vereinten Nationen gegenüber den in die Unabhängigkeit entlassenen südafrikanischen *homelands*', *Zeitschrift für ausländisches öffentliches Recht und Völkerrecht* 39 (1979), pp. 469–95, at p. 477; Théodore Christakis, 'Non-Reconnaissance', p. 127.

[57] Hersch Lauterpacht, *Recognition in International Law*, pp. 431 *et seq.*

[58] Jochen Abr. Frowein, 'Non-Recognition', p. 628.

[59] For an overview, see Théodore Christakis, 'Non-Reconnaissance', pp. 146 *et seq.*

[60] Cf Alexander Orakhelashvili, *Peremptory Norms*, pp. 386–8; in such a case, one would, however, need to be careful not to unduly infringe upon the human rights

However, we need to be careful not to turn an obligation of non-recognition into a concept requiring positive action.[61] It is true that under certain circumstances a failure to protest may come to imply acquiescence in a new legal claim.[62] However, protest is an active form of conduct and will thus not represent a typical means of non-recognition. Although a protest may express the position of non-recognition, it does not appear to be the case that an obligation of non-recognition would *require* a protest against a given form of conduct or even farther-reaching measures such as the suspension of treaty relations. In this sense, most authorities hold that the instrument of non-recognition is neither a countermeasure nor a sanction.[63] The ILC has referred to non-recognition and non-assistance as duties of abstention.[64] This categorisation appears to restrict too far-reaching interpretations of what non-recognition could require of States in the sense of Article 41(2) ASR.[65]

What is crucial for our purposes is to distinguish between the various emanations of non-recognition: the principle undoubtedly plays an important role where territorial questions or the right of self-

of the population which may be affected by such measures of isolation: see ICJ, *Legal Consequences for States of the Continued Presence of South Africa in Namibia (South West Africa) Notwithstanding Security Council Resolution 276 (1970)*, Advisory Opinion, ICJ Rep. 1971, 16, para. 122; see further Hersch Lauterpacht, *Recognition in International Law*, pp. 431–2; Antonelli Tancredi, 'A Normative "Due Process" in the Creation of States through Secession', in Marcelo G. Kohen (ed.), *Secession – International Law Perspectives* (Cambridge: Cambridge University Press, 2006), pp. 171–207, at p. 203.

[61] ICJ, *Legal Consequences for States of the Continued Presence of South Africa in Namibia (South West Africa) Notwithstanding Security Council Resolution 276 (1970)*, Advisory Opinion, ICJ Rep. 1971, 16, separate opinion of Judge Petrén, *ibid.*, p. 134.
[62] Cf Michael Byers, *Custom*, pp. 106–7.
[63] James Crawford, *Creation of States*, pp. 159, 173; Vera Gowlland-Debbas, *Collective Responses*, p. 277; Georges Abi-Saab, 'The Concept of "International Crimes" and Its Place in Contemporary International Law', in Joseph H. H. Weiler, Antonio Cassese and Marina Spinedi (eds.), *International Crimes of States – A Critical Analysis of the ILC's Draft Article 19 on State Responsibility* (Berlin: de Gruyter, 1989), pp. 141–50, at p. 149; Theodor Meron, *Humanization*, p. 283; David Turns, 'Stimson Doctrine', p. 135; see also Thilo Rensmann, 'Impact on the Immunity of States and Their Officials', in Menno T. Kamminga and Martin Scheinin (eds.), *The Impact of Human Rights Law on General International Law* (Oxford: Oxford University Press, 2009), pp. 151–70, at p. 165; for a different view, see Stefan Talmon, *Kollektive Nichtanerkennung*, pp. 295 *et seq.*; Stefan Talmon, *La non-reconnaissance collective*, pp. 59–60; undecided Willem A. Riphagen, 'State Responsibility', pp. 599, 607.
[64] ILC Commentary, Article 41, para. 4.
[65] See also the discussion by Andreas Zimmermann and Michael Teichmann on the relationship between non-recognition and a waiver of diplomatic protection, 'State Responsibility', p. 309.

determination are at stake. It is as true today as it was when the principle was first developed that acquisitions of territory by force will not be recognised by the international legal order. The same may hold true for the coming into existence of new States whose potential secession has been unlawfully supported by outside actors.[66] In these situations, non-recognition is mandatory for other States. If they nonetheless recognise the entity in question, they will have committed an independent internationally wrongful act *vis-à-vis* the legitimate sovereign.[67]

From this traditional function of non-recognition we need to distinguish what has emerged more recently: non-recognition as a principle which is attached to the effects of other violations of peremptory norms. In these cases, it is not apparent how recognition of, for example, the consequences of torture, would constitute an independent wrongful act. The essential difference relates to the original orientation of non-recognition of 'status', as Riphagen has described it.[68] With respect to these newer functions of non-recognition, status is not involved. A violation of the prohibition of torture, for example, has nothing to do with status. Rather, Article 41(2) ASR provides for a form of derivative responsibility along the lines of responsibility of a prohibition of complicity. If an obligation of non-recognition is conceptualised in terms of an obligation of abstention which covers a potentially unlimited range of measures which can imply recognition, it becomes similar to an obligation of non-assistance which is likewise derivative. In these matters which do not touch upon the traditional functions of non-recognition, this principle could thus find itself in competition with rules on non-assistance.[69]

3.1.2 The Namibia advisory opinion of the ICJ

In commenting upon Article 41(2) ASR, the ILC relied primarily on the approach of the ICJ in the *Namibia* advisory opinion.[70] In order to better understand how the ILC understood the relationship between

---

[66] Cf Georg Nolte, 'Secession and External Intervention', in Marcelo G. Kohen (ed.), *Secession – International Law Perspectives* (Cambridge: Cambridge University Press, 2006), pp. 65–93, at pp. 87 *et seq.*; Antonelli Tancredi, 'Normative Due Process', pp. 190, 194 *et seq.*
[67] James Crawford, *Creation of States*, p. 158; cf further Vera Gowlland-Debbas, *Collective Responses*, p. 323.
[68] Willem A. Riphagen, 'State Responsibility', p. 619, note 63.
[69] Similarly Jörg Künzli, *Unrechtsregimes*, p. 353.
[70] Cf Georges Abi-Saab, 'Que reste-t-il', p. 82.

non-recognition and non-assistance, the main arguments of the Court shall be briefly reconsidered. In its opinion, the Court made it clear that the precise determination of acts allowed or forbidden in the dealings of States with the South African government would fall within the competence of the appropriate organs of the UN.[71] Nevertheless, the Court pointed towards 'those dealings with the Government of South Africa which, under the Charter of the United Nations and general international law, should be considered as inconsistent with the declaration of illegality and invalidity made in paragraph 2 of resolution 276 (1970)', as they could be said to imply a recognition of South Africa's presence in Namibia.[72] In this respect, the Court held that UN Member States are under an obligation to abstain from entering into treaty relations with South Africa in all cases in which the South African government would purport to act on behalf of Namibia. Existing bilateral agreements would have to be applied or invoked in a manner which would not 'involve active intergovernmental cooperation'. The Court recognised an exception for multilateral treaties whose non-performance would affect the people of Namibia in an adverse manner.[73] Furthermore, the Court envisaged restrictions on diplomatic and consular relations[74] as well as on entering into economic and other forms of cooperation which would have entrenched South African authority over Namibia.[75]

In the Court's presentation of these consequences for UN Member States, they follow from the obligation of both non-recognition and non-assistance. However, they are easier to subsume under the heading of non-recognition than of non-assistance. The concept of non-assistance presupposes a close factual connection between the support rendered and the commission of a specific wrongful act.[76] The consequences the ICJ has mentioned, however, are more general and are envisaged to prevent a further entrenchment of an unlawful situation in general. In terms of what they require of UN Member States, they also go beyond what can be deduced from an obligation of non-assistance.

---

[71] ICJ, *Legal Consequences for States of the Continued Presence of South Africa in Namibia (South West Africa) Notwithstanding Security Council Resolution 276 (1970)*, Advisory Opinion, ICJ Rep. 1971, 16, para. 120.
[72] Ibid., para. 121. [73] Ibid., para. 122.
[74] Ibid., para. 123. [75] Ibid., para. 124.
[76] Cf Willem A. Riphagen, 'Third Report on the Content, Forms and Degrees of International Responsibility', UN Doc. A/CN.4/354 and Add.1-2, YBILC 1982, Vol. II, Part One, p. 22, commentary on Draft Article 6, para. 10.

Their defining element is the requirement that the measures which are to be refrained from could 'be said to imply recognition'.

3.1.3 Scholarly views on the distinction

A number of views are expressed in scholarly writings on the question of the relationship between the obligation of non-recognition and that pertaining to non-assistance. Some authors hold the view that a violation of the obligation of non-recognition would constitute a form of assistance.[77] This was, for example, the view held by Vera Gowlland-Debbas, who wrote that 'the granting of recognition to a regime which the United Nations was attempting to eliminate should surely be regarded as the giving of "assistance" to that regime'.[78] She discussed this question in the context of Article 2(5) of the UN Charter against the background of the question whether an obligation of non-recognition would flow from this provision. Similarly, Andreas Paulus has argued that the obligation of non-recognition could be brought within the scope of application of Article 16 ASR, thus assuming that 'aid or assistance' is the wider category of the two.[79] Another perspective on the delimitation between the two obligations is offered by Andrea Gattini, who wonders whether the obligation of non-recognition has any particular meaning in international law. Should a State violate the latter obligation, he posits, the result would have to be that its actual conduct contributed to the strengthening of the position of the State responsible for the creation of the situation. Accordingly, the State would have aided the responsible State.[80]

Santiago Villalpando, on the other hand, holds that the obligation of non-assistance can be entirely deduced from the obligation of non-recognition, which would seem to imply that non-assistance is a more specialised form of non-recognition.[81] Stefan Talmon has suggested that recognition cannot constitute a form of assistance. In this respect,

---

[77] Cf Michael Akehurst, 'State Responsibility for the Wrongful Acts of Rebels – An Aspect of the Southern Rhodesia Problem', *British Year Book of International Law* 43 (1968–9), pp. 49–70, at pp. 55–6; Zdenek Červenka, 'Rhodesia Five Years After the Unilateral Declaration of Independence', *Verfassung und Recht in Übersee* 4 (1971), pp. 9–30, at p. 28.
[78] Vera Gowlland-Debbas, *Collective Responses*, p. 289.
[79] Andreas L. Paulus, 'Jus Cogens', p. 315.
[80] Andrea Gattini, 'Return Ticket', p. 1191; in that regard, see similarly Eckart Klein, 'Nichtanerkennungspolitik', p. 493; see also Jörg Künzli, *Unrechtsregimes*, p. 353.
[81] Santiago Villalpando, *L'émergence*, p. 389.

Talmon has argued from the perspective of the declaratory theory of recognition in international law. By distinguishing non-recognition from Article 2(5) of the UN Charter and Article 41(2) ASR, he maintains that recognition would be only a form of psychological encouragement which would not therefore fall under recognised concepts of assistance.[82]

The position of the ILC on the issue does not necessarily clarify the matter.[83] Although, as the Commentary points out, the obligation of non-assistance could be seen as a logical extension of the obligation of non-recognition in some respects, it would have a separate scope of application.[84] The obligation of non-assistance would cover acts which would not imply recognition of the situation brought about by the serious breach of the peremptory norm under general international law. In this context, it should also be taken into account that the predecessor to Article 41(1) ASR in the Draft Articles as adopted on First Reading in 1996 did differentiate more clearly between non-recognition and non-assistance, as it postulated these obligations in Article 53(a) and (b) respectively.

3.1.4 Criteria for the distinction

While Villalpando's view is convincing insofar as it holds the obligation of non-assistance to be more specific, it is not clear whether non-assistance can be assimilated to non-recognition to the degree that it is to be derived from this broader category.[85] This is also doubtful as one should keep in mind that obligations of non-assistance do not exist only with respect to serious breaches of peremptory norms, but – as this study is concerned with in general – apply with respect to the whole spectrum of international law. In comparison, there is no obligation of non-recognition which generally prevents States from recognising the effects of wrongful conduct committed by other States.[86] Thus, if we follow the ILC which held that the obligation of non-assistance in Article 41(2) ASR needs to be viewed together with

---

[82] Stefan Talmon, *Kollektive Nichtanerkennung*, p. 334.
[83] With similar criticism Théodore Christakis, 'Non-Reconnaissance', p. 144; Stefan Talmon, 'Duty', p. 114.
[84] ILC Commentary, Article 41, para. 12.
[85] See also Stefan Talmon, 'Duty', p. 105.
[86] James Crawford, *Creation of States*, p. 159; Vera Gowlland-Debbas, *Collective Responses*, p. 281; Alain Pellet, 'Les articles', p. 17; exactly the contrary is suggested by Enrico Milano, *Unlawful Territorial Situations*, p. 186.

Article 16 ASR[87] – and may thus express a common principle[88] – it is hard to conceptualise a relationship between non-assistance and non-recognition within the serious breaches-regime which construes the former to be a subform of the latter. Rather, we subscribe to the view of Stefan Talmon who distinguishes between assistance which has a concrete impact upon the commission of a wrongful act and recognition which is not as closely connected to the wrongful situation.[89] One could object to the pertinence of Talmon's views for the interpretation of Article 41(2) ASR that he has developed his argument before the background of the traditional, territorial function of the doctrine of non-recognition. However, the specificities of this concept will always remain connected to this field as non-recognition was first developed in this regard. Arguably, the interpretation of non-recognition with respect to illegal territorial situations will thus also guide the interpretation of its newer forms as embodied in Article 41(2) ASR.

In light of these considerations, the following criteria should apply to distinguish between non-recognition and non-assistance in Article 41(2) ASR. First, the category of non-assistance needs to be viewed in the context of Article 16 ASR. Article 41(2) ASR can be considered as *lex specialis* to Article 16 ASR. Secondly, this entails that there should be some congruence between the criteria set out in Article 16 ASR to trigger responsibility for complicity and those for Article 41(2) ASR, save for special considerations the ILC had in mind with respect to the regime of serious breaches of peremptory norms under general international law. Thirdly, this means that responsibility for complicity under Article 41(2) ASR should also presuppose a certain factual and 'causal' connection between the support rendered and the maintenance of the situation brought about by the serious breach.[90] Fourthly, the category of non-recognition is wider than that of complicity. It covers more categories of support than is the case with complicity. It aims at eliminating forms of cooperation which do not make it materially easier for the responsible State to commit a specific wrongful act. Rather, the benefits of international recognition – here used in a

---

[87] ILC Commentary, Article 41, para. 11.
[88] See also Sandra Szurek, 'Responsabilité de protéger', p. 113.
[89] Stefan Talmon, *Kollektive Nichtanerkennung*, pp. 334–5.
[90] Cf Willem A. Riphagen, 'Third Report on the Content, Forms and Degrees of International Responsibility', UN Doc. A/CN.4/354 and Add.1–2, YBILC 1982, Vol. II, Part One, p. 22, Commentary on Draft Article 6, para. 10.

non-technical sense – will not materialise. The State responsible for the wrongful situation is to be isolated.[91] This becomes apparent from the examples the ICJ has given in its *Namibia* advisory opinion.[92] The way non-recognition would impact on treaty relations and the entry into further diplomatic and economic channels of cooperation is farther reaching than is usually required by an obligation of non-assistance.[93] Furthermore, there is a qualitative difference between a mere recognition of an illegal status and active participation therein.[94] The consequences of the latter activity should outweigh the former. The obligation of non-recognition is itself the legal consequence of another violation of international law whereas, in general, complicity is something parallel to the commission of a wrongful act. Measures of recognition would not trigger responsibility under Article 16 ASR which should be used as a guiding provision for the interpretation of Article 41(2) ASR. This begs the question, finally, whether there is a separate field of application for non-assistance if non-recognition is the broader concept. The answer is yes, and the rationale is here provided by the Commentary of the ILC: some measures of concrete support for the maintenance of the situation brought about by the serious breach will not be identifiable as recognition of a legal situation.[95] Nonetheless, they have the potential to entrench the unlawful state of affairs. It is to these forms of support to which the obligation of non-assistance under Article 41(2) ASR is applicable.

The two obligations thus complement each other: whereas non-assistance tackles concrete measures of help which impact directly upon the wrongful situation which is to be brought to an end, non-recognition addresses the more general, political forms of support. This does not mean to say that there may not be some overlap between the two obligations. For the sake of conceptual clarity, it is, however, preferable that the two categories be distinguishable.[96]

---

[91] Théodore Christakis, 'Non-Reconnaissance', p. 146; Nina Jørgensen, 'The Obligation of Non-Assistance to the Responsible State', in James Crawford, Alain Pellet and Simon Olleson (eds.), *The International Law of Responsibility* (Oxford: Oxford University Press, 2010), pp. 687–93, at p. 691.
[92] See above notes 72 *et seq.*   [93] Cf Alain Pellet, 'Conclusions', p. 421.
[94] Stefan Talmon, *Kollektive Nichtanerkennung*, p. 334.
[95] ILC Commentary, Article 41, para. 12; see also Stefan Talmon, 'The Cyprus Question before the European Court of Justice', *European Journal of International Law* 12 (2001), pp. 727–50, at p. 743; contra: Alexander Orakhelashvili, *Peremptory Norms*, p. 387.
[96] See also Stefan Talmon, *Kollektive Nichtanerkennung*, p. 335.

3.2 The concept of complicity in Articles 16 and 41(2) ASR

The next question is whether, and if so how, different criteria exist which render a complicit State responsible under Articles 16 and 41(2) ASR.

3.2.1 Aid or assistance 'after the fact'

The first notable difference between Article 16 ASR and Article 41(2) ASR is that the latter applies 'after the fact'.[97] Accordingly, the concept of complicity as developed in Article 41(2) ASR 'extends beyond the commission of the serious breach, and it applies whether or not the breach itself is a continuing one'.[98] The issue of continuing wrongful acts is a difficult one.[99] This group of situations would also be covered by Article 16 ASR. Article 14(2) ASR provides that '[t]he breach of an international obligation by an act of a State having a continuing character extends over the entire period during which the act continues and remains not in conformity with the international obligation'. In its Commentary, the ILC explains that a wrongful act is not of a continuing character because its effects or consequences extend in time.[100] The examples the ILC gives for acts of a continuing character relate to the maintenance in effect of legislative provisions which are incompatible with international law, an unlawful detention, the unlawful occupation of territory or of premises of embassies or the stationing of armed forces in another State without its consent.[101] In such cases, Article 41(2) ASR would apply alongside Article 16 ASR whose applicability is not excluded by the fact that the aid or assistance is rendered continuously. However, the ILC has also remarked that Article 41(2) ASR applies regardless of whether the obligation is of a continuing character. Hence, it must be presumed that there are other effects of serious breaches of peremptory norms which continue to have an impact although they have terminated as

---

[97] Cf Christian Tomuschat, 'International Crimes', p. 259; Alessandra Gianelli, 'Le conseguenze delle gravi violazioni di obblighi posti da norme imperative tra norme primarie e norme secondarie', in Marina Spinedi, Alessandra Gianelli and Maria Luisa Alaimo (eds.), *La codificazione della responsabilità internazionale degli stati alla prova dei fatti – Probleme e spunti di riflessione* (Milan: Giuffrè, 2006), pp. 245–90, at p. 278.
[98] ILC Commentary, Article 41, para. 11.
[99] For a thorough assessment, see Giovanni DiStefano, 'Fait continu, fait composé et fait complexe dans le droit de la responsabilité', *Annuaire Français de Droit International* 52 (2006), pp. 1–54.
[100] ILC Commentary, Article 14, para. 6. [101] *Ibid.*, para. 3.

such in their quality as wrongful acts. Here, the overlap with the obligation of non-recognition is particularly obvious and we can refer to our discussion on the distinguishing features of the two obligations.

But the question remains how one can identify situations which would not involve continuing wrongful acts and which would nonetheless call for a separate obligation of non-assistance which applies after the commission of the actual wrongful act. Christian Tomuschat has found that such a provision

> only makes sense with regard to instances where the wrongdoing State has obtained some valuable asset by perpetrating the crime. Where the result of its conduct is only death and destruction, the issue of maintaining the situation brought about by it does not arise.[102]

Tomuschat concludes that the obligation of non-assistance after the fact will have little practical relevance and also that the practice upon which the ILC relied is rather misleading – if analysed closely, the relevant UN Security Council resolutions on South Africa and Portugal rather concern ongoing violations of the law and would therefore aim at the elimination of direct participation in the commission of these wrongful acts.[103] In light of these considerations, it is important to note that the ILC is apparently not very strict with the concept of assistance after the fact, as it considers the obligation of non-assistance in Article 41(2) ASR to be applicable in the case of wrongful acts of a continuing character.[104] As Article 16 ASR also applies in these cases, it is indeed the case that, *stricto sensu*, the additional impact of Article 41(2) ASR is rather limited in terms of its temporal applicability.[105] One such scenario has been analysed by the Joint Committee on Human Rights of the UK House of Lords and House of Commons. In its report on 'Allegations of UK Complicity in Torture', the Committee considered that a 'general practice of passively receiving intelligence information which has or may have been obtained under torture' would be 'likely to be in breach of the UK's international law obligation not to render aid or assistance to other States which are in serious breach of their obligation not to torture'.[106] This would be aid or assistance which

---

[102] Christian Tomuschat, 'International Crimes', p. 259.
[103] *Ibid.*, pp. 259–60.   [104] See above note 99.
[105] See also Marina Spinedi, 'International Crimes of States', p. 99.
[106] UK House of Lords/House of Commons, Joint Committee on Human Rights, 'Allegations of UK Complicity in Torture', Twenty-Third Report of Session 2008–9, HL Paper 152, HC 230, published on 4 August 2009, para. 42.

would help that other State to maintain the wrongful situation. The Committee based its reasoning expressly on Article 41(2) ASR.[107]

In addition, it may be affirmed that Article 41(2) ASR retains some significance due to further modifications of the concept of complicity for situations involving serious breaches of peremptory norms to which we shall turn now.

3.2.2 The nexus between assistance and the wrongful situation

Some commentators have argued that the ILC has relaxed the requirement of a causal connection between the support rendered and the commission or maintenance of the unlawful act/situation.[108] This argument is deduced from the fact that the aid or assistance is to be rendered for the maintenance of the situation brought about by the serious breach which would require, according to these commentators, a less direct impact of the support rendered than is the case with Article 16 ASR.[109] However, in the view of the present author, this is not necessarily true. For one, we have discussed in Chapter 5 how problematic notions of causality are with respect to Article 16 ASR. It is not causality in a strict technical sense which is required in order to trigger responsibility under that provision. Rather, it is the impact of the aid or assistance on the way the main actor was able to carry out its wrongful act which characterises the special nexus between the aid or assistance rendered and the commission of the wrongful act.[110] As this criterion is not too demanding in its own right, it would be problematic to further loosen these ties with respect to Article 41(2) ASR. This 'causal' relationship will of course have to be modified. The requisite impact of the aid or assistance cannot be measured as to its effect upon the commission of the wrongful act, but with respect to its contribution to the maintenance of the situation brought about by the serious breach. However, the ILC has left no indications in its Commentary of a loosening of this nexus between assistance and the maintenance of the situation. It should thus not be too readily assumed that the relationship between the aid or assistance and the maintenance of the

---

[107] *Ibid.*
[108] Alexandra Boivin, 'Complicity and Beyond', p. 493; Andreas Felder, *Die Beihilfe*, p. 140; Jörg Künzli, *Unrechtsregimes*, p. 354.
[109] Alexandra Boivin, 'Complicity and Beyond', p. 493.
[110] See above in Chapter 5, text accompanying notes 102 *et seq.*

wrongful situation is in any form different from the way it is understood in Article 16 ASR. This is also supported by the fact that such a criterion cannot be found in international practice.

Secondly, following the criteria we have suggested for the distinction between non-recognition and non-assistance, such general support which has no specific nexus with the wrongful situation itself should preferably be discussed with respect to the obligation of non-recognition.[111] If the support in question has no direct linkage with the maintenance of the situation brought about by the serious breach, we enter the realm of rather symbolic measures by States to contribute to the isolation of the wrongdoer.[112] With Hersch Lauterpacht, we can hold that this is precisely the domain of non-recognition which he described as 'a somewhat symbolic instrument for upholding the challenged authority of international law'.[113]

3.2.3 The relaxed subjective requirement

A marked difference between Article 16 ASR and Article 41(2) ASR could, however, lie in an attenuated subjective requirement of the latter provision. The ILC has stipulated that distinctions apply in this regard: there is no requirement of knowledge or intent set out in Article 41(2) ASR or in the commentary thereto. In this regard, the Commission expressly held that 'it is hardly conceivable that a State would not have notice of the commission of a serious breach by another State'.[114]

On the face of it, the ILC's reasoning is convincing insofar as serious breaches of obligations under peremptory norms should not go unnoticed and that therefore the intent requirement postulated by Article 16 ASR need not be upheld.[115] This differential treatment of the subjective requirement can also be justified in light of the importance of the legal values protected by peremptory norms.[116] Directed against aggression, slavery, genocide, racial discrimination, *apartheid* and torture as well as comprising the most basic rules of international humanitarian and

---

[111] Cf Willem A. Riphagen, 'Third Report on the Content, Forms and Degrees of International Responsibility', UN Doc. A/CN.4/354 and Add.1–2, YBILC 1982, Vol. II, Part One, p. 22, Commentary on Draft Article 6, para. 10.
[112] Nina Jørgensen, 'The Obligation of Non-Assistance', p. 691.
[113] Hersch Lauterpacht, *Recognition in International Law*, p. 433.
[114] ILC Commentary, Article 41, para. 11.
[115] See also Sandra Szurek, 'Responsabilité de protéger', p. 113.
[116] Cf Alessandra Gianelli, 'Le conseguenze', p. 286.

human rights law,[117] *jus cogens* norms define the bottom line of an *ordre public international*. It is, from a viewpoint of logical construction, only proper to demand of third States a higher degree of vigilance when obligations triggered by *jus cogens* rules are at stake.[118] Further support for such an attenuation can be found in the limited applicability of Article 41(2) ASR to assistance rendered 'after the fact'. Although we have just discussed that this category is not unproblematic, at least from a conceptual point of view it is plausible to hold States to higher standards of vigilance if the wrongful act has already been committed and has now led to a situation by which the unlawful conduct is perpetuated. Here, States will have had more time to deliberate their legal position towards this conduct, whereas, amidst ongoing events, it will at times be difficult to clearly assess the lawfulness of the conduct of another State and the precise implications of assistance rendered thereto.

However, one should not expect too much of this explanation. As the ILC itself remarked in a different context, '[i]nternationally wrongful acts usually take some time to happen'.[119] Accordingly, no black and white distinction between complicity which occurs prior to and in parallel to the commission of a wrongful act and assistance which is rendered thereafter will be possible. It could of course be argued that due to the seriousness of the breach, i.e., its 'gross or systematic' character (cf Article 40(2) ASR), it will be easier for third States to assess the situation. However, experience shows that debates about what actually happens in a given situation are not made easier just because *jus cogens* makes an appearance.[120] Quite to the contrary, some would argue rather that the inherent uncertainty of this concept will impede greater legal clarity[121] and will thus also render the additional obligation of non-assistance which is embodied in Article 41(2) ASR if not meaningless then at least much less important than it may appear at first sight.[122]

---

[117] Andreas L. Paulus, 'Jus Cogens', p. 316.
[118] Cf James Crawford, 'First Report on State Responsibility', UN Doc. A/CN.490/Add.3, 4, para. 83.
[119] ILC Commentary, Article 14, para. 2.
[120] See ICJ, *Case Concerning the Application of the Convention on the Prevention and Punishment of the Crime of Genocide*, Judgment, para. 207, for the position that heightened standards of proof apply for exceptionally grave allegations. This will almost always apply to serious breaches of peremptory norms.
[121] Cf Martti Koskenniemi, 'Fate', pp. 15, 19.
[122] Dinah Shelton, 'Righting Wrongs: Reparations in the Articles on State Responsibility', *American Journal of International Law* 96 (2002), pp. 832–56, at p. 844.

3.2.4 The legal status of Article 41(2) ASR

It is quite another matter whether Article 41(2) ASR represents customary international law.[123] It should be noted that the ILC posited that the regime of serious breaches is in a state of development, thus implying that these additional consequences for third States do not necessarily represent customary international law.[124] However, it should also be noted that the ILC has not directly called the customary status of Article 41(2) into question, as it has done with respect to Article 41(1) ASR.[125] Assessing the legal status of paragraph 2 requires us to take into account various factors. A good example of how confusion reigns on these legal consequences for third States is the treatment of the issue by the ICJ in its *Wall* opinion. As will be remembered, the Court found that:

> [g]iven the character and the importance of the rights involved, the Court is of the view that all States are under an obligation not to recognize the illegal situation resulting from the construction of the wall in the Occupied Palestinian Territory, including in and around East Jerusalem. They are also under an obligation not to render aid or assistance in maintaining the situation created by such a construction.[126]

The character and importance of the rights involved did not relate to their possible character as *jus cogens* norms, but rather to their being obligations *erga omnes* – an unexpected twist which earned the Court much criticism.[127] The exact reasons for this position will be difficult to elucidate, although Alain Pellet has attributed the Court's position to 'la vigilance sourcilleuse (ou faudrait-il parler de terrorisme intellectuel?) des Juges français ... qui ont imposé à leurs collègues

---

[123] See Jörg Künzli, *Unrechtsregimes*, p. 354; Christian J. Tams, 'Probleme', p. 344; Alexander Orakhelashvili, *Peremptory Norms*, p. 287; see also Bruno Simma, 'From Bilateralism to Community Interest', pp. 317–18; see generally Carlo Focarelli, 'Promotional Jus Cogens: A Critical Appraisal of Jus Cogens' Legal Effects', *Nordic Journal of International Law* 77 (2008), pp. 429–59, at p. 442.
[124] ILC Commentary, Article 41, para. 14. [125] *Ibid.*, para. 3.
[126] ICJ, *Legal Consequences of the Construction of a Wall in the Occupied Palestinian Territory*, Advisory Opinion, ICJ Rep. 2004, 136, para. 159.
[127] For criticism in this regard, see *ibid.*, separate opinion of Judge Higgins, para. 37; *ibid.*, separate opinion of Judge Koijmans, para. 40; as well as James Crawford, 'Multilateral', p. 475; Ardi Imseis, 'Critical Reflections', pp. 114 *et seq.*; Alexander Orakhelashvili, 'Construction of a Wall', p. 248; Alexander Orakhelashvili, *Peremptory Norms*, pp. 286–7; Daniel-Erasmus Khan, 'Sicherheitszaun', pp. 368–9; Andreas L. Paulus, 'Jus Cogens', p. 315.

un tabou sur le mot'.[128] These terminological aspects are, however, not the most pressing ones. Rather, as President (then Judge) Higgins has found in her separate opinion, it is unclear how obligations *erga omnes* may bring about such duties for third States. Rather, she argued, the case would appear to be that it is 'self-evident' that 'an illegal situation is not to be recognized or assisted by third parties'.[129] From these findings, one could infer support by Judge Higgins for general obligations of non-recognition and non-assistance if not for the fact that she referred expressly to UN Members at the end of the very same passage for whom reliance upon obligations *erga omnes* would not be necessary to ground such obligations.[130] In light of this entangled situation, it is thus neither possible to infer direct support for the construction of the ILC from the Court's findings nor to hold that the two provisions undoubtedly represent customary international law.

At the same time, it is remarkable how frequently Article 41(2) ASR has been mentioned by domestic courts. The invocation of a provision of the ASR in domestic court proceedings may very well strengthen a so far doubtful quality as customary international law. Article 41(2) ASR has been mentioned in decisions by the UK House of Lords,[131] by the Italian Court of Cassation[132] and by the German Federal Constitutional Court.[133] While these cases by themselves do not suffice to constitute a general practice required to establish the customary character of Article 41(2) ASR, they may point towards a normative development which may eventually crystallise in a norm of customary international law as spelled out in the provision drafted by the ILC. In the course of this development, it is to be expected that relevant decision-makers will pick up upon the attenuated subjective requirement set out in Article 41(2) ASR. In the meantime, it is only possible to accept the Commission's findings in this regard as a matter of logical construction.

---

[128] Alain Pellet, 'Conclusions', p. 418.
[129] ICJ, *Legal Consequences of the Construction of a Wall in the Occupied Palestinian Territory*, Advisory Opinion, ICJ Rep. 2004, 136, separate opinion of Judge Higgins, *ibid.*, para. 38.
[130] *Ibid.*
[131] UK House of Lords, *A and others* v. *Secretary of State for the Home Department (No 2)*, opinion of Lord Bingham, para. 34.
[132] Italian Court of Cassation, *Ferrini* v. *Federal Republic of Germany*, 128 ILR 658, 669.
[133] German Federal Constitutional Court, BVerfGE 112, 1, 35 (para. 121).

3.3 Further distinctions

In addition to the modifications directly envisaged by the ILC's conception of Article 41(2) ASR, another question is whether further distinctions apply between complicity in violations of international law in general and those in which support is rendered to the breach of an obligation under a peremptory norm.[134] Such a development is not blocked by the work of the ILC. Quite to the contrary, it is directly mentioned in Article 41(3) ASR that Article 41(1) and (2) are without prejudice 'to such further consequences that a breach to which this Chapter applies may entail under international law'.[135] This proviso was introduced deliberately to reflect 'the conviction that the legal regime of serious breaches is itself in a state of development. By setting out certain basic legal consequences of serious breaches', it was not intended to 'preclude the further development of a more elaborate regime of consequences entailed by such breaches'.[136] Whereas it has been rightly questioned in the literature whether the inclusion of this clause was really necessary – given that Article 56 ASR already stipulates in general that the Articles are without prejudice to other rules of general international law[137] – the inclusion of this paragraph is understandable in light of the considerable uncertainty over the state of the law in this respect. The Commission, being generally regarded as a rather conservative body,[138] would have inevitably faced criticism for having codified only very meagre consequences of serious breaches of peremptory norms.[139] With Article 41(3) ASR, the Commission makes it clear that it does not want to prevent the further development of international law in this regard.[140]

In order to find such additional consequences, a careful analysis is called for in this regard as special consequences of *jus cogens* are more

---

[134] Cf James Crawford, 'First Report on State Responsibility', UN Doc. A/CN.4/490/Add.3, 4, para. 83; Bruno Simma, Statement at the 2578th Meeting of the ILC, YBILC 1999, Vol. I, Part One, p. 79, para. 40.
[135] See also Jörg Künzli, *Unrechtsregimes*, pp. 356-7; Alain Pellet, 'Les articles', p. 18.
[136] ILC Commentary, Article 41, para. 14.
[137] Andrea Gattini, 'Return Ticket', p. 1192.
[138] Cf Philip Allott, 'State Responsibility', p. 10.
[139] Which has happened despite the inclusion of this disclaimer: cf Andreas Paulus, 'Jus Cogens', p. 315.
[140] See further Santiago Villalpando, *L'émergence*, pp. 392 *et seq.*

often assumed than based on the current state of the law.[141] Roberto Ago rightly held that:

> the prohibition of any derogation from certain rules does not necessarily and automatically imply that the breach of the obligations arising therefrom should be subject to a regime of responsibility different from that associated with the breach of the obligations created by other rules.[142]

It has been noted[143] that international law has a tradition of aggravating responsibility in certain contexts.[144] The prime example of such an aggravation dates back to the *Corfu Channel* case, in which the United Kingdom qualified Albania's violations of the obligation to warn the UK of the existence of the mines in the strait as an 'offence against humanity'.[145] Although the Court did not follow this qualification, it echoed its substance when it discussed 'elementary considerations of humanity' which spoke in favour of an obligation on Albania to warn the United Kingdom of the mines.[146] In more recent times, the *Furundžija* judgment of the International Criminal Tribunal for the former Yugoslavia (ICTY) has given expression to the various possible consequences of peremptory norms which exceed the framework of the law of treaties.[147] At issue were the 'main features' of the prohibition against torture. After having found that this norm would enjoy the rank of *jus cogens* in international law,[148] the Tribunal discussed the effects of this finding. Besides its 'deterrent effect' in terms of clearly stating the prohibition of torture as an 'absolute value',[149] its *jus cogens* status would serve 'to internationally de-legitimize any legislative, administrative or judicial act authorizing torture'.[150] The Tribunal went on to state:

> It would be senseless to argue, on the one hand, that on account of the *jus cogens* value of the prohibition against torture, treaties or customary rules

---

[141] Carlo Focarelli, 'Promotional Jus Cogens', pp. 440 *et seq.*
[142] Roberto Ago, 'Fifth Report on State Responsibility', UN Doc. A/CN.4/291 and Add.1–2, YBILC 1976, Vol. II, pp. 3, 32, para. 99.
[143] Alexander Orakhelashvili, *Peremptory Norms*, p. 273.
[144] Antônio Augusto Cançado Trindade, 'International Law for Humankind: Towards a New Jus Gentium (II), General Course on Public International Law', *Recueil des Cours* 317 (2006), pp. 9–312, at pp. 100–1.
[145] ICJ, *Corfu Channel Case*, ICJ Pleadings 1949, 40, para. 72.
[146] ICJ, *Corfu Channel Case*, Judgment, ICJ Rep. 1949, 4, 22.
[147] ICTY, *Prosecutor v. Furundžija*, Case IT-95-17/1, 121 ILR 213.
[148] *Ibid.*, para. 153.   [149] *Ibid.*, para. 154.   [150] *Ibid.*, para. 155.

providing for torture would be null and void *ab initio*, and then be unmindful of a State say, taking national measures authorizing or condoning torture or absolving its perpetrators through an amnesty law.[151]

It is noteworthy that the Tribunal includes the condoning of torture in that passage. Although there is no indication that the ICTY had State complicity in another State's perpetration of torture in mind when it included that reference, the underlying reasoning can arguably not be that different: due to the absolute value the Appeals Chamber ascribes to the *jus cogens* prohibition of torture, stricter standards should apply as to the judgment of State conduct which can potentially impact on the perpetration of torture. Similar lines of thought were expressed in the separate opinion of Judge ad hoc Elihu Lauterpacht in the *Genocide Convention* case. Discussing the question whether or not the arms embargo against the whole of the Federal Republic of Yugoslavia and its former constituent parts in Security Council Resolution 713 could indirectly contribute to a genocide potentially occurring in Bosnia, Judge ad hoc Lauterpacht emphasised the *jus cogens* nature of the prohibition of genocide and highlighted the potential conflict between the resolution and the *jus cogens* rule.[152] Without going too much into the details of this conflict, Judge ad hoc Lauterpacht appeared to embrace a position which ascribed public order functions to the category of *jus cogens* rules.

The crucial question for the present study is, however, how one could arrive at attenuated criteria for holding complicit States responsible due to the fact that *jus cogens* norms are at stake. In one particular instance, the ILC has itself considered this to be warranted, namely, with respect to the subjective requirement of Article 41(2) ASR. This attenuation can be explained on various grounds: as plausible as it is to assume that it is the importance of the legal values protected by peremptory norms that caused the Commission to effect this change, one can also hold that it is rather the factual element, i.e., the sheer magnitude of what has happened, that prevents any State from being in a position to ignore to what it is contributing aid or assistance. In case the first explanation was the more important one, it would be convincing to argue for a less strict standard in terms of the subjective

---

[151] Ibid.
[152] ICJ, *Application of the Convention of the Prevention and Punishment of the Crime of Genocide*, Provisional Measures, ICJ Rep. 1993, 325, separate opinion of Judge ad hoc Elihu Lauterpacht, 407, para. 102.

requirement for all cases which involve violations of *jus cogens* and not just the ones covered by Article 41(2) ASR. Apart from such general expressions of view as the one by the ICTY, it is difficult to identify elements of international practice which would speak for such a move. It might, however, be possible to explain such a modification of the subjective requirement by reference to systemic considerations. In more concrete terms, further-reaching standards for complicit States when violations of *jus cogens* are involved could be based on an analogy with what is at times called the problem of 'subsequent validation' of breaches of *jus cogens*.[153] Subsequent validation is understood to comprise mechanisms such as acquiescence, estoppel and consent.[154] Under ordinary circumstances, the validly expressed consent of a State is a circumstance precluding wrongfulness in international law.[155] The ILC has put limits on the validity of consent for the case of a wrongful act which is not in conformity with an obligation arising under a peremptory norm of general international law (Article 26 ASR).[156] This provision implicitly affirms the effects of *jus cogens* outside of the law of treaties. The understanding that *jus cogens* norms could be affected by individual breaches of the law tells us that the concept of *jus cogens*, according to the ILC, exerts influence on the legal qualification of the conduct of individual States.[157]

This argument could further build on insights into the law-making processes in international law. In its present stage of development, international law still has to live with the apparent paradox that a

---

[153] Alexander Orakhelashvili, *Peremptory Norms*, p. 360.
[154] See also Ian Brownlie, 'Recognition', p. 201.
[155] Article 20 ASR; see also Georg Nolte, *Eingreifen auf Einladung*, pp. 133 *et seq.*, especially on *jus cogens* at pp. 137 *et seq.*; Mindia Vashakmadze, *Die Stationierung fremder Truppen im Völkerrecht und ihre demokratische Kontrolle – Eine Untersuchung unter besonderer Berücksichtigung Georgiens* (Berlin: Duncker & Humblot, 2008), pp. 67 *et seq.*; Andrea Gattini, 'La renonciation au droit d'invoquer la responsabilité', in Pierre-Marie Dupuy, Bardo Fassbender, Malcolm N. Shaw and Karl-Peter Sommermann (eds.), *Völkerrecht als Wertordnung – Festschrift für Christian Tomuschat* (Kehl: N. P. Engel, 2006), pp. 317–40.
[156] See also Ian Brownlie, *Principles*, p. 512.
[157] See further Guiding Principle No. 8 applicable to Unilateral Declarations of States capable of creating legal obligations, 'Report of the ILC of Its 61st Session', UN Doc. A/61/10, at p. 378; see also ICJ, *Armed Activities on the Territory of the Congo (New Application: 2002)*, Judgment, ICJ Rep. 2006, 5, para. 69; Theodor Meron, 'Age of Human Rights', p. 421; a traditional position held the view that *jus cogens* obligations were only concerned with derogation and not with violation: see Jerzy Sztucki, *Jus Cogens and the Vienna Convention on the Law of Treaties* (Vienna: Springer, 1974), p. 68.

breach of the law on one day can pave the way for the development of new rules of customary international law the next.[158] Accordingly, a violation of the law has an inherent potential to contribute to the creation of new rules. Not much consideration has so far been given to the role complicit States may play in this regard.[159] It is plausible to assume that complicit States may contribute to these processes if they do not dissociate themselves clearly from the legal position which is embodied in the wrongful act they are supporting. This hypothesis has two alternative implications for cases in which peremptory norms are at stake: one could either assume that the practice thus generated does not count in the first place given that international law does not allow for a 'derogation' from the standard embodied in the peremptory norm.[160] The other possible reading is that international law should aim at not allowing for such practice in the first place. A stricter rule on complicity in the context of breaches of *jus cogens* would serve this purpose. As it is nearly inconceivable that such practice could derogate from *jus cogens* rules,[161] this reading would amount to the construction of a barrier against the factual undermining of the normative basis of peremptory norms. It would aim at defending the effectiveness of peremptory norms which, despite their to some extent non-consensual origin, have to rely on an entrenchment in international practice in order not be reduced to mere rhetoric.[162]

This construction follows closely the arguments put forward for *jus cogens* limitations on recognition in international law.[163] As is the case with studies which deduce wide-ranging *jus cogens* limitations for the doctrine of non-recognition,[164] it remains ultimately unclear how *jus cogens* really impacts upon the standards of vigilance potentially

---

[158] Alfred Verdross and Bruno Simma, *Universelles Völkerrecht*, § 574; Georg Nolte, 'Die USA und das Völkerrecht', *Die Friedens-Warte* 78 (2003), pp. 119–40, at p. 128.
[159] But see Georg Nolte and Helmut Philipp Aust, 'Equivocal Helpers', pp. 19 *et seq.*
[160] See, *mutatis mutandis*, Stefan Talmon, 'Duty', p. 107.
[161] Alexander Orakhelashvili, *Peremptory Norms*, p. 385 (with respect to recognition of breaches of *jus cogens* rules); for the conditions pertaining to the change of peremptory norms, see Article 53 of the Vienna Convention on the Law of Treaties.
[162] On the subtle interplay between the normative basis and factual validation of *jus cogens*, see Theodor Meron, 'Age of Human Rights', p. 420; Carlo Focarelli, 'Promotional Jus Cogens', pp. 429 *et seq.*; Andreas L. Paulus, 'The International Legal System', p. 90, at note 80; these considerations also apply to international law in general: see Hersch Lauterpacht, *Recognition in International Law*, p. 427.
[163] See Alexander Orakhelashvili, *Peremptory Norms*, pp. 372 *et seq.*
[164] See, e.g., John Dugard, *Recognition*, pp. 132 *et seq.*

complicit States have to comply with. Rather, a vague feeling persists that international law *should* provide for stricter standards for situations in which *jus cogens* rules are at stake.[165] As Andreas Paulus has remarked in a different context, although *jus cogens* seems well entrenched in contemporary international law, its sweeping effects are not yet matched by conceptual clarity.[166] However, the question is warranted whether systemic considerations may make a difference here.[167] What might be understood by that is explained in a separate opinion of Judge ad hoc Dugard:

> The judicial decision is essentially an exercise in choice. Where authorities are divided or different general principles compete for priority, or different rules of interpretation lead to different conclusions, or State practices conflict, the judge is required to make a choice. In exercising this choice, the judge will be guided by principles (propositions that describe rights) and policies (propositions that describe goals) in order to arrive at a coherent conclusion that most effectively furthers the integrity of the international legal order.
>
> Norms of *jus cogens* are a blend of principle and policy. On the one hand, they affirm the high principles of international law, which recognize the most important rights of the international order … This explains why they enjoy a hierarchical superiority to other norms in the international legal order. The fact that norms of *jus cogens* advance both principle and policy means that they must inevitably play a dominant role in the process of judicial choice.[168]

This interpretation of the role *jus cogens* may play in the international legal order is convincing insofar as it does not assume a simple 'trumping' of established principles of international law by *jus cogens*,[169] but rather pleads for a subtle introduction of the category of *jus cogens* into the interpretive process of international law wherever it is suitable.[170] Dugard's position is also particularly appealing as it puts an emphasis on the judicial development of *jus cogens*. The development of the law in that regard will depend, in a large measure, on judicial pronouncements.[171] There is no shortage of doctrinal comments on the

---

[165] Similarly Carlo Focarelli, 'Promotional Jus Cogens', p. 442.
[166] Andreas L. Paulus, 'Jus Cogens', p. 330; see further Andrea Bianchi, 'Magic of Jus Cogens', p. 501.
[167] *Ibid.*, p. 497.
[168] ICJ, *Armed Activities on the Territory of the Congo (New Application: 2002)*, Judgment, ICJ Rep. 2006, 5, separate opinion of Judge ad hoc John Dugard, p. 86, para. 10.
[169] That is reaffirmed by Judge ad hoc Dugard, *ibid.*, para. 13.
[170] Similarly Andrea Bianchi, 'Magic of Jus Cogens', p. 503.
[171] Cf Alain Pellet, 'Conclusions', p. 420.

potential influence of *jus cogens* across the whole field of international law. The development of the law will, however, depend on instances of State practice and on the further entrenchment of this category in pronouncements of international as well as domestic courts and tribunals.[172]

Judicial pronouncements may thus contribute to a 'promotional' role of *jus cogens*. Carlo Focarelli, who is highly sceptical of the current state of debate with respect to peremptory norms, understands *jus cogens* as solely promotional in terms of its effects. By this he means that the existence of *jus cogens* in international law could not properly be understood in terms of the traditional doctrine of sources. However, he does not wish to do away with *jus cogens* but suggests to lay open its meta-juridical functions. In his view, *jus cogens* 'is not concerned with existing law, but rather with the process of bringing into existence a different international law in the future. In other words, *jus cogens* is inherently *promotional* and is to be properly situated in the *dynamics* (rather than in the statics) of international law.'[173] In this regard, Focarelli also places a particular emphasis on the role of courts which, when applying *jus cogens*, wish to emphasise that 'the underlying value, owing to its importance, is to be protected at any cost'.[174]

We need not enter into a general debate on whether Focarelli's analysis is correct in all aspects. It may suffice to call into question whether *jus cogens* is exclusively promotional. A more nuanced analysis would be better placed to do justice to the phenomenon of *jus cogens* as some of its effects are clearly provided for in international law and this applies, of course, first and foremost to its original provenance in the law of treaties. However, Focarelli is certainly right in addressing the aspirational character of much of the other uses of *jus cogens*.[175]

In essence, the ILC was not of a different view when it commented on the progressive character of Articles 40 and 41 ASR. The legal status

---

[172] Cf Christian J. Tams, 'Probleme', p. 349; Theodor Meron, 'Age of Human Rights', p. 416; see also Ian Brownlie, 'Discussion Statement', p. 110.
[173] Carlo Focarelli, 'Promotional Jus Cogens', p. 455.   [174] *Ibid.*, p. 456.
[175] See also Martti Koskenniemi, 'International Law in Europe: Between Tradition and Renewal', *European Journal of International Law* 16 (2005), pp. 113-24, at p. 122; on Koskenniemi's position in this regard, see Andreas L. Paulus, 'The Emergence of the International Community and the Divide Between International and Domestic Law', in Janne Nijman and André Nollkaemper (eds.), *New Perspectives on the Divide Between National and International Law* (Oxford: Oxford University Press, 2007), pp. 216-50, at p. 216, note 2.

of the two provisions is difficult to ascertain as they offer a mixture of well-recognised ingredients such as non-recognition (with respect to unlawful acquisition of territory) and obligations of non-assistance on the one hand and some more innovative features such as the expansion of non-recognition beyond its traditional field of application or the obligation of cooperation on the other. Considerations of the impact of *jus cogens* on situations of complicity may thus help judges and other decision-makers to push the boundaries of responsibility for complicity a bit further. It provides them with a tool for argument which they can deploy in order to maximise the protection of the most deeply entrenched values of the international community. In this respect, *jus cogens* may play a helpful role in holding complicit States responsible. One should, however, not regard the category of peremptory norms as a panacea in this regard: there is only so much room for the constructive development of the law. The dispute over decisions by the Italian Court of Cassation[176] shows that a well-intended contribution to the development of international law may raise objections even among close allies, as it is evidenced by the ongoing dispute before the ICJ between Germany and Italy.[177]

4 Complicity and obligations of cooperation

In addition to the duties of abstention included in Article 41(2) ASR, Article 41(1) ASR provides that: 'States shall cooperate to bring to an end through lawful means any serious breach within the meaning of article 40.'

4.1 The obligation of cooperation in the ASR

The concrete content and scope of that obligation of cooperation is not self-evident.[178] It may thus be useful to briefly situate Article 41(1) ASR in the context of other obligations of cooperation in international law.

---

[176] Italian Court of Cassation, *Ferrini v. Federal Republic of Germany* and *Federal Republic of Germany v. Giovanni Mantelli and others*.
[177] See ICJ, *Jurisdictional Immunities of the State*, Order of 6 July 2010.
[178] Cf Alessandra Gianelli, 'Le conseguenze', p. 275; Jörg Künzli, *Unrechtsregimes*, p. 356; Alain Pellet, 'Les articles', p. 17; Thilo Rensmann, *Wertordnung und Grundgesetz*, p. 384; Thilo Rensmann, 'Die Humanisierung des Völkerrechts durch das ius in bello – Von der Marten'schen Klausel zur Responsibility to Protect', *Zeitschrift für ausländisches öffentliches Recht und Völkerrecht* 68 (2008), pp. 111–28, at p. 122.

4.1.1 Antecedents and related concepts

International law knows general duties of cooperation, as set out, for example, in the UN General Assembly Resolution on Friendly Relations.[179] However, these remain fairly vague and arguably cannot impose concrete obligations upon States to cooperate in the face of serious breaches of obligations under peremptory norms of general international law.[180] Moreover, the issue of obligations of cooperation was for a long time associated with the struggle between the Western States, the communist States and the non-aligned countries which all read differing ideological elements into the concept of cooperation. While the Western States' primary concern was to restrict the scope of such an obligation to the obligations they had already entered into, the communist States and the non-aligned movement concentrated on a more pro-active understanding of cooperation, *bien compris* in line with their respective political agendas.[181]

That being said, a distinction should be made between the 'old' debates on cooperation in international law and the 'new' obligation of cooperation in the face of serious breaches of peremptory norms under general international law. This distinction should of course not divert attention from the fact that some lines of continuity exist between contemporary debates and their antecedents. For instance, the discussion on an obligation of cooperation may be connected with the French solidarist school of international lawyers in the inter-war period, as Martti Koskenniemi has described them.[182] However, one should also not forget that, as Koskenniemi puts it, 'French international lawyers had always stressed the indissociability of French interests from those of the world at large.'[183] Intimately connected with French thoughts

---

[179] UN Doc. A/RES/2625 (XXV) of 24 October 1970.
[180] Cf Gaetano Arangio-Ruiz, 'The Normative Role of the General Assembly of the United Nations and the Declaration of Principles of Friendly Relations', *Recueil des Cours* 137 (1972-III), pp. 419–742, at pp. 572–3; Alfred Verdross and Bruno Simma, *Universelles Völkerrecht*, § 452; Hanspeter Neuhold, 'Die Pflicht zur Zusammenarbeit zwischen den Staaten: Moralisches Postulat oder völkerrechtliche Norm?', in H. Miehsler, E. Mock, B. Simma and I. Tammelo (eds.), *Ius Humanitas – Festschrift zum 90. Geburtstag von Alfred Verdross* (Berlin: Duncker & Humblot, 1980), pp. 575–606, at p. 598; Georg Nolte, 'Zusammenarbeit', pp. 20–1; Alain Pellet, 'Les articles', p. 17; for a different assessment, see Andrea Gattini, 'Return Ticket', p. 1186.
[181] For an overview of the pertinent discussions, see Hanspeter Neuhold, 'Pflicht zur Zusammenarbeit', pp. 575 *et seq*.
[182] Martti Koskenniemi, *The Gentle Civilizer of Nations*, pp. 266 *et seq*.
[183] *Ibid.*, p. 270.

on solidarity in general, for this school of thought (which comprises international lawyers as distinct as Duguit and Scelle as well as the expatriates Alvarez and Politis), 'solidarism was characterised less by a definitive agenda than by a general aversion to the absolutism of individual rights and an emotional preference for social responsibility'.[184] One could even go back further to Hugo Grotius and connect the issue with his preference for solidarity over individual State concerns.[185] No genealogical lines should, however, be drawn from these historical forerunners to the contemporary state of the law. We should nonetheless be aware of the fact that solidarity in international law was neither an invention of the non-aligned movement or of the communist states in the Cold War nor was it a new idea when it entered the inventory of the law of State responsibility. Rather, international solidarity is a recurring pattern of discourse which is meant to counter-balance overly individualistic expressions of State sovereignty.[186] This tradition should be kept in mind when interpreting Article 41(1) ASR which can be read as an expression of this tradition.[187]

In addition to these historical forerunners, mention should also be made of some contemporary developments: first of all, international law knows positive obligations which could also border closely on a general obligation of cooperation. As we will discuss in the further progress of this section, Article I of the Genocide Convention requires States to prevent genocide insofar as it is possible for them to do so.[188] This obligation could very well be understood as calling for international cooperation which will arguably be more effective than the efforts of a single State to prevent a genocide from occurring.

---

[184] *Ibid.*, p. 289.
[185] Andrea Gattini, 'Return Ticket', p. 1185.
[186] See also Hersch Lauterpacht, *The Function of Law*, pp. 286 *et seq.*; for a contemporary view on solidarity as an emerging principle of international law, see Rüdiger Wolfrum, 'Solidarity Among States: An Emerging Structural Principle of International Law', in Pierre-Marie Dupuy, Bardo Fassbender, Malcolm N. Shaw and Karl-Peter Sommermann (eds.), *Völkerrecht als Wertordnung – Festschrift für Christian Tomuschat* (Kehl: N. P. Engel, 2006), pp. 1087–1101; for current philosophical underpinnings, see Hauke Brunkhorst, *Solidarität – Von der Bürgerfreundschaft zur globalen Rechtsgenossenschaft* (Frankfurt/Main: Suhrkamp, 2002), pp. 139 *et seq.*; a more sceptical position is held by Richard Rorty, *Contingency, Irony and Solidarity* (Cambridge: Cambridge University Press, 1989), pp. 189 *et seq.*
[187] Cf Alain Pellet, 'Les articles', p. 17.
[188] ICJ, *Case Concerning the Application of the Convention on the Prevention and Punishment of the Crime of Genocide*, Judgment, paras. 430 *et seq.*

Secondly, we should not forget the ambiguous politico-juridical concept of the 'responsibility to protect' ('R2P').[189] Developed as an attempt to frame the debate on the legality and legitimacy of humanitarian intervention after Kosovo in 1999,[190] it continues to inspire politicians, international relations scholars and international lawyers alike. In its most authoritative guise, the concept was recognised by the World Summit Outcome Document in 2005.[191] In this form, its scope is, however, somewhat reduced and the potentially rash consequences of a superficially plausible equation along the lines of 'if a State does not fulfil its responsibility to protect its own population, others may step in' have been tamed and inserted into reaffirmations of the pre-eminence of the mechanisms of collective decision-making under the UN Charter. At the same time, it has been remarked in the literature that the responsibility to protect comes fairly close to the idea of cooperation as embodied in Article 41(1) ASR.[192] However, it should be noted in this regard that for the applicability of Article 41(1) ASR the same strict criteria apply as to Article 41(2) ASR: there needs to be a serious breach of a peremptory norm under general international law – a threshold which may not necessarily be embodied in the concept of the 'R2P'. Furthermore, the obligation of cooperation only applies *a posteriori* – arguably, 'R2P' would kick in at an earlier point in time.

All this has not prevented international lawyers from arguing that the responsibility to protect and the obligation of cooperation of Article 41(1) ASR would mutually reinforce each other. Taken together, they would 'send a clear message: no State may stand idly by when genocide, war crimes or crimes against humanity are being perpetrated'.[193]

---

[189] See generally Carsten Stahn, 'Responsibility to Protect: Political Rhetoric or Emerging Norm?', *American Journal of International Law* 101 (2007), pp. 99–120; Andrew Clapham, 'Responsibility to Protect – "Some Sort of Commitment"', in Vincent Chetail (ed.), *Conflits, sécurité et coopération – Liber Amicorum Victor-Yves Ghebali* (Brussels: Bruylant, 2007), pp. 169–92, at p. 188.

[190] International Commission on Intervention and State Sovereignty, 'The Responsibility to Protect', 2001, available at www.iciss.ca/report-en.asp (last visited 1 November 2010).

[191] 2005 World Summit Outcome, UN Doc. A/RES/60/1, paras. 138–9.

[192] Carsten Stahn, 'Responsibility to Protect', p. 115; for a different view, see Peter-Tobias Stoll, 'Responsibility, Sovereignty and Cooperation – Reflections on the "Responsibility to Protect"', in Doris König, Peter-Tobias Stoll, Volker Röben and Nele Matz-Lück (eds.), *International Law Today – New Challenges and the Need for Reform?* (Berlin: Springer, 2008), pp. 1–16, at p. 8.

[193] Jutta Brunnée, 'International Law and Collective Concerns: Reflections on the Responsibility to Protect', in Tafsir Malick Ndiaye and Rüdiger Wolfrum (eds.), *Law*

Whereas it is too early at this stage to pass judgment on this position, it can be observed that the exact interaction between the two concepts is not always carefully established. However, we feel that 'R2P' is an important part of the conceptual environment in which the obligation of cooperation of Article 41(1) ASR needs to be situated. It can also not be ruled out that further reliance on Article 41(1) ASR may help to provide 'R2P' with a bedrock of more substantial international practice which could help this concept to mature into a binding legal obligation.[194]

4.1.2 The obligation of solidarity in the work of the ILC

The ILC Commentary is not particularly illuminating as to the precise meaning of this obligation of cooperation. It speaks of a 'positive duty' of States to cooperate, and mentions that cooperation could be organised in the framework of a competent international organisation such as the UN but need not be limited to institutionalised forms.[195] The ILC reckons that the diversity of circumstances would be too great to be able to prescribe in more detail which forms this cooperation should take and also what measures States should take in order to comply with Article 41(1) ASR.[196] In addition, the Commission points out, it is not clear whether Article 41(1) ASR reflects general international law or has to be seen as a form of the progressive development of the law.[197]

Prior to the final adoption of the ASR, the duty of cooperation was formulated in a somewhat milder form. Article 53(c) and (d) of the Draft Articles adopted at First Reading in 1996 provided that an international crime would entail an obligation by every other State '[c] to cooperate with other States in carrying out the obligations under subparagraphs (a) and (b); and (d) to cooperate with other States in the application of measures designed to eliminate the consequences of the crime.' This is arguably a less demanding formulation than the one which is now included in Article 41(1) ASR.[198] At the time, the Commentary to the Draft Articles of 1996 spoke clearly about these two subparagraphs being an expression of an obligation of solidarity in international law.

---

of the Sea, Environmental Law and Settlement of Disputes: Liber Amicorum Judge Thomas A. Mensah (Leiden: Nijhoff, 2007), pp. 35–51, at p. 50.
[194] Cf Sandra Szurek, 'Responsabilité de protéger', pp. 113–14.
[195] ILC Commentary, Article 41, para. 2.   [196] Ibid., paras. 2–3.
[197] Ibid., para. 3.
[198] Andrea Gattini, 'Return Ticket', p. 1185; Jörg Künzli, Unrechtsregimes, p. 355.

Cooperation would in most cases occur within the confines of the United Nations, but the Commission wanted to reiterate 'that a certain minimum response to a crime is called for on the part of all States'.[199] Article 53 of the 1996 Draft would be formulated in a way to give expression to that expectation and, at the same time, 'reinforce and support any more extensive measures which may be taken by States through international organizations in response to a crime'.[200]

Despite its more assertive wording, Article 41(1) ASR does not automatically require further-reaching measures of States than its 1996 predecessor.[201] In this respect, particular attention needs to be paid to the requirement that measures taken for the effort of cooperation need to be 'lawful'.[202] The interpretation of what 'lawful measures' can mean raises the same uncertainties as in the case of Article 54 ASR dealing with the problematic issue of countermeasures in the collective interest.[203] By referring to the lawfulness of these measures, the ILC is leaving it open whether the measures of cooperation or the countermeasures in question have the potential to justify conduct which would otherwise be considered wrongful.[204] That the obligation of cooperation could give rise to conflicts with existing legal obligations was a concern expressed by Giorgio Gaja, Chairman of the ILC's Drafting Committee in 2000. In his address to the Commission, he referred to a potential conflict between the obligation of cooperation and the laws on neutrality in the case where a serious breach of the peremptory norm against aggression would be at stake.[205] At that stage, Article 42 as then provisionally adopted by the Drafting Committee

---

[199] YBILC 1996, Vol. II, Part Two, p. 72, Commentary on Draft Article 53, para. 3.
[200] *Ibid.* At the same time, however, the 1996 Draft Articles recognised a general right of non-injured States to resort to countermeasures when an international crime had been committed. In this respect, the ASR as adopted in 2001 are more careful, as the ambiguously drafted Article 54 ASR makes clear: see section 5 below on complicity and countermeasures in the collective interest.
[201] Andreas L. Paulus, 'Jus Cogens', p. 315.
[202] Alessandra Gianelli, 'Le conseguenze', p. 277; Alain Pellet, 'Les articles', p. 17.
[203] Santiago Villalpando, *L'émergence*, p. 385; this relationship also troubled States as evidenced by the comments of Spain, UN Doc. A/CN.4/515, 54, and Austria, *ibid.*, 57.
[204] Alessandra Gianelli, 'Le conseguenze', p. 277.
[205] Statement of the Chairman of the Drafting Committee Mr Giorgio Gaja at the 2662nd Meeting of the ILC, 17 August 2000, at p. 28, available at www.lcil.cam.ac.uk/projects/state_responsibility_document_collection.php (last visited 1 November 2010); see also Nina Jørgensen, 'The Obligation of Cooperation', in James Crawford, Alain Pellet and Simon Olleson (eds.), *The International Law of Responsibility* (Oxford: Oxford University Press, 2010), pp. 695–701, at p. 700.

read '[t]o cooperate as far as possible to bring the breach to an end'.[206] The words 'as far as possible' were meant to accommodate these potentially conflicting obligations of the States required to cooperate.[207]

4.2 The Genocide Convention case

Given the rather unclear state of the law with respect to this obligation of cooperation, one could, for the moment, leave it to one side and consider it as not highly relevant for a study on complicity. However, the ICJ's *Genocide Convention* case, with its detailed treatment of the relationship between complicity in genocide and the obligation to prevent a genocide from occurring, warrants further examination.[208] From the outset, it has to be remarked that the obligation of cooperation in Article 41(1) ASR and an obligation to prevent genocide (Article I of the Genocide Convention) are technically distinct matters. Whereas the former applies after the fact and envisages States cooperating to bring the situation to an end, the latter applies before a genocide has taken place. However, as is the case with the separate obligation of non-assistance embodied in Article 41(2) ASR, it is possible to call into question whether the boundaries between what is just materialising and what has already happened will always be easy to identify. In addition, in terms of the means States will have to employ in order to comply with these obligations, some overlap can be found.[209]

In the *Genocide Convention* case, as will be recalled, the ICJ was dealing with the claim that Serbia was responsible for the commission of genocide in Bosnia and Herzegovina. Not being able to find conclusive evidence of a genocidal plan for the whole of Bosnia and Herzegovina, the Court's findings in terms of Serbian State responsibility were eventually confined to the killing of several thousand civilians in Srebrenica.[210] These killings were not perpetrated by Serbian State organs but rather by various factions and militias of the Bosnian Serbs. Accordingly, questions of attribution of this conduct to Serbia

---

[206] Draft Articles provisionally adopted by the Drafting Committee on Second Reading, UN Doc. A/CN.4/L.600 of 21 August 2000.
[207] See Andrea Gattini, 'Return Ticket', p. 1188.
[208] ICJ, *Case Concerning the Application of the Convention on the Prevention and Punishment of the Crime of Genocide*, Judgment.
[209] Similarly Marko Milanovic, 'State Responsibility for Genocide', *European Journal of International Law* 17 (2006), pp. 553–604, at p. 570.
[210] ICJ, *Case Concerning the Application of the Convention on the Prevention and Punishment of the Crime of Genocide*, Judgment, para. 297.

and Montenegro had to be determined. For that purpose, the Court was considering the various bases for attribution of the conduct of non-State actors but was unable to establish Serbian responsibility on the basis of a theory of *de facto* organs or under the 'effective control' test embodied in Article 8 ASR.[211] This left the Court with two further options: either it could find Serbian complicity in the genocide which occurred in Srebrenica or it could have recourse to the obligation of prevention and punishment of genocide as embodied in Article I of the Genocide Convention. In this respect, it should be noted that several points were controversial with respect to these two bases of State responsibility for genocide. The concept of complicity in genocide is included in Article III(e) of the Genocide Convention. Article III is generally about crimes for which States are required to establish criminal jurisdiction and which they must prosecute accordingly.[212] It was thus not self-explanatory to assume that a State could be held responsible for complicity in genocide by virtue of Article III(e) of the Genocide Convention.[213] Similarly, the scope of Article I of the Convention was not generally understood to mean that States could incur responsibility for the fact of not having prevented a genocide from occurring. An at least equally plausible interpretation of Article I was to read it as a *chapeau* for the Convention as a whole, giving a more general expression of the legal commitment States had undertaken by virtue of their ratification of the Convention.[214]

In order to interpret Article III(e) of the Convention, the Court had recourse to Article 16 ASR, which it found to be similar to the category of complicity in genocide.[215] According to the Court, Article 16 ASR would have provided guidance on the matter whether organs of Serbia and Montenegro furnished aid or assistance to the commission of the

---

[211] *Ibid.*, para. 413.
[212] Cf William A. Schabas, *Genocide in International Law*, pp. 285 *et seq.*
[213] Andreas Felder, *Die Beihilfe*, p. 146.
[214] See Nina Jørgensen, 'State Responsibility and the 1948 Genocide Convention', in Guy S. Goodwin-Gill and Stefan Talmon (eds.), *The Reality of International Law - Essays in Honour of Ian Brownlie* (Oxford: Oxford University Press, 1999), pp. 273-91, at pp. 275 *et seq.*; Antonio Cassese, 'Criminal Law Notions', pp. 876-7; John Quigley, *The Genocide Convention - An International Law Analysis* (Aldershot: Ashgate, 2006), pp. 222 *et seq.*; John Quigley, 'International Court of Justice as a Forum for Genocide Cases', *Case Western Reserve Journal of International Law* 40 (2007-8), pp. 243-63, at pp. 257 *et seq.*; Thilo Rensmann, 'Humanisierung', pp. 124-5.
[215] ICJ, *Case Concerning the Application of the Convention on the Prevention and Punishment of the Crime of Genocide*, Judgment, para. 419.

genocide in Srebrenica.[216] Before the Court determined that issue, however, it turned to the link between the specific intent (*dolus specialis*) of the perpetrators of the genocide and the 'motives which inspire the accomplice'.[217] The Court did not consider it necessary to determine whether the accomplice needs to share the specific intent as it did not find a preliminary condition satisfied, namely, that the organ or the person of the State in question acted knowingly, 'that is to say, in particular, was aware of the specific intent (*dolus specialis*) of the principal perpetrator'.[218] Here again, the Court borrowed from the formulation of Article 16 ASR. Thus having declined to find Serbian responsibility for complicity in genocide, the Court turned to the obligation to prevent genocide under Article I of the Genocide Convention.

The Court made it clear that the obligation to prevent genocide is one of conduct and not of result. In the process of determining whether a State has complied with this obligation, the notion of due diligence would be of crucial importance. Various parameters would operate against which a State's compliance with Article I could be measured. The Court especially mentioned a State's capacity to influence effectively the action of persons likely to commit or already committing genocide. This capacity could, *inter alia*, depend on geographical factors, for example the proximity of the State to the scene of events, as well as on political factors such as links between the authorities of the State with the actors committing the genocide. Furthermore, 'every State may only act within the limits permitted by international law' which could entail differences in terms of the legal rights a State would enjoy to take action to influence the situation.[219]

With respect to the relationship between the obligation of prevention and complicity, the Court noted that complicity would always require

that some positive action has been taken to furnish aid or assistance to the perpetrators of genocide, while a violation of the obligation to prevent results from the mere failure to adopt and implement suitable measures to prevent genocide from being committed. In other words, while complicity results from commission, violation of the obligation to prevent results from omission.[220]

In addition, the Court distinguished the two obligations on the basis of different conditions of knowledge about the genocide:

---

[216] Ibid., para. 420. [217] Ibid., para. 421. [218] Ibid.
[219] Ibid., para. 430. [220] Ibid., para. 432.

an accomplice must have given support in perpetrating genocide with full knowledge of the facts. By contrast, a State may be found to have violated its obligation to prevent even though it had no certainty, at the time when it should have acted, but failed to do so, that genocide was about to be committed or was under way; for it to incur responsibility on this basis it is enough that the State was aware, or should normally have been, of the serious danger that acts of genocide would be committed.[221]

On the basis of these requirements, the Court was able to find a breach by Serbia and Montenegro of its obligations under Article I of the Genocide Convention.[222] The reasoning of the Court is noteworthy for several reasons. It should first be noted that the Court canvassed the obligation to prevent genocide in a way which is not limited territorially.[223] Accordingly, it is conceivable that States which are far removed from the place in which a genocide is about to occur could face responsibility for having breached their obligation under Article I of the Genocide Convention.[224] At least prior to the Court's decision, it was not at all clear whether Article I could be construed in this way.[225]

It is even more remarkable, however, how the Court distinguished a failure to comply with the obligation to prevent from a breach of the prohibition of complicity in genocide.[226] It has not convinced all legal commentators that the Court deemed the very same knowledge on the part of the Serbian authorities to be insufficient to trigger responsibility for complicity whereas it was sufficiently concrete in order to find a

---

[221] Ibid.   [222] Ibid., para. 438.
[223] See Andreas L. Paulus, 'Zur Zukunft der Völkerrechtswissenschaft in Deutschland: Zwischen Konstitutionalisierung und Fragmentierung des Völkerrechts', Zeitschrift für ausländisches öffentliches Recht und Völkerrecht 67 (2007), pp. 695–719, at p. 704; Olivier Corten, 'L'arrêt', pp. 277–8.
[224] See Georg Nolte, 'Zusammenarbeit', p. 23; Andreas Zimmermann, 'Durchsetzung des Völkerrechts zwischen Fragmentierung, Multilateralisierung und Individualisierung', in Andreas Fischer-Lescano, Hans-Peter Gasser, Thilo Marauhn and Natalino Ronzitti (eds.), Frieden in Freiheit – Festschrift für Michael Bothe (Baden-Baden: Nomos, 2008), pp. 1077–88, at p. 1084.
[225] Marko Milanovic, 'Follow-Up', p. 685; it should be noted that the Court addressed this issue already in its 1996 decision on the preliminary objections. Whereas the Court held in that decision that 'the obligation each State … has to prevent and punish the crime of genocide is not territorially limited by the Convention', it was not entirely clear whether that actually meant that States can incur responsibility for not having prevented a genocide from occurring in another State's territory without their own *direct* involvement, ICJ, Application of the Convention on the Prevention and Punishment of the Crime of Genocide, Preliminary Objections, ICJ Rep. 1996, 595, para. 31.
[226] See Eduardo Savarese, 'Complicité', pp. 280 et seq.

breach of Article I of the Genocide Convention.[227] Antonio Cassese has remarked in that regard that

[i]t seems illogical (besides being unsupported by any authority or legal rule or principle) to hold that the foresight of a risk of genocide is relevant to the obligation to prevent whereas it is irrelevant to the crime of (or to state responsibility for) complicity in genocide.[228]

Cassese further argues that, if a State is becoming aware of the fact that there is a serious danger of its support given to other entities being used for acts of genocide, it should as a minimum discontinue this assistance. If it fails to do so, it would become an 'accomplice' to genocide.[229] According to some, it would follow from the general structure of domestic criminal legal systems that the threshold for liability for omissions would generally be higher than for complicity.[230]

Although this may be appealing as a matter of intuition and logic for international law, this analogy does not in itself lead to reliable results for the determination of State responsibility. Yet, there is some force in the argument that it is not entirely clear why the same degree of knowledge on the part of a third State would not render it responsible for complicity in genocide while it would at the same time be required to adopt measures in order to prevent the genocide.[231] Potentially, the latter form of conduct is more intrusive as it requires positive action. Common sense would rather suggest that States should first suspend forms of aid or assistance which could be used in the commission of genocide before they take measures of prevention.

If we assume for a moment that the findings of the Court would also apply within the confines of the secondary rules of State responsibility, it appears questionable whether similar results could be obtained with respect to the relationship between responsibility for complicity according to Articles 16 and 41(2) ASR and responsibility for not

---

[227] Andrea Gattini, 'Breach', p. 705; Mark Gibney, 'Genocide and State Responsibility', *Human Rights Law Review* 7 (2007), pp. 760–73, at p. 772; Sandesh Sivakumaran, 'Application of the Convention on the Prevention and Punishment of the Crime of Genocide (Bosnia and Herzegovina v. Serbia and Montenegro)', *International and Comparative Law Quarterly* 56 (2007), pp. 695–708, at p. 705; Philippe Weckel, 'L'arrêt', p. 327.
[228] Antonio Cassese, 'Criminal Law Notions', p. 887.
[229] Ibid.   [230] Andrea Gattini, 'Breach', p. 703.
[231] See also ICJ, *Case Concerning the Application of the Convention on the Prevention and Punishment of the Crime of Genocide*, Judgment, dissenting opinion of Judge ad hoc Mahiou, para. 127; similarly, *ibid.*, Declaration of Judge Keith.

having complied with the obligation of cooperation under Article 41(1) ASR. The obligation not to assist in the commission of an internationally wrongful act is more clearly entrenched in contemporary international law as compared to wide-ranging obligations of prevention.[232] Under this premise, one may very well inquire whether it makes sense to affirm a State's responsibility for not having complied with an obligation of prevention whereas its responsibility for complicity is denied. One possible way to explain the reasoning of the Court in the concrete case is a look at the legal consequences it attached to Serbia's wrongful act. It held that compensation would not be an appropriate remedy in the case at hand and confined itself to finding a breach of Serbia's obligation under international law which it considered to be an appropriate form of satisfaction.[233]

It is a matter of debate whether the Court's findings in this regard were owed to the general character of genocide as a crime which does not lend itself to financial remuneration or whether they were owed to the more remote responsibility of Serbia and Montenegro 'only' having been found responsible for the breach of the obligation of prevention.[234] At least under the second assumption, different consequences could have been attached to a finding of complicity. We have discussed in Chapter 6 of this study that the legal consequences of complicity are not devoid of problematic issues. Nonetheless, it would have been easier to award a financial form of reparation in the case of complicity than in the case of a violation of the obligation of prevention. However, it appears questionable to deduce findings on the basis of responsibility out of comparative analyses of their consequences.

Although the Court confined its findings expressly to the case at hand and to the Genocide Convention,[235] it will be difficult to limit the effects of the judgment in this manner. The question is to what extent the Court's findings are transposable to other obligations to prevent in the field of human rights law.[236] Why should there be a qualitative

---

[232] But see Andreas Zimmermann, 'Durchsetzung', p. 1084.
[233] ICJ, *Case Concerning the Application of the Convention on the Prevention and Punishment of the Crime of Genocide*, Judgment, paras. 462–3.
[234] For a discussion of these issues, see Andrea Gattini, 'Breach', pp. 706 *et seq.*; Christian Tomuschat, 'Reparation', pp. 905 *et seq.*
[235] ICJ, *Case Concerning the Application of the Convention on the Prevention and Punishment of the Crime of Genocide*, Judgment, para. 429.
[236] Mark Gibney, 'Genocide', p. 769; Thilo Rensmann, 'Humanisierung', p. 126, with footnote 89.

difference between the obligation to prevent genocide and a similar obligation to prevent torture?[237] And, finally, is it possible to interpret the Court's *dictum* on the obligation to prevent genocide as a push towards the development of Article 41(1) ASR into something more akin to hard law? In the course of the future development of the law, similar pronouncements of the ICJ may trigger such a development.

4.3 Interim conclusions

The *Genocide Convention* case thus points to the potential of developing Article 41(1) ASR. The Court's decision underlines how obligations of cooperation and prevention may be able to establish the responsibility of complicit States even where it is technically not possible to affirm responsibility for complicity itself. Thus, obligations of prevention and cooperation may be seen as functional equivalents to the prohibition of complicity in international law. Viewing the two mechanisms together is also appealing for another reason: the element of cooperation shows a way that States under an obligation of prevention can follow. Instead of mobilising their resources in a unilateral manner, channelling them through measures of cooperation is attractive insofar as it potentially increases the effectiveness of the measures taken and also frees a State from the suspicion of unilateral assertions. Credible attempts at prevention through cooperation will also constitute an effective defence against claims of complicity with a serious breach of a peremptory norm.

At the same time, it is important to note that these functional equivalents can only be found in distinct areas of international law. States are only required to prevent the wrongful acts of other actors with respect to obligations of particular importance. The same applies with respect to hard obligations of cooperation. While it is of course possible to stipulate a general and all-encompassing principle of cooperation, this would hardly entail significant legal consequences. A hard obligation of cooperation may, however, crystallise along the lines provided for in Article 41(1) ASR. In this connection, it is also warranted to look for additional bases to hold complicit States responsible even though this would not be possible under Article 16 ASR. Article 41(1) ASR fits this picture as it envisages an obligation of cooperation to bring to an end situations brought about by serious breaches of peremptory norms

---

[237] Georg Nolte, 'Zusammenarbeit', p. 24.

under general international law. If developed further through international practice, this provision will thus have to be read in connection with the obligation of non-assistance established in Article 41(2) ASR. In this respect, the two obligations form two sides of the same coin: the solidarity of the international community in the face of the most serious attacks on the rules meant to protect this community's fundamental values.

5 Complicity and countermeasures in the collective interest

At times, there is no clear borderline between State behaviour which could be seen as a consequence of the prohibition of complicity and the adoption of countermeasures in the collective interest. For example, the United States distanced itself from the regime of Idi Amin in Uganda after the serious human rights violations which occurred in 1978. Section 5(b) of the Uganda Embargo Act for a prohibition of export of goods and technology provided that 'the United States should take steps to dissociate itself from any foreign government which engages in the international crime of genocide'.[238] The Netherlands reacted in a similar way when a new military government in Surinam was blamed for massive human rights violations in 1982. Under agreements concluded in 1975, the Netherlands had agreed to deliver economic subsidies and financial assistance for the maintenance of the Surinam military. The Dutch government suspended the 1975 treaties and protested against the human rights violations.[239] In a diplomatic note of 14 December 1982 presented to Surinam, it made reference to its position that the granting of development assistance shall not entail co-responsibility for serious human rights violations.[240] These cases are usually analysed with respect to the problem of countermeasures in the collective interest. However, they may also be seen as important elements of international practice on complicity.

The existence of certain treaty or contractual ties between States may be seen as fostering violations of international law, for example with respect to arms deliveries or economic and military cooperation. If a sufficiently close nexus between the contractually guaranteed support and the commission of internationally wrongful acts exists, States

---

[238] 22 USC § 2151 (1978).
[239] Christian J. Tams, *Enforcing Obligations Erga Omnes*, p. 227.
[240] A German translation of the note is reprinted in Hans-Heinrich Lindemann, 'Auswirkungen', pp. 67–8, note 17.

may have to sever these treaty or contractual relationships in order not to become complicit.[241] Suspension or termination of these agreements[242] may, however, also amount to the taking of countermeasures, possibly even in the general or collective interest if the State in question is not an injured State within the meaning of Article 42 ASR. How can the relationship between complicity and countermeasures in the collective interest be understood?

Countermeasures constitute a permitted form of self-help by which a State, in non-compliance with its own obligations under international law, aims to induce another State to resume compliance with an obligation which has previously been violated.[243] Previously called 'reprisals',[244] their exercise is tied to a certain set of conditions. These include the prior violation of an obligation under international law by the target State, an unsuccessful attempt to invoke the responsibility of that State, compliance of the countermeasures with conditions of proportionality and the non-infringement of certain rules of international law such as the basic human rights of individuals, the prohibition of the use of force and peremptory norms in general.[245] Traditionally, the concept of countermeasures would apply according to the bilateral structure of the law of State responsibility. The injured State would thus be entitled to take countermeasures against the State directly responsible for the wrongful act. It is, however, an over-simplification to state that it was never considered in international law whether third States also could step in and take reprisals or countermeasures in lieu of or in addition to measures adopted by the injured State.[246] Over the course of time, such a right was recognised, but only under strictly limited circumstances. Michael Akehurst, for example, was willing to acknowledge the existence of such a right

---

[241] Cf Marina Spinedi, 'International Crimes of States', pp. 122–3.
[242] See Articles 60–62 of the Vienna Convention on the Law of Treaties.
[243] Cf ILC Commentary, Article 49, para. 1; Christian J. Tams, *Enforcing Obligations Erga Omnes*, pp. 19–20; Mary Ellen O'Connell, *Power and Purpose*, p. 232.
[244] *Naulilaa Incident Arbitration*, RIAA II, 1011.
[245] The restrictions upon the taking of countermeasures are spelt out in greater detail in ICJ, *Case Concerning the Gabcikovo-Nagymaros Project*, Judgment, ICJ Rep. 1997, 7, paras. 82 *et seq.*; Articles 49–53 ASR; see further Thomas M. Franck, 'On Proportionality of Countermeasures in International Law', *American Journal of International Law* 102 (2008), pp. 715–67.
[246] For a concise historical overview, see Georg Nolte, 'From Dionisio Anzilotti', pp. 1084 *et seq.*, with further references on the positions of, among others, Grotius, Vattel, Bynkershoek, Heffter, Bluntschli and Bulmerinq.

in three circumstances: in the case of enforcement of decisions of international courts and tribunals, in the case of Article 60(2)(a) of the Vienna Convention on the Law of Treaties (termination or suspension of a multilateral treaty in case of a material breach) and in case of violations of the rules pertaining to the prohibition of the use of force in international law.[247] The coming into existence of obligations *erga omnes* and the category of peremptory norms were challenges to this traditional view.[248] If all States are held to have an interest in the observation of certain rules, why should they not also have the right to take countermeasures in defence of these rules?

In order to understand more fully the relationship between complicity and the taking of countermeasures in the collective interest, a brief overview of the debate on countermeasures in the collective interest is called for. Following that, their relationship with the prohibition of complicity will be analysed.

5.1 Countermeasures in the collective interest

5.1.1 The position of the ILC and reactions towards it

As Denis Alland has noted, the treatment of the issue of countermeasures in the collective interest has gone through various cycles.[249] Initially, it was seen almost as a matter of logical consistency that the introduction of international crimes into the law of State responsibility would entail the possibility of States not directly injured to take countermeasures in order to protect the common interest.[250] At the same time, the Commission was of course well aware of the problematic features of countermeasures in their traditional bilateral form. These problems promised to be exacerbated if countermeasures were to be taken by third States.

Accordingly, Special Rapporteur Willem Riphagen shared much of the criticism levelled against countermeasures in the collective interest. According to him, 'a single State cannot take upon itself the role of "policeman" of the international community'.[251] Hence, he proposed a

---

[247] Michael Akehurst, 'Reprisals', p. 15.
[248] See, e.g., Jochen Abr. Frowein, 'Verpflichtungen', pp. 241 *et seq.*
[249] Denis Alland, 'Countermeasures of General Interest', *European Journal of International Law* 13 (2002), pp. 1221–39, at pp. 1228–9.
[250] See Alain Pellet, 'Les articles', p. 19.
[251] Willem Riphagen, 'Third Report on the Content, Forms and Degrees of International Responsibility', UN Doc. A/CN.4/354 and Add.1-2, YBILC 1982, Vol. II, Part One, pp. 22, 45, para. 140.

system in which the enforcement of aggravated responsibility would be linked to the existing procedures of the UN Security Council under Chapter VII of the UN Charter.[252] Riphagen's proposals met with criticism over the different functions of UN Security Council action and the enforcement of international responsibility.[253] However, this criticism did not prompt his successor as Special Rapporteur, Gaetano Arangio-Ruiz, to shy away from developing further ties with the UN system of collective security. Arangio-Ruiz envisaged an even more ambitious scheme involving either the General Assembly or the Security Council in a first step and the ICJ in a second step to determine the existence of an international crime.[254] However, in the form of the Draft Articles as they were adopted on First Reading in 1996, in the case of an international crime, every State was considered to be injured, which thus triggered the possibility of taking countermeasures.[255]

Under Special Rapporteur James Crawford, the whole regime of aggravated responsibility was redesigned. This did not leave the provisions on countermeasures unaffected. The position of the ILC was changing fast insofar as the Special Rapporteur first developed a differentiated regime for countermeasures in the collective interest which distinguished between situations in which there was an injured State to express its consent to the countermeasures by third States and situations in which there was no injured State.[256] During its fifty-second session, however, the Commission decided to expand this right of countermeasures in the collective interest and formulated a Draft Article

---

[252] Willem Riphagen, 'Sixth Report on the Content, Forms and Degrees of International Responsibility', UN Doc. A/CN.4/389, YBILC 1985, Vol. II, Part One, pp. 3, 11 *et seq.*

[253] See further Martin Dawidowicz, 'Public Law Enforcement', p. 345; Pierre Klein, 'Responsibility for Serious Breaches of Obligations Deriving from Peremptory Norms of International Law and United Nations Law', *European Journal of International Law* 13 (2002), pp. 1241–55, at pp. 1244 *et seq.*; Matthias Forteau, *Droit de la sécurité collective*, pp. 528 *et seq.*

[254] Cf Gaetano Arangio-Ruiz, 'Fifth Report on State Responsibility', UN Doc. A/CN.4/454 and Add.1–3, YBILC 1993, Vol. II, Part One, p. 1.

[255] On the 1996 solution of the ILC and its relation to Arangio-Ruiz' proposals, see Bruno Simma, 'From Bilateralism to Community Interest', p. 316; Mark Toufayan, 'A Return to Communitarianism? Reacting to "Serious Breaches of Obligations under Peremptory Norms of General International Law" under the Law of State Responsibility and United Nations Law', *Canadian Yearbook of International Law* 42 (2004), pp. 197–251, at pp. 218–19.

[256] James Crawford, 'Third Report on State Responsibility', UN Doc. A/CN.4/507/Add.4, para. 402.

54(2) stating that all States could take countermeasures in the case of serious breaches of obligations *erga omnes*.[257] This provision provoked a relative flood of governmental comments which were, on balance, considered to be unfavourable to the inclusion of this wide-ranging competence of third States to take countermeasures in the collective interest.[258] Christian Tams, who has analysed the governmental comments in greater detail, has come to the conclusion that they were not as negative as was portrayed by Special Rapporteur James Crawford and as can often be found in scholarly writings.[259] Be that as it may, the Commission ultimately decided to include the saving clause which is Article 54 ASR, which leaves it open whether or not international law currently gives third States a right to take countermeasures in the collective interest.

Two studies have carefully assembled the international practice with respect to countermeasures in the collective interest.[260] It is not necessary to report their findings here at great lengths. The studies came to the conclusion that there is indeed more practice available than the ILC has taken into consideration, that it is more widespread and also that it cannot be reduced to the practice of Western States, as for example African States had recourse to countermeasures *vis-à-vis apartheid* South Africa. In the context of colonialism and *apartheid*, G77 countries and socialist States have also participated in countermeasures.[261] Both studies have shown at least that it is more plausible than not to assume that third States today enjoy the right to take countermeasures in the collective interest.[262]

5.1.2 Remaining concerns

The question remains whether a faculty to take countermeasures in the collective interest is to be welcomed. As one commentator has noted, the discussion about the issue whether or not third States are entitled to take countermeasures in the collective interest builds upon

---

[257] See Statement of the Chairman of the Drafting Committee, Giorgio Gaja, at the 2662nd Meeting of the ILC, note 206 above.
[258] See the comments of governments in UN Doc. A/CN.4/515, at pp. 87 *et seq.*; see also Alain Pellet, 'Les articles', p. 20.
[259] Christian J. Tams, *Enforcing Obligations Erga Omnes*, p. 246.
[260] *Ibid.*, pp. 207 *et seq.*; Martin Dawidowicz, 'Public Law Enforcement', pp. 333 *et seq.*
[261] Christian J. Tams, *Enforcing Obligations Erga Omnes*, p. 236.
[262] See also Christian Hillgruber, 'Third States', p. 292; Santiago Villalpando, *L'émergence*, p. 412; Alexander Orakhelashvili, *Peremptory Norms*, p. 272; Christian Tomuschat, *Human Rights*, pp. 274–5.

'the inherent tension between the need for a more effective legal order in spite of decentralisation, and the risks of abuse relating to the allocation of enforcement authority to individual States, even if limited to the most serious illegalities'.[263] Michael Akehurst formulated his objections as follows:

> [T]here are sound policy reasons for considering that third States are not, as a general rule, allowed to take reprisals. In international disputes of a legal character, *both* sides usually accuse each other of breaking international law; if third States were able to intervene, there is a serious danger that they would be biased and that they would tend to support their allies, rather than the side which was objectively in the right. The result would be more likely to weaken international law than to strengthen it; and it would certainly cause a very disturbing increase in international tension.[264]

Although the state of the law has changed since Akehurst formulated these concerns in 1970, they still capture the general atmosphere of the debate. Martti Koskenniemi entertained fairly similar considerations just before the ILC completed its work on State responsibility in 2001: interested and powerful States, he wrote, would be transformed into something akin to a world police. As intervention in the form of countermeasures would be within their discretion, they could form a world order to their liking.[265] At the same time, one should not overestimate the willingness of third States to have recourse to third party countermeasures in the first place.[266] Injecting notions of international public order into the law of State responsibility without at the same time providing for the faculty to take countermeasures in the collective interest would indeed appear half-hearted.[267] However, even for authors who support the assumption that third States have the faculty to take countermeasures in the collective interest, it is nearly a truism that the potential for abuse exists[268] and that, in terms of the

---

[263] Martin Dawidowicz, 'Public Law Enforcement', p. 347.
[264] Michael Akehurst, 'Reprisals', pp. 15–16.
[265] Martti Koskenniemi, 'Solidarity Measures', p. 344.
[266] Christian J. Tams, *Enforcing Obligations Erga Omnes*, p. 230; Mark Toufayan, 'A Return', p. 248.
[267] Giorgio Gaja, 'Obligations Erga Omnes, International Crimes and Jus Cogens: A Tentative Analysis of Three Related Concepts', in Joseph H. H. Weiler, Antonio Cassese and Marina Spinedi (eds.), *International Crimes of State* (Berlin: de Gruyter, 1989), pp. 151–60, at pp. 155–6; see also Bruno Simma, 'From Bilateralism to Community Interest', p. 317; Santiago Villalpando, *L'émergence*, p. 371.
[268] Christian J. Tams, *Enforcing Obligations Erga Omnes*, p. 250 (but see also his position at p. 230).

development of international law, the idea of one State coming to the rescue of another and taking the enforcement of international law into its own hands remains a rather primitive one.[269]

5.2 Complicity and countermeasures in the collective interest

In more or less clear terms, it has been argued in the literature that there may be some overlap between questions concerning complicity and countermeasures in the collective interest.[270] A particularly promising road of inquiry could be how considerations of complicity could provide a better structure for the debate on countermeasures in the collective interest.[271]

5.2.1 Overlap of the two concepts

Such benefits may be obtained only with respect to some of the situation in which countermeasures in the collective interest could be deployed. These cases pertain to the scenario in which the treaty or contractual relationship which the third State (State A) wishes to suspend or terminate (i.e., the object of the countermeasure) is actually contributing to the violation of the serious breach of a peremptory norm under international law by State B *vis-à-vis* State C (and/or 'the international community as a whole', cf Article 48(1)(b) ASR). Such a contribution could either materialise directly, i.e., through the mere execution of the treaty, or through a close factual nexus between the assistance thus rendered and the commission of the wrongful act. In such a situation, considerations of the complicity of State A would arguably be an additional basis of legitimacy for the suspension or termination of treaty relationships.[272] Under the premises we have just discussed, State A would also be entitled to adopt such measures under the general state of the law on countermeasures. However, in the case where State A did not adopt the countermeasures, if State A were also

---

[269] Cf Bardo Fassbender, *The United Nations Charter*, p. 128.
[270] Marina Spinedi, 'International Crimes of States', p. 122; Alessandra Gianelli, 'Le conseguenze', p. 288; see also Willem A. Riphagen, 'Preliminary Report on the Content, Forms and Degrees of International Responsibility', UN Doc. A/CN.4/330, YBILC 1980, Vol. II, Part One, p. 107, at p. 121, para. 71.
[271] Tentatively in this direction Alessandra Gianelli, 'Le conseguenze', p. 288; Margo Kaplan, 'Using Collective Interests to Ensure Human Rights: An Analysis of the Articles on State Responsibility', *New York University Law Review* 79 (2002), pp. 1902-33, at p. 1928.
[272] See also Frank Hoffmeister, *Menschenrechts- und Demokratieklauseln*, p. 205.

to incur responsibility for having aided or assisted in the commission of the serious breach, it would arguably be compelled to take such measures. State A would still be free to violate international law and, *nota bene*, incur responsibility for its wrongful act.[273] State A could point to its obligation to State B to continue, for instance, to provide military material which it owes under the respective treaty. If, however, the norm breached by State B is a norm of *jus cogens*, it will be hard for State A to adhere to this position. Instead, its obligation not to become complicit in the wrongful act committed by State B would outweigh its treaty obligations towards the latter.

We do not mean to argue here that there exists a duty to take countermeasures in the collective interest.[274] However, considerations of possible complicity may exert an influence on third States which may lead them to believe that they are under an obligation to take countermeasures. Accordingly, the concept of complicity could contribute a first step towards an obligation of States to take countermeasures in the collective interest.[275] Understood correctly, this construction could help to rationalise a part of the debate on such countermeasures. Where responsibility for complicity with a serious breach of a peremptory norm would otherwise ensue, a State should obviously be considered as entitled to adopt countermeasures in the form of suspension or termination of agreements with the wrongdoer. One could object to this finding that, in such situations, these are not countermeasures in the *collective* interest, as the complicit State is simply guarding its own interest, i.e., the wish not to incur responsibility for complicity. However, this is at least partially a terminological matter. Countermeasures in the collective interest are also known under other denominations, be it 'in the general interest', countermeasures by 'third States' or by States 'not (directly) injured'. What is more important, however, is the fact that there is no available evidence that the taking of countermeasures in the collective interest may not also be motivated by other concerns.[276]

---

[273] Cf Vaughan Lowe, *International Law*, p. 33; Joost Pauwelyn, *Conflict of Norms*, pp. 98–9, 418 *et seq*.

[274] Cf Roger S. Clark, 'Obligations', pp. 631 *et seq*.; Giorgio Gaja, 'Do States Have a Duty to Ensure Compliance with Obligations Erga Omnes by Other States?', in Maurizio Ragazzi (ed.), *International Responsibility Today – Essays in Memory of Oscar Schachter* (Leiden: Nijhoff, 2005), pp. 31–6; Eckart Klein, 'Gegenmaßnahmen', p. 64.

[275] For a sceptical position in this regard, see Eckart Klein, 'Gegenmaßnahmen', p. 64.

[276] Christian J. Tams, *Enforcing Obligations Erga Omnes*, pp. 208–9.

5.2.2 Rationalising the countermeasures debate

So what are the merits of introducing considerations of complicity into the debate on countermeasures? In the view of the present author, two benefits may be identified. First of all, a clear understanding of when a State would incur responsibility for complicity could lower the threshold at which such complicit States may consider the taking of countermeasures. Despite the potential of abuse which is inherent in the taking of countermeasures, they remain a vital instrument for the enforcement of international law. If it is possible to provide for more readily apparent criteria justifying such measures, it could be expected that States would be more willing to have recourse to this instrument.

However – and this could prove to be a second benefit of the introduction of complicity considerations – there is no way around the recognition of this potential for abuse. In this perspective, considerations of complicity may help to distinguish between situations in which countermeasures are clearly warranted and others in which this is not the case. Greater awareness of State responsibility for complicity may also render countermeasures obsolete in some situations. If States begin to review their own conduct at an earlier stage, they may recognise risks inherent in their conduct which could render them responsible.

In this perspective, the impact of considerations of complicity on the debate on countermeasures is two-fold: it may help to justify countermeasures in situations in which they are clearly warranted and may, at the same time, be an attractive conceptual alternative to mechanisms which are widely considered as dangerous due to their undesirable side effects.

6 Conclusion

These considerations about the relationship between measures to avoid complicity and the faculty of taking countermeasures in the collective interest may show how closely the issue of complicity is related to the upholding of international public order. The various aspects on which the existence of peremptory norms and obligations *erga omnes* in the law of State responsibility have impacted, warrant the assumption that States face stronger obligations not to become complicit when the regime of aggravated responsibility is triggered. These considerations may also pave the way towards a more integrated understanding of the general complex of 'enforcing the community interest' in international law.[277] As we have seen in this chapter, various concepts are on offer in this regard. Besides the instruments which relate to the law of State responsibility *stricto sensu*, we have mentioned obligations of prevention established on the level of primary norms (Article I of the Genocide Convention, for instance) and the ambiguous concept of the 'responsibility to protect'.

These different concepts are pervaded by the same general idea: that it is no longer tolerable for 'third States' to stand by when serious violations of international law are committed. International lawyers are grappling with the various standards these concepts and obligations entail. A reading which combines these various factors may help to provide for a more effective, but also morally less charged, enforcement of international law in general, and of the community interest in particular. The concept of complicity lends itself to this exercise in a particular way: it defines what is at times referred to as the 'minimum response' to serious breaches of international law. This 'smallness' does not, however, mean that the obligation not to render aid or assistance to wrongful conduct is always closely complied with by States. If we look at the more demanding concepts such as obligations of prevention and countermeasures in the collective interest, we see that, for instance, the ICJ has tried to define criteria establishing when this obligation of prevention arises for States. Among other factors, 'the capacity to influence effectively the action of persons likely to commit, or already committing genocide' is to be taken into account, as are 'the strengths of the political links' between the entities in question.[278] With respect to the obligation of cooperation set out in Article 41(1) ASR and the formulation in Article 54 on countermeasures in the collective interest, it is noteworthy that both provisions speak of 'lawful measures' which are to be taken. In such situations, a clear and convincing analysis that a third State could face the risk of becoming implicated in serious breaches of peremptory norms would help both the relevant decision-makers *ex ante* and possibly international courts and tribunals *ex post* to assess whether positive measures finally taken were in conformity

---

[277] See also Christian Tomuschat, *Human Rights*, p. 274 (for similar considerations with respect to the relation between Articles 40 and 41 on the one hand and Article 54 on the other).

[278] ICJ, *Case Concerning the Application of the Convention on the Prevention and Punishment of the Crime of Genocide*, Judgment, para. 430.

with international law. The existence of a relationship of complicity between two States may, at the same time, fulfil the requisite degree of proximity required by the ICJ and explain the nature of certain forms of conduct as lawful such as to fulfil the criteria established by the ILC in Articles 41(1) and 54 ASR.

These considerations may be met with the objection that, if responsibility for complicity is already present, determining whether an obligation of prevention has been breached would make no sense. This is a technically correct view, but one which centres solely on the *ex post* perspective. The exact boundaries between action and abstention, mere isolation and the taking of positive measures may not always be easy to trace. Whereas the concept of complicity is frequently associated with a duty of abstention, the examples we have discussed in this chapter show that a positive action can very well be required, for example when a treaty needs to be severed in order to avoid complicity. In construing the interplay between these various concepts, one has to dissociate oneself from a purely remedial perspective. Furthermore, it needs to be kept in mind that these concepts do not exist merely in order to satisfy the demands for conceptual clarity of international lawyers, but should be construed in a way which reduces most effectively the immense human suffering which is the very reason for the introduction of notions of public order into international law. To this overarching goal of the international community, the relatively modest concept of complicity could thus contribute more than other, more demanding concepts.

8 A network of rules on complicity

We have now surveyed the core aspects of the international law of complicity. At this point, the reader might feel a certain sense of disappointment. Given the structure of Article 16 ASR and the obstacles attached to its implementation, especially before international courts and tribunals, Article 16 ASR may appear as some form of 'window dressing', pretending to tackle a pressing issue but offering modest returns in terms of concrete and practical consequences. This feeling is only slightly mollified by the comforting effects of *jus cogens* which could lead international lawyers to believe that, when the 'real important' issues are at stake, international law provides stronger rules on State complicity.[1] This mollification is doubly precarious as the general scope of application of peremptory norms in international law is a fairly modest one, too.[2] Stronger rules on complicity in the system of aggravated responsibility could be only one further component of the aforementioned 'window dressing'.

However, this assessment could be too negative. International law may provide for further rules which technically deal with different scenarios but have the potential to hold complicit States responsible as well, albeit under a 'different label'. This chapter will look into some of these possibilities. We will consider both primary and more specialised rules on complicity as well as alternative mechanisms for holding complicit States responsible (section 2). Subsequently, we will discuss

---

[1] One could refer here to the classification of *jus cogens* as 'Kitsch' by Martti Koskenniemi, 'Tradition and Renewal', pp. 121 *et seq.*; on this view, see Pierre-Marie Dupuy, 'Some Reflections on Contemporary International Law and the Appeal to Universal Values', *European Journal of International Law* 16 (2005), pp. 131–7, at pp. 135 *et seq.*

[2] Malcolm D. Evans, 'State Responsibility', p. 142.

their relationship to the general rule that is Article 16 ASR (section 3). In order to contextualise these efforts, we will first summarise weaknesses attached to the general rules on complicity.

1 Shortcomings of the general and secondary rules on complicity

If we look for shortcomings of the general rules on complicity included in the law of State responsibility, we can distinguish between normative features of the rules and structural obstacles to hold complicit States responsible.

1.1 Inherent normative weaknesses

Article 16 ASR presents some normative features which make it difficult to hold complicit States responsible. The main problem in that regard will be to distinguish between conduct which deserves to be classified as complicity and forms of international cooperation which should not be discouraged by a rule which is too strict.[3] This will require some balancing between situations which represent State complicity and those which do not. The crucial criterion in this regard will be the one which addresses the intent of the supporting State. Some authors are willing to go around this requirement and describe it as rendering the whole complicity provision unworkable.[4] The analysis of the customary character of Article 16 ASR has, however, shown that, at the current stage of the development of the law, there is no way around the requirement of intent.[5] Difficulties in proving the intent in question should thus not lead to the abandonment of intent as a requirement for triggering responsibility under Article 16 ASR.[6] It is another issue how international practice will deal with this requirement in pertinent situations. In diplomatic environments, it will prevent States from being confronted with unreasonable claims of complicity whereas greater

---

[3] Georg Nolte and Helmut Philipp Aust, 'Equivocal Helpers', p. 15; Sigrun I. Skogly, *Beyond National Borders*, p. 35.
[4] Andreas Felder, *Die Beihilfe*, p. 261; Bernhard Graefrath, 'Complicity', p. 375; Kate Nahapetian, 'Confronting State Complicity', p. 106; John Quigley, 'Complicity', p. 109; Sigrun I. Skogly, *Beyond National Borders*, pp. 38-9; Bruno Simma, 'Grundfragen', p. 380.
[5] See Chapter 5, text accompanying notes 221 *et seq*.
[6] Similarly Jörg Künzli, *Unrechtsregimes*, pp. 408 and 414; Maya Brehm, 'The Arms Trade', p. 385; see further Georg Nolte and Helmut Philipp Aust, 'Equivocal Helpers', p. 15.

latitude can be expected if courts or tribunals are to explore it. That said, it is equally clear that the criterion of intent could well stand in the way of holding complicit States responsible in a number of cases. This may even be the case when perceptions of justice and fairness militate for a finding of responsibility of the complicit State. It is, however, submitted here that this shortcoming has to be remedied by further developments in international practice. In this respect, only a few pertinent cases could suffice to trigger a development in this direction, especially if they emanate from authoritative bodies such as the ICJ.

1.2 Structural obstacles to holding complicit states responsible

Structural obstacles could prove to be even more of a hindrance to an effective implementation of responsibility for complicity than the inherent normative features of Article 16 ASR. In this regard, the main obstacle is the orientation of international judicial proceedings towards bilateral settings. The rules on the ICJ's jurisdiction are ill-equipped to deal with disputes which involve a multiplicity of actors. At times, the Court is willing to ignore the involvement of other actors, as has been the case in both the *Corfu Channel* case[7] and the more recent *Case Concerning Armed Activities on the Territory of the Congo*[8] between the Democratic Republic of the Congo and Uganda. Neglecting the impact third States may have had upon a case can, however, very well contribute to judgments which lack acceptance and legitimacy as they are perceived to oversimplify complex situations and press them into narrow bilateral confines.[9] This narrowing down of a dispute is, in any case, the exception rather than the rule: it is likely that, in most complicity cases, the *Monetary Gold* rule[10] would stand in the way of the Court exercising its jurisdiction. Other courts and tribunals may be more flexible in that regard but international law's preference for a consent-oriented system of the settlement of international disputes will prevent a good number of complicity cases from ever reaching the courts.

In addition, other aspects of the ICJ's jurisprudence may have contributed to developing further obstacles to holding complicit States

---

[7] ICJ, *Corfu Channel Case*, Judgment, ICJ Rep. 1949, 4.
[8] ICJ, *Armed Activities on the Territory of the Congo (Democratic Republic of the Congo v. Uganda)*, Judgment, ICJ Rep. 2005, 168.
[9] For criticism of the Court's approach in the *Congo v. Uganda* case, see Phoebe N. Okowa, 'Congo's War: The Legal Dimension of a Protracted Conflict', *British Year Book of International Law* 77 (2006), pp. 203–55, at p. 209.
[10] ICJ, *Monetary Gold Removed from Rome in 1943*, Judgment, ICJ Rep. 1954, 19, 32.

responsible. Whereas the requirement of intent is not included in the ILC's provisions on serious breaches of peremptory norms under general international law, the ICJ has considerably raised the threshold in terms of the burden of proof where exceptionally grave charges against States are at stake.[11] Although understandable from the perspective of the 'incriminated' State, this very high burden of proof takes away what the ILC has conceded, namely, that serious breaches of peremptory norms in international law will in most cases not go unnoticed.[12]

2 Special rules and alternative mechanisms

However, an examination of the problem of complicit States in international law which stops here would be incomplete. The rules of the law of State responsibility constitute only the basic framework of international law in that regard.[13] They are supplemented by subject-specific provisions which may establish the responsibility of complicit States in situations in which this would not be possible under the general rules which are Articles 16 and 41(2) ASR.[14] That specialised rules on complicity may go further than the general ones is plausible on an intuitive basis: States have agreed to these constraints in specific international agreements.[15] This section will give an overview of especially pertinent primary rules which address the problem of complicit States and will also look into neighbouring concepts which can supplement rules on complicity. The next section will explore their relation to the general rules in the law of State responsibility. This treatment is exploratory in the sense that the norms and concepts we are discussing in this chapter could very well warrant in-depth treatments of their own. We will only be able to present their most pertinent features and develop some thoughts on their relationship to the general rules on complicity on which this study focuses.

---

[11] ICJ, *Case Concerning the Application of the Convention on the Prevention and Punishment of the Crime of Genocide*, Judgment, para. 207.
[12] ILC Commentary, Article 41, para. 11; see further Georg Nolte and Helmut Philipp Aust, 'Equivocal Helpers', pp. 16–17.
[13] See Article 55 ASR on the principle of *lex specialis*; on its application in the law of State responsibility, see Bruno Simma and Dirk Pulkowski, 'Planets and the Universe', pp. 483 *et seq.*
[14] Cf John Cerone, 'Re-examining', p. 533.
[15] Georg Nolte and Helmut Philipp Aust, 'Equivocal Helpers', p. 17.

If we survey the field of international law, three areas are especially relevant for our study as they include special rules on complicit State behaviour. These are the rules on the use of force and the system of collective security, international humanitarian law and human rights law.

2.1 The use of force and collective security

The rules pertaining to the use of force and collective security are at the same time considered to form the very centre of today's international legal order and to be the most precarious rules in terms of compliance and enforcement. As issues of the *jus ad bellum* were always perceived to be most important, the role of third States and their relation to a war between two other States also received considerable attention.[16] In Chapter 2, we surveyed the developments of the law which oscillated over the centuries between an affirmation of just war theory and more positivist emanations of the *liberté à la guerre*. Under just war theory, restrictions were placed upon third States not to assist the party to a conflict which was waging an unjust war. In contrast, the international law of the classic, positivist period in the nineteenth century reaffirmed the law of neutrality as an option of choice, for example a third State having the right to remain aloof from a conflict and to keep an equal distance from the belligerents.[17] With the coming into existence of mechanisms of collective security, first of the League of Nations and then of the United Nations, these questions had to be embedded in the interpretation of the Covenant and the Charter respectively. Would it still be conceivable to opt for traditional neutrality in a system which (first partially, later comprehensively) outlawed the use of force in international relations? And how would the answer to the question be affected by the poor performance of these mechanisms of international public order?

If we try to assemble the pertinent rules on the role of third States with respect to the use of force, we are faced with the following layer of rules:[18] first, the general rule on aid or assistance to the commission of an internationally wrongful act which is Article 16 ASR applies. It is,

---

[16] Cf Carl Schmitt, *Die Wendung*, pp. 32 *et seq.* (on neutrality as the all-important issue in determining the characteristics of the 'institution' war).
[17] For a concise overview of the historical developments, see Stephen C. Neff, *War and the Law of Nations*, at pp. 59 and 191 *et seq.*
[18] For a similar classification, see Olivier Corten, *Le droit contre la guerre*, pp. 268 *et seq.*

secondly, supplemented by Article 41(2) ASR which provides that, after the commission of a serious breach of the international prohibition against aggression, States are under a special obligation not to render aid or assistance in the maintenance of the situation brought about by the serious breach.

Thirdly, Article 3(f) of the Definition of Aggression of 1974 provides that States shall not allow their territory, which they have placed at the disposal of another State, to be used by that State for the perpetration of an act of aggression against a third State.[19] Responsibility under this provision is potentially more compelling than Article 16 ASR as it does not require a special form of intent or knowledge on the part of the assisting State.[20] As the Definition of Aggression posits that the assisting State also commits an aggression through this form of assistance, it does not benefit from the relative 'privileges' the complicit State enjoys under Article 16 ASR. Instead, the supportive State runs the full risk of being held responsible: it need not have the 'wish' to contribute to the commission of the aggression. The mere factual establishment that it has granted the permission to make use of its territory for the commission of aggression suffices to trigger its responsibility and to expose it to the severe consequences attached to that act, which include the possibility of being targeted by measures of self-defence.[21]

Fourthly, this strict and objective form of responsibility for the permission to make use of territory for the commission of an unlawful use of force is further supplemented by the general obligation on States to control their own territory.[22] As Arbitrator Max Huber has put it in the *Island of Palmas* case, sovereignty over territory presupposes the effective exercise thereof which includes an obligation not to allow for unlawful conduct harming other States to take place on one's own territory.[23] This obligation thus requires the exercise of due diligence on the part of States over the uses to which their territory is put.[24] This obligation may also apply with respect to cases which

---

[19] Declaration on the Definition of Aggression, UN Doc. A/RES/3314 (XXIX) of 14 December 1974.
[20] See further Georg Nolte and Helmut Philipp Aust, 'Equivocal Helpers', p. 6.
[21] See also Alexander Orakhelashvili, 'Overlap and Convergence: The Interaction Between Jus ad Bellum and Jus in Bello', *Journal of Conflict and Security Law* 12 (2007), pp. 157–96, at p. 193.
[22] Olivier Corten, *Le droit contre la guerre*, p. 269.
[23] *Island of Palmas Case*, RIAA II, 839.
[24] On due diligence as a standard for complicit States, see generally Stefan Talmon, 'Plurality', p. 219.

technically do not fall within the scope of application of Article 3(f) of the Definition of Aggression. As will be recalled, the Definition limits itself to regulating the placing of territory at the disposal of another State. If interpreted narrowly, this would not include the granting of overflight rights which may, of course, be crucial for the effective use of force against another State.[25] Although it is debatable whether or not the granting of overflight rights would thus also fall within the purview of the Definition of Aggression, they would certainly violate a State's obligation not to allow its territory (that is, its airspace) to be used to the detriment of another State under the general obligation as affirmed by the *Island of Palmas* case.[26]

Fifthly, further obligations not to become complicit in the unlawful use of force may be triggered once the UN Security Council has taken preventive or enforcement action under Chapter VII of the Charter. In addition to concrete obligations of non-assistance which may be provided for in the operative parts of individual resolutions, Article 2(5) of the UN Charter provides that States are under an obligation to 'refrain from giving any assistance to any State against which the United Nations is taking preventive or enforcement action'. Arguably, the same obligation would apply when the Security Council simply finds that an act of aggression or of the unlawful use of force has been taken by a State without then deciding upon further action under Chapter VII.[27] The relevant point in both situations is that enhanced duties of isolation apply once the Security Council has taken a position on who is responsible for the bringing about of a situation which threatens international peace or security or may even constitute a breach of the peace or an act of aggression.

Finally, a sixth layer of obligations may apply for third States through the application of the traditional laws of neutrality.[28] This will, arguably, only be possible in situations in which the UN Security Council has not made any determination as to the party to a conflict which

---

[25] For the related discussion of the question whether or not different standards apply for States immediately neighbouring an attacked State and States more remote from the theatre of conflict, see Olivier Corten, *Le droit contre la guerre*, p. 284.

[26] Cf German Federal Administrative Court, 2 WD 12.04 = ILDC 483 (DE 2005), para. 4.1.4.1.4.

[27] In this regard, the obligation in Article 2(2) to apply the UN Charter in good faith could play a role.

[28] See Vaughan Lowe, 'Responsibility', p. 13; Jörg Künzli, *Unrechtsregimes*, p. 416; Georg Nolte and Helmut Philipp Aust, 'Equivocal Helpers', p. 6, note 19.

bears responsibility for its outbreak. However, as international practice shows, most cases will fall into this category. In this situation, most authorities are willing to accord States the privilege to adopt a neutral position and not to side with one party to an ongoing armed conflict.[29] Once applicable, the laws of neutrality trigger a special form of rules against complicity which aim to prevent the neutral State from rendering support to both sides of the conflict and to receive, in return, the benefit of remaining unaffected by the conflict.[30] In order to uphold this status, neutral States are required to refrain from supporting any of the parties to a conflict in an unequivocal manner and are subject to losing the status of a neutral State if they consistently violate their obligations of neutrality.[31]

The gist of the assembly of these six layers of obligations of States potentially complicit with violations of Article 2(4) of the UN Charter is to show that differentiated consequences apply for third States in situations which involve the use of force. Of these six layers, Article 16 ASR is only the most basic one.[32] Its strict criteria will mean that, in most cases concerning the unlawful use of force, it will not be the crucial rule upon which determinations of responsibility for complicit States will depend. There is a good chance that either more far-reaching primary and direct obligations such as that stemming from the Definition of Aggression or the general obligation not to allow territory to be used to the detriment of another State will apply or that the UN Security Council will have made a determination with respect to the conflict. Even in the default situation of the applicability of the laws of neutrality, States have to remain aloof from a conflict as long as they wish to retain the benefits of this position.[33] In this respect, a final twist can

---

[29] Ian Brownlie, *Use of Force*, p. 404; Yoram Dinstein, *War, Aggression and Self-Defence*, p. 164; Alfred Verdross and Bruno Simma, *Universelles Völkerrecht*, § 239; Christopher Greenwood, 'Concept of War', pp. 297 *et seq.*
[30] Cf Alexander Orakhelashvili, 'Overlap and Convergence', p. 193.
[31] Yoram Dinstein, *War, Aggression and Self-Defence*, p. 25.
[32] Cf Olivier Corten, *Le droit contre la guerre*, p. 268.
[33] Recurrent attempts by States to rely on a position of 'benevolent neutrality' or 'non-belligerency' which would allow limited forms of support to the party to a conflict which has the right to use force have not been successful: see Wolff Heintschel von Heinegg, 'Benevolent Third States', pp. 543 *et seq.*; Natalino Ronzitti, 'Italy's Non-Belligerency', pp. 197 *et seq.*; Yoram Dinstein, *War, Aggression and Self-Defence*, p. 168. Different considerations apply when the UN Security Council has taken enforcement action, cf Article 2(5) of the Charter: see further Stephen C. Neff, *Rights and Duties*, p. 193.

be identified which could help to further the effectiveness of Article 16 ASR: a third State to a conflict which decides *not* to remain neutral in a given conflict will in most cases be aware of the exact factual situation in this conflict. If it wishes to support one side of a conflict, it will have made a *prima facie* assessment that it also wished to further the commission of the acts of the State to which it is rendering aid or assistance. In this perspective, a decision of a third State *not* to remain neutral in a given conflict will help to establish the responsibility of that State under the general rule of Article 16 ASR. This is, partially, also owed to a functional overlap between Article 16 ASR and the traditional rules on neutrality: both are aimed to limit the consequences of international conflicts to the degree absolutely necessary.[34] The law of neutrality is doing so in a way which is more directly inspired by the characteristics of the traditional decentralised international legal system where the determination of the wrongdoer will not be obvious. The provision on complicity assumes that it will be possible to determine who has committed the internationally wrongful act. In a time when these two different historic layers of international law overlap and are applicable at the same time, it is only natural that they should be applied in a mutually supportive way. In this light, the laws of neutrality may be a safeguard available for third States to avoid claims of complicity. Due to their character as *lex specialis*, they will allow a third State to defend its position by pointing towards its strict impartiality. As a reflex, these rules will then also prevent the participation in violations of international law occurring in an armed conflict.[35]

In the case of the unlawful use of force, it is thus warranted to speak of a 'network' of rules on State complicity which mutually complement and reinforce each other if explored systematically. The systematic relationship between these rules deserves to be highlighted not only due to the fact that, in general, international rules should be interpreted with a view to their respective normative environment (Article 31(3)(c) of the Vienna Convention on the Law of Treaties[36]), but also because of

---

[34] See further Vaughan Lowe, 'Responsibility', p. 13.
[35] Jörg Künzli, *Unrechtsregimes*, p. 416.
[36] This rule is, of course, technically confined to the interpretation of treaties. It may, however, play a role as a further emanation of the principle of systemic integration for the interpretation of international law: see 'Fragmentation of International Law: Difficulties Arising from the Diversification and Expansion of International Law', Report of the Study Group of the International Law Commission, finalized by Martti Koskenniemi, UN Doc. A/CN.4/L.682, paras. 206 *et seq.*

the prime importance the international legal system attaches to the prohibition of the use of force in international relations.[37] At the same time, this systematic interpretation is a viable alternative to wide-ranging interpretations of Article 16 ASR which go beyond the current state of the law.[38]

2.2 International humanitarian law

In the field of international humanitarian law, no direct provision on complicity in violations of the rules of this body of law exists.[39] However, Common Article 1 of the 1949 Geneva Conventions I–IV is frequently interpreted as giving rise to an obligation of non-assistance with respect to the content of the Conventions.[40] The Article provides: 'The High Contracting Parties undertake to respect and to ensure respect for the present Convention in all circumstances.' It has been referred to as the 'nucleus for a system of collective responsibility'.[41] The provision had its antecedents in international law, most notably Article 25 of the Convention for the Protection of the Sick and Wounded of 1929:

1. The provisions of the present Convention shall be respected by the High Contracting Parties in all circumstances.

2. If, in time of war, a belligerent is not a party to the Convention, its provisions shall, nevertheless, be binding as between all the belligerents who are parties thereto.

---

[37] Humphrey Waldock, 'Regulations', p. 492; Christine Gray, *International Law*, p. 30; Albrecht Randelzhofer, 'Article 2(4)', para. 12; ICJ, *Armed Activities on the Territory of the Congo (Democratic Republic of Congo v. Uganda)*, Judgment of 19 December 2005, ICJ Rep. 2005, 168, para. 148.

[38] See also John Cerone, 'Re-examining', p. 534.

[39] See generally William A. Schabas, 'Enforcing International Humanitarian Law: Catching the Accomplices', *International Review of the Red Cross* 83 (2001), No. 842, pp. 439–59.

[40] See, e.g., Fateh Azzam, 'The Duty of Third States to Implement and Enforce International Humanitarian Law', *Nordic Journal of International Law* 66 (1997), pp. 55–75, at p. 70; Ardi Imseis, 'Critical Reflections', p. 115; Birgit Kessler, 'The Duty to "Ensure Respect" under Common Article 1 of the Geneva Conventions: Its Implications on International and Non-International Armed Conflicts', *German Yearbook of International Law* 44 (2001), pp. 489–516, at p. 503; Marco Sassòli, 'State Responsibility for Violations of International Humanitarian Law', *International Review of the Red Cross* 84 (2002), No. 846, pp. 401–34, at p. 413.

[41] Laurence Boisson de Chazournes and Luigi Condorelli, 'Common Article 1 of the Geneva Conventions Revisited: Protecting Collective Interests', *International Review of the Red Cross* 82 (2000), No. 837, pp. 67–87, at p. 68.

This provision conveyed a clear message: the binding force of the Convention was no longer to be subjected to the *si omnes* clause, i.e., the requirement that the Convention only applies if all parties to a conflict are bound by the instrument.[42] Furthermore, the reference to 'all circumstances' was meant to elucidate that some rules of the Convention would have to be implemented in times of peace as well. The second paragraph of the provision thus constituted a rebuttal of the argument that the Convention would have only started to become applicable with the commencement of war.[43]

Diverging views exist, however, on the reason why a similar provision was inserted into the 1949 Conventions and what it, accordingly, entails. Whereas Article 25 of the 1929 Convention was characterised by a close interplay between its two paragraphs, the second one of them was introduced into a substantive Article of its own in 1949 (Common Article 2(3)).[44] Hotly contested, and for our purposes the relevant issue, is the question whether the wording 'to ensure respect' is supposed to establish an obligation on States and what its precise scope would be. Some authors have held the view that it merely provides for a faculty of States to insist upon the application of the relevant rules of the Geneva Conventions in armed conflicts to which they are not a direct party.[45] It has also been shown in the literature that Common Article 1 can be deconstructed into its various parts – an exercise which leads to the result that the provision has no sensible meaning at all and rather constitutes a 'soap bubble'.[46] However, several factors point in the other direction. In the 'semi-official' commentary to the Conventions, edited by Jean Pictet, it is stated that:

Le système de protection prévu par la Convention exige en effet, pour être efficace, que les Parties contractantes ne se bornent pas à appliquer elles-mêmes

---

[42] Paul des Gouttes, *La Convention de Genève pour l'amélioration du sort des blessés et des malades dans les armées en campagne, Commentaire* (Geneva: International Committee of the Red Cross, 1930), pp. 187–8.

[43] Frits Kalshoven, 'The Undertaking to Respect and Ensure Respect in All Circumstances: From Tiny Seed to Ripening Fruit', *Yearbook of International Humanitarian Law* 2 (1999), pp. 3–61, at p. 9.

[44] Luigi Condorelli and Laurence Boisson de Chazournes, 'Quelques remarques à propos de l'obligation des Etats de "respecter et faire respecter" le droit international humanitaire "en toutes circonstances"', in Christophe Swinarski (ed.), *Etudes et essais sur le droit international humanitaire et sur les principes de la Croix-Rouge en l'honneur de Jean Pictet* (Leiden: Nijhoff, 1984), pp. 17–35, at p. 19.

[45] Frits Kalshoven, 'Respect and Ensure', p. 60.

[46] Carlo Focarelli, 'Common Article 1 of the 1949 Geneva Conventions: A Soap Bubble?', *European Journal of International Law* 21 (2010), pp. 125–71.

la Convention, mais qu'elle fassent également tout ce qui est en leur pouvoir pour que les principes humanitaires qui sont à la base des Conventions soient universellement appliqués.[47]

In addition, the view that Common Article I comprises an obligation 'to ensure respect' was also held at the Teheran Conference on Human Rights in 1968 which adopted, without opposition, a resolution in which it was recognised that 'States parties to the Red Cross Geneva Conventions sometimes fail to appreciate their responsibility to take steps to ensure the respect of these humanitarian rules in all circumstances by other States, even if they are not themselves directly involved in an armed conflict'.[48] The International Court of Justice has interpreted the obligation 'to ensure respect' as having its roots in customary international law and as requiring States not to encourage violations of international humanitarian law by others.[49] The Court was even more explicit in its *Wall* opinion, where it held that Common Article 1 provides that 'every State party to that Convention, whether or not it is a party to the specific conflict, is under an obligation to ensure that the requirements of the instruments in question are complied with'.[50] Finally, reference can be made to the recent study on customary international humanitarian law conducted by the ICRC.[51] Rule 144 provides:

States may not encourage violations of international humanitarian law by parties to an armed conflict. They must exert their influence, to the degree possible to stop violations of international humanitarian law.

The commentary to this rule expressly points to Article 16 ASR which would support the customary status of Rule 144.[52] In this

---

[47] Jean Pictet (ed.), *Commentaire – IV La Convention de Genève relative à la protection des personnes civiles en temps de guerre* (Geneva: International Committee of the Red Cross, 1956), p. 21.
[48] International Conference on Human Rights, Teheran, 1968, Resolution XXIII of 12 May 1968, preambular para. 9, available at www.icrc.org/ihl.nsf/WebPrint/430-FULL?OpenDocument (last visited 1 November 2010).
[49] ICJ, *Military and Paramilitary Activities In and Against Nicaragua*, Merits, ICJ Rep. 1986, 14, paras. 220, 255; for criticism in this regard, see *ibid.*, separate opinion of Judge Ago, para. 6.
[50] ICJ, *Legal Consequences of the Construction of a Wall in the Occupied Palestinian Territories*, Advisory Opinion, ICJ Rep. 2004, 136, para. 158.
[51] Jean-Marie Henckaerts and Louise Doswald-Beck, *Customary International Humanitarian Law*, Vol. I, *Rules* (Cambridge: Cambridge University Press, 2005), pp. 509 *et seq.*
[52] *Ibid.*, p. 511; see further David Turns, 'Implementation and Compliance', in Elizabeth Wilmshurst and Susan Breau (eds.), *Perspectives on the ICRC Study on*

respect, the study finds itself in line with those voices in the literature which affirm that Common Article 1 does indeed impose an obligation 'to ensure respect' for the Convention,[53] but would not require States to take countermeasures or even forcible measures in order to live up to this obligation. Rather, the concrete content of Common Article 1 could, in this respect, be understood as at least requiring States not to render aid or assistance to violations of the Geneva Conventions.[54] In this respect, there is some debate whether Article 16 ASR could be said to imply the general principle which is underlying this interpretation of Common Article 1.[55] A problematic feature of this debate is the conflation of encouragement with complicity, which occurs frequently. In the general law on State responsibility, incitement or encouragement do not render a State responsible.[56] In the context of international humanitarian law, the ICJ has, however, deduced the prohibition to encourage violations of the law from Common Article 1.[57] Accordingly, responsibility of third parties under Common Article 1 may commence at a lower

Customary International Humanitarian Law (Cambridge: Cambridge University Press, 2007), pp. 354-76, at pp. 364-5.

[53] See, first and foremost, Luigi Condorelli and Laurence Boisson de Chazournes, 'Quelques remarques', pp. 24 and 26; see further: Theodor Meron, *Human Rights and Humanitarian Norms as Customary Law* (Oxford: Clarendon Press, 1989), pp. 30-1; Maya Brehm, 'The Arms Trade', pp. 385-6; Birgit Kessler, *Durchsetzung*, p. 109; Birgit Kessler, 'Ensure Respect', pp. 502-3; Dieter Fleck, 'International Accountability for Violations of the Ius in Bello: The Impact of the ICRC Study on Customary International Humanitarian Law', *Journal of Conflict and Security Law* 11 (2006), pp. 179-99, at p. 182; Fateh Azzam, 'Duty of Third States', pp. 58-9; Marco Sassòli, 'State Responsibility', p. 421; Thilo Rensmann, 'Humanisierung', p. 120.

[54] Dietrich Schindler, 'Die erga omnes-Wirkung des humanitären Völkerrechts', in U. Beyerlin, M. Bothe and R. Hofmann (eds.), *Recht zwischen Umbruch und Bewährung – Festschrift für Rudolf Bernhardt* (Berlin: Springer, 1995), pp. 199-211, at p. 204; Fateh Azzam, 'Duty of Third States', p. 70; Ardi Imseis, 'Critical Reflections', p. 115; Marco Sassòli and Antoine Bouvier, *How Does Law Protect in War? Cases, Documents and Teaching Materials on Contemporary Practice in International Humanitarian Law*, 2nd edn (Geneva: International Committee of the Red Cross, 2006), p. 284; Andreas Felder, *Die Beihilfe*, p. 149; Jörg Künzli, *Unrechtsregimes*, pp. 329-30.

[55] See, e.g., Birgit Kessler, *Durchsetzung*, pp. 106 *et seq.*

[56] Roberto Ago, 'Seventh Report on State Responsibility', YBILC 1978, Vol. II, Part One, p. 30, 55, para. 63; ICJ, *Military and Paramilitary Activities In and Against Nicaragua*, Merits, ICJ Rep. 1986, 14, dissenting opinion of Judge Schwebel, pp. 388-9; Bernhard Graefrath, 'Complicity', p. 373; Jörg Künzli, *Unrechtsregimes*, p. 407; Georg Nolte and Helmut Philipp Aust, 'Equivocal Helpers', p. 13.

[57] ICJ, *Military and Paramilitary Activities In and Against Nicaragua*, Merits, ICJ Rep. 1986, 14, paras. 220, 255.

threshold than is the case with Article 16 ASR.[58] However, for those cases in which assistance to violations of international humanitarian law is at stake, it is very possible to construe Article 16 ASR as the *lex generalis* and Common Article 1 as *lex specialis*.[59] The strict criteria embodied in Article 16 ASR, especially with respect to the requisite degree of intent, may then be attenuated once complicity enters the scope of Common Article 1.[60]

Assistance to violations of international humanitarian law can thus be seen as an example where more demanding standards change the interpretation of Article 16 ASR. The obligation to ensure respect for the observance of international humanitarian law thus impacts upon the required vigilance of the complicit State. Marco Sassòli has described this with respect to the transfer of weapons in a situation in which systematic violations of international humanitarian law would occur in the State to which the weapons are transferred. Under the strict rules of Article 16 ASR, it would need to be established with certainty that the weapons were used for the concrete violations and the transferring State could possibly maintain that it rendered the support not for the violation of the international humanitarian law. However, such a narrow understanding of the obligations incumbent upon the assisting State would no longer be possible under the heightened standard imposed by Common Article 1: ensuring respect for international humanitarian law would thus demand more of the complicit State than the general rule which is Article 16 ASR.[61] However, one should also note scepticism with respect to the practical impact of Common Article 1, a provision which would only rarely be used.[62] At least in theory, Common Article 1 is, however, a valuable addition to the rules on complicity. It may thus contribute to further 'encircle' complicit State action with normative barriers.

---

[58] David Turns, 'Implementation', p. 365.
[59] Maya Brehm, 'The Arms Trade', pp. 385-6; Marco Sassòli, 'State Responsibility', p. 413; see also Luigi Condorelli and Laurence Boisson de Chazournes, 'Quelques remarques', p. 22; sceptical: Carlo Focarelli, 'Common Article 1', p. 169.
[60] Maya Brehm, 'The Arms Trade', p. 386.
[61] Marco Sassòli, 'State Responsibility', p. 413; Maya Brehm, 'The Arms Trade', p. 386; Birgit Kessler, *Durchsetzung*, p. 110.
[62] Cf Luigi Condorelli and Laurence Boisson de Chazournes, 'Quelques remarques', p. 27; Robert Kolb, *Ius in bello: Le droit international des conflits armés* (Basel: Helbing, 2003), p. 243; Carlo Focarelli, 'Common Article 1', p. 129.

2.3 Human rights law

The field of human rights law is too diverse to allow us to point to a single mechanism by which the problem of complicit States is expressly addressed and responsibility of States is established beyond the general state of the law as embodied in the ASR. However, three different mechanisms can be identified by which, in special areas of the law, more far-reaching responsibility for complicit States is established. These three mechanisms comprise special rules on complicity, obligations which cover different forms of State conduct which is, however, similar to complicity and the existence of positive obligations in several human rights treaties. Furthermore, complicity may have a role to play in determinations whether a given violation of the law took place within the jurisdiction of a State.

2.3.1 Special rules on complicity in human rights law

Article III(e) of the Genocide Convention of 1948 provides that 'complicity in genocide' shall be punishable. The wording of this provision indicates that originally it was intended to require States to provide for the criminal prosecution of individuals who have been complicit in genocide. In general, the Convention was traditionally interpreted as one by which States agreed to prosecute those responsible for the commission of genocide and the ancillary acts set out in Article III. Article III(e) was thus not so much understood as a provision under which responsibility of States for complicity would be established.[63] However, this interpretation of the Genocide Convention has been called into question step by step. In its 1951 advisory opinion on reservations to the Convention, the ICJ emphasised the special character of the obligations States have accepted by becoming party to the Convention. In its opinion, the Court interpreted the Convention in a strongly teleological manner. It pointed out that 'in a convention of this type one cannot speak of individual advantages or disadvantages of States, or of the maintenance of a perfect contractual balance between rights and duties'.[64] Although not directly connected to the question to what extent the Convention would establish State responsibility for genocide and the ancillary breaches, this line of interpretation is favourable

---

[63] Andreas Felder, *Die Beihilfe*, p. 146; William Schabas, *Genocide in International Law*, pp. 285 et seq.
[64] ICJ, *Reservations to the Convention on the Prevention and Punishment of the Crime of Genocide*, Advisory Opinion, ICJ Rep. 1951, 15, 23.

to an answer which puts an emphasis on a wide-ranging understanding of the obligations set out in the Convention.[65] What is more, the Court also underlined that the States party to the Convention did not enter *new* obligations by ratifying the Convention but that the principles underlying the Convention were principles which would be recognised as binding upon States by 'civilised nations' even without any conventional obligation.[66] More than fifty years later, the Court was able to expand on that jurisprudence and to establish with greater clarity why it considered the Convention to directly impose obligations under Articles I and III for States party to the Convention. With respect to Article I of the Convention, the Court held that it would be

> paradoxical if States were thus under an obligation to prevent, so far as within their power, commission of genocide by persons over whom they have a certain influence, but were not forbidden to commit such acts through their own organs, or persons over whom they have such firm control that their conduct is attributable to the State concerned under international law. In short, the obligation to prevent genocide necessarily implies the prohibition of the commission of genocide.[67]

At the next step, the Court extended this finding to the acts enumerated in Article III. While the Court recognised the fact that

> the concepts used in paragraphs (b) to (e) of Article III, and particularly that of 'complicity', refer to well known categories of criminal law and, as such, appear particularly well adapted to the exercise of penal sanctions against individuals ... it would not be in keeping with the object and purpose of the Convention to deny that the international responsibility of a State – even though quite different in nature from criminal responsibility – can be engaged through one of the acts, other than genocide itself, enumerated in Article III.[68]

Accordingly, Article III(e) of the Genocide Convention imposes upon States an additional obligation not to become complicit in genocide. The crucial question then is how this obligation differs from the general obligation not to aid or assist in the commission of a genocide

---

[65] See also Orna Ben-Naftali, 'The Obligations to Prevent and Punish Genocide', in Paola Gaeta (ed.), *The UN Genocide Convention – A Commentary* (Oxford: Oxford University Press, 2009), pp. 27–57, at p. 33.
[66] ICJ, *Reservations to the Convention on the Prevention and Punishment of the Crime of Genocide*, Advisory Opinion, ICJ Rep. 1951, 15, 23.
[67] ICJ, *Case Concerning the Application of the Convention on the Prevention and Punishment of the Crime of Genocide*, Judgment, para. 166.
[68] *Ibid.*, para. 167.

under Article 16 ASR. In this regard, the judgment of the Court in its *Genocide Convention* case sends ambiguous signals. In order to interpret Article III(e) of the Genocide Convention, the Court had recourse to Article 16 ASR. It noted that, although conceptually distinct from the situation it had to pass judgment on, Article 16 would merit consideration as there would be no apparent reason 'to make any distinction of substance between "complicity in genocide", within the meaning of Article III, paragraph (e), of the Convention and the "aid or assistance" of a State in the commission of a wrongful act by another State within the meaning of ... Article 16'.[69] This statement could be interpreted to mean that, with respect to genocide, no 'stricter' standards with respect to complicity apply than the ones embodied in Article 16 ASR.

This may appear to be disconcerting at first sight, but there is a reasonable explanation for this position. Article 16 ASR may indeed be suitable as a blueprint for responsibility for complicity in genocide under the Genocide Convention as the rules against genocide are among those rare examples in international law where intent on the part of a State is required in order to trigger responsibility. In order to hold a State responsible for the commission of genocide, it needs to be shown that the requisite *dolus specialis* – the special intent to destroy, in whole or in part, a national, ethnical racial or religious group (see Article II of the Genocide Convention) – was present.[70] The ICJ has interpreted this requirement in the context of complicity in a way such that an accomplice must have, *at the least*, awareness of the special intent of the perpetrators of genocide. The words 'at the least' suggest that, normally, the accomplice should have more than this awareness.[71] This is ultimately a convincing interpretation as it would run against all logic to require a lesser degree of intent for the complicit State than of the main actor. Thus, the strict interpretation of Article III(e) of the Genocide Convention appears to be warranted.

Although the provision on complicity in the Genocide Convention thus does not establish a stricter standard for complicit States, we have already seen how the ICJ has compensated for this finding in the form of a wide interpretation of the obligation to prevent genocide under Article I of the Genocide Convention – an issue to which we will return later in this section.

---

[69] *Ibid.*, para. 420.
[70] William A. Schabas, *Genocide in International Law*, pp. 206 *et seq.*
[71] Georg Nolte and Helmut Philipp Aust, 'Equivocal Helpers', p. 14.

A related case is Article 4(1) of the UN Convention Against Torture (CAT)[72] which provides that '[e]ach State Party shall ensure that all acts of torture are offences under its criminal law. The same shall apply to an attempt to commit torture and to an act by any person which constitutes complicity or participation in torture.' *Prima facie*, it is not apparent why it should not be possible to have recourse to a similar teleological reasoning such as the one effected by the ICJ with respect to Article III(e) of the Genocide Convention. After all, it could be argued that, if States are under a general obligation not to torture and to prevent torture from happening, they should also not become complicit in it. However, the argument is more difficult to construct in the case of the CAT as the duty of prevention which is envisaged by Article 2(1) CAT is expressly limited to 'acts of torture in any territory under its jurisdiction', i.e., the jurisdiction of the State Party. Although the term 'complicity' is interpreted rather widely in the context of Article 4(1) CAT,[73] it is difficult to extend its reach to cases of inter-State complicity in torture. With respect to torture, it is rather a different special rule which is promising in order to hold complicit States responsible.

2.3.2 Functionally similar rules: the prohibition of refoulement

Although technically dealing with situations which do not fall within the category of complicity as understood in the law of State responsibility, functionally similar rules may provide opportunities to hold complicit States responsible. In this regard, the concept of *non-refoulement* is an eminent example.[74] In general terms, the rule of *non-refoulement* prohibits States from returning a person to territories where there is a risk to his or her life or freedom.[75] The concept has various emanations

---

[72] UN Convention Against Torture of 10 December 1984, entered into force on 26 June 1987, 1465 UNTS 85.
[73] See Manfred Nowak and Elizabeth McArthur, *The United Nations Convention Against Torture – A Commentary* (Oxford: Oxford University Press, 2008), Article 4, para. 47.
[74] For support for the close relationship between complicity and *non-refoulement*, see Christian J. Tams, 'Abuse', p. 318. This position can also be found in the report by the UK House of Lords/House of Commons, Joint Committee on Human Rights, 'Allegations of UK Complicity in Torture', Twenty-Third Report of Session 2008–9, HL Paper 152, HC 230, published on 4 August 2009, para. 23.
[75] Cf Guy S. Goodwin-Gill and Jane McAdam, *The Refugee in International Law*, 3rd edn (Oxford: Oxford University Press, 2007), p. 201; Elihu Lauterpacht and Daniel Bethlehem, 'The Scope and Content', p. 89; Erika de Wet, 'Prohibition of Torture', p. 101.

among which, most notably, one can distinguish between the fields of refugee law and human rights law. The two are, however, not unrelated and mutually influence each other. In the field of international refugee law, the relevant provision on *non-refoulement* is Article 33 of the 1951 United Nations Convention relating to the Status of Refugees. It provides:

1. No contracting State shall expel or return (*refouler*) a refugee in any manner whatsoever to the frontiers of territories where his life or freedom would be threatened on account of his race, religion, nationality, membership of a particular social group or political opinion.

2. The benefit of the present provision may not, however, be claimed by a refugee whom there are reasonable grounds for regarding as a danger to the security of the country in which he is, or who, having been convicted by a final judgment of a particularly serious crime, constitutes a danger to the community of that country.

Article 33(2) of the Refugee Convention thus makes it clear that within its scope of application the protection against *refoulement* is not absolute.[76] It is, however, imposing stricter conditions upon expelling or returning a refugee than are provided for in Article 1F of the Refugee Convention which relates to the general grounds on which a State may refuse to accord refugee status.[77]

Human rights provisions against *refoulement* are more far-reaching than Article 33 of the Refugee Convention, but only insofar as they relate to the prohibition of torture.[78] In this regard, several pertinent norms exist at the international level. Most directly, the prohibition of *refoulement* is set out by Article 3(1) of the UN Convention Against Torture (CAT), according to which '[n]o State Party shall expel, return (*refouler*) or extradite a person to another State where there are substantial grounds for believing that he would be in danger of being subjected to torture'. In addition, the principle of *non-refoulement* is considered to be implicit in the various human rights provisions which generally provide for the freedom of the individual from torture. In interpreting Article 7 of the ICCPR, the Human Rights Committee has found that 'States parties must not expose individuals to the danger of torture ... upon return to another country by way of extradition,

---

[76] Guy S. Goodwin-Gill and Jane McAdam, *The Refugee in International Law*, p. 234.
[77] Rene Bruin and Kees Wouters, 'Terrorism and the Non-Derogability of Non-Refoulement', *International Journal of Refugee Law* 15 (2003), pp. 5–29, at p. 16.
[78] Cf ECtHR, *Saadi v. Italy*, para. 138.

expulsion or refoulement'.[79] Similar interpretations have been made with respect to the various international treaty rules against torture such as Article 3 of the European Convention on Human Rights, Article 5 of the African Charter on Human and Peoples' Rights[80] and Article 5(2) of the American Convention on Human Rights.[81]

The understanding according to which *refoulement* to a country where there exists a danger of torture itself constitutes a violation of the law has most clearly been developed by the European Court of Human Rights in its *Soering* case. In this decision, which involved the extradition of a German national by the United Kingdom to the United States, it was at issue whether the fact that the applicant would possibly face the so-called 'death row phenomenon' before an execution in the United States could trigger the responsibility of the United Kingdom. It is readily apparent that the inhuman or degrading treatment to which the applicant could be exposed would not have been inflicted by the United Kingdom. The Court held, however, that '[t]hese considerations cannot ... absolve the Contracting Parties from responsibility under Article 3 for all and any foreseeable consequences of extradition suffered outside their jurisdiction'.[82] The pertinent question would be

whether the extradition of a person to another State where he would be subjected or be likely to be subjected to torture or inhuman or degrading treatment or punishment would itself engage the responsibility of a Contracting State under Article 3.[83]

The Court remarked that

[i]t would hardly be compatible with the underlying values of the Convention ... were a Contracting State knowingly to surrender a fugitive to another State where there were substantial grounds for believing that he would be in danger of being subjected to torture, however heinous the crime allegedly committed. Extradition in such circumstances, while not explicitly referred to in the brief and general wording of article 3, would plainly be contrary to the spirit and intendment of the Article.[84]

---

[79] Human Rights Committee, CCPR General Comment No. 20, Replaces General Comment 7 Concerning Prohibition of Torture and Cruel Treatment of Punishment, para. 9.
[80] African Charter on Human and Peoples' Rights (Banjul Charta) of 27 June 1981, entered into force on 21 October 1986, 1520 UNTS 217.
[81] Rene Bruin and Kees Wouters, 'Terrorism', p. 23.
[82] ECtHR, *Soering v. United Kingdom*, Series A, No. 161, para. 86.
[83] *Ibid.*, para. 88. [84] *Ibid.*

The Court also extended this reasoning to the (as compared to torture less severe[85]) categories of inhuman or degrading treatment.[86] For the present study, the topical issue is the relationship between the principle of *non-refoulement* and the concept of complicity. The *Soering* type of situation is frequently distinguished from the situations covered by Article 16 ASR by the fact that *Soering* would involve an independently wrongful conduct involving another State whereas in the situation of complicity the very wrongfulness of the aid or assistance depends on the wrongfulness of the main actor's conduct.[87] To some extent, this distinction merits being upheld and underlined. The responsibility of the State which has extradited or repelled the person is not triggered for the reason of its support to the eventual maltreatment, but for the fact that it exposed the individual to that danger. In addition, an infringement upon the prohibition of *refoulement* triggers the responsibility of the extraditing State regardless of whether the torture or inhuman and degrading treatment eventually materialises. In situations covered by the concept of complicity, no responsibility would intervene if the wrongful act of the main actor was never committed as there is no such concept as an attempted internationally wrongful act.[88]

However, two considerations should be taken into account which may qualify this assessment. First, it needs to be borne in mind that States may extradite or transfer a person to another State with a view to having that person subjected to harsh interrogation procedures.[89] Whereas in this scenario the requirements of Article 16 ASR will most likely be met, there is no apparent reason why this conduct should not also trigger responsibility under the relevant provisions of human

---

[85] On the various theories concerning the delimitation between torture and inhuman and degrading treatment, see Walter Kälin and Jörg Künzli, *Universeller Menschenrechtsschutz*, 2nd edn (Basel/Baden-Baden: Helbig and Nomos, 2008), pp. 365 et seq.

[86] ECtHR, *Soering v. United Kingdom*, Series A, No. 161, para. 88.

[87] James Crawford, 'Second Report on State Responsibility', UN Doc. A/CN.4/498/Add.1, 3, para. 159; Andreas Felder, *Die Beihilfe*, p. 127.

[88] On attempt and complicity, see John Quigley, 'Complicity', p. 86; see also for the related issue of obligations of prevention and non-materialising wrongful acts ICJ, *Case Concerning the Application of the Prevention and Punishment of the Crime of Genocide*, Judgment, para. 431.

[89] For a legal assessment under the ECHR, see European Commission for Democracy through Law (Venice Commission), 'Opinion on the International Legal Obligations of Council of Europe Member States in Respect of Secret Detention Facilities and Inter-State Transfer of Detainees', Opinion No. 363/2005 of 17 March 2006, CDL-AD(2006)009, para. 68, on *refoulement*.

rights law.[90] In this light, provisions on *non-refoulement* could be seen as *leges speciales* to the general rule on complicity.[91]

This interpretation could be challenged by pointing towards the conceptually different structures of provisions which deal with complicity and those which address *refoulement*.[92] To argue that the two concepts are fundamentally different presupposes an understanding of complicity which is defined solely along the very narrow confines of Article 16 ASR. While Article 16 ASR is the generally recognised form in which States may incur responsibility for complicity in international law, other forms of complicity exist and do not fall within the scope of this provision.[93] In a broader perspective, the principle of *non-refoulement* may be seen as establishing a form of 'risk-based responsibility for complicity'. If examined more closely, the structural differences between complicity and *refoulement* are not that great. Under both concepts, the wrongfulness eventually depends on third State conduct. If State A is about to extradite Person B to State C in which B is likely to suffer torture or inhuman and degrading treatment, the conduct of State C is decisive for both responsibility for complicity and *refoulement*. The difference lies in the fact that in the complicity scenario it needs to be established that the wrongful treatment of B has actually intervened whereas in the *refoulement* scenario it is sufficient that there are serious grounds to believe that B will be subjected to these forms of treatment.

It is thus doubtful whether there exists a qualitative difference between these two conditions which would exclude the interpretation of the principle of *non-refoulement* as a form of *lex specialis* for complicity. Rather, the risk-based assessment of *non-refoulement* may also be understood as a precautionary mechanism which is set in place in order to prevent responsibility for complicity from coming into existence. The change from an assessment whether or not wrongful conduct has actually been committed to the assessment of an intervening risk is warranted from the viewpoint of an optimum protection of susceptible victims of torture: whereas a general rule of complicity may of course

---

[90] Cf Article 19 ASR: 'This Chapter [Chapter IV of Part One] is without prejudice to the international responsibility, under other provisions of these articles, of the State which commits the act in question, or any other State.'
[91] Christian J. Tams, 'Abuse', p. 318; see also Maurice Kamto, 'Fifth Report on the Expulsion of Aliens', UN Doc. A/CN.4/611, para. 78.
[92] Andreas Felder, *Die Beihilfe*, p. 133.
[93] Cf John Cerone, 'Re-examining', p. 533.

protect potential victims of torture as it could deter States from participating in such acts, the lowering of the threshold in order to find State responsibility in the situation when an individual is about to be deported is necessary in order to prevent the torture taking place in the first place. These functional arguments therefore militate for an interpretation which views the more general concept of complicity and the principle of *non-refoulement* together as two concepts which complement each other.

Secondly, the principle of *non-refoulement* may be seen as an important example where the standard of vigilance of potentially complicit States is raised due to the involvement of legal values being protected by a norm of peremptory status. There is widespread support for the finding that the prohibition of torture enjoys the rank of *jus cogens*.[94] This does not also automatically entail that the principle of *non-refoulement* is of the same status.[95] The manner in which the European Court of Human Rights has underlined the essential character of *non-refoulement* to the prohibition of torture[96] would, however, lend support to the view that *non-refoulement* indeed also benefits from the *jus cogens* nature of the prohibition of torture.[97] Being closely connected with the prohibition of torture itself, it benefits from the non-derogability under the CAT, the ECHR and the ICCPR. This interpretation has, however, recently been challenged in two court proceedings.

In the case of *Suresh* v. *Canada* before the Canadian Supreme Court, the non-derogability of the norm was at issue.[98] In this case, Suresh, a refugee from Sri Lanka, was about to be deported to his home country on grounds of national security, as he was a member of the Liberation Tigers of Tamil Eelam. He claimed that he would face a serious risk of

---

[94] ICTY, *Prosecutor* v. *Furundžija*, Case IT-95–17/1, 121 ILR 213, para. 153; ECtHR, *Al-Adsani* v. *United Kingdom*, ECHR 2001-XI, 79, para. 61; ILC Commentary, Article 26, para. 4; Alexander Orakhelashvili, *Peremptory Norms*, p. 54; Erika de Wet, 'Prohibition of Torture', pp. 97 *et seq.*

[95] Cautious in that regard are Elihu Lauterpacht and Daniel Bethlehem, 'Scope and Content', p. 141 (in the context of refugee law); the New Zealand Supreme Court has denied the *jus cogens* nature of *non-refoulement*: *Attorney General* v. *Ahmed Zaoui*, para. 51.

[96] ECtHR, *Soering* v. *United Kingdom*, Series A, No. 161, para. 88.

[97] See similarly Erika de Wet, 'Prohibition of Torture', p. 118; Jean Allain, 'The Jus Cogens Nature of Non-Refoulement', *International Journal of Refugee Law* 13 (2002), pp. 533–58; Rene Bruin and Kees Wouters, 'Terrorism', pp. 24–5.

[98] Supreme Court of Canada, *Suresh* v. *Canada (Minister of Citizenship and Immigration and Others)*, 124 ILR 343.

being tortured and invoked a violation of both international law and the Canadian Charter of Rights and Freedoms. The Canadian Supreme Court decided the case primarily on the basis of domestic law although it based 'its inquiry into the principles of fundamental justice' not only on Canadian law but also on 'international law, including *jus cogens*'.[99] The Court adopted a highly questionable approach in that regard, stipulating that:

> [d]etermining whether deportation to torture violates the principles of fundamental justice requires us to balance Canada's interest in combating terrorism and the Convention refugee's interest in not being deported to torture.[100]

The Court admitted, however, that some outcomes of balancing and testing the proportionality of decisions would be so extreme as to be ruled out in the first place.[101] The Court then indeed went on to confirm that the protection from torture under section 7 of the Canadian Charter of Rights and Freedoms applied not only domestically, but was also applicable to:

> deprivations of life, liberty or security effected by actors other than our government, if there is a sufficient causal connection between our government's participation and the deprivation ultimately effected … At least where Canada's participation is a necessary precondition for the deprivation and where the deprivation is an entirely foreseeable consequence of Canada's participation, the government does not avoid the guarantee of fundamental justice merely because the deprivation would be effected by someone else's hand.[102]

The Court then approached the matter from an international perspective.[103] It found substantial support for the assumption that the prohibition against torture constitutes a peremptory norm under international law which 'suggests that it cannot be easily derogated from'.[104] Although this may sound half-heartedly, one has to acknowledge that the Court eventually sided with a strict interpretation of Article 3 CAT. In sum, the Court affirmed a 'virtually categoric' rejection of State action leading to torture in general and deportation to torture specifically.[105] The Court left the Canadian government a certain leeway for

---

[99] *Ibid.*, p. 359, para. 46.   [100] *Ibid.*, para. 47.
[101] *Ibid.*   [102] *Ibid.*, p. 362, para. 54.
[103] The Court did not apply international law as a matter of obligation but rather to inform itself about principles of fundamental justice: 'We look to international law as evidence of these principles and not as controlling itself': *ibid.*, p. 363, para. 60.
[104] *Ibid.*, p. 365, para. 65.   [105] *Ibid.*, p. 368, para. 76.

'exceptional circumstances' in which deportation to face torture may be justified.[106]

In the *Saadi* case against Italy before the European Court of Human Rights, it was the United Kingdom government which intervened to argue for a development of the Court's case law away from its strict jurisprudence[107] into the direction of the more flexible approach adopted by the Canadian Supreme Court. In particular, the United Kingdom wished to establish a balancing process between the risk assessment concerning the possible torture of the person to be extradited and the security interests of the community of citizens in the country from which the person was to be deported. It argued that:

> in the event of expulsion, the treatment in question would be inflicted not by the signatory State but by the authorities of another State. The signatory State was then bound by a positive obligation of protection against torture implicitly derived from Article 3. Yet in the field of implied positive obligations the Court had accepted that the applicant's rights must be weighed against the interests of the community as a whole.[108]

The Court considered this argument to be 'misconceived'[109] and was not willing to accept that a distinction would have to be drawn between treatment directly inflicted by a signatory State and that of the authorities of another State.[110] In the words of the Court:

> Since protection against the treatment prohibited by Article 3 is absolute, that provision imposes an obligation not to extradite or expel any person who, in the receiving country, would run the real risk of being subjected to such treatment. As the Court has repeatedly held, there can be no derogation from that rule.[111]

The Court thus refused to view the principle of *non-refoulement* primarily as a matter deriving from positive obligations of the Contracting States under Article 1 ECHR and firmly anchored it in Article 3 ECHR.[112] In addition, its absolute character has been reaffirmed which excludes derogation according to Article 15(2) ECHR.[113] For the purposes of the

---

[106] Ibid., p. 369, para. 78.
[107] Identified with ECtHR, *Chahal v. United Kingdom*, ECHR 1996-V, 1831.
[108] ECtHR, *Saadi v. Italy*, para. 120.   [109] Ibid., para. 139.
[110] Ibid., para. 138.   [111] Ibid.
[112] Daniel Möckli, 'Saadi v. Italy – The Rules of the Game Have Not Changed', *Human Rights Law Review* 8 (2008), pp. 534–48, at p. 542.
[113] See also in this respect ECtHR, *Al-Saadoon and Mufdhi v. United Kingdom*, Merits and Just Satisfaction, para. 123.

present study, this means that within the scope of application of the ECHR, a strong, *jus cogens*-driven rule against a particular form of complicity exists which triggers risk-based responsibility and cannot be derogated from. Arguably, similar conclusions apply on the universal level for the Contracting States of the CAT where, likewise, Article 3 is not subject to derogation. That the UN Committee Against Torture is willing to apply equally cogent standards is shown by its decision in the case of *Agiza v. Sweden*. In that case, the Committee adopted a broad view of the obligations which are entailed by Article 3 CAT.[114] The Committee was especially sceptical about the value of a diplomatic assurance given by Egypt to Sweden that Mr Agiza would not be tortured.[115] Similar problems also arise in the jurisprudence of the ECtHR which has generally accepted that diplomatic assurances may considerably reduce the risk that a person will be subjected to torture once extradited.[116] However, one should hold with the Venice Commission of the Council of Europe that, although diplomatic assurances are in principle an 'expression of the necessary good faith and mutual trust between friendly States, … this general mutual trust must not prevail over the accurate examination of each specific situation'.[117]

2.3.3 Functionally similar rules: obligations of prevention

Another type of functionally similar rules may be seen in those human rights obligations which provide for positive duties on the side of Contracting States or establish obligations of prevention.[118] At first sight, there is no self-explanatory connection between the concept of positive obligations or obligations of prevention and the issue of complicity. However, as we have already seen,[119] the approach of the ICJ in its *Genocide Convention* case has provided a strong precedent which points in the direction of overlapping functions of the two categories.[120]

---

[114] Committee Against Torture, *Agiza v. Sweden*, CAT/C/34/D/233/2003, Decision of 20 May 2005.
[115] *Ibid.*, para. 13.4.
[116] ECtHR, *Mamatkulov and Askarov v. Turkey*, ECHR 2005-II, 293, para. 77.
[117] European Commission for Democracy through Law (Venice Commission), 'Opinion on the International Legal Obligations of Council of Europe Member States in respect of Secret Detention Facilities and Inter-State Transfer of Prisoners', Opinion No. 363/2005, CDL-AD(2006)009, paras. 141–2.
[118] John Cerone, 'Re-examining', pp. 527 and 532–3.
[119] See the discussion above in Chapter 7, text accompanying notes 209 *et seq.*
[120] ICJ, *Case Concerning the Application of the Convention on the Prevention and Punishment of the Crime of Genocide*, Judgment, para. 432.

The findings of the ICJ on Serbia's responsibility for not having complied with its obligation to prevent genocide under Article I of the Genocide Convention have already been discussed in Chapter 7 of this study. However, it deserves to be mentioned again briefly that the Court was not able to find responsibility of Serbia for complicity in genocide under Article III(e) of the Genocide Convention. This was due to the fact that the Court was not able to establish awareness on the part of the Serbian authorities of the genocidal intent of the perpetrators of the genocide in Srebrenica. At the same time, the overall amount of support for the authorities of the Republika Srpska by Serbia underlined the special relationship between the two entities.[121] In its judgment, the Court pointed to two main differences between the situation of complicity in genocide and a violation of the obligation to prevent which would 'make it impossible to treat the two types of violation in the same way'.[122] These two differences have to be seen, according to the Court, first in the fact that complicity would always require positive action whereas a violation of the obligation to prevent would result from a mere failure to act and, secondly, in the different standards pertaining to the knowledge of the State in question: 'an accomplice must have given support in perpetrating genocide with full knowledge of the facts', while 'a State may be found to have violated its obligation to prevent even though it had no certainty, at the time when it should have acted, but failed to do so, that genocide was about to be committed or was under way'.[123]

The amount of criticism the Court has been confronted with over this distinction shows that it is not at all inconceivable to see at least a close connection between a situation in which a State may incur responsibility for complicity and one in which it has violated an obligation of prevention.[124] One of the peculiarities of the reasoning of the ICJ in its *Genocide Convention* case is that the Court had to rely on the strength of the political, military and financial links between the Federal Republic of Yugoslavia and the Republika Srpska in order to find a violation of the obligation to prevent. The same links were at issue when the Court had to determine the responsibility for complicity.[125] In the end, the

---

[121] Ibid., para. 434.　[122] Ibid., para. 432.　[123] Ibid.
[124] Antonio Cassese, 'Criminal Law Notions', p. 885; Mark Gibney, 'Genocide', pp. 769 et seq.; Sandesh Sivakumaran, 'Application', p. 705; Philippe Weckel, 'L'arrêt', p. 326; Orna Ben-Naftali, 'The Obligations to Prevent and Punish Genocide', p. 41.
[125] Cf Monica Hakimi, 'State Bystander Responsibility', p. 364.

Court's reasoning thus boils down to a difference between the degree of awareness between complicity and the obligation to prevent on the one hand, and a complex distinction between mere support and support plus non-reaction on the other.

Seen from this perspective, positive obligations and obligations of prevention may also prove to be viable functional alternatives to Article 16 ASR which may in some cases make it easier to establish the responsibility of a complicit State. This may appear to be counterintuitive. Andrea Gattini has pointed out that in domestic legal systems, it usually takes more to incur responsibility for an omission than is the case with respect to complicity.[126] However, positive obligations and obligations of prevention could prove to be more flexible than a rigidly applied concept of complicity: first, determining the direct responsibility of a contracting party under a human rights instrument with respect to the compliance with positive obligations may absolve a court, tribunal or committee from having to consider the conduct of another State. Although no *Monetary Gold* principle in the technical sense would arguably hinder an international human rights body from doing so, it can safely be assumed that most courts would be reluctant to engage in such an assessment.[127]

Secondly, the criteria for a breach of a positive obligation are almost by definition vague; more so than this is the case with complicity. Accordingly, they allow for the consideration of policy questions. International courts and tribunals will have leeway to find a breach of these obligations if they consider the result of a negative finding on responsibility to be unjust in other regards.[128] Whether or not this would be a positive development is open to debate.[129] In fact, this 'relative benefit' of the inherently vague positive obligations over the restricted possibilities to find responsibility for complicity may once again prove the critics of positive obligations right, who never tire of pointing to the pitfalls of this concept. According to their sceptical position, positive obligations are a trigger mechanism for judicial activism, translating political choices into law.[130] With respect to the *Genocide Convention*

---

[126] Andrea Gattini, 'Breach', p. 703.
[127] See, e.g., ECtHR, *Saadi v. Italy*, para. 126.
[128] Monica Hakimi, 'State Bystander Responsibility', p. 366.
[129] For critical remarks in this context, see Jörg Künzli, *Unrechtsregimes*, p. 395.
[130] From the viewpoint of constitutional theory, see Bernhard Schlink, 'Freiheit durch Eingriffsabwehr – Rekonstruktion der klassischen Grundrechtsfunktion', *Europäische Grundrechte-Zeitschrift* 11 (1984), pp. 457–68; for similar criticism with

case, Antonio Cassese has spoken of a 'consolation prize' the Court has awarded.[131] This negative characterisation implies that the Court was not compelled by the state of the law to take this route but felt inclined to do so in order to offer the injured State something.

By pointing to these potential factors which could help to hold complicit States responsible more easily, it is understood that positive obligations will not be a panacea in that regard. They are rather understood as structural advantages positive obligations may have in some respects over the concept of complicity. These structural advantages will play out in some circumstances and will have no relevance in others. Arguably, they will come to the fore in a case where some form of implication of a contracting State to a human rights convention is apparent, but a finding of direct responsibility is not possible. A conceivable scenario could include a European State which is a party to the ECHR and which has cooperated with the United States in the programme of extraordinary renditions.[132] It may have sent some of its police officers to a third State where the alleged terrorist, a national of the European State, was held and potentially exposed to torture or inhuman and degrading treatment. These officers participated in an interrogation. It will be difficult to argue that this participation was relevant support to the commission of the unlawful interrogation methods in the form that would trigger responsibility under Article 16 ASR. Likewise, it is not clear whether the presence of these officers in an interrogation of a person held by another State could qualify as establishing the jurisdiction of the European State. In such a scenario, it is at least conceivable that the finding of a breach of a positive obligation could provide a way out of the dilemma of how to hold the complicit European State responsible. While it is counter-intuitive to assume that the requirements to find jurisdiction may be easier with respect to positive obligations than to the traditional, 'negative dimension' of human rights, some paradoxical elements of the jurisprudence of the ECtHR may indeed point in this direction.[133] It is to this issue that we shall now turn our attention.

---

respect to international law and the *Genocide Convention* case in particular, see Alexander Orakhelashvili, *The Interpretation of Acts and Rules*, pp. 147–8.

[131] Antonio Cassese, 'A Judicial Massacre', *The Guardian*, 27 February 2007.

[132] Cf UK High Court of Justice, *R (on the Application of Binyan Mohammed) v. Secretary of State for Foreign and Commonwealth Affairs*, para. 87.

[133] Olivier De Schutter, 'Globalization and Jurisdiction', p. 247.

2.3.4 Complicity and issues of jurisdiction

The relationship between complicity and the issue of jurisdiction in the meaning of human rights treaties has so far not been afforded a great deal of attention.[134]

2.3.4.1 General observations

Obligations incumbent upon States under human rights treaties are frequently limited to persons within the jurisdiction of a State. For example, Article 1 ECHR provides that '[t]he High Contracting Parties shall secure to everyone within their jurisdiction the rights and freedoms defined in Section I of this Convention'. Article 2(1) ICCPR provides that '[e]ach State Party to the present Covenant undertakes to respect and to ensure to all individuals within its territory and subject to its jurisdiction the rights recognized in the present Covenant'.[135] Apart from the various problems attached to the finding of the appropriate understandings of jurisdiction in these and other treaty regimes,[136] the interesting question for our study is whether State complicity with the

---

[134] But see Jörg Künzli, *Unrechtsregimes*, p. 395; Olivier De Schutter, 'Globalization and Jurisdiction', pp. 236 *et seq.*

[135] Other general jurisdiction clauses in human rights treaties include Article 7 of the International Convention on the Protection of the Rights of All Migrant Workers and Members of Their Families of 18 December 1990, entered into force on 1 July 2003, UN Doc. A/RES/45/158; Article 1(1) of the American Convention on Human Rights; Article 2(1) of the UN Convention on the Rights of the Child of 20 November 1989, entered into force on 2 September 1990, 1577 UNTS 3. Other treaties feature specific jurisdiction clauses: see, e.g., Article 3 of the Convention on the Elimination of All Racial Discrimination of 21 December 1965, entered into force on 4 January 1969, 660 UNTS 195, and the UN Convention Against Torture of 10 December 1984, which contains jurisdiction clauses in Articles 2(1), 5(1)(a), 5(2), 7(1), 11–13, 16 and 22(1), for an overview and comparison of these clauses, see Marko Milanovic, 'From Compromise to Principle: Clarifying the Concept of State Jurisdiction in Human Rights Treaties', *Human Rights Law Review* 8 (2008), pp. 411–48, at pp. 412 *et seq.*

[136] See generally on the notion of jurisdiction in this respect, Dirk Lorenz, *Der territoriale Anwendungsbereich der Grund- und Menschenrechte – Zugleich ein Beitrag zum Individualschutz in bewaffneten Konflikten* (Berlin: Berliner Wissenschafts-Verlag, 2005), pp. 62 *et seq.*; Marko Milanovic, 'From Compromise to Principle'; Georg Nolte, 'Das Verfassungsrecht vor den Herausforderungen der Globalisierung', *Veröffentlichungen der Vereinigung deutscher Staatsrechtslehrer* 67 (2007), pp. 129–59, at pp. 143 *et seq.*; Christian Tomuschat, *Human Rights*, pp. 126 *et seq.*; on the interpretation of the relationship between jurisdiction and territory in Article 2(1) ICCPR, see Human Rights Committee, General Comment 31, Nature of the General Legal Obligation on States Parties to the Covenant, UN Doc. CCPR/C/21/Rev.1/Add.13 (2004), para. 11.

conduct of another State which is both committed outside of the territory of the complicit State and constitutes a breach of a relevant human rights obligation takes place within the 'jurisdiction' of the complicit State under the human rights treaty in question. It is understood in this regard that generally human rights law applies extraterritorially if certain requirements are met;[137] despite this near-consensus, difficult questions arise in individual cases.

The problem is not only academic: the conduct of parties to the ECHR such as Poland or the Netherlands in arresting individuals and handing them over to the United Kingdom in Iraq for investigation or interrogation may serve as an example.[138] However, other scenarios are also conceivable in which it is by no means clear whether a person is within the jurisdiction of a complicit State: whereas generally human rights law applies on the national territories of the contracting States,[139] it is at least imaginable that a foreign State, be it a Member State of the ECHR or not, violates the human rights of an individual on the territory of the guest State with a degree of participation or collusion by the latter. In this respect, only a rebuttable presumption exists that a State exercises jurisdiction over its territory.[140] If it is prevented from doing so, infringements upon human rights taking place on a part of its territory over which it exercises no control may escape its jurisdiction.[141]

However, difficult cases may also arise in situations where a State is not generally prevented from exercising its jurisdiction on its territory. If we take, for instance, an abduction: is the home State which may have furnished intelligence and generally 'looked the other way' exercising jurisdiction? Whereas the answer in the latter scenario would

---

[137] See, with respect to the ICCPR, ICJ, *Legal Consequences of the Construction of a Wall in the Occupied Palestinian Territory*, Advisory Opinion, ICJ Rep. 2004, 136, para. 107; see generally Christian J. Tams, 'Abuse', p. 316.

[138] See, e.g., Michael Gondek, 'Extraterritorial Application of the European Convention on Human Rights: Territorial Focus in the Age of Globalization?', *Netherlands International Law Review* 52 (2003), pp. 349–87, at p. 350.

[139] ECtHR, *Ilascu and Others v. Moldova and Russia*, ECHR 2004-VII, 179, partly dissenting opinion of Judge Bratza, joined by Judges Rozakis, Hedigan, Thomassan and Pantiru, *ibid.*, p. 317, para. 3.

[140] Kjetil Mujezinovic Larsen, '"Territorial Non-Application" of the European Convention on Human Rights', *Nordic Journal of International Law* 78 (2009), pp. 73–93, at p. 79.

[141] Cf the reasoning in ECtHR, *Cyprus v. Turkey*, ECHR 2001-IV, 1, para. 78; see further Olivier De Schutter, 'Globalization and Jurisdiction', pp. 217 *et seq.*

most likely have to be in the affirmative,[142] it is also imaginable that the foreign State just profits from a generally permissive environment in which the conduct of foreign actors is not closely scrutinised. These considerations may suffice to show that difficult questions arise once several States participate in a violation of the human rights of an individual person.[143]

In this context, it should be understood that this issue is not simply a rehearsal where complicity incidentally plays a role; rather, it is crucial to understand how considerations of complicity may play a role in the field of human rights law in order to grasp more fully how primary rules in the field of human rights law and the general rule on complicity may complement each other and be part of the possible 'network' of rules on complicity.

2.3.4.2 The case law of the ECtHR: from Loizidou to Bankovic
Given the diversity of existing jurisdiction clauses and courts and treaty bodies which are responsible for the monitoring of compliance with their respective human rights agreements, it would exceed the scope of this study to provide for an exhaustive overview. Rather, we will focus here on the ECHR, the case law of the ECtHR being 'an excellent laboratory'[144] in this regard: the density of the jurisprudence of the Strasbourg Court and also the multitude of interactions between the contracting States of the ECHR promise potentially rich insights into the construction of the concept of jurisdiction.

Despite the wording of Article 1 ECHR, it has been held for a long time that the obligations of the States parties to the Convention are not limited to their national territory.[145] The early leading case in this regard is the Court's judgment in the *Loizidou* case.[146] In the case,

---

[142] Cf European Commission for Democracy through Law (Venice Commission), 'Opinion on the International Legal Obligations of Council of Europe Member States in respect of Secret Detention Facilities and Inter-State Transfer of Prisoners', Opinion No. 363/2005, CDL-AD(2006)009, para. 127.
[143] Cf Olivier De Schutter, 'Globalization and Jurisdiction', p. 191.
[144] *Ibid.*, p. 188.
[145] ECtHR, *Drozd and Janousek v. France and Spain*, Series A, No. 240, para. 91; European Commission for Human Rights, *Stocké v. Federal Republic of Germany*, Series A, No. 199, 24, para. 166; Jochen Abr. Frowein and Wolfgang Peukert, *Europäische Menschenrechtskonvention*, 3rd edn (Kehl: N. P. Engel, 2009), Article 1, paras. 4 *et seq.*; Christian Tomuschat, *Human Rights*, p. 126.
[146] ECtHR, *Loizidou v. Turkey*, Preliminary Objections, Series A, No, 310.

the Court recalls that, although Article 1 sets limits on the reach of the Convention, the concept of 'jurisdiction' under this provision is not restricted to the national territory of the High Contracting Parties ... the responsibility of Contracting Parties can be involved because of acts of their authorities, whether performed within or outside of national boundaries, which produce effects outside of their own territory.[147]

In order to further determine what these findings entailed in the concrete case – in which Turkey occupied the northern part of Cyprus and substantially backed the 'Turkish Republic of Northern Cyprus' – the Court explained:

Bearing in mind the object and purpose of the Convention, the responsibility of a contracting Party may also arise when as a consequence of military action – whether lawful or unlawful – it exercises effective control of an area outside of its national territory. The obligation to secure, in such an area, the rights and freedoms set out in the Convention derives from the fact of such control whether it be exercised directly, through its armed forces, or through a subordinate local administration.[148]

Hence, the Court established a connection between jurisdiction and the exercise of 'effective control' over a given territory. However, by this term the Court did not have in mind 'effective control' in the sense of the ICJ's *Nicaragua* case: rather, it elaborated, effective control was meant to be 'effective overall control'.[149] Implicitly, it also made clear that the notion of jurisdiction as understood in Article 1 ECHR differs from the general international law concept of jurisdiction with its component parts, i.e., jurisdiction to prescribe, enforce and adjudicate. Whereas the latter general concept of jurisdiction is meant to regulate when a State may *lawfully* exercise jurisdiction beyond its national borders – as these are the controversial situations – jurisdiction in the sense of Article 1 ECHR was meant to be understood in terms of a factual relationship between the exercise of public authority and the individual who is exposed to this exercise.[150]

---

[147] *Ibid.*, p. 23, para. 62.   [148] *Ibid.*
[149] ECtHR, *Loizidou* v. *Turkey*, Merits, ECHR 1996-VI, 2216, para. 56.
[150] See Olivier De Schutter, 'Globalization and Jurisdiction', pp. 196–7; Ralph Wilde, 'Triggering State Obligations Extraterritorially: The Spatial Test in Certain Human Rights Treaties', in Roberta Arnold and Noëlle Quénivet (eds.), *International Humanitarian Law and Human Rights Law – Towards a New Merger in International Law* (Leiden: Nijhoff, 2008), pp. 133–53, at pp. 138–9; Kjetil Mujezinovic Larsen, 'Territorial Non-Application', p. 78; cf further ICJ, *Legal Consequences for States of the Continued Presence of South Africa in Namibia (South West Africa) Notwithstanding Security*

All the more surprising then was the alternative route the Court took in its *Bankovic* case, decided in 2001. Dealing with air strikes against the former Yugoslavia by several NATO Member States, the Court literally made a U-turn and short-circuited the concept of jurisdiction in Article 1 ECHR with the one prevailing in general international law.[151] This interpretation was owed, in the opinion of the Court, to the requirement to interpret the Convention in light of 'any relevant rules of international law applicable in the relation between the parties' (Article 31(3)(c) of the Vienna Convention on the Law of Treaties).[152] In this perspective, the Court held the jurisdiction of States to be primarily territorial, reflecting the ordinary meaning of the term in general international law.[153] The Court acknowledged, of course, its previous jurisprudence on the extraterritorial effects of the Convention but distinguished it from the *Bankovic* case on various grounds relating, *inter alia*, to the notion of the *'espace juridique'* of the Convention to which the Federal Republic of Yugoslavia did not belong and to which the reach of the *ordre public* of the Convention thus did not extend.[154]

2.3.4.3 A normative and flexible concept of jurisdiction?
The picture which emerges from these two leading cases is thus mixed: whereas extraterritorial application of the Convention is possible, indeed even if conduct within the jurisdiction of the State causes

---

Council Resolution 276 (1970), Advisory Opinion, ICJ Rep. 1971, 16, para. 118: 'Physical control of a territory, and not sovereignty or legitimacy of title, is the basis of State liability for acts affecting other States.'

[151] Cf Marko Milanovic, 'From Compromise to Principle', pp. 417 *et seq.*
[152] ECtHR, *Bankovic and others v. Belgium and others*, ECHR 2001-XII, 334, para. 57.
[153] *Ibid.*, para. 61.
[154] *Ibid.*, para. 80; see on the *Bankovic* decision Heike Krieger, 'Die Verantwortlichkeit Deutschlands nach der EMRK für seine Streitkräfte im Auslandseinsatz', *Zeitschrift für ausländisches öffentliches Recht und Völkerrecht* 62 (2002), pp. 669–702, at pp. 670 *et seq.* (for a rather favourable commentary) and Alexander Orakhelashvili, 'Restrictive Interpretation of Human Rights Treaties in the Recent Jurisprudence of the European Court of Human Rights', *European Journal of International Law* 14 (2003), pp. 529–68, at pp. 538 *et seq.* (for critical remarks); see further Rick Lawson, 'Life After Bankovic: On the Extraterritorial Application of the European Convention on Human Rights', in Fons Coomans and Menno T. Kamminga (eds.), *Extraterritorial Application of Human Rights Treaties* (Antwerp: Intersentia, 2004), pp. 85–123; Dirk Lorenz, *Der territoriale Anwendungsbereich*, pp. 28 *et seq.* (and pp. 62 *et seq.* for further references); see also Cornelia Janik and Thomas Kleinlein, 'When Soering Went to Iraq ... Problems of Jurisdiction, Extraterritorial Effect and Norm Conflicts in Light of the European Court of Human Rights' Al-Saadoon Case', *Goettingen Journal of International Law* 1 (2009), pp. 459–518, at pp. 473 *et seq.*

effects beyond its borders, it is also limited to the *espace juridique* of the Convention, and even more importantly, the extraterritorial application should not be presumed. However, the picture changes, once again, if we take into consideration the *Ilascu* case the Court decided in 2004, a decision which is considered by some experts as the leading authority on the concept of jurisdiction in the sense of Article 1 ECHR.[155]

The ECtHR highlighted in *Ilascu* that support may entail jurisdictional control.[156] Here, Russia was, among other reasons, found to be responsible due to the presence of its military in the separatist region of Transdniestria and also due to support it gave to the separatist regime, the Moldovan Republic of Transdniestria (MRT).[157] The Court attached 'particular importance to the financial support enjoyed by the "MRT"'.[158] Furthermore, it held that:

the 'MRT', set up in 1991–92 with the support of the Russian Federation, vested with organs of power and its own administration, remains under the effective authority, or at the very least under the decisive influence, of the Russian Federation, and in any event that it survives by virtue of the military, economic, financial and political support given to it by the Russian Federation.

That being so, the Court considers that there is a continuous and uninterrupted link of responsibility on the part of the Russian Federation for the applicants' fate, as the Russian Federation's policy of support for the regime and collaboration with it continued beyond 5 May 1998, and after that date the Russian Federation made no attempt to put an end to the applicants' situation brought about by its agents, and did not act to prevent the violations allegedly committed after 5 May 1998.[159]

Accordingly, the Court considered the amount of support furnished by the Russian Federation to the MRT to be the decisive element in establishing Russian responsibility.[160] It may be wondered whether the

---

[155] Clare Ovey and Robin C. A. White, *The European Convention on Human Rights*, 4th edn (Oxford: Oxford University Press, 2006), p. 24; cf also Ioana Petculescu, 'Droit international de la responsabilité et droits de l'homme – A propos de l'arrêt de la Cour européenne des droits de l'homme du 8 juillet 2004 dans l'affaire Ilascu et autres c. la République de Moldova et la Fédération de Russie', *Revue générale de droit international public* 109 (2005), pp. 581–607, at p. 583; others consider it to be an isolated case, see Carlo Focarelli, 'Common Article 1', p. 140.
[156] See also Jörg Künzli, *Unrechtsregimes*, p. 395.
[157] ECtHR, *Ilascu and Others* v. *Moldova and Russia*, ECHR 2004-VII, 179.
[158] *Ibid.*, para. 390.   [159] *Ibid.*, paras. 392–3.
[160] See also Robert McCorquodale, 'Impact on State Responsibility', in Menno T. Kamminga and Martin Scheinin (eds.), *The Impact of Human Rights Law on General International Law* (Oxford: Oxford University Press, 2009), pp. 235–54, at p. 242.

influence of this case for our study is limited due to the fact that it was support to non-State actors which was at stake. However, it appears that the boundaries could be fluent in this regard. The regime in Transdniestria can be considered a stabilised *de facto* regime.[161] In such a case, the rules on inter-State complicity could arguably apply.[162] One could also be inclined to regard this finding of the Court as a mere continuation of its jurisprudence along the lines of *Loizidou*. However, the gradual mentioning of effective control, 'or at least decisive influence' and finally the considerations of support which contribute 'in any event' to the survival of the MRT show that the Court has applied an approach which is more flexible than its previous case law.

This image of jurisdiction turning into a relative concept is further corroborated by the treatment by the Court of the responsibility of Moldova. Although the Court acknowledged that the Moldovan government was not in a position to exercise effective control over Transdniestria due to the absolute control of the MRT,[163] it found Moldovan jurisdiction and ultimately considered that Moldova had not lived up to its positive obligations under the Convention:

> even in the absence of effective control over the Transdniestrian region, Moldova still has a positive obligation under Article 1 of the Convention to take the diplomatic, economic, judicial or other measures that it is in its powers to take and are in accordance with international law to secure to the applicants the rights guaranteed by the Convention.[164]

The Court's findings show considerable flexibility with respect to the notion of jurisdiction.[165] Jurisdiction finds itself decoupled from any understanding of effective control – a tendency which can also be found in other decisions of the Court.[166] Arguably, the category of jurisdiction

---

[161] Cf Ioana Petculescu, 'Droit international', p. 584.
[162] Cf Jochen Abr. Frowein, *Das de facto-Regime im Völkerrecht: eine Untersuchung zur Rechtsstellung 'nichtanerkannter' Staaten und ähnliche Gebilde* (Cologne: Heymanns, 1968), p. 86, on the general applicability of the law of State responsibility to *de facto* regimes; see also the application of Georgia instituting the case *Application of the International Convention on the Elimination of All Forms of Racial Discrimination (Georgia v. Russia)*, Application of 12 August 2008, para. 81, sub-paragraph (e) on the support of the Russian Federation for racial discrimination effected by the '*de facto* South Ossetian and Abkhaz separatist authorities'.
[163] ECtHR, *Ilascu and Others v. Moldova and Russia*, ECHR 2004-VII, 179, para. 330.
[164] Ibid., para. 331.   [165] Jörg Künzli, *Unrechtsregimes*, p. 395.
[166] ECtHR, *Agim Behrami and Bekir Behrami v. France* and *Ruzhdi Saramati v. France, Germany and Norway*; see on this case and the issue of extraterritorial application Heike Krieger, 'A Credibility Gap: The Behrami and Saramati Decision of the

is thus turned into a normative one, being a matter of degree.[167] The Court assesses for each situation whether specific State action was called for in light of the positive obligations as posited by the Convention. It also openly accounts for policy considerations whether or not a given conduct falls within the jurisdiction of a contracting party.[168] We may thus learn from *Ilascu* that support (i.e., complicity) may bring a situation within the jurisdiction of a State even though the main action is committed by a different actor. The question is, however, whether this jurisprudence will have repercussions beyond this scheme. Russia was held responsible not least due to its support for the separatist movement in Transdniestria. However, this situation did not equal the most typical complicity-type situations. Instead, it bordered on the edge of dependency.[169] Although some authors have vehemently argued for an expansion of the concept of State jurisdiction to cover complicity situations in extraterritorial contexts,[170] it remains to be seen whether the Court will prove to be responsive in that regard.

The further development of the Court's jurisprudence since the *Ilascu* case confirm the finding that the Court is rather flexible in its approach. Whereas the *Issa* case brought about some qualifications of the *Bankovic* ruling,[171] the decision on jurisdiction and admissibility in the *al-Saadoon* case has confirmed the Court's earlier position on jurisdiction in cases which involve physical control over individuals.[172] In the words of two commentators, the Court's case law is 'far from consistent – oscillating between normative and factual criteria'.[173] It is thus ultimately the Court's ultra-flexible approach which makes predictions unreliable whether State jurisdiction can be found in situations which involve complicity.[174] Obviously, any assessment will have to be made with respect to the facts of the individual case.

European Court of Human Rights', *Journal of International Peacekeeping* 13 (2009), pp. 159–80, at pp. 162 *et seq.*

[167] Cf Olivier De Schutter, 'Globalization and Jurisdiction', p. 222.
[168] ECtHR, *Assanidze v. Georgia*, ECHR 2004-II, 221, para. 142.
[169] See also Cornelia Janik and Thomas Kleinlein, 'When Soering Went to Iraq', p. 480.
[170] Mark Gibney, Katarina Tomasevski and Jens Vedsted-Hansen, 'Transnational State Responsibility', pp. 267–8; Sigrun I. Skogly, *Beyond National Borders*, pp. 35 *et seq.*
[171] ECtHR, *Issa and Others v. Turkey*, especially at paras. 67 *et seq.*
[172] ECtHR, *Al-Saadoon and Mufdhi v. United Kingdom*, Decision on Admissibility, paras. 84 *et seq.*
[173] Cornelia Janik and Thomas Kleinlein, 'When Soering Went to Iraq', p. 482.
[174] Jörg Künzli, *Unrechtsregimes*, p. 395; for criticism on the Court's arbitrariness, see also Alexander Orakhelashvili, *The Interpretation of Acts and Rules*, p. 143.

2.3.4.4 Cooperation in Iraq: the case of Saddam Hussein

The closest the Court so far came to evaluating a genuine complicity-type situation was the case of *Saddam Hussein v. Albania and Others*.[175] The former Iraqi president brought an individual complaint against several members of the informal coalition which had attacked Iraq. Hussein alleged violations of the Convention rights in the form of his arrest, detention, handover and ongoing trial. Without developing an argument of complicity, he held that the coalition States exercised *de facto* power in Iraq even after the June 2004 transfer of authority to the transitional government. The Court did not find the complaint to be admissible due to a lack of exercise of jurisdiction on the part of the States concerned. It argued:

> the Court considers that the applicant has not established that he fell within the jurisdiction of the respondent States on any of the bases alleged. The Court considers that he has not demonstrated that those States had jurisdiction on the basis of their control of the territory where the alleged violations took place ... Even if he could have fallen within a State's jurisdiction because of his detention by it, he has not shown that any one of the respondent States had any responsibility for, or any involvement or role in, his arrest and subsequent detention ... This failure to substantiate any such involvement also constitutes a response to his final submission to the effect that the respondent States were responsible for the acts of their military agents abroad. Finally, there is no basis in the Convention's jurisprudence and the applicant has not invoked any established principle of international law which would mean that he fell within the respondent States' jurisdiction on the sole basis that those States allegedly formed part (at varying unspecified levels) of a coalition with the US, when the impugned actions were carried out by the US, when security in the zone in which those actions took place was assigned to the US and when the overall command of the coalition was vested in the US.[176]

The reasoning of the Court thus appears to imply that jurisdiction will not be extended to a complicit State due solely to the fact that a State forms part of a coalition with another State. At the same time, it mentioned that the applicant failed to point to an established principle of international law. This could be meant to imply that in a case

---

[175] ECtHR, *Saddam Hussein v. Albania, Bulgaria, Croatia, Czech Republic, Denmark, Estonia, Hungary, Iceland, Ireland, Italy, Latvia, Lithuania, the Netherlands, Poland, Portugal, Romania, Slovakia, Slovenia, Turkey, Ukraine and the United Kingdom.*
[176] *Ibid.*

which falls squarely under Article 16 ASR – as the *Saddam Hussein* case arguably did not – it could reconsider its jurisprudence.

2.3.4.5 *The jurisprudence of the Canadian Supreme Court*

If the Court was willing to engage in some form of judicial borrowing, it could find inspiration in the jurisprudence of the Canadian Supreme Court. We have already discussed how this Court finds the Canadian Charter of Rights and Freedoms to be applicable if Canada acts extraterritorially and if, in that context, Canada participates in the commission of internationally wrongful acts.[177] The Canadian Supreme Court did not directly refer to Article 16 ASR but appeared to apply a principle which comes close to it.

While this jurisprudence needs to be distinguished from the question whether an international human rights treaty applies extraterritorially, there are some linkages between the two questions. What is noteworthy is that the reason why the Canadian Charter of Rights and Freedoms does not generally apply extraterritorially is, according to the Canadian Supreme Court, comity. In this context, the Court understands comity to embody the idea that Canada cannot prescribe the content of its laws for actions which are not covered by its bases of jurisdiction.[178] This position is fairly close to that of the ECtHR in *Bankovic* where the Court conflated the concept of jurisdiction in Article 1 ECHR with the issue whether a State is allowed to exercise prescriptive and enforcement jurisdiction.[179] To a certain extent, a decision not to apply the ECHR beyond the *'espace juridique'* of the Convention could also be seen as a form of comity, i.e., a form of self-restraint not to impose the *ordre public européen* beyond its original borders.

Borrowing from the Canadian jurisprudence would, however, be a fruitful exercise as there the limits of comity have now been clearly defined. If Canadian agents participate in activities by other States which are clearly wrongful under international law, comity does not apply. If the ECtHR is to further develop the lines of its *Bankovic* jurisprudence, the construction of the Canadian Supreme Court could help it to minimise some of the adverse consequences, i.e., that a large

---

[177] Supreme Court of Canada, *Canada (Justice) v. Khadr*, 2008 SCC 28, paras. 24 *et seq.*; see further the presentation of the case in Chapter 4 above, text accompanying notes 121 *et seq.*
[178] Supreme Court of Canada, *R v. Hape*, 2007 SCC 26, para. 50.
[179] See the text accompanying note 150 above.

number of situations will fall outside of the scope of its jurisdiction. Whether this is a policy objective shared by a majority of the judges of the Court is another question. However, it could help to translate the prohibition of complicity into human rights law.

2.3.5 Interim conclusion

The foregoing considerations on issues of human rights law may not warrant the belief that international law has brought about a general 'obligation to prevent'[180] human rights violations. Nonetheless, we can hold with Christian Tams that a general tendency is discernible: under human rights law, states are ever more frequently held responsible for human rights violations they have not themselves committed.[181] In general, it has been observed that human rights bodies have a liberal recourse to the rules of State responsibility and find responsibility in situations where this would not normally be the case.[182] This may be owed, especially in the context of the Inter-American and the European system of human rights protection, to the tendencies towards dynamic interpretation of the relevant treaty instruments.[183] The examples we have discussed show that human rights law may provide for alternative bases of responsibility for complicity (for example, *non-refoulement*, obligations of prevention) or that it may find creative ways around barriers such as the notion of jurisdiction which could, *prima facie*, rule out the possibility of responsibility for complicity in a majority of cases.

3 Conclusion

The analysis of three distinct areas of international law should not lead us to draw overly broad general conclusions. However, our examinations of the rules of the *jus ad bellum*, international humanitarian law and human rights law have all shown that international law may provide for more far-reaching rules on State complicity which cure some

---

[180] See, however, Monica Hakimi, 'State Bystander Responsibility'.
[181] Christian J. Tams, 'Abuse', p. 317.
[182] Malcolm D. Evans, 'State Responsibility', p. 140; Kjetil Mujezinovic Larsen, 'Attribution', p. 518.
[183] On the dynamic interpretation of the ECHR Constance Grewe, 'Vergleich zwischen den Interpretationsmethoden europäischer Verfassungsgerichte und des Europäischen Gerichtshofs für Menschenrechte', *Zeitschrift für ausländisches öffentliches Recht und Völkerrecht* 61 (2001), pp. 461–73, at pp. 466 *et seq.*

of the deficiencies which are attached to Article 16 ASR. We have seen different modes of a mutual reinforcement: whereas the rules pertaining to the use of force provide for differentiated consequences for complicit State behaviour, depending on various factors at play, international humanitarian law provides for a functionally similar rule, the obligation 'to ensure respect' for the 1949 Geneva Conventions which demands more of complicit States than is the case with Article 16 ASR. In the field of human rights law, the picture is more diverse: special rules on complicity complement each other with functionally similar rules. This leaves us with the question whether these developments, desirable as they may be, do not considerably reduce the scope of application of Article 16 ASR. In other words, how important can a provision be which, due to its inherent normative features, excludes a great number of cases from its applicability, and needs to be supplemented by other rules which go considerably further? In this respect, one should not be too pessimistic about the impact of Article 16 ASR; and that for a number of reasons.

First, it is by no means the case that the picture we have portrayed in this chapter holds true for the majority of other parts of international law. We have canvassed three fields in which other rules come to apply. However, in the vast majority of cases, such special rules will not be at the disposal of an injured State which wishes to bring a claim against a complicit State. One need only consider the enormously important areas of the law of consular and diplomatic relations, international economic law in all its facets, air and space law or the law of the sea where no such functional equivalents to Article 16 ASR can be identified. Accordingly, the scope of application of Article 16 ASR will remain large enough if only for this reason.

Secondly, the relationship between Article 16 ASR and the more special rules which we have discussed fits perfectly well the conception of the law of international responsibility which has inspired the ILC in its work. The prevalence of more special rules is expressly recognised in Article 55 ASR.[184] Special Rapporteur James Crawford has defended the inclusion of Article 16 ASR as a secondary rule by reference to its relation to more demanding primary rules. The relationship between primary and secondary (or 'special' and 'general' rules, as we prefer to

---

[184] The provision also applies to the whole of the ASR and not just with respect to Part Two, as was the case with Draft Article 37 as adopted in 1996, see ILC Commentary, Article 55, para. 6.

call them in this study) was explained by him in terms of the stricter standards to which States have committed themselves in primary (special) rules on complicity.[185] The application of the *lex specialis* principle to our examples may seem less obvious than in other cases. After all, one could say that, for example, positive obligations cannot be viewed as more special emanations of a rule on complicity. While this is true in the abstract, this view would cling too much to the general distinction between primary and secondary rules as it is said to underlie the construction of the ASR. We have already noted above that, for Article 16 ASR, this distinction was applied in a less rigorous manner than with respect to the other rules of State responsibility.[186] In this perspective, Article 16 ASR is a form of hybrid rule, sitting somewhere in between the categories of primary and secondary rules. Seen from this angle, it is only natural that emanations of *lex specialis* may have roots in both primary and secondary rules.

This leads to a third reason why the general rule on complicity is important despite the presence of more specialised and stringent rules on the same matter: through their existence, the general rules of the law of State responsibility continue to represent an important part of the normative environment in which more specialised rules need to be seen. The special can only be defined in terms of its reference to the general. By existing as a matrix for other mechanisms in the field of State responsibility, they provide guidance for the making and application of international law.[187] Although they may not expressly be referred to, they represent a source of potential inspiration for other fields of the law.[188] In the absence of an express derogation (i.e., the direct provision of a rule on complicity), they will continue to represent the applicable law and will determine how primary rules are to be interpreted when complicity is at stake.[189] Even if other rules take precedence and are deemed to be applicable instead of the general rule on complicity, Article 16 ASR may provide a yardstick of 'no return beyond this point'.

---

[185] James Crawford, Statement at the 2578th Meeting of 28 May 1999, YBILC 1999, Vol. I, p. 78, para. 39.
[186] See the text accompanying notes 432 *et seq.* in Chapter 4 above.
[187] Christian J. Tams, 'Unity and Diversity', p. 459.
[188] 'Fragmentation of International Law: Difficulties Arising from the Diversification and Expansion of International Law', Report of the Study Group of the International Law Commission, finalized by Martti Koskenniemi, UN Doc. A/CN.4/L.682, para. 102.
[189] Cf, *mutatis mutandis*, ICJ, *North Sea Continental Shelf Cases*, Judgment, ICJ Rep. 1969, 3, para. 63; ICJ, *Elettronica Sicula SpA (ELSI)*, Judgment, ICJ Rep. 1989, 15, para. 50.

States are of course free to modify the existing rules on international responsibility *inter se*. For example, a group of States may agree to apply, between them, a different standard of responsibility which does not provide possibilities for holding complicit States responsible. However, such an agreement would have no effect *vis-à-vis* third States, and it is also doubtful whether this could apply with respect to human rights guarantees which protect the rights and interests of individuals. On the universal level, it is conceivable only that the UN Security Council may derogate from the general law of responsibility and absolve States of their responsibility for complicity.[190] Although not spelled out directly, one may infer such an objective on the part of the Security Council in the way it allowed for cooperation with the occupying powers in Iraq after the 2003 invasion.[191]

A fourth reason for the importance of a general rule on complicity exceeds the realm of positivist analysis. Although Article 16 ASR is primarily targeted at the inter-State level, its existence may play an important role beyond that level. The 'language' of complicity is especially powerful, as it has strong moral undercurrents:[192] international law is no longer solely used by traditional and recognised international actors. It is also an important part of domestic and international discourses in civil society. It enhances the capability of individual citizens and NGOs to attack the conduct of governments in the language of law.[193] It connects with the expectation nurtured by the concept of an international rule of law that international law will no longer tolerate complicit State behaviour.

---

[190] Generally on the possibilities the Security Council may have in this regard, see Giorgio Gaja, 'The Impact of Security Council Resolutions on State Responsibility', in Georg Nolte (ed.), *Peace Through International Law – The Role of the International Law Commission* (Berlin: Springer, 2009), pp. 53–60.
[191] UN Doc. S/RES/1483 (2003).
[192] See Vaughan Lowe, 'Responsibility', pp. 14–15.
[193] See further Christine Chinkin, 'Continuing Occupation?', p. 183; Andreas Fischer-Lescano, *Globalverfassung*, pp. 89 *et seq.*

General conclusions

We will present our general conclusions in two steps: first we will summarise our findings with respect to the status of Article 16 ASR in international law as well as its application and interpretation, before turning to its wider, conceptual implications in a second step.

1 Summary of the main findings

1. Article 16 ASR is an expression of customary international law. Although this status was already affirmed by the International Court of Justice in the *Genocide Convention* case, it remained open to doubt whether State practice and *opinio juris* met the requisite criteria for this finding. The analysis of the customary law status of Article 16 ASR has shown that the practice of States is general and of a sufficient density to allow one to speak of a customary rule. This finding is supplemented by an analysis of governmental comments and statements which help to establish the requisite *opinio juris*.

2. With respect to the concept of 'aid or assistance' in Article 16 ASR, it can be noted that a close nexus between the support and the eventual wrongful act of the main actor is required. This is owing to a comparative analysis of special rules on complicity which do not allow one to speak of assistance in the case of mere association. In other words, more than cooperation alone is required in order to bring about responsibility for complicity.

3. Although the ILC requires some form of causality between the support rendered and the commission of the wrongful act, caution needs to be applied in this regard. Notions of causality are not easily applicable with respect to complicity as too demanding criteria in this regard would effectively mean treating joint main actors as

accomplices. Nevertheless, a substantial effect of the aid or assistance upon the commission of the wrongful act is required. This can be understood to mean that the aid or assistance must have made a difference for the main actor, rendering it materially easier to commit the wrongful act.

4. Aid or assistance can also consist of omissions. Although the ICJ has commented negatively on this issue, it is not apparent from the work of the ILC that omissions could not trigger responsibility for complicity. High standards will have to be met in order to find responsibility in such cases. Nonetheless, situations are conceivable where this will be practically relevant.

5. With respect to the subjective requirement in Article 16 ASR, intent on the part of the complicit State is required. This follows both from the analysis of international practice as well as from considerations concerning the construction of Article 16 ASR. The intent need not be focused on the eventual effect of the wrongful act of the main actor, but on the contribution of the complicit State to the commission of the wrongful act. This does not require the complicit State to actually wish for the outcome of the wrongful act. The establishment of the intent of the helping State will have to be determined in the specific case at hand. Inferences can be drawn from the circumstances in which its conduct took place. However, this does not mean that intent can, as a rule, always be inferred from supportive conduct. This would effectively mean that the helping State would need to prove that it did not wish to render aid or assistance to the commission of an internationally wrongful act. Such a reversal of the burden of proof for situations of complicity is not warranted.

6. Article 16(b) ASR requires that the complicit State needs to be bound by the obligation that the main actor has violated. For the majority of situations, this requirement will not pose particular problems. In the case of largely parallel obligations emanating from different sources, for example human rights obligations rooted in different regional agreements, it is, however, difficult to determine whether this criterion is fulfilled. Whereas this issue raises complex questions of legal theory (the identity or difference between rules, norms and sources), it can be observed with the ICJ that different rules representing nearly identical norms remain distinct in international law. However, where a common principle underlies the distinct rules or norms, it is argued that Article 16(b) ASR should be applied more liberally. It would run counter to the object and purpose of human rights treaties if States

could defend support for violations of human rights by pointing to the fact that the main actor would be technically violating a different human rights obligation which is, however, identical in substance to the one to which the complicit State is bound.

7. With respect to the consequences of responsibility for complicity, it can be observed that complicity does not lead to joint and several responsibility. Rather, the complicit State will only have to compensate for a share of the injury. In the case of monetary compensation, this will almost necessarily lead to difficult exercises in determining the shares of responsibility. Hence, satisfaction appears to be an appropriate remedy for cases of complicity as it is easier to decouple from these difficult calculations. In order not to turn into a symbolic basis for responsibility, courts, arbitrators and other decision-makers should make use of the possibility of awarding a monetary form of satisfaction.

8. Furthermore, difficulties exist in holding complicit States responsible before international courts and tribunals. As their jurisdiction is regularly based on the principle of consent, it is problematic that disputes between the complicit State and the injured State implicitly involve a third party, i.e., the main actor. Under the *Monetary Gold* principle of the ICJ, it will thus in many cases be difficult to bring a complicit State before the Court. However, the jurisprudence of the ICJ is diverse enough to allow for a reconsideration of this issue in the future. Moreover, other international courts and tribunals do not have such a strict rule on the indispensable third party. In addition, the growing willingness of domestic courts to apply the rules of State responsibility promises to be an alternative avenue for considerations of State complicity.

9. In the regime of 'aggravated responsibility' which is constituted by Articles 40 and 41 ASR, a separate obligation of non-assistance applies 'after the fact'. In this respect, it needs to be distinguished from the obligation of non-recognition to which it is closely related. The ILC understood the obligations of non-assistance in Articles 16 and 41(2) ASR to be closely related. This suggests that a close nexus between the assistance and the maintenance of the situation brought about by the serious breach of the peremptory norm is required also for complicity under Article 41(2) ASR. This provides a criterion to distinguish it from non-recognition which focuses on more general forms of cooperation which are not susceptible to contribute directly to the maintenance of the situation.

10. The concept of complicity is modified in further respects when violations of *jus cogens* norms have been supported. In these cases, Article 41(2) ASR presupposes no intent on the part of the complicit State. In addition, it may be questioned whether the fact that complicity with violations of *jus cogens* is at stake entails further modifications. These are not readily identifiable in the current state of the law. With respect to the progressive development of the law, one should, however, take account of the 'promotional' role of *jus cogens* which would allow judges of international courts and tribunals to contribute to the development of stricter standards for complicity when *jus cogens* is at stake.

11. With respect to other aspects of the regime of aggravated responsibility, an integrated view of its elements is desirable. As the approach of the ICJ in the *Genocide Convention* case has shown, a close relation exists between obligations of prevention and the issue of complicity. Obligations of prevention may provide the means to hold a State responsible where the less flexible criteria for complicity rule out such a finding. In addition, the concept of complicity is a valuable addition to the discussion on countermeasures in the collective interest. For some cases, it may be argued that States not only have the faculty to adopt such countermeasures, but that they are under a heightened expectation to do so as they would otherwise incur responsibility for complicity. While this does not amount to a duty to react to serious breaches of peremptory norms, it is a first step in this direction. Furthermore, introducing considerations of complicity into the debate on countermeasures in the collective interest may help to rationalise this debate and to distinguish between situations in which the taking of such countermeasures is clearly warranted and others in which this is not the case.

12. Furthermore, the general rules on complicity embodied in the ASR need to be seen as part of a larger network on rules against complicity. Other rules may be found in primary norms which directly establish responsibility for complicity. Functionally similar rules such as the obligation of *non-refoulement* or positive obligations in the field of human rights law may complement the general rule on complicity. With respect to the use of force in international relations, both the *jus ad bellum* and the *jus in bello* provide for additional rules which provide for more demanding criteria States need to respect in order not to face responsibility for complicity. Where there exist special rules on complicity in international law, Article 16 continues to provide a matrix for

the interpretation of these special rules. These special rules need not technically address the issue of complicity. For example, obligations of prevention have a different focus. However, they allow to attribute responsibility in situations where States are supporting other violations of international law under different conditions as would be the case for responsibility for complicity.

2 Complicity and the international rule of law

The present study has considered the problem of complicity through a particular prism – the international rule of law. This concept has not so much a fixed content; rather the rule of law was presented here as a particular approach to understanding the international legal system as materially complete, and thus as able to answer practical questions from an informed and principled standpoint. This concept is thus more an analytical tool than a blueprint which would entail direct normative consequences. It was used in order to show that, from a systemic viewpoint, there would be a presumption for the existence of rules on complicity in today's international legal system. This presumption has been derived from the finding that otherwise a situation of conflict of rights would exist between the freedom of the helping State to engage in supportive conduct, which would otherwise not be directly prohibited, and the freedom of the State injured by the conduct of the main actor and, indirectly, the complicit State. Such a situation could be solved by recourse to the principle of abuse of rights which is, however, vague and would not present a significant step forward in the direction of a legal system which offers differentiated responses to such situations. As we have been able to confirm the presumption for the existence of a rule on complicity in terms of positive law, the question remains what use there is for a continuing reference to the international rule of law and abuse of rights as concepts and principles sitting in the background of the norms on complicity.

The answer is that the rule of law underlines the significance and importance of the problem of complicity. It becomes apparent that the issue of complicity has more to do with the general development of the international legal system than might be suspected at first sight. The rule of law offers us a conceptual perspective on complicity which is attractive and, at the same time, less prone to evoking ideological cleavages than the saga of the evolution of international law from bilateralism to community interest. The international rule of law is an ideal which is shared by many different voices in academia and practice. It also has the benefit of being generally recognised by States as a principle for the organisation of international relations.[1] Critics may say that the concept of the rule of law is inherently vague. Through the connection with concrete problems such as complicity in international law, it may, however, become more definite and help to push the development of international law in the direction of a more encompassing form of compliance with the law.

The potential of rules on complicity to contribute to this development lies in the fact that they are on the one hand a fairly modest instrument. Rules on complicity do not depend on grand themes or designs in order to justify their existence. On the other hand, we have also shown that they are able to impact upon the very same issues that the concepts deal with which are usually associated with the protection of the community interest. Through its defining features, the concept of complicity is also better suited to dealing with the deficiencies which still characterise the international legal system. It aims at suppressing participation in wrongful acts. It thus entails 'a negative', whereas the means to enforce the community interest, such as countermeasures in the collective interest or the 'responsibility to protect', require positive action. In this respect, the latter instruments are more vulnerable to abuse and give States which take the enforcement of the law into their own hands a certain leeway which sits uneasily with the concept of the international rule of law. After all, the rule of law has always been conceived of as something directed against arbitrariness and overbroad margins of discretion. Incidentally, our position is an expression of a preference for a more formal understanding of the rule of law at the international level. In the philosophical debate, Joseph Raz has called the rule of law an 'essentially negative value'.[2] Some commentators in the international debate have maintained that the international rule of law will have to confine itself to a formal notion.[3] A focus on complicity as a rule requiring abstention connects well with these positions. Complicity operates under the umbrella of a 'principle of legality': either there is responsibility or there is not.

This 'negative' direction of a norm on complicity is noteworthy in its own right. When Wolfgang Friedmann described the development

---

[1] See the UN World Summit Outcome Document, A/RES/60/1, para. 134.
[2] Joseph Raz, 'The Rule of Law and Its Virtue', p. 224.
[3] Simon Chesterman, 'An International Rule of Law?', p. 333.

of international law from a stage of coexistence to one of cooperation in 1964, he also identified a 'move of international society', namely, 'from an essentially negative code of rules of abstention to positive rules of cooperation'.[4] Friedmann readily admitted, however, that this move towards cooperation had not yet taken root in the whole universe of international law. Rather, it was confined to some sectoral areas. International law in general could be characterised by a duality between coexistence and cooperation.[5] Nearly fifty years later, this is still a fitting analysis. As James Crawford has written:

> Institutions have been created, have changed and developed, many new rules and arrangements have come into existence. But, in principle, the foundations do not appear to have changed (statehood, treaty, custom, consent, acquiescence ...). Thus we have the apparent paradox of rapidly expanding horizons and a simple, not to say, elemental set of underpinnings.[6]

The particular charm of the concept of complicity is, in this perspective, that it offers answers to problems which are community-related: it determines the degree of necessary international solidarity in the face of violations of international law. At the same time, an obligation not to engage in complicity does not have to leave behind the traditional 'code of abstention'. It is thus an instrument for the promotion of the community interest in traditional guise; or, to paraphrase the formulation of Bruno Simma, an emanation of 'community interest on a bilateralist grounding'.[7]

In order to make a difference in 'real life', this analysis has to rest on a further assumption, namely, the understanding that the interdependence of today's world is large enough to make non-assistance a powerful tool in international relations. Serious violations of international law also occur without the involvement of other States. In such a situation, considerations of complicity obviously have no role to play. If, for example, an oppressive regime carries out massacres among its internal opposition and no outside intervention is possible, the international community will have to resort to other lawful mechanisms in order to bring the situation to an end. A look at major contemporary crises reveals, however, that, more often than not, there is external influence upon a situation. Whether it is Rwanda in 1994 or Darfur

---

[4] Wolfgang Friedmann, *The Changing Structure*, p. 62.   [5] *Ibid.*, p. 367.
[6] James Crawford, *International Law as an Open System*, p. 17.
[7] Bruno Simma, 'From Bilateralism to Community Interest', pp. 248–9.

today, it will in most cases be possible to point to outside actors which have a decisive influence upon the way these tragedies unfold.

A further point needs to be addressed: is it not deeply disappointing that, instead of proposing solidarity in terms of more active involvement in the life and fate of others, mere abstention is argued for? Is this not a step back beyond what international law has already achieved? In response to these questions, it should first of all be remarked that this study does not argue that complicity is 'the' new tool for the enforcement of the community interest in international law. It is not stipulated here that reliance upon a prohibition of complicity will always be enough. If an imminent genocide is to be prevented, it is obviously no choice to sit back and take comfort in the fact that one is not directly complicit in it. The ICJ itself has made it clear that all States parties to the Genocide Convention have an obligation to prevent genocide from occurring. Depending on the intensity of the links they have with a State about to commit genocide, this may call for positive action,[8] especially if the UN Security Council has taken further action. This study is not directed at necessary forms of cooperative international action in the face of ongoing or imminent tragedies. Rather, it argues for a shift of focus. The magnitude of the catastrophes often coincides with the grandeur of the legal concepts in which refuge is sought: humanitarian intervention, the responsibility to protect or countermeasures in the collective interest. In this perspective, the issue of complicity is frequently overlooked. The magnitude of such crises may, however, be reduced if more emphasis is put on the concept of complicity. If States scrutinise their connections with wrongful conduct at an earlier stage, the need for recourse to more intrusive mechanisms may be reduced. One could also argue that, before States take positive enforcement action, they should have scrutinised possible complicity with the situation they wish to affect. When they are not complicit themselves, they may remind other States of their obligation not to assist the wrongful acts of the State engaged in the commission. In this light, a prohibition of complicity could become part of a larger principle of proportionality in the enforcement of the community interest.[9]

---

[8] ICJ, *Case Concerning the Application of the Convention on the Prevention and Punishment of the Crime of Genocide*, Judgment, paras. 432 et seq.

[9] On proportionality as a limit to the enforcement of the community interest in international law, see also, *mutatis mutandis*, Georg Nolte, 'Article 2(7)', in Bruno

This would require a greater awareness of the issue of complicity among international lawyers and decision-makers. It is not intended here to oversell the issue of complicity. However, it is true that as a legal concept, the importance of complicity is not always properly understood. Its current significance still lags behind the scope of its potential application. While it is not a primary task for the academic international lawyer to change this state of affairs, an awareness of the existing state of the law may help to bring issues of complicity to the fore in a larger number of situations. In recent years, we have seen important steps in this direction. It has been argued here that it is no longer possible to deny the existence of a rule against complicity in customary international law. The contours of this rule may still be unclear in some areas. Whereas this study has, for example, argued that the current state of the law requires the finding of a subjective element on the part of the complicit State, i.e., its intent, it is of course possible for international practice to challenge this finding and to develop the rule further in the direction of a more objective form of responsibility for complicity. Arguably, such a more objective form of responsibility would presuppose progress on the institutional side of the law as well. There is no better recipe for disappointment than an immense development of international law in substantive terms which then falls foul of a lack of accompanying steps on the procedural level.

In this light, some caution in the interpretation of Article 16 ASR is no kowtow in the face of power politics. Intercourse between States is so dense as to have the potential to bring a large number of situations within the realm of a norm on complicity which should not entail responsibility in this regard. Proponents who argue for 'more' responsibility for complicity should be aware of potentially adverse consequences. If States become too timid about cooperation with other States, the result would be more isolationism than can be considered healthy for the development of international relations. In the end, this could amount to what Adorno has held in his *Minima Moralia*: 'Mere affability is participation in injustice.'[10] For the context in which Adorno wrote in 1951, this view is understandable, to say the least. However,

---

Simma (ed.), *The Charter of the United Nations – A Commentary*, 2nd edn (Oxford: Oxford University Press, 2002), para. 75.

[10] Theodor W. Adorno, *Minima Moralia – Reflexionen aus dem beschädigten Leben* (Frankfurt/Main: Suhrkamp, 2003), p. 26 ('Umgänglichkeit selber ist Teilhabe am Unrecht'; translation by the author).

it is an assessment too sweeping for the needs of international law. If all States were complicit with one another all of the time, the need for legal rules to differentiate between what is wrongful and what is not would disappear. If international law is to draw sensible lines between behaviour which entails responsibility and which does not, it should not contribute to the feeling that it is eventually unavoidable to incur responsibility for mere association with other States.

The issues here are similar to the larger question how the international system is to be organised: is a 'League of Democracies' to be preferred over the system of the UN? Moral rigour would answer in the affirmative: why should 'we' deal with States which flagrantly violate human rights and other obligations? So far, however, the better arguments appear to militate for an inclusive approach to world politics. As one philosopher, Tamar Schapiro, put it, 'insisting on strict adherence to high-minded standards of conduct in the face of others' wrongdoing can be naïve at best, and at worst tragically misguided'.[11]

The striking of a subtle balance is thus required: keeping the channels of cooperation and communication between States open while not allowing such forms of intercourse to stray into complicity.

---

[11] Tamar Schapiro, 'Compliance, Complicity, and the Nature of Nonideal Conditions', *Journal of Philosophy* 100 (2003), pp. 329–55, at p. 329.

Bibliography

Abi-Saab, Georges, 'The Concept of "International Crimes" and Its Place in Contemporary International Law', in Joseph H. H. Weiler, Antonio Cassese and Marina Spinedi (eds.), *International Crimes of States – A Critical Analysis of the ILC's Draft Article 19 on State Responsibility* (Berlin: de Gruyter, 1989), pp. 141–50.
  'Que reste-t-il du "crime international"?', in *Droit du pouvoir – Pouvoir du droit: Mélanges offerts à Jean Salmon* (Brussels: Bruylant, 2007), pp. 69–91.
Adorno, Theodor W., *Minima Moralia – Reflexionen aus dem beschädigten Leben* (Frankfurt/Main: Suhrkamp, 2003, paperback edition, originally published in 1951).
Ago, Roberto, 'Le délit international', *Recueil des Cours* 68 (1939-II), pp. 415–554.
  'Das Verschulden im völkerrechtlichen Unrecht', *Zeitschrift für öffentliches Recht* 20 (1940), pp. 449–84.
Akande, Dapo, 'Nuclear Weapons, Unclear Law? Deciphering the Nuclear Weapons Advisory Opinion of the International Court of Justice', *British Year Book of International Law* 68 (1997), pp. 165–217.
Akehurst, Michael, 'State Responsibility for the Wrongful Acts of Rebels – An Aspect of the Southern Rhodesia Problem', *British Year Book of International Law* 43 (1968-9), pp. 49–70.
  'Reprisals by Third States', *British Year Book of International Law* 44 (1970), pp. 1–18.
  'Custom as a Source in International Law', *British Year Book of International Law* 47 (1974-5), pp. 1–53.
  'Equity and General Principles of Law', *International and Comparative Law Quarterly* 25 (1976), pp. 801–25.
Alexy, Helmut, 'Völkerrechtliche Praxis der Bundesrepublik Deutschland im Jahre 1958', *Zeitschrift für ausländisches öffentliches Recht und Völkerrecht* 20 (1960), pp. 636–82.
Allain, Jean, 'The Jus Cogens Nature of Non-Refoulement', *International Journal of Refugee Law* 13 (2002), pp. 533–58.

Alland, Denis, 'Countermeasures of General Interest', *European Journal of International Law* 13 (2002), pp. 1221-39.
Allott, Philip, 'State Responsibility and the Unmaking of International Law', *Harvard International Law Journal* 29 (1988), pp. 1-26.
  Eunomia – New Order for a New World (Oxford: Oxford University Press, 1990).
  The Health of Nations – Society and Law Beyond the State (Cambridge: Cambridge University Press, 2002).
Alvarez, Alejandro, *Le droit international nouveau dans ses rapports avec la vie actuelle des peuples* (Paris: Pedone, 1959).
Ambos, Kai, *Der Allgemeine Teil des Völkerstrafrechts – Ansätze einer Dogmatisierung* (Berlin: Duncker & Humblot, 2002).
  'Article 25', in Otto Triffterer (ed.), *Commentary on the Rome Statute of the International Criminal Court – Observers' Notes, Article by Article*, 2nd edn (Munich/Oxford: C. H. Beck and Hart, 2008), pp. 743-77.
Amerasinghe, Chittharanjan F., *Evidence in International Litigation* (Leiden: Nijhoff, 2005).
  Diplomatic Protection (Oxford: Oxford University Press, 2008).
Anghie, Antony, *Imperialism, Sovereignty and the Making of International Law* (Cambridge: Cambridge University Press, 2005).
Anzilotti, Dionisio, 'La responsabilité internationale des Etats à raison des dommages soufferts par des étrangers', *Revue générale de droit international public* 13 (1906), pp. 5-29 and pp. 285-309.
  Lehrbuch des Völkerrechts, Vol. 1, *Einführung – Allgemeine Lehren, Übersetzung der 3. erweiterten und revidierten italienischen Ausgabe* (Berlin/Leipzig: de Gruyter, 1929).
Appelbaum, Christian, *Einschränkungen der Staatenimmunität in Fällen schwerer Menschenrechtsverletzungen – Klagen von Bürgern gegen einen fremden Staat oder ausländische staatliche Funktionsträger vor nationalen Gerichten* (Berlin: Duncker & Humblot, 2007).
Arangio-Ruiz, Gaetano, 'The Normative Role of the General Assembly of the United Nations and the Declaration of Principles of Friendly Relations', *Recueil des Cours* 137 (1972-III), pp. 419-742.
Arend, Katrin, 'Article 10 DSU', in Rüdiger Wolfrum, Peter-Tobias Stoll and Karen Kaiser (eds.), *Max Planck Commentaries on World Trade Law*, Vol. 2, *WTO – Institutions and Dispute Settlement* (Leiden: Nijhoff, 2006), pp. 373-85.
Aust, Anthony, *Modern Treaty Law and Practice*, 2nd edn (Cambridge: Cambridge University Press, 2007).
Aust, Helmut Philipp, 'Through the Prism of Diversity – The Articles on State Responsibility in the Light of the ILC Fragmentation Report', *German Yearbook of International Law* 49 (2006), pp. 165-200.
  'German Constitutional Law Cases 2004-2006', *European Public Law* 13 (2007), pp. 205-21.
  'The Normative Environment for Peace – On the Contribution of the ILC's Articles on State Responsibility', in Georg Nolte (ed.), *Peace Through*

International Law – The Role of the International Law Commission (Berlin: Springer, 2009), pp. 13-46.
Aust, Helmut Philipp and Georg Nolte, 'International Law and the Rule of Law of the National Level', in André Nollkaemper, Randy Peerenboom and Michael Zürn (eds.), *The Dynamics of the Rule of Law*, forthcoming.
Aust, Helmut Philipp and Mindia Vashakmadze, 'Parliamentary Consent to the Use of the German Armed Forces Abroad: The 2008 AWACS Decision of the Federal Constitutional Court', *German Law Journal* 9 (2008), pp. 2223-36.
Azzam, Fateh, 'The Duty of Third States to Implement and Enforce International Humanitarian Law', *Nordic Journal of International Law* 66 (1997), pp. 55-75.
Ballreich, Hans, 'Treaties, Effects on Third States', in Rudolf Bernhardt (ed.), *Encyclopedia of Public International Law*, Vol. 4 (Amsterdam: Elsevier, 2000), pp. 945-9.
Barker, J. Craig, *The Abuse of Diplomatic Privileges and Immunities – A Necessary Evil?* (Aldershot: Ashgate, 1996).
Barnidge, Robert P., 'Questioning the Legitimacy of Jus Cogens in the Global Legal Order', *Israel Yearbook of Human Rights* 38 (2008), pp. 199-225.
Bartels, Lorand, 'Article XX of GATT and the Problem of Extraterritorial Jurisdiction – The Case of Trade Measures for the Protection of Human Rights', *Journal of World Trade* 36 (2002), pp. 353-403.
  Human Rights Conditionality in the EU's International Agreements (Oxford: Oxford University Press, 2005).
Bassiouni, M. Cherif, 'A Functional Approach to "General Principles of International Law"', *Michigan Journal of International Law* 11 (1990), pp. 768-818.
Bastid, Suzanne, *Les traités dans la vie internationale – Conclusion et effets* (Paris: Economica, 1985).
Bauer, Andreas F., *Effektivität und Legitimität – Die Entwicklung der Friedenssicherung durch Zwang nach Kapitel VII der Charta der Vereinten Nationen unter besonderer Berücksichtigung der neueren Praxis des Sicherheitsrates* (Berlin: Duncker & Humblot, 1996).
Bauer, Franz J., *Das 'lange' 19. Jahrhundert – Profil einer Epoche* (Stuttgart: Reclam, 2004).
Beaulac, Stéphane, 'The Rule of Law in International Law Today', in Gianluigi Palombella and Neil Walker (eds.), *Relocating the Rule of Law* (Oxford: Hart, 2009), pp. 197-223.
Becker, Tal, *Terrorism and the State – Rethinking the Rules of State Responsibility* (Oxford: Hart, 2006).
Bederman, David J., 'Counterintuiting Countermeasures', *American Journal of International Law* 96 (2002), pp. 817-32.
Ben-Naftali, Orna, 'The Obligations to Prevent and Punish Genocide', in Paola Gaeta (ed.), *The UN Genocide Convention – A Commentary* (Oxford: Oxford University Press, 2009), pp. 27-57.

Benvenisti, Eyal, 'The Conception of International Law as a Legal System', *German Yearbook of International Law* 50 (2007), pp. 393–405.
Benvenisti, Eyal and George W. Downs, 'The Emperor's New Clothes: Political Economy and the Fragmentation of International Law', *Stanford Law Review* 60 (2007), pp. 595–631.
Berber, Friedrich, *Die Rechtsquellen des internationalen Wassernutzungsrechts* (München: Oldenbourg, 1955).
Bernhardt, Rudolf, 'Article 103', in Bruno Simma (ed.), *The Charter of the United Nations – A Commentary*, 2nd edn (Oxford: Oxford University Press, 2002), pp. 1292–1302.
  'Article 59', in Andreas Zimmermann, Christian Tomuschat and Karin Oellers-Frahm (eds.), *The Statute of the International Court of Justice – A Commentary* (Oxford: Oxford University Press, 2006), pp. 1231–51.
Bernstorff, Jochen von, *Der Glaube an das universale Recht – Zur Völkerrechtstheorie Hans Kelsens und seiner Schüler* (Baden-Baden: Nomos, 2001).
Besson, Samantha, 'La pluralité d'Etats responsable – Vers une solidarité internationale?', *Schweizerische Zeitschrift für Internationales und Europäisches Recht* 17 (2007), pp. 13–38.
Bethlehem, Daniel L. (ed.), *The Kuwait Crisis: Sanctions and Their Economic Consequences*, Part I (Cambridge: Cambridge University Press, 1991).
Bianchi, Andrea, 'Denying State Immunity to Violators of Human Rights', *Austrian Journal of Public and International Law* 46 (1994), pp. 195–229.
  'L'immunité des Etats et les violations graves des droits de l'homme: la fonction de l'interprète dans la détermination du droit international', *Revue générale de droit international public* 108 (2004), pp. 63–101.
  'Ferrini v. Federal Republic of Germany', *American Journal of International Law* 99 (2005), pp. 242–8.
  'Human Rights and the Magic of Jus Cogens', *European Journal of International Law* 19 (2008), pp. 491–508.
Bindschedler, Rudolf L., 'Neutrality, Concept and General Rules', in Rudolf Bernhardt (ed.), *Encyclopedia of Public International Law*, Vol. III, J–P (Amsterdam: Elsevier, 1997), pp. 549–53.
Birnie, Patricia W., Alan E. Boyle and Catherine Redgwell, *International Law and the Environment*, 3rd edn (Oxford: Oxford University Press, 2009).
Bleckmann, Albert, 'Die Handlungsfreiheit der Staaten – System und Struktur der Völkerrechtsordnung', *Österreichische Zeitschrift für öffentliches Recht und Völkerrecht* 29 (1978), pp. 173–96.
Blum, Gabriella, 'Bilateralism, Multilateralism, and the Architecture of International Law', *Harvard International Law Journal* 49 (2008), pp. 323–79.
Bluntschli, Johann Casper, *Das moderne Völkerrecht der civilisirten Staaten als Rechtsbuch dargestellt* (Nördlingen: C. H. Beck, 1868).
Bodansky, Daniel, 'Non Liquet and the Incompleteness of International Law', in Laurence Boisson de Chazournes and Philippe Sands (eds.), *The International Court of Justice, International Law and Nuclear Weapons* (Cambridge: Cambridge University Press, 1999), pp. 153–70.

Bodeau-Livinec, Pierre, Gionata P. Buzzini and Santiago Villalpando, 'Case Note (on Behrami and Behrami v. France, Samarati v. France, Germany and Norway)', *American Journal of International Law* 102 (2008), pp. 323–31.

Boeck, Charles de, 'L'expulsion et les difficultés internationales qu'en soulève la pratique', *Recueil des Cours* 18 (1927-III), pp. 443–650.

Bogdandy, Armin von, 'The Telos of International Law', in Pierre-Marie Dupuy, Bardo Fassbender, Malcolm N. Shaw and Karl-Peter Sommermann (eds.), *Völkerrecht als Wertordnung – Festschrift für Christian Tomuschat* (Kehl: N. P. Engel, 2006), pp. 703–21.

Bogdandy, Armin von and Markus Rau, 'The Lotus', in Rüdiger Wolfrum (ed.), *Max Planck Encyclopedia of Public International Law*, online edition (Oxford: Oxford University Press, 2008), available at www.mpepil.com (last visited 1 November 2010).

Boisson de Chazournes, Laurence and Luigi Condorelli, 'Common Article 1 of the Geneva Conventions Revisited: Protecting Collective Interests', *International Review of the Red Cross* 82 (2000), No. 837, pp. 67–87.

Boivin, Alexandra, 'Complicity and Beyond: International Law and the Transfer of Small Arms and Light Weapons', *International Review of the Red Cross* 87 (2005), No. 887, pp. 467–96.

Bollecker-Stern, Brigitte, *Le préjudice dans la théorie de la responsabilité internationale* (Paris: Pedone, 1973).

Bonafè, Beatrice I., *The Relationship Between State and Individual Responsibility for International Crimes* (Leiden: Nijhoff, 2009).

Borchard, Edwin M., 'War, Neutrality and Non-Belligerency', *American Journal of International Law* 35 (1941), pp. 618–25.

Bothe, Michael, 'Neutrality', in Dieter Fleck (ed.), *The Handbook of Humanitarian Law in Armed Conflict* (Oxford: Oxford University Press, 1995), pp. 485–515.

'Der Irak-Krieg und das völkerrechtliche Gewaltverbot', *Archiv des Völkerrechts* 41 (2003), pp. 255–71.

Boyle, Alan and Christine Chinkin, *The Making of International Law* (Oxford: Oxford University Press, 2007).

Brehm, Maya, 'The Arms Trade and States' Duty to Ensure Respect for Humanitarian and Human Rights Law', *Journal of Conflict and Security Law* 12 (2008), pp. 359–87.

Brierly, J. L., 'The Theory of Implied State Complicity in International Claims', *British Year Book of International Law* 9 (1928), pp. 42–9.

Briggs, Herbert W., 'Neglected Aspects of the Destroyer Deal', *American Journal of International Law* 34 (1940), pp. 569–87.

Brownlie, Ian, *International Law and the Use of Force by States* (Oxford: Clarendon Press, 1963).

'Recognition in Theory and Practice', *British Year Book of International Law* 53 (1982), pp. 197–211.

State Responsibility (Oxford: Oxford University Press, 1983).

'Discussion Statement', in Antonio Cassese and Joseph H. H. Weiler (eds.), *Change and Stability in International Law-Making* (Berlin: de Gruyter, 1988), pp. 108–10.

The Rule of Law in International Affairs (The Hague: Nijhoff, 1998).
Principles of Public International Law, 7th edn (Oxford: Oxford University Press, 2008).
Bruin, Rene and Kees Wouters, 'Terrorism and the Non-Derogability of Non-Refoulement', *International Journal of Refugee Law* 15 (2003), pp. 5–29.
Brunkhorst, Hauke, *Solidarität – Von der Bürgerfreundschaft zur globalen Rechtsgenossenschaft* (Frankfurt/Main: Suhrkamp, 2002).
Brunnée, Jutta, 'International Law and Collective Concerns: Reflections on the Responsibility to Protect', in Tafsir Malick Ndiaye and Rüdiger Wolfrum (eds.), *Law of the Sea, Environmental Law and Settlement of Disputes: Liber Amicorum Judge Thomas A. Mensah* (Leiden: Nijhoff, 2007), pp. 35–51.
Buchwald, Todd F. and Michael J. Matheson, 'US Security Assistance and Related Programs', in John Norton Moore and Robert F. Turner (eds.), *National Security Law* (Durham, NC: Carolina Academic Press, 2005), pp. 1179–1206.
Burri, Thomas, 'The Kosovo Opinion and Secession: The Sounds of Silence and Missing Links', *German Law Journal* 11 (2010), pp. 881–9.
Buzzini, Gionata P., 'La théorie des sources face au droit international général: réflexions sur l'émergence du droit objectif dans l'ordre juridique internationale', *Revue générale de droit international public* 106 (2002), pp. 581–617.
Byers, Michael, 'Conceptualising the Relationship Between Jus Cogens and Erga Omnes Rules', *Nordic Journal of International Law* 66 (1997), pp. 211–39.
Custom, Power and the Power of Rules – International Relations and Customary International Law (Cambridge: Cambridge University Press, 1999).
'Abuse of Rights: An Old Principle, a New Age', *McGill Law Review* 47 (2001–2), pp. 389–431.
'Afghanistan: We Cannot Risk Complicity in Torture', *Globe and Mail*, 27 September 2005, p. A17.
'Extraditing Schreiber Now Violates International Law', *Globe and Mail*, 30 January 2008, available at www.theglobeandmail.com (commercial archives).
Bynkershoek, Cornelius van, *Quaestionum Juris Publici Libri Duo*, translated by Tenney Frank, No. 14 of 'The Classics of International Law', Vol. 2 (Oxford: Clarendon Press, 1930, originally published 1737).
Caflisch, Lucius, 'La pratique suisse en matière de droit international public 2005', *Schweizerische Zeitschrift für Internationales und Europäisches Recht* 16 (2006), pp. 605–57.
Cançado Trindade, Antônio Augusto, 'The Development of International Human Rights Law by the Operation and Case-Law of the European and the Inter-American Courts of Human Rights', *Human Rights Law Journal* 25 (2004), pp. 157–60.
'International Law for Humankind: Towards a New Jus Gentium (I), General Course on Public International Law', *Recueil des Cours* 316 (2006), pp. 9–440.

'International Law for Humankind: Towards a New Jus Gentium (II), General Course on Public International Law', *Recueil des Cours* 317 (2006), pp. 9–312.
Caplan, Lee M., 'State Immunity, Human Rights, and Jus Cogens: A Critique of the Normative Hierarchy Theory', *American Journal of International Law* 97 (2003), pp. 741–81.
Capotorti, Francesco, 'Cours général de droit international public', *Recueil des Cours* 248 (1994-IV), pp. 9–344.
Caron, David D., 'The Basis of Responsibility: Attribution and Other Transsubstantive Rules', in Richard B. Lillich and Daniel Barstow Magraw (eds.), *The Iran–United States Claims Tribunal: Its Contribution to the Law of State Responsibility* (Irvington-on-Hudson, NY: Transnational, 1998), pp. 109–84.
  'The ILC Articles on State Responsibility: The Paradoxical Relationship Between Authority and Form', *American Journal of International Law* 96 (2002), pp. 857–73.
Carty, Anthony, *Philosophy of International Law* (Edinburgh: Edinburgh University Press, 2007).
Cassese, Antonio, 'Foreign Economic Assistance and Respect for Civil and Political Rights: Chile – A Case Study', *Texas International Law Journal* 14 (1979), pp. 251–63.
  International Law in a Divided World (Oxford: Clarendon Press, 1986).
  'Statement', in Antonio Cassese and Joseph H. H. Weiler (eds.), *Change and Stability in International Law-Making* (Berlin: de Gruyter, 1988), pp. 112–13.
  'Remarks on Scelle's Theory of "Role-Splitting" (Dédoublement Fonctionnel) in International Law', *European Journal of International Law* 1 (1990), pp. 210–31.
  International Law, 2nd edn (Oxford: Oxford University Press, 2005).
  'A Judicial Massacre', *The Guardian*, 27 February 2007, available at http://commentisfree.guardian.co.uk/antonio_cassese/2007/02/the_judicial_massacre_of_srebr.html (last visited 1 November 2010).
  'On the Use of Criminal Law Notions in Determining State Responsibility for Genocide', *Journal of International Criminal Justice* 5 (2007), pp. 875–87.
  'The Nicaragua and Tadic Tests Revisited in Light of the ICJ Judgment on Genocide in Bosnia', *European Journal of International Law* 18 (2007), pp. 649–68.
  International Criminal Law, 3rd edn (Oxford: Oxford University Press, 2008).
Cerone, John, 'Re-examining International Responsibility: "Complicity" in the Context of Human Rights Violations', *ILSA Journal of International and Comparative Law* 14 (2008), pp. 525–34.
Červenka, Zdenek, 'Rhodesia Five Years After the Unilateral Declaration of Independence', *Verfassung und Recht in Übersee* 4 (1971), pp. 9–30.
Chadwick, Elizabeth, *Traditional Neutrality Revisited* (The Hague: Kluwer, 2002).

Charney, Jonathan I., 'The Persistent Objector Rule and the Development of Customary International Law', *British Year Book of International Law* 56 (1985), pp. 1–24.
  'Universal International Law', *American Journal of International Law* 87 (1993), pp. 529–51.
Cheng, Bin, *General Principles of Law as Applied by International Courts and Tribunals* (London: Stevens, 1953).
  'Custom: The Future of General State Practice in a Divided World', in Ronald St John Macdonald and Douglas M. Johnston (eds.), *The Structure and Process of International Law* (Dordrecht: Martinus Nijhoff, 1986), pp. 513–54.
Chesterman, Simon, 'An International Rule of Law?', *American Journal of Comparative Law* 56 (2008), pp. 331–61.
  'The Turn to Ethics: Disinvestment from Multinational Corporations for Human Rights Violations – The Case of Norway's Sovereign Wealth Fund', *American University International Law Review* 23 (2008), pp. 577–615.
  'Rule of Law', in Rüdiger Wolfrum (ed.), *Max Planck Encyclopedia of Public International Law*, online edition (Oxford: Oxford University Press, 2008).
Chinkin, Christine, *Third Parties in International Law* (Oxford: Clarendon Press, 1993).
  'The East Timor Case', *International and Comparative Law Quarterly* 45 (1996), pp. 712–25.
  'Article 62', in Andreas Zimmermann, Christian Tomuschat and Karin Oellers-Frahm (eds.), *The Statute of the International Court of Justice – A Commentary* (Oxford: Oxford University Press, 2006), pp. 1331–68.
  'The Continuing Occupation? Issues of Joint and Several Liability and Effective Control', in Phil Shiner and Andrew Williams (eds.), *The Iraq War and International Law* (Oxford: Hart, 2008), pp. 161–83.
Christakis, Théodore, 'L'obligation de non-reconnaissance des situations créés par le recours illicite à la force ou d'autres actes enfreignant des règles fondamentales', in Christian Tomuschat and Jean-Marc Thouvenin (eds.), *The Fundamental Rules of the International Legal Order – Jus Cogens and Obligations Erga Omnes* (Leiden: Nijhoff, 2006), pp. 127–66.
Christenson, Gordon A., 'Attributing Acts of Omission to the State', *Michigan Journal of International Law* 12 (1991), pp. 312–70.
Clapham, Andrew, 'Symbiosis in International Human Rights Law: The Öcalan Case and the Evolving Law on the Death Penalty', *Journal of International Criminal Justice* 1 (2003), pp. 475–89.
  'Responsibility to Protect – "Some Sort of Commitment"', in Vincent Chetail (ed.), *Conflits, sécurité et coopération – Liber Amicorum Victor-Yves Ghebali* (Brussels: Bruylant, 2007), pp. 169–92.
  'The Jus Cogens Prohibition of Torture and the Importance of Sovereign State Immunity', in Marcelo G. Kohen (ed.), *Promoting Justice, Human Rights and Conflict Resolution Through International Law – Liber Amicorum Lucius Caflisch* (Leiden: Nijhoff, 2007), pp. 151–69.

Clapham, Andrew and Scott Jerbi, 'Categories of Corporate Complicity in Human Rights Abuses', *Hastings International and Comparative Law Review* 24 (2001), pp. 339-49.

Clark, Roger S., 'Obligations of Third States in the Face of Illegality – Ruminations Inspired by the Weeramantry Dissent in the Case Concerning East Timor', in Antony Anghie (ed.), *Legal Visions of the 21st Century – Essays in Honour of Judge Christopher Weeramantry* (The Hague: Kluwer, 1998), pp. 631-51.

Cohen, Stephen B., 'Conditioning US Security Assistance on Human Rights Practices', *American Journal of International Law* 76 (1982), pp. 246-79.

Combacau, Jean, *Le pouvoir de sanction de l'ONU – Etude théorique de la coercition non militaire* (Paris: Pedone, 1974).

Combacau, Jean and Serge Sur, *Droit international public*, 7th edn (Paris: Montchrestien, 2006).

Condorelli, Luigi and Laurence Boisson de Chazournes, 'Quelques remarques à propos de l'obligation des Etats de "respecter et faire respecter" le droit international humanitaire "en toutes circonstances"', in Christophe Swinarski (ed.), *Etudes et essais sur le droit international humanitaire et sur les principes de la Croix-Rouge en l'honneur de Jean Pictet* (Leiden: Nijhoff, 1984), pp. 17-35.

Conforti, Benedetto, 'Cours général de droit international public', *Recueil des Cours* 212 (1988-V), pp. 9-210.

The Law and Practice of the United Nations, 3rd edn (Leiden: Nijhoff, 2005).

Corten, Olivier, 'Quels droits et quels devoirs pour les Etats tiers? Les effets juridiques d'une assistance à un acte d'aggression', in Karine Bannelier, Théodore Christakis, Olivier Corten and Pierre Klein (eds.), *L'intervention en Irak et le droit international* (Paris: Pedone, 2004), pp. 105-28.

'L'arrêt rendu par la CIJ dans l'affaire du crime de génocide (Bosnie-Herzégovine c. Serbie): Vers un assouplissement des conditions permettant d'engager la responsabilité d'un Etat pour génocide?', *Annuaire français de droit international* 53 (2007), pp. 249-79.

Le droit contre la guerre (Paris: Pedone, 2008).

Corten, Olivier and Pierre Klein (eds.), *Les Conventions de Vienne sur le droit des traités – Commentaire article par article*, Vols. I-III (Brussels: Bruylant, 2006).

Craig, Paul, 'Formal and Substantive Conceptions of the Rule of Law: An Analytical Framework', *Public Law* (1997), pp. 467-87.

Crawford, James, 'Revising the Draft Articles on State Responsibility', *European Journal of International Law* 10 (1999), pp. 435-60.

International Law as an Open System (London: Cameron May, 2002).

'The ILC Articles on State Responsibility: A Retrospect', *American Journal of International Law* 96 (2002), pp. 874-90.

(ed.), *The International Law Commission's Articles on State Responsibility, Introduction, Text and Commentaries* (Cambridge: Cambridge University Press, 2002).

'International Law and the Rule of Law', *Adelaide Law Review* 24 (2003), pp. 3-12.

'Responsibility of States and Non-State Actors', Speech at the Biennial Conference of the Japanese Association of International Law, Tokyo, 14 May 2005, manuscript on file with the author.

The Creation of States in International Law, 2nd edn (Oxford: Oxford University Press, 2006).

'Multilateral Rights and Obligations in International Law', *Recueil des Cours* 319 (2007), pp. 325-482.

Cryer, Robert, Hakan Friman, Darryl Robinson and Elizabeth Wilmshurst, *An Introduction to International Criminal Law and Procedure* (Cambridge: Cambridge University Press, 2007).

Dahm, Georg, Jost Delbrück and Rüdiger Wolfrum, *Völkerrecht*, Vol. I/1, 2nd edn (Berlin: de Gruyter, 1989).

Völkerrecht, Vol. I/3, 2nd edn (Berlin: de Gruyter, 2002).

Dallaire, Romeo, Kishan Manocha and Nishan Degnarain, 'The Major Powers on Trial', *Journal of International Criminal Justice* 3 (2005), pp. 861-78.

D'Amato, Anthony, *The Concept of Custom in International Law* (Ithaca, NY: Cornell University Press, 1971).

'Trashing Customary International Law', *American Journal of International Law* 81 (1987), pp. 101-5.

d'Argent, Pierre, *Les réparations de guerre en droit international public. La responsabilité internationale des Etats à l'épreuve de la guerre* (Brussels: Bruylant, 2002).

d'Aspremont, Jean, 'Softness in International Law: A Self-Serving Quest for New Legal Materials', *European Journal of International Law* 19 (2008), pp. 1075-93.

'Rebellion and State Responsibility: Wrongdoing by Democratically Elected Insurgents', *International and Comparative Law Quarterly* 58 (2009), pp. 427-42.

David, Eric, 'Article 34', in Olivier Corten and Pierre Klein (eds.), *Les Conventions de Vienne sur le droit des traités – Commentaire article par article*, Vols. I-III (Brussels: Bruylant, 2006), 1403-15.

'Primary and Secondary Rules', in James Crawford, Alain Pellet and Simon Olleson (eds.), *The Law of International Responsibility* (Oxford: Oxford University Press, 2010), pp. 27-33.

Dawidowicz, Martin, 'Public Law Enforcement without Public Law Safeguards? An Analysis of State Practice on Third-Party Countermeasures and Their Relationship to the UN Security Council', *British Year Book of International Law* 77 (2006), pp. 333-418.

'The Obligation of Non-Recognition of an Unlawful Situation', in James Crawford, Alain Pellet and Simon Olleson (eds.), *The Law of International Responsibility* (Oxford: Oxford University Press, 2010), pp. 677-86.

De Hoogh, André J. J., *Obligations Erga Omnes and International Crimes – A Theoretical Inquiry into the Implementation and Enforcement of the International Responsibility of States* (The Hague: Kluwer, 1996).

'Australia and East Timor – Rights Erga Omnes, Complicity and Non-Recognition', *Australian International Law Journal* 1999, pp. 63–90.
Delbrück, Jost, 'Collective Security', in Rudolf Bernhardt (ed.), *Encyclopedia of Public International Law*, Vol. 1, A–D (Amsterdam: Elsevier, 1992), pp. 646–56.
'Laws in the Public Interest – Some Observations on the Foundations and Identification of Erga Omnes Norms in International Law', in Volkmar Götz, Günther Jaenicke and Peter Selmer (eds.), *Liber amicorum Günther Jaenicke – zum 85. Geburtstag* (Berlin: Springer, 1998), pp. 17–36.
De Schutter, Olivier, 'Globalization and Jurisdiction: Lessons from the European Convention on Human Rights', *Baltic Yearbook of International Law* 6 (2006), pp. 185–247.
De Wet, Erika, *The Chapter VII Powers of the United Nations Security Council* (Oxford: Hart, 2004).
'The Prohibition of Torture as an International Norm of Jus Cogens and Its Implications for National and Customary Law', *European Journal of International Law* 15 (2004), pp. 97–121.
'The Emergence of International and Regional Value Systems as Manifestations of the Emerging International Constitutional Order', *Leiden Journal of International Law* 19 (2006), pp. 611–32.
Dicey, A. V., *An Introduction to the Study of the Law of the Constitution*, 10th edn, ed. by E. C. S. Wade (London: Macmillan, 1961)
Dinstein, Yoram, *War, Aggression and Self-Defence*, 4th edn (Cambridge: Cambridge University Press, 2005).
'Customary International Law and Treaties', *Recueil des Cours* 322 (2006), pp. 243–427.
DiStefano, Giovanni, 'Fait continu, fait composé et fait complexe dans le droit de la responsabilité', *Annuaire Français de Droit International* 52 (2006), pp. 1–54.
Doehring, Karl, 'Neutralität und Gewaltverbot', *Archiv des Völkerrechts* 31 (1993), pp. 193–205.
Dominicé, Christian, 'La question du droit de la neutralité', in Laurence Boisson de Chazournes and Philippe Sands (eds.), *International Law, the International Court of Justice and Nuclear Weapons* (Cambridge: Cambridge University Press, 1999), pp. 200–8.
'Responsabilité des Etats et responsabilité internationale: commentaires sur l'approche de la Commission; exposé', in United Nations (ed.), *The International Law Commission Fifty Years After: An Evaluation* (New York: United Nations, 2000), pp. 30–42.
'Attribution of Conduct to Multiple States and the Implication of a State in the Act of Another State', in James Crawford, Alain Pellet and Simon Olleson (eds.), *The International Law of Responsibility* (Oxford: Oxford University Press, 2010), pp. 282–9.
Dopagne, Frédéric and Pierre Klein, 'L'attitude des Etats tiers et de l'ONU à l'égard de l'occupation de l'Irak', in Karine Bannelier, Théodore

Christakis, Olivier Corten and Pierre Klein (eds.), *L'intervention en Irak et le droit international* (Paris: Pedone, 2004), pp. 325–41.
Dörr, Oliver, 'Staats- und völkerrechtliche Aspekte des Irak-Krieges 2003', *Informationsschriften zum Humanitären Völkerrecht* 16 (2003), pp. 181–8.
  'Codifying and Developing Meta-Rules: The ILC and the Law of Treaties', *German Yearbook of International Law* 49 (2006), pp. 129–64.
Dubber, Markus D., 'Criminalizing Complicity – A Comparative Analysis', *Journal of International Criminal Justice* 5 (2007), pp. 977–1001.
Dugard, John, *Recognition and the United Nations* (Cambridge: Grotius, 1987).
Dupuy, Pierre-Marie, 'Le fait générateur de la responsabilité internationale', *Recueil des Cours* 188 (1984-V), pp. 9–134.
  'The Danger of Fragmentation or Unification of the International Legal System and the International Court of Justice', *New York University Journal of International Law and Politics* 31 (1999), pp. 791–807.
  'A General Stocktaking of the Connections between the Multilateral Dimension of Obligations and Codification of the Law of State Responsibility', *European Journal of International Law* 13 (2002), pp. 1053–81.
  'L'unité de l'ordre juridique internationale. Cours général de droit international public', *Recueil des Cours* 297 (2002), pp. 9–490.
  'Quarante ans de codification du droit de la responsabilité internationale des Etats. Un bilan', *Revue générale de droit international public* 107 (2003), pp. 305–47.
  'Some Reflections on Contemporary International Law and the Appeal to Universal Values', *European Journal of International Law* 16 (2005), pp. 131–7.
  'Crime sans châtiment ou mission accomplie', *Revue générale de droit international public* 111 (2007), pp. 243–57.
Dupuy, René-Jean, 'Coutume sage et coutume sauvage', in *Mélanges offerts à Charles Rousseau* (Paris: Pedone, 1974), pp. 75–87.
Dworkin, Ronald, *A Matter of Principle* (Cambridge, MA: Harvard University Press, 1985).
Dyzenhaus, David, 'The Rule of (Administrative) Law in International Law', *Law and Contemporary Problems* 68 (2005), Autumn Issue, pp. 127–66.
  The Constitution of Law – Legality in a Time of Emergency (Cambridge: Cambridge University Press, 2006).
Eboe-Osuji, Chile, '"Complicity in Genocide" Versus "Aiding and Abetting in Genocide"', *Journal of International Criminal Justice* 3 (2005), pp. 56–81.
Egli, Patricia, 'Rechtliche Schranken des Handels mit Kriegsmaterial', *Schweizerische Zeitschrift für Internationales und Europäisches Recht* 15 (2005), pp. 665–83.
Eick, Christophe, 'Die Anerkennung der obligatorischen Gerichtsbarkeit des Internationalen Gerichtshofs durch Deutschland', *Zeitschrift für ausländisches öffentliches Recht und Völkerrecht* 68 (2008), pp. 763–77.
Elias, Olufemi, 'The Nature of the Subjective Element in Customary International Law', *International and Comparative Law Quarterly* 44 (1995), pp. 501–20.

Elver, Hilal, 'World Commission on Dams Report Challenges Financing for Ilisu Dam', *Turkish Daily News*, 20 March 2001.

Enoch, David, 'Intending, Foreseeing, and the State', *Legal Theory* 13 (2007), pp. 69-99.

Epiney, Astrid, 'Nachbarrechtliche Pflichten im internationalen Wasserrecht und Implikationen von Drittstaaten', *Archiv des Völkerrechts* 39 (2001), pp. 1-56.

'Umweltvölkerrechtliche Rahmenbedingungen für Entwicklungsprojekte', *Berichte der Deutschen Gesellschaft für Völkerrecht* 41 (2005), pp. 329-77.

Eser, Albin, 'Individual Criminal Responsibility', in Antonio Cassese, Paola Gaeta and John R. W. D. Jones (eds.), *The Rome Statute of the International Criminal Court, A Commentary*, Vol. I (Oxford: Oxford University Press, 2002), pp. 767-822.

Evans, Malcolm D., 'State Responsibility and the European Convention on Human Rights: Role and Realm', in Malgosia Fitzmaurice and Dan Sarooshi (eds.), *Issues of State Responsibility before International Judicial Institutions* (Oxford: Hart, 2004), pp. 139-60.

Farrall, Jeremy Matam, *United Nations Sanctions and the Rule of Law* (Cambridge: Cambridge University Press, 2007).

Fassbender, Bardo, 'The United Nations Charter as Constitution of the International Community', *Columbia Journal of Transnational Law* 36 (1998), pp. 529-619.

UN Security Council Reform and the Right of Veto: A Constitutional Perspective (The Hague: Kluwer, 1998).

'Der Schutz der Menschenrechte als zentraler Inhalt des völkerrechtlichen Gemeinwohls', *Europäische Grundrechte-Zeitschrift* 30 (2003), pp. 1-15.

'Die Gegenwartskrise des völkerrechtlichen Gewaltverbots vor dem Hintergrund der geschichtlichen Entwicklung', *Europäische Grundrechte-Zeitschrift* 31 (2004), pp. 241-56.

The Charter of the United Nations as the Constitution of the International Community (Leiden: Nijhoff, 2009).

Fastenrath, Ulrich, *Lücken im Völkerrecht - Zu Rechtscharakter, Quellen, Systemzusammenhang, Methodenlehre und Funktionen des Völkerrechts* (Berlin: Duncker & Humblot, 1991).

Felder, Andreas, *Die Beihilfe in der völkerrechtlichen Staatenverantwortlichkeit* (Zurich: Schulthess, 2007).

Fenwick, C. G., 'Is Neutrality Still a Term of Present Law?', *American Journal of International Law* 63 (1969), pp. 100-2.

Fife, Rolf Einar, 'Elements of Nordic Practice 2001/2003: Norway', *Nordic Journal of International Law* 73 (2004), pp. 551-7.

Fink, Udo, 'Artikel 26', in Hermann von Mangoldt, Friedrich Klein and Christian Starck (eds.), *Das Bonner Grundgesetz - Kommentar*, Vol. 2, *Artikel 20 bis 78*, 5th edn (Munich: Vahlen, 2005), pp. 517-40.

Fischer, Horst, 'Friedenssicherung und friedliche Streitbeilegung', in Knut Ipsen, *Völkerrecht*, 5th edn (Munich: C. H. Beck, 2004), pp. 1065–1194.
Fischer-Lescano, Andreas, *Globalverfassung – Die Geltungsbegründung der Menschenrechte* (Weilerswirst: Velbrück, 2005).
Fischer-Lescano, Andreas and Gunther Teubner, 'Regime-Collisions: The Vain Search for Legal Unity in the Fragmentation of Global Law', *Michigan Journal of International Law* 25 (2003–4), pp. 999–1046.
  Regime-Kollisionen: Zur Fragmentierung des globalen Rechts (Frankfurt/Main: Suhrkamp, 2006).
Fisher Williams, John, 'Sanctions Under the Covenant', *British Year Book of International Law* 17 (1936), pp. 130–49.
Fitzmaurice, Gerald, 'The Law and Procedure of the International Court of Justice: General Principles and Substantive Law', *British Year Book of International Law* 27 (1950), pp. 1–41.
  'The Law and Procedure of the International Court of Justice, 1951–54: General Principles and Sources of Law', *British Year Book of International Law* 30 (1953), pp. 1–70.
  'The General Principles of International Law Considered from the Standpoint of the Rule of Law', *Recueil des Cours* 92 (1957-II), pp. 1–227.
  'Some Problems Regarding the Formal Sources of International Law', in Frederik Mari van Asbeck (ed.), *Symbolae Verzijl: présentées au professeur J. H. W. Verzijl à l'occasion de son LXX-ième anniversaire* (The Hague: Nijhoff, 1958), pp. 153–76.
Fitzmaurice, Malgosia, 'Third Parties and the Law of Treaties', *Max Planck Yearbook of United Nations Law* 6 (2002), pp. 37–137.
Fleck, Dieter, 'International Accountability for Violations of the Ius in Bello: The Impact of the ICRC Study on Customary International Humanitarian Law', *Journal of Conflict and Security Law* 11 (2006), pp. 179–99.
Focarelli, Carlo, 'Promotional Jus Cogens: A Critical Appraisal of Jus Cogens' Legal Effects', *Nordic Journal of International Law* 77 (2008), pp. 429–59.
  'Case Note (Federal Republic of Germany v. Giovanni Mantelli and Others)', *American Journal of International Law* 103 (2009), pp. 122–31.
  'Common Article 1 of the 1949 Geneva Conventions: A Soap Bubble?', *European Journal of International Law* 21 (2010), pp. 125–71.
Forteau, Mathias, *Droit de la sécurité collective et droit de la responsabilité internationale de l'Etat* (Paris: Pedone, 2006).
Fox, Gregory H., *Humanitarian Occupation* (Cambridge: Cambridge University Press, 2008).
Fox, Hazel, *The Law of State Immunity*, 1st edn (Oxford: Oxford University Press, 2002).
  The Law of State Immunity, 2nd edn (Oxford: Oxford University Press 2008).
Franck, Thomas M., *Fairness in International Law and Institutions* (Oxford: Clarendon Press, 1995).
  'On Proportionality of Countermeasures in International Law', *American Journal of International Law* 102 (2008), pp. 715–67.

Friedmann, Wolfgang, 'The Uses of "General Principles" in the Development of International Law', *American Journal of International Law* 57 (1963), pp. 279–99.
  The Changing Structure of International Law (London: Stevens, 1964).
Frowein, Jochen Abr., *Das de facto-Regime im Völkerrecht: eine Untersuchung zur Rechtsstellung 'nichtanerkannter' Staaten und ähnlicher Gebilde* (Cologne: Heymanns, 1968).
  'Die Verpflichtungen erga omnes im Völkerrecht und ihre Durchsetzung', in Rudolf Bernhardt et al. (eds.), *Völkerrecht als Rechtsordnung – Internationale Gerichtsbarkeit – Menschenrechte. Festschrift für Hermann Mosler* (Berlin: Springer, 1984), pp. 241–62.
  'Collective Enforcement of International Obligations', *Zeitschrift für ausländisches öffentliches Recht und Völkerrecht* 47 (1987), pp. 67–79.
  'Reactions by Not Directly Affected States to Breaches of Public International Law', *Recueil des Cours* 248 (1994-IV), pp. 345–438.
  'Non-Recognition', in Rudolf Bernhardt (ed.), *Encyclopedia of Public International Law*, Vol. III (Amsterdam: Elsevier, 1995), pp. 627–9.
  'Konstitutionalisierung des Völkerrechts', *Berichte der Deutschen Gesellschaft für Völkerrecht* 39 (2000), pp. 427–45.
Frowein, Jochen Abr. and Nico Krisch, 'Article 2(5)', in Bruno Simma (ed.), *The Charter of the United Nations – A Commentary*, 2nd edn (Oxford: Oxford University Press, 2002), pp. 136–9.
Frowein, Jochen Abr. and Wolfgang Peukert, *Europäische Menschenrechtskonvention*, 3rd edn (Kehl: N. P. Engel, 2009).
Fry, James D., 'Coercion, Causation and the Fictional Elements of Indirect State Responsibility', *Vanderbilt Journal of Transnational Law* 40 (2007), pp. 611–41.
Gaja, Giorgio, 'Jus Cogens Beyond the Vienna Convention', *Recueil des Cours* 172 (1981-III), pp. 271–316.
  'Obligations Erga Omnes, International Crimes and Jus Cogens: A Tentative Analysis of Three Related Concepts', in Joseph H. H. Weiler, Antonio Cassese and Marina Spinedi (eds.), *International Crimes of State* (Berlin: de Gruyter, 1989), pp. 151–60.
  'Réflexions sur le rôle du Conseil de Sécurité dans le nouvel ordre mondial', *Revue générale de droit international public* 97 (1993), pp. 297–319.
  'Do States Have a Duty to Ensure Compliance with Obligations Erga Omnes by Other States?', in Maurizio Ragazzi (ed.), *International Responsibility Today – Essays in Memory of Oscar Schachter* (Leiden: Nijhoff, 2005), pp. 31–6.
  'Obligations and Rights Erga Omnes in International Law', *Annuaire de l'Institut de Droit International* 71 (2005), pp. 117–51.
  'The Impact of Security Council Resolutions on State Responsibility', in Georg Nolte (ed.), *Peace Through International Law – The Role of the International Law Commission* (Berlin: Springer, 2009), pp. 53–60.

Gattini, Andrea, *Zufall und force majeure im System der Staatenverantwortlichkeit anhand der ILC-Kodifikationsarbeit* (Berlin: Duncker & Humblot, 1991).
  'A Return Ticket to "Communitarisme", Please', *European Journal of International Law* 13 (2002), pp. 1181–99.
  'War Crimes and State Immunity in the *Ferrini* Decision', *Journal of International Criminal Justice* 3 (2005), pp. 224–42.
  'La renonciation au droit d'invoquer la responsabilité', in Pierre-Marie Dupuy, Bardo Fassbender, Malcolm N. Shaw and Karl-Peter Sommermann (eds.), *Völkerrecht als Wertordnung – Festschrift für Christian Tomuschat* (Kehl: N. P. Engel, 2006), pp. 317–40.
  'Un regard procédural sur la fragmentation du droit international', *Revue générale de droit international public* 110 (2006), pp. 303–36.
  'Breach of the Obligation to Prevent and Reparation Thereof in the ICJ's Genocide Convention Judgment', *European Journal of International Law* 18 (2007), pp. 695–713.
  'Post 1945 German International Law and State Responsibility', *German Yearbook of International Law* 50 (2007), pp. 407–14.
Gaurier, Dominique, *Histoire du droit international* (Rennes: Presses universitaires de Rennes, 2005).
Gianelli, Alessandra, 'Le conseguenze delle gravi violazioni di obblighi posti da norme imperative tra norme primarie e norme secondarie', in Marina Spinedi, Alessandra Gianelli and Maria Luisa Alaimo (eds.), *La codificazione della responsabilità internazionale degli stati alla prova dei fatti – Probleme e spunti di riflessione* (Milan: Giuffrè, 2006), pp. 245–90.
Gibney, Mark, 'Genocide and State Responsibility', *Human Rights Law Review* 7 (2007), pp. 760–73.
Gibney, Mark and Erik Roxstrom, 'The Status of State Apologies', *Human Rights Quarterly* 23 (2001), pp. 911–39.
Gibney, Mark, Katarina Tomasevski and Jens Vedsted-Hansen, 'Transnational State Responsibility for Violations of Human Rights', *Harvard Human Rights Law Journal* 12 (1999), pp. 267–95.
Giegerich, Thomas, 'Do Damage Claims Arising from Jus Cogens Violations Override State Immunity from the Jurisdiction of Foreign Courts?', in Christian Tomuschat and Jean-Marc Thouvenin (eds.), *The Fundamental Rules of the International Legal Order – Jus Cogens and Obligations Erga Omnes* (Leiden: Nijhoff, 2006), pp. 203–38.
Goldsmith, Jack L., *The Terror Presidency: Law and Judgment Inside the Bush Administration* (New York: Norton, 2007).
Gondek, Michael, 'Extraterritorial Application of the European Convention on Human Rights: Territorial Focus in the Age of Globalization?', *Netherlands International Law Review* 52 (2003), pp. 349–87.
Goodhart, Arthur L., 'The Rule of Law and Absolute Sovereignty', *University of Pennsylvania Law Review* 106 (1958), pp. 943–63.
Goodrich, Leland M., Edvard Hambro and Anne Patricia Simons, *Charter of the United Nations – Commentary and Documents*, 3rd edn (New York: Columbia University Press, 1969).

Goodwin-Gill, Guy S. and Jane McAdam, *The Refugee in International Law*, 3rd edn (Oxford: Oxford University Press, 2007).
Gouttes, Paul des, *La Convention de Genève pour l'amélioration du sort des blessés et des malades dans les armées en campagne, Commentaire* (Geneva: International Committee of the Red Cross, 1930).
Gowlland-Debbas, Vera, *Collective Responses to Illegal Acts in International Law – United Nations Action in the Question of Southern Rhodesia* (Dordrecht: Nijhoff, 1990).
  'Security Council Enforcement Action and Issues of State Responsibility', *International and Comparative Law Quarterly* 43 (1994), pp. 55–98.
Grabenwarter, Christoph, *Europäische Menschenrechtskonvention*, 3rd edn (Munich: C. H. Beck, 2008).
Graefrath, Bernhard, 'Complicity in the Law of International Responsibility', *Revue Belge de Droit International* 29 (1996), pp. 370–80.
Gray, Christine D., *Judicial Remedies in International Law* (Oxford: Clarendon Press, 1988).
  International Law and the Use of Force, 3rd edn (Oxford: Oxford University Press, 2008).
Green, Leslie, 'Law and Obligations', in Jules Coleman and Scott Shapiro (eds.), *The Oxford Handbook of Jurisprudence and Philosophy of Law* (Oxford: Oxford University Press, 2002), pp. 514–47.
Greenwood, Christopher, 'The Concept of War in Modern International Law', *International and Comparative Law Quarterly* 36 (1987), pp. 283–306.
Grewe, Constance, 'Vergleich zwischen den Interpretationsmethoden europäischer Verfassungsgerichte und des Europäischen Gerichtshofs für Menschenrechte', *Zeitschrift für ausländisches öffentliches Recht und Völkerrecht* 61 (2001), pp. 461–73.
Grewe, Wilhelm G., *Epochen der Völkerrechtsgeschichte* (Baden-Baden: Nomos, 1984).
Grote, Rainer, 'Völkerrechtspraxis der Bundesrepublik Deutschland im Jahre 1995', *Zeitschrift für ausländisches öffentliches Recht und Völkerrecht* 57 (1997), pp. 923–1164.
  'Rule of Law, Rechtsstaat and "Etat de Droit"', in Christian Starck (ed.), *Constitutionalism, Universalism and Democracy – A Comparative Analysis* (Baden-Baden: Nomos, 1999), pp. 269–306.
Grotius, Hugo, *De jure belli ac pacis libri tres*, translated by Francis W. Kelsey, No. 3 of 'The Classics of International Law', Vol. 2 (Oxford: Clarendon Press, 1925).
Grünfeld, Fred and Anke Huijboom, *The Failure to Prevent Genocide in Rwanda: The Role of Bystanders* (Leiden: Nijhoff, 2007).
Guggenheim, Paul, 'Documentation – Droit international public', *Schweizerisches Jahrbuch für Internationales Recht* 10 (1953), pp. 191–254.
Hafner, Gerhard, 'The Rule of Law and International Organizations', in Klaus Dicke, Stephan Hobe, Karl U. Meyn *et al.* (eds.), *Weltinnenrecht – Liber amicorum Jost Delbrück* (Berlin: Duncker & Humblot, 2005), pp. 307–14.

Hailbronner, Kay, 'Sanctions and Third Parties and the Concept of International Public Order', *Archiv des Völkerrechts* 30 (1992), pp. 2-15.
Hakimi, Monica, 'State Bystander Responsibility', *European Journal of International Law* 21 (2010), pp. 341-85.
Hart, H. L. A., *The Concept of Law*, 2nd edn (Oxford: Oxford University Press, 1994).
Hart, H. L. A. and Tony Honoré, *Causation in the Law*, 2nd edn (Oxford: Clarendon Press, 1985, reprint 2002).
Hartwig, Matthias, 'Völkerrechtliche Praxis der Bundesrepublik Deutschland im Jahr 2003', *Zeitschrift für ausländisches öffentliches Recht und Völkerrecht* 65 (2005), pp. 741-88.
Heffter, August Wilhelm, *Europäisches Völkerrecht der Gegenwart auf den bisherigen Grundlagen*, 8th edn, edited by F. Heinrich Geffcken (Berlin: Schroeder, 1888).
Heintschel von Heinegg, Wolff, 'Die völkerrechtlichen Verträge als Hauptrechtsquelle des Völkerrechts', in Knut Ipsen, *Völkerrecht*, 5th edn (Munich: C. H. Beck, 2004), pp. 112-209.
  'Die weiteren Quellen des Völkerrechts', in Knut Ipsen, *Völkerrecht*, 5th edn (Munich: C. H. Beck, 2004), pp. 210-56.
  'Wider die Mär vom Tod des Neutralitätsrechts', in Horst Fischer, Ulrike Froissart, Wolff Heintschel von Heinegg and Christian Raap (eds.), *Krisensicherung und Humanitärer Schutz/Crisis Management and Humanitarian Protection, Festschrift für Dieter Fleck* (Berlin: Berliner Wissenschafts-Verlag, 2004), pp. 221-41.
  '"Benevolent" Third States in International Armed Conflicts: The Myth of the Irrelevance of the Law of Neutrality', in Michael N. Schmitt and Jelena Pejic (eds.), *International Law and Armed Conflict: Exploring the Faultlines. Essays in Honour of Yoram Dinstein* (Leiden: Nijhoff, 2007), pp. 543-68.
Heinzelmann, Kate, 'Towards Common Interests and Responsibilities: The US-India Civil Nuclear Deal and the International Nonproliferation Regime', *Yale Journal of International Law* 33 (2008), pp. 447-78.
Heller, Kevin Jon, 'Retreat from Nuremberg: The Leadership Requirement in the Crime of Aggression', *European Journal of International Law* 18 (2007), pp. 477-97.
Henckaerts, Jean-Marie and Louise Doswald-Beck, *Customary International Humanitarian Law*, Vol. I, *Rules* (Cambridge: Cambridge University Press, 2005).
Henkin, Louis, 'Force, Intervention and Neutrality in Contemporary International Law', *Proceedings of the American Society of International Law* 1963, pp. 147-62.
Herdegen, Matthias, *Internationales Wirtschaftsrecht*, 7th edn (Munich: C. H. Beck, 2008).
Heuschling, Luc, *Etat de Droit, Rechtsstaat, Rule of Law* (Paris: Dalloz, 2002).

Heydte, August Freiherr von der, 'Die Erscheinungsformen des zwischenstaatlichen Rechts: jus cogens und jus dispositivum im Völkerrecht', *Zeitschrift für Völkerrecht* 16 (1932), pp. 461–78.
Higgins, Rosalyn, *Of Problems and Process* (Oxford: Clarendon Press, 1994).
'The Rule of Law: Some Sceptical Thoughts', in Rosalyn Higgins, *Themes and Theories. Selected Essays, Speeches and Writings in International Law*, Vol. 2 (Oxford: Oxford University Press, 2009), pp. 1330–9.
Hilf, Meinhard and Stefan Oeter, *WTO-Recht – Rechtsordnung des Welthandels* (Baden-Baden: Nomos, 2005).
Hillgruber, Christian, 'The Right of Third States to Take Countermeasures', in Christian Tomuschat and Jean-Marc Thouvenin (eds.), *The Fundamental Rules of the International Legal Order – Jus Cogens and Obligations Erga Omnes* (Leiden: Nijhoff, 2006), pp. 265–94.
Hilpold, Peter, *Der Osttimor-Fall* (Frankfurt/Main: Peter Lang, 1996).
Hobe, Stephan, *Einführung in das Völkerrecht*, 9th edn (Tübingen: Francke, 2008).
Hoffmeister, Frank, *Menschenrechts- und Demokratieklauseln in den vertraglichen Außenbeziehungen der Europäischen Gemeinschaft* (Berlin: Springer, 1998).
Hofmann, Rainer, 'Art. 25 GG und die Anwendung völkerrechtswidrigen ausländischen Rechts', *Zeitschrift für ausländisches öffentliches Recht und Völkerrecht* 49 (1989), pp. 41–60.
Howard, Jessica, 'Invoking State Responsibility for Aiding the Commission of International Crimes – Australia, the United States and East Timor', *Melbourne Journal of International Law* 2001, online edition, available at http://mjil.law.unimelb.edu.au/go/issues/issue-archive/volume-2-1 (last visited 1 November 2010).
Howse, Robert L. and Jared M. Genser, 'Are EU Trade Sanctions on Burma Compatible with WTO Law?', *Michigan Journal of International Law* 29 (2008), pp. 165–96.
Huber, Max, 'Observations (sur le rapport de Louis Le Fur sur Reconnaissance, détermination et signification en droit international du domaine laissé par ce dernier à la compétence exclusive de l'Etat)', *Annuaire de l'Institut de Droit International* 31 (1936-1), pp. 77–81.
Hulme, Karen, 'The 2008 Cluster Munitions Convention: Stepping Outside the CCW Framework (Again)', *International and Comparative Law Quarterly* 58 (2009), pp. 219–27.
Imseis, Ardi, 'Critical Reflections on the International Humanitarian Law Aspects of the ICJ Wall Advisory Opinion', *American Journal of International Law* 99 (2005), pp. 102–18.
International Law Association (ed.), *Report of the 41st Conference* (Cambridge: International Law Association, 1946).
Ipsen, Knut, 'Völkerrechtliche Verantwortlichkeit und Völkerstrafrecht', in Knut Ipsen, *Völkerrecht*, 5th edn (Munich: C. H. Beck, 2004), pp. 615–73.

Jackson, Robert H., 'Address to the Inter-American Bar Association, Havana, Cuba, 27 March 1941', *American Journal of International Law* 35 (1941), pp. 348–59.
Janik, Cornelia and Thomas Kleinlein, 'When Soering Went to Iraq ... Problems of Jurisdiction, Extraterritorial Effect and Norm Conflicts in Light of the European Court of Human Rights' Al-Saadoon Case', *Goettingen Journal of International Law* 1 (2009), pp. 459–518.
Jennings, Robert and Arthur Watts, *Oppenheim's International Law*, Vol. 1, *The Law of Peace*, 9th edn (London: Longman, 1992).
Jimenez de Arechaga, Eduardo, 'International Law in the Past Third of a Century', *Recueil des Cours* 159 (1978-I), pp. 1–344.
Johnson, D. H. N., 'The Case of the Monetary Gold Removed from Rome in 1943', *International and Comparative Law Quarterly* 4 (1955), pp. 98–115.
Jørgensen, Nina, 'State Responsibility and the 1948 Genocide Convention', in Guy S. Goodwin-Gill and Stefan Talmon (eds.), *The Reality of International Law – Essays in Honour of Ian Brownlie* (Oxford: Oxford University Press, 1999), pp. 273–91.
  The Responsibility of States for International Crimes (Oxford: Oxford University Press, 2000).
  'The Obligation of Cooperation', in James Crawford, Alain Pellet and Simon Olleson (eds.), *The International Law of Responsibility* (Oxford: Oxford University Press, 2010), pp. 695–701.
  'The Obligation of Non-Assistance to the Responsible State', in James Crawford, Alain Pellet and Simon Olleson (eds.), *The International Law of Responsibility* (Oxford: Oxford University Press, 2010), pp. 687–93.
Jouannet, Emmanuelle, 'Le principe de l'or monétaire à propos de l'arrêt de la Cour du 30 juin 1995 dans l'affaire du Timor Oriental (Portugal c. Australie)', *Revue générale de droit international public* 100 (1996), pp. 673–714.
Jowell, Jeffrey, 'The Rule of Law and Its Underlying Values', in Jeffrey Jowell and Dawn Oliver (eds.), *The Changing Constitution*, 7th edn (Oxford: Oxford University Press, 2007), pp. 5–24.
Justen, Detlev, *Der Oslo-Prozess zum Verbot von Streumunition* (Berlin: Stiftung Wissenschaft und Politik, 2008).
Kadelbach, Stefan, *Zwingendes Völkerrecht* (Berlin: Duncker & Humblot, 1992).
  'Staatenverantwortlichkeit für Angriffskriege und Verbrechen gegen die Menschlichkeit', *Berichte der Deutschen Gesellschaft für Völkerrecht* 40 (2001), pp. 63–102.
  'Jus Cogens, Obligations Erga Omnes and Other Rules: The Identification of Fundamental Rules', in Christian Tomuschat and Jean-Marc Thouvenin (eds.), *The Fundamental Rules of the International Legal Order: Jus Cogens and Obligations Erga Omnes* (Leiden: Nijhoff, 2006), pp. 21–40.

Kadelbach, Stefan and Thomas Kleinlein, 'International Law – A Constitution for Mankind? An Attempt at a Re-Appraisal with an Analysis of Constitutional Principles', *German Yearbook of International Law* 50 (2007), pp. 303–47.

Kadish, Sanford H., 'Complicity, Cause and Blame: A Study in the Interpretation of Doctrine', *California Law Review* 73 (1985), pp. 323–410.

Kälin, Walter and Jörg Künzli, *Universeller Menschenrechtsschutz*, 2nd edn (Basel/Baden-Baden: Helbig and Nomos, 2008).

Kälin, Walter and Erika Schläppi, *Schweizerische Wirtschaftshilfe und internationale Menschenrechte: Konflikte und Konvergenzen aus völkerrechtlicher Sicht, Studie im Rahmen des NFP 'Außenpolitik', Synthesebericht vom 3. März 2000* (Bern: Sekretariat Nationalfonds, 2000).

Kalshoven, Frits, 'The Undertaking to Respect and Ensure Respect in All Circumstances: From Tiny Seed to Ripening Fruit', *Yearbook of International Humanitarian Law* 2 (1999), pp. 3–61.

Kaplan, Margo, 'Using Collective Interests to Ensure Human Rights: An Analysis of the Articles on State Responsibility', *New York University Law Review* 79 (2002), pp. 1902–33.

Katselli, Elena, *The Problem of Enforcement in International Law – Countermeasures, the Non-Injured State and the Idea of International Community* (London: Routledge, 2010).

Kaufmann, Daniel, Aart Kray and Massimo Matruzzi, 'Governance Matters VI: Governance Indicators 1996–2006', World Bank Policy Research Paper No. 4280, July 2007, available at http://papers.ssrn.com/sol3/papers.cfm?abstract_id=999979 (last visited 1 November 2010).

Kelsen, Hans, 'Unrecht und Unrechtsfolge im Völkerrecht', *Zeitschrift für öffentliches Recht* 12 (1932), pp. 481–608.

'Théorie du droit coutumier', reprinted in Nicoletta Bersier Ladavac, *Hans Kelsen à Genève (1933–1940)* (Geneva: Thémis, 1996), pp. 33–64.

Peace Through Law (Chapel Hill, NC: University of North Carolina Press, 1944).

'The Draft Declaration on Rights and Duties of States – Critical Remarks', *American Journal of International Law* 44 (1950), pp. 259–76.

The Law of the United Nations – A Critical Analysis of Its Fundamental Problems (London: Stevens, 1951).

Principles of International Law (New York: Rinehart, 1952).

'Théorie du droit international public', *Recueil des Cours* 84 (1953-III), pp. 1–202.

Reine Rechtslehre, 2nd edn (Vienna: Franz Deuticke, 1960).

Kennedy, David, *The Dark Sides of Virtue – Reassessing International Humanitarianism* (Princeton, NJ: Princeton University Press, 2004).

Kennedy, Duncan, 'Form and Substance in Private Law Adjudication', *Harvard Law Review* 89 (1976), pp. 1685–1778.

'Toward a Critical Phenomenology of Judging', in Allan C. Hutchinson and Patrick Monahan (eds.), *The Rule of Law – Ideal or Ideology?* (Toronto: Transnational, 1987), pp. 141–67.
Kessler, Birgit, *Die Durchsetzung der Genfer Abkommen von 1949 in nicht-internationalen bewaffneten Konflikten auf Grundlage ihres gemeinsamen Art. 1* (Berlin: Duncker & Humblot, 2001).
  'The Duty to "Ensure Respect" Under Common Article 1 of the Geneva Conventions: Its Implications on International and Non-International Armed Conflicts', *German Yearbook of International Law* 44 (2001), pp. 489–516.
Khaliq, Urfan, *Ethical Dimensions of the Foreign Policy of the European Union – A Legal Appraisal* (Cambridge: Cambridge University Press, 2008).
Khan, Daniel-Erasmus, 'Sicherheitszaun oder Apartheidmauer? Das Gutachten des Internationalen Gerichtshofs vom 9. Juli 2004 zu den israelischen Sperranlagen gegenüber dem Westjordanland', *Die Friedenswarte* 79 (2004), pp. 345–70.
Kirgis, Frederic L., 'Custom on a Sliding Scale', *American Journal of International Law* 81 (1987), pp. 146–51.
Kiss, Alexandre, 'Abuse of Rights', in Rüdiger Wolfrum (ed.), *Max Planck Encyclopedia of Public International Law*, online edition (Oxford: Oxford University Press, 2008).
Kleen, Richard, *Lois et usages de la neutralité d'après le droit international conventionnel et coutumier des Etats civilizes*, Vol. I, *Principes fondamentaux – Devoirs des neutres* (Paris: Chevalier-Marescq, 1898).
Klein, Eckart, 'Die Nichtanerkennungspolitik der Vereinten Nationen gegenüber den in die Unabhängigkeit entlassenen südafrikanischen homelands', *Zeitschrift für ausländisches öffentliches Recht und Völkerrecht* 39 (1979), pp. 469–95.
  Statusverträge im Völkerrecht – Rechtsfragen territorialer Sonderregime (Berlin: Springer, 1980).
  'Beihilfe zum Völkerrechtsdelikt', in Ingo von Münch (ed.), *Staatsrecht – Völkerrecht – Europarecht. Festschrift für Hans-Jürgen Schlochauer* (Berlin: de Gruyter, 1981), pp. 425–38.
  'Gegenmaßnahmen', *Berichte der Deutschen Gesellschaft für Völkerrecht* 37 (1997), pp. 39–71.
Klein, Friedrich, *Die mittelbare Haftung im Völkerrecht* (Frankfurt/Main: Klostermann, 1941).
Klein, Pierre, 'Responsibility for Serious Breaches of Obligations Deriving from Peremptory Norms of International Law and United Nations Law', *European Journal of International Law* 13 (2002), pp. 1241–55.
Kleinlein, Thomas, 'The Language of Public International Law', in Société Française pour le droit international (ed.), *Droit international et diversité des cultures juridiques* (Paris: Pedone, 2008), pp. 199–208.
  Konstitutionalisierung im Völkerrecht: Konstruktion und Elemente einer idealistischen Völkerrechtslehre (Berlin: Springer, 2011, forthcoming).

Koh, Harold H., 'Why Do Nations Obey International Law?', *Yale Law Journal* 106 (1997), pp. 2598–2659.
Kok, Erik, 'The Principle of Complicity in the Law of State Responsibility and in International Criminal Law', in Larissa van den Herik and Carsten Stahn (eds.), *The Diversification and Fragmentation of International Law* (Cambridge: T. M. C. Asser Press, 2011), forthcoming, manuscript on file with the author.
Kolb, Robert, *La bonne foi en droit international public: contribution à l'étude des principes généraux de droit* (Paris: Presses universitaires de France, 2000).
  Théorie du ius cogens international: essai du relecture du concept (Paris: Presses universitaires de France, 2001).
  Ius in bello: Le droit international des conflits armés (Basel: Helbing, 2003).
  'Selected Problems in the Theory of Customary International Law', *Netherlands International Law Review* 50 (2003), pp. 119–50.
  Interprétation et création du droit international – Esquisse d'une herméneutique juridique moderne pour le droit international public (Brussels: Bruylant, 2006).
  'Principles as Sources of International Law (With Special Reference to Good Faith)', *Netherlands International Law Review* 53 (2006), pp. 1–36.
Koskenniemi, Martti, 'The Politics of International Law', *European Journal of International Law* 1 (1990), pp. 4–32.
  'The Silence of the Law/the Voice of Justice', in Laurence Boisson de Chazournes and Philippe Sands (eds.), *The International Court of Justice, International Law and Nuclear Weapons* (Cambridge: Cambridge University Press, 1999), pp. 488–510.
  'Introduction', in Martti Koskenniemi (ed.), *Sources of International Law* (Aldershot: Ashgate, 2000), pp. xi–xxviii.
  'Solidarity Measures: State Responsibility as a New International Order?', *British Year Book of International Law* 72 (2001), pp. 337–56.
  The Gentle Civilizer of Nations – The Rise and Fall of International Law 1870–1960 (Cambridge: Cambridge University Press, 2002).
  From Apology to Utopia – The Structure of International Legal Argument, Reissue with a New Epilogue (Cambridge: Cambridge University Press, 2005).
  'International Law in Europe: Between Tradition and Renewal', *European Journal of International Law* 16 (2005), pp. 113–24.
  'The Fate of Public International Law: Between Technique and Politics', *Modern Law Review* 70 (2007), pp. 1–30.
  'History of International Law, World War I to World War II', in Rüdiger Wolfrum (ed.), *Max Planck Encyclopedia of Public International Law*, online edition (Oxford: Oxford University Press, 2008).
  'The Politics of International Law – 20 Years Later', *European Journal of International Law* 20 (2009), pp. 7–19.
  'Doctrines of State Responsibility', in James Crawford, Alain Pellet and Simon Olleson (eds.), *The Law of International Responsibility* (Oxford: Oxford University Press, 2010), pp. 45–51.

Koskenniemi, Martti and Päivi Leino, 'Fragmentation of International Law? Postmodern Anxieties', *Leiden Journal of International Law* 15 (2002), pp. 553-79.
Kramer, Matthew, 'On the Moral Status of the Rule of Law', *Cambridge Law Journal* 63 (2004), pp. 65-97.
Kress, Claus, 'Anmerkung zu Generalbundesanwalt, Entschließung v. 21.3.2003 zu § 80 StGB', *Juristenzeitung* (2003), pp. 911-16.
  'The German Chief Federal Prosecutor's Decision Not to Investigate the Alleged Crime of Preparing Aggression Against Iraq', *Journal of International Criminal Justice* 2 (2004), pp. 245-64.
Krieger, Heike, *Das Effektivitätsprinzip im Völkerrecht* (Berlin: Duncker & Humblot, 2000).
  'Die Verantwortlichkeit Deutschlands nach der EMRK für seine Streitkräfte im Auslandseinsatz', *Zeitschrift für ausländisches öffentliches Recht und Völkerrecht* 62 (2002), pp. 669-702.
  'A Credibility Gap: The Behrami and Saramati Decision of the European Court of Human Rights', *Journal of International Peacekeeping* 13 (2009), pp. 159-80.
Krisch, Nico, *Selbstverteidigung und kollektive Sicherheit* (Berlin: Springer, 2001).
Kumm, Matthias, 'International Law in National Courts: The International Rule of Law and the Limits of the Internationalist Model', *Virginia Journal of International Law* 44 (2003-4), pp. 19-32.
Kunz, Josef L., 'The Nottebohm Judgment (Second Phase)', *American Journal of International Law* 54 (1960), pp. 536-71.
  'The "Vienna School" and International Law', in Josef L. Kunz, *The Changing Law of Nations* (Columbus, OH: Ohio State University Press, 1968), pp. 59-124 (originally published 1934).
  'The Nature of Customary International Law', in Josef L. Kunz, *The Changing Law of Nations* (Columbus, OH: Ohio State University Press, 1968), pp. 335-46 (originally published 1953).
  'Sanctions in International Law', in Josef L. Kunz, *The Changing Law of Nations* (Columbus, OH: Ohio State University Press, 1968), pp. 621-60 (originally published 1961).
Künzli, Jörg, *Vom Umgang des Rechtsstaats mit Unrechtsregimes – Völker- und landesrechtliche Grenzen des Verhaltensspielraums der schweizerischen Außenpolitik gegenüber Völkerrecht missachtenden Staaten* (Bern: Stämpfli, 2008).
Kutz, Christopher, *Complicity – Ethics and Law for a Collective Age* (Cambridge: Cambridge University Press, 2000).
  'Responsibility', in Jules Coleman and Scott Shapiro (eds.), *The Oxford Handbook of Jurisprudence and Philosophy of Law* (Oxford: Oxford University Press, 2002), pp. 548-87.
Lackner, Karl and Kristian Kühl, *Strafgesetzbuch mit Erläuterungen*, 26th edn (Munich: C. H. Beck, 2007).

Lagrange, Philippe, 'Responsabilité des Etats pour actes accomplis en application du Chapitre VII de la Charte des Nations Unies', *Revue générale de droit international public* 112 (2008), pp. 85-109.

Larsen, Kjetil Mujezinovic, 'Attribution of Conduct in Peace Operations: The "Ultimate Authority and Control" Test', *European Journal of International Law* 19 (2008), pp. 509-31.

'"Territorial Non-Application" of the European Convention on Human Rights', *Nordic Journal of International Law* 78 (2009), pp. 73-93.

Lauterpacht, Elihu, 'The Contemporary Practice of the United Kingdom in the Field of International Law - Survey and Comment', *International and Comparative Law Quarterly* 7 (1958), pp. 514-76.

(ed.), *British Practice in International Law in 1965* (London: British Institute for International and Comparative Law, 1967).

Lauterpacht, Elihu and Daniel Bethlehem, 'The Scope and Content of the Principle of Non-Refoulement: Opinion', in Erika Feller, Volker Türk and Frances Nicholson (eds.), *Refugee Protection in International Law - UNHCR's Global Consultations on International Protection* (Cambridge: Cambridge University Press, 2003), pp. 87-177.

Lauterpacht, Hersch, *Private Law Sources and Analogies in International Law* (London: Longmans, Green and Co., 1927).

The Function of Law in the International Community (Oxford: Clarendon Press, 1933).

'Neutrality and Collective Security', in Elihu Lauterpacht (ed.), *International Law Being the Collected Papers of Hersch Lauterpacht*, Vol. 5, *Disputes, War and Neutrality* (Cambridge: Cambridge University Press, 2005), pp. 611-31 (originally published in *Politica* 2 (1936), pp. 133-55).

'Contract to Breach a Contract', in Elihu Lauterpacht (ed.), *International Law Being the Collected Papers of Hersch Lauterpacht*, Vol. 4, *The Law of Peace, Parts VII-VIII* (Cambridge: Cambridge University Press, 1978), pp. 340-75 (originally published in *Law Quarterly Review* 52 (1936)).

'General Rules of the Law of Peace', in Elihu Lauterpacht (ed.), *International Law Being the Collected Papers of Hersch Lauterpacht*, Vol. 1, *The General Works* (Cambridge: Cambridge University Press, 1970), pp. 179-443 (originally published in French in *Recueil des Cours* 62 (1937-IV)).

'The Grotian Tradition in International Law', *British Year Book of International Law* 23 (1946), pp. 1-53.

Recognition in International Law (Cambridge: Cambridge University Press, 1948).

The Development of International Law by the International Court (London: Stevens, 1958).

Lawson, Rick, 'Life After Bankovic: On the Extraterritorial Application of the European Convention on Human Rights', in Fons Coomans and Menno T. Kamminga (eds.), *Extraterritorial Application of Human Rights Treaties* (Antwerp: Intersentia, 2004), pp. 85-123.

Lehnardt, Chia, 'Individual Liability of Private Military Personnel under International Criminal Law', *European Journal of International Law* 19 (2008), pp. 1015–34.

Leibholz, Gerhard, 'Das Verbot der Willkür und des Ermessensmißbrauchs im völkerrechtlichen Verkehr der Staaten', *Zeitschrift für ausländisches öffentliches Recht und Völkerrecht* 1 (1929), pp. 77–125.

Lerner, Nathan, 'Comment: Third States and International Measures Against Terrorism', *Archiv des Völkerrechts* 30 (1992), pp. 55–62.

Lindemann, Hans-Heinrich, 'Die Auswirkungen der Menschenrechtsverletzungen in Surinam auf die Vertragsbeziehungen zwischen den Niederlanden und Surinam', *Zeitschrift für ausländisches öffentliches Recht und Völkerrecht* 44 (1984), pp. 64–93.

'Völkerrechtliche Praxis der Bundesrepublik Deutschland im Jahre 1982', *Zeitschrift für ausländisches öffentliches Recht und Völkerrecht* 44 (1984), pp. 495–584.

Linderfalk, Ulf, 'State Responsibility and the Primary–Secondary Rules Terminology – The Role of Language for an Understanding of the International Legal System', *Nordic Journal of International Law* 78 (2009), pp. 53–72.

Liszt, Franz von, *Das Völkerrecht systematisch dargestellt*, 3rd edn (Berlin: Haering, 1904).

Lorenz, Dirk, *Der territoriale Anwendungsbereich der Grund- und Menschenrechte – Zugleich ein Beitrag zum Individualschutz in bewaffneten Konflikten* (Berlin: Berliner Wissenschafts-Verlag, 2005).

Lowe, Vaughan, 'The Politics of Law-Making: Are the Method and Character of Norm Creation Changing?', in Michael Byers (ed.), *The Role of Law in International Politics – Essays in International Relations and International Law* (Oxford: Oxford University Press, 2000), pp. 207–26.

'Responsibility for the Conduct of Other States', *Kokusaiho Gaiko Zassi* 101 (2002), pp. 1–15.

'The Iraq Crisis: What Now?', *International and Comparative Law Quarterly* 52 (2003), pp. 859–71.

International Law (Oxford: Oxford University Press, 2007).

Macdonald, Ronald St John, 'Fundamental Norms in Contemporary International Law', *Canadian Yearbook of International Law* 25 (1987), pp. 115–49.

Mahiou, Ahmed, 'Article 2, paragraphe 5', in Jean-Pierre Cot, Alain Pellet and Mathias Forteau (eds.), *La Charte des Nations Unies – Commentaire article par article*, 3rd edn (Paris: Economica, 2005), pp. 467–73.

Malanczuk, Peter, 'Haftung', in Karl-Heinz Böckstiegel (ed.), *Handbuch des Weltraumrechts* (Cologne: Heymanns, 1991), pp. 755–803.

Martens, Fedor de, *Traité de droit international, tome III*, traduit du russe par Alfred Léo (Paris: Marescqains, 1887).

Maslen, Stuart, *Commentaries on Arms Control Treaties*, Vol. I, *The Convention on the Stockpiling, Production, and Transfer of Anti-Personnel Mines and on Their Destruction*, 2nd edn (Oxford: Oxford University Press, 2005).
Matz, Nele, *Wege zur Koordinierung völkerrechtlicher Verträge – Völkervertragsrechtliche und institutionelle Ansätze* (Berlin: Springer, 2005).
McCorquodale, Robert, 'Impact on State Responsibility', in Menno T. Kamminga and Martin Scheinin (eds.), *The Impact of Human Rights Law on General International Law* (Oxford: Oxford University Press, 2009), pp. 235–54.
McCorquodale, Robert and Penelope Simons, 'Responsibility Beyond Borders: State Responsibility for Extraterritorial Violations by Corporations of International Human Rights Law', *Modern Law Review* 70 (2007), pp. 598–625.
McGregor, Lorna, 'State Immunity and Jus Cogens', *International and Comparative Law Quarterly* 55 (2006), pp. 437–46.
McNair, Arnold, *The Law of Treaties* (Oxford: Clarendon Press, 1961).
Mégret, Frédéric, 'Epilogue to an Endless Debate: The International Criminal Court's Third Party Jurisdiction and the Looming Revolution of International Law', *European Journal of International Law* 12 (2001), pp. 247–68.
Mehr, Farhang, 'Neutrality in the Gulf War', *Ocean Development and International Law* 20 (1989), pp. 105–6.
Meiertöns, Heiko, *Die Doktrinen US-amerikanischer Sicherheitspolitik – Völkerrechtliche Bewertung und ihr Einfluss auf das Völkerrecht* (Baden-Baden: Nomos, 2006).
Mendelson, Maurice H., 'The Formation of Customary International Law', *Recueil des Cours* 272 (1998), pp. 155–410.
Menzel, Jörg, 'Domestizierung des Leviathan? Südostasiens Verfassungen und ASEAN's neues Homogenitätskriterium demokratischer Verfassungsstaatlichkeit', *Verfassung und Recht in Übersee* 41 (2008), pp. 534–59.
Meron, Theodor, *Human Rights and Humanitarian Norms as Customary Law* (Oxford: Clarendon Press, 1989).
  'International Law in the Age of Human Rights – General Course on Public International Law', *Recueil des Cours* 301 (2003), pp. 9–490.
  The Humanization of International Law (Leiden: Nijhoff, 2006).
Milano, Enrico, *Unlawful Territorial Situations in International Law – Reconciling Effectiveness, Legality and Legitimacy* (Leiden: Nijhoff, 2006).
Milanovic, Marko, 'State Responsibility for Genocide', *European Journal of International Law* 17 (2006), pp. 553–604.
  'State Responsibility for Genocide: A Follow-Up', *European Journal of International Law* 18 (2007), pp. 669–94.
  'From Compromise to Principle: Clarifying the Concept of State Jurisdiction in Human Rights Treaties', *Human Rights Law Review* 8 (2008), pp. 411–48.

Mistelis, Loukas A., 'Confidentiality and Third Party Participation – UPS v. Canada and Methanex Corporation v. United States of America', *Arbitration International* 21 (2005), pp. 211–32.
Möckli, Daniel, 'Saadi v. Italy – The Rules of the Game Have Not Changed', *Human Rights Law Review* 8 (2008), pp. 534–48.
Moore, John Bassett (ed.), *History and Digest of the International Arbitrations to Which the United States Has Been a Party* (Washington DC: Government Printing Office, 1898).
Moore, Michael S., *Causation and Responsibility – An Essay in Law, Morals and Metaphysics* (Oxford: Oxford University Press, 2009).
Morrison, Fred L., 'Legal Issues in the Nicaragua Opinion', *American Journal of International Law* 81 (1987), pp. 160–6.
Morvay, Werner, 'Völkerrechtliche Praxis der Bundesrepublik Deutschland im Jahre 1959', *Zeitschrift für ausländisches öffentliches Recht und Völkerrecht* 21 (1961), pp. 259–300.
Mosler, Hermann, 'The International Society as a Legal Community', *Recueil des Cours* 140 (1974-IV), pp. 1–320.
  The International Society as a Legal Community (Alphen aan den Rijn: Kluwer, 1980).
  'General Principles of Law', in Rudolf Bernhardt (ed.), *Encyclopedia of Public International Law*, Vol. II, E-I (Amsterdam: Elsevier, 1999), pp. 511–27.
Müller, Jörg P. and Robert Kolb, 'Article 2(2)', in Bruno Simma (ed.), *The Charter of the United Nations – A Commentary*, 2nd edn (Oxford: Oxford University Press, 2002), pp. 91–101.
Müller, Jörn, 'The Signing of the US–India Agreement Concerning Peaceful Uses of Nuclear Energy', *Goettingen Journal of International Law* 1 (2009), pp. 179–98.
Müllerson, Rein, 'The Interplay of Objective and Subjective Elements in Customary International Law', in Karel Wellens (ed.), *International Law: Theory and Practice. Essays in Honour of Eric Suy* (The Hague: Nijhoff, 1998), pp. 161–78.
Nahapetian, Kate, 'Confronting State Complicity in International Law', *UCLA Journal of International Law and Foreign Affairs* 7 (2002), pp. 99–127.
Nakatani, Kazuhiro, 'Diplomacy and State Responsibility', in Maurizio Ragazzi (ed.), *International Responsibility Today – Essays in Memory of Oscar Schachter* (Leiden: Nijhoff, 2005), pp. 37–47.
Nardin, Terry, 'International Pluralism and the Rule of Law', *Review of International Studies* 26 (2000), pp. 95–110.
  'Theorising the International Rule of Law', *Review of International Studies* 34 (2008), pp. 385–401.
Neff, Stephen C., *The Rights and Duties of Neutrals – A General History* (Manchester: Manchester University Press, 2000).
  War and the Law of Nations – A General History (Cambridge: Cambridge University Press, 2005).

Neuhaus, Rupert Klaus, *Das Rechtsmißbrauchsverbot im heutigen Völkerrecht – Eine Untersuchung zur Entwicklung und Anwendbarkeit eines Begriffes* (Berlin: Duncker & Humblot, 1984).
Neuhold, Hanspeter, 'Die Pflicht zur Zusammenarbeit zwischen den Staaten: Moralisches Postulat oder völkerrechtliche Norm?', in H. Miehsler, E. Mock, B. Simma and I. Tammelo (eds.), *Ius Humanitas – Festschrift zum 90. Geburtstag von Alfred Verdross* (Berlin: Duncker & Humblot, 1980), pp. 575–606.
'Völkerrechtlicher Vertrag und "Drittstaaten"', *Berichte der Deutschen Gesellschaft für Völkerrecht* 29 (1988), pp. 51–103.
Niyungeko, Gérard, *La preuve devant les juridictions internationales* (Brussels: Bruylant, 2005).
Nollkaemper, André, 'Concurrence Between Individual Responsibility and State Responsibility in International Law', *International and Comparative Law Quarterly* 52 (2003), pp. 615–40.
'Internationally Wrongful Acts in Domestic Courts', *American Journal of International Law* 101 (2007), pp. 760–99.
'The Internationalized Rule of Law', *Hague Journal on the Rule of Law* 1 (2009), pp. 74–8.
Nolte, Georg, *Eingreifen auf Einladung – Zur Zulässigkeit des Einsatzes fremder Truppen im internen Konflikt auf Einladung der Regierung* (Berlin: Springer, 1999).
'Kosovo und Konstitutionalisierung: Zur humanitären Intervention der NATO-Staaten', *Zeitschrift für ausländisches öffentliches Recht und Völkerrecht* 59 (1999), pp. 941–60.
'The Limits of the Security Council's Powers and Its Functions in the International Legal System', in Michael Byers (ed.), *The Role of Law in International Politics* (Oxford: Oxford University Press, 2000), pp. 315–26.
'Article 2(7)', in Bruno Simma (ed.), *The Charter of the United Nations – A Commentary*, 2nd edn (Oxford: Oxford University Press, 2002), pp. 148–71.
'From Dionisio Anzilotti to Roberto Ago: The Classical International Law of State Responsibility and the Traditional Primacy of a Bilateral Conception of Inter-State Relations', *European Journal of International Law* 13 (2002), pp. 1083–98.
'Die USA und das Völkerrecht', *Die Friedens-Warte* 78 (2003), pp. 119–40.
'Sovereignty as Responsibility?', *Proceedings of the American Society of International Law* 99 (2005), pp. 389–93.
'Zum Wandel des Souveränitätsbegriffs', *Frankfurter Allgemeine Zeitung*, 6 April 2005, p. 8.
'With a Little Help from My Friends', *Frankfurter Allgemeine Zeitung*, 17 December 2005, p. 8.
'Secession and External Intervention', in Marcelo G. Kohen (ed.), *Secession – International Law Perspectives* (Cambridge: Cambridge University Press, 2006), pp. 65–93.

'Das Verfassungsrecht vor den Herausforderungen der Globalisierung', *Veröffentlichungen der Vereinigung deutscher Staatsrechtslehrer* 67 (2007), pp. 129–59.

'Zusammenarbeit der Staaten bei der Friedenssicherung – Steuerung durch Haftungsrecht', in Marten Breuer, Astrid Epiney, Andreas Haratsch, Stefanie Schmahl and Norman Weiß (eds.), *Im Dienste des Menschen: Recht, Staat und Staatengemeinschaft. Forschungskolloquium anlässlich der Emeritierung von Eckart Klein* (Berlin: Duncker & Humblot, 2009), pp. 19–35.

Nolte, Georg and Helmut Philipp Aust, 'Equivocal Helpers – Complicit States, Mixed Messages, and International Law', *International and Comparative Law Quarterly* 58 (2009), pp. 1–30.

Nowak, Manfred and Elizabeth McArthur, *The United Nations Convention Against Torture – A Commentary* (Oxford: Oxford University Press, 2008).

Noyes, John E. and Brian D. Smith, 'State Responsibility and the Principle of Joint and Severable Liability', *Yale Journal of International Law* 13 (1988), pp. 225–67.

O'Connell, Mary Ellen, 'Who Helps the Hegemon?', *Austrian Review of International and European Law* 8 (2003), pp. 91–100 (published 2005).

The Power and Purpose of International Law – Insights from the Theory and Practice of Enforcement (Oxford: Oxford University Press, 2008).

Oellers-Frahm, Karin, 'Phosphate Lands in Nauru Case (Nauru v. Australia)', in Rüdiger Bernhardt (ed.), *Encyclopedia of Public International Law*, Vol. III, J–P (Amsterdam: Elsevier, 1997), pp. 1025–7.

'Multiplication of International Courts and Tribunals and Conflicting Jurisdictions – Problems and Possible Solutions', *Max Planck Yearbook of United Nations Law* 5 (2001), pp. 67–104.

Oeter, Stefan, 'Ursprünge der Neutralität. Die Herausbildung des Instituts der Neutralität im Völkerrecht der frühen Neuzeit', *Zeitschrift für ausländisches öffentliches Recht und Völkerrecht* 48 (1988), pp. 447–88.

Neutralität und Waffenhandel (Berlin: Springer, 1992).

'Neutrality and Alliances', in *Le droit international de Vattel vu du XXIème siècle*, forthcoming, manuscript on file with the author.

Okowa, Phoebe N., *State Responsibility for Transboundary Air Pollution in International Law* (Oxford: Oxford University Press, 2000).

'Congo's War: The Legal Dimension of a Protracted Conflict', *British Year Book of International Law* 77 (2006), pp. 203–55.

Oliver, Covey T., 'The Monetary Gold Decision in Perspective', *American Journal of International Law* 49 (1955), pp. 216–21.

Oppenheim, Lassa, *International Law – A Treatise*, Vol. I, *Peace*, 2nd edn (London: Longmans, 1912).

International Law – A Treatise, Vol. II, *War and Neutrality*, 2nd edn (London: Longmans, 1912).

International Law – A Treatise, Vol. I, *Peace* (ed. by Hersch Lauterpacht) (London: Longmans, 1955).

Orakhelashvili, Alexander, 'State Immunity and International Public Order', *German Yearbook of International Law* 45 (2002), pp. 227-67.
  'Restrictive Interpretation of Human Rights Treaties in the Recent Jurisprudence of the European Court of Human Rights', *European Journal of International Law* 14 (2003), pp. 529-68.
  'International Public Order and the International Court's Advisory Opinion on the Legal Consequences of the Construction of a Wall in the Occupied Palestinian Territory', *Archiv des Völkerrechts* 43 (2005), pp. 240-56.
  Peremptory Norms in International Law (Oxford: Oxford University Press, 2006).
  'State Immunity and International Public Order Revisited', *German Yearbook of International Law* 49 (2006), pp. 327-65.
  'Overlap and Convergence: The Interaction Between Jus ad Bellum and Jus in Bello', *Journal of Conflict and Security Law* 12 (2007), pp. 157-96.
  'State Immunity and Hierarchy of Norms: Why the House of Lords Got It Wrong', *European Journal of International Law* 18 (2007), pp. 955-70.
  The Interpretation of Acts and Rules in Public International Law (Oxford: Oxford University Press, 2008).
  'Division of Reparation Between Responsible Entities', in James Crawford, Alain Pellet and Simon Olleson (eds.), *The Law of International Responsibility* (Oxford: Oxford University Press, 2010), pp. 647-65.
Ovey, Clare and Robin C. A. White, *The European Convention on Human Rights*, 4th edn (Oxford: Oxford University Press, 2006).
Padelletti, Maria Luisa, *Pluralità di Stati Nel Fatto Illecito Internazionale* (Milan: Giuffrè, 1990).
Palchetti, Paolo, 'State Responsibility for Complicity in Genocide', in Paola Gaeta (ed.), *The UN Genocide Convention - A Commentary* (Oxford: Oxford University Press, 2009), pp. 381-93.
Palombella, Gianluigi, 'The Abuse of Rights and the Rule of Law', in András Sajo (ed.), *Abuse - The Dark Side of Fundamental Rights* (Utrecht: Eleven, 2006), pp. 5-28.
  'The Rule of Law Beyond the State: Failures, Promises, and Theory', *International Journal of Constitutional Law* 7 (2009), pp. 442-67.
Paollilo, Felipe, 'Article 30 - Convention de 1969', in Olivier Corten and Pierre Klein (eds.), *Les Conventions de Vienne sur le droit des traités - Commentaire article par article*, Vols. I-III (Brussels: Bruylant, 2006), pp. 1247-83.
Parry, Clive, *The Sources and Evidence of International Law* (Manchester: Manchester University Press, 1965).
Paulus, Andreas L., *Die internationale Gemeinschaft im Völkerrecht: eine Untersuchung zur Entwicklung des Völkerrechts im Zeitalter der Globalisierung* (Munich: C. H. Beck, 2001).
  'International Law After Postmodernism: Towards Renewal or Decline of International Law?', *Leiden Journal of International Law* 14 (2001), pp. 727-55.

'The War Against Iraq and the Future of International Law: Hegemony or Pluralism?', *Michigan Journal of International Law* 25 (2004), pp. 691–733.
'Jus Cogens in a Time of Hegemony and Fragmentation', *Nordic Journal of International Law* 74 (2005), pp. 297–334.
'The Emergence of the International Community and the Divide Between International and Domestic Law', in Janne Nijman and André Nollkaemper (eds.), *New Perspectives on the Divide Between National and International Law* (Oxford: Oxford University Press, 2007), pp. 216–50.
'Zur Zukunft der Völkerrechtswissenschaft in Deutschland: Zwischen Konstitutionalisierung und Fragmentierung des Völkerrechts', *Zeitschrift für ausländisches öffentliches Recht und Völkerrecht* 67 (2007), pp. 695–719.
'The International Legal System as a Constitution', in Jeffrey L. Dunoff and Joel P. Trachtman (eds.), *Ruling the World – Constitutionalism, International Law, and Global Government* (Cambridge: Cambridge University Press, 2009), pp. 69–109.
Paust, Jordan J., 'Federal Jurisdiction over Extraterritorial Acts of Terrorism and Nonimmunity for Foreign Violators of International Law under the FISA and the Act of State Doctrine', *Virginia Journal of International Law* 23 (1983), pp. 191–249.
Pauwelyn, Joost, *Conflict of Norms in Public International Law – How WTO Law Relates to Other Rules of International Law* (Cambridge: Cambridge University Press, 2003).
Peerenboom, Randall, 'Human Rights and the Rule of Law – What's the Relationship?', *Georgetown Journal of International Law* 36 (2005), pp. 810–945.
Pellet, Alain, 'Can a State Commit a Crime? Definitely, Yes!', *European Journal of International Law* 10 (1999), pp. 425–34.
'Les articles de la CDI sur la responsabilité internationale de l'Etat pour fait internationalement illicite suite – et fin?', *Annuaire français de droit international* 43 (2002), pp. 1–23.
'Article 38', in Andreas Zimmermann, Christian Tomuschat and Karin Oellers-Frahm (eds.), *The Statute of the International Court of Justice – A Commentary* (Oxford: Oxford University Press, 2006), pp. 677–792.
'Conclusions', in Christian Tomuschat and Jean-Marc Thouvenin (eds.), *The Fundamental Rules of the International Legal Order – Jus Cogens and Obligations Erga Omnes* (Leiden: Nijhoff, 2006), pp. 417–24.
Petculescu, Ioana, 'Droit international de la responsabilité et droits de l'homme – A propos de l'arrêt de la Cour européenne des droits de l'homme du 8 juillet 2004 dans l'affaire Ilascu et autres c. la République de Moldova et la Fédération de Russie', *Revue générale de droit international public* 109 (2005), pp. 581–607.
Peters, Anne, 'The Growth of International Law between Globalization and the Great Power', *Austrian Review of International and European Law* 8 (2003), pp. 109–40 (published 2005).

'Compensatory Constitutionalism: The Function and Potential of Fundamental International Norms and Structures', *Leiden Journal of International Law* 19 (2006), pp. 579-610.

'Humanity as the A and Ω of Sovereignty', *European Journal of International Law* 20 (2009), pp. 513-44.

Petersen, Niels, 'Der Wandel des ungeschriebenen Völkerrechts im Zuge der Konstitutionalisierung', *Archiv des Völkerrechts* 46 (2008), pp. 502-23.

Pictet, Jean (ed.), *Commentaire – IV La Convention de Genève relative à la protection des personnes civiles en temps de guerre* (Geneva: International Committee of the Red Cross, 1956).

Pisillo Mazzeschi, Riccardo, 'The Due Diligence Rule and the Nature of International Responsibility of States', *German Yearbook of International Law* 35 (1992), pp. 9-51.

Politis, Nicolas, 'Le problème des limitations de la souveraineté et la théorie de l'abus des droit dans les rapports internationaux', *Recueil des Cours* 6 (1925-I), pp. 1-121.

Quigley, John, 'Complicity in International Law: A New Direction in the Law of State Responsibility', *British Year Book of International Law* 57 (1986), pp. 77-131.

'State Responsibility for Ethnic Cleansing', *UC Davis Law Review* 32 (1999), pp. 341-85.

The Genocide Convention – An International Law Analysis (Aldershot: Ashgate, 2006).

Soviet Legal Innovation and the Law of the Western World (Cambridge: Cambridge University Press, 2007).

'International Court of Justice as a Forum for Genocide Cases', *Case Western Reserve Journal of International Law* 40 (2007-8), pp. 243-63.

Ragazzi, Maurizio, *The Concept of International Obligations 'Erga Omnes'* (Oxford: Oxford University Press, 1997).

Randelzhofer, Albrecht, 'Article 2(4)', in Bruno Simma (ed.), *The Charter of the United Nations – A Commentary*, 2nd edn (Oxford: Oxford University Press, 2002), pp. 112-36.

Ratner, Steven R., 'Corporations and Human Rights: A Theory of Legal Responsibility', *Yale Law Journal* 111 (2003), pp. 443-545.

'Predator and Prey: Seizing and Killing Suspected Terrorists Abroad', *Journal of Political Philosophy* 15 (2007), pp. 251-75.

Rauschning, Dietrich, 'Allgemeine Völkerrechtsregeln zum Schutz gegen grenzüberschreitende Umweltbeinträchtigungen', in Ingo von Münch (ed.), *Staatsrecht – Völkerrecht – Europarecht: Festschrift für Hans-Jürgen Schlochauer* (Berlin: de Gruyter, 1981), pp. 557-76.

'Verantwortlichkeit der Staaten für völkerrechtswidriges Verhalten', *Berichte der Deutschen Gesellschaft für Völkerrecht* 24 (1984), pp. 7-34.

Raz, Joseph, 'The Rule of Law and Its Virtue', in Joseph Raz, *The Authority of Law – Essays on Law and Morality* (Oxford: Clarendon Press, 1979), pp. 210-29.

'The Politics of the Rule of Law', in Joseph Raz, *Ethics in the Public Domain* (Oxford: Clarendon Press, 1994), pp. 354–62.
Redslob, Robert, *Théorie de la Société des Nations* (Paris: Rousseau, 1927).
Reisman, W. Michael, *Nullity and Revision – The Review and Enforcement of International Judgments and Awards* (New Haven, CT: Yale University Press, 1971).
Reisman, W. Michael and Andrew R. Willard (eds.), *International Incidents* (Princeton, NJ: Princeton University Press, 1988).
Rensmann, Thilo, *Wertordnung und Grundgesetz – Das Grundgesetz im Kontext grenzüberschreitender Konstitutionalisierung* (Tübingen: Mohr Siebeck, 2007).
'Die Humanisierung des Völkerrechts durch das ius in bello – Von der Marten'schen Klausel zur Responsibility to Protect', *Zeitschrift für ausländisches öffentliches Recht und Völkerrecht* 68 (2008), pp. 111–28.
'Impact on the Immunity of States and Their Officials', in Menno T. Kamminga and Martin Scheinin (eds.), *The Impact of Human Rights Law on General International Law* (Oxford: Oxford University Press, 2009), pp. 151–70.
Reyes-Knoche, Susanne and Katrin Arend, 'Article XX lit d GATT', in Rüdiger Wolfrum, Peter-Tobias Stoll and Anja Seibert-Fohr (eds.), *Max Planck Commentaries on World Trade Law*, Vol. 3, *WTO – Technical Barriers and SPS Measures* (Leiden: Nijhoff, 2007), pp. 124–33.
Rigaux, François, 'International Responsibility and the Principle of Causality', in Maurizio Ragazzi (ed.), *International Responsibility Today: Essays in Memory of Oscar Schachter* (Leiden: Nijhoff, 2005), pp. 81–92.
Riphagen, Willem A., 'State Responsibility: New Theories of Obligation in Interstate Relations', in Ronald St John Macdonald and Douglas M. Johnston (eds.), *The Structure and Process of International Law: Essays in Legal Philosophy, Doctrine and Theory* (The Hague: Nijhoff, 1983), pp. 581–625.
'General Principles of Law', in Antonio Cassese and Joseph H. H. Weiler (eds.), *Change and Stability in International Law-Making* (Berlin: de Gruyter, 1988), pp. 33–7.
Rodiles, Alejandro, 'Coaliciones of the Willing: Coyuntura, Contexto y Propriedades. Un primer esbozo', *Anuario Mexicano de Derecho Internacional* 7 (2007), pp. 675–702.
Ronzitti, Natalino, 'Italy's Non-Belligerency During the Iraq War', in Maurizio Ragazzi (ed.), *International Responsibility Today – Essays in Memory of Oscar Schachter* (Leiden: Nijhoff, 2005), pp. 197–207.
Rorty, Richard, *Contingency, Irony and Solidarity* (Cambridge: Cambridge University Press, 1989).
Rosenne, Shabtai, *The Law and Practice of the International Court of Justice 1920–2005*, 4 vols., 4th edn (Leiden: Nijhoff, 2006).
'International Courts and Tribunals, Jurisdiction and Admissibility of Inter-State Applications', in Rüdiger Wolfrum (ed.), *Max Planck Encyclopedia of Public International Law*, online edition (Oxford: Oxford University Press, 2008).

Roulet, Jean-David, *Le caractère artificiel de la théorie de l'abus de droit en droit international public* (Neuchâtel: Editions de la Baconnière, 1958).
Rozakis, Christos L., 'Treaties and Third States: A Study in the Reinforcement of the Consensual Standards in International Law', *Zeitschrift für ausländisches öffentliches Recht und Völkerrecht* 35 (1975), pp. 1–40.
  The Concept of Jus Cogens in the Law of Treaties (Amsterdam: North-Holland Publishing Company, 1976).
Ruffert, Matthias, 'Zusammenarbeit der Staaten bei der Friedenssicherung: Kommentar', in Marten Breuer, Astrid Epiney, Andreas Haratsch, Stefanie Schmahl and Norman Weiß (eds.), *Im Dienste des Menschen: Recht, Staat und Staatengemeinschaft. Forschungskolloquium anlässlich der Emeritierung von Eckart Klein* (Berlin: Duncker & Humblot, 2009), pp. 37–42.
Russo, Francis V., 'Neutrality at Sea in Transition: State Practice in the Gulf War as Emerging International Customary Law', *Ocean Development and International Law* 19 (1988), pp. 381–99.
Ryngaert, Cedric, *Jurisdiction in International Law* (Oxford: Oxford University Press, 2008).
Salacuse, Jeswald W. and Nicholas P. Sullivan, 'Do BITs Really Work? An Evaluation of Bilateral Investment Treaties and Their Grand Bargain', *Harvard International Law Journal* 46 (2005), pp. 67–130.
Salvioli, Gabriele, 'Les règles générales de la paix', *Recueil des Cours* 46 (1933-IV), pp. 1–164.
Sand, Peter H., *United States and Britain in Diego Garcia* (New York: Palgrave Macmillan, 2009).
Sands, Philippe, 'International Rule of Law: Extraordinary Rendition, Complicity and Its Consequences', *European Human Rights Law Review* (2006), pp. 411–21.
Santos, Alvaro, 'The World Bank's Uses of the "Rule of Law" Promise in Economic Development', in David M. Trubek and Alvaro Santos (eds.), *The New Law and Economic Development* (Cambridge: Cambridge University Press, 2006), pp. 253–302.
Sari, Aurel, 'Jurisdiction and International Responsibility in Peace Support Operations: The Behrami and Saramati Cases', *Human Rights Law Review* 8 (2008), pp. 151–70.
Sassòli, Marc, 'State Responsibility for Violations of International Humanitarian Law', *International Review of the Red Cross* 84 (2002), No. 846, pp. 401–34.
Sassòli, Marc and Antoine Bouvier, 'How Does Law Protect in War? Cases, Documents and Teaching Materials on Contemporary Practice in International Humanitarian Law', 2nd edn (Geneva: International Committee of the Red Cross, 2006).
Saul, Ben, 'Attempts to Define Terrorism in International Law', *Netherlands International Law Review* 52 (2003), pp. 57–83.

Savarese, Eduardo, 'Complicité de l'Etat dans la perpétration d'actes de génocide: Les notions contiguës et la nature de la norme', *Annuaire français de droit international* 53 (2007), pp. 280–90.

Scalia, Antonin, 'The Rule of Law as a Law of Rules', *University of Chicago Law Review* 56 (1989), pp. 1175–88.

Scelle, Georges, *Précis de droit des gens – Principes et systématique*, Vol. I, *Introduction – Le milieu intersocial* (Paris: Recueil Sirey, 1932).

  'Le phénomène juridique du dédoublement fonctionnel', in Wolfgang Schätzel and Hans-Jürgen Schlochauer (eds.), *Rechtsfragen der internationalen Organisation. Festschrift für Hans Wehberg* (Frankfurt/Main: Klostermann, 1956), pp. 324–42.

Schabas, William A., *Genocide in International Law* (Cambridge: Cambridge University Press, 2000).

  'Enforcing International Humanitarian Law: Catching the Accomplices', *International Review of the Red Cross* 83 (2001), No. 842, pp. 439–59.

  An Introduction to the International Criminal Court, 3rd edn (Cambridge: Cambridge University Press, 2007).

Schapiro, Tamar, 'Compliance, Complicity, and the Nature of Nonideal Conditions', *Journal of Philosophy* 100 (2003), pp. 329–55.

Scheuner, Ulrich, 'Naturrechtliche Strömungen im heutigen Völkerrecht', *Zeitschrift für ausländisches öffentliches Recht und Völkerrecht* 13 (1950–1), pp. 556–619.

Schindler, Dietrich, 'Die erga omnes-Wirkung des humanitären Völkerrechts', in U. Beyerlin, M. Bothe and R. Hofmann (eds.), *Recht zwischen Umbruch und Bewährung – Festschrift für Rudolf Bernhardt* (Berlin: Springer, 1995), pp. 199–211.

Schlink, Bernhard, 'Freiheit durch Eingriffsabwehr – Rekonstruktion der klassischen Grundrechtsfunktion', *Europäische Grundrechte-Zeitschrift* 11 (1984), pp. 457–68.

Schlochauer, Hans-Jürgen, 'Die Theorie des abus de droit im Völkerrecht', *Zeitschrift für Völkerrecht* 17 (1933), pp. 373–94.

Schmitt, Carl, *Verfassungslehre*, 9th edn (Berlin: Duncker & Humblot, 2003) (originally published 1928).

  Die Wendung zum diskriminierenden Kriegsbegriff, 3rd edn (Berlin: Duncker & Humblot, 2003) (originally published 1938).

  Der Nomos der Erde im Völkerrecht des Jus Publicum Europaeum, 4th edn (Berlin: Duncker & Humblot, 1997) (originally published 1950).

Schoen, Paul, *Die völkerrechtliche Haftung der Staaten aus unerlaubten Handlungen* (Breslau: Kern, 1917).

Schorer, Sabine, *Das Konsensprinzip in der internationalen Gerichtsbarkeit* (Frankfurt/Main: Peter Lang, 2003).

Schreuer, Christoph, 'Unjust Enrichment', in Rudolf Bernhardt (ed.), *Encyclopedia of Public International Law*, Vol. IV, Q–Z (Amsterdam: Elsevier, 2000), pp. 1243–6.

Schücking, Walther, *Der Staatenverband der Haager Konferenzen* (Munich: Duncker & Humblot, 1912).
  Internationale Rechtsgarantien – Ausbau und Sicherung der zwischenstaatlichen Beziehungen (Hamburg: Broschek, 1918).
Schücking, Walther and Hans Wehberg, *Die Satzung des Völkerbundes*, 2nd edn (Berlin: Vahlen, 1924).
Schultz, Nikolaus, 'Ist Lotus verblüht? Anmerkung zum Urteil des IGH vom 14. Februar 2002 im Fall betreffend den Haftbefehl vom 11. April 2000 (Demokratische Republik Kongo gegen Belgien)', *Zeitschrift für ausländisches öffentliches Recht und Völkerrecht* 62 (2002), pp. 703–58.
Schwarzenberger, Georg, 'Uses and Abuses of the "Abuse of Rights", in International Law', *Transactions of the Grotius Society* 46 (1952), pp. 147–79.
Schwarzenberger, Georg and Edward Duncan Brown, *A Manual of International Law*, 6th edn (Milton: Professional Books, 1976).
Schweisfurth, Theodor, 'Aggression', *Frankfurter Allgemeine Zeitung*, 28 April 2003, p. 10.
Scobbie, Iain and Catriona Drew, 'Self-Determination Undetermined: The Case of East Timor', *Leiden Journal of International Law* 9 (1996), pp. 185–211.
Shaker, Mohamed Ibrahim, 'The Evolving International Regime of Nuclear Non-Proliferation', *Recueil des Cours* 321 (2006), pp. 9–202.
Shaw, Malcolm N., *International Law*, 6th edn (Cambridge: Cambridge University Press, 2008).
Sheehan, James J., *Kontinent der Gewalt – Europas langer Weg zum Frieden*, translated by Martin Richter (Bonn: Bundeszentrale für politische Bildung, 2008).
Shelton, Dinah, 'Righting Wrongs: Reparations in the Articles on State Responsibility', *American Journal of International Law* 96 (2002), pp. 832–56.
  'International Law and "Normative Relativity"', in Malcolm D. Evans (ed.), *International Law*, 2nd edn (Oxford: Oxford University Press, 2006), pp. 159–85.
  'Normative Hierarchy in International Law', *American Journal of International Law* 100 (2006), pp. 291–323.
Shklar, Judith N., 'Political Theory and the Rule of Law', in Allan C. Hutchinson and Patrick Monahan (eds.), *The Rule of Law – Ideal or Ideology?* (Toronto: Transnational, 1987), pp. 1–16.
Sicilianos, Linos-Alexandre, *Les réactions décentralisées à l'illicite – Des contremesures à la légitime défense* (Paris: LGDJ, 1990).
Simma, Bruno, *Das Reziprozitätselement in der Entstehung des Völkergewohnheitsrechts* (Munich: Fink, 1970).
  'Grundfragen der Staatenverantwortlichkeit in der Arbeit der International Law Commission', *Archiv des Völkerrechts* 24 (1985), pp. 357–407.
  'Self-Contained Regimes', *Netherlands Yearbook of International Law* 16 (1985), pp. 111–36.

'The Antarctic Treaty as a Treaty Providing for an "Objective Régime"', *Cornell International Law Journal* 19 (1986), pp. 189–209.

'Bilateralism and Community Interest in the Law of State Responsibility', in Yoram Dinstein (ed.), *International Law at a Time of Perplexity – Essays in Honour of Shabtai Rosenne* (Dordrecht: Nijhoff, 1989), pp. 821–44.

'From Bilateralism to Community Interest in International Law', *Recueil des Cours* 250 (1994-VI), pp. 217–384.

'Comment', in Andreas Zimmermann and Rainer Hofmann (eds.), *Unity and Diversity in International Law* (Berlin: Duncker & Humblot, 2006), pp. 467–70.

Simma, Bruno and Philip Alston, 'The Sources of Human Rights Law: Custom, Jus Cogens, and General Principles', *Australian Yearbook of International Law* 12 (1992), pp. 82–108.

Simma, Bruno and Daniel-Erasmus Khan, 'Verwaltungshandeln im Außenwirtschaftsrecht – Die Berücksichtigung menschenrechtlicher Gesichtspunkte bei der Auslegung und Anwendung nationaler Vorschriften zur Steuerung der grenzüberschreitenden Wirtschaftstätigkeit', in B. Großfeld, R. Sack and Th J. Möllers (eds.), *Festschrift für Wolfgang Fikentscher zum 70. Geburtstag* (Tübingen: Mohr Siebeck, 1998), pp. 1009–29.

Simma, Bruno and Dirk Pulkowski, 'Of Planets and the Universe: Self-Contained Regimes in International Law', *European Journal of International Law* 17 (2006), pp. 483–530.

Simpson, Gerry, *Great Powers and Outlaw States: Unequal Sovereigns in the International Legal Order* (Cambridge: Cambridge University Press, 2004).

Singer, P. W., 'Corporate Warriors: The Rise of the Privatized Military Industry and Its Ramifications for International Security', *International Security* 26, No. 3 (2001-2), pp. 186–220.

Sivakumaran, Sandesh, 'Application of the Convention on the Prevention and Punishment of the Crime of Genocide (Bosnia and Herzegovina v. Serbia and Montenegro)', *International and Comparative Law Quarterly* 56 (2007), pp. 695–708.

'Impact on the Structure of International Obligations', in Menno T. Kamminga and Martin Scheinin (eds.), *The Impact of Human Rights Law on General International Law* (Oxford: Oxford University Press, 2009), pp. 133–50.

Skogly, Sigrun I., *Beyond National Borders: States' Human Rights Obligations in International Cooperation* (Antwerp: Intersentia, 2006).

Slaughter, Anne-Marie, *A New World Order* (Princeton, NJ: Princeton University Press, 2004).

Smend, Rudolf, *Staatsrechtliche Abhandlungen und andere Aufsätze*, 3rd edn (Berlin: Duncker & Humblot, 1994).

Smith, Brian D., *State Responsibility and the Marine Environment – The Rules of Decision* (Oxford: Oxford University Press, 1988).

Smith, K. J. M., *A Modern Treatise on the Law of Criminal Complicity* (Oxford: Clarendon Press, 1991).
Somek, Alexander, 'From the Rule of Law to the Constitutionalist Makeover: Changing European Conceptions of Public International Law', University of Iowa Legal Studies Research Paper No. 09-25, May 2009, available at http://ssrn.com/abstract=1397249 (last visited 1 November 2010).
Sørensen, Max, *Les sources du droit international – Etude sur la jurisprudence de la Cour permanente de la Justice internationale* (Copenhagen: Munskgaard, 1946).
  'Principes de droit international public', *Recueil des Cours* 101 (1960-III), pp. 5–254.
Spiermann, Ole, 'Lotus and the Double Structure of International Legal Argument', in Laurence Boisson de Chazournes and Philippe Sands (eds.), *International Law, the International Court of Justice and Nuclear Weapons* (Cambridge: Cambridge University Press, 1999), pp. 131–52.
Spinedi, Marina, 'International Crimes of State: The Legislative History', in Joseph H. H. Weiler, Antonio Cassese and Marina Spinedi (eds.), *International Crimes of State: A Critical Analysis of the ILC's Draft Article 19 on State Responsibility* (Berlin: de Gruyter, 1989), pp. 7–138.
  'From One Codification to Another: Bilateralism and Multilateralism in the Genesis of the Codification of the Law of Treaties and the Law of State Responsibility', *European Journal of International Law* 13 (2002), pp. 1099–1125.
Stahn, Carsten, 'Responsibility to Protect: Political Rhetoric or Emerging Norm?', *American Journal of International Law* 101 (2007), pp. 99–120.
Stein, Torsten, 'International Measures Against Terrorism and Sanctions By and Against Third States', *Archiv des Völkerrechts* 30 (1992), pp. 38–54.
Stern, Brigitte, 'La France et le droit de la responsabilité internationale des Etats', in Gérard Cahin, Florence Poirat and Sandra Szurek (eds.), *La France et le droit international*, Vol. I, *Ouverture* (Paris: Pedone, 2007), pp. 169–95.
Stoll, Peter-Tobias, 'Responsibility, Sovereignty and Cooperation – Reflections on the "Responsibility to Protect"', in Doris König, Peter-Tobias Stoll, Volker Röben and Nele Matz-Lück (eds.), *International Law Today – New Challenges and the Need for Reform?* (Berlin: Springer, 2008), pp. 1–16.
Stowell, Ellery C., *International Law* (New York: Henry Holt, 1931).
Streinz, Rudolf, 'Artikel 26', in Michael Sachs (ed.), *Grundgesetz – Kommentar*, 5th edn (Munich: C. H. Beck, 2009), pp. 978–93.
Strupp, Karl, *Das völkerrechtliche Delikt* (= *Handbuch des Völkerrechts, Dritter Band, Erste Abteilung a*) (Stuttgart: Kohlhammer, 1920).
  'Les règles générales du droit de la paix', *Recueil des Cours* 47 (1934), pp. 259–595.
Sztucki, Jerzy, *Jus Cogens and the Vienna Convention on the Law of Treaties* (Vienna: Springer, 1974).

Szurek, Sandra, 'Responsabilité de protéger, nature de l'obligation et responsabilité internationale', in Société française pour le droit international (ed.), *La responsabilité de protéger* (Paris: Pedone, 2008), pp. 91–134.
Talmon, Stefan, 'The Cyprus Question before the European Court of Justice', *European Journal of International Law* 12 (2001), pp. 727–50.
  Kollektive Nichtanerkennung illegaler Staaten (Tübingen: Mohr Siebeck, 2006).
  'The Obligation Not to "Recognize as Lawful" a Situation Created by the Illegal Use of Force or Other Serious Breaches of a Jus Cogens Obligation: An Obligation without Real Substance?', in Christian Tomuschat and Jean-Marc Thouvenin (eds.), *The Fundamental Rules of the International Legal Order: Jus Cogens and Obligations Erga Omnes* (Leiden: Nijhoff, 2006), pp. 99–125.
  La non-reconnaissance collective des Etats illégaux (Paris: Pedone, 2007).
  'A Plurality of Responsible Actors: International Responsibility for Acts of the Coalition Provisional Authority in Iraq', in Phil Shiner and Andrew Williams (eds.), *The Iraq War and International Law* (Oxford: Hart, 2008), pp. 185–230.
Tamanaha, Brian Z., *On the Rule of Law – History, Politics, Theory* (Cambridge: Cambridge University Press, 2004).
Tams, Christian J., 'All's Well That Ends Well – Comments on the ILC Articles on State Responsibility', *Zeitschrift für ausländisches öffentliches Recht und Völkerrecht* 62 (2002), pp. 759–96.
  'Do Serious Breaches Give Rise to Any Specific Obligations of the Responsible State?', *European Journal of International Law* 13 (2002), pp. 1161–80.
  'Probleme mit dem Ius Cogens', *Archiv des Völkerrechts* 40 (2002), pp. 331–49.
  Enforcing Obligations Erga Omnes in International Law (Cambridge: Cambridge University Press, 2005).
  'Article 49', in Andreas Zimmermann, Christian Tomuschat and Karin Oellers-Frahm (eds.), *The Statute of the International Court of Justice – A Commentary* (Oxford: Oxford University Press, 2006), pp. 1099–1108.
  'Unity and Diversity in the Law of State Responsibility', in Andreas Zimmermann and Rainer Hofmann (eds.), *Unity and Diversity in International Law* (Berlin: Duncker & Humblot, 2006), pp. 437–60.
  'Buchbesprechung (Alexander Orakhelashvili, Peremptory Norms, 2006)', *Verfassung und Recht in Übersee* 40 (2007), pp. 380–3.
  'The Abuse of Executive Powers: What Remedies?', in Andrea Bianchi and Alexis Keller (eds.), *Counterterrorism: Democracy's Challenge* (Oxford: Hart, 2008), pp. 313–34.
Tams, Christian J. and Andreas Zimmermann, '"The Federation Shall Accede to Agreements Providing for General and Compulsory International Arbitration" – The German Optional Clause Declaration of 1 May 2008', *German Yearbook of International Law* 51 (2008), pp. 391–416.

Tancredi, Antonelli, 'A Normative "Due Process", in the Creation of States through Secession', in Marcelo G. Kohen (ed.), *Secession – International Law Perspectives* (Cambridge: Cambridge University Press, 2006), pp. 171–207.
Tange, P. C., 'Netherlands State Practice for the Parliamentary Year 2002–2003', *Netherlands Yearbook of International Law* 35 (2004), pp. 317–94.
'Netherlands State Practice for the Parliamentary Year 2005–2006', *Netherlands Yearbook of International Law* 38 (2007), pp. 263–366.
Taylor, G. D. S., 'The Content of the Rule Against Abuse of Rights in International Law', *British Year Book of International Law* 46 (1972–3), pp. 323–52.
Teitel, Ruti G., 'Humanity's Law: Rule of Law for the New Global Politics', *Cornell International Law Journal* 35 (2002), pp. 355–87.
Téson, Fernando R., 'The Liberal Case for Humanitarian Intervention', in J. L. Holzgrefe and Robert O. Keohane (eds.), *Humanitarian Intervention – Ethical, Legal and Political Dilemmas* (Cambridge: Cambridge University Press, 2003), pp. 93–129.
Thienel, Tobias, 'The Admissibility of Evidence Obtained by Torture under International Law', *European Journal of International Law* 17 (2006), pp. 349–67.
'The Burden and Standard of Proof in the European Court of Human Rights', *German Yearbook of International Law* 50 (2007), pp. 543–88.
Thirlway, Hugh, 'The Law and Procedure of the International Court of Justice, Part Nine', *British Year Book of International Law* 69 (1998), pp. 1–83.
'Injured and Non-Injured States Before the International Court of Justice', in Maurizio Ragazzi (ed.), *International Responsibility Today – Essays in Memory of Oscar Schachter* (Leiden: Nijhoff, 2005), pp. 311–28.
Tigoudra, Hélène, 'La Cour européenne de droits de l'homme et les immunités juridictionelles d'Etats – Observations sous les arrêts McElhinney, Fogarty et al-Adsani', *Revue belge de droit international* 34 (2001), pp. 526–48.
'Le régime d'occupation en Iraq', *Annuaire français de droit international* 50 (2004), pp. 77–101.
Tomuschat, Christian, 'Völkerrechtlicher Vertrag und Drittstaaten', *Berichte der Deutschen Gesellschaft für Völkerrecht* 28 (1988), pp. 9–49.
'Obligations Arising for States Without or Against Their Will', *Recueil des Cours* 241 (1993-IV), pp. 195–374.
'Die internationale Gemeinschaft', *Archiv des Völkerrechts* 33 (1995), pp. 1–20.
'International Crimes by States: An Endangered Species?', in Karel Wellens (ed.), *International Law: Theory and Practice. Essays in Honour of Eric Suy* (The Hague: Kluwer, 1998), pp. 253–74.
'International Law: Ensuring the Survival of Mankind on the Eve of a New Century: General Course on Public International Law', *Recueil des Cours* 281 (1999), pp. 9–438.
'L'immunité des Etats en cas de violations graves des droits de l'homme', *Revue générale de droit international public* 109 (2005), pp. 51–74.

'Article 36', in Andreas Zimmermann, Christian Tomuschat and Karin Oellers-Frahm (eds.), *The Statute of the International Court of Justice – A Commentary* (Oxford: Oxford University Press, 2006), pp. 589–657.

'Internationale Terrorismusbekämpfung als Herausforderung für das Völkerrecht', *Die Öffentliche Verwaltung* (2006), pp. 357–69.

'Reconceptualizing the Debate on Jus Cogens and Obligations Erga Omnes – Concluding Observations', in Christian Tomuschat and Jean-Marc Thouvenin (eds.), *The Fundamental Rules of the International Legal Order – Jus Cogens and Obligations Erga Omnes* (Leiden: Nijhoff, 2006), pp. 425–36.

'Reparation in Cases of Genocide', *Journal of International Criminal Justice* 5 (2007), pp. 905–12.

'Case Note: R (on the Application of al-Jedda) v. Secretary of State for Defence – Human Rights in a Multi-Level System of Governance and the Internment of Suspected Terrorists', *Melbourne Journal of International Law* 10 (2008), available at http://mjil.law.unimelb.edu.au/go/issues/issue-archive/volume-9-2 (last visited 1 November 2010).

Human Rights – Between Idealism and Realism, 2nd edn (Oxford: Oxford University Press, 2008).

Torres Bernárdez, Santiago, 'The New Theory of "Indispensable Parties" under the Statute of the International Court of Justice', in Karel Wellens (ed.), *International Law: Theory and Practice. Essays in Honour of Eric Suy* (The Hague: Kluwer, 1998), pp. 737–50.

Toufayan, Mark, 'A Return to Communitarianism? Reacting to "Serious Breaches of Obligations under Peremptory Norms of General International Law" under the Law of State Responsibility and United Nations Law', *Canadian Yearbook of International Law* 42 (2004), pp. 197–251.

Treves, Tullio, 'Customary International Law', in Rüdiger Wolfrum (ed.), *Max Planck Encyclopedia of Public International Law*, online edition (Oxford: Oxford University Press, 2008).

Triepel, Heinrich, *Völkerrecht und Landesrecht* (Leipzig: Hirschfeld, 1899).

Trubek, David M., 'The "Rule of Law", in Development Assistance: Past, Present, and Future', in David M. Trubek and Alvaro Santos (eds.), *The New Law and Economic Development* (Cambridge: Cambridge University Press, 2006), pp. 74–94.

Tsagourias, Nicholas, 'Globalization, Order and the Rule of Law', *Finnish Yearbook of International Law* 11 (2000), pp. 247–64.

Turns, David, 'The Stimson Doctrine of Non-Recognition: Its Historical Genesis and Influence on Contemporary International Law', *Chinese Journal of International Law* 2 (2003), pp. 105–44.

'Implementation and Compliance', in Elizabeth Wilmshurst and Susan Breau (eds.), *Perspectives on the ICRC Study on Customary International Humanitarian Law* (Cambridge: Cambridge University Press, 2007), pp. 354–76.

Ugrekhelidze, Mindia, 'Causation: Reflection in the Mirror of the European Convention on Human Rights (A Sketch)', in L. Caflisch, J. Callewaert, R. Liddell, P. Mahoney and M. Villiger (eds.), *Liber Amicorum Luzius Wildhaber: Human Rights – Strasbourg Views* (Kehl: N. P. Engel, 2007), pp. 469–81.

UK Ministry of Defence (ed.), *The Manual of the Law of Armed Conflict* (Oxford: Oxford University Press, 2004).

Vagts, Detlev F., 'The Traditional Law of Neutrality in a Changing Environment', *American University International Law Review* 14 (1998), pp. 83–102.

Vashakmadze, Mindia, *Die Stationierung fremder Truppen im Völkerrecht und ihre demokratische Kontrolle – Eine Untersuchung unter besonderer Berücksichtigung Georgiens* (Berlin: Duncker & Humblot, 2008).

Vattel, Emer de, *Le droit des gens ou principes de la loi naturelle appliqués à la conduite et aux affaires des Nations et de Souverains*, Classics of International Law, ed. by James Brown Scott (Washington, DC: Carnegie Endowment for International Peace, 1916) (originally published in 1758).

Verdross, Alfred, 'Forbidden Treaties in International Law', *American Journal of International Law* 31 (1937), pp. 571–7.

'La neutralité dans le cadre de l'ONU particulièrement celle de la République d'Autriche', *Revue générale de droit international public* 61 (1957), pp. 177–92.

'Entstehungsweisen und Geltungsgrund des universellen völkerrechtlichen Gewohnheitsrechts', *Zeitschrift für ausländisches öffentliches Recht und Völkerrecht* 29 (1969), pp. 635–53.

Die Quellen des universellen Völkerrechts – Eine Einführung (Freiburg: Rombach, 1973).

Verdross, Alfred and Bruno Simma, *Universelles Völkerrecht – Theorie und Praxis*, 3rd edn (Berlin: Duncker & Humblot, 1984).

Verhoeven, Joe, *La reconnaissance internationale dans la pratique contemporaine – Les relations publiques internationales* (Paris: Pedone, 1973).

'La reconnaissance internationale: déclin ou renouveau?', *Annuaire Français de Droit International* 39 (1993), pp. 7–40.

Droit international public (Brussels: Larcier, 2000).

Vermeer-Künzli, Annemarieke, 'Exercising Diplomatic Protection – The Fine Line Between Litigation, Demarches and Consular Assistance', *Zeitschrift für ausländisches öffentliches Recht und Völkerrecht* 66 (2006), pp. 321–50.

Villalpando, Santiago, *L'émergence de la communauté internationale dans la responsabilité des Etats* (Paris: Presses universitaires de France, 2005).

'The Legal Dimension of the International Community: How Community Interests Are Protected in International Law', *European Journal of International Law* 21 (2010), 387–419.

Villiger, Mark E., *Customary International Law and Treaties – A Manual on the Theory and Practice of the Interrelation of Sources*, 2nd edn (The Hague: Kluwer, 1997).

Vitzthum, Wolfgang Graf (ed.), *Handbuch des Seerechts* (Munich: C. H. Beck, 2006).
  (ed.), *Völkerrecht*, 4th edn (Berlin: de Gruyter, 2007).
Waldock, C. Humphrey M., 'The Regulation of the Use of Force by Individual States in International Law', *Recueil des Cours* 81 (1952-II), pp. 451-517.
Waldron, Jeremy, 'The Rule of International Law', *Harvard Journal of Law and Public Policy* 30 (2006-7), pp. 15-30.
  'Are Sovereigns Entitled to the Benefit of the International Rule of Law?', Institute of International Law and Justice Working Paper 2009/3, available at http://papers.ssrn.com/sol3/papers.cfm?abstract_id=1323383 (last visited 1 November 2010).
Wallis, Andrew, *Silent Accomplice – The Untold Story of France's Role in Rwandan Genocide* (London: I. B. Tauris, 2006).
Watts, Arthur, 'The International Rule of Law', *German Yearbook of International Law* 36 (1993), pp. 15-45.
Weckel, Philippe, 'L'arrêt sur le génocide: Le souffle de l'avis de 1951 n'a pas transporté la Cour', *Revue générale de droit international public* 111 (2007), pp. 305-31.
Wedgwood, Ruth, 'The International Criminal Court: An American View', *European Journal of International Law* 10 (1999), pp. 93-107.
Weil, Prosper, 'Towards Relative Normativity in International Law?', *American Journal of International Law* 77 (1983), pp. 413-42.
  'Cours général de droit international public: le droit international en quête de son identité', *Recueil des Cours* 237 (1992-VI), pp. 9-370.
Weiss, Leonard, 'US–India Nuclear Cooperation – Better Later Than Sooner', *Nonproliferation Review* 14 (2007), pp. 429-57.
Weiß, Wolfgang, 'Allgemeine Rechtsgrundsätze des Völkerrechts', *Archiv des Völkerrechts* 39 (2001), pp. 394-431.
Wengler, Wilhelm, *Völkerrecht*, Vol. 1 (Berlin: Springer, 1964).
Wenzel, Nicola, 'Article XX lit a GATT', in Rüdiger Wolfrum, Peter-Tobias Stoll and Anja Seibert-Fohr (eds.), *Max Planck Commentaries on World Trade Law*, Vol. 3, *WTO – Technical Barriers and SPS Measures* (Leiden: Nijhoff, 2007), pp. 80-95.
Werle, Gerhard, *Völkerstrafrecht*, 2nd edn (Tübingen: Mohr Siebeck, 2007).
Westlake, John, *International Law*, Part II, *War* (Cambridge: Cambridge University Press, 1907).
Wiebringhaus, Hans, *Das Gesetz der funktionellen Verdoppelung: Beitrag zu einer universalistischen Theorie des Internationalprivat- und Völkerrechts*, 2nd edn (Saarbrücken: West-Ost-Verlag, 1955).
Wilde, Ralph, *International Territorial Administration: How Trusteeship and the Civilizing Mission Never Went Away* (Oxford: Oxford University Press, 2008).
  'Triggering State Obligations Extraterritorially: The Spatial Test in Certain Human Rights Treaties', in Roberta Arnold and Noëlle Quénivet (eds.),

International Humanitarian Law and Human Rights Law – Towards a New Merger in International Law (Leiden: Nijhoff, 2008), pp. 133–53.
Willrich, Mason, *Non-Proliferation Treaty: Framework for Nuclear Arms Control* (Charlottesville, VA: Michie Company, 1969).
Wittich, Stephan, 'Joint Tortfeasors in Investment Law', in Christina Binder, Ursula Kriebaum, August Reinisch and Stephan Wittich (eds.), *International Investment Law for the 21st Century – Essays in Honour of Christoph Schreuer* (Oxford: Oxford University Press, 2009), pp. 708–23.
Wolfrum, Rüdiger, 'Intervention in the Proceedings before the International Court of Justice and the International Tribunal for the Law of the Sea', in Volkmar Götz, Günther Jaenicke and Peter Selmer (eds.), *Liber amicorum Günther Jaenicke – Zum 85. Geburtstag* (Berlin: Springer, 1998), pp. 427–42.
  'Das Streitbeilegungssystem des VN-Seerechtsübereinkommens', in Wolfgang Graf Vitzthum (ed.), *Handbuch des Seerechts* (Munich: C. H. Beck, 2006), pp. 463–97.
  'Solidarity Among States: An Emerging Structural Principle of International Law', in Pierre-Marie Dupuy, Bardo Fassbender, Malcolm N. Shaw and Karl-Peter Sommermann (eds.), *Völkerrecht als Wertordnung – Festschrift für Christian Tomuschat* (Kehl: N. P. Engel, 2006), pp. 1087–1101.
  'Taking and Assessing Evidence in International Adjudication', in Tafsir Malick Ndiaye and Rüdiger Wolfrum (eds.), *Law of the Sea, Environmental Law and Settlement of Disputes – Liber Amicorum Judge Thomas A. Mensah* (Leiden: Nijhoff, 2007), pp. 341–56.
Wühler, Norbert, 'Monetary Gold Case', in Rudolf Bernhardt (ed.), *Encyclopedia of Public International Law*, Vol. III, J–P (Amsterdam: Elsevier, 1997), pp. 445–7.
Wulf, Herbert, 'The Federal Republic of Germany', in Ian Anthony (ed.), *Arms Export Regulations* (Oxford: Oxford University Press, 1991), pp. 72–85.
Wyler, Eric, 'From "State Crime" to "Serious Breaches of Obligations under Peremptory Norms of General International Law"', *European Journal of International Law* 13 (2002), pp. 1147–60.
Yee, Sienho, 'The News That Opinio Juris "Is Not a Necessary Element of Customary [International] Law" Is Greatly Exaggerated', *German Yearbook of International Law* 43 (2000), pp. 227–38.
  Towards an International Law of Co-Progressiveness (Leiden: Nijhoff, 2004).
Yihdego, Zeray, *The Arms Trade and International Law* (Oxford: Hart, 2007).
Zimmermann, Andreas, 'Die Zuständigkeit des Internationalen Gerichtshofs zur Entscheidung über Ansprüche gegen am Verfahren nicht beteiligte Staaten', *Zeitschrift für ausländisches öffentliches Recht und Völkerrecht* 55 (1995), pp. 1051–76.
  'Durchsetzung des Völkerrechts zwischen Fragmentierung, Multilateralisierung und Individualisierung', in Andreas Fischer-Lescano, Hans-Peter Gasser, Thilo Marauhn and Natalino Ronzitti (eds.), *Frieden in Freiheit – Festschrift für Michael Bothe* (Baden-Baden: Nomos, 2008), pp. 1077–88.

Zimmermann, Andreas and Michael Teichmann, 'State Responsibility for International Crimes', in André Nollkaemper and Harmen van der Wilt (eds.), *System Criminality in International Law* (Cambridge: Cambridge University Press, 2009), pp. 298–313.

Zobel, Katharina, 'Judge Alejandro Álvarez at the International Court of Justice (1946–1955): His Theory of a "New International Law" and Judicial Law-Making', *Leiden Journal of International Law* 19 (2006), pp. 1017–40.

Index

abstention duty as to non-assistance/non-recognition 326, 425-6
abuse of rights
  application of principle
    generally 69
    problems with 76
  as contested notion 71
  contribution to development of international law 75-7
  detriment of third parties 82
  as general principle of international law 71
  importance 77-8
  intent requirement 83
  meaning generally 70
  as 'norm-source' 75
  principle of
    debate as to legal status of 71
    overuse 94-5
    recognition of 73-5
    support for 72-3
    transformative role 76
  relationship to complicity, arguments for 81-3
  and rule of law 77-8, 81-3
  and State responsibility 83-5
  subjective element, problem of establishing 83
Afghanistan, detainees transfer 126-7
aggravated responsibility
  and collective security 367-8
  development of rules 320-5
  and *erga omnes* obligations generally 319-20
  general issues 319-20
  impact of rules 325
  and *jus cogens* generally 319-20
  main finding 421, 422
  summary of issues 373-5

aid, foreign, international law violations 145-6
'aid or assistance' *see also* non-assistance
  'after the fact' 338-40
  assessment of practice 174-91
  'assistance', meaning of in special rules 200-10
  causality
    assessment 218-19
    criminal law 213-14
    distinctions 215-16
    factors 216-18
    general issues 210-12
    ILC commentary 212-13
    main finding 419-20
  debate as to scope 195-7
  definition
    abstractness 198
    assessment of practice 209-10
    general issues 197-8
    negative criteria 219-30
    in primary rules of law 200-10
    scope 195
  ILC Draft Articles, governmental statements
    analysis 182
    constructive criticism 172
    generally 169-70
    objections 170-1
    support 173
  main finding 419
  omission as 225-30, 420
  related bases for responsibility 219-21
  for serious breaches of peremptory norms 156, 338-52
  wrongful situation, nexus with 340-1
aircraft *see* military aircraft
al-Adsani case, State immunity ruling 38-40

475

Albania
  Corfu Channel case see Corfu Channel case
  Monetary Gold case see Monetary Gold
    principle
Angola
  contribution to practice 177
  South African occupation 133
anti-personnel land mines, use, meaning
    of 'assistance' 200
Arar case, compensation 124
arbitrariness and rule of law 77-8, 79, 80-1
arbitration 314-15
Argentina
  termination of German arms supplies
    133
armaments see weapons
armed forces interoperability 203-7
Arms Trade Treaty (ATT), preparatory
    conference 137
Article 16 ASR
  'aid or assistance' see 'aid or assistance'
  development 100-3
  general issues 192-5
  intent requirement see intent
    requirement
  interpretation, subjective element
    235-7
  opinio juris see opinio juris
  and pacta tertiis rule see pacta tertiis rule
  primary/secondary rules distinction 4-5,
    187-90, 415-18
  as secondary rule 6
  State responsibility provisions see State
    responsibility
  subjective element
    debate as to 232-5
    general issues 230-1
    intent requirement 237-41, 244-9
    interpretation of provision 235-7
    main finding 419-20
    need for 230-1
    practical issues 241-4
    relaxation of requirement 244-9, 341-2
    summary of issues 249
  summary of issues 266-8
  UN Charter provisions compared 30-2
Articles on State Responsibility (ASR)
    see also State responsibility
  Article 16 see Article 16 ASR
  content of responsibility
    provisions 269
  domestic application 178, 180-1, 317,
    344
  implementation, consequences 269, 286
  and jus cogens see jus cogens
  obligation of cooperation
    see cooperation
'assistance' see 'aid or assistance'

Australia
  military support policy 141-2
  Nauru case 287, 291, 300-2
  Ottawa Convention, meaning of 'assist'
    201
Austria
  Ilisu Dam 148
  Iraq war 115
  military support policy 141-2

Barcelona Traction case, recognition of erga
    omnes obligations 41, 321
Belgium
  Barcelona Traction case 321
  Chile, withdrawal of military support
    145-6
  extradition 164
  Stanleyville incident 110-11
bilateralism
  and complicity
    summary of issues 47-9
  movement away from see community-
    oriented law
  and neutrality see neutral States;
    neutrality, law of
  'serial bilateralism' 260-1
  and State responsibility, conceptual
    constraints 4-5, 12-15
  and third parties see third parties
  traditional bilateralism
    general issues 12
    overview 13-14
Bosnia and Herzegovina
  extraordinary renditions investigations
    125
  genocide see Genocide Convention
Brazil, Ottawa Convention, meaning of
    'assist' 202
Bulgaria
  claims against 281
Burma/Myanmar, EU trade sanctions
    151

Canada
  Arar case 125
  detainees transferred in Afghanistan
    126-7
  extraordinary renditions 125-6
  Germany, legal cooperation 167-8
  and Guantanamo Bay human rights
    violations 125-6
  ILC Draft Articles statement 172
  jurisdiction issues 414-15
  Khadr case 125-6
  legal cooperation
    general principles 166-7
    Schreiber case 167-8, 258-60
  military support policy 142

case law and practice generally
    see also Table of cases
  arbitration 314–15
  domestic courts 178, 180–1, 317, 344
cessation, expectation of 85, 274
chemical weapons supply, protests 134
Chile, withdrawal of military support
    145–6
China
  ILC Draft Articles statement 172–4
  Ilisu Dam 149
  Japan, Manchuria annexation 326–7
  military support policy 141–2
Chorzów Factory case
  restitution ruling 276–7
cluster munitions
  convention 203–7, 218
  use
    'assistance', meaning 203–7
    responsibility concerns 2
coercion, responsibility for 222
collective security
  and aggravated responsibility 367–8
  and complicity generally 30–2, 380–5
  and neutrality 26–30
  and use of force 380–5
community-oriented law
  collective security *see* collective security
  countermeasures *see* countermeasures
  development of 23, 320
  international crimes, controversy over
    concept 320
  and *jus cogens* 36–41, 419
  public interest norms *see* public interest
    norms
  and rule of law 86–9
  and third parties 87–8
compensation for State responsibility
  extraordinary renditions 124–5
  generally 278–84
completeness of law *see* international law
compliance
  with customary law 179–81
  dispute 152
  GATT obligations 151
  of other State, responsibility for
    scrutiny 246–9
  rule of law as 7, 63–5
complicit State, meaning 9–10
complicity *see also* State responsibility
  abuse of rights *see* abuse of rights
  aggravated responsibility *see* aggravated
    responsibility
  Article 16 ASR *see* Articles on State
    Responsibility (ASR)
  bilateralism *see* bilateralism
  case law and practice *see* case law and
    practice generally

collective security *see* collective security
community-oriented law
    see community-oriented law
cooperation *see* cooperation
criminal law origin 9–10
customary law *see* customary law
enforcement of laws *see* enforcement
    of laws
exoneration for 162–4
extent, question of 1
governmental statements as *opinio juris*
    182
greater role 1
greater scope, consequences of 427–8
international law *see* international law
network of rules *see* network of rules
neutrality, law of *see* neutrality, law of
and 'new legal relationship' 271–4
omission as 225–6
pacta tertiis rule *see* *pacta tertiis* rule
paradigms 11–12
practical impact 425–6
responsibility *see* State responsibility
rule of law *see* rule of law
studies 4
summary of issues 419
use of force *see* use of force
use of term 9–10
conflicting rights, problem of 69
Congo (Democratic Republic), Stanleyville
    incident 110–11
control and direction, responsibility for
    222
cooperation *see also* community-oriented
    law
  balance with complicity 428
  as consolidation of unlawful events 152
  economic cooperation 147–9
  effectiveness 364
  generally 353
  obligation
    ASR provisions generally 352
    general issues 352
    Genocide Convention 354
    Genocide Convention case 358–64
    obligation of solidarity 356–8
    origins 353
    related concepts 353
    summary of issues 364
Corfu Channel case
  aggravated responsibility 346
  compensation ruling 281, 282
  complicity through omission 226–7
  intent requirement 245
  plurality of responsible actors 290
  UK claims 108
Council of Europe
  contribution to practice 177–9

478 INDEX

Council of Europe (*cont.*)
  extraordinary renditions investigations 124–5
countermeasures
  as complicity issue generally 371
  conceptual overlap 371
  current issues 369–71
  general issues 365
  ILC position 367
  ongoing debate 373
  overview 367
  potential abuse 88
criminal law
  case law and practice 213–14, 225–6, 315–16, 346
  causality *see* 'aid or assistance'
  complicity originating in 9–10
  components of international regime of 323
  legal consequences of international crimes, views on 33
Cuba
  Angola protests 133
  contribution to practice 177–9
customary law
  chapter summary 7
  compliance 179–81
  consistency 179–81
  evaluation 174–7
  general issues 97–100
  motivation for practice 181–2
  opinio juris see *opinio juris*
  overview 103–7
  practice, general issues 107–8
  relevance of peremptory norms to practice 190–1
  representativeness of practice 177–9
  standards for establishing 174–7
  summary of issues 191
Cyprus, ILC Draft Articles statement 172
Czech Republic/Czechoslovakia
  contribution to practice 177–9
  ILC Draft Articles statement 172
  Ottawa Convention, meaning of 'assist' 201–2
  suspension of arms supplies to Iraq 133

dédoublement fonctionnel theory and rule of law 59
Denmark, ILC Draft Articles statement 173
detention *see* extraordinary renditions
direction and control, responsibility for 222
duality of functions and rule of law 59
duty of abstention as to non-assistance/non-recognition 326

East Germany
  ILC Draft Articles statement 170–1
  Soviet Union expropriations 154
East Timor, ICJ case 302–4, 307
Eastern Carelia principle 309
economic cooperation, practice 147–9
Egypt, *Agiza* case 316–17
ELSI case, arbitrariness concept applied 80–1
enforcement of laws
  alternative models, need for 88–9
  and complicity 88–9
  main finding 421
  potential abuse 88
  and rule of law 83–5
Entebbe, Israeli operation 169
erga omnes obligations *see* obligations *erga omnes*
Ethiopia, ILC Draft Articles statement 173
Europe
  Ilisu Dam, responsibility concerns as to international law violations 1
  Iraq war, extent of complicity 1
European Union/European Community (EU/EC)
  arms exports Code of Conduct 143
  Burma/Myanmar trade sanctions 151
  contribution to practice 177–9
  extraordinary renditions investigations 120
  foreign aid 146–7
  Turkey customs union 152
  Turkey textiles dispute 312–13
  'Uganda Guidelines' 146–7
Eurotunnel arbitration, plurality of responsibility 291
export credit guarantees 147–9
extradition
  practice 164–5
  Soering case 395
extraordinary renditions
  complicity, question of extent 1
  investigations
    by international organisations 120
    by specific countries 122–4
  issue 120
  practice 120

Finland, ILC Draft Articles statement 173
Fisheries case, *Lotus* principle critiqued 66–8
force, right to use *see* use of force
foreign aid, international law violations 145–6
France
  Cluster Munitions Convention, meaning of 'assistance' 205

contribution to practice 177-9
Eurotunnel arbitration 291
ILC Draft Articles statement 171, 182
Iranian protests 134
military support policy 141-2
Monetary Gold case *see Monetary Gold* principle
Rainbow Warrior case 286
Rwandan investigation 134
solidarist school of international law 353
Tripartite Declaration 1950 130
US attacks on Libya 112-13

GATT obligations, compliance 151
genocide, investigation of complicity 134
Genocide Convention
  application 9
  ICJ case
    compensation ruling 282-4
    complicity through omission 225-6
    intent requirement 235-6, 239
    obligation of cooperation 358-64
    ruling 9
    satisfaction ruling 285
  obligation of cooperation 354
Georgia-Russia war
  complicity, question of extent 2
  Ukrainian arms supplies 135-6
Germany *see also* East Germany
  Argentina, withdrawal of arms supplies 133
  and Article 16 ASR 183
  Canada, legal cooperation 167-8, 258-60
  Chile, withdrawal of military support 145-6
  Chorzów Factory case 276-7
  Cluster Munitions Convention, meaning of 'assistance' 205
  contribution to practice 177-9
  extradition 164-5
  Greece, war crimes in 155
  ILC Draft Articles statement 171, 183
  Ilisu Dam 148
  Iraq war
    Chief Federal Prosecutor's decision 118
    complicity, question of extent 1
    Federal Administrative Court's decision 118
    overflight rights 216
    practice 117-18
  Italian military internees case 156
  military forces exception to ICJ jurisdiction 305

military support
  domestic law 140, 142
  Turkey 134
Monetary Gold case *see Monetary Gold* principle
opinio juris 183
Poland, *Chorzów Factory* case 276-7
Soviet Union protest 109-10
Turkey
  Ilisu Dam 148
  military support 134
  unlawful cooperation policy 154
governmental statements as *opinio juris* 182
Greece
  German war crimes 155
  ILC Draft Articles statement 173
  State immunity, ruling as to 37
Grotius, Hugo, just war theory 16-17
Guantanamo Bay, human rights violation 125-6
Guinea
  contribution to practice 177-9
  Stanleyville incident 110-11

human rights law
  case law and practice 38, 57-8, 206-7, 223-4, 240, 246, 284, 314, 316-17, 396, 398, 399-400
  extraordinary renditions
    see extraordinary renditions
  and GATT 151
  and Guantanamo Bay human rights violations 125-6
  intent requirement 246
  jurisdiction issues 405-15
  obligation of prevention 401-4
  refoulement, prohibition 393-401
  risk of violation 224-5, 316-17
  scrutiny of other State's compliance, responsibility for 246-9
  special rules generally 390
  specific special rules 390-3
  summary of issues 415
humanitarian law, use 385-9
Hungary, US claims against 168-9, 281

Ilisu Dam 1, 147-9
immunity
  for serious breaches of peremptory norms 155
impartiality, duty of strict 20-2
incitement, responsibility for 221-2
India
  Sri Lanka conflict 2009 2
  US nuclear agreement 208-9
indispensable third party *see also Monetary Gold* principle

indispensable third party (*cont.*)
  case law generally 297–8
  specific cases 305
  summary of issues 310–11
individualism and rule of law 59
Indonesia, *East Timor* case 302–4, 307
intent requirement
  importance 237–41
  modifications to 244–9
inter-State relations
  dédoublement fonctionnel theory 59
  rule of law 59
International Committee of the Red Cross, Arms Trade Treaty conference 137–8
International Court of Justice (ICJ)
  abuse of rights principle, recognition of 74–5
  and arbitrariness 80–1
  and Article 16 ASR 2
  and Genocide Convention *see* Genocide Convention
  and *Monetary Gold* principle 8, 298–300
  Namibia Advisory Opinion 332–4
  obligations of third parties, ruling 40–1
  peremptory norms, recognition 44–5
  State responsibility 83–5
international crimes *see* criminal law
International Criminal Court (ICC), case law and practice generally 315–16
International Criminal Tribunal for Rwanda (ICTR), case law and practice generally 225–6
International Criminal Tribunal for the former Yugoslavia (ICTY)
  aggravated responsibility ruling 346
  case law and practice generally 213–14
international law *see also* customary law; *opinio juris*
  abuse of rights *see* abuse of rights
  capability to be obeyed, need for 81–3
  'classic' period 18–19, 22
  completeness 6, 61–2, 91–2
  customary law *see* customary law
  framework 11
  future organisation 428
  impact on complicity, questions of 50–2
  and law of neutrality
    compatibility with obligations 26–7
    relationship generally 22
  legal relationships 14
  peremptory norms *see* peremptory norms
  primary rules *see* primary rules of law
  public order concept 36–7
  rule of law *see* rule of law
  secondary rules *see* secondary rules of law
  solidarist school 353
  States as agents of 61–2
  structural arguments 14–15
  substantive obligations *see* primary rules of law
International Law Commission (ILC), Articles *see* Articles on State Responsibility (ASR)
international organisations
  exclusion from study 9–10
  investigations into extraordinary renditions 120
international rule of law *see* rule of law
interoperability of armed forces 203–7
interrogation of terrorist suspects, extraordinary renditions
  see extraordinary renditions
Iran
  contribution to practice 177–9
  hypothetical Israeli air strike 114–15, 227–9
  ILC Draft Articles statement 172
  Oil Platforms case *see Oil Platforms* case
  protests to UK and France 134
  US hostage rescue 169
Iraq
  chemical weapons supply 134
  contribution to practice 177–9
  cooperation 413–14
  Ilisu Dam 148
  Iraq war, coalition complicity
    joint responsibility 220–1
    landing rights 192
    overflight rights 115, 216
    question of extent 1
  Israeli air strike on Iran 114–15, 227–9
  Kuwait invasion 133
  Osirak incident 112
  termination of Czech arms supplies 133
  UN sanctions, ending 162–4
  weapons manufacture in Sudan 128
Ireland
  Cluster Munitions Convention, meaning of 'assistance' 205
  Iraq war 116, 192
Israel
  Bulgaria claims 281
  Entebbe operation 169
  hypothetical Iran air strike 114–15, 227–9
  Israeli Wall case 42, 152–3, 309, 343–4
  military support policy 141–2
  Osirak incident 112

Soviet Union protest 109-10
Swiss arms supplies, withdrawal 133
UN policy 161-2
Italy
  Chile, withdrawal of military support 145-6
  contribution to practice 177-9
  ELSI case 81
  Germany, military internees case 156
  ILC Draft Articles statement 172
  Monetary Gold case *see Monetary Gold* principle
  non-belligerency 29-30
  Soviet Union protest 109-10

Jamaica, ILC Draft Articles statement 173
Japan
  ILC Draft Articles statement 172
  Manchuria annexation 326-7
joint responsibility
  adjudication, means of 293-4
  compensation as to 281
  example 219-21
  implementation of 288-93
  main finding 421
  right to internal recourse 294-5
jurisdiction issues
  conceptual issues 409-12
  cooperation 413-14
  ECtHR case law 407-9
  general issues 405-7
  human rights law 405-15
  national jurisprudence, example 414-15
jus cogens see also peremptory norms
  adoption 320
  and aggravated responsibility generally 319-20
  application 345-52
  and practice 190-1, 349
  main finding 422
  and non-recognition 327-8
  and public interest norms 36-7
just war theory, development of 16-17

Kazakhstan, military support policy 141-2
Kenya
  contribution to practice 177-9
  Entebbe, Israeli operation 169
Khadr case 125-6
knowledge requirement for serious breaches 245, 341-2
Korea
  ILC Draft Articles statement 172
  military support policy 141-2
  Korean War, UN resolutions 109

Kuwait, Iraqi invasion 133
Kyrgyzstan, Iraq war 116

land mines convention 200
Lauterpacht, Hersch
  on abuse of rights 70, 72-3, 80-1, 82
  on international law 6
  on *Lotus* principle 62-3, 65-6
  on neutrality 27
  on non-recognition 327
  on *pacta tertiis* rule 252
  on rule of law 62-3, 65-6
  on use of force 19
lawfulness, and *Lotus* principle 6
League of Arab States
  contribution to practice 177-9
  Israeli Wall case 152-3
League of Nations, law of neutrality 26-7
Lebanon, Soviet Union protest at US attacks 109-10
legal cooperation, practice 165-8
liberté à la guerre see use of force
Libya
  contribution to practice 177-9
  US attacks 112-13
Lotus principle
  application 6
  and conflicting rights 69
  critique 60-2, 65-6
  and material completeness of law 91-2

Mali
  contribution to practice 177-9
  ILC Draft Articles statement 173
  Stanleyville incident 110-11
Manchuria, Japan's annexation 326-7
material completeness of law
  see international law
Mauritania, Cluster Munitions Convention, meaning of 'assistance' 205
Mexico
  Arms Trade Treaty conference 137
  Cluster Munitions Convention 206
  ILC Draft Articles statement 172
  military support policy 141-2
  NAFTA dispute with US 152
Middle East *see also specific countries e.g.* Iraq
  Tripartite Declaration 1950 on Near East security 130
military aircraft
  landing rights 192
  overflight rights 115, 216, 227-9
military support
  assessment of practice 142
  general issues 129-30

military support (cont.)
  international law practice 130
  soft law 142
Moldova, Transdniestria ruling 284, 410
Monetary Gold principle
  application 8, 298–300
  generally 298–300
  indispensable third party rule 305
Montenegro, *Genocide Convention* case
  see Genocide Convention
moral values and rule of law 79
Morocco, Cluster Munitions Convention, meaning of 'assistance' 205
Movement of Non-Aligned States, contribution to practice 177–9
munitions *see* weapons
Myanmar/Burma, EU trade sanctions 151

NAFTA, legal compliance dispute 152
Namibia
  ICJ Advisory Opinion 308–9, 332–4
  South African occupation, non-recognition 159, 327
Nauru, ICJ case 287, 291, 300–2, 307
Near East *see* Middle East
Netherlands
  Chile, withdrawal of military support 145–6
  contribution to practice 177–9
  extraordinary renditions 124
  ILC Draft Articles statement 170–1, 172, 183
  Iraqi reconstruction 163–4
  Surinam, withdrawal of military support 132, 365
network of rules *see also* primary rules of law; secondary rules of law
  chapter summary 9
  general issues 376
  main finding 422
  summary of issues 415–18
neutral States 15–16
  collective security 26–7
  and *liberté à la guerre* 19–22
  and positivist theories 19–22
  rules on conduct of 5
  summary of issues 22
neutrality, law of
  and bilateralism 15
  and 'classic' international law 18–19, 22
  and complicity 15
  development of 16
  impartiality duty 20–2
  and international law
    compatibility with obligations 26–7
    relationship generally 22
  and just war theory 16–17

non-belligerency 29–30
obligations, structure of 22
origins of complicity in 15
UN Charter, compatibility with 28–32
and use of force 19
New Zealand
  Arms Trade Treaty conference 137
  Cluster Munitions Convention 206
  ILC Draft Articles statement 173
  Nauru trusteeship 301
  Rainbow Warrior case 286
Nicaragua, ICJ case 263–4
Nigeria, ILC Draft Articles statement 173
non-assistance
  duty of abstention 326
  non-recognition distinguished
    criteria 335–7
    scholarly debate 334–5
  obligation
    legal basis for obligation in UN practice 160–1
    requirement 13–14, 91–2, 121, 161–2, 374
  rescue operations 169
  UN practice 158–62
non-belligerency policy 29–30
non-recognition
  case law and practice 332–4
  distinguishing features 329–30
  domestic application 329–30
  duty of abstention 326
  further application of 332
  international application 329
  and *jus cogens* 327–8
  as mandatory action 331
  non-assistance distinguished
    criteria 335–7
    scholarly debate 334–5
  overview 326–7
  protest as 331
  scope 327–8
  Stimson Doctrine 326–7
non-refoulement, breach of prohibition, responsibility for 224–5, 239–41, 393–401
non-State actors, exclusion from study 9–10
'norm-source', abuse of rights principle as 75
norms
  negative direction 424–5
  peremptory *see* peremptory norms
  public interest *see* public interest norms
  qualified, as to practice 190–1
  and rule of law 57
Norway
  Arms Trade Treaty conference 137

INDEX 483

Chile, withdrawal of military support 145-6
Cluster Munitions Convention 206
contribution to practice 177-9
Fisheries case 66-8
Iraq war 119-20
Iraqi reconstruction 162-3
wealth fund 149
Nuclear Non-Proliferation Treaty (NPT), meaning of 'assistance' 207-8

obligations *erga omnes*
  and aggravated responsibility generally 41-5, 46-9, 319-20
  conflict as to serious breaches 357-8
  and practice 190-1
  and peremptory norms 35-6, 44-6
  third parties 40-1, 303, 307
obligations of protection 355-6
obligations of solidarity 356-8
Oil Platforms case
  Iranian claims 113
  plurality of responsibility 290
  reparation ruling 275-6
omission, complicity via, as to 'aid or assistance' 225-6
opinio juris
  assessment 185-6
  governmental statements 182
  as to motivation for practice 181-2
  need for 181
  standards for establishing 174-7
organs of State, responsibility for actions on behalf of another State 223-4
Osirak incident 112
Ottawa Convention on anti-personnel land mines, meaning of 'assistance' 200
overflight rights, grant or refusal 115, 216, 227-9

pacta tertiis rule
  and complicity generally 250-5
  general issues 249
  norms 261-5
  objective regimes 255-8
  obligations 258-65
  sources of law 261-5
  summary of issues 265-6
Pakistan, US nuclear security assistance 208
peremptory norms *see also jus cogens*
  and aggravated responsibility 46, 319-20, 421
  application, scope 376
  contrary acts
    non-toleration of 39-40
    recognition of 37

and *erga omnes* obligations 35-6, 44-6
hierarchical effects 36-7
maximising effect of 39-40
as 'new' international law 40-1
non-assistance *see* non-assistance
non-compliance, measures against 47
non-recognition *see* non-recognition
recognition of 44-5
relevance of practice to 349
serious breaches
  aggravated responsibility 46
  ASR provisions 8
  assistance for 156
  categories 323
  and conflicting obligations 357-8
  cooperation in response to 353
  cooperative prevention, effectiveness 364
  countermeasures 365
  distinctions other than non-recognition/non-assistance 345-52
  and *erga omnes* obligations 44-6
  general issues 325
  intent requirement 245, 341-2
  knowledge requirement 245, 341-2
  meaning 326
  response to, duty of 422
  seriousness, levels of 270
  summary of issues 47-9, 373-5
Peru, Cluster Munitions Convention 206
plurality of responsibility *see* joint responsibility
Poland, *Chorzów Factory* case 276-7
Portugal, *East Timor* case 302-4, 307
positivism and neutrality 19-22
prevention, obligation of 401-4
primary rules of law
  Article 16 ASR as primary rule 5-6
  'assistance', meaning 200-10
  normative weaknesses 377-8
  secondary rules distinguished 4-5
  structural weaknesses 378
  substantive obligations 4-5
  weaknesses 377-8
protest as non-recognition 331
public interest norms
  development of 25
  general issues 35-6
  and *jus cogens* 36-7
  State responsibility law developments 45-6
public order concept in international law 36-7

Rainbow Warrior case, satisfaction ruling 286
reduced share of responsibility, provision for 295

refoulement, prohibition 393-401
renditions see extraordinary renditions
reparation for State responsibility
  expectation of claim 85
  generally 274-6
rescue operations, non-assistance 169
responsibility for complicity see State responsibility
responsibility to protect (R2P) and obligation of cooperation 355-6
restitution for State responsibility 276-7
Rhodesia
  non-recognition 327
  UN sanctions 159
right of war see use of force
rights see also abuse of rights
  conflicting rights, problem of 69
  obligations as mirror of 13-14
risk of unlawful treatment, responsibility for creation 224-5
role splitting and rule of law 59
Romania, ILC Draft Articles statement 173
rule by law as rule of law 7, 64
rule of law
  abstractness 57
  and abuse of rights 77-8, 81-3
  and arbitrariness 77-8, 79, 80-1
  as 'background constitution' 80-1
  balanced conception 80
  chapter summary 5-7, 52
  as 'climate of legality' 65-6
  and community-oriented law 86-7
  as compliance 7, 63-5
  and complicity generally 89-91
  conceptions 78
  contribution to understanding of international law 56
  and dédoublement fonctionnel theory 59
  definition
    approaches to 53
    comparative approach 54-5
    problem of 53
    study approach 53
  discussion on, main features 57-8
  and enforcement of laws 83-5, 88-9
  formal conceptions 78
  highlighting of complicity problem 423-4
  impact, ability to 424
  and individualism 59
  inter-State relations 59
  and legal norms 57
  in legal systems generally 54-5
  and Lotus principle see Lotus principle
  and moral values 79
  rule by law as 7, 64
  and State responsibility 83-5

as study viewpoint 423
substantive conceptions 79
summary of issues 95-6
vagueness 424
Russia see also Soviet Union
  contribution to practice 177-9
  Georgia-Russia war see Georgia-Russia war
  ILC Draft Articles statement 173
  Swiss legal cooperation 165-8
  Transdniestria ruling 284, 410
Rwanda
  contribution to practice 177-9
  France investigation 134
  ICTR case law and practice generally 226

safe haven, provision of as complicity 128
satisfaction for State responsibility
  expectation of claim 85
  generally 284
Saudi Arabia
  contribution to practice 177-9
  Israeli Wall case 152-3
  United Arab Republic attack 111
Schreiber case 167-8, 258-60
scrutiny of other State's compliance, responsibility for 246-9
secondary rules of law
  Article 16 ASR as example 6
  primary rules distinguished 4-5, 415-18
  special rules generally 379-80
Senegal, Cluster Munitions Convention, meaning of 'assistance' 205
Serbia, Genocide Convention case 9, 235, 358-64, 391-2
'serial bilateralism' 260-1
serious breaches see peremptory norms
shelter, provision of as complicity 128
Slovenia, ILC Draft Articles statement 173
Soering case 314, 395
solidarist school of international law 353
solidarity 356-8
  abstention opposed to 426
  obligation 356-8
South Africa
  military support policy 141-2
  Namibia occupation 159, 308-9, 327
  US support 133
Southern Rhodesia see Rhodesia
Soviet Union
  Angola protests 133
  contribution to practice 177-9
  expropriations from East Germany 154
  protests by 109-10
  US claims against 168, 281

space objects, liability for damage caused by 292-3
Spain, *Barcelona Traction* case 41, 321
Sri Lanka conflict 2009, extent of complicity 2
Stanleyville incident 110-11
State immunity *see* immunity
State organs, responsibility for actions on behalf of another State 223-4
State responsibility
  aggravated responsibility *see* aggravated responsibility
  Articles *see* Articles on State Responsibility (ASR)
  assessment of consequences 274
  attribution of conduct by private actors 92-4
  and bilateralism *see* bilateralism
  and community-oriented law 320
    see also community-oriented law
  compensation 278-9
  complicit State, meaning 9-10
  consequences generally 271
  content 269, 271
  contribution to 'climate of legality' 85-6
  extent of responsibility 296
  further development of law of 295
  implementation of 269, 286-95
  incitement 221-2
  joint responsibility *see* joint responsibility
  plurality *see* joint responsibility
  policy considerations 295
  reduced share, provision for 295
  reparation generally 274-6
  restitution 276-7
  and rule of law 83-5
  satisfaction 284
States as agents of international law 61-2
Stimson Doctrine as to non-recognition 326-7
strict impartiality, duty of 20-2
subjective element *see* Article 16 ASR
Sudan, US protest 128
Surinam, withdrawal of Dutch military support 132, 365
Swaziland, ILC Draft Articles statement 172
Sweden
  Agiza case 316-17
  contribution to practice 177-9
  ILC Draft Articles statement 172
  Israeli Wall case 152-3
Switzerland
  Arms Trade Treaty conference 137
  contribution to practice 177-9

extradition 164
ILC Draft Articles statement 171, 183
Ilisu Dam 148
Iraq war 115
military support policy 133, 141-2
Russia, legal cooperation 165-6
Syria
  contribution to practice 177-9
  Ilisu Dam 147-9

terrorism
  national policies 128
  UN policy 128-9
terrorist suspects
  extraordinary renditions *see* extraordinary renditions
third parties *see also* indispensable third party
  abuse of rights to detriment of 82
  and bilateralism 12
  case law and practice 297-8
  and community-oriented law 87-8
  countermeasures by *see* countermeasures
  erga omnes obligations 40-1
  and *Monetary Gold* principle 8, 304
  neutrality *see* neutral States
  overflight rights 115
  and public interest norms 40-1
  refoulement prohibition 396
tort, breach of legal obligation as 14
Trinidad and Tobago
  Arms Trade Treaty conference 137
  ILC Draft Articles statement 173
Tripartite Declaration 1950 on Near East security 130
Tunisia, ILC Draft Articles statement 173
Turkey
  EC customs union 152
  German military support 134
  Ilisu Dam
    export credit guarantees 147-9
    responsibility concerns as to international law violations 1
  Iraq war 116-17
  Soviet Union protest 109-10
  textiles dispute with EC 312-13

Uganda
  EC Guidelines on assistance 146-7
  Entebbe, Israeli operation 169
  US suspension of relations with 365
Ukraine
  arms supplies to Georgia 135-6
  ILC Draft Articles statement 173
United Arab Republic (UAR), Saudi Arabia attack 111

486   INDEX

United Kingdom (UK)
  al-Adsani case 38
  Bulgaria claims 281
  Chile, withdrawal of military support 145–6
  Cluster Munitions Convention, meaning of 'assistance' 205
  contribution to practice 177–9
  Corfu Channel case see Corfu Channel case
  Eurotunnel arbitration 291
  extraordinary renditions 122–4
  Fisheries case 66–8
  ILC Draft Articles statement 172
  Ilisu Dam 147–9
  Iranian protests 134
  Iraq war see Iraq
  Iraqi reconstruction 162–4
  military support policy 131–2, 141–2
  Monetary Gold case see Monetary Gold principle
  Nauru trusteeship 300–2
  non-recognition jurisprudence 329–30
  Ottawa Convention, meaning of 'assist' 202
  Stanleyville incident 110–11
  terrorism policy 128
  torture, complicity allegations 339–40
  Tripartite Declaration 1950 130
  'Uganda Guidelines' 146–7
  unlawful cooperation policy 156
  US attacks on Libya 112–13
  US extradition, Soering case 314, 395
  Yemen dispute 111
United Nations (UN)
  Arms Trade Treaty conference 137
  Charter provisions compared with Article 16 ASR 30–2
  exonerating practice 162–4
  Korean War 108–9
  military support practice 136
  neutrality, law of 27–8, 30–2
  non-assistance practice 158–62
  resolutions as to non-recognition 327, 329
  terrorism policy 128–9
United Nations Convention on the Law of the Sea (UNCLOS)
  abuse of rights principle, recognition of 74–5
  dispute settlement 313
United States (US)
  Bulgaria claims 281
  ELSI case 81
  extradition case 164–5
  Georgia-Russia war 2
  Guantanamo Bay human rights violations 125–6
  Hungary, claims against 168, 281
  hypothetical Israeli air strike on Iran 114–15, 227–9
  ILC Draft Articles statement 172
  India nuclear agreement 208–9
  Iran
    hostage rescue 169
    Oil Platforms case see Oil Platforms case
  Iraq war see Iraq
  Lebanon attacks, Soviet Union protest 109–10
  Libya attacks 112–13
  Mexico, NAFTA dispute 152
  military support policy 138
  Monetary Gold case see Monetary Gold principle
  Nicaragua case 263–4
  non-belligerency 29
  observation balloons, Soviet Union protest 109–10
  Pakistan, nuclear security assistance 208–9
  South Africa, support for 133
  Soviet Union, claims against 168, 281
  Stimson Doctrine 326–7
  Sudan protest 128
  terrorism policy 128
  Tripartite Declaration 1950 130
  Uganda, withdrawal of relations 365
  UK extradition, Soering case 314, 395
  Yemen, extradition case 164–5
unlawful treatment, risk of, responsibility for creation 224–5, 316–17
unlawful use of force, assistance, practice 108
use of force
  assistance to
    case law and practice 108
    frequency of complicity 108
  and collective security 380–5
  and neutrality 19
  Nicaragua case 263–4
  and positivist theories 19–21

Vattel, Emer de, just war theory 16–17
Venezuela, ILC Draft Articles statement 173

Wassenaar Arrangement 143–5
weapons see also military support
  aircraft see military aircraft
  chemical weapons supply 134
  cluster munitions see cluster munitions
  conventions and treaties, meaning of 'assistance' 200–10
  land mines convention 200
  nuclear non-proliferation 207–8

supplies, withdrawal of 133
trade treaty, preparatory conference 137
Wassenaar Arrangement 143-5
World Trade Organization (WTO)
abuse of rights principle, recognition of 74-5
dispute settlement 312-13
GATT obligations 151
wrongful conduct
aiding of *see* 'aid or assistance'
committing of, assessment as to 397
deterrence to 268
early scrutiny 426
implication in 297-8
joint responsibility, compensation as to 281
non-assistance *see* non-assistance
by third parties *see* third parties
wrongful situation, nexus with 'aid or assistance' 340-1

Yemen
extradition case 164-5
UK protests 111
Yugoslavia *see also* International Criminal Tribunal for the former Yugoslavia (ICTY)
Corfu Channel case 245
Genocide Convention case 9, 235, 358-64, 391-2
ILC Draft Articles statement 172

Zaire *see* Congo (Democratic Republic)
Zimbabwe, Ottawa Convention, meaning of 'assist' 202

CAMBRIDGE STUDIES IN INTERNATIONAL AND COMPARATIVE LAW

Books in the series

Complicity and the Law of State Responsibility
Helmut Philipp Aust

State Control over Private Military and Security Companies in Armed Conflict
Hannah Tonkin

The UN and Human Rights: Who Guards the Guardians?
Guglielmo Verdirame

Sovereign Defaults before International Courts and Tribunals
Michael Waibel

Making the Law of the Sea: A Study in the Development of International Law
James Harrison

'Fair and Equitable Treatment' in International Investment Law
Roland Kläger

Legal Aspects of Transition from Illegal Territorial Regimes in International Law
Yaël Ronen

Access to Asylum: International Refugee Law and the Globalisation of Migration Control
Thomas Gammeltoft-Hansen

Trading Fish, Saving Fish: The Interaction between Regimes in International Law
Margaret Young

The Individual in the International Legal System: State-Centrism, History and Change in International Law
Kate Parlett

The Participation of States in International Organisations: The Role of Human Rights and Democracy
Alison Duxbury

Theatre of the Rule of Law: The Theory, History and Practice of Transnational Legal Intervention
Stephen Humphreys

'Armed Attack' and Article 51 of the UN Charter: Evolutions in Customary Law and Practice
Tom Ruys

Science and Risk Regulation in International Law: The Role of Science, Uncertainty and Values
Jacqueline Peel

The Public International Law Theory of Hans Kelsen: Believing in Universal Law
Jochen von Bernstorff

Vicarious Liability in Tort: A Comparative Perspective
Paula Giliker

Legal Personality in International Law
Roland Portmann

Legitimacy and Legality in International Law: An Interactional Account
Jutta Brunnée and Stephen J. Toope

The Concept of Non-International Armed Conflict in International Humanitarian Law
Anthony Cullen

The Challenge of Child Labour in International Law
Franziska Humbert

Shipping Interdiction and the Law of the Sea
Douglas Guilfoyle

International Courts and Environmental Protection
Tim Stephens

Legal Principles in WTO Disputes
Andrew D. Mitchell

War Crimes in Internal Armed Conflicts
Eve La Haye

Humanitarian Occupation
Gregory H. Fox

The International Law of Environmental Impact Assessment: Process, Substance and Integration
Neil Craik

The Law and Practice of International Territorial Administration: Versailles, Iraq and Beyond
Carsten Stahn

Cultural Products and the World Trade Organization
Tania Voon

United Nations Sanctions and the Rule of Law
Jeremy Farrall

National Law in WTO Law: Effectiveness and Good Governance in the World Trading System
Sharif Bhuiyan

The Threat of Force in International Law
Nikolas Stürchler

Indigenous Rights and United Nations Standards
Alexandra Xanthaki

International Refugee Law and Socio-Economic Rights
Michelle Foster

The Protection of Cultural Property in Armed Conflict
Roger O'Keefe

Interpretation and Revision of International Boundary Decisions
Kaiyan Homi Kaikobad

Multinationals and Corporate Social Responsibility: Limitations and Opportunities in International Law
Jennifer A. Zerk

Judiciaries within Europe: A Comparative Review
John Bell

Law in Times of Crisis: Emergency Powers in Theory and Practice
Oren Gross and Fionnuala Ní Aoláin

Vessel-Source Marine Pollution: The Law and Politics of International Regulation
Alan Tan

Enforcing Obligations Erga Omnes *in International Law*
Christian J. Tams

Non-Governmental Organisations in International Law
Anna-Karin Lindblom

Democracy, Minorities and International Law
Steven Wheatley

Prosecuting International Crimes: Selectivity and the International Law Regime
Robert Cryer

Compensation for Personal Injury in English, German and Italian Law: A Comparative Outline
Basil Markesinis, Michael Coester, Guido Alpa and Augustus Ullstein

Dispute Settlement in the UN Convention on the Law of the Sea
Natalie Klein

The International Protection of Internally Displaced Persons
Catherine Phuong

Imperialism, Sovereignty and the Making of International Law
Antony Anghie

Necessity, Proportionality and the Use of Force by States
Judith Gardam

International Legal Argument in the Permanent Court of International Justice: The Rise of the International Judiciary
Ole Spiermann

Great Powers and Outlaw States: Unequal Sovereigns in the International Legal Order
Gerry Simpson

Local Remedies in International Law
C. F. Amerasinghe

Reading Humanitarian Intervention: Human Rights and the Use of Force in International Law
Anne Orford

Conflict of Norms in Public International Law: How WTO Law Relates to Other Rules of International Law
Joost Pauwelyn

Transboundary Damage in International Law
Hanqin Xue

European Criminal Procedures
Edited by Mireille Delmas-Marty and John Spencer

The Accountability of Armed Opposition Groups in International Law
Liesbeth Zegveld

Sharing Transboundary Resources: International Law and Optimal Resource Use
Eyal Benvenisti

International Human Rights and Humanitarian Law
René Provost

Remedies Against International Organisations
Karel Wellens

Diversity and Self-Determination in International Law
Karen Knop

The Law of Internal Armed Conflict
Lindsay Moir

International Commercial Arbitration and African States: Practice, Participation and Institutional Development
Amazu A. Asouzu

The Enforceability of Promises in European Contract Law
James Gordley

International Law in Antiquity
David J. Bederman

Money Laundering: A New International Law Enforcement Model
Guy Stessens

On Civil Procedure
J. A. Jolowicz

Trusts: A Comparative Study
Maurizio Lupoi

The Right to Property in Commonwealth Constitutions
Tom Allen

International Organizations Before National Courts
August Reinisch

The Changing International Law of High Seas Fisheries
Francisco Orrego Vicuña

Trade and the Environment: A Comparative Study of EC and US Law
Damien Geradin

Unjust Enrichment: A Study of Private Law and Public Values
Hanoch Dagan

Religious Liberty and International Law in Europe
Malcolm D. Evans

Ethics and Authority in International Law
Alfred P. Rubin

Sovereignty Over Natural Resources: Balancing Rights and Duties
Nico Schrijver

The Polar Regions and the Development of International Law
Donald R. Rothwell

Fragmentation and the International Relations of Micro-States: Self-determination and Statehood
Jorri Duursma

Principles of the Institutional Law of International Organizations
C. F. Amerasinghe

For EU product safety concerns, contact us at Calle de José Abascal, 56–1°,
28003 Madrid, Spain or eugpsr@cambridge.org.

www.ingramcontent.com/pod-product-compliance
Ingram Content Group UK Ltd.
Pitfield, Milton Keynes, MK11 3LW, UK
UKHW020348060825
461487UK00008B/578